D1714014

Hunger Models

Hunger Models

Computable Theory of Feeding Control

Edited by

D. A. Booth

Department of Psychology,
University of Birmingham, England.

1978

ACADEMIC PRESS
London · New York · San Francisco
A Subsidiary of Harcourt Brace Jovanovich, Publishers.

U.K. Edition published and distributed by
ACADEMIC PRESS INC. (LONDON) LTD.
24/28 Oval Road
London NW1

United States Edition published and distributed by
ACADEMIC PRESS INC.
111 Fifth Avenue
New York, New York 10003

Library of Congress Catalog Card Number: 77 81383
ISBN: 0 12 115950 7

Printed in Gt. Britain by
Page Bros (Norwich) Ltd, Norwich

CONTRIBUTORS

J. S. Armstrong, *Commonwealth Scientific and Industrial Organisation, Canberra, Australia.*

G. M. Barnwell, *Department of Bioengineering, University of Texas, Health Science Center, San Antonio, Texas, USA.*

D. A. Booth, *Department of Psychology, The University of Birmingham, Elms Road, P.O. Box 363, Birmingham, England.*

G. A. Bray, *Department of Medicine, Harbor General Hospital, Torrance, California, U.S.A.*

F. R. Calaresu, *Department of Psychology, University of Western Ontario, London, Canada.*

L. A. Campfield, *Engineering Systems Department, School of Engineering and Applied Science, University of California, California, USA.*

B. J. Collins, *Department of Psychology, University of Illinois, Chicago, USA.*

A. O. Cromer, *Psychology Department, University of Louisville, Louisville, Kentucky, USA.*

J. D. Davis, *Department of Psychology, University of Illinois, Chicago, USA.*

J. M. Forbes, *Department of Animal Physiology and Nutrition, University of Leeds, Leeds, England.*

J. Hirsh, *The Rockefeller University, New York, NY 10021, USA.*

M. W. Levine, *Department of Psychology, University of Illinois, Chicago, USA.*

P. Mather, *Department of Psychology, The University of Birmingham, Elms Road, Birmingham, England.*

D. J. McFarland, *Animal Behaviour Research Group, Department of Zoology, Oxford, England.*

G. J. Mogenson, *Department of Physiology, University of Western Ontario, London, Canada.*

G. Pask, *Systems Research Ltd., 16, Montague Road, Richmond, Surrey, England.*

J. Panksepp, *Department of Psychology, Bowling Green State University, Bowling Green, Ohio, USA.*

M. RUSSEK, *Department of Psychology, Escuela Nacional de Ciencias Biologicas, Instituto Politecnico Nacional, Mexico.*

A. J. SCHILSTRA, *Zoological Laboratory of the State University at Groningen, Haren (Gr.), The Netherlands.*

J. B. THURMOND, *Psychology Department, University of Louisville, Louisville, Kentucky, USA.*

A. J. STUNKARD, *Philadelphia General Hospital, Philadelphia, Pennsylvania, U.S.A.*

F. M. TOATES, *Division of Psychology, Preston Polytechnic, Preston, England.*

E. C. ZEEMAN, *Mathematics Institute, University of Warwick, Coventry, England.*

PREFACE

Theories of the mechanisms controlling food intake in animals and human beings have only recently become sufficiently systematic and complete for it to be possible to construct quantitative or logically precise computer simulations of hunger. This book provides a comprehensive review of the hunger models available to date.

The book begins and ends with discussions of systems analysis and its application to hunger modelling. The first model for food intake and obesity is described, and then a variety of different later models. Some of these are based on central or peripheral interaction between a facilitatory factor and an inhibitory factor. Others involve several major components interacting outside and inside the central nervous system. The book includes discussions of computable aspects of the interaction of hunger and other motivation and of the concept of hunger itself. Some of the clinical implications of hunger modelling are also discussed.

Many different logical or mathematical styles of simulation are available, and simulation is new in this field. Thus, the chapters and the models they describe vary a great deal in their approach. Each contributor offers a non-technical explanation of his approach and some justification for it. No knowledge of modelling, computing or mathematics is assumed: the contributors were asked to make extensive use of diagrams and verbal description rather than algebra in order to explain how a model works.

The book is intended to indicate the potential value of modelling as a technique in theory construction. The contributors are mainly experimentalists who believe that theory, based on experimental analysis of normal and disordered feeding control systems, should be disciplined by attempts at computable theoretical synthesis. The various hunger models offered and the theories they embody must compete for a while, to see which sorts of experimental data, which hypothetical postulates, and which programming techniques are most likely to bring current research nearest the truth about the mechanisms controlling food intake and body composition.

I am greatly indebted to my co-authors for their industry and patience during the long process of preparing this book, to Eileen Brookes and Barbara Hudson for all their meticulous typing and retyping, and to Academic Press for their care with the detail of a slightly unusual production.

June, 1978 David Booth

CONTENTS

A*

5. A Dynamical System Theory Approach to Food Intake Control

GEORGE M. BARNWELL

6. Types of Modelling with an Initial Structural Analysis of the Neural Control of Feeding

L. ARTHUR CAMPFIELD

7. The Interaction Between Gustatory Stimulation and Gut Feedback in the Control of the Ingestion of Liquid Diets

JOHN D. DAVIS, BARBARA J. COLLINS AND MICHAEL W. LEVINE

8. Analysis of Feeding Patterns: Data Reduction and Theoretical Implications

JAAK PANKSEPP

9. Simulation of Feeding Behaviour: Comparison of Deterministic and Stochastic Models Incorporating a Minimum of Presuppositions

A. J. SCHILSTRA

10. Semi-quantitative Simulation of Food Intake Control and Weight Regulation

MAURICIO RUSSEK

11. Prediction of Feeding Behaviour from Energy Flows in the Rat

D. A. BOOTH

12. Prototype Model of Human Feeding, Growth and Obesity

D. A. BOOTH AND P. MATHER

13. Models of the Control of Food Intake and Energy Balance in Ruminants

J. M. FORBES

14. A Physiological Control Theory of the Hunger–Thirst Interaction

F. M. TOATES

15. Hunger in Interaction with Other Aspects of Motivation

D. J. MCFARLAND

16. A Catastrophe Theory of Anorexia Nervosa

E. C. ZEEMAN

17. The Regulation of General Evolving Systems: Needs and Hunger in a Formal Ecology

G. PASK

18. Hunger Modelling: A Discussion of the State of the Art

G. A. BRAY, D. A. BOOTH, L. A. CAMPFIELD, G. J. MOGENSON AND A. J. STUNKARD

1

Food Intake Considered from the Viewpoint of Systems Analysis

GORDON J. MOGENSON AND FRANCO R. CALARESU
Departments of Physiology and Psychology, University of Western Ontario, London, Canada

"All vital mechanisms, varied as they are, have only one object, that of preserving constant conditions of life in the internal environment."

(Claude Bernard)

I. Introduction

Animals, as self-regulating, adaptive systems, require food as a source of energy for work and heat production and as a source of "building blocks" for tissue growth and maintenance. Complex mechanisms, under the control of the central nervous system, have evolved for the initiation of feeding behaviour as well as for regulating the processing of nutrients and the expenditure of energy. The neural and endocrine control systems ensure that food intake approximates energy expenditure in the adult animal as reflected by the relative stability of body weight, an indicator of the constancy of body energy content (Fig. 1). Accordingly food intake has been considered for a number of years from the viewpoint of regulatory physiology and feeding as a self-regulatory behaviour that contributes to body energy homeostasis (Richter, 1943). This approach using systems analysis has provided new insights into the factors controlling feeding behaviour. The emphasis here will be on the neural components of this control system. Endocrine factors are certainly very important and are known to interact with neural factors but they will not be considered in this chapter. The reader is referred to recent reviews by Bray and Campfield (1975) and Frohman (1971) as well as to Booth *et al.* (1976: see Fig. 1, p. 131).

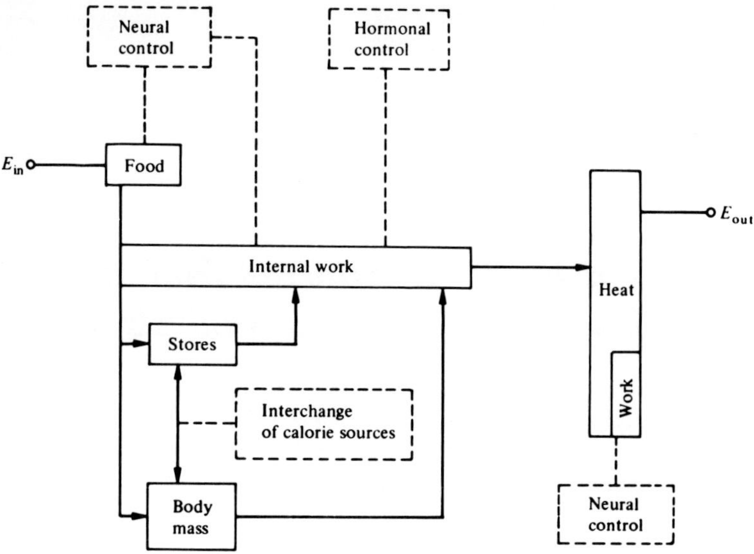

Fig. 1. A simplified model showing the principal pathways from energy intake (E in) to energy output (E out). Food, the source of energy, is either stored (as glycogen or fat), or utilized for growth which adds to body mass, or energy expended as work or heat. In the adult animal body weight is relatively constant over long periods of time, an indication that body energy content is being regulated. Food intake and energy expenditure are under neural and endocrine control in response to a variety of signals. Food intake is periodic, since many animals are meal eaters, but the metabolic machinery is organized so that energy is expended continuously (Carlson and Hsieh, 1970).

In the first section of this chapter the literature on the control of food intake and energy balance will be reviewed briefly in order to provide an appropriate framework for enumerating, in subsequent sections, the signals and feedback loops which influence and control feeding behaviour in relation to body energy homeostasis. In later chapters other contributors will present examples of applications of systems analysis to this field.

II. Food Intake and Body Energy Homeostasis

A. *Defence of Intake*

The basal energy requirements in man are approximately 1800 kcal per day or 1·2 kcal per kg body weight per hour (1·4 W per kg). For the rat, used extensively in laboratory studies of food intake and energy balance, the basal energy requirements are higher, about 5 kcal per kg body weight per hour. In the normally active man energy requirements are about 2500–3000kcal per day and they are higher during intense exercise and physical work and in a cold environment. They are also increased during rapid growth and during gestation and lactation (Ota and Yokoyama, 1967). In order to provide for and replenish such expenditures, energy is taken into the body as food.

It is widely known that depriving an animal of food for several hours is a reliable way to ensure that feeding behaviour will occur. Food intake has been considered the response to energy deficits and it has been widely assumed that animals eat for calories. When the caloric content or energy density of the diet is altered, as in the classical diet dilution experiments (Adolph, 1947), rats readily adjust their food intake and maintain a caloric intake appropriate to their energy expenditure. Similarly when energy requirements are increased by placing the animal in a cold environment, its food intake increases in relation to the increased energy expenditure (Stevenson, 1954).

B. *Complications in Energy Control*

These observations suggest that an animal monitors energy expenditure (energy deficits) and responds by ingesting an appropriate number of calories of food for body energy regulation. It apparently does not do this in a simple and direct manner. There are three complicating factors in attempting to account for food intake in terms of a simple feedback mechanism that reflects current energy expenditure.

1. *Delay in Energy Availability*

The first is that there is a delay between the ingestion of food and the subsequent availability of energy to the cells and tissues of the body. The delay is because of the time for digestion, absorption and transport of the energy constituents. If food intake was regulated by a simple feedback control from energy depletion this time lag would result in an excess or overshooting of food intake. Apparently there are other signals and feedback loops that enable an animal to turn feeding off before the food is digested and the energy made available for utilization by the tissues.

2. *Energy Storage*

The second complicating factor is that the body can store appreciable amounts of energy (Fig. 1). There are sufficient glycogen reserves, as a readily utilizable short term energy source, for about a day and enough fat stores for about a month. As a consequence, although energy expenditure is continuous, feeding is usually periodic; man and higher animals are meal eaters. The metabolic machinery is so organized that energy stored in the body can be made available in the intervals between meals so that the animal is free to engage in other activities. Energy intake does not need to equal energy expenditure precisely in the short term even though in the long term energy expenditure is balanced by energy intake, since body weight (that is body energy content) remains relatively constant. There is a long time-constant for energy balance (Hervey, 1971: p. 113).

There are a number of cases in which energy intake does not match energy expenditure in the short term. Edholm *et al.* (1955) reported that there was no or only a low correlation between energy intake and energy expenditure of individual military cadets as determined for 24-hour periods but a good correlation when these measures were averaged over periods of two weeks. Rats take in more calories than they expend at night and take in less than they expend in the daytime (Le Magnen, 1975). Plasma levels of amino acids have also been reported to show circadian rhythms unrelated to the intake of dietary proteins (Feigin *et al.* 1971). Man may overeat on weekends and holidays but takes fewer calories than expended during part of the periods between. As noted some years ago by Strominger and Brobeck (1953: p. 383),

> "What an animal eats and how much are usually thought to be determined by the energy requirements of the body; but every careful observer who has conducted feeding experiments knows that there are many circumstances in which the amount of food eaten is not related to energy expenditure".

Panksepp (1973: p. 93) has suggested that

> "the free-feeding pattern of rats is generated by an internal signal of body nutrient depletion–repletion which varies in a circadian fashion".

3. *Environmental Modulations*

The third complicating factor in attempting to account for food intake in terms of a simple feedback mechanism that reflects current expenditure is that the animal lives in an external environment that is frequently complex and variable and sometimes even hostile. Feeding is one of a number of behaviours that the animal exhibits as it adapts to a changing environment. Feeding, like drinking, thermoregulatory and other self-regulatory behaviours, is periodic as well as purposive and persistent (Richter, 1943).

Feeding behaviour is periodic, in part, because the signals for its onset and termination wax and wane with the availability of body energy and, in part, because of events occurring in the external environment. As a consequence feeding competes with other behaviours; "time sharing" is a prominent feature of motivated behaviours (McFarland, 1974b). In certain circumstances food intake is postponed even in the presence of strong "hunger signals" because of the higher priority of another activity, such as sexual behaviour in the oestrous female rat or escape from a predator. The great tit *Papus Major*, which eats two or three meals per hour during the day, does not feed at night and is presumably very hungry in the morning. Yet at dawn feeding is postponed while it first engages in territorial behaviour (McFarland, pers. comm.). "Motivational time sharing" may appear to operate on a competitive basis as suggested by Adolph's (1947) concept of "priorities and compromises" but, as proposed by McFarland (1974a,b), there is an overall organization for the initiation of motivated behaviours so that they contribute to "biological fitness" and survival (see Chapter 5).

Feeding behaviour is not only postponed in spite of the presence of homeostatic deficit signals, as indicated in the previous paragraph, but may also occur in the absence of deficit signals. When laboratory animals are fed a highly palatable diet they increase their food intake, gain body weight and accumulate fat (Hamilton, 1964). In man, social and cultural factors, as well as palatability, may result in a marked increase in food intake (Rozin, 1976). Furthermore, since feeding behaviour follows a circadian rhythm in some species, energy intake may exceed energy expenditure during certain periods of the day. For example, as indicated earlier, in the rat which eats 80—90% of its total daily intake during the dark period more energy is taken in than expended at night and lipogenesis occurs (Le Magnen, 1975). During the light period the rat expends more energy than taken in by feeding and lipolysis occurs.

C. *Implications*

These considerations have led several investigators to suggest that food intake is determined by a number of signals and is under multifactor control (Adolph, 1947; Stevenson, 1964b). In the short term some of these signals may result in an intake of food and thus of energy that either exceeds or is less than current energy expenditure. However, in the long term, food intake is brought into line with energy expenditure and body weight remains constant. The fact that feeding behaviour is not always related directly to current energy expenditure and to the presence of deficit signals has important implications for the systems analysis of feeding behaviour. The task of the systems analyst or model builder is made more difficult and requires the use of feedforward mechanisms as well as feedback mechanisms.

III. Signals that Influence and Control Food Intake

One of the first factors to be emphasized was oropharyngeal sensations; von Haller (1764) proposed that feeding is initiated because of the taste, smell and other pleasurable oropharyngeal sensations of food. A century later Cannon and Washburn (1912) attributed hunger to the occurrence of stomach contractions. Subsequently, it was demonstrated that rhythmical stomach contractions were not the cause, but merely a consequence of hunger. However, signals from the gastrointestinal tract resulting from gastric and duodenal distension were shown to have an important role, for the cessation rather than for the initiation of feeding (Davis *et al.,* 1976; Janowitz and Grossman, 1949; Paintal, 1954). In the 1950s following fundamental observations of the effects on ingestive behaviour of lesions and stimulation of the hypothalamus using stereotactic techniques, which were the basis of a neurology of hunger (Mogenson, 1976), three major signals were recognized (see Fig. 2). These signals soon became associated with the three classical theories: thermostatic (Brobeck, 1948), glucostatic (Mayer, 1952) and lipostatic (Kennedy, 1953).

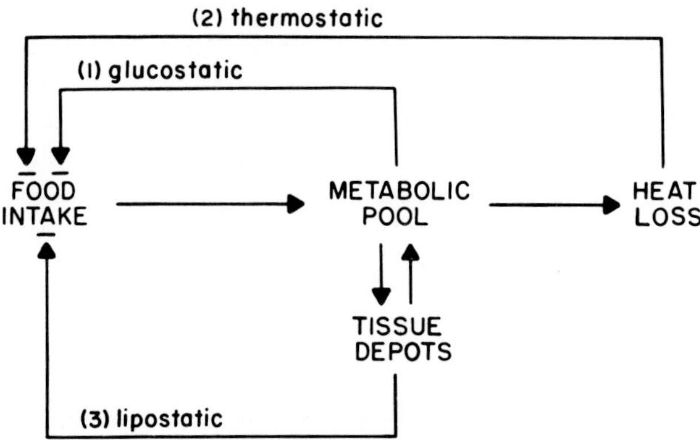

Fig. 2. Since the early 1950s three major signals (glucostatic, thermostatic, lipostatic) for the control of food intake have been emphasized and they have become associated with three classic theories.

A number of other signals, summarized in Table I, have been implicated over the years in the initiation, modulation and termination of feeding. These include the level of amino acids (or the concentration of certain amino acids) in the blood (Harper, 1976; Harper and Boyle, 1976; Mellinkoff *et al.,* 1956), osmolarity of the extracellular fluid (McCleary, 1953), gastrointestinal chemical signals (Sharma, 1967), duodenal distension (Davis *et al.,* 1976), duodenal hormones

Table I
Signals involved in the control of feeding behaviour

	Initiate	Modulate	Terminate
External			
Olfactory		20, 45	
Visual	19		
Temperature (ambient)		13,38, 49	
Social and cultural factors		37, 39	

Table I *contd.*

	Initiate	Modulate	Terminate
Internal			
1. Pre-absorptive			
Mechanical			
Oropharyngeal (taste, texture)	1, 17, 48	24, 25	
GI tract			
stomach contractions	2		
stomach distension			3, 4, 31
intestinal distension			8, 10
Hormonal factors			
insulin	18, 32	11	
prostaglandins		26, 27	29
cholecystokinin			9
other gut hormones		9, 47	
Humoral factors		42, 43	
2. Post-absorptive			
plasma glucose	11, 18		
plasma free fatty acids		23	
plasma amino acids		5, 6, 33	
lipid mobilizing substances		36	30, 35
plasma glycerol		41	
3. Long term feeding controls			
fat stores	21	14	
hormones		16	
insulin		22	
growth hormone		40	
sex hormones		12, 15, 28	
thyroxine		41	
glucagon		34, 46	
corticosteroids		44	
4. Other factors		7	

1. von Haller, 1764; 2. Cannon and Washburn, 1912, 3. Janowitz and Grossman, 1949; 4. Paintal, 1954; 5. Mellinkoff *et al.*, 1956; 6. Harper, 1976; 7. Scott and Quint, 1946; 8, Davis *et al.*, 1976; 9. Smith *et al.*, 1974; 10. Hill *et al.*, 1952; 11. Mayer, 1955; 12. Fishman, 1976; 13. Brobeck, 1948; 14. Kennedy, 1953; 15. Wade, 1972; 16. Bray, 1974; 17. Mickelsen *et al.*, 1955; 18. Steffens, 1969; 19. Schachter, 1971a; 20. Pfaffmann, 1956; 21. Cabanac *et al.*, 1971; 22. Panksepp and Nance, 1972; 23. Walker and Remley, 1970; 24. Jacobs, 1962; 25. Corbit and Stellar, 1964; 26. Baile and Martin, 1973; 27. Baile *et al.*, 1973; 28. Simpson and Dicara, 1973; 29. Baile and Grovum, 1974; 30. Kastin *et al.*, 1974; 31. Snowdon, 1970; 32. MacKay *et al.*, 1940; 33. Panksepp and Booth, 1971; 34. Schulman *et al.*, 1957; 35. Beaton *et al.*, 1964; 36. Russek *et al.*, 1968; 37. Rozin, 1976; 38. Hamilton, 1975; 39. Schachter, 1971b; 40. Frohman, 1971; 41. Bray and Campfield, 1975; 42. Davis *et al.*, 1971; 43. Fleming, 1969; 44. Stevenson and Franklin, 1970; 45. Cabanac and Duclaux, 1970b; 46. Sudsaneh and Mayer, 1959; 47. Schally *et al.*, 1967; 48. Nicolaïdis, 1969; 49. Kraly and Blass, 1976.

(Smith *et al.,* 1974), insulin (Woods *et al.*, 1974), hepatic energy reserves (Russek, 1963) and energy flow (Booth *et al.,* 1976). A consensus has not yet been reached among workers in this field as to which signals are fundamental and essential. Some of these signals may merely modify food intake but not play a critical role in the regulation of energy balance. This lack of consensus will be reflected in subsequent chapters by the emphasis given by different authors to the various signals. However, the application of control systems analysis to the mechanisms for food intake and body energy regulation should eventually help to identify the relevant factors and signals and to indicate which are fundamental and which modulatory.

IV. Regulation of Food Intake and Energy Balance Considered from the Viewpoint of Systems Analysis

This section is a concise review of experimental data selected in relation to the approach of systems analysis. The purpose is not to be comprehensive but rather to provide a background and orientation to the issues dealt with in subsequent chapters. The relevant material is organized in relation to the simplified diagram shown in Fig. 3.

A. *Output*

When considering hunger and energy balance according to systems analysis the output is feeding behaviour, normally expressed quantitatively as amount of food eaten per unit of time (see right side of Fig. 3). Amount of time engaged in feeding and the performance of a lever press or other operant response, which can be very precisely quantified, may also be used but if one is interested in

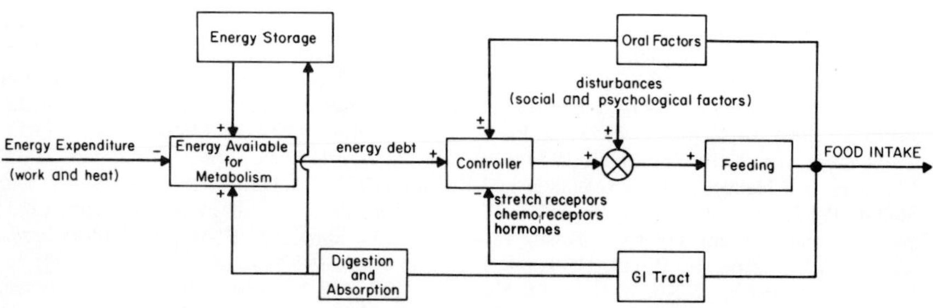

Fig. 3. A simplified diagram illustrating some of the signals and feedback loops which contribute to the control of food intake and the regulation of energy balance in the body.

energy balance as well as in the control of feeding then grams of food intake per unit of time is a more appropriate measure. If the energy density of the food is known it is then easy to calculate energy intake in calories.

The output of energy varies not only from person to person depending on the type of activity but also in the same person depending on the climatic conditions, patterns of metabolic demands and other factors. To ensure that energy intake as food equals energy expenditure, so that at least in the long term energy balance is maintained, several variables are monitored and signals are integrated by the CNS to generate command signals to the motor system which controls the seeking and ingestion of food. The signals which initiate and terminate feeding (that is the signals for hunger and satiety) will be considered in the next section followed by a discussion of feedback loops to the controller.

B. *Input*

Energy is required for metabolic processes necessary for the various functions of the body. Some energy is liberated as heat which is often a by-product contributing to body temperature regulation. Stated simply, energy is expended as work and heat (see left side of Fig. 3). Nutrients and energy are also required for the maintenance and repair of body tissues. However, with the exception of special situations such as growth, pregnancy and lactation, and when nutrients are being stored as excess fat, energy intake equals energy expenditure and body weight remains constant.

The most readily utilized sources of energy in the body are carbohydrates, especially blood glucose, and free fatty acids. Fats and proteins may also be utilized but involve intervening metabolic processes (Bray and Campfield, 1975; Frohman, 1971). Glucose is the major source of energy for the brain and the metabolite in highest concentration in the plasma and, therefore, it is not surprising that one of the first signals for food intake to be suggested was the level of blood sugar (Mayer, 1952), subsequently considered to be the availability of blood sugar to body tissues (arterial venous glucose difference; Mayer, 1955). Later, other signals for the initiation of feeding were proposed, some related to nutrient or energy deficits and some to palatability either because of their hedonic characteristics or because of conditioning or past experience.

One of the major issues in this field for a number of years, which has not yet been resolved, concerns the nature of the signal or signals essential for the regulation of food intake and body energy balance. More than two decades ago three proposals were made concerning the essential signal: changes in plasma glucose concentration and availability as indicated in the previous paragraph (Mayer, 1952, 1955), changes in body temperature (Brobeck, 1948) and in body fat content (Kennedy, 1953) (see Fig. 2). Subsequently other signals were suggested, such as levels and patterns of plasma amino acids (Harper *et al.*,

1970; Mellinkoff *et al.,* 1956), and the modulating effects of taste and habit or experience, and social and emotional factors (Rozin, 1976; Schachter, 1971a,b; Young, 1959) on food intake were recognized. Following a period of debate about the merits of these three theories, designated glucostatic, thermostatic and lipostatic theories (and to a lesser extent a fourth, the aminostatic theory, Harper *et al.,* (1970)) of food intake regulation, many workers in this field came to accept the view that food intake, like water intake, is under the control of multiple factors (Adolph, 1947; Brobeck, 1960; Stevenson, 1964a,b). However, the possibility of a unifactor model could not be rejected and recently there has been renewed interest in this possibility and in particular in the suggestion that a signal reflecting the "current supply of energy for intermediary metabolism" controls food intake (Booth, 1972; Russek, 1971). Toates and Booth (1974) have suggested in their computer model that the primary control of food intake is the inhibition of feeding by readily metabolizable energy (energy flow from the gut and to or from fat stores). After critically reviewing the evidence for several theories of food intake regulation, Russek (1971) rejected the multifactor approach on the grounds that it was merely a reflection of our lack of understanding of the basic mechanisms, and presented a good deal of evidence for an essential role of hepatic glucoammonium receptors.

An important consideration in trying to choose between unifactor and multifactor models for the investigation of food intake and body energy regulation is the long "time constant" for energy balance (Hervey, 1971: p. 113). Although the regulation of energy balance is good over a long time period (e.g. 2–4 weeks) it is frequently poor over the short term (e.g. 12–24 hours). For example, there was no or only a very low correlation between energy intake and energy expenditure of individual military cadets determined for 24-hour periods but a good correlation when these measures were averaged over periods of two weeks (Edholm *et al.,* 1955). Accordingly there may be different signals, feedback loops and integrative control mechanisms for short- and long-term regulation. The original proposal of this sort was by Mayer (1952) who suggested that a glucostatic system was concerned with short-term regulation and a lipostatic system with long-term regulation; a short-term "glucostatic signal" could be modified by a "lipostatic signal" (Mayer and Thomas, 1967) so that errors of short-term regulation would be corrected in the long term.

The receptors for signals for which there is relatively good evidence of a role in the regulation of food intake, such as lipostatic and glucostatic signals, are unknown or controversial. On the other hand, for some of the receptors that are known, such as those for temperature (both peripheral and central) and taste, they either do not play an important role in the control of feeding in normal circumstances (e.g. temperature receptor) or may have a secondary rather than a primary role (e.g. taste receptor). According to the lipostatic hypothesis the plasma concentration of some metabolite related to fat reserves could be the signal controlling food intake (Kennedy, 1950; Kennedy and Mitra, 1963) but the nature and location of the receptors are not known. Glucoreception in the hypothalamus has been postulated and the results of experiments utilizing goldthioglucose (Marshall *et al.,* 1955) and electrophysiological techniques (Anand *et al.,* 1962; Oomura, 1969) have been considered evidence for their presence in the ventromedial and possibly lateral hypothalamus. However, this evidence is far from conclusive, and glucoreceptors, if present in the brain, may not be concerned with the initiation of feeding but rather with autonomic and endocrine regulations for the control of glucose metabolism and blood glucose levels (Epstein *et al.,* 1975; Russek, 1971). Feeding has been induced by infusing 2-deoxy-D-glucose, a compound that produces glucoprivation of glucoreceptive cells, into the hepatic portal system (Novin *et al.,* 1973; Russell and Mogenson, 1975) and satiety has been induced by similar infusions of glucose (Russek, 1975; Vanderweele *et al.,* 1974) suggesting the presence of glucoreceptors in the liver but additional experiments are needed to identify and characterize these receptors and to assess their role in the control of spontaneous, day-to-day food intake. Russek's hypothesis that liver receptors, which he designates glucoammonium receptors, monitor the availability and utilization of both glucose and amino acids deserves further investigation. Since satiety has been reported following infusions of glucose into the duodenum (Novin *et al.,* 1976; Snowdon, 1975), the possibility of duodenal glucoreceptors must also be considered.

It has been postulated that gastric distension is an important satiety signal (see Fig. 3) and that stretch receptors in the stomach (Paintal, 1954) send signals to the CNS, possibly to the ventromedial nucleus of the hypothalamus (Brobeck *et al.,* 1956). One of the possible reasons that animals eat larger meals following lesions of the ventromedial hypothalamus (VMH) and become hyperphagic is that this satiety signal is defective or lost. The ventromedial hypothalamus may also receive and integrate some signal related to body fat reserves (Le Magnen, 1971; Panksepp, 1974). Another suggestion is that neurons of the VMH might increase their fat content in parallel with peripheral adipose cells and serve as central "witness cells" (Nicolaïdis *et al.,* 1974) signalling the level of fat stores in the body. These are only speculations, however, and there is a lack of consensus about the role of the VMH in satiety (Blundell, 1975; Booth *et al.,* 1976; Mogenson, 1974).

For more detailed discussions of signals and receptors the reader is referred to Mogenson (1976), Russek (1971) and Stevenson (1964b, 1967).

C. *Feedback Loops*

The food ingested passes through the oropharyngeal cavity, along the gastrointestinal tract and is eventually digested and absorbed; blood levels of glucose, amino acids and fats will then gradually increase thereby removing the signal or signals that had previously activated the feeding system (see Fig. 3). An appreciable period of time is required for digestion and absorption and as a consequence the deficit nutrient signals do not disappear as soon as the food is ingested. Feeding terminates, however, because food intake is monitored at the oral, alimentary and systemic levels and signals from all three contribute to satiety (see Fig. 3). Signals from chemoreceptors in the mouth (oral level) and in the gastrointestinal tract as well as signals from stomach distension (alimentary level) contribute to pre-absorptive satiation and the diminution or even cessation of feeding prior to any significant change in blood nutrient levels (systemic level). There are multiple signals or factors in satiety and, as pointed out by McFarland (1970), the relative importance or weighting of these factors varies considerably among species.

> "Thus, while the delays involved in digestion and absorption entail some sort of short-term satiation mechanism, it appears that different species have solved the problem in different ways" (McFarland, 1970: p. 230).

Taste and other oropharyngeal sensations may also facilitate feeding through positive feedback loops so that feeding once initiated is more likely to continue for some time (De Ruiter *et al.,* 1974; Wiepkema, 1971). Le Magnen (1971) reported that food intake could be increased substantially during a two-hour feeding period by changing the taste of the food every few minutes. Such positive feedbacks from taste and oral stimuli are shown by a positive sign in Fig. 3. These oropharyngeal stimuli which are intially pleasant may become unpleasant as the animal is satiated with food. A good example is a study by Cabanac and Duclaux (1970a) in which human subjects who rated certain foods highly pleasant rated the same foods as unpleasant after being given a gastric load of 100 ml of glucose.

As pointed out by Van Sommers (1972: p. 82) the feedback loops involved in the control of food intake are organized in a hierarchy. They comprise

> "a system of superimposed controls operating in the mouth and stomach during eating, in the bloodstream as food is absorbed, and throughout the body as food is stored as fat or as body weight increases. Each successive level of control involves detection of changes over a longer time period and each serves to compensate for errors in the adjustment of the others. Finally, the further dimension of palatability must be added to these controls".

Clearly such feedback loops, particularly those involving negative feedback, are important in food intake regulation. But are they also responsible for regulation of energy balance and body weight regulation? For some years there have been two points of view on this issue. According to Brobeck (1960: p. 1200),

> ". . . although the end result of regulation is control of energy intake, animals apparently have no mechanisms for measuring energy *per se*. They do not meter calories ingested but attain energy balance indirectly through reactions that are related to or proportional to energy need".

Russek (1971) agrees with Brobeck's view that fat stores and body weight are not regulated, and cites the major problem of obesity as evidence that food intake frequently does not merely compensate for a deficit in overall energy balance of the body. On the other hand a few years later Hervey (1971: p. 112), in discussing the accuracy of adjustment of food intake in diet-dilution experiments, stated

> "It is difficult to see what could bring about the corrective changes in food intake in [diet dilution] experiments such as these, other than a feedback regulation using some signal which indicated the current state of energy balance".

However, as pointed out by Hoebel (1971: p. 539) in the same year

> "In spite of twenty years of searching, no one has yet managed to specify the stimulus which is correlated with body weight and serves such an important role in food intake".

D. *Set Point*

> "When provided with a diet that is adequate in amino acids, vitamins, minerals and essential free fatty acids, mature animals ingest amounts of energy sufficient to maintain constant body weight and young animals to maintain normal rate of growth. Further, when body weight is experimentally displaced from age-appropriate levels, energy intake is adjusted in such a fashion as to ultimately restore energy balance at appropriate body weight for age" (Harper and Boyle, 1976: p. 1).

In order to account for the remarkable constancy of body weight, which is frequently observed, a "ponderostat" or set point for the regulation of body fat stores has been postulated (Cabanac *et al.,* 1971). The effects of lesions of the hypothalamus on food intake and body weight have been attributed to a shifting of the set point. For example, Powley and Keesey (1970) pointed out that rats recovered from the aphagia and anorexia after bilateral lesions of the lateral hypothalamus "persist in maintaining their body weight at levels substantially below those of controls" and they suggest that there is not a deficit in the motivation to eat or in the motor responses for feeding, as typically suggested, but rather the "set-point for weight regulation is lowered by lesions of the lateral hypothalamus" (p. 26). In support of this view, Powley and Keesey showed that if body weight was reduced by starving the rats before making the lateral hypothalamic lesions the aphagia and weight loss did not occur following surgery. On the other hand, the increased food intake and body weight following lesions of the ventromedial hypothalamus have been attributed to an elevation of the set point for body weight regulation (Woods *et al.,* 1974). That hypothalamic hyperphagic rats are in fact regulating their body weight, but at a higher level, has been demonstrated by force-feeding them and observing that they reduce their body weight to the former level by reducing food intake at the termination of force-feeding (Hoebel and Teitelbaum, 1966). Recently Nisbett (1972) has speculated that overweight people have a higher set point for body weight regulation and because of dieting in response to social pressure they are below their normal set point and thus actually are in a state of deprivation; this could be an important factor in accounting for the difficulty of obese people reducing their body weight by dieting.

Cabanac (1971) has suggested that body weight (or energy stores) in relation to the set point may determine the palatability of food and thus the amount eaten. Subjective ratings of the pleasantness of the taste and smell of food were reduced in human subjects following a stomach load of 100g of glucose. Cabanac suggests that it may be difficult for obese subjects, in whom the set point for body weight regulation is abnormally high, to remain lean after losing weight because their body weight is now below the set point, and since the palatability of the food is thereby increased, they gradually let their body weight drift up again.

The term set point has been used by Powley and Keesey and by Cabanac and other investigators in a descriptive sense without considering its appropriateness or validity from the viewpoint of systems analysis. The mechanism that establishes the set point has not been identified and, until it is, a more parsimonious alternative is to assume body weight regulation (in the normal animal as well as in animals with hypothalamic lesions) is due to the interaction of two balanced systems operating with proportional control. Booth *et al.,* (1976) and Peck (1976) have recently suggested that the concept "set point" is unnecessary and potentially misleading since its use will "encourage experimenters to look for unnecessarily complex systems in biology" (Booth *et al.,* 1976, p. 138). Booth and co-workers comment (p. 138) that

> "The stability of such a system of fat store size could be mathematically equivalent to a set-point function, but there is no set-point mechanism involved, no receptor specific to a signal from the fat store, no system to generate a precise reference value, and no comparator mechanism to compute the error value".

Some years ago Engelberg (1966) also referred to the potential pitfalls of the concept of set point and noted that ". . . the controlled variable in a regulatory system can be changed by an adjustment of the characteristics of any one of a number of components in the system" (p. 83).

A clue concerning the mechanism for the regulation of body fat stores and body weight is the observation that obese animals, including man, have a larger number of adipose cells than non-obese (Hirsch and Han, 1969). The number of adipose cells determined by genetic factors and early nutritional experience remains constant throughout the life of the animal irrespective of body weight changes with variations in food intake. This "cellular imprinting", or constancy of number of adipose cells, may be an important determinant of body weight.

> "We have to assume that depleted adipose cells somehow 'scream' for food till they are replenished to a certain level, while overloaded fat cells reduce somehow the amount of food ingested till they reach their 'set point' (which is actually the body weight 'set point')". (Russek, 1975: p. 130.)

If this is the mechanism then the adipose cells must in some way provide a signal to the CNS regarding their content of fat. Russek has speculated that prostaglandins might be the signal, which is consistent with earlier observations that the lipostatic signal is blood borne (Hervey, 1969).

According to another recent speculative hypothesis the set point for determining body fat stores and therefore body weight regulation depends on the ratio of plasma levels of insulin (I) and growth hormone (GH). Woods *et al.* (1974) suggest that when the I/GH ratio increases, food intake and body weight increase, whereas when this ratio decreases, food intake and body weight decrease. In support of their hypothesis they review experimental evidence showing that plasma insulin levels are high and plasma growth hormone levels low in spontaneously obese and hypothalamic hyperphagic animals and that the administration of insulin or growth hormone to alter the I/GH ratio influences food intake and body weight. Panksepp (1975) has criticized the proposal that the I/GH ratio determines regulatory feeding and thereby body weight regulation and in particular questions whether plasma levels of insulin and growth hormone are "causes or consequences of feeding" (p. 158).

E. *Feedforward*

Figure 3 and the presentation which appeared in the last few pages are based on a homeostatic model utilizing negative feedback loops and on the assumption that feeding is initiated by "hunger (deficit) signals". However, as indicated earlier, feeding is not always directly associated with energy deficit signals. In some cases food intake may be postponed in the presence of strong "hunger signals" because of the higher priority of another activity and in other cases food intake may occur in the absence of "hunger signals" (see Fig. 3, disturbances). Food intake of the latter type has been called "anticipatory feeding". It is clearly recognized by ethologists but has received little attention in laboratory studies and as a consequence has usually been ignored in theoretical and neural models of ingestive behaviour.

Since anticipatory feeding may be the sort of spontaneous food intake which frequently occurs in the natural environment of the animal, it is important that it not be ignored when the control of food intake is being considered from the viewpoint of systems analysis. The major implication is the necessity to include feedforward mechanisms in addition to feedback loops of the kind discussed in the previous section. "Feed-forward enables the animal to anticipate the long-term consequences of behaviour and to take appropriate action to forestall such consequences" (Fitzsimons, 1972: p. 494). How this is accomplished by the central nervous system is at present unknown but it involves learning and memory; in Oatley's (1973) words it involves "representational processes of the environment deployed not in the feedback mode so that deficits are corrected, but in a feedforward mode so that they can be anticipated" (p. 221).

When food intake is in response to energy deficit signals resulting from energy expenditure (left side of Fig. 3) it has been designated regulatory feeding since it directly restores an imbalance of body energy homeostasis. In contrast when food intake is initiated not by energy deficit signals, but by palatable food, social or other stimuli (right side of Fig. 3, disturbance factors) it has been called non-regulatory feeding. The latter term is rather ambiguous, however, since it may apply in one case to feeding which anticipates energy deficits but which maintains an energy intake equivalent to energy expenditure and in another case to feeding which results in energy intake in excess of expenditure. The term non-regulatory is confusing, therefore, because it designates anticipatory feeding that contributes to body energy homeostasis as well as feeding which results in a positive energy balance.

V. The Virtues and Defects of Systems Analysis and Models of Food Intake

The investigation of a biological system eventually requires the formulation of a model that simulates the dynamic characteristics of the system (Waterman, 1968). Although model building is unavoidable, physiologists have, in the past, preferred to use verbal models rather than attempting to develop formal quantitative models. This has been particularly true for the study of feeding behaviour. This reticence of physiologists to use mathematics in model building reflects an attitude dating back to Claude Bernard:

> "The most useful path for physiology and medicine to follow now is to seek to discover new facts instead of trying to reduce to equations the facts which science already possesses" (Bernard, 1878).

The main virtues of systems analysis and of modelling in the study of feeding behaviour (as well as for the study of any biological or behavioural system) are:

(i) a very complex system can be looked at in functional terms in its entirety and the properties of the system that emerge from its organization because of connectivity relations will become obvious (Guyton *et al.*, 1972);

(ii) gaps in knowledge and imprecise thinking are easily detected under the demands of a precise mathematical formulation;

(iii) when the model is completed more experiments may be suggested either because gaps in knowledge become obvious, or because the model makes predictions about the mode of operation of the system which can be tested experimentally;

(iv) models introduce a new theoretical way to look at systems, using powerful computational techniques.

One of the goals of systems analysis and model building is to produce a symbolic representation of functional relations based on experimental findings that can be represented by a computer program. The model that has reached the stage of a program may then be tested on a computer to study the effects of changing parameters in the performance of the system. This process, called simulation, may produce predictions that are not intuitively obvious and may be tested experimentally.

Formal models, on the other hand, have some defects, the most obvious being that the distributed character of physiological systems, their nonlinearities, their variability with time, their memory for past events, and their ability to adjust their performance to a change in the environment of the system, demand mathematical techniques that may not be available. Other often cited criticisms of physiological models are that they may be remote from the reality they are supposed to represent and that they are too complicated for the human mind to comprehend. This is often the case, but the painstaking efforts that have gone into model building are really aimed at producing a symbolic representation of functional relations based on experimental findings that is sufficiently unambiguous for computer simulation. The evidence to date is that building mathematical models is a useful exercise; the rigour of mathematical notation reduces the imprecision of descriptive models, points to obvious gaps in knowledge of physiological mechanisms and may suggest critical experiments to be done (Hardy and Stolwijk, 1968). Control theory and systems analysis therefore seem to offer the potential for understanding and prediction in very complex systems.

VI. Summary

There has been a strong inclination over the years to consider food intake from the viewpoint of regulatory physiology. Food is the source of energy required for the various functions of animals and feeding is a self-regulatory behaviour in the sense that energy intake tends to match energy expenditure thereby contributing to body energy homeostasis. Feeding behaviour is a topic, therefore, which may be profitably investigated with the assistance of control theory and systems analysis.

Feeding behaviour cannot be accounted for in terms of a simple feedback mechanism reflecting current energy expenditures. There is a delay between the ingestion of food and the subsequent availability of energy to body tissues. Also the body can store an appreciable amount of energy so that feeding behaviour does not need to occur continuously and is normally periodic. The metabolic machinery of the body is organized to provide a continuous supply of energy even though many animals are meal eaters. A further complication is that feeding behaviour occurs in a complex and changing external environment and must compete with other activities so that the overall organization of behaviour contributes to "biological fitness" and survival. Laboratory studies of feeding are typically performed in highly artificial circumstances, involving constant conditions of illumination, temperature and humidity with food freely available. The animals do not experience the usual seasonal changes in food availability or rhythms of hibernation and reproduction. We must therefore add these factors and produce realistic models which accommodate the behavioural as well as the physiological evidence. Our experimental preparations are of necessity simplified and exclude environmental factors that may have important influences on feeding behaviour in the natural habitat and normal ecological niche of the animal. The approach of systems analysis provides a framework and strategy for dealing with such factors while at the same time dealing rigorously with the mechanisms of body energy homeostasis.

Feeding behaviour is under multifactor control and the multiplicity of signals means that there are a number of feedback loops for the initiation and termination of food intake. Many of these operate according to negative feedback, but some operate in the feedforward mode since feeding also occurs in the absence of energy deficit signals. Signals reflecting energy deficits and energy stores are very important and may play a vital role for long term body energy homeostasis. The stimulus characteristics of food which determine its palatability are also important. Past experience, social and cultural factors influence food intake, particularly in man. Furthermore, as the food is ingested and digested, signals from the oropharyngeal cavity, the stomach and the intestines contribute to satiety so that feeding behaviour terminates before the deficit signals have been eliminated by the nutrients reaching body cells.

Since the pioneering studies on hypothalamic hyperphagia there has been a strong interest in investigating and speculating about the central neural mechanisms that control food intake. Much effort has been devoted to developing neurological models of the brain mechanisms for hunger and feeding behaviour. Unfortunately the formulation of such models has been premature, based primarily on evidence of the effects of lesions and stimulation of the hypothalamus and associated neural structures on food intake. Empirical evidence is lacking on a number of fundamental issues—concerning the physiologically relevant signals and receptors, the neural pathways, and the interface of integrative systems for hunger and satiety signals and the neural systems for "action" (that is, for the motor control of feeding behaviour). We lack a "neurology of hunger" and it is unlikely that we will have one for some time (Mogenson, 1976). Systems analysis, by providing a clearer picture of what is known and by suggesting experiments to fill the gaps in the available experimental evidence, should assist in the task of eventually understanding how the brain controls feeding behaviour.

Acknowledgements

The assistance of Miss Blanche Box with the references and with Table I, of Miss Rebecca Woodside with the illustrations, and of Miss Marilyn Allen with the typing of the manuscript is acknowledged. The research of the authors' laboratories has been supported by grants from the Medical Research Council of Canada and the National Research Council of Canada. During the preparation of this chapter the senior author was a Visiting Fellow of Wolfson College, Oxford University.

References

Adolph, E. F. (1947). Urges to eat and drink in rats. *Am. J. Physiol.* **151**, 110–125.

Anand, B. K., Chhina, G. S. and Singh, B. (1962). Effect of glucose on the activity of hypothalamic "feeding centers". *Science, N.Y.* **138**, 597–598.

Baile, C. A. and Grovum, W. L. (1974). Pentagastrin, secretin, cholecystokinin and coerulein and feeding in sheep. Proc. Vth Int. Conf. on Physiology of Food and Fluid Intake, Jerusalem, p. 39.

Baile, C. A. and Martin, F. H. (1973). Relationship between prostaglandin E_1, polyphloretin phosphate and adrenoceptor-bound feeding loci in the hypothalamus of sheep. *Pharmacol. Biochem. Behav.* **1**, 539–545.

Baile, C. A., Simpson, C. W., Bean, S. M., McLaughlin, C. L. and Jacobs, H. L. (1973). Prostaglandins and food intake of rats: a component of energy balance regulation? *Physiol. Behav.* **10**, 1077–1086.

Beaton, J. R., Szlavko, A. J., Box, B. M. and Stevenson, J. A. F. (1964). Biological effects of anorectic and fat-mobilizing substances from rat urine. *Can. J. Physiol. Pharmacol* **42**, 657–664.

Bernard, C. (1878). La Science Expérimentale, Baillière, Paris. *In* "An Introduction to the Study of Experimental Medicine" by Claude Bernard [trans. by H. C. Green], 1957, p. 130. Dover, New York.

Blundell, J. E. (1975). Anorexic drugs, food intake and the study of obesity. *Nutrition, Lond.* **29**, 5–18.

Booth, D. A. (1972). Postabsorptively induced suppression of appetite and the energostatic control of feeding. *Physiol. Behav.* **9**, 199–202.

Booth, D. A., Toates, F. M. and Platt, S. V. (1976). Control system for hunger and its implications in animals and man. *In* "Hunger: Basic Mechanisms and Clinical Implications" (D. Novin, W. Wyrwicka and G. A. Bray, eds), pp. 127–143. Raven Press, New York.

Bray, G. A. (1974). Endocrine factors in the control of food intake. *Fed. Proc.,* **33**, 1140–1145.

Bray, G. A. and Campfield, L. A. (1975). Metabolic factors in the control of energy stores. *Metabolism* **24**, 99–117.

Brobeck, J. R. (1948). Food intake as a mechanism of temperature regulation. *Yale J. Biol. Med.* **20**, 545–552.

Brobeck, J. R. (1960). Regulation of feeding and drinking. *In* "Handbook of Physiology" Section I, Neurophysiology, Vol. II, (J. Field, ed.), pp. 1197–1206. American Physiological Society, Washington, D.C.

Brobeck, J. R., Larsson, S. and Reyes, E. (1956). A study of the electrical activity of the hypothalamic feeding mechanism. *J. Physiol., Lond.* **132**, 358–364.

Cabanac, M. (1971). Physiological role of pleasure. *Science, N.Y.* **173**, 1103–1107.

Cabanac, M. and Duclaux, R. (1970a). Obesity: absence of satiety aversion to sucrose. *Science, N.Y.* **168**, 496–497.

Cabanac, M. and Duclaux, R. (1970b). Specificity of internal signals in producing satiety for taste stimuli. *Nature, Lond.* **227**, 966–967.

Cabanac, M., Duclaux, R. and Spector, N. H. (1971). Sensory feedback regulation of body weight: is there a ponderostat? *Nature, Lond.* **229**, 125–127.

Cannon, W. B. and Washburn, A. L. (1912). An explanation of hunger. *Am. J. Physiol.* **29**, 441–454.

Carlson, L. D. and Hsieh, A. C. L. (1970). "Control of Energy Exchange". Macmillan, New York.

Corbit, J. D. and Stellar, E. (1964). Palatability, food intake and obesity in normal and hyperphagic rats. *J. comp. physiol. Psychol.* **58**, 63–67.

Davis, J. D., Campbell, C. S., Gallagher, R. J. and Zurakov, M. A. (1971). Disappearance of a humoral satiety factor during food deprivation. *J. comp. physiol. Psychol.* **75**, 476–482.

Davis, J. D., Collins, B. J. and Levine, M. W. (1976). Peripheral control of meal size: interaction of gustatory stimulation and postingestional feedback. *In* "Hunger: Basic Mechanisms and Clinical Implications" (D. Novin, W. Wyrwicka and G. A. Bray, eds), pp. 395–408. Raven Press, New York.

De Ruiter, L., Wiepkema, P. R. and Veening, J. G. (1974). Models of behaviour and the hypothalamus. *In* "Progress in Brain Research" Vol. 41, Integrative Hypothalamic Activity, pp. 481–507. Elsevier, Amsterdam.

Edholm, O. G., Fletcher, J. G., Widdowson, E. M. and McCance, R. A. (1955). The energy expenditure and food intake of individual men. *Br. J. Nutr.* **9**, 286–300.

Engelberg, J. (1966). Physiological regulation. The steady state. *Physiologist, Wash.* **9**, 69–88.

Epstein, A. N., Nicolaïdis, S. and Miselis, R. (1975). The glucoprivic control of food intake and the glucostatic theory of feeding behaviour. *In* "Neural Integration of Physiological Mechanisms and Behaviour" (G. J. Mogenson and F. R. Calaresu, eds), pp. 148–168. University of Toronto Press, Toronto.

Feigin, R. D., Beisel, W. R. and Wannemacher, R. W., Jr. (1971). Rhythmicity of plasma amino acids and relation to dietary intake. *Am. J. clin. Nutr.* **24**, 329–341.

Fishman, J. (1976). Appetite and sex hormones. *In* "Appetite and Food Intake" (T. Silverstone, ed.), pp. 207–218. Dahlem Konferenzen, West Berlin.

Fitzsimons, J. T. (1972). Thirst. *Physiol. Rev.* **52**, 468–561.

Fleming, D. G. (1969). Food intake in parabiotic rats. *Ann. N.Y. Acad. Sci.* **157**, 985–1003.

Frohman, L. A. (1971). The hypothalamus and metabolic control. *Pathol. A.* **1**, 353–372.

Guyton, A. C., Coleman, T. G. and Granger, H. J. (1972). Circulation: overall regulation. *A. Rev. Physiol.* **34**, 13–41.

von Haller, A. (1764). Fames et Sitis. *Elementa Physiol Corp. Humani* **6**, 164–187.

Hamilton, C. L. (1964). Rat's preference for high fat diets. *J. comp. physiol. Psychol.* **58**, 459–460.

Hamilton, C. L. (1975). Feeding and temperature. *In* "Neural Integration of Physiological Mechanisms and Behaviour" (G. J. Mogenson and F. R. Calaresu, eds), pp. 186–193. University of Toronto Press, Toronto.

Hardy, J. D. and Stolwijk, J. A. J. (1968). Regulation and control in physiology. *In* "Medical Physiology" (V. B. Mountcastle, ed.), pp. 591–610. Mosby, St. Louis.

Harper, A. E. (1976). Protein and amino acids in the regulation of food intake. *In* "Hunger: Basic Mechanisms and Clinical Implications" (D. Novin, W. Wyrwicka and G. A. Bray, eds), pp. 103–114. Raven Press, New York.

Harper, A. E. and Boyle, P. C. (1976). Nutrients and food intake. *In* "Appetite and Food Intake" (T. Silverstone, ed.), pp. 177–206. Dahlem Konferenzen, West Berlin.

Harper, A. E., Benevenga, N. J. and Wohlheuter, R. M. (1970). Effects of ingestion of disproportionate amounts of amino acids. *Physiol. Rev.* **50**, 428–558.

Hervey, G. R. (1969). Regulation of energy balance. *Nature, Lond.* **223**, 629–631.

Hervey, G. R. (1971). Physiological mechanisms for the regulation of energy balance. *Proc. Nutr. Soc.* **30**, 109–116.

Hill, R. G., Isn, E. C., Jones, W. W. and Archdeacon, J. W. (1952). The small intestine as a factor in regulation of eating. *Am. J. Physiol.* **170**, 201–205.

Hirsch, J. and Han, P. W. (1969). Cellularity of rat adipose tissue: effects of growth, starvation and obesity. *J. Lipid Res.* **10**, 77–82.

Hoebel, B. G. (1971). Feeding: neural control of intake. *A. Rev. Physiol.* **33**, 533–568.

Hoebel, B. G. and Teitelbaum, P. (1966). Weight regulation in normal and hypothalamic hyperphagic rats. *J. comp. physiol. Psychol.* **61**, 189–193.

Jacobs, H. L. (1962). Physical, metabolic and sensory components in the appetite for glucose. *Am. J. Physiol* **203**, 1043–1054.

Janowitz, H. D. and Grossman, M. E. (1949). Effect of variations in nutritive density on intake of food of dogs and rats. *Am. J. Physiol.* **158**, 184–193.

Kastin, A., Dempsey, G. L., LeBlanc, B., Dyster-Aas, K. and Schally, A. V. (1974). Extinction of an appetitive operant response after administration of MSH. *Horm. Behav.* **5**, 135–139.

Kennedy, G. C. (1950). The hypothalamic control of food intake in rats. *Proc. R. Soc., Lond.* (Biol.) **137**, 535–549.

Kennedy, G. C. (1953). The role of depot fat in the hypothalamic control of food intake in the rat. *Proc. R. Soc., Lond.* (Biol.) **140**, 578–592.

Kennedy, G. C. and Mitra, J. (1963). Hypothalamic control of energy balance and the reproductive cycle in the rat. *J. Physiol., Lond.* **166**, 395–407.

Kraly, F. S. and Blass, E. M. (1976). Increased feeding in rats in a low ambient temperature. *In* "Hunger: Basic Mechanisms and Clinical Implications" (D. Novin, W. Wyrwicka and G. A. Bray, eds), pp. 77–87. Raven Press, New York.

Le Magnen, J. (1971). Advances in studies on the physiological control and regulation of food intake. *In* "Progress in Physiological Psychology" (E. Stellar and J. M. Sprague, eds), Vol. 4, pp. 204–261. Academic Press, London and New York.

Le Magnen, J. (1975). Current concepts in energy balance. *In* "Neural Integration of Physiological Mechanisms and Behaviour" (G. J. Mogenson and F. R. Calaresu, eds), pp. 95–108. University of Toronto Press, Toronto.

MacKay, E. M., Calloway, J. W. and Barnes, R. H. (1940). Hyperalimentation in normal animals produced by protamine insulin. *J. Nutr.* **20**, 59–66.

McCleary, R. A. (1953). Taste and post-ingestion factors in specific-hunger behaviour. *J. comp. physiol. Psychol.* **46**, 411–421.

McFarland, D. J. (1970). Recent developments in the study of feeding and drinking in animals. *J. psychosom. Res.* **14**, 229–237.

McFarland, D. J. (1974a). "Motivational Control Systems Analysis". Academic Press, London and New York.

McFarland, D. J. (1974b). Time-sharing as a behavioral phenomenon. *Adv. Study Behav.* **5**, 201–225.

Marshall, N. B., Barrnett, R. J. and Mayer, J. (1955). Hypothalamic lesions in goldthioglucose-injected mice. *Proc. Soc. exp. Biol. Med.* **90**, 240–244.

Mayer, J. (1952). The glucostatic theory of regulation of food intake and the problem of obesity. *Bull. New Engl. Med. Cent.* **14**, 43–49.

Mayer, J. (1955). Regulation of energy intake and body weight, the glucostatic theory and the lipostatic hypothesis. *Ann. N.Y. Acad. Sci.* **63**, 15–43.

Mayer, J. and Thomas, D. W. (1967). Regulation of food intake and obesity. *Science, N.Y.* **156**, 328–337.

Mellinkoff, S. M., Frankland, M., Boyle, D. and Greipel, M. (1956). Relationship between serum amino acid concentration and fluctuations in appetite. *J. appl. Physiol.* **8**, 535–538.

Mickelsen, O., Takahashi, H. and Craig, C. (1955). Experimental obesity. I. Production of obesity in rats by feeding high fat diets. *J. Nutr.* **57**, 541–554.

Mogenson, G. J. (1974). Changing views of the role of the hypothalamus in the control of ingestive behaviour. *In* "Recent Studies of Hypothalamic Function" (K. Lederis and K. Cooper, eds), pp. 268–293. Karger, Basel.

Mogenson, G. J. (1976). Neural mechanisms of hunger: current status and future prospects. *In* "Hunger: Basic Mechanisms and Clinical Implications" (D. Novin, W. Wyrwicka and G. A. Bray, eds), pp. 473–485. Raven Press, New York.

Nicolaïdis, S. (1969). Early systemic responses to orogastric stimulation in the regulation of food and water balance: functional and electrophysiological data. *Ann. N.Y. Acad. Sci.* **157**, 1176–1203.

Nicolaïdis, S., Petit, M. and Polonowski, J. (1974). Etude du rapport entre la régulation de la masse adipeuse corporelle et la composition lipidique de ses centres régulateurs. *C.R. hebd. Séanc. Acad. Sci., (D) Paris* **278**, 1393–1396.

Nisbett, R. E. (1972). Hunger, obesity and the ventromedial hypothalamus. *Psychol. Rev.* **79**, 433–453.

Novin, D., Vanderweele, D. A. and Rezek, M. (1973). Infusion of 2-deoxy-D-glucose into the hepatic-portal system causes eating: evidence for peripheral glucoreceptors. *Science, N.Y.* **181**, 858–860.

Novin, D., Gonzalez, M. F. and Sanderson, J. D. (1976). Paradoxical increased feeding following glucose infusions in recovered lateral rats. *Am. J. Physiol.* **230**: 1084–1089.

Oatley, K. (1972). "Brain Mechanisms and Mind". Dutton, New York.

Oatley, K. (1973). Simulation and theory of thirst. *In* "The Neuropsychology of Thirst: New Findings and Advances in Concepts" (A. N. Epstein, H. R. Kissileff and E. Stellar, eds), pp. 199–223. Winston, Washington, D.C.

Oomura, Y., Ooyama, H., Naka, F., Yamamoto, T., Ono, T. and Kobayashi, N. (1969). Some stochastical patterns of single unit discharges in the cat hypothalamus under chronic conditions. *Ann. N.Y. Acad. Sci.* **157**, 666–689.

Ota, K. and Yokoyama, A. (1967). Body weight and food consumption of lactating rats nursing various sizes of litters. *J. Endocr.* **38**, 263–268.

Paintal, A. S. (1954). A study of gastric stretch receptors: their role in the peripheral mechanism of saturation of hunger and thirst. *J. Physiol., Lond.* **126**, 255–270.

Panksepp, L. (1973). Reanalysis of feeding patterns in the rat. *J. comp. physiol. Psychol.* **82**, 78–94.

Panksepp, J. (1974). The ventromedial hypothalamus and metabolic control of feeding behavior. *Fed. Proc.* **33**, 1150–1165.

Panksepp, J. (1975). Metabolic hormones and regulation of feeding: a reply to Woods, Decke and Vasselli. *Psychol. Rev.* **82**, 158–164.

Panksepp, J. and Booth, D. A. (1971). Decreased feeding after injection of aminoacids into the hypothalamus. *Nature, Lond.* **233**, 341–342.

Panksepp, J. and Nance, D. M. (1972). Insulin, glucose and hypothalamic regulation of feeding. *Physiol. Behav.* **9**, 447–451.

Peck, J. W. (1976). Situational determinants of the body weights defended by normal rats and rats with hypothalamic lesions. *In* "Hunger: Basic Mechanisms and Clinical Implications" (D. Novin, W. Wyrwicka and G. A. Bray, eds), pp. 297–311. Raven Press, New York.

Pfaffmann, C. (1956). Taste and smell. *A. Rev. Psychol.* **7**, 391–408.

Powley, T. L. and Keesey, R. E. (1970). Relationship of body weight to the lateral hypothalamic feeding syndrome. *J. comp. physiol. Psychol.* **70**, 25–36.

Richter, C. P. (1942–43). Total self-regulatory functions in animals and human beings. *Harvey Lectures* **38**, 63–103.

Rozin, P. (1976). The psychobiological and cultural basis of food selection. *In* "Appetite and Food Intake" (T. Silverstone, ed.), pp. 285–312. Dahlem Konferenzen, West Berlin.

Russek, M. (1963). Participation of hepatic glucoreceptors in the control of intake of food. *Nature, Lond.* **197**, 79–80.

Russek, M. (1971). Hepatic receptors and the neurophysiological mechanisms controlling feeding behavior. *In* "Neurosciences Research" Vol. 4. (S. Ehrenpreis and O. C. Solnitsky, eds), pp. 214–282. Academic Press, New York and London.

Russek, M. (1975). Current hypotheses in the control of feeding behavior. *In* "Neural Integration of Physiological Mechanisms and Behaviour" (G. J. Mogenson and F. R. Calaresu, eds), pp. 128–147. University of Toronto Press, Toronto.

Russek, M., Stevenson, J. A. F. and Mogenson, G. J. (1968). Anorexigenic effects of adrenaline, amphetamine and FMSIA. *Can. J. Physiol. Pharmacol.* **46**, 635–638.

Russell, P. J. D. and Mogenson, G. J. (1975). Drinking and feeding induced by jugular and portal infusions of 2–deoxy-D-glucose. *Am. J. Physiol.* **229**, 1014–1018.

Schachter, S. (1971a). Some extraordinary facts about obese humans and rats. *Am. Psychol.* **26**, 129–144.

Schachter, S. (1971b). "Emotion, Obesity and Crime". Academic Press, New York and London.

Schally, A. V., Redding, T. W., Lucien, H. W. and Meyer, J. (1967). Enterogastrone inhibits feeding by fasted mice. *Science, N.Y.* **157**, 210–211.

Schulman, J. L., Carleton, J. L., Whitney, G. and Whitehorn, J. C. (1957). Effect of glucagon on food intake and body weight in man. *J. appl. Physiol.* **11**, 419–421.

Scott, E. M. and Quint, E. (1946). Self selection of diet. III. Appetites for B vitamins. *J. Nutr.* **32**, 285–291.

Sharma, K. N. (1967). Receptor mechanisms in the alimentary tract: their excitations and functions. *In* "Handbook of Physiology", Section 6, Alimentary Canal, Vol. I, Control of Food and Water Intake (C. F. Code, ed.), pp. 225–238. American Physiological Society, Washington, D.C.

Simpson, C. W. and Dicara, L. V. (1973). Estradiol inhibition of catecholamine elicited eating in the female rat. *Pharmacol. Biochem. Behav.* **1**, 413–419.

Smith, G. P., Gibbs, J. and Young, R. C. (1974). Cholecystokinin and intestinal satiety. *Fed. Proc.* **33**, 1146–1149.

Snowdon, C. T. (1970). Gastrointestinal, sensory and motor control of food intake. *J. comp. physiol. Psychol.* **71**, 68–76.

Snowdon, C. T. (1975). Production of satiety with small intraduodenal infusions in the rat. *J. comp. physiol. Psychol.* **88**, 231–238.

Steffens, A. B. (1969). Blood glucose and FFA levels in relation to the meal pattern in the normal rat and the VMH hypothalamic lesioned rat. *Physiol. Behav.* **4**, 212–225.

Stevenson, J. A. F. (1954). Diet and survival. *In* "Cold Injury", Transactions of the Third Conference (M. I. Ferrer, ed.), pp. 165–188. Josiah Macy Jr. Foundation, New York.

Stevenson, J. A. F. (1964a). Current reassessment of the relative functions of various hypothalamic mechanisms in the regulation of water intake. *In* "Thirst", Proceedings of the First International Symposium on Thirst in the Regulation of Body Water (M. J. Wayner, ed.), pp. 553–567. Pergamon, New York.

Stevenson, J. A. F. (1964b). The hypothalamus in the regulation of energy and water balance. *Physiologist* **7**, 305–318.

Stevenson, J. A. F. (1967). Central mechanisms controlling water intake. *In* "Handbook of Physiology", Section 6, Alimentary Canal, Vol. I, Control of Food and Water Intake (C. F. Code, ed.), pp. 173–190. American Physiological Society, Washington, D.C.

Stevenson, J. A. F. and Franklin, C. (1970). Effects of ACTH and corticosteroids in the regulation of food and water intake. *Prog. Brain Res.* **32**, 141–151.

Strominger, J. L. and Brobeck, J. R. (1953). A mechanism of regulation of food intake. *Yale J. Biol. Med.* **25**, 383–390.

Sudsaneh, S. and Mayer, J. (1959). Relation of metabolic events to gastric contractions in the rat. *Am. J. Physiol.* **197**, 269–273.

Toates, F. M. and Booth, D. A. (1974). Control of food intake by energy supply. *Nature, Lond.* **251**, 710–711.

Vanderweele, D. A., Novin, D. and Rezek, M. (1974). Duodenal or hepatic-portal glucose perfusion: evidence for duodenally-based satiety. *Physiol. Behav.* **12**, 467–473.

Van Sommers, P. (1972). "The Biology of Behaviour". Wiley, New York.

Wade, G. N. (1972). Interaction between estradiol and growth hormone in control of food intake in weanling rats. *J. comp. physiol. Psychol.* **86**, 359–362.

Walker, D. W. and Remley, N. R. (1970). The relationships among percentage body weight loss, circulating free fatty acids and consumatory behavior in rats. *Physiol. Behav.* **5**, 301–309.

Waterman, T. H. (1968). Systems theory and biology—view of a biologist. *In* "Systems Theory and Biology" (M. D. Mesarovic, ed.), pp. 1–37. Springer-Verlag, New York.

Wiepkema, P. R. (1971). Positive feedbacks at work during feeding. *Behaviour* **39**, 266–273.

Woods, S. C., Decke, E. and Vasselli, J. R. (1974). Metabolic hormones and regulation of body weight. *Psychol. Rev.* **81**, 26–43.

Young, P. T. (1959). The role of affective processes in learning and motivation. *Psychol. Rev.* **66**, 104–125.

2

*Getting Models off the Ground**

J. S. ARMSTRONG
Commonwealth Scientific and Industrial Research Organisation, Canberra, Australia

I. Systems Analysis

Learning a new skill can be an exciting experience. It can also be a frustrating one. The traditional method of learning through observing an expert at work has its drawbacks. For it is just as difficult for an expert to make fundamental mistakes as it is for the beginner to avoid making them. Fortunately skills can be improved by manual and mental effort.

One way of attacking problems is to use the "systems approach". This paper is an introduction to the practical side of the approach. The main concern is with the initial stages of model building, hence the title. The systems approach works as follows. A model of the problem (system) under investigation is defined for purposes of discussion and experiment. This can be a scale model, as used with wind tunnels, or it may be in a completely abstract form such as a series of mathematical equations.

Models are used in problem solving and decision making in two ways. Firstly, the formal definition of the system to be studied is conducive to clear thinking and improved communication and, in many cases, gives sufficient insight into the system to indicate lines of action. Secondly, the model can be used as a basis for experiments which will predict the response of the real system. This technique is known as simulation and is particularly useful for those problems which, due to their complexity or nonlinearity, are not amenable to direct analysis, or which contain elements that are subject to random variation. It is, of course, only one of a band of techniques which have arisen with the growth of the discipline known as Systems Analysis. The general adoption of the systems approach to problem solving† has been delayed, mainly by difficulties in model

* An edited version of Armstrong (1972) reprinted with permission.
†In the context of agricultural systems, at least.

definition due to a lack of data, and by the difficulty of validating the model.

In the context of systems analysis, a system is defined as an arrangement of component parts which together perform some function. Further, the relations between the components can be functions of time and other external variables and of the values of the components. In other words, the system is dynamic. From this it follows that for all except the very simple systems, the definitions of the system response to all the variations in component values is a formidable task.

II. The Aim

The first step in model building is to define the purpose and scope of the model in relation to the overall problem. This will determine the scale or level of the model. Although the real system includes all levels of processes and quantities, the model will be an abstraction to some particular level. The choice of the level then determines the components which are to be included in the model, and it also indicates the relevant forcing functions (inputs) and the data required for them.

It is at this point that the quantities in the system will be seen to fall into several distinct groups. Some, like hours of daylight, will be variable, but will be known accurately. Others, while having a constant value, will be known only approximately. Other variables will be subject to random variation and this randomness may be an essential part of the model. As a general rule however, in the initial stages, the model should incline towards simplicity and reasonableness rather than complexity and realism. The introduction of stochastic (random) variables at the beginning will only obscure the main aim which is to construct a feasible model.

III. Draft and Block Diagrams

The next stage, assuming a simulation model is to be used, is to draw up a draft diagram of the model. This will show the basic quantities and the processes by which they are connected.

The thing to avoid at this stage is to call a halt to modelling while everyone busies themselves recording measurements on all the unknown processes. Instead, the processes should be defined in an empirical way using the data and estimates of people experienced with the problem. Then translate the block diagram into a computer program and run this version of the model. After correcting any gross errors, the model should be run with variations in those parameters considered to be dominant. The results will show how responsive the model is to these changes and this will strengthen or throw doubt on your initial assessment. In any case you should now concentrate on those parts of the model which appear to have the most effect. It may mean expansion of the block diagram, a literature search or the setting up of field and laboratory trials. The point is that the model is refined, and research resources allocated, only as and where the model is shown to be inadequate for its purpose.

IV. Requirements for Modelling

The application of systems analysis techniques is itself a problem in resource allocation. There is some need to evolve special skills and to use specialized equipment.

A. *The Team Approach*

The scope of most models requires a co-operative effort by a team. Whilst a group of experts may be necessary to cover all aspects of a problem, there is also an enhancement effect of working in a team because interaction in discussion plays an important part in the integration of the components of the system.

Projects handled by teams do require resources to be allocated to the organizational aspects. These are mainly concerned with communication. There is a definite need to issue regular reports on the projects and for formal contact between groups doing similar work.

B. *Special Equipment*

There are two categories to be considered; equipment to aid the modelling phase and equipment for the field or laboratory.

Special equipment for the modelling phase means *computers*. The minimum requirements are easy access to the computing system and the availability of a high level programming language such as Fortran or Algol. There are many desirable extras. For example, special purpose programming languages have their place. Simscript is a powerful simulation language designed for discrete applications. It is particularly valuable in problems where the scheduling and cancelling of future events has a complex structure. For the user whose problems are defined in terms of differential equations, languages such as CSMP or Dynamo are suitable. The beginner is advised to use the local common language which will normally be Fortran or Algol. The main reason for this advice is the ease in obtaining instruction and debugging facilities. Some specialist languages are restricted to a particular computer manufacturer, and limitations of this sort can inhibit communication between groups using different computing systems.

Then there are special input–output devices which enable the user to communicate directly with his model. Using graphical output, a simulation model can be manipulated in the same way as an ordinary laboratory experiment. The user can view the effect of different parameter settings in the model or of different model layouts, and thus gain insight into the overall model behaviour.

As a result of initial work in the modelling phase it is frequently found that there are certain key elements in the model. At the same time it is found that these key elements are lacking good data. This leads to further experiments and it may also require special equipment. One of the usual requirements is to sample a particular variation intensively. This could involve *automatic data collecting.*

V. A Developing Model

There is always a danger when looking at the final production that the stages leading up to it will be discounted. It is not unknown for the early practitioners to do this, probably out of a sense of guilt that their early efforts were (as it now appears) so crude. This effect is particularly relevant with models which are bound to pass through many revisions in their development.

The following section describes the development of a particular process in a model of a grazing system.

A. *Eating*

A model of a grazing system (Freer *et al.,* 1970; Christian *et al.,* 1972) has been developed sporadically since 1967. One particular and important process is the reduction in the available pasture by the sheep eating it.

In the original model the only representation of pasture was by dry material. Intake was simply proportional to availability until an upper limit to intake was reached.

In the next development, rain produced green material, and as this aged it passed through a succession of digestibility classes until a residual quantity was added to the pool of dry material. At first, the intake of food was calculated from the total material available and the mean digestibility of the selected diet. To predict the latter value, the proportion of green in the diet was calculated as a function of the production of green in the available food, and the mean digestibility was the weighted mean of the components, biased upwards in proportion to the amounts available to allow for selective grazing. However, the predicted proportion of green in the diet was insensitive to the absolute amounts of green and dry if these changed in proportion.

To overcome this, the sheep were considered to be satisfying their appetite successively from green and dry material. A change in the intake of green with respect to its availability was proportional not only to its availability but also to the extent to which the animals' potential intake of green had not already been satisfied. Integrating this function gives the potential intake of green, and this value was taken from the appetite of the animals before calculating the potential intake of dry in the same way. The actual amounts eaten were calculated by multiplying the potential values by the digestibility coefficients.

The most recent development is to allow for both reduction in hunger and reduction in availability during each day's grazing. The equations describing the eating process are given in more detail by Freer *et al.*, (1970) and in a companion paper (Armstrong, 1971).

B. *Implications*

There are two lessons which emerge from this and similar work. They concern relations and data.

Consider, first, the *relations* used in this part of the model. As our experience in modelling increased, and as we found the proposed equations had deficiencies, so the equations were refined. We have developed this part of the model from a simple description to the point where the mathematical equations approach biological reality.

Secondly, although the supporting *data* were neither detailed, generalized, nor precise, that did not impede model development. We will almost certainly find it necessary to undertake experiments to obtain better data for these relationships, but before we do the need must be seen to exist.

References

Armstrong, J. S. (1971). Modelling a grazing system. *Proc. Ecol. Soc. Aust.* **6**, 194–202.

Armstrong, J. S. (1972). Getting models off the ground. *Proc. Aust. Soc. Anim. Prod.* **9**, 104–111.

Christian, K. R., Armstrong, J. S., Donnelly, J. R., Davidson, J. L. and Freer, M. (1972). Optimization of a grazing management system. *Proc. Aust. Soc. Anim. Prod.* **9**, 124–129.

Freer, M., Davidson, J. L., Armstrong, J. S. and Donnelly, J. R. (1970). Simulation of summer grazing. *Proc. 11th Int. Grassl. Cong., Surfers Paradise,* 913.

Reading List

Anderson, J. R. (1974). Simulation: methodology and application in agricultural economics. *Review of Marketing and Agricultural Economics.*

Christian, K. R., Freer, M., Donnelly, F. R., Davidson, J. L. and Armstrong, J. S. (1978). "Simulation of Grazing Systems." Pudoc, Wageningen, Netherlands.

Dent, J. B. and Anderson, J. R. (1971). "Systems Analysis in Agricultural Management". Wiley, Sydney.

Emshoff, J. R. and Sisson, R. L. (1970). "Design and Use of Computer Simulation Models". Macmillan, New York.

Forrester, J. W. (1968). "Principles of Systems" 2nd Prelim. Edn. Wright-Allen, Cambridge, Mass.

Gordon, G. (1969). "System Simulation". Prentice-Hall, New Jersey.

Jeffers, J. N. R. (1971). "Mathematical Models in Ecology". Blackwell, Oxford.

Naylor, T. H. (1969). "The Design of Computer Simulation Experiments". Duke University Press, Durham. N.C.

Naylor, T. H., Balintfy, J. L., Burdick, D. S. and Chu, K. (1966). "Computer Simulation Techniques". Wiley, New York.

Patten, B. C. (1971). "Systems Analysis and Simulation in Ecology". Academic Press, New York and London.

Ramo, S. (1969). "Cure for Chaos". D. McKay, New York.

de Wit, C. T. and Goudriaan, J. (1974). "Simulation of Ecological Processes". Centre for Agricultural Publications and Documentation, Wageningen, Netherlands.

Wright, A. (1970). Systems research and grazing systems management-oriented simulation. *In* "Bulletin of Farm Management, No. 4". University of New England, Armidale, Australia.

3

Computer Modelling of Hunger for Purposes of Teaching and Research

JOHN B. THURMOND AND ARTHUR O. CROMER
Psychology Department, University of Louisville, Louisville, Kentucky. U.S.A.

In the typical class-related laboratory experiment, the student acquires an isolated experience with the effects of variables operating under one rigid set of conditions. Recent approaches have been developed which use computer models in order to expand the student's experience to include the entire range of conditions in the cause-and-effect relationships associated with a particular phenomenon under study (Main, 1972; Shure and Brainerd, 1975; Stout, 1975; Thurmond and Cromer, 1972, 1975). One system which permits the implementation of this approach is the Louisville Experiment Simulation System (LESS) Compared with other systems, it is moderately complex. This system permits the instructor or researcher, without programming knowledge, to prepare a computer model that can be called up by students or research planners as a simulated experiment.

I. Teaching

The main purpose of LESS as a general system is to permit instructors in any discipline to use data-generating computer models in their classes as an aid to learning the concepts of good research strategy. The data generated by a model used in class are not intended to replace the traditional methods of teaching, e.g. class lectures, demonstrations and experiments. Rather, the computer-generated data allow students an experience of the phenomena dealt with in the course that would not otherwise be possible. The use of data-generating models to supplement course content, demonstrations and laboratory experiments, improves instruction in at least four ways.

(i) Computer models simulate different experimental or other situations without the need of expensive equipment and without using valuable time in the class or laboratory.

(ii) They enhance the student's understanding of the content of the course by permitting him to conduct many experiments in different areas covered by the subject matter of the course.

(iii) They teach the student to use good scientific research strategy by putting him in a situation where he must formulate hypotheses in order to obtain meaningful results and where he must examine results carefully in order to draw meaningful conclusions.

(iv) Finally, they increase motivation by involving the student in an active learning process in which he interacts with the computer model in order to understand the phenomena under study.

The student is introduced to the problem area by reading appropriate background material. He is then presented with a list of potentially important variables in the problem area and told to choose how he would collect relevant data if he could make choices among the variables. The student selects the variables he wishes to investigate and their specific levels. The computer model calculates the results, presenting the data as if the specified experiment has just been run. The data produced by the computer contain random errors, as would be the case if a real experiment had been conducted; thus, the results of an experiment run on the computer vary, even if an experiment is repeated. Along with this output, the programs give an "experimental cost" based on the parameter values chosen. The student then may ask for summary statistics and the error of this run as compared to the preceding run, to aid in analysis.

By combining the simulations with live experiments, where the emphasis is on the techniques necessary for running the experiments and collecting the data, a balanced coverage is provided for the entire range of research training. Since the variables that are specified for conditions in the data-generating model are the same as those covered by the content of the course, the student can, if he desires, replicate his laboratory experience by specifying the conditions of his experiment to the computer and then go on to investigate many other conditions as well. The conditions under which the variables are to have effects are given to the computer, and the data are generated all in a matter of minutes.

II. The Modelling System

In order to build a computer model such as the one in the system on human obesity, all that is needed is a description of the cause and effect relationships which relate changes in the variables under study to typical experimental data.

This does not mean that one must understand the processes by which the variables control feeding; one only needs to know what the data should look like, given certain conditions. With the modular system of LESS, one need not understand computer programming in order to build a data-generating model and to use it in teaching or in research. A non-programmer may build up and revise his own set of models for his course (or his research). Since new models can be added easily or old ones removed, a simple model can be constructed to accompany a laboratory experiment or to account for a set of data, replaced later with a better one or left intact while new models are added.

LESS is a set of four core programs (LESS, LESSIN, LESPUT, and LESTES) and a data file (LESDAT). The data file, LESDAT, can be cleared by running LESSIN. Then, after carefully planning a data-generating model, a session of 10–30 minutes using LESPUT is required to add the model to the system. It may then be tested using LESTES, or deleted by LESSIN in order to make major changes by re-entering the model. The user is only aware of one program, LESS, which he calls up and runs. This main program calls up whichever model the user selects by chaining to the appropriate model program.

A. *General Model Builder*

An important feature of the system is the ability for a non-programmer to add a model to the system using the general model builder (GMB). In a second mode, the author is expected to write his own program to generate data. In both modes, the LESPUT program asks a series of identical questions about general characteristics of the model, such as how many variables there will be, what values will be "legal" or recognized for each variable, etc. When the program reaches the point where it begins asking for values that will be used as effects or costs in the data generator, in Mode 1 the questions are very simple. The author is asked how many costs and how many effects values there will be and then is asked to give them. From there on, the two modes are nearly identical. In the second or general model builder mode, the questions are more elaborate. If the model can be expressed as the sum of a weighted combination of terms (the GMB will accept up to a seven-way interaction) plus a constant, then it is easier to use the general model builder. However, if the model requires a series of logical branches of varying complexity and depth, it is more efficient, both in execution time and computer core requirements, to write the model program. An advantage of writing the model is that almost anything can be done before returning to the main program. The main program serves the function of accepting variable specifications from the user, checking them for legality and proper form, and passing the "sanitized" specifications to the model. It also can output simple statistics (mean, variance and correlations) before cycling again to accept more specifications or start another model.

B. *Variables*

The system handles a number of different types of variables. Each variable can be controlled or randomized by the author of the model to have from no effect to a great effect. In addition, a cost function may be used to approximate the cost of running particular variables or combinations of variables.

Parameter variables are general variables, such as number of cases, sample size, number of time periods, etc. which determine how many values of a dependent variable will be generated in one run.

Discrete variables must take on whole number values only, where the number may just be a label of a category, such as 1 = male, 2 = female, or may have more meaning, such as 1 = below \$5000, 2 = \$5000–\$10 000, 3 = \$10 000–\$20 000, etc.

Continuous variables may be used in an author-written model program directly or may be broken up into discrete sections before use.

X variables are unknown variables which may represent one or more specific variables important to the model which the students are to discover, or may be any variable(s) the author did not include in the original model.

Secondary variables are the specific variables mentioned above which are important to the model but were not originally revealed to the student until he had examined the relationships among the initial set of variables.

Dependent variables represent the results of the measurements or observations on the simulated experiment.

III. Obesity Model

The computer model of human obesity that was constructed with the system and presented here was designed purely for instructional purposes. It is not intended to be an authoritative representation of the processes underlying human obesity, although the variables and effects it employs are based on findings reported in the literature which apparently are related to feeding in human beings. Nor was it intended for use in research, although rigorous models of hunger could be constructed and added to the system for the purpose of evaluating the differences between outcomes produced by the model and empirical findings. The system presently in use contains a number of different models, each of which simulates a different phenomenon. Some of the models have relatively few variables and are conceptually rather simple; others have many variables and are conceptually quite complex. Each was created to meet a particular tutorial need. The model of human obesity was added to the system in order to encourage the student to begin to do some thinking on his own, i.e. to formulate hypotheses and deduce outcomes based on his knowledge of obesity and the factors that ought to influence it. The area of human obesity was chosen for simulation because it is rich in factors which are likely to be familiar to the student, including genetic, endocrine, environmental, and psychological variables related to human obesity; thus, the student is provided initially with a framework for approaching a research area in which the possibility of some success is maximized.

In order to use computer models effectively as aids in learning the concepts of good research strategy, information must be provided to the student concerning the relevant problem area and the variables in the model, and information must be provided to the instructor explaining the effects of the variables. On the pages that follow, the information given to the student is presented first, followed by the instructor's information and samples of computer output based on actual simulation runs.

The Student's Side of Model Use

A. *Characteristics of the Problem Description*

The problem description is relatively brief, it puts the area of investigation into a meaningful context for the student, it is informative with regard to the variables actually contained in the model to be used in studying the problems, and it motivates the student to want to ask questions about the problem and hence seek solutions to his questions. Concerning this last principle, enough information is given in the problem description to permit the student to develop some meaningful questions concerning the effects of the variables in the model, but then he should be encouraged to find the answers to his questions by stating hypotheses relevant to his questions, deducing the effects the variables in the model must have in order to support his hypotheses, designing one or more experiments which manipulate the variables of the model in such a way as to provide a meaningful test of his hypotheses, and finally, examining the results of his investigation carefully in order to determine whether in fact his hypotheses should be accepted or rejected. Our problem description for the obesity model is given in the next Section. As an alternative to providing a problem description, readings in the student's textbook or in the literature can be assigned to familiarize him with the problem.

B. *Student's Problem Description for the Obesity Model in LESS*

There are many stresses on the obese person in our society. Part of the stress is due to the fact that overeating, and hence overweight, is associated with a lack of "will power." As a result, the obese individual may feel ashamed of his inability to control his overeating. The guilt engendered in the obese person by these attitudes of society may cause him to worry about his performance and behaviour more than normal. By being sure that he performs on tasks as well or better than the average person, and by being careful to behave correctly according to the *mores* of society, he counteracts any negative attitudes that society may have concerning his will power. In support of this line of reasoning it might be noted that fat people, when interviewed, typically will not give accurate reports about how much they eat or exercise. Indeed, chronic obese patients who have been fed everything that, in interviews, they admitted to eating daily, all steadily lost weight. This is not surprising since in three or four such self-report studies, fat people have reported eating considerably less than normal people report.

Why do obese people eat more than those of normal weight? It is an interesting observation that obese people have a relatively easy time fasting when they are not near food but a difficult time in its presence. This may be because they experience some confusion in deciding whether or not they are hungry. If so, then the obese person may think he is hungry when food is nearby though he may not be hungry at all. This idea may not be as far fetched as it sounds. We tend to think of hunger as an unmistakable feeling that arises because of the state of our body, states such as an empty stomach and low blood sugar. But it could be that the feeling of hunger does not automatically occur with these body states. It could be rather that people learn to attach the label "hunger" to certain body feelings and behave accordingly. As a consequence, if a person learns to attach "hunger" to body feelings which in fact do not correspond to the need for food, he will eat whether he is hungry or not.

The results of several different kinds of experiments indicate that obese people do have trouble associating hunger with the appropriate body states. It has been found, for example, that the normal-sized person is likely to report hunger when his stomach contracts and is likely to say that he does not feel hungry when his stomach is quiescent. The obese person, on the other hand, shows little correspondence between gastric motility and self-report of hunger. Whether or not the fat person describes himself as being hungry seems to have almost nothing to do with what is going on in his stomach. But, it may be that this is only true if we are dealing with an empty stomach.

What happens when the stomach is full? Dr Stanley Schachter and his associates at Columbia University designed an experiment to find out. The experiment was disguised as a study of taste, and they asked their subjects (normal and obese) to do without the meal (lunch or dinner) that preceded the experiment. When they arrived, half the subjects were fed roast beef sandwiches; the other half were fed nothing. Then, all subjects participated in the "taste" experiment. Each one was seated in front of five bowls of crackers, asked to judge the taste of the crackers and told, "taste as many or as few of the crackers of each type as you want in making your judgments; the important thing is that your rating be as accurate as possible." It comes as no surprise that the normal weight subjects ate considerably fewer crackers when their stomachs were full of roast beef sandwiches than when their stomachs were empty. The obese subjects, however, ate as much, in fact slightly more, when their stomachs were full as when they were empty.

What about other things like blood sugar and states of fear that ought to be related to hunger? It has been demonstrated that both the state of fear and the injection of adrenalin will inhibit gastric motility and increase blood sugar, and that both of these physiological changes are associated with low hunger. It turns out that while these manipulations do affect the amounts eaten by normal weight subjects, they have no effect at all on the amounts eaten by obese subjects.

In addition to the differences between obese and normal-sized people concerning hunger and body states, there appear to be some other rather odd differences. In one experiment, subjects were asked to look at slides which presented an object or a word. After a number of such slides, each of which was exposed for five seconds, the subjects were asked to recall what they saw. Fat subjects recalled more objects than the normal subjects did. In another experiment, it was found that the obese are better at proof-reading than normal subjects as long as there are no distractions. However, the results are different if the subjects are asked to correct proof while listening to recorded tapes that have been prepared to grip a subject's attention, and therefore distract him. Under these distracting conditions, the performance of the obese subjects has been found to be considerably worse than that of normals.

In another experiment, the subjects were led to believe that they were taking part in a study of thinking. On the table at which the subjects sat were a variety of objects among which was a large tin of shelled cashew nuts. The subjects did their thinking under two conditions of illumination: in one condition the table was illuminated by an unshaded table lamp with a 40-watt bulb, whereas in the other condition the lamp was shaded and contained a $7\frac{1}{2}$-watt red bulb. When the dim $7\frac{1}{2}$-watt light was on, the normal subjects ate 25 g of nuts and the obese subjects ate 17 g. Under the other condition, where the brighter 40–watt light was on, the normal subjects ate 20 g of nuts and the obese subjects ate 37 g.

Normal-sized people and obese people seem to approach food differently when they have to work for it. To get food, subjects in one experiment had to use their index finger to pull for 12 minutes on a ring that was attached by a wire to a seven-pound (3·2 kg) weight. The subject did not get something to eat every time he successfully pulled the ring. Instead, in a way similar to the pay-off of a slot machine, a subject received a quarter of a sandwich, on the average, for every 50 pulls of the ring. To encourage his subjects to work, the experimenter placed the sandwich the subject would eventually get (if he kept pulling the weight) beside the subject. Sometimes the sandwich was covered in a transparent wrap, but just as often, the sandwiches were wrapped in white, non-transparent shelf paper. All subjects were fed something before they started to work; half of them were given a quarter of a very good sandwich, while the remaining subjects ate a roughly equivalent portion of plain white bread. The normal subjects seemed to take little encouragement from anything the experimenter did, like setting the sandwich beside them while they were pulling on the weight, and pulled about 400 responses regardless. The obese subjects pulled less than the normal weight subjects without any of these encouraging kinds of factors but pulled more than the normals if they had them.

Generally speaking, however, obese subjects do not seem willing to work as hard as normal weight subjects in order to get something to eat. Subjects in another experiment were asked to sit at the experimenter's desk and fill out a variety of personality tests and questionnaires. Besides the usual stuff on a desk, there was also a bag of almonds. After the subject was seated at the desk, the experimenter left him alone with his tests and questionnaires for 15 minutes. But, as she left, the experimenter helped herself to a nut, and invited the subject to do the same. Under one condition of the experiment, the nuts had shells on them; there were no shells on the nuts in the other condition. Only about half of the normal weight subjects ate any nuts at all. However, if you look at the normal-sized subject who did eat the nuts, it did not seem to matter if the nuts had shells on them because the number of normal-sized subjects who ate the nuts when they had to shell them was the same as the number who ate the nuts with no shells. Almost all of the obese subjects ate the nuts on the desk when they had no shells, but only one fat subject ate the nuts when they had not been shelled.

Dr Schachter points out that there seem to be astonishing parallels between the plump people we have been discussing and animals who have had a lesion made in the ventromedial nucleus of their hypothalamus. If bilateral lesions are made in these hypothalmic nuclei, the result is an animal that will eat prodigious amounts of food – and the effect has been demonstrated with mice, rats, cats, monkeys, rabbits, goats, dogs and sparrows. The lesioned animal also shows emotional behaviour that is markedly different from normal. Does this have any direct relation to obesity in humans? There is at least one case study suggesting that it does – a lady who had a precisely localized neoplasm that destroyed her ventromedial hypothalamus. Dr Schachter says that, "she ate immense amounts of food, as much as 10 000 calories a day, grew impressively fat and was apparently a wildly emotional creature given to frequent outbursts of laughing, crying and rage." Does this mean that obese people have a lesion in their hypothalamus? Most probably not. More likely, if their obesity is related to hypothalamic function, then perhaps the ventromedial nucleus is not as functionally active as it should be. Some evidence that might be used to support this point of view comes from examinations of the hypothalamus of a strain of mice that grow to be very fat due to a gene they inherit from their parents. Even though these genetically obese mice are as fat as any hypothalamically lesioned rat or any obese person you will ever hope to see, if you look at their hypothalami you will see nothing to indicate that they are different from mice who grow to normal size. However, it is entirely possible that the hypothalamus of the genetically obese mouse could look perfectly normal and still contain a functionally quiescent ventromedial nucleus.

Some striking parallels apparently exist between obese people and obese lesioned hypothalamic animals. When left alone, the lesioned rats show little emotion and are quite lethargic, but when handled they are vicious. In two experiments with humans, the emotional behaviour of the subjects indicated that analogous differences seem to exist between obese and normal people. In one experiment, fear was manipulated in the subjects by threat of painful electric shock; of course, this was only a threat, and none of the subjects ever received a painful shock. Even so, when the subjects were asked to rate the degree of their emotional reactions to the threat, it turned out that the acknowledgements of the fat subjects on the rating scales indicated that they were somewhat more frightened and anxious than the normal weight subjects. Subjects in another experiment listened to an audio tape while they worked at a task. Some of the tapes were neutral and required the subject to think about either rain or seashells; others were emotionally charged and required the subject to think about his own death or about the bombing of Hiroshima. The effects produced by these tapes on the obese and normal subjects were dramatically different. The obese described themselves on a variety of rating scales as being considerably more upset and disturbed by the emotionally-charged tapes than the normal subjects. They also indicated that they had more palpitations and changes in breathing in response to the emotional tapes than the normal subjects did. Moreover, there was a dramatic deterioration in performance of the obese subjects on the monitoring and proof-reading tasks used when they listened to the emotional tapes; deteriorations in task performance were not nearly as great for the normals.

Another parallel between lesioned rats and obese humans has to do with the taste of food. People in an experiment concerned with the effect of taste were given either a good vanilla milk shake or a vanilla shake that had been laced with quinine. The results of the study indicated that the obese subjects drank more than normal weight subjects when the milk shake was good, but they drank considerably less than normals when the milk shake had some quinine in it. The results from studies with lesioned rats look very similar. Normally, the lesioned animal is hyperphagic (an excessive eater), but if quinine is added to its food, it drastically decreases its food intake to levels far below what the normal animal eats when the same amount of quinine is added to its food. If instead the food is made more tasty to the rat by adding something that it apparently likes such as dextrose or lard, then the lesioned animal eats a lot more than it normally would.

That is, the lesioned rat not only eats more of the tasty food than a normal rat would eat, it eats even considerably more than a control lesioned rat whose food has also been enriched but not with something as tasty as dextrose or lard.

We have already seen that obese humans are not as inclined to eat as much as normals when some work is required to get at the food, like the work required to shell a nut. What about the lesioned hyperphagic rat? Will these fat rats work as hard as normals to get food? The evidence indicates that they definitely will not. The results of an experiment that required rats to uncover a weighted food dish are typical. In this experiment, it was found that whereas lesioned rats ate more than normal weight controls when an unweighted lid covered the food dish, they ate less than the normals when the lid of the food dish was weighted down by fastening a 75-g weight to it.

A difference has been found between obese and normal weight people concerning the number of fat cells in their bodies. The excess of fat cells is not present in the newborn baby, but these cells apparently start to develop before the age of two. Overeating at any age causes an increase in the size and number of fat cells in the body which continually crave nourishment. When acquired at an early age and maintained, these extra fat cells become increasingly difficult to shed. When people have a higher than normal number of large fat cells, cutting down on calories reduces pounds but does not reduce the number of fat cells.

Still, reducing the number of pounds is a good idea. The weight of scientific evidence indicates that the overweight are likely to have a shorter life span. A thin child physiologically stands a better chance of developing into a more healthy adult. Unfortunately, in our culture a fat baby is considered to be a healthy, happy baby. The trouble is that fat babies have a tendency to turn into fat children and then fat adults—unhealthy and unhappy.

C. *Student's Description of Variables*

1. *A general parameter in the model*

a. *Number of subjects in any given condition* (n). The amount eaten by human subjects will be obtained in grams for each of n subjects in any experimental condition, where n equals the number of subjects in any given group. For this problem, the range of n is from 10 to 20. If the group size is left unspecified, an n of 15 will be generated.

2. *Discrete controllable variables in the model.*

Below is a set of factors that are conceived of as having an influence on the amount of food eaten by subjects. Each factor may have a more or less potent effect, depending on the type or the level chosen and the interrelated influence of the remaining variables.

b. *Size of subject* (SIZE). You may choose whether to test subjects who are normal in size, or obese.
c. *Age of subject* (AGE). The test subjects you choose must be specified as being either adults, or children.
d. *Number of fat cells* (CELLS). You can choose subjects who have a normal number of fat cells or fatty cells in significantly greater numbers than normals.
e. *Level of hunger induced by different methods* (HUNGER). There are four ways that the level of hunger of the test subjects can be specified. You are concerned here with the state that the subjects are in at the beginning of the experiment, and how they got in that state. Thus, the subjects can be specified as being in one of the four following states when the experiment begins.

(i) Comfortable—i.e. not hungry but not having just eaten.

(ii) Empty stomach—i.e. not having eaten for several hours and ready for a meal.

(iii) Low hunger—simulated by injecting with adrenalin, producing low gastric motility and high blood sugar.

(iv) Full stomach–preloaded with food by having just been fed a meal.

f. *Amount of work to get at food* (WORK). You may choose whether to make the food readily accessible to the subject where no work is required to get at the food (1), or harder to get at so that he must work in order to obtain the food (2).

3. *Unknown variable*

g. Variable (*X*). This simulation will permit you to investigate the effect of any of the variables mentioned above on the amount of food that people eat. In addition the simulation contains an *X* or "unknown" variable that you may replace with a variable that you think should have an important effect on feeding behaviour. If you choose to ignore the *X* variable, its effects will simply show up in your data as random variations as do the effects of any uncontrolled variable. The procedure for using the *X* variable is as follows: The *X* variable may take on any name and any value (including decimal fractions). If you want to ignore it (the default case), enter a 0 and any effects it may have on the experimental results will be completely random. If you want to study the effects of some variable on the amount of food eaten by your subjects, enter a "1" for the level of *X*. The computer will then ask you to give the name of your variable, its code (*which you must get from your instructor*), the upper and lower limits of the range of values over which you wish to measure the effects of your variable (this can be some range on an arbitrary psychological scale if required), and the value you want your variable to have in the range you have specified.

An example would be if you desired to measure the effects of "anxiety" on the amount of food eaten. In this case, the name of the variable might be ANXIOUS, the range of values might be specified on a psychological scale from 1 to 100.

Then if you want to measure the effects of a low level of anxiety, a relatively low value of ANXIOUS could be specified, e.g. a value of ANXIOUS = 10 in the range from 1 to 100. Of course, ANXIOUS could take on any value from 1 to 100, and if it is effective in changing the amount eaten, one could reasonably expect the degree of effect to be a function of its value. Thus, if the value of ANXIOUS was set at 90 instead of 10, the data obtained could be quite different.

D. *Description of Costs for Student*

The BASE cost to run any experiment is 50 points. All other costs are related to selection procedures, and to treating subjects before and during the experiments; these costs are assessed for each subject. Note that the WORK variable does not affect the costs.

AGE. If you use children as subjects, each one will cost 1 point. Adults are three times as expensive, and each one will cost 3 points.

SIZE. There are no extra costs for using normal subjects. However, if the subjects are to be obese, an additional cost of 2 points is charged.

CELLS. If obese subjects are used who have been determined to have extra fat cells, the additional cost is 4 points for each subject.

HUNGER. If subjects are to be fed before the test (stomach preload with food), the cost will be 1 point for each subject. Also, a charge of 1 point will be assessed if subjects are to be administered adrenalin before the test. Subjects who are not fed before the experiment result in no additional costs.

X. If you wish to specify an unlisted variable, it will cost an additional 5 points for each subject run in the experiment.

The cost of a run is then calculated according to the formula: $\text{COST} = \text{BASE} + n \times (\text{AGE} + \text{SIZE} + \text{CELLS} + \text{HUNGER} + X)$ where the code names refer to the associated costs as described above, and the cost is stated on the print-out of results.

The Instructor's Side of Model Use

The main purpose of the Obesity Model is to encourage the student to engage in some independent thinking through the use of the "*X*" variable, or unknown variable, concept. The problem description suggests numerous factors which should affect the dependent measure (the amount eaten by the subjects). Some of these are "subject" variables, characteristics that can be used to classify subjects, like their tendency to perform poorly under distracting conditions or the degree to which they are upset by emotionally distrubing conditions. There are also genetic factors and endocrine disturbances that are related to obesity. There are in addition many "environmental" variables such as the amount of exercise engaged in by the subjects, how they were fed as children, etc. An explanation of how the instructor manages the "*X*" variable follows the description given below of the explicit variables in the model.

A. *Explanation of Variables for the Instructor*

n. The number of observations (subjects run) desired in the experiment; it is a general parameter, not a variable.

SIZE. Generally, subjects who are normal in size eat less than subjects who are obese. However, there are exceptions to this depending on the level of the other variables in the simulation (i.e. the levels chosen for the HUNGER and WORK variables). The specific ways that each of the levels of these variables affect the normal and obese subjects in the model is given below.

AGE. If children are chosen for use as subjects instead of adults, there is a general decrease in the amount of food eaten for each subject. There are no effects that are obtained with children that are not also obtained with adults, i.e. the variables in the simulation affect the eating behaviour of children in essentially the same ways as they affect the eating behaviour of adults.

CELLS. Among the researchers who have studied the relation of fatty cells to obesity are Drs Jerome L. Kittle, head of pediatric nutrition at Mt Sinai School of Medicine and Jules Hirsch of Rockefeller University. They have found that obese children and adults of all ages from two to 26 have a greater number of fatty cells. Obese children by age seven had a fat cell number equal to or greater than non-obese adults.

It is important to keep in mind that a person without an extraordinarily high number of fat cells may eat more than normal and not be obese because of a hyperthyroid (high metabolic rate) condition. On the other hand, a person may have a hypothyroid condition and eat very little and yet be obese. In choosing subjects according to the number of fatty cells they have, we are choosing between subjects who have more fat cells than normal (and should therefore eat more than normal) and subjects who have a normal number of fat cells (and who may, or may not, eat more than normal depending on the levels of other variables in the model).

HUNGER. A fundamental difference between normal weight subjects and obese subjects, according to the work of Dr Stanley Schachter and his associates (Schachter, 1971), is that the eating behaviour of normals is under internal control (hunger) whereas the eating behaviour of obese subjects is under external control (sight of food, taste, smell, etc.). Thus normal subjects will not eat much when they are comfortable (not hungry but not having just eaten either), when they are under conditions of simulated low hunger (injected with adrenalin) or when they have a full stomach (preloaded with food). The normals do eat a good deal when they have an empty stomach, i.e. when they are hungry. The amount of food eaten by obese subjects is unaffected by any of these internal conditions.

WORK. Normal subjects will work to obtain food provided they are hungry (i.e. HUNGER = empty stomach). Obese subjects will not work to obtain food. Thus, if a moderate amount of work is required to obtain food (like shelling nuts for example), the amount of food eaten by obese subjects is decreased. The obese subject would work to obtain food if enough positive external cues were available (e.g., if the food were visible, attractive, etc.) but a variable dealing with external cues is not in the model. Variables dealing with external cues can be specified as the X variable (see explanation of X variable below).

X. The student has been given some of the more obvious variables (SIZE, CELLS, HUNGER and WORK) but his problem description stresses the importance of other variables, and provides him with indications of what they are and the effects they ought to have.

The student can test his hypothesis about the effects of a variable he believes should affect the amount eaten by his subjects by entering a "1" for X when the computer asks for its level. If the student sets $X = 1$, the computer asks for the name of the variable, the code, and the upper and lower limits. The name the student gives his X variable has no effect whatsoever and should be selected to be representative of the effect the student desired to examine. After listening to the student's explanation of the variable he wants to assign to X and why he thinks it should be effective, the instructor gives the student a three-digit code *which will determine the effectiveness of his variable.*

The code is very simple. It must be an even number to be effective. Although it has 3 digits, the second 2 digits have no other effect except to insure that the code is long enough so that the student will not catch on to it; thus, the second digit of the code is a "dummy" and may vary from 0 to 9. Depending on the number of the first digit, if the code is an even number, the computer will apply the function specified by the first digit to the range specified by the student. Thus, the effect that the student gets from his X variable is a function of the value he gives the computer for his variable.

B. *Code for the Unknown Variable*

Only the first digit of the three-digit code is effective, provided that the third digit is *even*. The functions specified by the first digit of the code are listed below:

Positive linear (1). Values in the upper two quartiles of the range increase the dependent measure from zero (for values of X at midrange) to a maximum of about 10% above normal (at values near the upper end of the range). Values for X in the lower two quartiles of the range specified have no effect. This code (one of which might be 196) is useful when the variable the student wants to investigate should logically only increase values of the dependent measure in a somewhat linear fashion. In other words, for the conditions specified by the student concerning the variable he wants to examine, if a decrease in the dependent measure is not logical as an outcome, when for a linear function this code is useful.

Positive linear (2). Values in the upper two quartiles of the range specified increase the dependent measure from zero (for values of X at midrange) to a maximum of about 10% above normal; at values near the lower end of the range, the dependent measure is decreased from 0% (at midrange X values) to a minimum of about 10% below normal. This code (one of which might be 254) is useful when the variable the student wants to investigate should logically increase values of the dependent measure at high values, but decrease the dependent measure at low values.

Negative linear (3). Values in the upper two quartiles of the range decrease the dependent measure from zero (for X values at midrange) to a minimum of about 10% below normal (at values near the upper end of the range). Values for X in the lower two quartiles of the range specified have no effect. The same logic applies to using this code (an effective value might be 322) as in using the first positive linear code except that the function is negative instead of positive.

Negative linear (4). Values in the upper two quartiles of the range decrease the dependent measure from zero (for X values at midrange) to a minimum of about 10% below normal (at values near the upper end of the range). Values of X in the lower two quartiles of the range specified increase the dependent measure from zero (for values of X at midrange) to a maximum of about 10% above normal (at values near the lower end of the range). The same logic applies using this code (an effective value might be 478) as in using the second positive linear code except that the function is negative instead of positive.

Positive normal (5). Values of X at midrange increase the dependent measure about 10% above normal. Values for X in the upper or lower quartiles result in less and less increase in the dependent measure as the upper and lower ends of the range are approached. This code (an effective one might be 536) is useful when the student's *X* variable ought to produce an increase in the dependent measure only in the midrange of values.

Negative normal (6). Values of *X* at midrange decrease the dependent measure about 10% below normal. Values of *X* in the upper and lower quartiles result in less and less decrease in the dependent measure as the upper and lower ends of the range are approached. This code (an effective one might be 644) is useful when the student's *X* variable ought to produce a decrease in the dependent measure only in the midrange of values.

Positive exponential, rate of change increasing (7). Values of *X* in the lower quartiles of the range specified and at midrange have little or no effect. Increases in the value of the *X* variable increase the dependent measure exponentially to about 20% above normal as the upper end of the range is approached. This code (an effective one of which might be 762) is useful as an alternative to the first positive linear code when the student's *X* variable should logically produce an increase in the dependent measure greater than 10% above normal.

Positive exponential, rate of change decreasing (8). Increases in values of *X* in the lower quartiles increase the dependent measure exponentially to about 20% above the normal as the midrange is reached. The function levels off at midrange so that values of *X* in the upper quartiles of the range specified have little or no effect in further increasing the dependent measure. This code (an effective one of which might be 888) is useful if the student's *X* variable should logically produce initial large increases in the dependent measure.

Negative exponential, rate of change increasing (9). Values of *X* in the lower quartiles of the range specified and at midrange have little or no effect. Increases in values of *X* in the upper quartiles decrease the dependent measure exponentially to about 20% below normal as the upper end of the range is approached. This code (an effective one of which might be 932) is useful as an alternative to the first negative linear code (3-negative linear) if increases in value of the student's *X* variable should logically decrease the dependent measure by more than 10% below normal.

Negative exponential, rate of change decreasing (0). Increases in values of *X* in the lower quartiles of the range specified decrease the dependent measure exponentially to almost 20% below normal as the midrange is reached. The function levels off at midrange so that values of *X* in the upper quartiles of the range have little or no effect in further decreasing the dependent measure. This code (an effective one of which might be 016) is useful if the student's *X* variable should logically produce initial large decreases in the dependent measure.

C. *Calculations*

The calculation processes by which specified levels of variables are converted into the food intake value in the output are provided in the model program by the following equation. This equation is not intended to rest on theoretical formulations. Rather, it is intended to produce the desired differences between levels of the variables that will support hypotheses the student should develop from his problem description.

Amount eaten (in g) $= f(\text{AGE}) \times f(\text{CELLS}) \times [f(\text{SIZE} \times \text{HUNGER}) + f(\text{SIZE} \times \text{WORK})] + 65$

The functions of the variables are not specified. Instead, a value for the function is obtained from a matrix in a computer data file for the levels of the variables and their interactions. For example, the values from the data file necessary to calculate the effects of the variables when all levels = 1 are as follows (see summary of parameters on p. 49):

Variable level			(Data file) Matrix value
SIZE = 1, HUNGER = 1	f(SIZE × HUNGER)	=	20
SIZE = 1, WORK = 1	f(SIZE × WORK)	=	50
AGE = 1	f(AGE)	=	6
CELLS = 1	f(CELLS)	=	0·5

Thus the calculation for the parameters of the variable levels specified as 12, 1, 1, 1, 1, 1, 0 would be as follows (SIZE = 1, AGE = 1, CELLS = 1, HUNGER = 1, WORK = 1, $X = 0$):

Amount eaten (in g) $= f(\text{AGE}) \times f(\text{CELLS}) \times (f(\text{SIZE} \times \text{HUNGER}) + f(\text{SIZE} \times \text{WORK})) + 65$
$= 6 \times 0{\cdot}5 \times (20 + 50) + 65 = 275.$

The data file for the Obesity Model is given in Table I. From this it is possible to determine how the different main effects and interaction effects of the variables in the model are calculated. The names of the variables in the model appear in the first two lines of the table. The pairs of numbers in the third and fourth lines specify such things as the location of certain types of values in the matrix (e.g. where the values for costs are located), where the last value of the matrix is located (at 1, 55), number of variables of each type, number of variables the student will be allowed to control, lower and upper limit of each variable, number of costs, number of effects, and the values used in the cost computations. The last line of the table gives the values of the effects for the variable levels. Taken in order as they appear in the table, they are (in parentheses) as follows: AGE = 1(6), AGE = 2(1), CELLS = 1(0·5), CELLS = 2(0·6), SIZE = 1 and HUNGER = 1(20), SIZE = 2 and HUN-

Table I
Data file for the obesity model

```
"n SIZE CELLS HUNGER WORK X GRAMS",
"OBESITY",
0,0,0,0,1,33,1,39,1,55,1,5,0,0,1,0,1,7,15,1,2,1,1,1,0,0,10,20,
0,2,0,2,0,2,0,4,0,2,0,99,0,1,0,4,16,3,1,0,4,
6,1,-5,-6,20,245,212,245,20,245,20,245,50,50,50,0
```

GER = 1(245), SIZE = 1 and HUNGER = 2 (212), SIZE = 2 and HUNGER = 2(245), SIZE = 1 and HUNGER = 3(20), SIZE = 2 and HUNGER = 3(245), SIZE = 1 and HUNGER = 4(20), SIZE = 2 and HUNGER = 4 (245), SIZE = 1 and WORK = 1(50), SIZE = 2 and WORK = 1(50), SIZE = 1 and WORK = 2(50), SIZE = 2 and WORK = 2(0).

It is not necessary for the model's subroutine program in the system to access a data file to obtain the values for the variable effects. We have models in which the calculations are made by equations in the program. The reason for doing it this way is that most of the phenomena we simulate with our models are realistically complex, and the easiest way to model the phenomena is to obtain the effect the variable would have at the level specified, from a data file.

Computer Output from Obesity Model

Any model constructed and run with LESS handles all of the variables in essentially the same way in terms of the specification of the value of the variable for the computer. For each variable, the computer must be given a number which indicates the value the variable is to have under the conditions of the experiment being simulated. Each run with the computer model simulates only one set of conditions at a time. Thus, in order to see the effects of changing a variable, the simulation must be run with one set of conditions, and then those conditions run again with the value of the variable of interest changed between the first run and the second run.

From the background material given to the student in his problem description on human obesity, he could hypothesize that injecting obese subjects with adrenalin, producing a simulated state of low hunger by reducing gastric motility and raising the blood sugar, should not influence the amount of food they eat. On the other hand, producing a low hunger state by injecting adrenalin should reduce the amount of food eaten by normal subjects. To test this hypothesis, the student may decide to simulate an experiment with the obesity model in which the amount of food eaten by normal-sized subjects (SIZE = 1) and obese subjects (SIZE = 2) is obtained under conditions in which they should be hungry (HUNGER = 2, an empty stomach) and in which they should not be hungry (HUNGER = 3, adrenalin simulated low hunger). In order not to confound the experiment, all other variables are held constant across these experimental conditions. For this investigation suppose the student decides to obtain data on each of 12 subjects under the different experimental conditions ($n=12$), to use only adult subjects (AGE = 1, adult) with a number of fat cells in the normal range (CELLS = 1, normal number of fat cells) who do not have to work to obtain the food (WORK = 1, no work required). The effects of any additional variables, if they are important, will have random effects across the four conditions of the experiment ($X=0$, random).

The sample output which follows was obtained from actual runs with the obesity model when these conditions were specified. Note that before the levels of the variables in the model are specified, the computer asks:

DO YOU WANT TO BE PROMPTED ON VARIABLE ORDER (*Y* OR *N*)?

If a *Y* (=Yes) is entered, the computer prompts the investigator on each of the variable names. After one becomes more accustomed to the variables in a model, investigations can be conducted more efficiently by entering *N* (=No) in answer to this question; then, the computer comes back with the statement:

TYPE PARAMETERS.

This is the format used in specifying the levels of the variables in the obesity model shown below, after the first sample run. In order to specify the experimental conditions for a particular run, the level of each variable in the model is entered, separated by a comma.

For summary, the parameters of the Obesity Model are, in order:

(a) *n*: Number of subjects to be run (from 10 to 20).

(b) *SIZE*: Size of subject (1=normal; 2=obese).

(c) *AGE*: Age of subject (1=adult; 2=child).

(d) *CELLS*: Type of cells (1=normal number of fat cells; 2=abnormally high number of fatty cells).

(e) *HUNGER*: (1=comfortable; 2=empty stomach; 3=adrenalin simulated low hunger; 4=full preloaded stomach).

(f) *WORK*: Amount of work to get at food (1=no work required; 2=must work moderately hard).

(g) *X*: Variable (random if = 0; if used must = 1; give name, code, upper and lower limits, and value).

Note also that the summary statistics are provided if requested, as well as the standard error of the mean difference a particular run as compared to the preceding run.

A. *Runs Without the Unknown Variable Operative*

The first examples of output are for runs with $X=0$.

Twelve subjects are specified in each case, all adults with normal numbers of fat cells and no work to get food. Figure 1 gives the intake at a meal for normal-

```
GET-$LESS
RUN
LESS

WHICH OF THE FOLLOWING MODELS DO YOU WISH TO RUN?
FEAR
OBESE
IMPRNT
SCHIZ
PARTY
TOT
RT
ROTO
?OBESE

LOUISVILLE EXPERIMENT SIMULATION SYSTEM
OBESITY SIMULATION

DO YOU WANT TO BE PROMPTED ON VARIABLE ORDER (Y OR N)?Y
PLEASE GIVE VALUE FOR N
?12
SIZE     =?1
AGE      =?1
CELLS    =?1
HUNGER   =?2
WORK     =?1
X        =?0

AMOUNT EATEN (IN GRAMS)
 910
 809
 963
 861
 897
 748
 1026
 870
 1014
 931
 654
 897
COST FOR THIS RUN IS 86   POINTS

STATISTICS WANTED?Y
MEAN = 882.236
STANDARD DEVIATION = 106.368
VARIANCE = 11314.1
DO YOU WANT THE STANDARD ERROR OF THE MEAN DIFFERENCE(Y OR N)?N
```

Fig. 1. Output for normal-size subjects with an empty stomach.

```
DO YOU WANT TO BE PROMPTED ON VARIABLE ORDER (Y OR N)?N
TYPE 7    PARAMETERS
?12, 1, 1, 1, 3, 1, 0

AMOUNT EATEN (IN GRAMS)
 263
 300
 300
 272
 229
 283
 262
 280
 219
 250
 297
 272
COST FOR THIS RUN IS 98    POINTS

STATISTICS WANTED?Y
MEAN = 269.441
STANDARD DEVIATION = 26.154
VARIANCE = 684.03
DO YOU WANT THE STANDARD ERROR OF THE MEAN DIFFERENCE(Y OR N)?Y
STANDARD ERROR OF THE MEAN DIFFERENCE = 31.6203              DF= 22
```

Fig. 2. Output for normal-size subjects with adrenalin injection.

sized subjects with an empty stomach, and Fig. 2 the output for the same subjects with adrenalin injection. Figure 3, on the other hand is output for obese subjects under the same two conditions.

B. *Unknown Variables*

Unknown variables, termed X variables, represent a number of variables that are important to the phenomenon under study but which are not specified in the model. In this sense, they are not given to the student and thus they are "unknown" as far as he is concerned. Thus, X variables may represent one or more very important variables that the instructor left out of the model deliberately in order to encourage the students to discover and investigate them. Or, in a broader sense, they may be viewed as any variables the instructor did not include in the model whether they are importantly related or not. As will be seen below, by entering a 1 for the value of X in the model, the student can test the validity of hypotheses he has deduced from his knowledge of the problem. If the student sets $X = 1$, the computer asks for the name of the variable he wishes to investigate, and the upper and lower limits of the values the variable can assume. The computer then asks the student for the particular value of the variable for which he wishes to see the data. After giving the value, the computer provides the student with results that show the effect on the observations that his variable has had. The student may, if he wishes, run the model several times, each time giving the computer a different value for his variable in the range of values he has specified. Thus, the student can obtain the effects of his variable over a range of

```
DO YOU WANT TO BE PROMPTED ON VARIABLE ORDER (Y OR N)?N
TYPE 7    PARAMETERS
?12,2,1,1,2,1,0
```

(a)

```
AMOUNT EATEN (IN GRAMS)
 1056
 846
 1002
 802
 972
 937
 938
 1221
 1096
 782
 981
 909
COST FOR THIS RUN IS 110  POINTS

STATISTICS WANTED?Y
MEAN = 962.328
STANDARD DEVIATION = 124.69
VARIANCE = 15547.6
DO YOU WANT THE STANDARD ERROR OF THE MEAN DIFFERENCE(Y OR N)?N

DO YOU WANT TO BE PROMPTED ON VARIABLE ORDER (Y OR N)?N
TYPE 7    PARAMETERS
?12,2,1,1,3,1,0
```

(b)

```
AMOUNT EATEN (IN GRAMS)
 986
 1013
 890
 1005
 745
 1014
 1025
 1153
 861
 946
 823
 812
COST FOR THIS RUN IS 122  POINTS

STATISTICS WANTED?Y
MEAN = 939.864
STANDARD DEVIATION = 115.476
VARIANCE = 13334.7
DO YOU WANT THE STANDARD ERROR OF THE MEAN DIFFERENCE(Y OR N)?Y
STANDARD ERROR OF THE MEAN DIFFERENCE = 49.0593            DF= 22
```

Fig. 3. (a) Output for obese subjects with an empty stomach. (b) Output for obese subjects with adrenalin injection.

(a)

```
DO YOU WANT TO BE PROMPTED ON VARIABLE ORDER (Y OR N)?Y
PLEASE GIVE VALUE FOR N
?10
SIZE     =?1
AGE      =?1
CELLS    =?1
HUNGER   =?1
WORK     =?1
X        =?1

PLEASE INPUT NAME OF VARIABLE X?TASTE OF FOOD
NOW GIVE ITS CODE, LOWER AND UPPER LIMITS?495,0,10
NOW GIVE THE VALUE OF TASTE OF FOOD IN THE RANGE FROM 0     TO 10
?2

AMOUNT EATEN (IN GRAMS)
 281
 262
 284
 352
 270
 332
 287
 315
 313
 254
COST FOR THIS RUN IS 80    POINTS

STATISTICS WANTED?Y
MEAN = 295.493
STANDARD DEVIATION = 31.8036
VARIANCE = 1011.47
DO YOU WANT THE STANDARD ERROR OF THE MEAN DIFFERENCE(Y OR N)?N
```

(b)

```
DO YOU WANT TO BE PROMPTED ON VARIABLE ORDER (Y OR N)?N
TYPE 7     PARAMETERS
?10,1,1,1,1,1,1

PLEASE INPUT NAME OF VARIABLE X?TASTE OF FOOD
NOW GIVE ITS CODE, LOWER AND UPPER LIMITS?495,0,10
NOW GIVE THE VALUE OF TASTE OF FOOD IN THE RANGE FROM 0     TO 10
?8

AMOUNT EATEN (IN GRAMS)
 235
 264
 252
 281
 274
 285
 287
 305
 295
 300
COST FOR THIS RUN IS 80    POINTS

STATISTICS WANTED?Y
MEAN = 278.412
STANDARD DEVIATION = 22.1841
VARIANCE = 492.133
DO YOU WANT THE STANDARD ERROR OF THE MEAN DIFFERENCE(Y OR N)?Y
STANDARD ERROR OF THE MEAN DIFFERENCE = 12.2621                DF= 18
```

Fig. 4. (a) Output for normal size subjects with neutral taste of food. (b) Output for normal size subjects with good taste of food.

values, and he can plot these results to show how the observations are a function of the variable he is investigating.

Actually, unknown to the student, the name that he gives the computer for his variable has no effect whatsoever. The instructor gives the student a code which determines the effects that the student's variable will have. After listening to the student's explanation of the variable he wishes to investigate, the instructor helps the student decide on an appropriate name for his variable. Then the instructor refers to the codes (see p. 45) under the pretence that the computer must have a code to "understand" the exact conditions under which the student wishes to investigate his variable. What the instructor is really doing (and students never catch on to this) is deciding whether or not the student's variable should have an effect, and if so, what sort of function the variable would probably have. Having made this decision, he gives the student the code for his variable, which the student in turn gives the computer. Using the code, the computer then applies the function specified by the code to the range of values the student has specified for his variable. Two considerations make assigning a code for the student's X variable a fairly easy task. In the first place, the effects that the student's variable should have need only be generally approximated, so it is not important that exactly the correct function be applied to the student's variable. Secondly, since the instructor has decided what effects the X variable should have, he is in an ideal position to justify the outcome of the investigation to the student.

Example. Suppose the student indicates that he wants to use as an X variable food that ranges from a neutral taste to a very good taste. An appropriate name for the student's variable would be TASTE OF FOOD; range is arbitrary, say on a psychological scale from 0 to 10 where 0 is neutral. The student wishes to run the experiment with subjects who are normal (SIZE = 1) and obese (SIZE = 2). From the problem description provided by the student, it can be concluded that obese people are more affected than normal people by external stimuli such as the taste of food. For his runs with normal subjects (see Fig. 4), the amount of food eaten should not be affected much by the taste of food so the code could be any three digits as long as the third digit is odd, making the first digit ineffective as a code number (e.g. 311, 495, 929, etc.). For his runs with obese subjects (see Fig. 5), the amount of food eaten should depend on how good the food tastes. Since the student is not using any bad-tasting food, only increases in amount eaten should occur so the first digit could be "7" (positive exponential code, rate increasing) and it should be an even three-digit number (e.g. 712, 798, 742, etc.).

The effect that the student gets from his X variable is a function of the value the student gives for his variable. In the specified range for TASTE of 0 to 10, values of X from 0 to 5 will produce little or no effect (if the first digit of the code = 7) when obese subjects are used. Values of X from 5 to 10 will produce

```
DO YOU WANT TO BE PROMPTED ON VARIABLE ORDER (Y OR N)?N
TYPE 7     PARAMETERS
?10,2,1,1,1,1,1

PLEASE INPUT NAME OF VARIABLE X?TASTE OF FOOD
NOW GIVE ITS CODE, LOWER AND UPPER LIMITS?712,0,10
NOW GIVE THE VALUE OF TASTE OF FOOD IN THE RANGE FROM 0     TO 10
?8



AMOUNT EATEN (IN GRAMS)
 1136
 795
 1372
 1142
 1332
 1162
 1382
 1191
 1068
 1334
COST FOR THIS RUN IS 190   POINTS

STATISTICS WANTED?Y
MEAN = 1191.85
STANDARD DEVIATION = 178.841
VARIANCE = 31984
DO YOU WANT THE STANDARD ERROR OF THE MEAN DIFFERENCE(Y OR N)?Y
STANDARD ERROR OF THE MEAN DIFFERENCE = 59.7545                   DF= 18

DO YOU WANT TO BE PROMPTED ON VARIABLE ORDER (Y OR N)?N
TYPE 7     PARAMETERS
?10,2,1,1,1,1,1

PLEASE INPUT NAME OF VARIABLE X?TASTE OF FOOD
NOW GIVE ITS CODE, LOWER AND UPPER LIMITS?712,0,10
NOW GIVE THE VALUE OF TASTE OF FOOD IN THE RANGE FROM 0     TO 10
?2



AMOUNT EATEN (IN GRAMS)
 959
 930
 840
 917
 953
 979
 850
 849
 975
 1012
COST FOR THIS RUN IS 150   POINTS

STATISTICS WANTED?Y
MEAN = 926.973
STANDARD DEVIATION = 61.0078
VARIANCE = 3721.96
DO YOU WANT THE STANDARD ERROR OF THE MEAN DIFFERENCE(Y OR N)?N
```

Fig. 5. (a) Output for obese subjects with neutral taste of food. (b) Output for obese subjects with good taste of food.

increasingly large amounts of food eaten by the obese subjects. As mentioned earlier, the student could plot the function of the effects of his variable TASTE OF FOOD on the amount eaten by obese subjects by making successive runs and setting X at different values within the range specified.

```
LOUISVILLE EXPERIMENT SIMULATION SYSTEM
OBESITY SIMULATION


DO YOU WANT TO BE PROMPTED ON VARIABLE ORDER (Y OR N)?Y
PLEASE GIVE VALUE FOR N
?10
SIZE      =?2
AGE       =?1
CELLS     =?1
HUNGER    =?1
WORK      =?2
X         =?1

PLEASE INPUT NAME OF VARIABLE X?TASTE OF FOOD
NOW GIVE ITS CODE, LOWER AND UPPER LIMITS?712,0,10
NOW GIVE THE VALUE OF TASTE OF FOOD IN THE RANGE FROM 0      TO 10
?8



AMOUNT EATEN (IN GRAMS)
 711
 797
 690
 721
 805
 791
 900
 971
 644
 735
COST FOR THIS RUN IS 150  POINTS

STATISTICS WANTED?Y
MEAN = 776.89
STANDARD DEVIATION = 99.3123
VARIANCE = 9862.93
DO YOU WANT THE STANDARD ERROR OF THE MEAN DIFFERENCE(Y OR N)?N
```

Fig. 6. Output for obese subjects required to work moderately hard to get food with good taste.

Any effects the student obtains from his X variable will combine with effects from the other variables in the model. Thus, if he chooses to use obese subjects and gives a value of eight for TASTE OF FOOD, the amount of food eaten by his subjects will be less if he has also specified that the subjects must work moderately hard to obtain the food (see Fig. 6, WORK = 2). Alternatively, if the student specified that the subjects have a higher than normal number of fatty cells, the amount eaten by his subjects would be larger.

IV. Research

The Louisville Experiment Simulation System has been used in recent years mainly as a teaching system. Until very recently, this was necessary as the models the system contained were designed for teaching purposes. However, there was no logical requirement that the models the system contained should be designed for this purpose. Rather, this bias reflects the response of those individuals using it to the demands of teaching good scientific research strategy to students. Several features that have been added to the system enhance its potential use as a research tool for constructing and testing computer models.

A. *Linear Combination Models*

One of these features is the General Model Builder, which as indicated above permits an individual with no programming skills to construct and test a model. It should be noted, however, that the General Model Builder in LESS assumes a general linear model in which the model must be expressed as the *sum of a weighted combination of terms plus a constant.* Although many processes can be so expressed, many research workers would probably be inclined to write their own model program to simulate the processes of interest in the form specified by their experimental results and theoretical assumptions.

B. *Model Testing Routines*

Whether the researcher using LESS decides to employ the General Model Builder mode or to write his own model, a number of programs in various stages of development has been added to the system which serve to aid the modification and testing of a model. These are all interactive programs, and none require the user to be a programmer.

1. *Parameter File Adjustment*

Thus, one of them permits the author of a model to create a file containing a set of parameters for testing a model he has constructed. If desired, he can then

(i) create an entirely new set of parameters in the file for testing the model;
(ii) delete, change, or add particular values of parameters in the file;
(iii) delete an entire set of parameters for testing a particular model in the system;
(iv) list any portion of the parameter file for examination of its contents.

Another interactive program permits the author of a model to change particular values or effects in the file used by the model for generating the data. Hence, with no programming, the author of a model can employ a "means-end" analysis to obtain the desired results from the variables in his model. If the data generated by the model subroutine do not match the empirical values the author intended to achieve, he can change the effects or values in the file and test the model again.

2. *Comparison of Modelled with Expected Values of Output*

Testing a model which the author has added to the system is facilitated by running a test program (LESTES) which obtains the parameters specifying a set of conditions to be tested from the parameter file and an expected value that the model should generate if the model is "correct." This test program passes the set of parameters to the model subroutine program, which generates an observation based on the set of parameters (variable conditions) specified, and returns the value of this observation back to the test program. The test program then prints out line by line the set of parameters tested, the expected (empirical) value which the model program should generate given these parameters, and the value actually generated by the model program.

Table II
Test of the obesity model by LESTES

Parameters	Expected value	(Model) Theoretical value	
12, 1, 2, 1, 4, 2, 0,	100	60	Minimum value
12, 2, 1, 2, 2, 1, 0,	1127	1135	Maximum value
12, 1, 1, 1, 1, 1, 0,	275	276	Size effects
12, 2, 1, 1, 1, 1, 0,	950	952	
12, 1, 1, 1, 1, 1, 0,	275	282	Age effects
12, 1, 2, 1, 1, 1, 0,	100	59	
12, 1, 1, 1, 1, 1, 0,	275	285	Cells effects
12, 1, 1, 2, 1, 1, 0,	317	337	
12, 1, 1, 1, 1, 1, 0,	275	275	
12, 1, 1, 1, 2, 1, 0,	851	850	Hunger effects
12, 1, 1, 1, 3, 1, 0	275	279	(size=normal)
12, 1, 1, 1, 4, 1, 0	275	284	
12, 2, 1, 1, 1, 1, 0,	950	958	
12, 2, 1, 1, 2, 1, 0,	950	956	Hunger effects
12, 2, 1, 1, 3, 1, 0,	950	952	(size=obese)
12, 2, 1, 1, 4, 1, 0,	950	953	
12, 1, 1, 1, 1, 1, 0,	275	284	Work effects
12, 1, 1, 1, 1, 2, 0,	275	283	(size=normal)
12, 2, 1, 1, 1, 1, 0,	950	950	Work effects
12, 2, 1, 1, 1, 2, 0,	800	799	(size=obese)

The advantage of the test program is that the author of a model can, if he wishes, obtain the results that his model produces for many levels of variables in the model, or in fact for any set of conditions provided by the variables in the model, all in a matter of minutes. Furthermore, the print-out provided by the test program gives a ready comparison of expected values and the theoretical values produced by the model. Table II is the relevant part of the print-out from a test of the Obesity Model in LESS using a parameter file specifying systematic changes of each variable in the model. Note that although the parameter specifying the number of subjects for each run is 12, a single error-free mean value generated by the model is provided by the test program.

C. *Future Developments*

The Louisville Experiment Simulation System is thus a set of computer programs having considerable potential for further development in teaching and research, including specifically the modelling of intake under various condition such as obesity. Acquaintance with programming and the programmed details of LESS would probably be of considerable help in developing the system for application to particular research problems pertaining to hunger.

References

Main, D. B. (1972). Toward a future-oriented curriculum. *Am. Psychol.* **27**, 245–248.

Schachter, S. (1971). Some extraordinary facts about obese humans and rats. *Am. Psychol.* **26**, 129–144.

Shure, G. and Brainerd, K. (1975). MODELR: Model building and model modification for instruction. *Behav. Res. Meth. Instr.* **7**, 221–225.

Stout, R. (1975). Modelling on the simulation writer interactive program. *Behav. Res. Meth. Instr.* **7**, 226–228.

Thurmond, J. B. and Cromer, A. O. (1972). Toward the optimal use of computer simulations in teaching scientific research strategy. Proceedings of the Conference on Computers in the Undergraduate Curricula, Atlanta.

Thurmond, J. B. and Cromer, A. O. (1975). Models and modeling with the Louisville Experiment Simulation System (LESS). *Behav. Res. Meth. Instr.* **7**, 229–232.

4

*A Model for Feeding Behaviour and Obesity**

J. HIRSCH
Rockefeller University, New York, U.S.A.

An effort has been made to create a scheme to explain some known observations on food intake behaviour in man and animals. It must be made clear at the outset, that the word "explain" is not used in the sense of providing an ultimate and sure description of mechanism, but only the creation of a shorthand scheme to order currently available information. Some elements in the scheme will be compared to neural structures, but no assumption is made that there are, or will be found, precise, neural representation for each element in this scheme. Finally, it must be pointed out that such schemes are highly arbitrary. Other schemes might as well explain the phenomenology of obesity and weight regulation. Whatever value such a scheme may have must ultimately be left to the reader.

I. Outline of The Model

The approach used borrows heavily from the methods and language of systems analysis (Hardy and Stolwijk, 1968). It assumes that the fundamental variable to be controlled is body weight or the amount of stored calories. As shown in Fig. 1, stored calories are designated "Q". Q is changed both by ingested calories and by the energy requirements of the organism. Q remains constant only when these two forces are in balance. For the purposes of this discussion it is assumed that ingested calories vary and thereby control the magnitude of Q; energy requirements are kept constant.

* Abstracted from Hirsch, J. (1972). Discussion. *Adv. Psychosom. Med.* **7**, 229–242 (by permission of the author and publisher).

Control is achieved as follows: the quantity of stored calories, Q, generates a signal which is some function of Q shown as $f(Q)$. $f(Q)$ is compared with f("ideal" Q). f(ideal Q) is a set point or command signal assumed to be generated in the central nervous system. The algebraic expression f(ideal Q) minus $f(Q)$ acts as a governor of ingested changed calories. When Q is diminished by starvation, the governor changes so as to enhance food intake and restore Q.

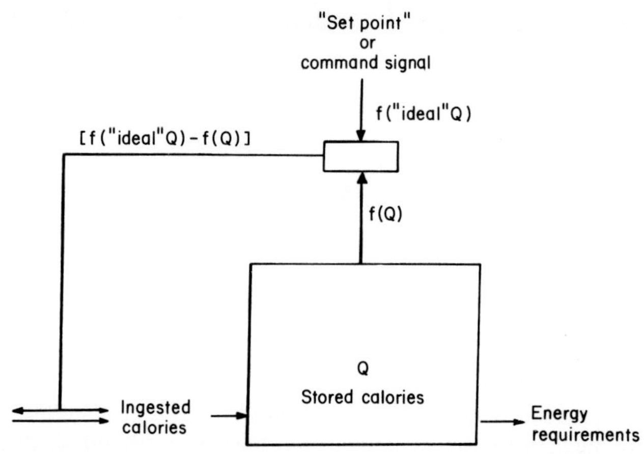

Fig. 1. General plan of a regulatory mechanism for the control of body weight.

When Q is enlarged by overfeeding, the difference between the two signals diminishes, food intake declines, and equilibrium is once again restored as Q approaches "ideal" Q. This is a system of set point regulation, analogous to current theories of body temperature regulation (Bard, 1968). The basic organizational pattern of Fig. 1 is easily extended to a more comprehensive scheme as shown in Fig. 2.

Again it is assumed that Q, the stored calories in adipose tissue, generate a signal, $f(Q)$, which can be transmitted to higher feeding centres. $f(Q)$ might also be affected by a variety of neural or humoral events relating to energy and carbohydrate metabolism, activity and muscle metabolism, heat production, etc. but ultimately $f(Q)$ is blended with signals from several central feeding centres: T, S and R. Each of these three centres is a set point which generates a signal proportional to "ideal" or "appropriate" body weight. Given the redundancy of many neural pathways, it is reasonable to consider that there may be many such centres. Indeed, the existence of hierarchies of control for food intake has been suggested. T can be conceptualized as the highest centre, in the sense of greatest involvement with external events such as cognition, perception and learned

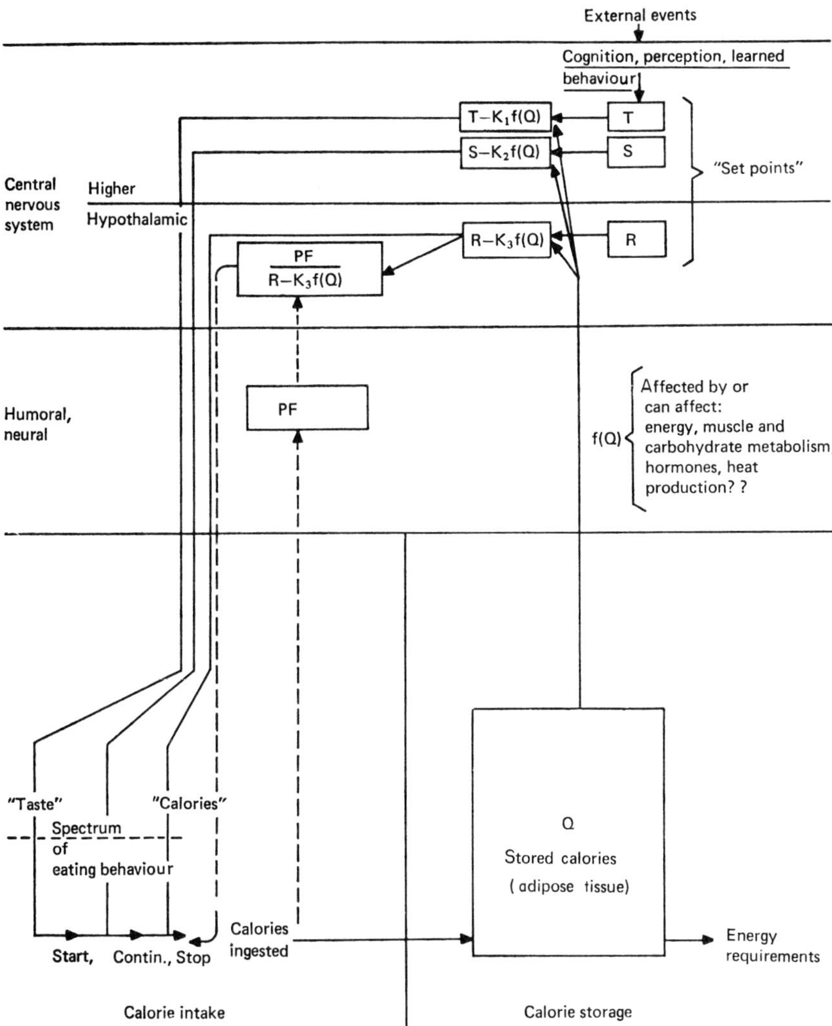

Fig. 2. A detailed scheme of a regulatory mechanism controlling Q, or body weight, by a series of set point and feedback controls.

behaviour; R, the lowest centre, is least involved with these factors and more affected by "internal" events such as the concentration of important metabolites or hormones. Yet each of these three signals, as was the case with the single signal in Fig. 1, interacts with $f(Q)$ to generate three drives for eating behaviour: $T-K_1f(Q)$, $S-K_2f(Q)$ and $R-K_3f(Q)$. The lowest centre, R, is considered to be most highly coupled with internal, metabolic and hormonal events and the uppermost centre, T, least coupled with these events; thus, the constants K_3, K_2 and K_1 are in descending order of magnitude with $K_3 > K_2 > K_1$. As shown in the lower left hand portion of Fig. 2, there is a spectrum of eating behaviours such that different modes of food acquisition can occur depending on the relative force of each of the three drives for food intake. When $T - K_1 f(Q)$ dominates, one would consider the organism eating more for "taste", i.e. olfaction, gustatory stimuli, and such externally modifiable forces as cognition, perception and learned behaviour. When $R - K_3 f(Q)$ dominates, a group of drives, here designated as "calories", are dominant; collectively these are the internal metabolic and physiological drives for acquisition of calories.

Eating behaviour is periodic or episodic in all complex organisms. A number of factors consequent to food ingestion create a sense of satiety and stop further intake of food. They include such factors as gastric filling, blood sugar levels and a variety of oropharyngeal sensations all of which lead to a sense of satiety. In the scheme of Fig. 2, this pathway is shown by dotted lines. As food is ingested, "PF" or peripheral factors leading to satiety increase. These factors are "sensed", according to this scheme, only at the lowest neural hierarchy. In a more complex scheme, upper hierarchies would also sense these factors. The signal which leads to the cessation of food intake is a blend of "PF" with the driving signal from the lowest neural hierarchy, i.e. PF divided by $R - K_3 f(Q)$. This is shown as a quotient to indicate that the total amount of stored calories may also modify the sense of satiety. Thus, the starved animal will eat more per meal than the normal or overfed animal. As $f(Q)$ declines consequent to diminution in stored calories, the denominator grows and a higher PF must be generated by more ingested calories in order to signal the cessation of food intake.

One should note that however complex this scheme seems to be, it probably is a gross over-simplification of the true state of affairs. Yet it is instructive to see what one can do with such a scheme. How much of what is known about food regulation and obesity can be explained or analogized?

II. Use of the Model

In order to demonstrate the operation of this scheme, arbitrary numerical values were assigned to the various constants and symbols shown in Fig. 2. Q was assigned the number 35, suggested by the fact that a normal man stores approximately 35-days worth of calories in adipose tissue. It was assumed that in the equilibrium condition, $\frac{1}{35}$ of this amount is lost per day and there is a repletion of $\frac{1}{35} \times 35$ or 1, by food intake. $f(Q)$, for simplicity, is indicated as being Q. i.e. the height of the signal is simply 1×35. R and T were arbitrarily given the values of 45 and 25 and K_1 and K_3 values of 0·1 and 0·5 respectively. PF was given the value 1347·5. This value multiplied by 1, the calories eaten each day generated a value. 1347·5 × 1, sufficient to counter the sum of all drives for food intake.

A program was written for a small digital computer (Hewlett-Packard Model 9100). The program enabled the calculation of Q, amount eaten, and the two expressions $T-K_1 f(Q)$ and $R-K_3 f(Q)$ each day or after each day's calories were consumed. The output of the computer was in the form of an x–y plot of these four variables each day. The "S" shown in Fig. 2 was totally eliminated from consideration in order to conserve space in this relatively small computer.

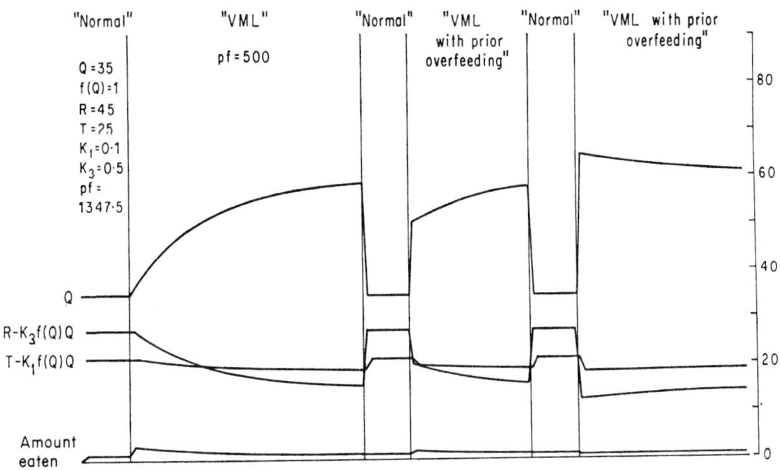

Fig. 3. Operation of the mechanism shown in Fig. 2. This figure is an x–y plot obtained from a Hewlett-Packard 9100 computer. The abscissa is time and the ordinates show solutions for Q, amount eaten, and two factors $R-K_3 f(Q)$ and $T-K_1 f(Q)$ which relate to modes of eating behaviour (see text). An hypothetical VML lesion is made by reducing PF (see text). The effect of such a "lesion" on eating behaviour is shown as well as the effects of prior "overfeeding" at two different levels.

A. *Ventromedial Hypothalamic Lesions*

Figure 3 shows a typical plot using this program. At the extreme left of the plot, the model is in equilibrium. Q is equal to 35. R and T "factors" [$R-K_3 f(Q)$ and $T-K_1 f(Q)$] do not change and the amount eaten is $\frac{1}{35}$ of the energy store per day. Then, a hypothetical ventromedial lesion is made. It is assumed that such a lesion might be equivalent to reducing PF, i.e. the generation or sensing of peripheral factors consequent to eating. PF is arbitrarily decreased from 1347·5 to 500. The results of this single manipulation on the model are shown. Clearly, the amount eaten increases rapidly; likewise, Q rises. Eventually, both Q and the amount eaten come into equilibrium. This occurs in about 50 "days". When Q reaches a new equilibrium, there is essentially normal intake, but Q is much higher with nearly a doubling in body weight. Concomitantly, R and T factors change. Since the R factor is more highly coupled with the amount of stored fat, it declines precipitously but T changes very little. It might be said then, to the extent that such a model represents a ventromedial lesion, that animals having such a lesion would become more "finicky"; that is, they would be driven in food-acquiring behaviour more by external events or factors designated T than those food drives schematized as R. The next panel of Fig. 3 shows the scheme again operating more "normally", and following this the effects of "ventromedial lesions" with prior overfeeding at two different levels. Obviously, the equilibrium position is the same regardless of the initial setting of Q. The extremely overfed "animal" declines in body weight after the lesion and to the same obese equilibrium position. Very similar regulation after ventromedial lesions in experimental animals has been described (Teitelbaum, 1955).

B. *Lateral Hypothalamic Lesions*

A similar consideration can be applied to the hypothetical case of lateral hypothalamic lesions. As shown in Fig. 4, it is assumed that the primary driving influence from the lower neural hierarchy, R, is reduced as an analogy to lateral

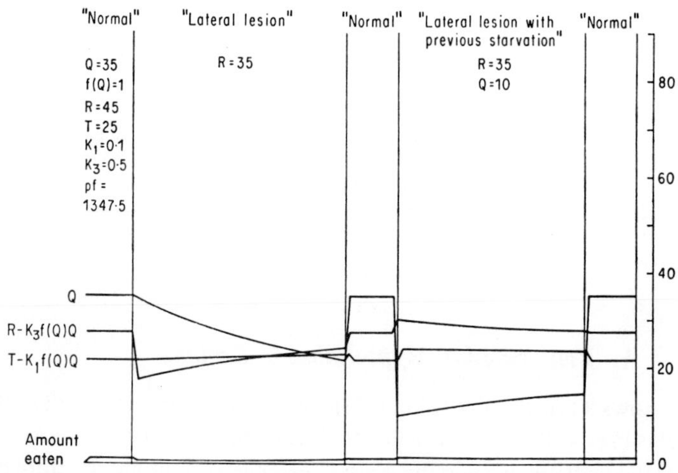

Fig. 4. A lateral hypothalamic lesion is analogized by a reduction in R. Prior underfeeding and its effects as also shown.

lesions being made. Reduction in R is arbitrarily from 45 to 35. The consequences are a sharp decline both in amount eaten and also in Q, the stored adipose. R shows a very spectacular decline and in this circumstance whatever feeding goes on is dominated by T or "external" factors. As shown in an additional panel of Fig. 4, a lateral lesion with previous starvation or previous reduction in adipose depot size can actually lead to a gain in weight. This is of particular interest since it mimics experimental findings on starved, lateral lesioned animals (Powley and Keesey, 1970).

C. *Overfeeding or "Genetic" Obesity*

Figure 5 shows the effect of overfeeding or starvation as represented in this scheme by an increase or decrease in Q.

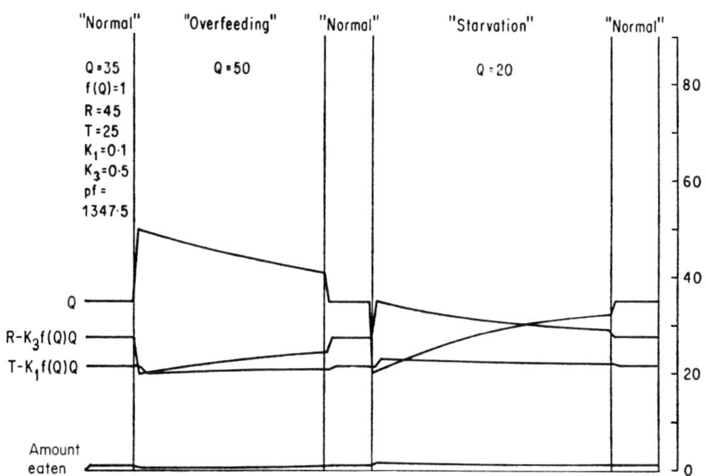

Fig. 5. The effects of manipulating Q as to simulate overfeeding and underfeeding.

Interestingly, in these circumstances the R and T factors change during the dynamic phase of restitution of body weight, but with restoration of body weight they again become normal. This would seem to indicate that consequent to any distortion in body weight, a disturbance of food-acquiring behaviour could occur. However, if obesity comes about by a reduction in $f(Q)$ alone, which is shown in Fig. 6 and termed "genetic" obesity, then in the equilibrium or obese state, R and T are completely normal. A change of $f(Q)$ is analogous to genetic obesity since it seems possible, although completely speculative, that such inborn errors of regulation creating obesity may be the result of a peripheral cellular change in which the signal generated by Q is in some way insufficient or inadequate. Recently, my associates and I (Greenwood *et al.*, 1971) have reported on the absence of "finickiness" in genetically obese rats and mice. This

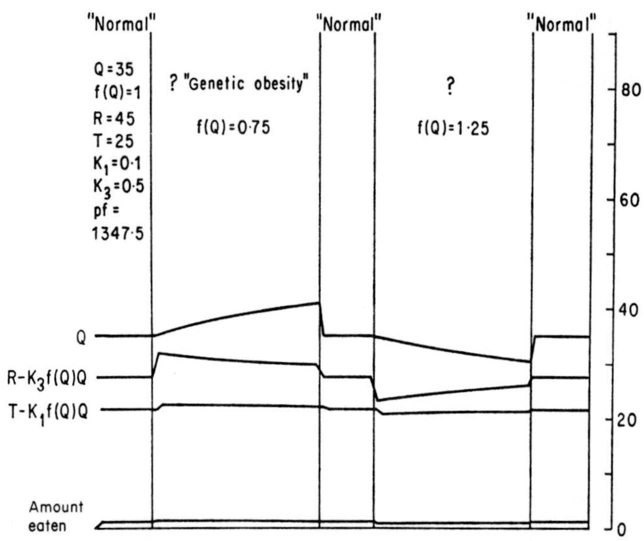

Fig. 6. Manipulations of $F(Q)$ are here termed genetic obesity to indicate that this form of obesity and its converse state of low $f(Q)$ are due to manipulations at the most peripheral and least externally modifiable portion of the scheme of Fig. 2.

is tantalizing support for the present scheme, although much more careful work must be done on feeding behaviour in both genetically obese and lesioned animals to clarify this issue. The next panel of Fig. 6 shows a hypothetical situation in which $f(Q)$ is increased. In this situation, the read-out of calorie storage is enhanced and weight reduction ensues. Could this be an analogy to the chronically thin but well individual who appears to have normal eating behaviour but simply "cannot" put on weight?

D. *Activity*

Figure 7 shows another hypothetical situation relating to under- and overactivity. This was done by a minor change in the computer program which reduced or increased energy output from 1·0 to 0·5 or from 1·0 to 1·5. The effects on amount eaten and body weight are shown, as well as the consequences on food-acquiring behaviour. Exercise appears to promote a shift in eating

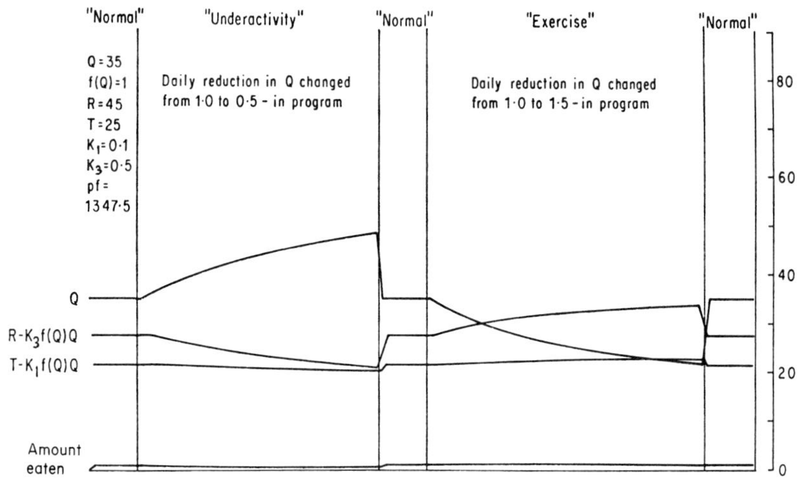

Fig. 7. The effects of varying caloric outflow from Q.

behaviour toward domination by "internal" factors; the reverse is found with inactivity. This is reminiscent of many speculations concerning the beneficial effects of exercise in the treatment of obesity. The benefits of exercise may be to change eating behaviour as well as the more obvious effect of increasing energy outgo and hence reducing fat storage.

III. Further Considerations

More theoretical work can be done with this scheme. It should be possible to add factors and interrelations governing meal size and frequency of taking meals. It should be possible to express energy requirements in terms of body size and amount of stored fat rather than as a constant. Similar additions and refinements may permit one to explain more experimental facts than is possible with this model and also to suggest further lines of laboratory inquiry. No such theoretical model can take the place of well-designed observations and experiments, yet such theoretical approaches may be useful to tie together currently available information and suggest new lines of study.

In reference to human obesity, what information is "explained" by this scheme? First, it demonstrates that both the obese and non-obese are in a state of regulation and thus the relative fixity of body weight is understandable. Starvation or removal of obese body weight, it might be predicted, would induce changes in food-acquiring behaviour. Thus, disturbance or disorder of regulation in terms of an exclusive reduction in Q would alter other forces in the direction of sensing starvation and restoring the previous obese weight. The difficulty of therapy with obese patients might be predicted by the realization that the only input into the system with present modes of dietary therapy is through *T*, the uppermost aspect of this regulatory system and a portion of the system which is least well coupled with internal or metabolic events. Thus, the correct idea that continuous, intensive group therapy and behavioural modification may be the most appropriate method for handling the problem of obesity certainly seems reasonable.

Obviously, the scheme predicts that there may be many aetiologies for an increase in *Q* or obesity. At the deepest or most cellular level there could be a change in cellularity or of $f(Q)$. This could be the case, particularly with juvenile onset obesity. In this circumstance, the individual is quite well regulated as long as *Q* is elevated; only when *Q* is reduced do feeding behaviour disturbances appear. Adult onset obesity might be much more related to higher factors designated *T* in this scheme. One must ask whether there are different types of regulatory disorders and whether the findings would change depending on whether or not the obese subject is at a regulated or upper weight rather than in some state of weight reduction?

An essential ingredient of this scheme is the idea that body weight can be sensed by the central nervous system and that the magnitude of *Q* can affect central nervous functioning. The nature of the signal which relays information about *Q* to the central nervous system is totally unknown and thus purely speculative. Perhaps this model makes the search for such a signal more imperative if a fuller understanding of food intake regulation is to be obtained. In any event, this model is one effort to order present information on obesity and food regulation into a single scheme. Undoubtedly, further investigation will elaborate on this scheme and may even necessitate fundamental changes in this type of conceptualization.

References

Bard, P. (1968). Body temperature regulation. *In* "Medical Physiology" (V. B. Mountcastle, ed.) 12th edn. St. Louis, Mosby.

Greenwood, M. R. C., Johnson, P. R., Cruce, J. A. F., Quartermain, D. and Hirsch, J. (1971). Is the ability to regulate good intake inpaired in genetic obesity? *Fed. Proc.* **30**, 579 Abs.

Hardy, J. O. and Stolwijk, J. A. J. (1968). Regulation and control in physiology. *In* "Medical Physiology" (V. B. Mountcastle, ed.) 12th edn. St. Louis, Mosby.

Powley, T. L. and Keesey, R. E. (1970). Relationship of body weight to the lateral hypothalamic feeding syndrome. *J. comp. physiol. Psychol.* **70**, 25–36.

Teitelbaum, P. (1955). Sensory control of hypothalamic hyperphagia. *J. comp. physiol. Psychol.* **48**, 158–163.

5

A Dynamical System Theory Approach to Food Intake Control

GEORGE M. BARNWELL
Department of Bioengineering, University of Texas Health Science Center at San Antonio, Texas, U.S.A.

I. Introduction

My interest in food intake control was initiated by a course on biological mechanisms of motivation, which I took as a graduate student in psychology. I realized the potential applicability of cybernetic, systems-theoretic and neural modelling concepts, and like many other psychologists, simultaneously developed a conditioned aversion to such "explanatory" terms as "drive", "motivation" and "emotion." I was also intrigued by the evidence for positive feedback mechanisms, which contradicted the then accepted dogma that homeostasis and negative feedback provided stability and gave sufficient account of the behaviour of biological systems. As a result, I went on to obtain my PhD in biomathematics but maintained my interest in neurobiology and in particular in food intake control. I have endeavoured to develop a mathematical modelling approach that could incorporate the multiplicity of factors involved in food intake control.

As every reader of this volume knows, numerous theories and experiments have attempted to elucidate the processes underlying food intake control. A few of the many factors that have been implicated in food intake control are gastric contractions, gastric distension, hunger hormones, temperature, blood glucose, calorie intake, intestinal absorption, circulating metabolites and oropharyngeal stimuli. Several of these factors have been advocated as primary explanations of the control of food intake, such viewpoints being named thermostatic, glucostatic or lipostatic theories. These single-factor theories all offer partial accounts of the complex processes involved in food intake control but none of them can successfully account for all the experimental evidence. Typically, each of the single-factor theories has been weakened by experiments demonstrating that food intake and body weight could be controlled with the factor of interest held constant or eliminated entirely (Anand, 1961).

The dual-centre theory, which maintained that hunger and food intake are initiated by activity of neurones in the lateral hypothalamic area (LH), while activity of ventromedial hypothalamic (VMH) neurones provides a satiety mechanism, attempted to integrate several of the single-factor theories to give a coherent account of neural control mechanisms. The dual centre theory and the concept of localized hypothalamic centres were challenged by evidence indicating involvement of extrahypothalamic regions in food intake control (e.g. Grossman, 1968; 1972). Indeed, accumulating evidence indicates interaction of many factors and subsystems in the brain, gastrointestinal tract, and other regions, from cellular to organ system to entire organism levels, as summarized in several recent reviews (Baile and Forbes, 1974; Grossman, 1975; Hoebel, 1971; Lepkovsky, 1973a, b; Liebelt *et al.,* 1973; Morgane and Jacobs, 1969; Nisbett, 1972; Teitelbaum, 1971; Woods and Porte, 1974).

In view of the multivariate nature of the food intake control system, the interaction of many variables, and the adaptability of the system in controlling food intake when one or more variables are held constant, the value of single factor theories has diminished, while the information yielded by single factor experiments is often difficult to interpret without the context of a guiding theoretical framework. As Morgane (1969) and Fleming (1969) have stated, there is a need for a quantitative, systems-theoretic approach to the food intake control system. What is needed is a general theory of food intake control that interrelates nutrient availability as reflected in the composition of the diet and the intracellular concentrations of nutrients and metabolites in various regions of the body, neuronal membrane potentials or firing rates, neuronal connective patterns, and behaviour of the whole organism, including the effects of temperature, hormones, body weight and composition, water intake, etc. A mathematical model based on such a theory would suggest new hypotheses and experiments, clearly indicate promising avenues of research, and predict results of very complex and costly experiments, which could then be conducted on a smaller scale. The theory and model should be of sufficient generality to be applicable to any mammalian species, account for both long- and short-term control of food intake and body weight, and integrate the various interacting subsystems in the food intake control hierarchy, from the biochemical to the behavioural level.

My approach to a general theory and mathematical model of the vertebrate food intake control system will be described here. My initial model of food intake control (Barnwell, 1972) primarily served to focus my attention on the problems raised by the model. I later abandoned the initial model for a different approach, to be elaborated below. Some general theoretical concepts will first be discussed as a background for the mathematical modelling approach. A mathematical model of two mutually inhibitory neural circuits and computer simulations based on the model will be presented and related to experimental evidence. The extension of the neural circuit model to interactions with the gastrointestinal tract, adipose tissue and feeding reflex systems will be considered. Finally, the applicability of the modelling approach to other behaviours will be discussed.

II. Basic Concepts

A. *Rates of Change and Steady States*

The concepts of rate of change and steady state are essential for understanding the dynamical systems approach. Figure 1 represents a tank of water, with the

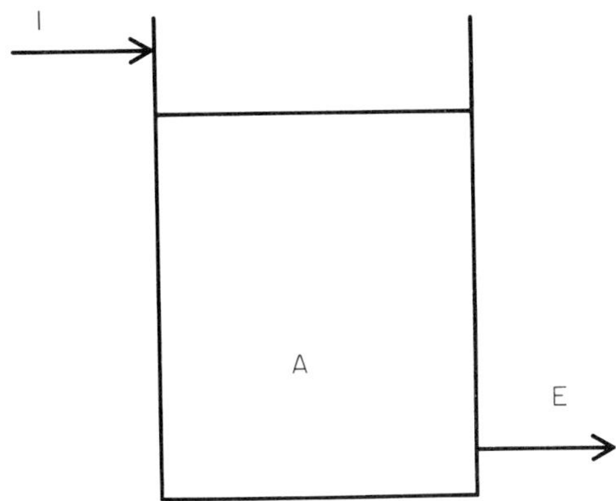

Fig. 1. Rates of change and steady state. A = Amount of water in the tank at a given time. I = Rate of water inflow. E = Rate of water outflow.

letter A denoting the amount of water in the tank at a given time, I denoting the rate at which water is added to the tank, and E denoting the rate at which water leaves the tank. Mathematically, the instantaneous rate of change in water contents (A) with respect to time is denoted by $\mathrm{d}A/\mathrm{d}t$, the derivative of A, or its differential with respect to time (t). An intuitive interpretation of this derivative follows. Suppose the reservoir were sealed so that no water could flow in or out, and every 60s a man dipped a bucket into the water and removed 4 litres of water. If he decided to lift smaller loads, he could still remove water at the same rate by removing 2 litres every 30s, or 1 litre every 15s. The rate of change in each case is a loss of 4 litres/60s = 2 litres/30s = 1 litre/15s. If smaller and smaller amounts of water were removed at shorter and shorter intervals, eventually a continuous flow would be approached. This is precisely how the derivative, or instantaneous rate of change, is defined. If we let ΔA denote the change in A in time interval Δt, and we take smaller and smaller time intervals until we approach an infinitesimally small time interval, the instantaneous rate of change of A is the limit of $\Delta A/\Delta t$ as Δt approaches zero. The rate of change of A equals the difference between the input flow I and the output flow E, or $\mathrm{d}A/\mathrm{d}t = I - E$. When water is being removed faster than it is added, the rate of change is negative; when water is added faster than it is removed, the rate of change is positive.

In the steady state situation, the input flow equals the output flow, $I = E$. Obviously, if there is exactly as much water flowing out of the reservoir as there is flowing into it, then the amount of water in the reservoir is not changing, or mathematically, $\mathrm{d}A/\mathrm{d}t = I - E = 0$, which defines the steady state condition of the reservoir.

B. *Thermodynamics and Natural Selection*

The second law of thermodynamics states that an isolated system tends to approach equilibrium, maximum entropy or disorganization. The organism is an open system; it can exchange matter and energy with its environment. Living systems avoid equilibrium states by extracting matter and energy from the environment, utilizing certain available portions of these, and returning waste to the environment. The net effect is to increase or preserve the organization, information and structure of the system (Morowitz, 1968). An equilibrium state can be avoided only by keeping the system *open* and maintaining a *flow* of matter and energy through the system. In the simplest case, a constant net flow rate for all substances would result in a steady state, generally a steady state far from equilibrium.

With respect to evolution and natural selection, there are at least four basic requirements for all living organisms.

(i) Obtain needed materials from environment.
(ii) Grow and reproduce.
(iii) Release waste to environment.
(iv) Avoid predators or other dangers.

The "successful" organisms, or those which are not eliminated by natural selection, are the ones that are able to meet these four requirements in the most efficient or *optimum* manner.

In considering how mammalian species meet the four basic requirements, one immediately notes several problems:

(a) Food intake is not a continuous process, but is a discrete act. Therefore, the flow of matter and energy through such organisms is discontinuous or non-uniform and no single steady state will suffice to keep the system from approaching equilibrium. This means either that there are no steady states and the entire system is continuously changing or that there is more than one steady state for the system, and that it can make transitions between the steady states. This point will be discussed in further detail below. Discrete food intake also necessitates an energy storage system to maintain the flows when food is unavailable.

(b) Water intake, mating, fighting, fleeing and waste elimination are also discrete processes which must be controlled in an optimum fashion for the organism to survive and contribute its offspring to the next generation. These discrete processes are (in general) mutually incompatible, distinct behavioural modes (Kilmer *et al.*, 1969; Bloch *et al.*, 1971).

(c) For a process or variable to be controlled, there must be input signals that give information about the state of the system, and there must be controlling output signals that can change the state of the system.

(d) Since the organism must meet all the essential requirements by discrete behavioural acts, there must be some means to integrate all available information on the state of the system and to select the appropriate behavioural mode at any given time, i.e. there must be an integrative decision-making centre for behavioural mode selection.

(e) Exigencies of the environment may change the availability of energy and nutrients, increase energy expenditure, etc. Therefore, the organism must be adaptive. It can adapt to a wide variety of situations, both by changing intracellular biochemical reaction patterns via adaptive enzyme systems and by changing behavioural patterns via decision-making neural circuits. Such a multivariate adaptive system is inherently nonlinear.

C. *Behavioural Modes and Neural Controls*

For an animal to meet the four basic survival requirements listed above, it must be able to respond to environmental and metabolic demands by selecting the appropriate behavioural mode. Food intake, water intake, sleep and aggression are examples of an estimated maximum of about 25 behavioural modes (Kilmer *et al.*, 1969). Once an animal has entered a behavioural mode, it must be able to persist in that mode until the environmental/metabolic demands are satisfied, i.e. the mode must be stable. Stability of a behavioural mode means that a distracting stimulus will not produce more than a transient change to another behavioural mode as long as conditions favouring that mode are present, unless the distracting stimulus signals that immediate action is necessary for survival. Thus, a chimpanzee feeding on fruit might stop to chase off a competitor, and then return to eating. In emergency situations, the animal must be able to rapidly change from one behavioural mode to another. If a leopard approached the feeding chimpanzee, the chimpanzee would have to forget about food for a while and flee.

The neural systems mediating behavioural mode selection and decision-making should therefore have two fundamental properties. They should maintain ongoing behaviour appropriate to meeting environmental/metabolic demands, and they should respond rapidly to significant shifts in demands. The neural systems must integrate incoming exteroceptive and interoceptive information, decide on the appropriate behavioural mode, implement the decision, and maintain the behaviour until it is no longer appropriate, due to changes in the stimulus situation. The organism can adapt to various situations by switching behavioural modes.

D. *Metabolism and Biochemical Controls*

It is well known that many adaptive enzyme systems exist, such that the activity of one or more enzymes in a pathway can be increased or decreased by a variety of nutrients or metabolites. For example, in feedback inhibition the end product, a metabolite, inhibits the initial enzyme in the reaction sequence. In feedback activation the initial enzyme is activated by a reaction product. Other mechanisms include parallel activation, precursor activation, and substrate activation (Monod, 1971). Such enzymes are termed allosteric enzymes, and in general, their activity is a function of the concentration of one or more controlling substances. Monod (1971) also notes that allosteric enzymes are generally controlled by several factors, so that a single enzyme might be activated by its substrate, inactivated by a terminal metabolite, and activated or inactivated by a metabolite from a parallel pathway.

Synthesis of messenger RNA and protein may be turned on or off by derepression and repression, giving further possibilities for adaptive control. For the purposes of this discussion, derepression v. repression and activation v. inactivation are both viewed as on–off switching mechanisms. The important concept is that changes in the concentration of one or more nutrients, metabolites, ions or other substances can alter the rate of synthesis and/or the relative activity of certain enzymes, which in turn results in a reaction pathway switching capability. The importance of the switching capability is that animals that exhibit modal behaviour patterns (e.g. discrete activities such as eating, drinking, sleeping) can also adjust their metabolic machinery to adapt to the extreme variations in nutrient and energy inputs to maintain availability of nutrients and energy at the cellular level in all tissues. Thus, meal pattern and diet composition produce a variety of adaptive enzyme responses in animals (Herman *et al.*, 1970; Leveille, 1970; Potter *et al.*, 1968; Rogers and Leung, 1973; Scott and Potter, 1970; Tepperman and Tepperman, 1970). The marked capability for adaptive response has been emphasized by Tepperman and Tepperman (1970) who noted that hepatic adaptive enzyme systems "reflect the composition of the diet with extraordinary fidelity and subtlety".

Adaptive enzyme systems are particularly important with respect to energy storage and release. Note that the switching capability of the adaptive enzyme systems results in discrete, mutually exclusive metabolic modes such as energy storage or energy release for glycogen and adipose tissue reserves. Thus, energy is stored when it is abundant, and released when it is scarce. But storage and release do not occur simultaneously, so a highly co-ordinated, complex metabolic control system operates by simultaneously inactivating an adaptive enzyme controlling energy storage and activating an adaptive enzyme controlling energy release, or vice versa, as the situation demands. Since multiple factors affect the activity of allosteric enzymes, the states of maximal activity (on) and complete inactivity (off) are not necessarily the only two states possible, and numerous intermediate possibilities could exist.

Although energy balance is important, the idea that caloric intake is the regulated factor in food intake control, and that energy balance determines body weight is an over-simplification. As mentioned above, diet composition affects both adaptive enzyme systems and the feeding process. In addition, there is evidence that the interaction of dietary components affects nutrient utilization patterns (Albanese and Orto, 1973; Herman *et al.*, 1970; Leveille, 1970). Amino acid imbalances, deficiencies or excesses can influence diet selection and amount of food ingested (Rogers and Leung, 1973). Similarly, animals deficient in salt, thiamine and other substances can learn to select diets containing these substances (Denton, 1967; Lat, 1967; Rozin, 1967).

E. *Hierarchical Systems*

A system may be defined as a collection of interacting elements. The word "hierarchy" implies an ordering or ranking of the elements of a system into different levels of structure, function or complexity. For example, a mammal may be viewed as a hierarchical system whose levels of function, from lowest to highest, are

(i) molecular interactions,
(ii) cell metabolism,
(iii) organ system function,
(iv) integrated function of the whole animal.

Within each level, there may be structural and functional relationships among elements that differ for different levels, and there may be groupings of elements into subsystems within a level (e.g. organ systems in the body). At the molecular and cellular levels there is a considerable degree of component redundancy, i.e. there are large numbers of macromolecular structures or cells performing identical functions. Such redundancy results in a high degree of reliability of the function, since reasonable performance continues if several components are removed or malfunctioning.

Structural and functional relationships among levels yield a new type of reliability, which enables the system to adapt to internal and external changes. If there are sufficient interrelationships among levels and subsystems, the system may still be able to function with the loss of an entire subsystem.

The concept of steady state was defined above and the discrete nature of food intake was cited as the basis for the existence of no steady states or many steady states. It is possible, although not likely, that if neural activity (defined as average firing frequency in a neural mass), heart rate, and other statistical averages were used, the entire organism might be able to attain a steady state for a brief time period. However, the overall steady state would be unstable because internal changes would occur in the biological system independently of any external variables that might be held constant. This property of living systems has been termed "marginal instability" (Bloch *et al.,* 1971). Thus, even if there are multiple steady states, the organism cannot remain at any single steady state, but will eventually drift away from it. However, animals can persist in a behavioural mode for a reasonable amount of time, and metabolic modes should persist under favourable conditions. Indeed, some mechanisms for stability and constancy in certain processes are necessary, e.g. a food-deprived animal must continue to eat rather than switching to a new behaviour, and fat storage must persist for some time following a meal.

If local steady states could be maintained in some subsystems while the variables characterizing other subsystems were changing in value, a compromise solution would be obtained. The existence of local, stable steady states of subsystems seems to be a mechanism by which the organism could minimize entropy production and extract a maximal amount of energy and information from available nutrients. In accordance with Prigogine's notion of minimum entropy production occurring at a steady state (Glansdorff and Prigogine, 1971; Prigogine and Nicolis, 1971), some subsystems could remain at steady states while others were varying, rather than all subsystems varying simultaneously. The notion of local steady states will be further developed in Section III.

F. *Overview*

The organism is viewed as a marginally unstable, nonlinear, multilevel, hierarchical control system that controls food intake and optimizes nutrient utilization according to environmental/metabolic demands. The control hierarchy is comprised of several levels, including biochemical pathways at the cellular level, organ system function, behaviour of the whole organism. The nervous system provides integrated control of all levels.

Periodic transitions between local stable steady states are a consequence of discrete food intake behaviour, one set of local steady states corresponding to hunger (nutrient deficits) and the other to satiety (sufficient nutrients), each of which may be attained by many different combinations of variable values in a mode-selecting optimization process. Nutrient utilization will eventually displace the system from the satiety state, necessitating further food intake, so cyclic processes result.

Nutrient intake (meal frequency and size) and nutrient utilization (energy storage, energy release, catabolism, anabolism) are optimized such that entropy production is minimized and the organism extracts a maximal amount of energy and information from the available supply of nutrients and allocates supplies according to environmental/metabolic demands. Such a system would have a high selective value, concurring with Eigen's (1971) approach of self-organization and evolution of systems.

Neural control of behavioural-mode selection arises from mutually interacting closed-loop, positive feedback neural circuits involving regions of the limbic system, medial forebrain bundle, reticular formation, lateral and ventromedial hypothalamus, and other areas. Mutually inhibitory positive feedback neural circuits containing subsets of neurones sensitive to the concentrations of nutrients or metabolites have a decision-making capability, and can initiate steady state transitions and behavioural mode changes. Since each local steady state can be achieved by optimizing over many variables, loss of information on one variable can be compensated for by a readjustment of the other variables, i.e. by defining a new steady state set point for one or more subsystems.

III. Mathematical Model of Interacting Neural Circuits

A. *Dynamical System Theory*

The engineering-oriented principles of control theory have been successfully applied to numerous biological subsystems. However, the limitations imposed by concepts of linear systems theory, negative feedback stability criteria, and biological homeostasis preclude such successful applications of control theory to studies of dynamics of entire biological systems. Milhorn (1966) notes some of the difficulties: technological systems are generally linear while physiological systems may be nonlinear, a physiological system may lack both a reference input and an error detector, and physiological systems may have multiple inputs and outputs. In addition, there are the problems of incorporating positive feedbacks and decision-making capabilities into linear systems models. For these reasons, a dynamical system theory approach seems to offer more possibilities and greater generality.

A dynamical system is simply a system that changes in time. The instantaneous state of a dynamical system is described by the values of a set of state variables characterizing the system. The behaviour of a dynamical system is described by a set of differential equations in which the rate of change of each state variable is a function of some subset of the other state variables. An introductory exposition of dynamical system theory is given by Rosen (1970).

B. *Components of the Model*

The first step in attempting to develop a dynamical system theory formulation of food intake control seemed to be to develop a model of the neural circuits that would exhibit the necessary decision-making properties.

Several investigators have suggested that positive feedback processes are involved in either the motivational arousal circuits that initiate feeding or in the stimulus properties that maintain and facilitate feeding (Le Magnen, 1969; de Ruiter, 1967). It has also been suggested that closed-loop reciprocating or reverberatory circuits of neurones selectively activated by different chemicals or transmitters could play a fundamental role in the biological basis of drive and motivation (Fisher, 1964, 1969; Fisher and Coury, 1964; Grossman, 1968, 1969; Morgane, 1969; Stein, 1968). The positive feedback circuits indicated by the evidence involve the medial forebrain bundle, reticular system, limbic system and other regions.

There is substantial evidence for mutually inhibitory interactions of LH and VMH (Anand *et al.,* 1961, 1964; Oomura *et al.,* 1964, 1969a,b). Anatomical evidence also indicates reciprocal relations between LH and VMH (Arees and Mayer, 1967; Millhouse, 1973a,b).

The simplest version of the model assumes that feeding and satiety decisions result from the interactions of a feeding circuit and a satiety circuit, each consisting of hypothalamic and extrahypothalamic neurones. Each circuit is assumed to consist of a large number of mutually excitatory neurones in a reverberatory circuit or positive feedback loop configuation, such that only excitatory synapses are formed between pairs of neurones in the circuit. The two reverberatory circuits are assumed to be mutually inhibitory, that is, the level of activity in one loop tends to reduce the level of activity in the other loop via inhibitory synapses.

1. *Characteristics of a Positive Feedback Loop*

A loop is shown schematically in Fig. 2. It is assumed to contain many path neurones. There is extensive axonal and dendritic branching, both in parallel and transversely to the path of the loop. Also, any external input (e.g. excitatory *A* or *B* or the inhibitory *C* or *D*) may provide collaterals to an extensive region of the loop. The component neurones are tonic neurones that tend to fire at some average frequency dependent on the existing conditions. Thus, although each circuit is spatially distributed, the tonic activity and diffuse connective patterns of component neurones make it difficult to define localized homogeneous compartments.

It is thus reasonable to assume that a given circuit will behave as an entity because of the collective statistical properties of the interconnected neurones. We are interested in von Neumann's "majority vote logic" and can concentrate on the loop's summated properties, ignoring the details of processes in individual neurones and synapses. As Pattee (1973) suggests, "function or control can arise only through some selective loss of detail" in complex, hierarchical systems.

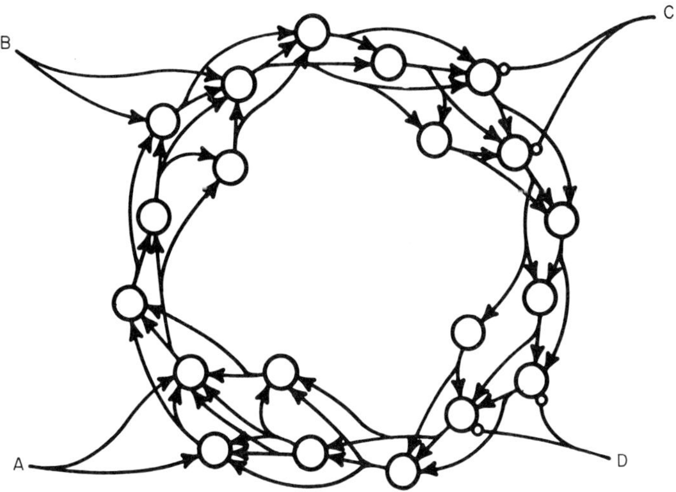

Fig. 2. A reverberatory circuit. *A* and *B*: External excitation. *C* and *D*: External inhibition. Other arrows: internal excitation or positive feedback.

The definitions and assumptions in the mathematical specification of a model positive feedback loop are as follows (Barnwell and Stafford, 1975a).

(a) *Level of activity or inactivity.* The activity in a loop is the average number of neural firings occurring per second, and is denoted by n. There is a saturation or maximal level of activity in a circuit, denoted by η, which is determined by certain properties of component neurones and their interconnections, e.g. degree of convergence and divergence, membrane time constant, refractory period, axonal transmission time. The activity cannot exceed η, so the degree of inactivity is denoted by $(\eta - n)$.

(b) *Rate of change of activity* (dn/dt). Activity may increase or decrease (positive or negative dn/dt), depending on the excitatory and inhibitory inputs, and will not change at steady state.

Increase in neural activity in the loop can arise from positive feedback within the loop and from excitation from neurones outside the loop. The internal connectivity contributing to a positive feed-back effect is represented by a factor γ. The average connectivity among neurones in the neural mass or network outside the loop and the average weighted effects of incoming excitatory fibres of chemical inputs to loop neurones are represented by the lumped term βE, where E is the magnitude of all externally originating excitation. The actual rate of increase of activity in the loop is assumed to be proportional to the product of these factors $(\gamma+\beta E)$ and the present activity (n) times the degree of inactivity $(\eta - n)$. The multiplier n denotes the proportionality of activity change to present activity. The relative activity of a circuit will be represented as a ratio to that circuit's saturation activity, i.e. the multiplier becomes n/η. The resulting

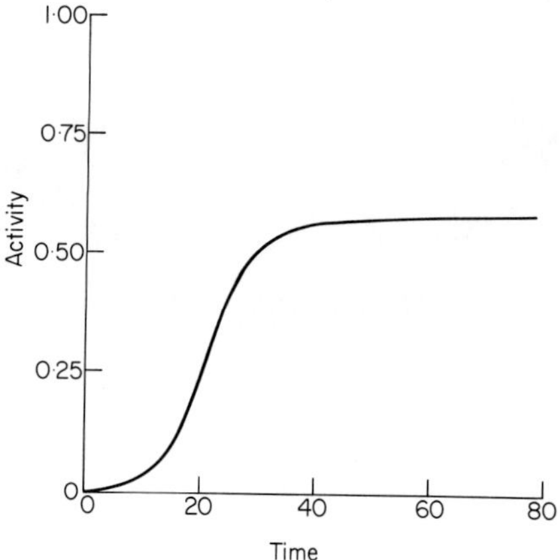

Fig. 3. A logistic function, showing increase of activity in a neural circuit.

equation $dn/dt = (\eta - n)(\gamma + \beta E)n/\eta$ is a form of the familiar sigmoid or logistic curve in population mathematics, as shown in Fig. 3. The saturation property (n cannot exceed η) results in a stable positive feedback system. If the values of γ, β or E are increased, the rate of increase in activity within the loop becomes greater, so that the slope of the curve in Fig. 3 becomes steeper and the asymptote is attained more rapidly.

Decrease in loop activity arises in part from externally arising inhibition of neurones which are active within the reverberatory system. This influence is represented as $-\delta I$, where δ is a neural connectivity parameter and I is a lumped term for external inhibition. It is also assumed that active neurones become inactive in the absence of other influences, at a proportional decay rate L. Hence the decreasing factors are $-\delta I$ and L. When these terms are included with the excitatory terms, they lower the asymptotic value reached by the logistic function of Fig. 3.

2. *Mutually Inhibitory Positive Feedback Loops*

When a pair of reverberatory circuits are connected together by inhibitory neurones, the inhibitory connective strength of one circuit on the other can be denoted by a parameter α. Then the inhibitory effect of that circuit on the loop will be the product of α and the activity in the inhibiting circuit ($-\alpha n$).

The feeding circuit has to be distinguished from the satiety circuit, so let subscript 1 denote feeding and subscript 2 denote satiety. Furthermore, we would need to distinguish between different classes of excitatory external input (classes 1, 2 . . . j) and inhibitory external input (1, 2 . . . k) to the loops, and then sum the effects of excitatory variables ($\Sigma_j \beta_j E_j$) and of inhibitory variables ($\Sigma_k \delta_k I_k$).

This gives a full equation for change in activity in the *feeding circuit*:

$$\frac{dn_1}{dt} = \frac{n_1}{\eta_1}\left[(\eta_1 - n_1)(\gamma_1 + \sum_j \beta_{1j} E_{1j}) - \alpha_1 n_2 - \sum_k \delta_{1k} I_{1k} - L_1\right] \tag{1}$$

Similarly, the equation for the *satiety circuit* changes is:

$$\frac{dn_2}{dt} = \frac{n_2}{\eta_2}\left[(\eta_2 - n_2)(\gamma_2 + \sum_j \beta_{2j} E_{2j}) - \alpha_2 n_1 - \sum_k \delta_{2k} I_{2k} - L_2\right] \tag{2}$$

The mathematical restriction is imposed that n_1 and n_2 be always positive-valued. This incorporates the biological intuition that activity in a neural circuit could become extremely small but never zero or less.

3. *Control of Feeding by the Feeding and Satiety Loops*

Eating is initiated and maintained whenever activity in the feeding circuit exceeds that in the satiety circuit, and eating is terminated if activity in the feeding circuit drops below that in the satiety circuit. Eating and not eating are the only modes: other aspects of behaviour are ignored in this model.

We are interested in the existence of stable steady states in such a system and in the mechanisms which initiate transition from one steady state to another. At a steady state, the rate of change of activity in each circuit is zero. Thus we can put the model initially into steady state by setting both equations (1) and (2) to zero. We can then study the steady state and transitional activity levels in each circuit simultaneously as a function of the parameters denoting the various neural, hormonal and metabolic influences on the component neurones. The relative importance of a particular type of excitatory input j is represented by β_{1j} or β_{2j}, and similarly each type of inhibitory input k by the δ factors. Each circuit responds to the total amount of input from all sources, and so the contribution of a particular input can be unimportant, i.e. decisions are made on the basis of totals. If information on one or more inputs is lost, somewhat larger values of inputs having similar effects will still produce the same behaviour. The feeding and satiety circuits are competing by virtue of their reciprocal inhibition: the circuit with the higher level of activity will become dominant with respect to behaviour mode selection, while the circuit with lower activity is suppressed.

The neural networks modelled should produce extended periods of eating alternating with extended periods of not eating, when coupled with a compartmental model of the gastrointestinal tract and other subsystems.

C. *Computer Simulation Results*

1. *Qualitative Properties*

Preliminary computer simulations were designed to examine the qualitative behaviour of the model, and have established that the behaviour corresponds to previous theoretical predictions (Barnwell, 1974a,b) and to several experimental observations. Since the purpose of the preliminary studies was to determine whether the model would exhibit behaviour qualitatively corresponding to certain experimental observations of LH–VMH interactions, the levels of excitation and inhibition and the parameter values were regarded as relative strengths of dimensionless numbers ranging from 0·0 to 1·0.

Our initial results were obtained by analogue computer simulations (Barnwell and Stafford, 1975a). In subsequent digital computer simulations, we first replicated the analogue simulations and then studied other situations (Barnwell and Stafford, 1975b), and portions of these results will be presented here.

Initial simulations showed that the circuit receiving the greatest net excitation would become dominant over the other circuit. Furthermore, very strong excitation or inhibition was necessary to reverse dominance of one circuit over the other; for a given set of steady states, a threshold amount of increased excitation to the suppressed circuit was necessary for a reversal to occur. Thus, the model integrates incoming inputs by summing excitatory and inhibitory inputs in each circuit and successfully makes decisions by comparing relative activity levels in each circuit, selecting the behavioural mode corresponding to the circuit with the highest relative activity. The decision-making capability is an inherent property of the model.

2. *Feeding Before Serious Deficit*

Barnwell (1972) suggested that a positive feedback reverberatory circuit configuration of chemosensitive neurones would be a more efficient deficit detector than a simple mass of chemosensitive neurones. If some type of neurones increased its firing rate in response to a decreased blood level of a nutrient, or possibly in response to an increased blood level of a metabolite produced by utilization of the nutrient, neurones of this type would serve as a deficit detector for this nutrient. It was suggested that if such a collection of neurones were organized into a positive feedback loop configuration, the deficit detector system would respond earlier and initiate food-seeking behaviour well before deficits became serious.

We have used the model to corroborate this suggestion theoretically, by comparing responses of the model for different values of the positive feedback parameter in one of the loops.

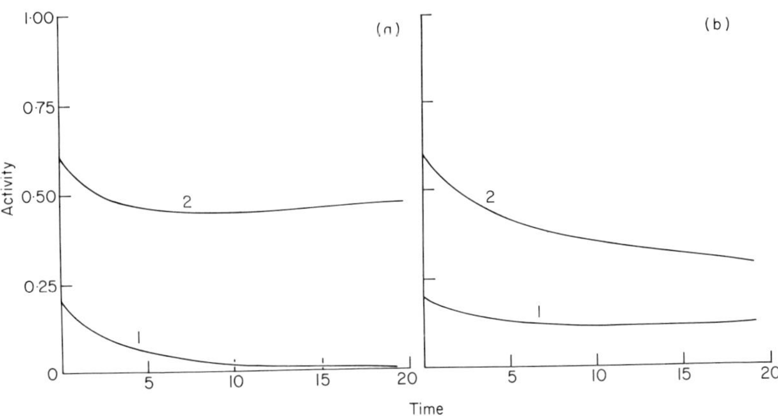

Fig. 4. (a) Activity in the model feeding circuit (1) and satiety circuit (2). External excitation is low and equal in both circuits ($\beta_1 E_1 = \beta_2 E_2 = 0{\cdot}1$), and internal positive feedback is put into the satiety circuit only ($\gamma_1 = 0$; $\gamma_2 = 0{\cdot}1$). Equal values are given in the mutual inhibition ($\alpha_1 = \alpha_2 = 0{\cdot}5$) and the decay terms ($L_1 = L_2 = 0{\cdot}1$), with no inhibition from external sources. (b) Parameter values as in (a) except that stronger external excitation is applied to the feeding loop ($\beta_1 E_1 = 0{\cdot}3$).

The results of a series of simulations are given in Figs 4–6. The satiety circuit was in all cases initially set at higher activity than the feeding circuit. For simplicity. inhibition from external sources was omitted, the inhibitory influences of the feeding and satiety circuits on each other were set equal. as were the loss terms for each circuit, representing spontaneous decay of activity.

The effects of various levels of the internal positive feedback factor of the feeding circuit (1) were calculated at two different values of excitation to feeding from sources outside the circuit. Without any positive feedback within the feeding loop, the final steady state values of activity in the two loops were both somewhat lower than the initial values, both at the lower (Fig. 4a) and the higher values (Fig. 4b) of external excitation. Although the stronger excitation produced greater steady state activity in the initially less active feeding loop (1) than did the lower excitation, and also decreased the steady state activity in the more active satiety loop (2), these effects were not sufficient to reverse the dominance of satiety over feeding.

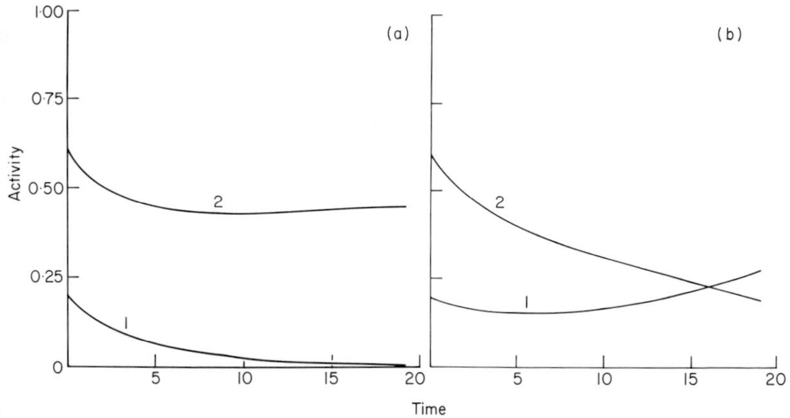

Fig. 5. Activity in feeding (1) and satiety (2) circuits set as in Fig. 4a and b, except that internal positive feedback is added to the feeding circuit, although at a value still lower than that of positive feedback in the satiety circuit ($\gamma_1 = 0 \cdot 05$). (a) Low external excitation to feeding ($\beta_1 E_1 = 0 \cdot 1$). (b) Greater excitatory input to feeding ($\beta_1 E_1 = 0 \cdot 3$).

However, when some internal positive feedback was provided in the feeding circuit, the stronger excitatory input to that loop did induce a reversal of dominance (Fig. 5b), although the weaker excitation did not (Fig. 5a). The probability of food seeking would be greatly increased in this situation.

With a still stronger positive feedback effect in feeding (equal to that given to satiety throughout), the results are qualitatively similar. Figure 6a shows the results of all three levels of positive feedback with external excitation at the lower value—reversal does not occur. Figure 6b gives the result of strong positive feedback with stronger external excitation—the reversal of relative activity occurs faster where the positive feedback effect is greater.

Thus, we have provided theoretical support for the suggestion that positive feedback deficit detector circuits would be more efficient than simple masses of deficit detector neurones. An immediate selective advantage would be that the animal would begin to seek food before energy stores had to be used.

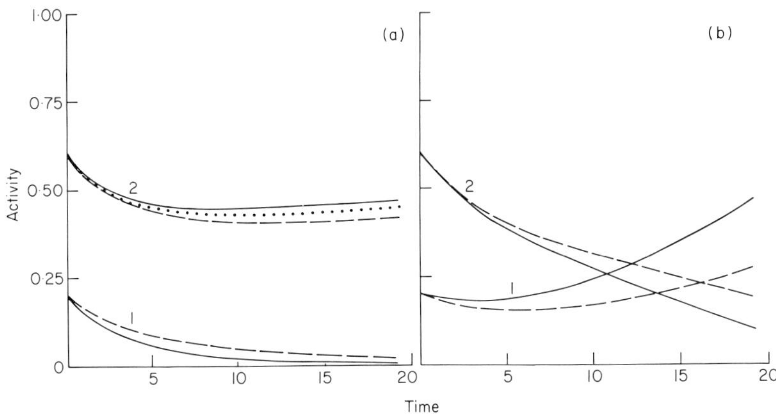

Fig. 6. Activity in feeding (1) and satiety (2) circuits with various levels of internal positive feedback within the feeding circuit. (a) External excitation as in Figs 4 and 5a ($\beta_1 E_1 = 0{\cdot}1$); solid line, $\gamma_1 = 0$; dotted line, $\gamma_1 = 0{\cdot}05$; dashed line, $\gamma_1 = 0{\cdot}1$. (b) external excitation higher as in Fig. 5b ($\beta_1 E_1 = 0{\cdot}3$); dashed line, $\gamma_1 = 0{\cdot}05$; solid line $\gamma_1 = 0{\cdot}1$.

3. *Natural Slowly Changing Inputs*

The previous simulations have largely studied effects of step inputs beginning at steady state levels. Many simulations of this type are quite realistic in terms of simulating physiological/behavioural experiments in which the onset of some stimulus can be approximated by step inputs, e.g. effects of electrial or chemical stimulation in various brain regions. However, it is equally desirable to study the animal in its natural state to discover determinants of feeding patterns. To do this, one must consider continuous variables, especially exponential increases and decreases in various quantities that would be observed in flows of material between compartments, e.g. intestinal absorption of glucose after a meal.

Several simulations of this type were conducted. Two examples of the model behaviour in reponse to such exponential changes are seen in Fig. 7a and b. Figure 7a corresponds to beginning at initial conditions of $n_1 = 0{\cdot}333$ and $n_2 = 0{\cdot}001$ approximately, and allowing excitation to n_1 to decay exponentially according to the expression $E_1 = \exp(-0{\cdot}1t)$. The initial increase in n_1 resulted from an initial value of n_1 that was lower than the steady state value corresponding to the parameter values; it is rapidly reversed as the excitation begins to decay. Figure 7b corresponds to the opposite situation in which satiety activity in circuit 2 is initially higher and the exponential decay of activity in circuit 2 eventually results in a reversal.

When the model is enlarged in scope, to include the gastrointestinal tract, and energy storage and utilization, numerous variable inputs to the neural circuits will be of interest. The threshold properties of the model indicate that no mode change will occur in response to a small, slowly increasing or decreasing input (such as the tail or approximately linear portion of an exponential decay curve), but that when a threshold excitation level is reached, a reversal, and hence a mode change, will occur rapidly. This suggests that the system ignores small inputs and remains in a stable steady state until significant changes occur.

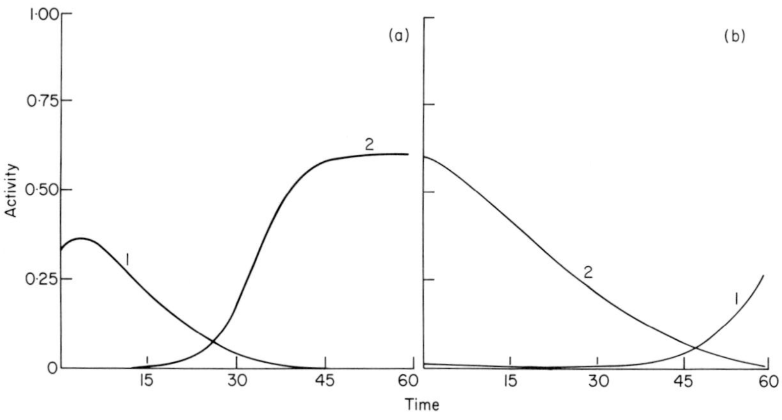

Fig. 7. Model response to exponential inputs. (a) Initial activity higher in feeding circuit, with exponential decay of excitation in that circuit. (b) Initial activity higher in satiety circuit, with exponential decay of excitation in that circuit.

4. *Oscillations*

Considerable emphasis has been placed on steady state activity in the neural circuits as a prerequisite for stability of a behavioural mode, and on the mechanism for steady state transitions, or mode changes. The scheme needs to be carried a step further, to consider oscillatory behaviour, i.e. feeding cycles. The two-circuit model is essentially a decision-making model in that it integrates all inputs, makes a decision, and sticks to that decision until significant stimulus changes occur. The two-circuit model does not exhibit intrinsic oscillatory behaviour, i.e. no combination of constant parameter values will produce oscillatory activity in the two circuits. However, external inputs corresponding to changing stimulus conditions can produce steady state transitions, and if sinusoidal inputs are employed, the model does exhibit oscillations. An example of oscillatory behaviour of the two-circuit model is shown in Fig. 8, in which a strong sinusoidal excitatory input to one circuit produced large amplitude oscillations in that circuit and smaller amplitude oscillations in the other circuit. Physiologically, oscillations in blood glucose levels or other factors could provide similar inputs to feeding and/or satiety circuits.

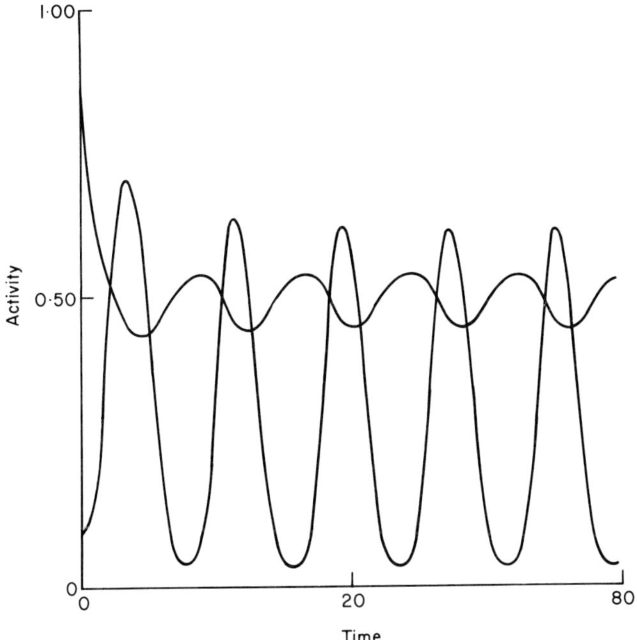

Fig. 8. Example of two-circuit model response to sinusoidal inputs, showing stable oscillations. A strong sinusoidal input to one circuit produced large oscillations in activity in that circuit, which in turn, led to smaller oscillations in the other circuit due to the inhibitory effects. Stable patterns of such oscillations were attained for various combinations of parameter values.

5. *Relation to Experimental Evidence*

The simulations have thus far shown that the model exhibits qualitative behaviour corresponding to a variety of experimental observations on LH-VMH interactions. At intermediate levels of activity in the two circuits, a moderate imbalance of excitation/inhibition drives the circuit with most excitation toward its saturation activity level. Thus, increasing the value of any variable or combination of variables that excites circuit 1 or inhibits circuit 2 will lead to increased activiation and dominance of circuit 1 over circuit 2 and hence results in feeding behaviour. Similarly, activity in circuit 2 could become stronger than circuit 1 by a reversed effect. Such behaviour is analogous to that of a moderately food-deprived animal which is exposed to food-associated stimuli and then begins to eat.

When activity in one circuit greatly exceeds that in the other circuit, very strong excitation of the suppressed circuit or very strong inhibition of the dominant circuit is necessary to reverse the situation and change the behaviour. Thus, the sight of food will have no effect, but electrical stimulation of the LH can produce feeding in a satiated animal. Rebound effects have also been demonstrated. A strong stimulus produces a mode change, but after the stimulus is removed, the system reverts to the original mode. Such effects are a consequence of the stable steady states.

Thresholds were shown to exist for steady state transitions involving reversals of circuit dominance. The thresholds are significant system properties since they are variable, they help guarantee that ongoing behaviour will not be disrupted by small fluctuations (e.g. a satiated animal will not begin to eat in response to the sight of food), and any combination of variable values that exceeds the existing threshold will reverse the dominance and result in the opposite behavioural mode. This latter property of thresholds corresponds to the suggestion that an optimization process controls decision making, in that the neural circuits are responding to a weighted sum of current values of all variables affecting food intake. Experimental modifications such as vagotomy or feeding with a gastric fistula correspond to eliminating one or more of the inputs in the summation so that higher values of the remaining variables are necessary to achieve the extant threshold level.

Positive feedback in the circuits not only contributes to deficit-detecting capability. but actually contributes to system stability by self-excitatory effects that help to maintain steady states and, thus, ongoing behaviour. For example, if $\gamma_1=0$ in equation (1), it is obvious that some constant level of excitation is necessary to prevent activity in the circuit from decreasing due to external inhibition and the decay term, L. McFarland (1971) suggested that a momentum for ongoing behaviour could be provided by positive feedback from the consequences of the behaviour, and noted the need for a momentum concept to account for persistence of a given behaviour in the presence of motivational competition. As shown above, the model presented here can account for persistence of a given behaviour in the presence of motivational competition. The consequences of behaviour are easily incorporated into the model as inputs to the two circuits. Thus, if food intake is initiated by a particular combination of relative activity levels in the circuits, the positive feedback effect of taste can be represented as a subsequent excitatory input to the feeding circuit. Computer simulations of this type have shown that the positive feedback input further increases activity in the feeding circuit, which, in turn, would increase the probability of repeating the behaviour and ensure persistence of the behavioural mode.

Obviously, the above discussion is over-simplified, in view of the numerous transmitters associated with the LH, VMH, MFB, and other regions and the numerous fibre systems coursing through the MFB (Morgane, 1975). Further complications include contradictory results of electrophysiological investigations (Sutin, 1973) and differences between species. If several distinct neural circuits are in anatomical juxtaposition, either electrical stimulation or lesions at a particular locus may affect several circuits, and the precise effect observed in a particular individual of a particular species will depend on the extant activity levels in both damaged and intact circuits. Furthermore, stimulation of, or recording from, a particular locus may yield opposite results at different time periods because of changes in relative activity levels in the circuits. Models may prove useful in interpretations of such experiments.

Just as the concepts of "feeding centre" and "satiety centre" were shown to be inadequate, the two-circuit model based on a "feeding circuit" and a "satiety circuit" will in all likelihood prove insufficient to account for the accumulated experimental observations on the biological bases of food intake control. At present, the two-circuit model is conceptually useful in showing how such reverberatory, mutually inhibitory circuits can integrate incoming information and make decisions that change an animal's behaviour. This, in itself, should be of considerable importance in providing insights into the fuction of neural control systems. However, if the contributions from other neural circuits cannot simply be considered as inputs to a feeding or satiety circuit or both, and food intake decisons are actually made by multiple circuits, the modelling approach is easily extended. Some examples of multiple-circuit models are discussed below.

6. *Set Points as Steady State Levels*

Before considering extensions of the model, some comments will be made on the nature of set points in physiology. Physiological systems are nonlinear and, in general, cannot be analysed in the standard linear control theory paradigm in which there is an internally specified reference input or set point and a negative feedback signal to correct for deviations from it. Instead, the mathemetical interpretation of a set point is the steady state point toward which the system moves asymptotically or around which the system oscillates, for a given combination of parameters. Varying the parameters shifts the steady state level, and hence, the externally observed "set point".

For example, consider the set point concept in body weight. If, on the average over some extended time period, the rate of fat storage in adipose tissue equals the rate of release (in mass units), the amount of adipose tissue does not change, and consequently it is at a steady state. This steady state amount has been regarded as the set point. Yet it is variable, and may be modified by any factor that affects either storage or release of reserves, including activity of adaptive enzymes, diet composition, neural activity and hormonal influences. Thus, as Panksepp (1974) implies, it is not sufficient to state that a set point is determined by LH—VMH interaction, or that the effect of some procedure is to lower the set point, because no information is given as to how the set point is determined or modified. Thus, the concept of set point as a steady state level is useful descriptively, but not in an explanatory sense.

It is of interest to note that Myers *et al.* (1972) used the steady state concept in relation to the set point in suggesting that the sodium to calcium ratio could modify the steady state firing rates of neurones controlling the set point for body weight regulation. Ionic alteration of steady state activity in neural circuits and the associated behaviours, as Myers and Veale (1971) or Myers *et al.* (1972) have accomplished, is in complete accord with our model.

IV. Extensions and Generality of the Model

As mentioned previously, the dynamical system theory approach was selected because it seems to offer the most promising quantitative insights into the nature of the complex systems mediating food intake control and other behavioural modes. Current views of the biological basis of drive and motivation favour the ideas that distinct neurochemical circuits may mediate different behaviours (Glickman and Schiff, 1967; Stein, 1968; also see papers in Myers and Drucker-Colín, 1974). The mathematical modelling approach described above is easily extended to any number of interacting neural circuits by simply adding a new equation for each additional circuit and representing excitatory or inhibitory connections between circuits with appropriate excitatory or inhibitory input terms. Such models have already been constructed, and computer simulations based on three and four mutually inhibitory positive feedback circuits have demonstrated that these systems behave qualitatively like two-circuit systems in achieving dominance and reversals of activity levels, with thresholds and stable steady states (Barnwell and Stafford, 1975c). A more complex and probably more realistic model defines a primary arousal circuit, and a secondary action circuit for each of three behaviour modes. The three primary circuits are mutually inhibitory, and each excites its corresponding secondary circuit and inhibits the other two secondary circuits. Similar system properties were again observed.

The most recent model consists of eight reverberatory circuits connected in the following fashion: two sets of four sequentially connected circuits correspond to the two mutually inhibitory behavioural modes, with each primary circuit exciting its secondary circuit and inhibiting both the opposing primary and secondary circuit, each secondary circuit exciting its tertiary circuit and inhibiting the opposing tertiary circuit, each tertiary circuit exciting its quaternary circuit and inhibiting the opposing quaternary circuit, and each quaternary circuit inhibiting its own primary circuit. The effect of such a connective pattern is that once the primary circuits have made the decision as to which behavioural mode to enter, the entire behaviour sequence of that mode is executed by the sequential activation of the secondary, tertiary and quaternary circits corresponding to that mode, and is then terminated via inhibition of the primary circuit by the quaternary circuit. External inputs and feedback inputs to intermediate circuits may be necessary for completion of a sequence in some cases, but not in others (intrinsic oscillations).

Models of this type may offer insights into possible physiological mechanisms of such ethological concepts as "innate releasing mechanisms", "fixed action patterns" an "displacement" behaviour. Such models exhibit both intrinsic oscillations and extrinsic or driven oscillatory behaviour. An example of intrinsic oscillations is given in Fig. 9. which shows only the activity in the first

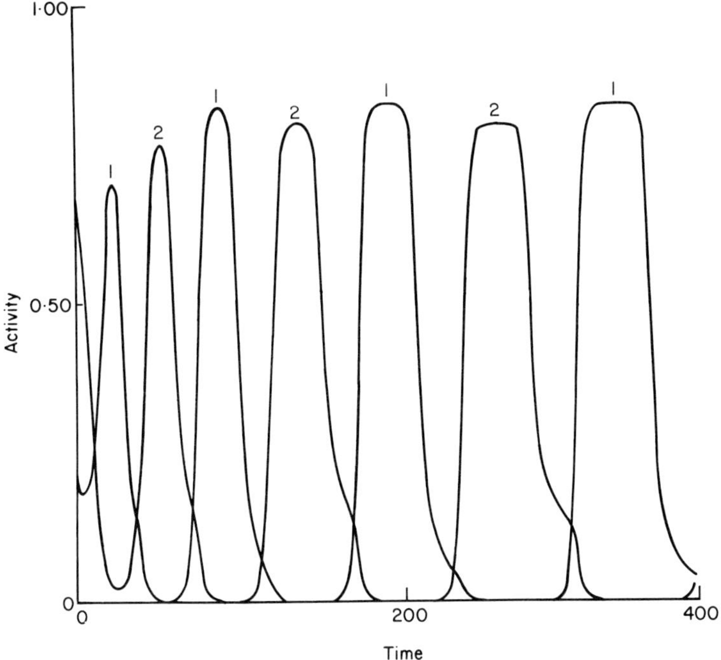

Fig. 9. Intrinsic oscillations in eight-circuit model. Only the activity levels for the first two circuits are shown. See text for details.

two circuits. Note that the peaks and troughs are flat, which means the activity in a circuit is indeed remaining at a stable steady state for an extended time period, and then making a very rapid transition to a new steady state in periodic fashion.

Multicircuit models offer a basis for a quantitative theory of behavioural mode selection as a function of measurable environmental and physiological variables. without the need for hypothetical constructs such as "drive" or "motivaton". Such models should be a valuable adjunct to experimental research on food intake control. water intake control, sleep and other behaviour. An interesting question, analogous to the genetic coding question of how many bases were necessary to code for an amino acid, is how many neurochemical circuits are necessary to specify each of the estimated 25 behavioural modes. Perhaps the answer will be suggested by models.

The mathematical model of decision-making neural circuits for food intake control will be extended to a large scale model that will include the neural control circuits, gastrointestinal trast, adipose tissue, glycogen stores and other factors. Such a model should be useful for investigating interactions of many variables known to affect food intake and body weight. In general, control and feedback effects of a variety of ions, nutrients, metabolites and hormones will be incorporated by treating these substances as modifiers of adaptive enzymes, where activity of the enzyme is a sigmoidal function of the concentration of one or more modifiers. Differential equations will describe rates of ingestion and flow through compartments in the gastrointestinal tract, and rates of storage and release. It seems that such a model would be capable of generating periodic food intake behaviour and adjusting meal size and frequency to changing demands. At any rate, an adaptive, decision-making model is the goal.

References

Albanese, A. A. and Orto, L. A. (1973). The proteins and amino acids. *In* "Modern Nutrition in Health and Disease" (R. S. Goodhart and M. E. Shils, eds), pp. 28–88. Lea and Fibiger, Philadelphia.

Anand, B. K. (1961). Nervous regulation of food intake. *Physiol. Rev.* **41**, 677–708.

Anand, B. K., Subberwal, U., Manchanda, S. K. and Singh, B. (1961). Glucoreceptor mechanism in the hypothalamic feeding centres. *Indian J. med. Res.* **49**, 717–724.

Anand, B. K., Chhina, G. S., Sharma, K. N., Dua, S. and Singh, B. (1964). Activity of single neurons in the hypothalamic feeding centres: effect of glucose. *Am. J. Physiol* **207**, 1146–1154.

Arees, E. A. and Mayer, J. (1967). Anatomical connections between medial and lateral regions of the hypothalamus concerned with food intake. *Science, N.Y.* **157**, 1574–1575.

Baile, C. A. and Forbes, J. M. (1974). Control of feed intake and regulation of energy balance in ruminants. *Psychol. Rev.* **54**, 160–214.

Barnwell, G. M. (1972). Neural control of food intake: a systems approach. Presented at International Congress of Cybernetics and Systems, Oxford, England, August, 1972. *In* "Progress in Cybernetics" (J. Rose, ed.), pp. 631–641. Gordon and Breach, New York.

Barnwell, G. M. (1974a). A theory and mathematical model of mammalian food intake control. Presented at 27th Annual Conference on Engineering in Medicine and Biology, Philadelphia, Pa., October, 1974.

Barnwell, G. M. (1974b). Mammalian food intake control: a theory and mathematical model. Presented at Vth International Conference on Physiology of Food and Fluid Intake, Jerusalem, Israel, October, 1974.

Barnwell, G. M. and Stafford, F. S. (1975a). Mathematical model for decision-making neural circuits controlling food intake. *Bull. Psychon. Soc.* **5**, 473–476.

Barnwell, G. M. and Stafford, F. S. (1975b). To eat or not to eat: properties of a mathematical model of mammalian food intake control. Presented at Eleventh Symposium on Biomathematics and Computer Science in the Life Sciences, Houston, Texas, April, 1975.

Barnwell, G. M. and Stafford, F. S. (1975c). A mathematical model of decision-making neural circuits controlling behavioural mode selection, Presented at First Meeting of the Society for Mathematical Biology, Bowling Green, Ohio, May, 1975. Also in *Bull. Math. Biol.* **39** 223–227, (1977).

Bloch, E., Cardon, S., Iberall, A., Jacobowitz, D., Kornacker, K., Lipetz, L., McCulloch, W., Urquhart, J., Weinberg, M. and Yates, F. (1971). "Introduction to a Biological Systems Science." NASA CR-1720.

Denton, D. A. (1967). Salt appetite. *In* "Handbook of Physiology Sect. 6: Alimentary Canal" (C. F. Code, ed.) Vol. I., pp. 433–459. American Physiological Society, Washington, DC.

Eigen, M. (1971). Self organization of matter and the evolution of biological macromolecules. *Die Naturwissenschaften* **10**, 465–523.

Fisher, A. E. (1964). Chemical stimulation of the brain. *Scient. Am.* **210**, 60–68.

Fisher, A. E. (1969). The role of limbic structures in the central regulation of feeding and drinking behaviour. *Ann. N.Y. Acad. Sci.* **157**, 894–901.

Fisher, A. E. and Coury, J. N. (1964). Chemical tracing of neural pathways mediating the thirst drive. *In* "Thirst" (M. J. Wayner ed.), pp. 515–531. MacMillan, New York.

Fleming, D. G. (1969). Food intake studies in parabiotic rats. *Ann. N.Y. Acad. Sci.* **157**, 985–1003.

Glansdorff, P. and Prigogine, I. (1971). "Thermodynamic Theory of Structure, Stability and Fluctuations". Wiley, New York.

Glickman, S. E. and Schiff, B. B. (1967). A biological theory of reinforcement. *Psychol. Rev.* **74**, 81–109.

Grossman, S. P. (1968). Hypothalamic and limbic influences on food intake. *Fed. Proc.* **27**, 1349–1360.

Grossman, S. P. (1969). A neuropharmacological analysis of hypothalamic and extrahypothalamic mechanisms concerned with the regulation of food and water intake. *Ann. N.Y. Acad. Sci.* **157**, 902–917.

Grossman, S. P. (1972). Neurophysiologic aspects: extrahypothalamic factors in the regulation of food intake. *Adv. psychosom. Med.* **7**, 49–72.

Grossman, S. P. (1975). Role of the hypothalamus in the regulation of food and water intake. *Psychol. Rev.* **82**, 200–224.

Herman, R. H., Zakim, D. and Stifel, F. B. (1970). Effect of diet on lipid metabolism in experimental animals and man. *Fed. Proc.* **29**, 1302–1307.

Hoebel, B. G. (1971). Feeding: neural control of intake. *Ann. Rev. Physiol.* **33**, 533–568.

Kilmer, W. L., McCulloch, W. S. and Blum J. (1969). An embodiment of some vertebrate command and control principles. *Trans. ASME J. basic Engin.* 295–304.

Lat, J. (1967). Self-selection of dietary components. *In* "Handbook of Physiology Sect. 6: Alimentary Canal" (C. F. Code, ed.) Vol. I, pp.367–386. American Physiological Society, Washington, DC.

Le Magnen, J. (1969). Peripheral and systemic actions of food in the caloric regulation of intake. *Ann. N.Y. Acad. Sci.* **157**, 1126–1157.

Lepkovsky, S. (1973a). Hypothalamic-adipose tissue interrelationships. *Fed. Proc.* **32**, 1705–1708.

Lepkovsky, S. (1973b). Newer concepts in the regulation of food intake. *Am. J. clin. Nutr.* **26**, 271–284.

Leveille, G. A. (1970). Adipose tissue metabolism: influence of periodicity of eating and diet composition. *Fed. Proc.* **29**, 1294–1301.

Liebelt, R. A., Bordelon, C. B. and Liebelt, A. G. (1973). The adipose tissue system and food intake. *In* "Progress in Physiological Psychology" (E. Stellar and J. M. Sprague, eds), pp. 211–252. Academic Press, New York and London.

McFarland, D. J. (1971). "Feedback Mechanisms in Animal Behaviour". Academic Press, London and New York.

Milhorn, H. T., jr. (1966). "The Application of Control Theory to Physiological Systems". W. B. Saunders, Philadelphia.

Millhouse, O. E. (1973a). The organization of the ventromedial hypothalamic nucleus. *Brain Res.* **55**, 71–87.

Millhouse, O. E. (1973b). Certain ventromedial hypothalamic afferents. *Brain Res.* **55**, 89–105.

Monod, J. (1971). "Chance and Necessity: an Essay on the Natural Philosophy of Modern Biology". Knopf. New York.

Morgane, P. J. (1969). The limbic and rhinic forebrain-limbic midbrain systems and reticular formation in the regulation of food and water intake. *Ann. N.Y. Acad. Sci.* **157**, 806–848.

Morgane, P. J. (1975). Anatomical and neurobiochemical bases of the central nervous control of physiological regulations and behaviour. *In* "Neural Integration of Physiological Mechanisms and Behaviour" (G. J. Morgenson and F. R. Calaresu, eds), pp. 24–67. University of Toronto Press, Toronto and Buffalo.

Morgane, P. J. and Jacobs, H. L. (1969). Hunger and satiety. *In* "World Review of Nutrition and Dietetics" (G. H. Bourne, ed.) Vol. 10, pp, 100–213. Karger, Basel and New York.

Morowitz, H. J. (1968). "Energy Flow in Biology". Academic Press, New York and London.

Myers, R. D. and Drucker-Colín, R. R. (eds) (1974). "Neurohumoral Coding of Brain Function". Plenum Press, New York and London.

Myers, R. D. and Veale, W. L. (1971). Spontaneous feeding in the satiated cat evoked by sodium or calcium ions perfused within the hypothalamus. *Physiol. Behav.* **6**, 507–512.

Myers, R. D., Bender, S. A., Krstic, M. K. and Brophy, P. D. (1972). Feeding produced in the satiated rat by elevating the concentration of calcium in the brain. *Science, N.Y.* **176**, 1124–1125.

Nisbett, R. E. (1972). Hunger, obesity, and the ventromedial hypothalamus. *Psychol. Rev.* **79**, 433–453.

Oomura, Y., Kimura, K., Ooyama, H., Maeno, H., Iki, M. and Kuniyoshi, M. (1964). Reciprocal activities of the ventromedial and lateral hypothalamic areas of cats. *Science, N.Y.* **143**, 484–485.

Oomura, Y., Ooyama, H., Yamamoto, T., Ono, T. and Kobayashi, N. (1969a). Behaviour of hypothalamic unit activity during electrophoretic application of drugs. *Ann. N.Y. Acad. Sci.* **157**, 642–665.

Oomura, Y., Ooyama, H., Naka, F., Yamamoto, T., Ono, T. and Kobayashi, N. (1969b). Some stochastical patterns of single unit discharges in the cat hypothalamus under chronic conditions. *Ann. N.Y. Acad. Sci.* **157**, 666–689.

Panksepp, J. (1974). Hypothalamic regulation of energy balance and feeding behaviour. *Fed. Proc.* **33**, 1150–1165.

Pattee, H. H. (1973). The physical basis and origin of hierarchical control. *In* "Hierarchy Theory" (H. H. Pattee, ed.), pp. 71–108. Braziller, New York.

Potter, V. R., Baril, E. F., Watanabe, M. and Whittle, E. D. (1968). Systematic oscillations in metabolic functions in liver from rats adapted to controlled feeding schedules. *Fed. Proc.* **27**, 1238–1245.

Prigogine, J. and Nicolis, G. (1971). Biological order, structure, and instabilities. *Q. Rev. Biophys.* **4**, 107–148.

Rogers, Q. R. and Leung, P. M. B. (1973). The influence of amino acids on the neuroregulation of food intake. *Fed. Proc.***32**, 1709–1719.

Rosen, R. (1970). Dynamical system theory in biology. Wiley-Interscience, New York and London.

Rozin, P. (1967). Thiamine specific hunger. *In* "Handbook of Physiology Sect. 6: Alimentary Canal" (C. F. Code, ed.) Vol I, pp. 411–431. American Physiological Society, Washington, DC.

Ruiter, L. de (1967). Feeding behaviour of vertebrates in the natural environment. *In* "Handbook of Physiology, Sect. 6: Alimentary Canal" (C. F. Code, ed.) Vol I, pp. 97–116. American Physiological Society, Washington, DC.

Scott, D. F. and Potter, V. R. (1970). Metabolic oscillations in lipid metabolism in rats on controlled feeding schedules. *Fed. Proc.* **29**, 1553–1559.

Stein, L. (1968). Chemistry of reward and punishment. *In* "Psychopharmacology, a Review of Progress: 1957–1967" (D. H. Efron, ed.), pp. 105–123. US Govt Printing Office, Washington, DC.

Sutin, J. (1973). Neural factors in the control of food intake. *In* "Obesity in Perspective" (G. A. Bray, ed.), pp. 1–11, DHEW Publication No. (NIH) 75–708, US Govt Printing Office, Washington, DC.

Teitelbaum, P. (1971). The encephalization of hunger. *Prog. physiol. Psychol* **4**, 319–350.

Tepperman, J. and Tepperman, H. M. (1970). Glucogenesis, lipogenesis and the Sherringtonian metaphor. *Fed. Proc.* **29**, 1284–1293.

Woods, S. C. and Porte, D., jr. (1974). Neural control of the endocrine pancreas. *Physiol. Rev.* **54**, 596–619.

6

Types of Modelling with an Initial Structural Analysis of the Neural Control of Feeding

L. ARTHUR CAMPFIELD
Biocybernetics Laboratory, School of Engineering and Applied Science, University of California, Los Angeles, California, U.S.A.

I. Systems Analysis and Mathematical Models

Systems analysis is that branch of science devoted to characterizing the properties of an existing collection of components connected or related in such a manner as to act as a unit or system. In technological applications, systems analysis is often performed to design a control system which meets specified performance criteria or to characterize and understand the performance of a existing control system. This latter application is appropriate for the investigation of adaptive, evolutionary designed biological control systems such as the feeding control system. A *control system* is an arrangement of components connected or related in such a manner that it dynamically or actively commands, directs or regulates itself or another system. The food intake control system is, therefore, the components that are connected or related such that the food intake of the animal is regulated. Analysis of this system has as its goal the characterization of the individual components, their couplings and interactions so that the mechanisms that result in food intake control can be understood.

The attainment of this understanding of a biological system consists of two processes: analysis and synthesis. The process of analysis is characterized by the experimental and theoretical decomposition of the system into a set of fundamental mechanisms described in terms of the laws of physics and chemistry. This decomposition is achieved by application of the scientific method, together with techniques of systems analysis for the design of experiments and for data analysis. The process of synthesis is characterized by explicit mathematical representation of these fundamental mechanisms together with their couplings and interactions in an isomorphic *mathematical model* of the system. The solution of these mathematical relationships (model simulation) as a function of time should result in model responses that agree with the observed dynamic responses of the biological system. When simulated responses of the model agree with *all* experimentally observed input–output pairs, then true *understanding* of the operation of the biological system will have been achieved. Therefore, mathematical models of the control of food intake should provide such a synthesis of mechanisms and couplings that will aid in determining the degree of our understanding of feeding control.

A. *Nonparametric Models*

The methods of systems analysis of biological systems require a collection of experimentally determined input–output pairs and a statement of what is known about the structure of the system. If nothing is known about the structure of the system or the structure is not of interest, then methods of classical control systems can be applied to this "black box" problem to obtain a model of the system that will reproduce the data set.

A *linear system* is a system which satisfies the following condition: if an input $u_1(t)$ is applied to the system with zero initial conditions and the output is $y_1(t)$, then if $\alpha u_1(t)$ is applied $\alpha y_1(t)$ will be observed, for all α. If the biological system is linear, or can be represented by a linear model over a particular range of operation, then the classical methods of linear control theory can be used to determine the weighting function or the transfer function which will allow the calculation of the response to any input. If the weighting function is $w(t,\tau)$, the "black box" can be represented by the convolution integral:

$$y(t) = \int_{t_0}^{t} w(t,\tau)u(\tau)d\tau.$$

If $Y(s)$ and $U(s)$ are the Laplace Transforms of $y(t)$ and $u(t)$ respectively, the system can be represented by the transfer function $TF(s)$:

$$Y(s) = TF(s)U(s).$$

Such representations of the system are called *empirical* or *non-parametric models*.

B. *Parametric Models*

If the system structure is partially or completely known, then mathematical equations can be derived from the specified structure. The model parameters, the unknown coefficients of these equations, must then be specified numerically before the model can be used to reproduce the input–output data set. The problem of assigning numerical values to the parameters on the input–output data is called the "grey box", the inverse, or the identification problem. Since the parameters of the model have significance in terms of the structure of the model and are potentially quantifiable, this class of models are called *parametric models*.

The analysis of parametric models of systems that can be represented by differential equations (*dynamical systems*) is enhanced and simplified by using the state variable approach of modern control theory. This approach is general in that one vector–matrix differential equation can represent all systems of a particular class. For example, all stationary, linear systems can be written as:

$$\dot{\mathbf{X}} = \mathbf{A}\mathbf{x} + \mathbf{B}\mathbf{u}$$

$$\mathbf{x}(t_0) = \mathbf{x}_0$$

where $\mathbf{x}$ is a vector of n state variables
$\mathbf{u}$ is a vector of m inputs
$\dot{\mathbf{x}}$ is a vector of n first derivatives of
$\mathbf{A} = n \times n$ system matrix
$\mathbf{B} = n \times m$ input matrix
$\mathbf{x}_0 =$ initial state at $t = t_0$

A *state equation model* of a particular system is characterized by the specification of its state variables, $\mathbf{x}$, and the matrices $\mathbf{A}$ and $\mathbf{B}$. The response of the model to any particular input, $\mathbf{u}$, depends upon that input, $\mathbf{u}$, and the numerical value $\mathbf{x}_0$ of the state $\mathbf{x}$ at the initial time. The concept of initial state is equivalent to the initial conditions of the experiment. For example, a lesioned animal will, in general, respond differently to an input than its non-lesioned control and this would be modelled by a different initial state in the "lesioned" and "non-lesioned" model. The elements of the state vector, $\mathbf{x}$, will typically be firing rates, concentrations, secretion rates, food intake, body weight, activity and other variables of interest. The parameters (elements of $\mathbf{A}$ and $\mathbf{B}$) will be theoretically measurable quantities with a direct correspondence to the biological system in an isomorphic, parametric mathematical model.

The state variable approach allows nonlinear and high order systems to be compactly modelled and analysed. It is important to note, however, that there is a direct correspondence between classical and state variable representations of linear systems.

II. Qualitative Classification of Systems

One of the objectives of systems analysis is to classify systems according to several qualitative categories. This account of classification follows DiStefano *et al.* (1967).

The definition of a *linear* system was given above; all other systems are *nonlinear*. A *time invariant* (or stationary) system is one in which the parameters are not explicit functions of time and, therefore, the response depends only upon the time interval between the present time, t, and the time of the application of the input, t_0. All other systems are *time varying*. A *deterministic* system is one which contains no random variables or processes; its response to a specified input is always identical. Conversely, a *stochastic* system is one in which random variables and/or processes cause the response of the system to several applications of a specified input to vary in a random manner. A *continuous* system is one in which the output is defined at every instant of time, while the variables and the output of a *discrete* system are defined only at specified instants of time. A *distributed-parameter* system is a system in which variables are functions of both time and space, while the variables in a *lumped-parameter* system are considered to be concentrated at one point and, therefore, can be considered as function of time only.

The biological control system that regulates feeding behaviour could be classified in these qualitative terms as a nonlinear, time varying, stochastic, discrete, distributed-parameter system. This is the antithesis of the hopes of the systems analyst, who has formidable analytical tools at his/her disposal for linear, time invariant, deterministic, continuous, lumped-parameter systems.

An important qualitative category of system performance is the determination of the *stability* of the system. A *stable* system is a system that if at rest, stays at rest, and if disturbed will return to rest. A more precise statement is that if a bounded (finite) input is applied to a stable system, a bounded output will result. Thus, the technical use of the term stability implies something about the dynamics of the system. Often, as is illustrated in several chapters of this volume, the word "stability" is used to imply either constancy of the output of the system or to indicate that the system is in a steady state ("rest") condition. Therefore, it is important to indicate clearly the intended meanings when stability is being discussed.

Identifiability is a qualitative property of a system model and a specific experimental protocol. Given a particular model structure and set of experiments, if all the unknown parameters can be uniquely determined, then the model is identifiable from those experiments. For example, if the purpose of our experimental studies is to estimate a parameter of the feeding control system such as ventromedial hypothalamic activity, then we can use the available information about the control system together with identifiability analysis (DiStefano, 1976) to design a set of feasible experiments that will allow us uniquely to determine VMH activity.

Another qualitative system classification is based on the existence of *feed-*

back. Feedback is the property of the system which allows the input to be compared with the output so that the appropriate control system response is generated as a function of both signals. If the feedback is either structurally or functionally absent, then the output is a function of the input only and the system is called *open loop*; if present, the output is a function of both input and output and the system is called *closed loop*. Feedback can be either negative or positive.

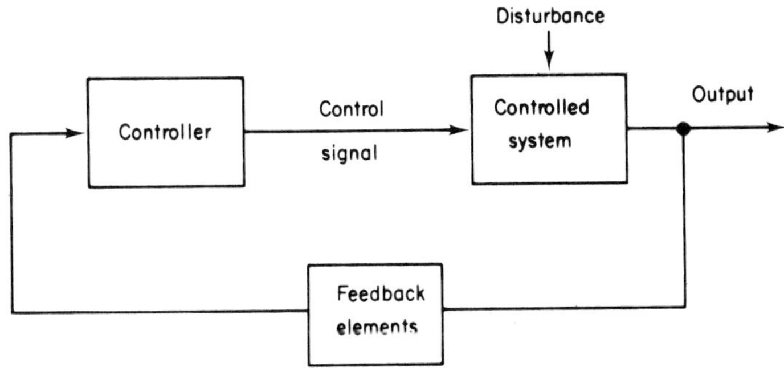

Fig. 1. Generalized block diagram of a biological feedback control system.

A closed loop feedback control system can be represesented graphically in block diagram form as shown in Fig. 1. A feedback control system has three major components: the controlled system, the controller and the feedback elements. The controlled system consists of those elements of the control system that produce or generate the output. The controller consists of those elements generating an appropriate control signal that modifies the magnitude of response of the controlled system. The feedback elements are those elements that transform the output into the feedback signal. A disturbance is an undesired input signal that affects the magnitude of the output. The summing point and reference input (set point) usually included in block diagrams of technical systems have been omitted in Fig. 1 and the feedback signals act directly on the controller. In contrast to technological systems, the interpretation of feedback signals in biological systems can be considered to reside within the controller rather than be externally imposed on the system. The systems analyst measures the effectiveness of the feedback loop in a closed loop system by determining the non-dimensional *loop gain*. The larger the loop gain, the more effective the feedback loop. One of the still unresolved issues of feeding control is the magnitude of the loop gain of the hypothesized feedback loop from energy storage or body mass to food intake.

Application of system analysis and mathematical modelling to the food intake control system should result in the qualitative classification of the system, specification of the assumptions necessary to apply methods of linear system theory to its analysis and modelling, a discussion of the stability of the system, the use of identifiability analysis as a tool for experimental design and a resolution of the issue of a feedback loop between body energy storage and feeding.

III. Uses of Mathematical Models

The primary use of mathematical models in biology is to aid in the synthesis necessary for the achievement of complete understanding of the biological system. Although complete understanding is a goal that is not yet attained for any biological system, at any particular stage of its evolution the model is the most complete and explicit synthesis of the system. As a result of an explicit and systematic process of model development, areas of missing or incomplete knowledge are identified and specific experimental studies necessary for continued model development are suggested. Models can be used to test explicitly hypotheses as to the structural organization of the system, either by testing the logical consistency of a proposed model structure with the experimental data base or by testing potential sites of action of an input or inputs known to affect the output. The objective of this process is the systematic rejection of most structural hypotheses as infeasible, resulting in only a small number of feasible structural alternatives. This process requires an extensive experimental data base and usually requires simulation of the model on a digital computer.

Another use of models of biological systems is experimental design. Identifiability analysis of composite parametric models has not been utilized as a tool for the design of experiments in most biological systems. Nevertheless, this approach should be applied widely in future because it helps the investigator make maximum use of the accumulated prior knowledge about the system. It also indicates possible directions for methodological development in order to increase the set of feasible experiments.

Because of their unique ability to reproduce the dynamic behaviour of biological systems, mathematical models are increasingly being used to design and to optimize clinical therapeutic regimes and as teaching tools.

IV. Neural Control of Feeding

Most of the issues in the control of food intake and/or body energy storage posed by Mogenson and Calaresu in Chapter 1 of this book (i.e. set point, feedback from energy stores, multifactor/unitary factor control) are discussed in several of the chapters. However, the hypothesized hypothalamic signal processing between potential control signals (e.g. glucose) and feeding are not discussed or included in any of the models.

I have recently begun to apply a technique for testing hypotheses of structural organization to the extended glucostatic hypothesis of food intake control. The technique is based on determining the logical consistency of the proposed structures with the experimental data base and was formally developed by Gann, Cryer and Schoeffler (1973). The 3-h cumulative food intake data following centrally or peripherally administered glucose or 2-deoxyglucose (2-DG) to intact, lateral hypothalamus (LH) lesion or vagotomized rats and rabbits published by Novin and co-workers (Novin *et al.*, 1973, 1974, 1976; Vanderweele *et al.*, 1974) were used as the experimental data base. Glucose infusions were assumed to increase the glucose concentrations, while 2-DG infusions were assumed to decrease intracellular glucose concentrations.

A block diagram model indicating the connectivity and functional relations between inputs (hypothalamic and duodenal/hepatic glucose concentrations, GH and GD), model subsystems (vagus nerve, VMH, LH and motor systems), unmeasurable internal variables (vagal nerve activity, VMH and LH activity) and outputs (food intake) together with a set of experimental data (initial state, inputs and outputs) was used to test for logical consistency. The block diagram model must be constructed so that functional relationships are monotonic for all subsystems and so that one-to-one relationships exist between subsystem inputs and outputs. Each variable (inputs, internal variables, outputs) must be quantized, that is, assigned to one of a finite number of levels. For example, 3-h cumulative food intake data were quantized into eight levels, by normalizing the food intake of an experimental group with the intake of a control group. Experimental states of the model subsystems (vagus, VMH, LH) were specified as: lesioned (0), intact (1) or stimulated (2). The quantized inputs, subsystem states and output levels for each experiment were entered into a truth table; the internal variables were subscripted with the appropriate experiment number. The block diagram, the subsystem states and inputs were then used to *predict* the relationships between the internal variables and, ultimately, the food intake for each experiment. If, following an exhaustive search of the truth table, all model

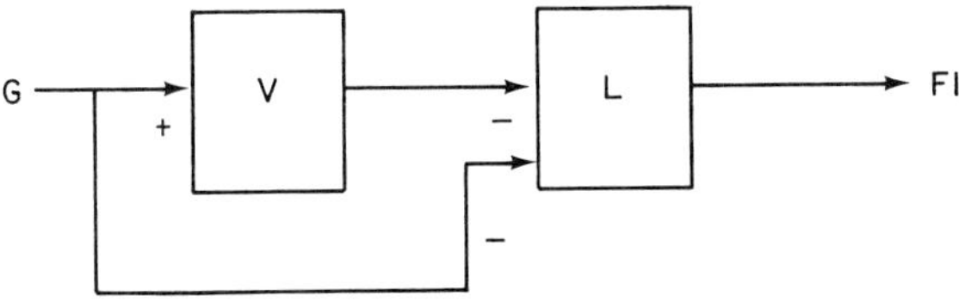

Fig. 2. Series structure.

predictions were consistent with the experimental data, the model was accepted as a possible structure.

As an illustration of this logical technique, consider the structure shown in Fig. 2. Glucose (G) increases VMH activity (V) and decreases LH activity (L). VMH activity inhibits LH activity which generates the output, food intake (FI).

Table I shows a truth table of the quantized data. Consider experiments 1 and 2 (effect of glucose infusion on intact animals): $G_1 < G_2$ which implies $V_1 < V_2$. The effect of G on L (L_G) gives $L_{G_1} > L_{G_2}$ and the effect of V on L (L_V) gives $L_{V_1} > L_{V_2}$. Therefore $L_1 > L_2$, which implies $FI_1 > FI_2$, which agrees with the measured food intakes ($FI_1 = 3$; $FI_2 = 2$).

Now, consider experiments 3 and 4 (effect of glucose in LH lesioned animals): $G_3 < G_4$ which implies $V_3 < V_4$, $L_{G3} > L_{G4}$ and, thus, $L_{V_3} \;\; L_{V_4}$. Therefore, $L_3 > L_4$ which implies $FI_3 > FI_4$, which *does not* agree with the observed $FI_3 = 2$ and $FI_4 = 3$. A similar inconsistent prediction occurs when experiments 2 and 4 (effect of LH lesion) and 3 and 5 (effect of vagotomy) are considered. Therefore, this structure was judged not logically consistent and rejected.

Table I
Truth Table of Quantized Data

Expt no.	G	I_R	I_{LH}	V	L	FI
1	3	1	1	V_1	L_1	3
2	4	1	1	V_2	L_2	2
3	3	1	0	V_3	L_3	2
4	4	1	0	V_4	L_4	3
5	3	0	1	V_5	L_5	5

I_R: = 0 vagotomized
= 1 intact vagus

I_{LH}: = 0 LH lesioned
= 1 intact LH

This technique has been used on a data set consisting of 12 experiments and the structure shown in Fig. 3 has been accepted as a potential structure for the short term neural control of feeding by glucose.

This model suggests the following operational hypotheses: In intact animals, hypothalamic glucose concentration (GH) increases VMH activity and decreases LH activity. Duodenal–hepatic glucose concentration (GD), acting through a splanchnic receptor, decreases vagal activity (N). Vagal activity increases LH activity which, in turn, inhibits VMH activity. The LH acts on the motor subsystem to increase food intake, while the VMH acts to decrease food

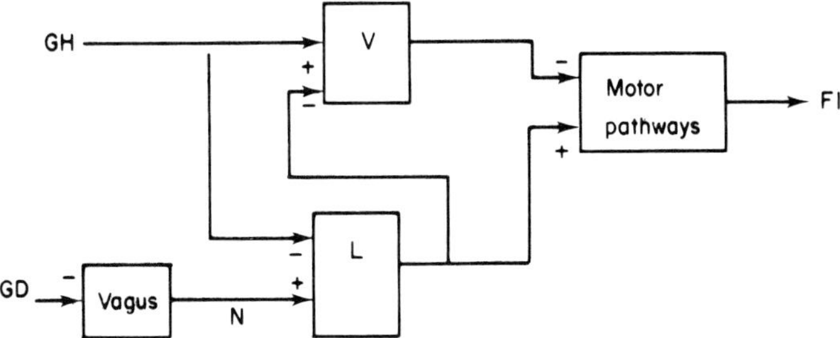

Fig. 3. Proposed structural hypothesis of the neural control of food intake.

intake. In LH lesioned or vagotomized animals, the *GH*-LH and *GD*-LH functional relationships are shifted downward one or more levels and the slopes are reversed.

As more experiments and more inputs are added to the truth table, this structure will be modified and other possible structures may emerge. The goal of these studies is to reject as many hypotheses as possible and then to design experiments that will differentiate among the remaining potential structures.

Acknowledgement

I wish to thank Mr Y. Saito for his research assistance with the modelling of the neural control of food intake. This research was funded in part by the National Science Foundation Research Grant 76-09619.

References

Bray, G. A. and Campfield, L. A. (1975). Metabolic factors in the regulation of body energy storage. *Metabolism* **24**, 99–117.

DiStefano, J. J., III (1976). Tracer experiment design for unique identification of nonlinear physiological systems. *Am. J. Physiol.* **230**, 476–485.

DiStefano, J. J., III, Stubberud, A. R. and Williams, I. J. (1967). "Feedback and Control Systems". McGraw-Hill, New York.

Gann, D. S., Cryer, G. L. and Schoeffler, J. D. (1973). Finite level models of biological systems. *Ann. biomed. Engin.* **1**, 385–445.

Novin, D., Vanderweele, D. A. and Rezek, M. (1973). Infusion of 2-deoxy-D-glucose into the hepatic-portal system causes eating: Evidence for peripheral glucoreceptors. *Science, N.Y.* **181**, 858–860.

Novin, D., Sanderson, J. D. and Vanderweele, D. A. (1974). The effect of isotonic glucose on eating as a function of feeding condition and infusion site. *Physiol. Behav.* **13**, 3–7.

Novin, D., Gonzalez, M. F. and Sanderson, J. D. (1976). Paradoxical increased feeding followed glucose infusions in recovered lateral rats. *Am. J. Physiol.* **230**, 1084–1088.

Vanderweele, D. A., Novin, D., Rezek, M. and Sanderson, J. D. (1974). Duodenal or hepatic-portal glucose perfusion: Evidence for duodenally-based satiety. *Physiol. Behav.* **12**, 467–473.

7

The Interaction Between Gustatory Stimulation and Gut Feedback in the Control of the Ingestion of Liquid Diets

JOHN D. DAVIS, BARBARA J. COLLINS AND MICHAEL W. LEVINE

Department of Psychology, University of Illinois at Chicago Circle, Chicago, U.S.A.

I. Control of Meal Size

The amount of food an animal eats in some fixed period of time is often taken as an index of the level of the animal's hunger. Experimental manipulations which, for example, raise the daily food intake are often viewed as increasing the animal's hunger, and manipulations which lower daily intake are often viewed as reducing it. Measuring daily intake as an index of hunger has been an acceptable practice for many decades and still appears to be widely used. Recording only the total amount an animal eats in a day, however, obscures an important characteristic of the feeding behaviour of most animals; with few exceptions, organisms eat discrete meals separated by varying intervals of abstinence. The size of each of these meals and the length of the intervals that separate them determine the total amount of food an animal will ingest in a day, a week, a month and its life time. Daily intake can be raised by increasing the average size of meals taken, by decreasing the average length of the intervals that separate them, or both. Each of these three possibilities implies something different about an experimental manipulation that leads to a change in daily intake. It thus seems clear that an understanding of those variables that control the size of a meal and those that control the intermeal interval will provide a better understanding of the problem of hunger than will measures which obscure this fundamental characteristic of the feeding behaviour of most organisms.

Of these two parameters of feeding behaviour, meal size has been by far the most thoroughly studied. It now appears possible because of this work to construct a specific quantitative model of control of liquid diet intake incorporating two of the classes of variables which have been clearly established as playing an important role in controlling the amount of a substance an organism will ingest during a bout of drinking nutritive or non-nutritive solutions. These two classes of variables are gustatory stimulation and the gastrointestinal consequences of ingestion. It is abundantly clear that these are not the only variables which influence meal or draught size, and we are making no claim for the comprehensiveness of the model described in this chapter. A complete quantitative model of draught size will include many more variables than these two. Nevertheless any ingestion model must include at least these two, and it seems reasonable to start with them, build the model, test its implications and then modify it as data demand. As will be seen, a feedback model incorporating only these two classes of variables provides a remarkably good quantitative description of the ingestion of carbohydrate solutions.

II Background

A. *Gustatory Control of Ingestion*

Richter and Campbell (1940) were probably the first to demonstrate the enormous effect gustatory stimulation can have on ingestion. In this classic study, rats were offered a choice between distilled water and solutions such as sucrose, glucose, maltose and galactose. They drank increasing amounts of the carbohydrate solution as its concentration was progressively increased above the detection threshold. The stimulating effect on ingestion of the carbohydrate solutions was so great that when the rats were offered a choice between an 0·6 mol/l glucose solution (the optimum concentration for that carbohydrate) and distilled water they drank on the average 85 ml of the glucose solution per day. Since the average daily distilled water intake of these animals was about 24 ml, it seems clear that the drinking of this amount of fluid was not a response to thirst; in fact, the animals must have been overhydrated much of the time. Nor is this excessive intake of carbohydrate a response to food deprivation, since the animals had free access at all times to a well balanced diet. The preference measure they used was the total daily intake and so it is unclear in this study whether the carbohydrate solutions were stimulating larger or more frequent draughts or both. Subsequent work using a variety of measures of ingestion has shown clearly that carbohydrate solutions are capable of stimulating and sustaining ingestion for relatively long periods of time (Ernits and Corbit, 1973; Hammer, 1968; McCleary, 1953). Moreover, Ernits and Corbit (1973) have recently shown that rats deprived of water for 16 hours drink only slightly more glucose or sucrose solutions in a one-hour period that the amount drunk by non water-deprived rats. Futhermore, since in their study the animals were deprived of food for only one hour prior to the drinking test, again it cannot be argued convincingly that the ingested carbohydrate solutions were being ingested to satisfy caloric need.

These studies lead necessarily to the conclusion that certain substances which taste sweet to humans are capable of stimulating a great deal of ingestive behaviour in rats quite apart from any state of hunger or thirst of the animal. One has only to look at the tremendous quantities of artificially and naturally sweetened beverages that are consumed each year by humans to realize that sweetness is a very potent ingestional stimulus for us as well.

B. *Negative Feedback*

While palatability clearly plays an important role in the control of ingestion the postingestional consequences of eating or drinking have also been shown to influence greatly how much of a particular substance an organism will ingest. It has been recognized for some time that the consequences of the accumulation of food or fluids in the gastrointestinal tract serve to slow down and eventually to stop ingestive behaviour. Recognition of this has lead to a considerable amount of research directed at identifying the origin and nature of the negative feedback signals, or as they are more commonly called, short term satiety signals. Evidence has now accumulated suggesting that a variety of different kinds of short-term satiety signals can operate under certain conditions to limit meal or draught size. Examples are gastrointestinal distension (Davis *et al.* 1975; Herrin and Meek, 1945; Herrin *et al.* 1933; Lepkovsky *et al.* 1971), the duodenal hormone cholecystokinin (Liebling *et al.*, 1975), chemospecific activity in the gastrointestinal tract (Novin *et al.*, 1974; Campbell and Davis, 1974), hepatic glucoreceptor activation (Russek, 1971), and an osmotic signal (McCleary, 1953). Which of these signals operate at any given time probably depends on a variety of conditions such as the nature and palatability of the diet, and deprivation and feeding conditions.

C. *Interaction of Ingestional Stimuli and Postingestional Inhibition*

While a great deal of attention has been paid to the problems of identifying the nature of the feedback signals which limit intake, relatively little attention has been devoted to the problem of how they interact with those factors such as deprivation and palatability which are presumed to augment or sustain ingestive activity. It is possible, as Cabanac (1971) has argued, that during the course of ingestion of a highly palatable substance the taste of the substance becomes gradually more unpleasant because of some consequence of the accumulation of the ingested substance in the gut. Another possibility is that as a consequence of ingestion the composition of the fluids bathing the gustatory receptors is altered, leading to a change in their adaptation level which lowers the afferent input. McCleary (1953) has argued that thirst caused by an osmotically induced influx of water to the intestinal lumen caused by hypertonic load inhibits further ingestion. Jacobs (1961) has argued that organisms monitor caloric input in some unknown way and adjust their intake accordingly. Finally, Le Magnen (1971) has argued that, because of prior learning, oral metering by itself plays an important role in limiting intake.

We (Davis, Collins and Levine, 1975) have proposed a model which is somewhat different from those mentioned above. The basic idea of our model is that excitatory afferent input from gustatory receptors combines algebraically in some CNS integration centre with inhibitory afferent input from distension of the intestinal tract. We have proposed that the output from this integration centre drives an ingestive mechanism controller in proportion to its magnitude. The ingestive mechanism controller is viewed as a complicated neural control circuit which converts the output from the integration centre into the motor activities involved in the act of ingestion. Thus if the output from the integration centre is large, either because of a small negative feedback signal from the gut or because of a large positive input from the gustatory receptors, the ingestive mechanism controller will direct a high rate of ingestion. If, on the other hand, the output from the integration centre is low, either because of a small positive signal from the gustatory receptors or because of a large negative input from the gut, then the ingestive mechanism controller will direct a low rate of ingestion. These ideas were made quantitatively explicit by constructing a control theory negative feedback model which will be described here in some detail.

Those readers familiar with Dethier's (1969) analysis of the control of food intake of the blowfly will recognize that our model bears more than a superficial similarity to his description of the control of ingestion in that animal. In his analysis, stimulation of tarsal hairs of the fly by carbohydrate solutions is responsible for initiating and sustaining ingestion; and activation of tension receptors in the foregut is responsible for blocking ingestion. Although the details of the control of ingestion of carbohydrate solutions by the blowfly and the rat appear to be different, the overall plans of control involving the interaction between an excitatory input and negative feedback from the gut are quite similar.

III. Feedback Model for the Control of Ingestion

A. *Descriptive Feedback Model*

McFarland (1971) has recently shown that control theory, which has been developed in detail in the field of engineering, can be applied with some success to the study of behaviour. In its simplest terms, control theory has been developed to analyse systems whose outputs influence their inputs by means of feedback control. Feeding behaviour clearly can be analysed within this context since it is easy to demonstrate that the consequences of ingestion act to limit further intake. Our model of the control of meal size is illustrated schematically in Fig. 1.

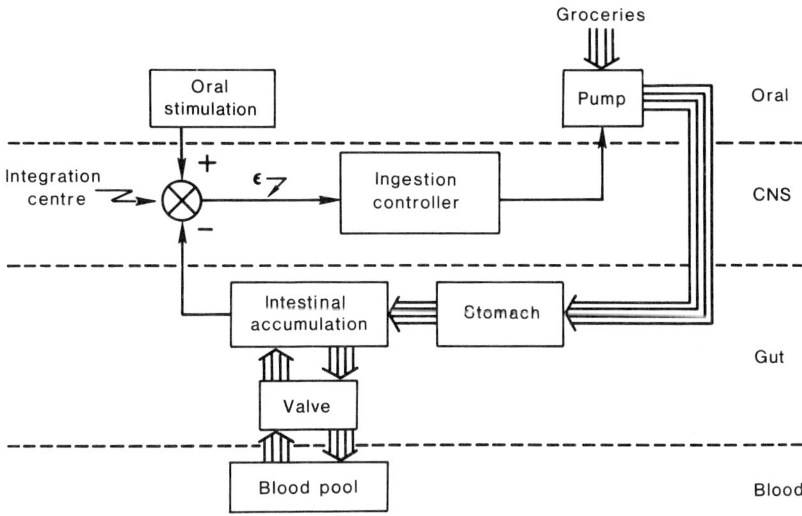

Fig. 1. Description of the model. The heavy lines show the flow of fluid through the body. The thin lines represent the pathways of neural information flow. The diagram is organized vertically according to the anatomical structures involved.

The diagram is organized vertically according to the various anatomical mechanisms involved in the control of feeding. The heavy lines indicate flow of fluids through the system while the thin lines represent the flow of neural information within the system. At the top on the right the mouth, the teeth, the tongue and the various oropharyngeal mechanisms involved in swallowing are represented by the box labelled *pump*. It is this apparatus which is responsible for transferring and transforming groceries from the environment to chyme in the gut. On the top left the box labelled *oral stimulation* represents all of those sensory inputs which are involved in controlling the feeding system once food is in the mouth. The most important of these are gustatory and olfactory stimulation, and our model at present is designed to take only these sensory inputs into consideration. Nevertheless, we are aware of the fact that a more fully developed model will have to include visual and auditory inputs, perhaps as conditioned stimuli, as well as inputs related to the state of energy balance of the organism.

At the next level in our diagram an integration centre and a controller are represented. The integration centre, represented as a summing point, combines inputs from two levels: a signal from sensory stimulation and a negative feedback signal from the gut. The output from this integration centre is simply the algebraic sum of the two inputs. If the signal from sensory input is greater than that from the gut, the controller will receive a positive signal whose magnitude will depend on the relative magnitudes of the positive and negative inputs to the integration centre. The sign and magnitude of this output signal is the key determinant in our model of whether or not the animal will eat and if so at what rate, since the controller converts this signal into one which controls the pump. If the input to the controller is positive, it activates the pump (i.e. the animal begins to eat) and drives it at a rate which is proportional to the magnitude of the input signal. A large positive input to the controller means a high rate of ingestion, and a small positive input means a slow rate of ingestion. If this input signal is zero or negative, the pump is not activated (i.e. the animal does not eat).

The next level is that of the gut. When an animal eats, the ingested substances begin to accumulate in the stomach and are there converted to chyme. From the stomach, chyme is transferred through the pylorus by peristaltic activity to the intestine, where much of it is absorbed across the intestinal wall to the blood and lymphatic system. When the contents of the intestinal lumen are hypertonic with respect to body fluids, the absorption process can be temporarily reversed leading to an influx of fluid into the intestine. Thus the fluid which is present in the intestine may be equal to, less than, or greater than the volume delivered to it by the stomach. This effect is represented in the diagram by a valve inserted between the box representing the accumulated contents of the intestine and that representing the blood pool of the body. Since substances are absorbed from the intestine at different rates depending on their chemical nature and concentration, this valve should be seen not only as a two-directional device letting fluid flow into as well as out of the intestine, but also as a modulator of the net rate of flow out of the intestine. The valve is intended to represent those physiochemical properties of the intestinal membrane which determine the net rate of transfer of fluid out of the intestine.

It can be seen that the setting of this valve, which depends on the concentration and nature of intestinal fluid, will determine the rate of accumulation of fluid in the intestine for a given rate of flow from the stomach. When the valve is wide open (that is, when the concentration of intestinal contents is low), all the fluid coming from the stomach will go directly to the blood and there will be little accumulation of fluid in the intestine. When the valve is almost closed, because of the presence of nearly isotonic fluid in the intestine, nearly all of the ingested fluid will accumulate there. And finally, when the valve is reversed because of the presence of hypertonic fluid in the intestine, there will be a net accumulation of fluid in the intestine amounting to more than is actually delivered by the stomach.

Leading from the box labelled intestinal accumulation is a thin line which terminates at the integration centre with a negative sign; this line is intended to represent information about the state of distension of the intestine. We visualize it as a neural pathway involving either sympathetic or parasympathetic afferents or both. It is this pathway which completes the negative feedback loop.

As fluid accumulates in the intestine, information conveyed along this channel provides a negative input to the integration centre in direct proportion to the degree of intestinal distension. Intestinal distension in turn will be a function of the rate of accumulation of fluid in the intestine. Thus if an organism is ingesting a substance which is rapidly absorbed this negative feedback signal will grow slowly. Since this signal combines with a relatively constant positive input from sensory input, the signal to the controller will decay slowly and ingestive behaviour will decline slowly, continuing for a relatively long period of time.

On the other hand, if the organism is ingesting a substance which is delivered fairly rapidly to the intestine but is slowly absorbed there will be a rapid accumulation of fluid in the intestine, accompanied by its distension. This will lead to a relatively rapidly increasing negative signal at the integration centre and consequently a rapid decline in the input signal to the controller, and ingestive behaviour will decline quickly to zero.

Note that it is the integration centre where the interaction between sensory input from the mouth and gut occurs, and that it is the joint effect of both signals which determines how rapidly and for how long the animal continues to drink. If we neglect a possible decrement in input due to sensory adaptation from sensory receptors on the tongue, we can assume a relatively constant positive signal from the gustatory receptors to the input to the integration centre throughout the course of a meal. Furthermore, if we assume that at the beginning of a meal the stomach and intestine are relatively empty, then the negative input from the gut to the integration centre will initially be zero. Thus ingestion will begin at a rate that depends entirely on the magnitude of the positive input which in turn will depend on the palatability of the tasted substance.

In short, the initial rate of ingestion will depend entirely on palatability, but the rate at which ingestive activity is slowed down and eventually terminated will depend entirely on how rapidly the intestine fills up.

B. *Quantitative Feedback Model*

The feedback model as described so far permits only rather general predictions about ingestion rate and amount consumed. Fortunately these general predictions can be made quantitatively explicit by the use of the mathematics of control theory. While it is our intention to keep mathematical expressions to a minimum in this paper, it will be necessary to introduce the concept of a transfer function and to describe two algebraic functions which summarize quantitatively the predictions made by the model in the preceding section. The derivation of the two functions is given in the appendix for those readers who prefer a more rigorous treatment.

The first step in deriving a mathematical function which describes the behaviour of the model is to translate the descriptive model into one which can be handled mathematically. This translation is illustrated in Fig. 2.

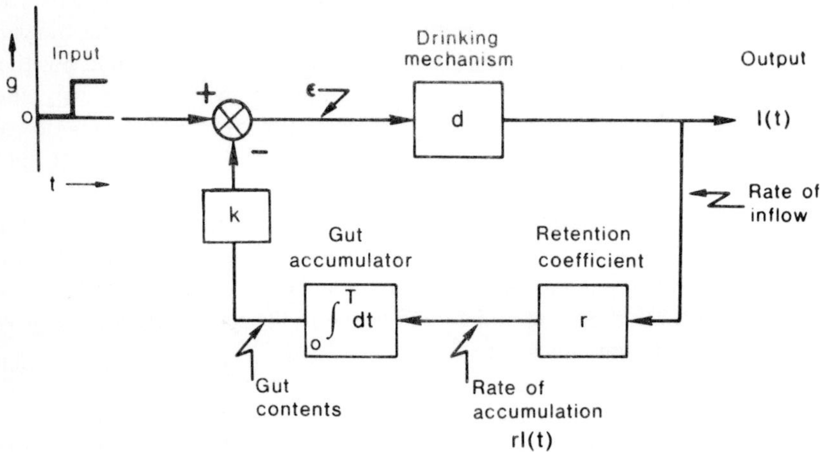

Fig. 2. Quantitative form of the model. In this form parameters and variables have been substituted for the descriptive terms used in Fig. 1.

Going from left to right in this figure the input (*oral stimulation*) has been replaced by a symbol indicating a step change in sensory input from 0 to some magnitude, g. This is intended to represent the fact that when an animal first makes gustatory contact with a fluid, afferent input from gustatory receptors goes immediately from zero to a level which is proportional to the stimulating effectiveness of the solution. The variable g represents the strength of the flavour, and we are assuming here that peripheral gustatory adaptation is minimal; that is, the value of the input variable g remains relatively constant throughout the meal. This simplifying assumption, while probably not strictly true, may not be too far wrong as far as total afferent input from the tongue is concerned. A weak sucrose solution would be represented by a small step, a small value of g, whereas a strong sucrose solution would be represented by a large step or large value of g.

Next the integration centre has been replaced by a symbol for a summing point. A summing point is simply a combination of a variety of inputs into a single output (ε), which is the algebraic sum of the inputs.The controller and the pump have been combined into a single parameter d. The parameter d, which stands for drinking mechanism, is the ratio of rate of ingestion, $I(t)$, to the input ε, and is the forward gain of the system. Its physical basis is neural excitation. The drinking mechanism itself is of course a very complicated system, but here we are only concerned with the input to it and the output from it, and this translation from input to output can be represented by a single parameter, d. The output of the system, designated $I(t)$, is ingestion rate and is measured in terms of licks or ml per minute.

The box in the negative feedback loop designated r replaces the valve in the conceptual model. It is a variable which we have called the retention coefficient. It represents the fact that different concentrations of different substances are retained in the intestine for different amounts of time. The input to this box is rate of inflow, which depends on the rate at which the animal is drinking. If absorption rate is rapid, that is, if the retention coefficient is small, there will be a slow rate of accumulation in the gut. If absorption is slow, the retention coefficient will be large, and there will be a more rapid rate of accumulation of fluid in the intestine. Thus the output from this box represents the rate at which fluid builds up in the gut. In effect, r represents the relative rate of inflow and outflow to the gut or the fraction of fluid delivered to the gut which is retained there. Being a fraction, r is dimensionless.

As pointed out above, we assume that the negative feedback signal depends not on the rate at which the intestine is filling but on the amount of fluid in it at any given time, since it is the amount of fluid in the intestine which determines how distended it is. The next box to the left, labelled "gut accumlulator" (which is simply the time integral of rate of accumulation), makes the conversion from rate to amount. *The signal returned to the summing point is a neural representation of this volume mediated by the activation of intestinal stretch receptors. This translation from volume to neural activation is accomplished by multiplying intestinal volume by the constant k represented in the next box.

Since distension depends on the amount of fluid in the gut, the output from this box is returned with a negative sign to the summing point and the loop is completed.

A *transfer function* for any system describes mathematically how the output of the system varies as the input is changed. Applying the assumed input (a step in g) to the transfer function for our model will describe how ingestion rate (the

*The total gut contents at any time T after the beginning of a draught is $\int_0^T r\, I(t)\mathrm{d}t$. Since this expression is exactly equal to $r \int_0^T I(t)\mathrm{d}t$ and since $\int_0^T I(t)\mathrm{d}t$ is the amount of fluid ingested at time T, r can be seen as representing the fraction of fluid ingested by time T that is still present in the gut.

output) changes over time after the animal first makes contact with a flavoured substance. This function, which is derived in the appendix, is:

$$I(t)=gde^{-drkt}.$$

In this function t is time in minutes, g represents the stimulating effectiveness of the tasted substance. The term d is the parameter in the model shown in Fig. 2 which represents the transformation from the input to the output of the ingestion mechanism; its value will depend on the individual characteristics of each organism. e is a constant, the base of the natural logarithms; its numerical value is 2·71 . . . The term r is the retention coefficient; its value will depend on the nature and concentration of the contents of the intestinal lumen. Fluids in the intestine which are absorbed as rapidly as they are delivered to the intestine have a retention coefficient of 0. Fluids which are not absorbed from the intestine at all are represented by retention coefficients of 1. Fluids sufficiently hypertonic to draw body fluids into the intestine will have retention coefficients greater than 1.

This function $I(t)$ represents a family of curves which differ according to the particular values of the independent variables g and r and the system parameter d. Some representative curves generated by this function when $I(t)$ is plotted against t are shown in Fig. 3a. The values chosed for gd and dr are representative of empirical values obtained in a variety of experiments carried out in our laboratory. These curves describe the decay of ingestion rate, $I(t)$, during a drinking bout after the animal first makes contact with the test fluid. The intial rate of drinking is defined by gd, since $I(t)=gd$ when $t=0$. This is to say that the initial rate of drinking is determined solely by the palatability of the solution (the value of g) and a factor which characterizes individual reactivity to gustatory stimulation (the value of d). Three pairs of curves are represented, with each pair beginning at a different point. If the same animal were to generate these six curves then d would be a constant and we could conclude that the top pair were generated by a highly palatable fluid, the middle pair by a fluid of intermediate palatability and the lowest pair by a fluid of low palatability.

Note that although each member of any pair of curves begins at the same value of $I(t)$ they decay at different rates. The rate of decay of the function $I(t)$ depends upon the value of the exponent dr. Small values of this exponent generate slow rates of decay, large values more rapid rates of decay. Note for example that the ingestion rates described by curves A, C or E are all practically zero 30 minutes after the animal has begun to drink whereas the ingestion rate described by curves B, D or F are still far from zero even 35 minutes after the initiation of drinking.

The numerical value of the exponents depends on three factors, the forward gain of the system d, the retention coefficient r and the constant of proportionaliy k. If we again assume that these six curves all describe the change in drinking rate over time by the same animal we would have to conclude that the top two described the drinking of two fluids which were equally palatable (they begin at the same point) but which were absorbed by the intestine at different rates. This follows from the fact that although d and k are constant (the same animal is used throughout) the values for drk are different for the two curves and thus the value of r must be different in the two cases. The same is true for the other two pairs of curves except that they describe the ingestion rate stimulated by an intermediate and low palatability fluid.

Since the curves A, C and E in Fig. 3a start from different initial values, it is not apparent that the rates of decline in drinking are the same and that together they are different from the rates of decline of funtions B, D and F. The fact that the rates of decline of the functions which have the same exponential numerical value are the same can be illustrated by plotting the curves similar to those represented in Fig. 3a on semilog paper as in Fig. 3b. Here the values of $I(t)$ have been scaled logarithmically and plotted against time. It is obvious that although curves A, C and E start from different points they are parallel in their decline. The same is true of curves B, D and F. This is perhaps a clearer way of showing that equal palatability generates equal initial drinking rates and that equal rates of intestinal accumulation generate equal rates of decline in drinking rate.

Up to this point we have been describing the change in drinking rate which occurs during a draught by describing the decay in rate of ingestion. While there is nothing really wrong with looking at the problem in this way, the conventional experimental approach has been to record cumulative intake rather than intake rate. To convert the ingestion rate function $I(t)$ into a cumulative intake function we simply take the time integral of $I(t)$. This generates a new function $C(t)$ which has the general form:

$$C(t)=g/rk\,(1\text{-}e^{-drkt})$$

The symbols in this function correspond exactly to symbols which describe the $I(t)$ function, but the form of the function is different. In this type of function the curves rise to a final value, or asymptote, defined by the value of g/rk at a rate which is given by the value of the exponent drk. Figure 4a,b illustrate families of curves of this general form. In Fig. 4a the exponents are all the same ($drk=0{\cdot}150$) but the asymptotes g/rk are different. If we assume that these five curves were all generated by the same animal then we could assume that d is constant, and therefore, since drk is constant across all five curves, the difference in the asymptotes (g/rk) depends entirely on the palatability (g) of the tasted substance. The top curve would describe the cumulative intake of a highly palatable fluid while the bottom curve would describe the cumulative intake of a relatively unpalatable fluid. In this situation variations in draught size (the value of the asymptote in ml) depend entirely on the palatability of the ingested fluid. The value of the negative feedback, or short term satiety signal, is the same in each case. Such a family of curves might be generated by offering an animal a

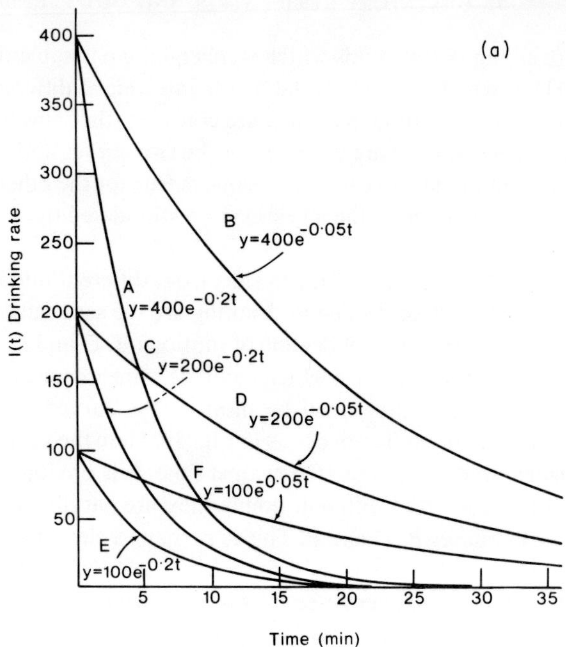

(a)
I(t) Drinking rate
400
350
300
250
200
150
100
50
B
y=400e$^{-0.05t}$
A
y=400e$^{-0.2t}$
C
y=200e$^{-0.2t}$
D
y=200e$^{-0.05t}$
F
y=100e$^{-0.05t}$
E
y=100e$^{-0.2t}$
5
10
15
20
25
30
35
Time (min)

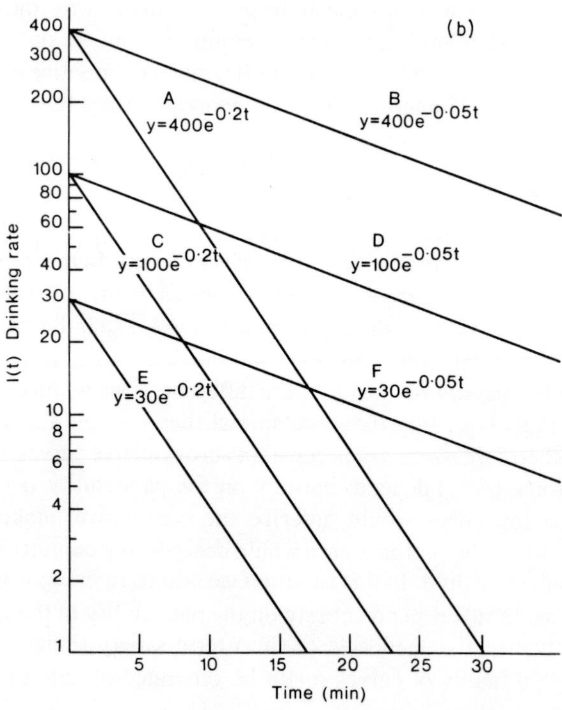

(b)
I(t) Drinking rate
400
300
200
100
80
60
40
30
20
10
8
6
4
2
1
A
y=400e$^{-0.2t}$
B
y=400e$^{-0.05t}$
C
y=100e$^{-0.2t}$
D
y=100e$^{-0.05t}$
E
y=30e$^{-0.2t}$
F
y=30e$^{-0.05t}$
5
10
15
20
25
30
Time (min)

series of sucrose solutions which are identical in concentration but are adulterated with various amounts of quinine.

Figure 4b shows the form of the cumulative intake function $I(t)$ in the situation where the asymptote (g/rk) is the constant, but the exponent (drk) is allowed to vary. Notice that all curves are headed for the same final value but that they approach it at different rates. Again, if we assume that all of these curves were generated by the same animal, then d and k would be constant, but since drk is a variable they must be generated by substances which vary in their retention by the intestine. We would also have to conclude that they vary in palatability as well. This follows from the fact that the asymptote g/rk is constant and r varies, and so g must vary with r to keep the ratio g/rk constant.

An example of a situation such as this, where the intake of two fluids is the same but for entirely different reasons, exists when one analyses the so-called preference aversion curve for sugars. Such a curve is shown in Fig. 5, where the 30–min intake of a sugar is plotted against its concentration. The data are hypothetical but are representative of the results of many published studies. The horizontal dashed line crosses the function at equal intakes of two different concentrations of sucrose. It is generally assumed that the lower concentration is less palatable than the higher concentration, and it is also generally assumed that the intake of the more concentrated solution is limited by the activation of a short term satiety signal. In terms of our model this is equivalent to saying that g_a is less than g_b and r_a is less than r_b. Curves A and B in Fig. 4b illustrate this situation. The asymptotes of the two curves are the same $g_a/r_a\ k_a = g_b/r_b\ k_b = 2000$). For A, however, $drk = 0{\cdot}08$ and for B $drk = 0{\cdot}30$. Since it is assumed that these curves were generated by the same animal, d will be the same in both and therefore r_a must be less than r_b. However, if that is the case, then g_a must be less than g_b in order for the ratio g_a/r_a to be equal to the ratio g_b/r_b. Notice that, although the asymptotes for the two functions are the same, the rates of reaching these asymptotes are different. Presumably the cumulative intake of solution A in Fig. 5 would look like curve A in Fig. 4b and that of solution B would look like curve B in Fig. 4b, but if total intake only is measured after some relatively long period of time, both curves will have reached the same value.

Fig. 3. Intake functions predicted by the model. The function which generated these curves is $I(t) = gde^{-drkt}$. (a) The values for the three pairs of curves A, B; C, D; and E, F were chosen to illustrate the situation where an animal is ingesting fluid of high palatability, (A,B) intermediate palatability (C,D) and a low palatability (E,F). Within each pair, the solutions differ with respect to their rate of clearance from the intestine. Curves B,D and F describe the change in drinking rate of solutions which clear rapidly from the intestine, while curves A, C and E describe the ingestion of solutions which clear slowly from the intestine. (b) Similar to curves shown in (a) but with drinking rate $I(t)$ plotted on a logarithmic scale. This is intended to illustrate the prediction made by the model that the decline of ingestion rate of solutions which are cleared at the same rate from the intestine is the same regardless of palatability.

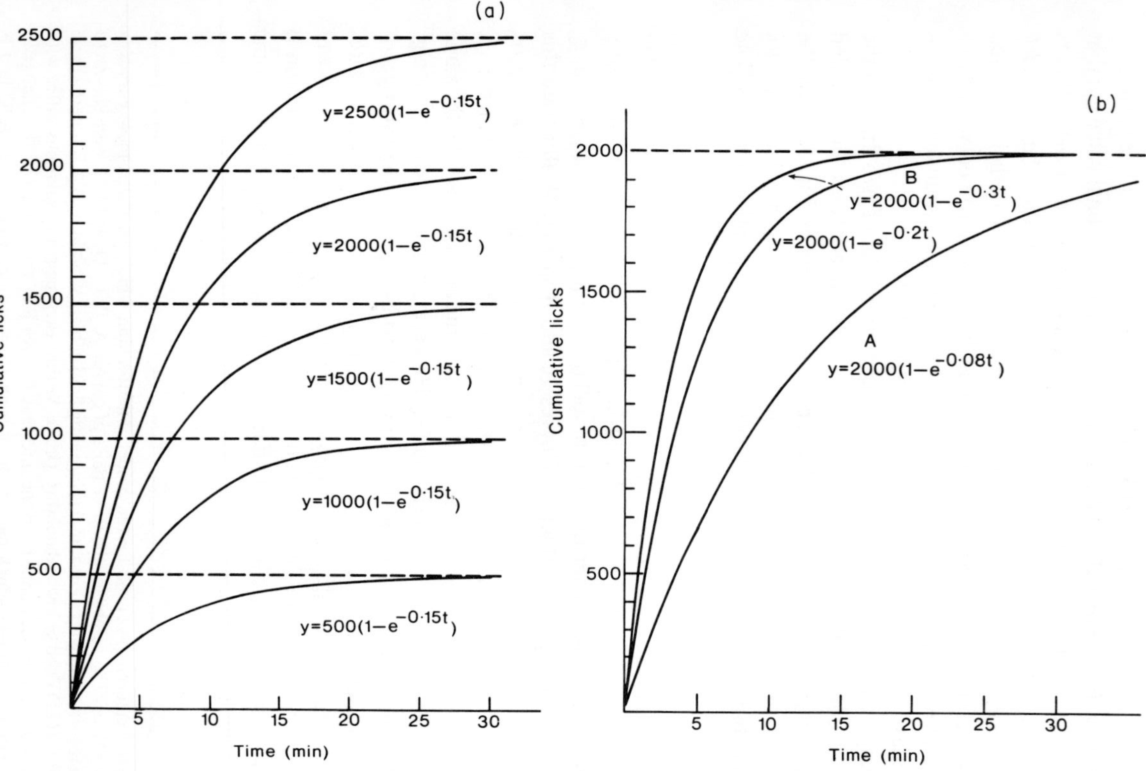

Fig. 4. Cumulative intake curves predicted by the model. The function which generated these curves is $C(t)=g/rk(1\text{-}e^{-drkt})$. (a) These curves illustrate the predicted form of cumulative intake functions for solutions that all have the same clearance rate from the intestine but differ in palatability. (b) These curves illustrate the predicted form of cumulative intake function for solutions which differ both in palatability and rate of clearance from the gut. Note that the three curves all have the same asymptote.

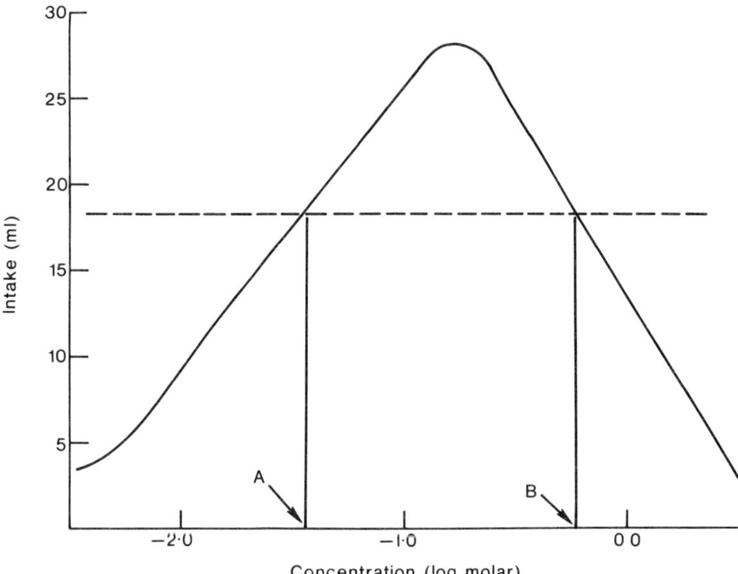

Fig. 5. An illustration of the "preference-aversion" function for a representative carbohydrate solution. The curve describes how total intake in a 30-min period varies with the concentration of the ingested fluid.

IV Experimental Tests of the Model

A. *Measurement of Ingestion Rate*

The model described above makes very specific predictions about the shape of intake functions, predictions which are stated precisely enough to be tested with relatively little ambiguity. How well then do the predictions conform to experimental data? Before considering the experimental evidence relevant to our model a word needs to be said about measurement of the major dependent variable $I(t)$ ingestion rate.

Rate of fluid ingestion can be measured in two ways. The more conventional way is to record the height of a column of the test fluid in a graduated drinking cylinder at fixed periods of time, such as every minute, during the course of a drinking bout. This generates a cumulative intake function with the absolute level of the fluid at any given time being the cumulative intake $C(t)$ at that time. When each of these successive measurements is subtracted from the preceding one and the successive differences are plotted against time the curves will have the general form shown in Fig. 3a starting at a relatively high level and decaying toward zero.

The other method is to record the number of tongue contacts an animal makes with the drinking tube during the drinking period. This method has a number of advantages. One is that it is a direct measure of the behaviour of the animal which determines how rapidly fluid is transferred to its gut. It can provide a reasonably accurate measure of the volume of fluid ingested, for while the actual amount ingested per lick is not exactly constant (Allison and Castellan, 1970), the variations are small. It is a well documented fact that lick rate is characterized by bursts of licking at a constant rate (e.g. Davis and Keehn, 1959; Stellar and Hill, 1952); both satiation and responsiveness to different concentrations of sugars are characterized by variations in burst length and interburst intervals. The number of licks which occur during successive minutes reflects these variations in burst length and interburst intervals and appears to be a very sensitive measure of gustatory responsiveness (Davis, 1973).

We have used this latter measure almost exclusively in our work for two reasons. First, it is technically simpler to make automatic records of tongue contacts than changes in the height of a column of fluid. But, more important, the tongue contact measure gives a much finer temporal resolution of the changes in drinking rate than do changes in the height of a column of fluid, even in a small diameter tube. Therefore in most of the work reported here we have recorded automatically on printing counters the number of licks which occur during each minute of a drinking period, measured from the first tongue contact. The drinkometers have either been phonograph cartridge types which are activated when the rat's tongue moves a small wire extending across the opening of a drinking spout or phototransistor types which are activated when the rat's tongue interrupts a beam of light from a light-emitting diode positioned across from the phototransistor at the tip of the tube.

Finally, our data are usually presented as cumulative intake functions $[C(t)]$ rather than drinking rate functions $[I(t)]$ because this is the more conventional form of presentation, and because this function shows directly the total amount drunk which the drinking rate function does not. This should cause no problems if it is remembered that $C(t)$ is simply the integral form of $I(t)$.

Now let us consider the evidence that is relevant to the model to see how well the data conform to the predictions made by the model.

B. *Open Loop Behaviour*

One of the most obvious and fundamental predictions is that, if the negative feedback loop is opened, drinking should continue indefinitely. This follows from the fact that under these conditions no signal with a negative sign will appear at the integration centre, or summing point, to diminish the magnitude of ε. Thus, drinking should begin at a rate determined solely by the palatability of the solution (g) and the factor d which describes the reactiveness to gustatory stimulation of the individual animal, and drinking should continue at this rate indefinitely.

This situation has been studied experimentally by the sham drinking technique implemented in a variety of ways (e. g. Davis and Campbell 1973; Mook, 1963; Young *et al.*, 1974). The data reported in these studies and others are

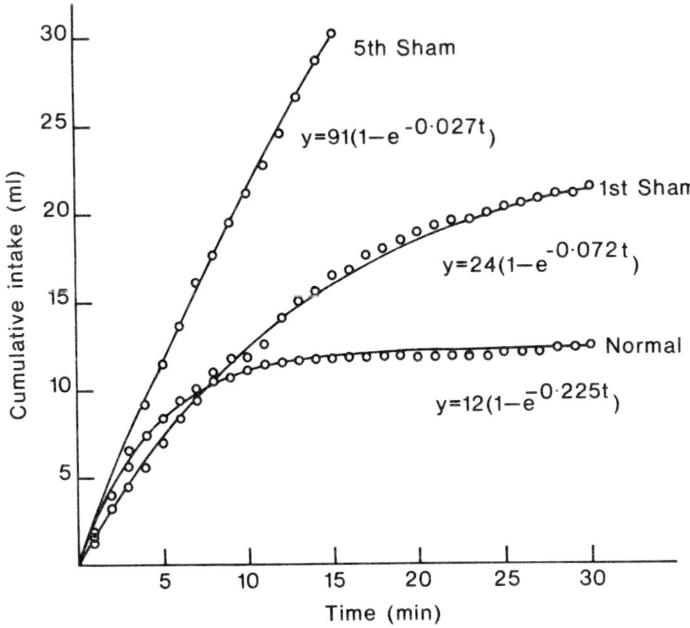

Fig. 6. Cumulative intake of milk under normal and sham drinking conditions. The lowest curve describes normal intake; the middle one intake on the first day of sham drinking; the top curve intake on the fifth consecutive day of sham drinking. The solid lines are the least squares fits to the data of the function $C(t)=g/rk(1\text{-}e^{-drkt})$.

consistent in showing that when ingested fluids do not accumulate in the gastrointestinal tract, drinking continues for a much longer period of time than normal. Figure 6, replotted from Davis and Campbell (1973), shows the cumulative mean intake of a group of animals drinking milk normally but with the ingested milk being aspirated from the stomach while they drink it. The solid lines in the figure are least squares fits of the general form of the cumulative intake function used in Fig. 4a, b: $C(t)=a(1-e^{-bt})$ where a corresponds in our model to g/rk and b to drk. Notice that the asymptotic value (g/rk) for the sham drinking situation is very much larger than it is when the animal is drinking normally, and that the value of the exponent (drk) for the sham drinking situation is very much smaller than it is for the normal drinking situation. Since milk is the test solution in both cases, g should be constant. Since the data are from the same group of animals, d should be constant. Therefore, the only way that g/rk can be large in the sham drinking and small in normal drinking is for r to be small in the first and large in the latter test situations. But this must be the case, since when the animals are sham drinking there is no fluid accumulation in the intestine, which is equivalent to saying that r must be zero or close to it. It may not be exactly zero: although ingested food is not accumulating in the stomach or intestine, the secretory glands of the digestive system still secrete in response to gustatory stimulation, and these fluids may accumulate to some extent in the intestine before they are absorbed.

An unexpected finding in this study was that during their first experience with open loop drinking the animals drank much more than normal in 30 minutes (22 ml v. 12 ml) but not nearly as much as they did on the fifth day of sham drinking. The cumulative intake functions for the first and fifth day of sham drinking are shown in Fig. 6. By the fifth day the cumulative intake function is almost linear as required by the model but on the first sham drinking day it is well described by an exponential function. This indicates to us that, even though the ingested milk is being removed from the stomach as rapidly as it is being delivered, there is still negative feedback operating during the course of the drinking bout—a negative feedback signal which is almost completely gone by the fifth day.

One possible explanation for this is that on the first sham drinking day there is appreciable intestinal and pancreatic secretion stimulated by the cephalic phase of secretion. The accumulation of these secretions could, by filling the intestine, activate the negative feedback loop. If these secretions were conditioned reactions and extinguished because of the absence of chyme in the intestine, then with experience in the sham drinking situation they would no longer activate the negative feedback loop.

An alternative explanation is that the progressive increase in amount consumed represents extinction of the conditioned oral metering proposed by Le Magnen (1967). This kind of control could be represented by an additional negative feedback loop in parallel with the one we have shown in Fig. 2. If such a mechanism exists, there should be a progressive rather than an abrupt increase in draught size with experience in a sham drinking situation. The response of our model with two negative feedback loops to a step input is derived in the appendix. Expressed as a cumulative intake, this model predicts the following function for cumulative intake:-

$$C(t) = \frac{g}{rk + a}\,(1 - e^{-d(rk+a)})$$

Note that the form of this function is indistinguishable from that obtained with only one negative feedback loop. When $r=0$, as in sham drinking, then the asymptote and exponent depend only on a in the same way they depended on rk in the original model and, since $a \leqslant rk+a$, the asymptote for sham feeding would be higher and the exponent lower than for normal drinking. If the value of a then decreases (by extinction) during successive sham drinking experiences, one would expect to obtain the family of curves that are illustrated in Fig. 6.

C. *Shape of Cumulative Intake Functions*

A second prediction which the model makes is that cumulative intake functions ($C(t)$] will have the general form described by the function $y=a(1-e^{-bt})$. The model predicts this to be the case regardless of the specific character of palatability or rate of absorption of the ingested substance from the intestine.

This prediction seems to be well supported by a variety of data we have collected. For example, the data summarized in Fig. 6 were fitted by the least squares method to the negatively accelerated exponential functions. These fits appear as solid lines in that figure; it is clear that the solid lines describe the average intake data quie well. The same can be said for the curves which were fitted by least squares to the data summarized in Fig. 7a. These data describe the average cumulative number of licks stimulated by a variety of solutions differing in palatability but equal in their rates of clearance from the intestine. The solid lines, as in Fig. 6, are the least squares exponential fits to these data. Figure 7b illustrates the cumulative intake function of solutions equal in palatability but differing in absorption rate from the intestine. Here again it is apparent that least squares exponential fits to these data describe the data remarkably well. Exponential fits to the cumulative intake functions of solutions which vary both in palatability and absorption rate from the intestine are also good.

Figure 8 shows the cumulative intake functions for three different concentrations of maltose solutions ranging from weak (0·1 mol/l) to intermediate (0·4 mol/l) to concentrated (1·6 mol/l). These three solutions vary both in palatability and short term satiety effects, both being increasing functions of concentration. The solid lines again are the least squares fits to exponential functions of the general form predicted by the model.

Thus it is clear that the intake functions of a variety of fluids, differing in palatability and in short term satiety effects, can all be described well by the same general function $y=a(1\text{-}e^{-bt})$.

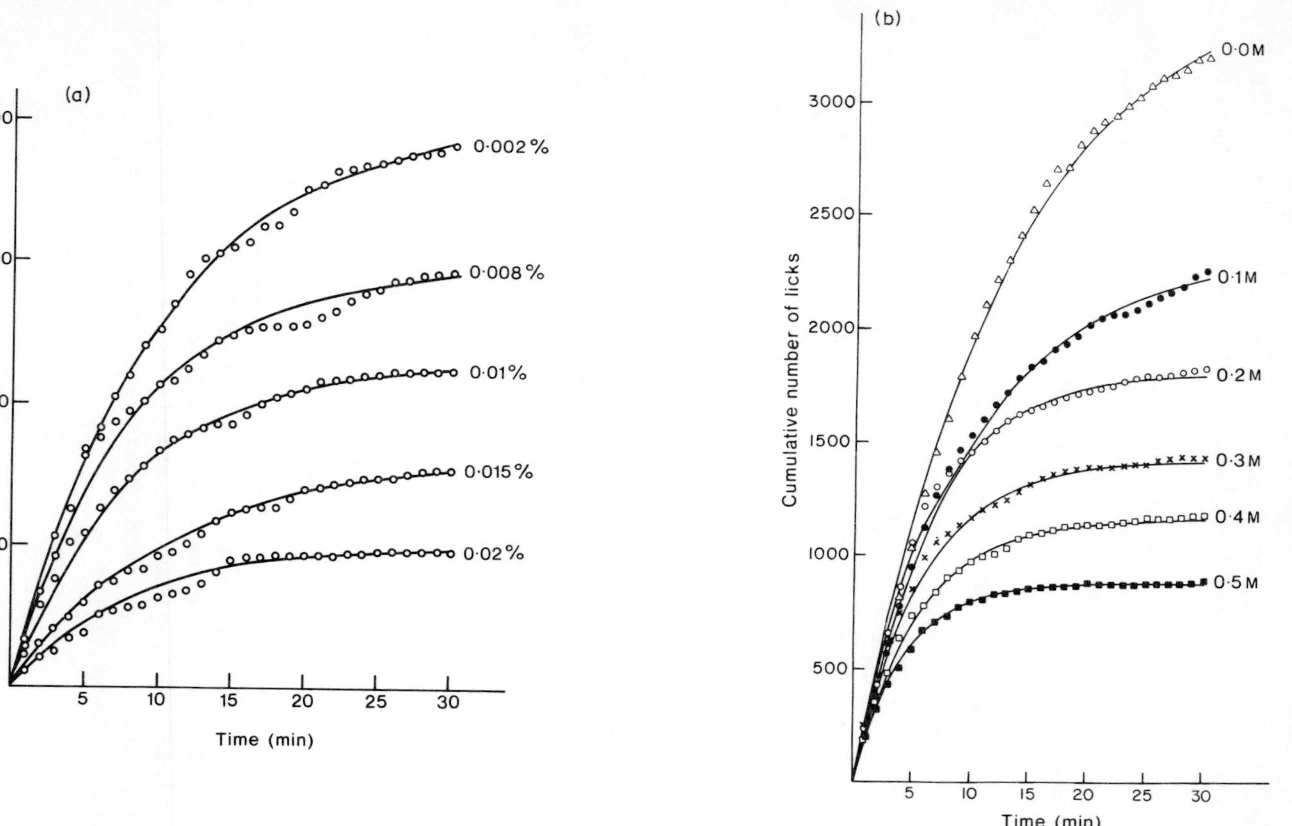

Fig. 7. Cumulative intake functions for the situations where (a) the ingested solutions vary in palatability (concentration of quinine in percentage concentration indicated at the right of each curve) but have a constant clearance rate from the gut, and (b) where palatability is constant but the solutions vary in their rate of clearance from the gut (concentration of mannitol in ingested fluid indicated at the right). The solid lines are the least squares fits to the data of the function $C(t)=g/rk(1\text{-}e^{-drkt})$.

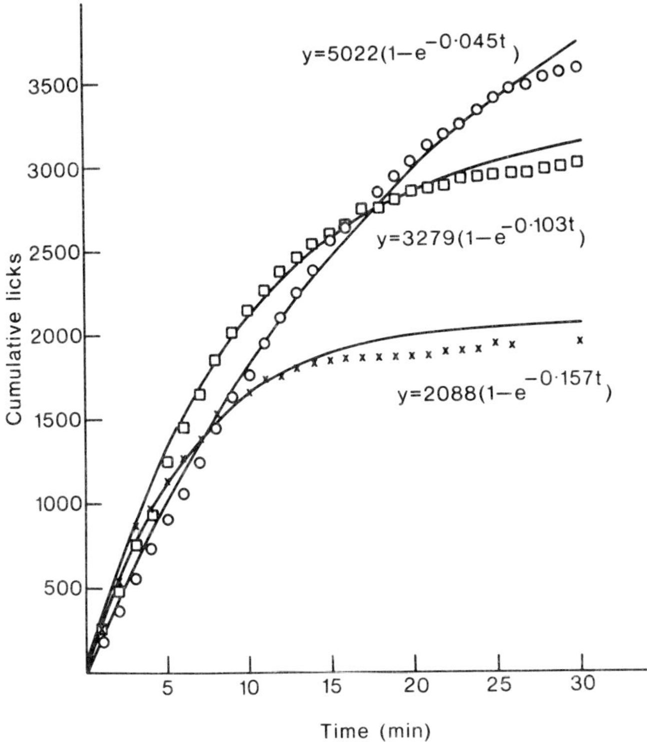

Fig. 8. Cumulative intake of three different concentrations of maltose solutions. The solid lines are the least squares fits to the data of the function $C(t)=g/rk(1\text{-}e^{-drkt})$. The concentrations of maltose are, from top to bottom at 30 min 0·1, 0·4 and 1·6 mol/l.

D. *Response to Differences in Palatability*

Still another prediction made by the model is that palatability will affect the value of the asymptote but not the rate at which drinking approaches that asymptote. This follows from the fact the g appears in the asymptote value g/rk but not in the exponent value drk. This fact perhaps can be seen more clearly in the intake functions $I(t)$ displayed in Fig. 3a, b. There it can be seen that the exponent drk determines the slope of the intake function but that the initial drinking rate gdk depends on the palatability of the solution for a particular animal. Given two solutions with the same retention coefficient (r) but with different palatabilities (g), the more palatable solution will be ingested at a faster rate at any given time than will the less palatable solution. However, the rate of decline of ingestion rate will be the same for both. Thus according to the model an animal will drink more of a more palatable solution than of a less palatable one, simply because he drinks the more palatable solution more rapidly than the less palatable solution at any given time in the drinking period.

This prediction was tested in a study which has not yet been published. In this study we varied palatability but kept the retention coefficient constant by training rats to drink a 0·3 mol/litre glucose solution. When intake had become asymptotic, we adulterated the glucose solution with various amounts of quinine. As the concentration of the test solution was constant at 0·3 mol/*l*, we assumed that the retention coefficient would be constant, and that the small amounts of quinine added to this solution would have no effect on intestinal absorption. On the other hand, it was assumed that the palatability variable g would depend directly on the concentration of quinine in the test solution.

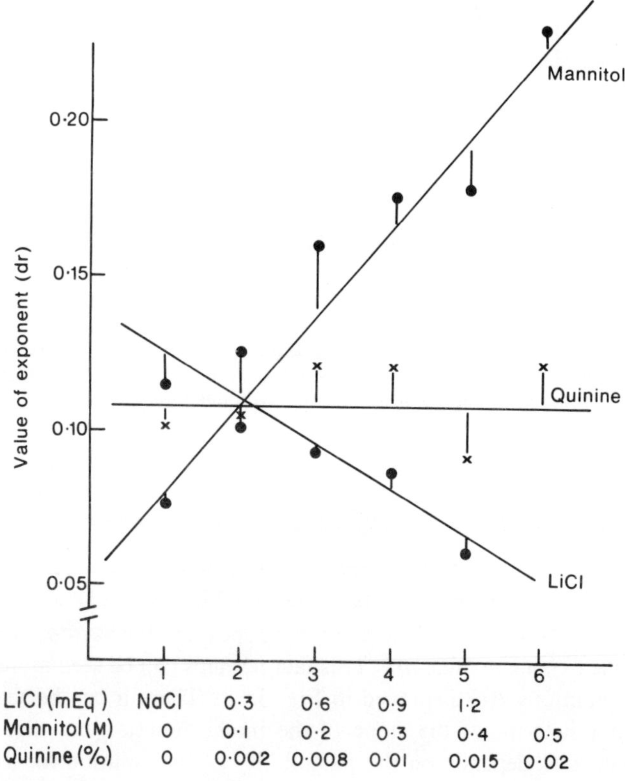

Fig. 9. A plot of the values of the exponents (drk) determined by least squares fit to the data from three different experiments. The solid lines are least squares linear fits for the three sets of derived values of drk. The specific concentrations of LiCl, (mEq/kg), mannitol (molar) and quinine (percentage) associated with the three sets of points are indicated below the abscissa.

The specific prediction was that the asymptotes (g/rk) of the cumulative intake functions would be inversely related to quinine concentration, but that the values of the exponent (drk) would be constant across all quinine adulterations.

The cumulative intake functions obtained in this study were given in Fig. 7a. Each curve was obtained with the same group of animals drinking a 0·3 mol/l glucose solution to which quinine was added, in concentrations indicated at the end of each curve. It is clear that, in agreement with many previously reported studies, total intake varies inversely with quinine concentration. What is not as apparent from an inspection of this figure is that the values of the exponents were not related in any systematic way to these asymptotes. Figure 9 shows the values of the exponents determined from least squares fits to data displayed in Fig. 7a. While they are not exactly constant, as demanded by the model, they do fall reasonably close to a horizontal line. The least squares fit to these data has a slope of only 0·002, which is virtually a horizontal line.

E. *Response to Differences in Intestinal Clearance Rate*

Another prediction made by the model is that, if palatability is kept constant across a variety of solutions which vary in their rates of clearance from the intestine, the total amount drunk and the rate at which this asymptote is approached will vary directly with the rate of clearance from the intestine. This follows from the fact that the asymptote of the cumulative intake function $C(t)$ is g/rk. Increasing r (decreasing rate of intestinal clearance) while keeping g constant decreases the value of this ratio. The prediction about the rate of approach to the asymptote follows from the fact that this rate is described by the magnitude of the exponent drk. Decreasing rates of clearance from the intestine imply increasing values for r and hence of the quantity drk.

This prediction was tested in a series of studies previously reported by the authors (Davis *et al.*, 1975). Absorption rate was manipulated by varying the concentration of mannitol in a very palatable saccharin–glucose mixture. Since mannitol is absorbed from the intestine very slowly if at all, and since the concentration of fluid absorbed from the intestine is isotonic with the luminal contents of the intestine, increasing the concentration of mannitol in the test solution is equivalent to increasing the value of r. The cumulative intake functions for these test solutions are displayed in Fig. 7b. Each curve is the average cumulative intake of solutions containing mannitol in concentrations indicated at the end of the intake functions. A previous study had shown that mannitol did not significantly affect the palatability of the saccharin–glucose solution, indicating that g was a constant across all of the test solutions. Given that g was constant, the asymptote g/rk should be an inverse function of mannitol concentration. This inverse relation is apparent in Fig. 7b and is shown directly in Fig. 10, which displays the values of the asymptotes of the curves in

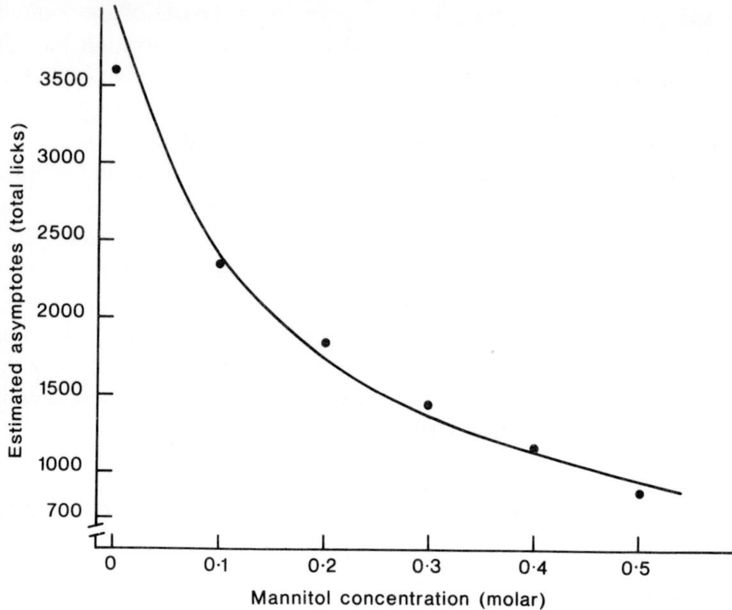

Fig. 10. A plot of the values of the asymptotes (g/rk) obtained by the least squares fits to the data obtained in the mannitol study. The solid line is the least squares fit of the form $y=1/x$.

Fig. 7b plotted against mannitol concentration. The solid line is a least squares hyperbolic function ($y=1/x$).

The other prediction, that the value of the exponent *drk* should be directly proportional to mannitol concentration, was also supported by the data. Figure 9 displays these values determined from the least squares fit to the functions displayed in Fig. 7b, plotted against mannitol concentration. Here the direct relationship between mannitol concentration and the exponent *drk* is clearly apparent.

It is interesting to compare the exponents for the 0·015% quinine curve shown in Fig. 7a and the 0·5 M mannitol curve shown in Fig. 7b. Their values are 0·092 and 0·231 respectively. The asymptotes for these two curves were almost identical, 855 and 822 licks respectively. Here again is an example of the fact that virtually the same amount of fluid can be ingested for quite different reasons. The important point to note is that the shape of the cumulative intake function as determined by the value of the exponent *drk* can provide insight into the factors determining draught size. A large value of the exponent implies that "satiety" is achieved rapidly whereas a relatively smaller value suggests that it is achieved more slowly. One of the merits of our model is that it may provide a way of determining whether an alteration in meal size is due to a change in palatability or gut feedback when it is not clear from the experimental manipulations what the alteration is due to. For example if a CNS lesion increases meal size but leaves the numerical value of *drk* the same, the model leads one to the conclusion that the lesion has somehow altered the palatability of the diet.

F. *Initial Rate of Drinking*

Another prediction of the model is that the initial rate of drinking depends on the palatability of the tasted substance and the forward gain of the drinking mechanism *d*. This follows from the fact that $I(t)=gd$ at $t=0$.

It is possible to get an estimate of this initial rate of drinking by offering rats a test solution for a brief period of time and recording the number of tongue contacts made (Davis, 1973; Young, 1967). Figure 11 shows the results of a

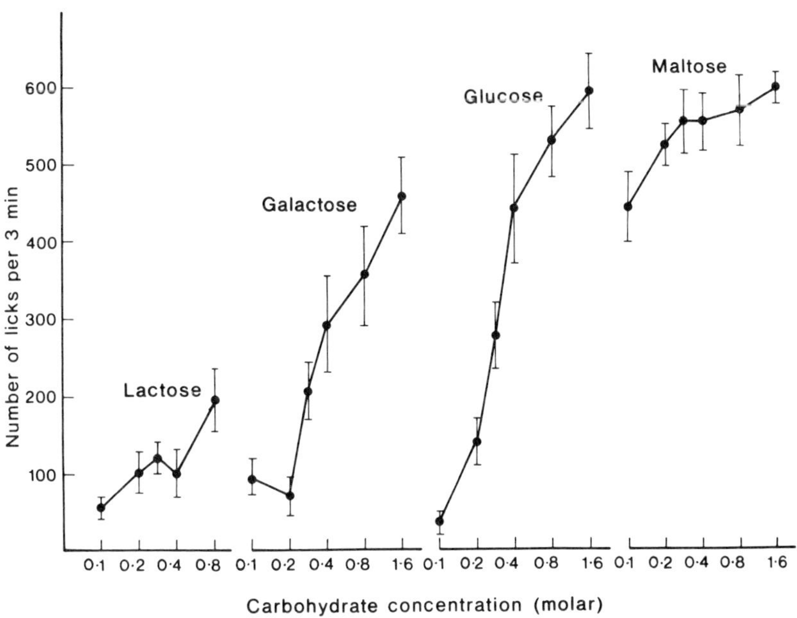

Fig. 11. The total number of licks made by rats during 3-min access periods to different concentrations of four common sugars.

study done in collaboration with Ann Rabinow, in which the same group of rats was offered contact with a variety of sugars at a variety of concentrations for 3 min. The numbers of tongue contacts made with the drinking tube during the 3-min access periods were recorded and are plotted against concentration for the four sugars lactose, galactose, glucose and maltose. It is clear from inspection that ingestion rate $[I(t)]$ increases directly with concentration in all cases, and that the slopes of the curves depend on the nature of the sugar used.

Since these curves were generated by the same group of animals, they can be interpreted as describing the way our gustatory variable g varies across concentration for a particular sugar, and across sugars for a particular concentration.

V. Implications

In general the model we have described seems to work rather well in predicting the outcome of a variety of different types of experiments. In a way this should not be particularly surprising because the model is basically a quantitatively explicit statement of the generally accepted and quite well documented view that the intake of flavoured fluids is controlled in part by the interaction of the palatability of the fluid and its postingestional consequences.

The major strength of our model is one that it shares with any quantitatively explicit model, namely that it generates specific predictions about the phenomena it simulates. Starting with a few quite reasonable assumptions about the nature of some of the major variables which control fluid intake and the ways in which they interact, the model makes specific predictions about the pattern of drinking—predictions which can be tested quantitatively. With a minimum number of parameters, the model described here is capable of describing a variety of phenomena which are characteristic of the behaviour of an animal ingesting palatable fluids.

Another advantage is that the model not only makes intuitive sense, but—more important—it explains some theories on the control of ingestion which have been generally accepted for some time. Many people have recognized that ingestion, like many other forms of behaviour, is controlled in part by its consequences. The so-called "short term satiety signals" is simply another label for negative feedback loops. Once this is recognized, it is relatively easy to translate such terms into quantitatively explicit variables and then apply the relatively well developed mathematics of control theory to the problem. By doing this and then conducting experiments to see how well the predictions conform to reality, it is easier to see the discrepancies between assumption and reality than when predictions are less explicitly stated.

A. *Other Proposed Cumulative Intake Functions*

Another advantage of this kind of approach to model building appears when we contrast the cumulative intake function $C(t)$ generated by our model with another approach to the quantitative description of ingestion patterns.In our model each of the variables and parameters refers specifically to identifiable physiological characteristics of the organism. An alternative approach has been to fit intake functions to arbitrarily selected mathematical functions. For example, Skinner (1932) reported that cumulative intake functions for the early part of a meal could be fitted by functions of the form $N=kt^n$, where N is the amount of food eaten at time t, and k and n are constants. Functions of this form fit his data well but we are left with the problem of the meaning of the constants k and n—a problem which he did not attempt to tackle. Furthermore, this type of function does not have an asymptote, which implies that once an animal begins a meal it will never completely stop eating; this is patently untrue.

Since the curves Skinner presented appeared to be similar to those we have presented here, we determined how well his data could be fitted by the function our model generates. Choosing the value of k to be 1 and taking the value of n to be 0·7 (the value he reported), a cumulative intake function was generated. This curve was then fitted by least squares to our cumulative intake function. The result was $C(t)= 15{\cdot}3\ (1\text{-e}^{-0{\cdot}04t})$. The coefficient of correlation for our fit was 0·997, which we interpret as indicating that an exponential function fits his data as well as the type he chose.

Indeed, Bousfield (1934) reported that the cumulative intake function describing the ingestion of whole wheat by chickens could be fitted well by functions of the form $f=c(1\text{-e}^{-mt})$, which is the general form of the cumulative intake function predicted by our model. Nevertheless, the interpretation of the variables c and m in his function differs from the corresponding ones (g/rk and drk respectively) in our model. He interpreted c as representing the physiological capacity of the organism, and m he called the "coefficient of voracity", implying motivational significance. Our work described above indicates that the asymptote of the intake function depends not on the capacity of the organism but rather jointly on palatability and the rate of absorption from the intestine. Our work also shows that the exponent in the equation, Bousfield's "coefficient of voracity", is identified with the system (d) that converts neural input to motor output in conjunction with a variable describing the rate of absorption of the ingested substance (r). Anyone, of course, is free to interpret these variables in any way he chooses, but a function generated by a specific model has a clear interpretative advantage over one derived from curve-fitting alone.

B. *Interpretation of Garcia Effect*

The model presented here may provide the means for identifying the nature of control of draught size in situations where it is not clear whether palatability or negative feedback from the consequences of ingestion is primarily responsible.

An example of this is the learned taste aversion phenomenon as described by Garcia. The typical finding is that draught size is reduced when ingestion is followed by a variety of procedures designed to induce gastrointestinal illness, such as the injection of lithium chloride or apomorphine. One explanation for the reduced draught size is that the flavour which preceded the onset of sickness becomes less palatable as a result of its association with sickness, and therefore the animal will drink less of it. In terms of our model, this explanation is equivalent to saying that the association of sickness with flavour reduces the magnitude of the variable g for that flavour. However, as should be clear now, changes in draught size can be accomplished by changing palatability or by altering the postingestional consequences of the ingested fluid. If only the total amount ingested is recorded it is not possible to distinguish between these two alternative explanations. However, the model provides a way to distinguish between the two using cumulative intake data, since alterations in palatability alone will be reflected in changes in the asymptote but not in the exponent, as was seen in the case of quinine study. Alterations in gastrointestinal feedback on the other hand will be reflected in changes in both the asymptote and the exponent.

We, in collaboration with Alice Formento, have begun some experiments to determine if the reduced intake following poisoning is due to variations in palatability or negative feedback. Nachman and Ashe (1973) have shown that it is possible to vary the magnitude of draught size reduction by varying the amount of lithium chloride injected following the ingestion of the test solution. They reported an inverse relation between the amount of lithium chloride injected following the ingestion of a sucrose solution and the amount of the test fluid which was ingested in a later test. We repeated their experiment, using a 0·3 mol/l glucose solution as the test fluid and injections of 0·3, 0·6, 0·9 and 1·2 mEq/kg of a 0·15 mol/l lithium chloride solution. Each concentration was administered to a separate group of animals. During the test following poisoning, the cumulative number of licks was recorded minute by minute. These data were then fitted by the least squares method to a curve of the form of our cumulative intake function, $C(t)$.

As expected, the asymptotes of these curves were in inverse relation to the concentration of lithium chloride. If poisoning affected only palatability and had no effect on negative feedback from the gut, then the exponents determined from curve fitting should have been constant. They are displayed in Fig. 9. It is clear that on the contrary, they follow a trend of decreasing magnitude with increasing lithium chloride concentration.

The interpretation of this is not clear at present. The experiment was a between-subjects design, and, since d is assumed to be an individual differences parameter, it is possible that by chance animals with smaller values of d were assigned to the larger lithium chloride treatment. Repeating the experiment will evaluate that possibility. If it turns out that sampling error is responsible for declining trend in the magnitude of the exponents and that a horizontal line describes these values well, then the Garcia effect can be ascribed to a change in the input variable g. If not, we will have to consider three other possibilities. One is that poisoning affects the absorption rate of the test solution. The others are that poisoning decreases forward gain (d) or volume feedback (k). Although our initial attempt at a better understanding of the Garcia effect through the application of our model did not provide the clear-cut interpretation we would have liked, the model does provide us with some very specific alternatives which can be tested experimentally. Future research should tell us which of these alternatives is correct.

C. *Some Limitations of the Model*

Quantitative models have the advantage of offering very specific hypotheses for testing. Although the model we have presented here shares that advantage with other quantitative models, it does have some important limitations. For one thing, it takes into account only two of the many variables which are known to affect draught or meal size. We have not yet included the effects of deprivation which play an important role in determining the amount an animal will ingest. Deprivation may interact with our input variable g, increasing it in some way as deprivation increases, or it may operate to change the forward gain of the system, d. It is possible that d varies not only across animals, but within a given animal with changes in deprivation level. Or it may be that the effects of deprivation on draught size will have to be brought into the model in an entirely different way. Future research should determine which of these various alternatives best describes the effect of deprivation on meal size.

Another limitation is that learning seems to exert an influence on ingestive behaviour in a way which has not been included in our model. Many studies now have confirmed Garcia's demonstration (Garcia *et al.*, 1966) that draught size can be decreased or increased through a long delayed conditioning mechanism (Garcia *et al.*, 1967). Most of these experiments have depended upon inducing gastrointestinal distress (Garcia *et al.*, 1974) so it is not clear what role this phenomenon plays, if any, in the normal control of the ingestion of flavoured fluids. However, it may be necessary to incorporate some kind of learning mechanism such as this in our model because we have recently obtained evidence which indicates that a similar kind of learning may be involved in the control of the ingestion of fluids containing mannitol. Preliminary results indicate that only after their first exposure to solutions containing mannitol do some rats reduce their intake of the fluid. Since these are preliminary results and since we have not yet explored the phenomena thoroughly, we do not know yet how to interpret the effect. Nevertheless, these results suggest that our model will have to be modified in some way to incorporate what appears to be some kind of learning based on gastrointestinal filling.

Another problem is that we are using a model which generates a continuous intake function to describe a non-continuous process. It is well known (e.g.

Davis and Keehn, 1959; Stellar and Hill, 1952) that drinking occurs in discrete bursts of relatively constant rate which become shorter and less frequent as satiety is approached. Our model successfully predicts mean cumulative intake functions averaged across a group of animals, but these curves obscure the fine grain on-off character of drinking. We have interpreted these averaged curves as describing the envelope or overall trend of the individual drinking pattern and our model should be seen as describing this trend, which it does very well. However, a fully developed model must take into account the details of the drinking pattern as well as its average trend. Oatley (1967) suggested that the drinking pattern shown by individual rats can be modelled by a hysteresis loop in the output. Some device of this sort will have to be included in a more fully developed model of drinking.

Close inspection of the intake functions we have obtained suggests that the initial rate of drinking is linear and not exponential. This implies that it may be necessary to incorporate a threshold in the negative feedback loop. That is, the negative input to the summing point may not appear until some time after a minimal accumulation of fluid has been achieved. The inclusion of such a threshold generates a different transfer function from the one we have presented; it also introduces two new parameters. We have not yet attempted to fit our data to these functions because we do not believe that the data we have at present warrant precise enough estimates of the parameters in this new model.

These are a few of the limitations of our model in its current state of development. Most likely more will be found as we gain a better understanding of the variables which control meal size and the ways in which they interact. As better understanding is achieved, it may be possible to modify our model appropriately. This is our current hope. Nevertheless, one must observe caution in model building, for probably the most serious problem of all with a model such as ours which gives a good first approximation to data is that one begins to take it too seriously. Our initial success was seductive, and there is a strong tendency under these circumstances to begin to believe that the model really does represent reality and that all that is needed is a little patching up here and there when discrepancies appear between theoretical predictions and experimental data. This is likely to make one blind to alternative, perhaps better, models and to look for confirmation rather than refutation of the basic assumptions. Quantitative model building has the distinct advantage of requiring clarification of concepts, and precision in the specification of the interrelations among variables. Yet it can also lead the model builder astray and obscure the subtleties and complexities of behaviour which do not fit easily into the model. This, however, may not be a serious problem in the field of the control of food intake, for the reader is presented in this volume with a variety of models, each emphasizing different aspects of the problem. Competition among these models should provide a healthy antidote for complacency.

Acknowledgement

The work described here was supported in part by National Science Foundation Grants GB25936 and BMS 75–17091.

References

Allison, J. and Castellan, N. J. (1970). Temporal characteristics of nutritive drinking in rats and humans. *J. comp. physiol. Psychol.* **70**, 116–125.

Bousfield, W. A. (1934). Certain quantitative aspects of chickens' behaviour toward food, *Am. J. Psychol.* **46**, 456–458

Cabanac, M. (1971). Physiological role of pleasure. *Science, N. Y.* **173**, 1103–1107.

Campbell, C. S. and Davis, J. D. (1974). Licking rate of rats is reduced by intraduodenal and introportal glucose infusion. *Physiol. Behav.* **12**, 357–365.

Davis, J. D. (1973). The effectiveness of some sugars in stimulating licking behaviour in the rat. *Physiol. Behav.* **11**, 39–45.

Davis, J. D. and Campbell, C. S. (1973). Peripheral control of meal size in the rat: Effect of sham feeding on meal size and drinking rate. *J. comp. physiol. Psychol.* **83**, 379–387.

Davis, J. D. and Keehn, J. D. (1959). Magnitude of reinforcement and consummatory behavior. *Science, N. Y.* **130**, 269–271.

Davis, J. D., Collins, B. J. and Levine, M. W. (1975). Peripheral control of drinking: Gastrointestinal filling as a negative feedback signal, a theoretical and experimental analysis. *J. comp. physiol. Psychol.* **89**, 985–1002.

Dethier, V. G. (1969). Feeding behaviour of the Blowfly. *In* "Advances in the Study of Behavior" (D. S. Lehrman, R. A. Hinde and E. Shaw, eds). Academic Press, New York and London.

Ernits, T. and Corbit, J. D. (1973). Taste as a dipsogenic stimulus. *J. comp. physiol. Psychol.* **83,** 27–31.

Garcia, J., Ervin, F. R. and Koelling, R. A. (1966). Conditioned aversion with prolonged delay of reinforcement. *Psychon. Sci.* **5**, 121–122.

Garcia, J. D., Ervin, F. R., Yorke, C. H. and Koelling, R. (1967). Conditioning with delayed vitamin injections. *Science, N. Y.* **155**, 716–718.

Garcia, J., Hankins, W. G. and Rusiniak, K. W. (1974). Behavioral regulation of the milieu interne in man and rat. *Science, N. Y.* **185**, 824–831

Hammer, L. R. (1968). Relationship of reinforcement value to consummatory behavior. *J. comp. physiol. Psychol.* **66**, 667–672

Herrin, R. C. and Meek, W. J. (1945). Afferent nerves excited by intestinal distention. *Am. J. Physiol.* **144**, 720–723.

Herrin, R. C., Meek, W. J. and Mathews, J. J. (1933). Some physiological responses following distention of isolated intestinal loops. *Am. J. Physiol.* **105**, 49–50.

Jacobs, H. L. (1961). The osmotic postingestion factor in the regulation of glucose appetite. *In* "The Physiological and Behavioral Aspects of Taste" (M. R. Kare and B. P. Halperin, eds). University of Chicago Press, Chicago and London.

Janowitz, H. D. and Grossman, M. I. (1949). Some factors affecting the food intake of normal dogs and dogs with esophagostomy and gastric fistula. *Am. J. Physiol.* **159**, 143–148.

Le Magnen, J. (1967). Habits and food intake. *In* "Handbook of Physiology Sect. 6: Alimentary Canal" (C. F. Code, ed.) Vol. I. American Physiological Society, Washington DC.

Le Magnen, J. (1971). Advances in studies on the physiological control and regulation of food intake. *In* "Progress in Physiological Psychology" (E. Stellar and J. M. Sprague, eds) Vol. 4. Academic Press, New York and London.

Lepkovsky, S. P., Bortfeld, M. K., Dimick, S. E., Feldman, F., Furuta, I. M., Sharon and Parks, R. (1971). Role of upper intestine in the regulation of food intake in parabiotic rats with their intestines "crossed" surgically. *Israeli J. med. Sci.* **7**, 639–646.

Liebling, D. S., Eisner, J. D., Gibbs, J. and Smith, G. P. (1975). Intestinal satiety in rats. *J. comp. physiol. Psychol.* **89**, 955–965.

McCleary, R. A. (1953). Taste and post-ingestive factors in specific hunger behavior. *J. comp. physiol. Psychol.* **46**, 411–421.

McFarland, D. J. (1971). "Feedback Mechanisms in Animal Behaviour." Academic Press, London and New York.

Mook, D. G. (1963). Oral and postingestinal determinants of the intake of various solutions in rats with esophageal fistulas. *J. comp. physiol. Psychol.* **56**, 645–659.

Nachman, M. and J. H. Ashe (1973). Learned taste aversions in rats as a function of dosage, concentration and route of administration. *Physiol. Behav.* **10**, 73–78.

Novin, D., Sanderson, J. D. and Vanderweele, D. A. (1974). The effect of isotonic glucose on eating as a function of feeding condition and infusion site. *Physiol. Behav.* **13**, 3–7.

Oatley, K. (1967). A control model of the physiological basis of thirst. *Med. biol. Engin.* **5**, 225–237.

Richter, C. P. and Campbell, K. H. (1940). Taste thresholds and taste preferences of rats for five common sugars. *J. Nutr.* **20**, 31–46.

Russek, M. (1971). Hepatic receptors and the nuerophysiological mechanisms controlling feeding behaviour. *Neurosci. Res.* Vol. **4**, 213–282.

Skinner, B. F. (1932). Drive and reflex strength. *J. gen. Psychol.* **6**, 22–37.

Stellar, E. and Hill, J. H. (1952). The rat's rate of drinking as a function of water deprivation. *J. comp. physiol. Psychol.* **45**, 96–102.

Young, P. T. (1967). The hedonic response to foodstuffs. *In* "Handbook of Physiology Sect. 6: Alimentary canal". (C. F. Code., ed.) Vol. I. American Physiological Society, Washington D. C.

Young, R. C., Gibbs, J., Antin, J., Holt, J. and Smith, G. P. (1974). Absence of satiety during sham feeding in the rat. *J. comp. physiol. Psychol.* **87**, 795–800.

Appendix

We wish to derive the mathematical relationship between the input $g(t)$ and the output $I(t)$ [or $C(t)$ which is the time integral of $I(t)$] for the model shown in Fig. 2; from this we may predict the output behaviour given an assumed input, a constant value of g from the time contact is first made with the test solution. It is very convenient to express all the variables as simple algebraic expressions, so the equations of the model may be manipulated with simple algebra instead of calculus. To do this, control engineers generally perform a LaPlace transform* and express the variables as functions of the LaPlace operator (or complex frequency), s. Thus, we express the input as the transformed function $g(s)$ and the output as $I(s)$. Constants are unaffected by the transformation; the integration in time, representing the accumulation of fluid in the gut, is expressed by division by s. (The functions in the LaPlace domain that correspond to their given counterparts in the time domain may be found either by performing the integration that defines the transform, or by finding the appropriate entries in a table of LaPlace transform pairs such as the one published by the Chemical Rubber Co.)

We may now write equations relating the variables of the model by noting that the output of any box (as a function of s) is simply the product of the input to the box (as a function of s) times the governing equation for the box (a function of s or a constant). $I(s)$ is simply d times $\varepsilon(s)$, where ε represents the "error" or command signal; that is

$$I(s) = d\varepsilon(s). \tag{1}$$

Similarly, the negative feedback signal (gut contents) is $1/s$ times r times k times the output $I(s)$, or $(rk/s)I(s)$. The error signal is the difference between the input, $g(s)$ and the gut contents:

$$\varepsilon(s) = g(s) - \frac{rk}{s} I(s). \tag{2}$$

Combining equations (1) and (2) gives

$$I(s) = dg(s) - \frac{drk}{s} I(s). \tag{3}$$

Which may be solved for $I(s)$:

$$I(s) = \frac{dg(s)}{1 + (drk/s)}$$

or

$$I(s) = \left(\frac{sd}{s + drk}\right) g(s). \tag{5}$$

(The expression in brackets is the transfer function for the model.)

To find the predicted behaviour, we now substitute an assumed function for $g(s)$. We assume that $g(t)$ is a step function:

$$g(t) = 0 \qquad (t < 0) \tag{6a}$$

$$g(t) = g \qquad (t > 0). \tag{6b}$$

---

*Readers not familiar with the LaPlace transforms need not take alarm: the transform is simply a mathematical trick for converting differential equations into algebra. For our purposes, one may consider the LaPlace operator, s, as a shorthand notation for the differential operator, d/dt. Looking ahead to equation (5), it may be rewritten as

$$(s + drk)I(s) = sdg(s)$$

or

$$sI(s) + drkI(s) = sdg(s).$$

Since s really just represents d/dt, this is the first order, non-homogeneous linear differential equation

$$\frac{d}{dt} I(t) + drkI(t) = d\frac{d}{dt} g(t)$$

whose solution is equation (9).

The LaPlace transform of this function is

$$g(s) = \frac{g}{s}. \tag{7}$$

Substitution in equation (5) gives

$$I(s) = \frac{gd}{s + drk}. \tag{8}$$

To convert back to the time domain we must take the inverse transform of (8), either by integration in the complex plane or by referring to a transform pair table. The resultant function is:

$$I(t) = gde^{-drkt} \tag{9}$$

where e is the base of the natural logarithms. This function may be integrated in time to give

$$C(t) = \frac{g}{rk}(1 - e^{-drkt}). \tag{10}$$

Let us now consider the case of nested or parallel feedback loops, in which a second accumulator acts in parallel with the feedback due to accumulated fluid in the gut. In the model, this would be a second branch linking the summation point with $I(s)$, and would look much like the feedback present in the original model: a coefficient, a, and an integrator. This additional loop would have no effect on equation (1), but equation (2) would have to be modified to include another negative term representing the second negative feedback:

$$\varepsilon(s) = g(s) - \frac{rk}{s}I(s) - \frac{a}{s}I(s). \tag{11}$$

Collecting terms:

$$\varepsilon(s) = g(s) - \frac{(rk + a)}{s}I(s).$$

This equation is of the same form as equation (2); the only difference is that r has been replaced by the sum of the feedback coefficients, $(rk + a)$, The derivation proceeds as before, with the exception of that one substitution. Equations (9) and (10) then become

$$I(t) = gd\, e^{-d(rk+a)t} \tag{13}$$

and

$$C(t) = \frac{g}{rk + a}(1 - e^{-d(rk+a)t}). \tag{14}$$

These two equations are of the same form as (9) and (10). If the values of r or a were manipulated (say by opening a feedback loop so that one coefficient goes to 0) the form of the functions would remain the same, but the rate constants and the asymptotic value for $C(t)$ would change (in the case of opening one of the loops, a longer time would elapse before drinking ceased, and a larger total quantity would be consumed).

8

Analysis of Feeding Patterns: Data Reduction and Theoretical Implications

JAAK PANKSEPP
Department of Psychology, Bowling Green State University, Bowling Green, Ohio, USA

To maintain a stable level of body energy, animals must consume as much food as they dissipate in metabolic activity (Fig. 1). Unlike energy utilization, however, the process of energy acquisition is not a continuous function. Like

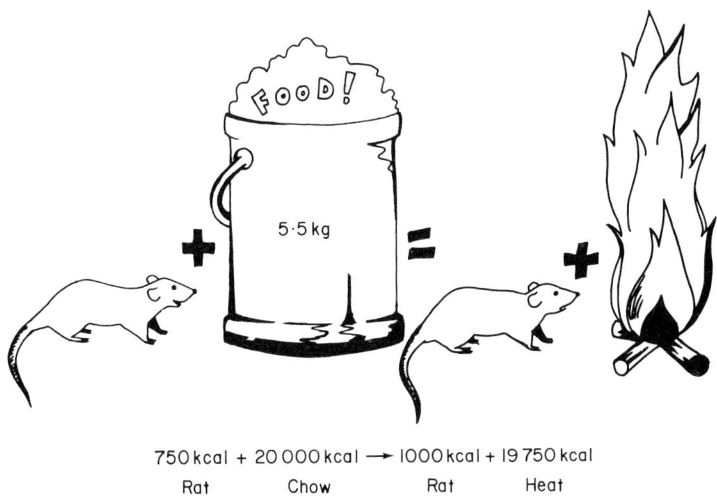

Fig. 1. Female rats' yearly energy balance. Daily intake error < 0·7kcal.

other behaviour sequences, feeding is a periodic series of discrete events, and the analysis of feeding patterns entails a detailed examination of the temporal structure of this series. At present, there exists more information on the feeding patterns of the laboratory rat than any other species, and this chapter focuses on the findings and controversies of that work. Although there is no assurance that a study of the rat will clarify the regulatory behaviours of other mammals, it can be argued that the observed similarities among the appetitive behaviours of omnivores, herbivores and carnivores (Collier *et al.* 1972; Hirsch and Collier, 1974; Kanarek, 1973) are more compelling than the differences. All mammals work to the same extremes when required to press a lever thousands of times for their food. Among the brain processes which ultimately govern food intake, behavioural differences among mammals may result from the degree to which common processes control ongoing feeding. Cats, because of their dependence on energy-rich sources of food, may govern intake more by long term regulatory mechanisms, while intake of herbivores, with their energy-poor sources of nourishment, may be guided more by shorter term controls such as gastric fill and intestinal passage. Omnivores may strike a balance between these extremes. In any case, findings from rats should provide an adequate conceptual base for comparative analysis.

I. What is a Meal?

Richter (1927) was the first to study systematically the daily feeding behaviour of the rat. Although he did not report his observations in detail, he did note that rats entered feeding tunnels attached to home cages about seven or eight times each day. The fact that each meal was heralded by ever increasing stomach contractions and bodily activity emphasized the integration of feeding with rhythmic physiological processes, reinforcing the belief that the causes of meal eating would be found among concurrent bodily changes.

Furthermore, the observation of distinct feeding bouts established a precedent for analysing the free feeding behaviour of rats in meal size and intermeal interval units, and it became widely recognized that all adjustments of daily food intake would have to be expressed by changes in either the frequency or the size of meals. Implicitly, it also came to be assumed that meal pattern analysis is the best behavioural tool for elucidating the nature of physiological processes which govern daily energy balance. This, however, remains an assumption that has not yet been demonstrated. Indeed, we cannot yet assert that dynamic physiological processes are major participants in determining how an animal distributes the details of its daily energy intake.

Even the procedural aspects of analysing feeding patterns remain matters of controversy. A central problem is that the definition of intermeal intervals depends on the definition of meals, and of meals on intermeal intervals. On the basis of apparent clustering of eating, the minimal length of intermeal intervals has been taken to range from 5 to 40 min by different investigators with 10- and 20-minute criteria being the most widely used. Although a majority of feeding bouts are separated by more than 40 min, and may be gratuitously considered as real meals, the number falling within the 5–40 min range could exert an undesirable bias if they were to be improperly included or excluded from certain types of analyses. Unfortunately, we presently have no established rules for designating what constitutes a proper intermeal interval.

Considering the extent to which a valid analysis of meal patterns hinges on the definition of a meal, surprisingly little effort has been expended in putting the intermeal interval on a sound conceptual rather than an arbitrary operational footing. Impressionistic criteria must ultimately be exchanged for precise mathematical and functional ones. As stated by Booth and Pain (1970)

> "The intuitive notion of a meal must not be applied to feeding patterns by using an arbitrarily chosen criterion of duration of feeding to define the end of the meal, as has been common practice. The meal-end criterion should be chosen for its functional significance as indicated by the characteristics of the feeding behaviour itself."

In the initial attempt to provide such criteria, Booth analysed the frequency distribution of interpellet intervals (plotted as absolute or log survivor functions—see Cox and Lewis (1966) for a discussion of procedures) for natural discontinuities which might "provide performance-based criteria by which to apply the concept of a 'meal' in the analysis of the rats' feeding" (Booth, 1972). On the basis of his analysis, Booth suggested that intervals between 1–10min reflect "development of satiety during a meal" while intervals longer than 10 min indicated true intermeal intervals. However, these conclusions can only be taken as tentative estimates. From the survivor plots presented, one could argue that important discontinuities occurred at intervals of 15–18 min (Fig. 1, Booth and Pain, 1970) and at approximately 30 min (Fig. 2, Booth, 1972). Another analysis of log survivor frequencies for intervals between feeding bouts has recently been completed for mice (Petersen, 1975), and the results indicated a major discontinuity at 20 min which may have indicated the break between within-meal pauses and intermeal intervals. Presently, it would appear that these simple stochastic analyses should be extended to a mathematically rigorous analysis of discontinuities in interpellet pauses within the range of 5–40 min. Such an analysis should be based on a large amount of data on a substantial sample of *individual* animals. Linear least squares equations should be fitted to small segments of the overall function to determine at which points statistically reliable discontinuities actually do occur.

Still, it should be emphasized that meals and intermeal intervals cannot be defined solely in terms of mathematical criteria. The decision must also be based on reasonable behavioural and physiological indices. It is possible that long pauses within meals may be due to drinking bouts, grooming or other competing behaviours. A striking example of the possible effects of competing behaviours is observed on the night of oestrus in female rats. During oestrus arousal, absolute food intake decreases by 25%, but this is accomplished by a greater than 50%

reduction in average meal size and a doubling of feeding frequency (10-min intermeal criterion) (Nance and Gorski, 1975). Ultimately, meal pattern analysis may have to construct subcategories within meal and intermeal interval concepts to make sense out of such behaviour patterns, and Petersen (1975) has already proposed that the concept of "feeding session" which would include several discrete "meals" may be useful in circumscribing functional boundaries in daily feeding. Of course, with no adequate definition of a meal, all further categorization becomes extremely thorny. For the present, it may still be best to aim for a unitary definition of a meal, a definition which is based on those behaviours and physiological processes which consistently precede and follow well differentiated bouts of eating (i.e. those separated by at least 40 min).

Before the onset of feeding bouts, rats show increased restlessness behaviourally reflected in heightened motor activity, and physiologically in increased stomach activity (Richter, 1927). Just before starting to eat, rats usually drink (Fitzsimons and Le Magnen, 1969). When the rat has eaten to satiety, it exhibits a different sequence consisting of a thorough bout of grooming, a short period of investigatory activity, and then sleep (Smith *et al.,* 1974). The presence of somnolence (or at least a certain amount of electrocortical synchrony) could serve as a reliable, easily measured and quantified indicator that an intermeal interval has really begun. It could then be argued that intervals which fail to contain a certain minimum level of satiety synchronization should not be categorized as intermeal intervals but as within-meal pauses. At the very least, they would be intervals of a different type. This kind of analysis, though arduous, could ground the concept of a meal and intermeal interval on a biobehaviourally relevant foundation. Without such data, it might at present behove investigators to utilize the more conservative of the traditional criteria (20 min and more) than the more liberal ones (10 min and less). This should tend to increase the error of the second kind (failure to observe a relationship when one actually exists) rather than errors of the first kind (the claim of functional relationships when none really exists).

Alternatively, one is tempted to abandon meal pattern analysis completely in preference for a criterion-free analysis, such as the systematic measurement of the frequency distribution of interpellet or interbite intervals (i.e. a continuous measure of rate of eating). Unfortunately, the gain in empirical clarity may be lost by the resulting conceptual poverty. The concepts of meals and intermeal intervals are probably essential for an adequate understanding of energy intake regulation, but it is surely true that any analysis would be enhanced by supplementary approaches such as log survivor plots of intervals, etc.

Until the concepts are empirically defined, each investigator should, in principle, be responsible for demonstrating that conclusions are not limited to specific, and potentially artifactual, sets of criteria. Of course, due to the expense of such extensive analysis, the principle has been generally disregarded (myself included). The only study which has heeded the dictum is the one that generated it. Kissileff (1970) found fairly stable distributions of meals with intermeal interval criteria ranging from 12 to 40 min whether animals had free access to food or whether they had to press a lever on a continuously reinforced schedule. Shorter criteria yielded different patterns of results, and Kissileff surmised that the minimum interval which should be taken to constitute a true intermeal interval, as opposed to a within-meal pause, was between 10 and 20 min.

II. The Basic Pattern of Meal Taking in the Rat

Although the exact definition of a true intermeal interval remains unresolved, the concept of a meal has become fundamental to the analysis of feeding patterns since Richter's initial studies. Richter's own results may have been well out of the range of ambiguity for what should constitute an intermeal interval. His animals ate recurrently "about every three hours throughout the day". Although this assertion is surprising considering our present knowledge that rats usually exhibit diurnal feeding rhythms—more being eaten at night than day—it should be clarified that Richter may have only been describing the period of nocturnal hyperphagia. Certainly his summary of frequency distribution of intermeal intervals indicated wide variability, with values being normally distributed and ranging from 40 min to over 8 h with a mode of about 4 h.

The first detailed mathematical treatment of feeding patterns was premised on the possibility that the rhythmicity in feeding described by Richter may have been due to entrainment of eating by uncontrolled environmental stimuli rather than physiological processes within the animal (Baker, 1953). Indeed, Baker found that under constant environmental conditions, rats do not eat at very consistent intervals (an intermeal interval was arbitrarily defined as 10 min without eating). In retrospect, this is actually quite consistent with the wide range of intermeal intervals reported (but not emphasized) by Richter. Still, Baker's notion that the meal-taking pattern of the rat might be haphazard in time did constitute a challenge to the basic assumption that meal taking is controlled primarily by dynamic internal stimuli. Even today such a possibility, as framed by ecological theories of feeding patterns (Collier *et al.* 1972; Hirsch and Collier, 1974), remains a viable alternative.

It should be noted, however, that Baker's notion of aperiodicity in feeding bouts (i.e. the lack of consistent meal interval durations) does not exclude the existence of an overriding cyclicity which may characterize the daily feeding rhythm. Indeed, Baker's analysis established the presence of an important asymmetry in meal patterns which is consistent with the presence of daily feeding rhythms. The variability of meal sizes was consistently smaller (the coefficient of variation being $\pm 32\%$) than that of intermeal intervals ($\pm 61\%$).

Although Baker did not elaborate on this finding, it probably indicated that meals were taken at twice the frequency during waking (usually the dark phase of the day) than during repose (usually the light phase), while meal size remained relatively stable. Quite directly, this would have indicated that the satiating value of food is less at certain times of day than others, and currently this single fact is providing the most important key to understanding the physiological processes which subserve the maintenance of stable daily energy balance.

III. The Postprandial Correlation: A Controversy

The major reason for studying the details of animals' feeding patterns is to understand both the behavioural and physiological processes which control feeding. What changes in the internal environment initiate eating? What determines how much is eaten? What changes are associated with the maintenance of satiety? How do environmental conditions modify feeding? As the first order of analysis, it is always reasonable to determine whether meals are systematically related to the length of intervals which precede and follow meals, and it is no wonder that the correlation of meal sizes with pre- and postprandial intervals has received considerable attention. In fact, Baker (1953) was the first to be disappointed by such an analysis. In attempting to determine whether his conclusion of aperiodicity in feeding might merely have been a consequence of focusing on meal times to the exclusion of amounts consumed, Baker calculated the correlation "between the amount of food ingested and the time of self-imposed deprivation" for each of 12 animals tested for four consecutive days. No reliable relationship was observed in any animal. Although not precisely clear from his description, it appears from the above quotation as well as the intent of the calculations that pairings were between meal sizes and postmeal intervals.

In view of those results, it is surprising that the presence of a reliable positive relationship between meal sizes and postprandial intervals was ultimately observed. The report by Le Magnen and Tallon (1966) was soon followed by confirmation from a large number of laboratories (Balagura and Coscina, 1968; Snowdon, 1969; Thomas and Mayer, 1968), followed by a failure to replicate by a number of others (Levitsky, 1974; Panksepp, 1973). It is clear now that conflicting findings are partially the result of how the data are handled statistically; the time spans for which the statistics are calculated (e.g. daily v. day and night separately); and the exact experimental conditions under which animals are tested (e.g. liquid v. solid food, diurnal v. continuous lighting, caloric density and palatability of diets, the degree of effort required to obtain food). Thus, although a reliable postprandial correlation can be demonstrated under certain conditions, since the measure is sensitive to a large number of variables, one cannot yet conclude that the relationship reflects a fundamental regulatory process in the daily feeding pattern of the rat.

A. *The Use of Correlational Statistics in the Analysis of Feeding Patterns.*

It can readily be shown that the original demonstration of a reliable correlation between meals and postmeal intervals was partially the result of mathematical bias. In the original analyses, the data from different subjects were considered simultaneously, and this may yield a correlation merely because some animals consume many small meals with short intermeal intervals while others take larger meals with long intervals. It is unlikely that this was a critical bias, however, for it should have yielded high postprandial correlations as well as high preprandial ones. Only a reliable postprandial correlation was observed.

Probably a more serious bias was the computation of statistics on pooled data rather than raw data. Specifically, meals were first rank ordered, and successive subsets (bins consisting of 10% of total meals) were averaged. These means, along with the corresponding average intermeal intervals, were used for computations. By this procedure, intermeal intervals are not pooled according to any predetermined pattern, and therefore the data reduction artificially maintains the natural variability of meal sizes but not of intermeal intervals. This bias is clearly depicted in Fig. 2, which represents the data of four of our animals analysed by

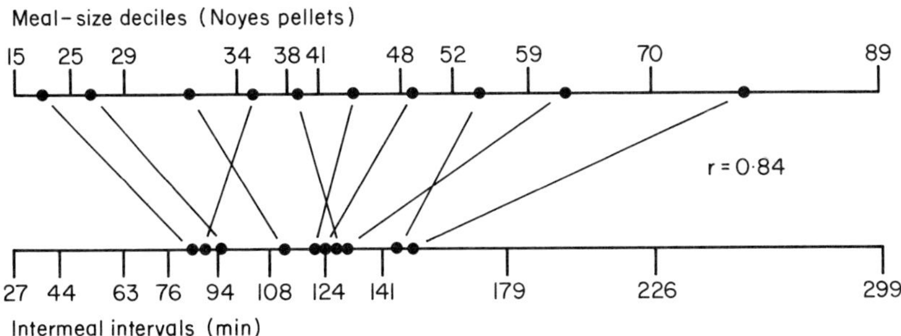

Fig. 2. Relationship between meals ordered into deciles for four individual animals averaged and the corresponding average postmeal intervals. Intermeal internal deciles are indicated.

the above procedures. When the meal sizes were pooled into deciles the average coefficient of variation (i.e. standard deviation as a percentage of mean) of meals was ±39%—a good estimate of the average raw data variation which was ±40%. However, by this manoeuvre, the average variability of intermeal intervals was reduced from ±55% to ±28%. Consequently, the average correlation of these animals rose from 0·22 computed on the raw data of individual animals to 0·84 when computed on the pooled data of all four animals. Clearly, this increase in the postprandial correlation must be attributed to the mathematical procedures employed rather than to any intrinsic relationship within the feeding pattern of the animals.

Important as these computational issues are, they do not account for the postprandial relationship completely. Recent data indicate that calculations on raw data of individual animals can yield modest postprandial correlations in most animals (de Castro, 1975; de Castro and Balagura, 1975; Snowdon and Wampler, 1974; Thomas and Mayer, 1968), or a small minority of animals (Balagura and Coscina, 1968; Levitsky, 1974; Panksepp, 1973; Panksepp and Ritter, 1975). The strength of this relationship as indicated by de Castro's recent work (using an intermeal criterion of 10 min) is 0·4 for all animals tested (day and night data considered separately). Accordingly, the relationship explains approximately 16% of the variance in half-day feeding periods. This value falls to 5% when the whole day's feeding is considered (Panksepp, 1973; Panksepp and Ritter, 1975). Although the values are usually quite a bit higher for animals tested with liquid food (Snowdon and Wampler, 1974, using a 6-min IMI criterion, and Thomas and Mayer, 1968 using a 20-min one), it is debatable whether those values can be properly considered to reflect processes underlying energy balance regulation as opposed to interactive fluid control mechanisms.

B. *Feeding Patterns with Reference to the Lighting Cycle.*

The reason an overall positive relationship between meals and postmeal intervals should not be obvious in daily feeding patterns is because rats take large frequent meals during the night and smaller less frequent ones during the day (Balagura and Coscina, 1968). Although a moderate correlation is observed fairly reliably when day and night feeding periods are considered separately, the relationship should not be taken to be reflective of *daily* feeding patterns. Thus, the postprandial relationship may be indicative of control processes occurring during limited segments of the day. Indeed, the effect is quite striking when a well controlled 3-hour segment of the day is considered (Panksepp, 1973).

The analysis of feeding separately for day and night periods can only be accomplished with enforced cyclic lighting schedules. In preference to such imposed conditions, several studies have employed a continuous low level of illumination (Baker, 1953; Panksepp, 1973; Panksepp and Ritter, 1975). Although this has been criticized by some, it is an open question which is the preferable approach. From the vantage of experimental control, it may be best to use constant conditions, since there is no assurance that changes in lighting and the consequent entrainment may not have its own unique effect on the patterning of feeding. Certainly the effects of lighting are sufficiently strong that rats will entrain their feeding rhythm to a short 2-h day (Borbely and Houston, 1974). Further, though diurnal illumination does simulate the succession of day and night, it probably fails to simulate the lighting rats would normally be exposed to in the wild. The ecologically appropriate illumination may resemble continuous low illumination more than the abrupt cycling of bright light with total darkness.

In any case, the use of unchanging illumination conditions provides the only lighting condition under which a clear analysis of circadian modulatory processes can be pursued. With enforced diurnal lighting there is no assurance that observed rhythms are endogenous (i.e. truly circadian), and hence that data should not be interpreted to reflect the circadian nature of feeding patterns. The term diurnal should be applied.

C. *Liquid v. Solid Food.*

Studies which have employed liquid diets are purposely de-emphasized in the present discussion. Although the highest post-prandial correlations are observed in those experiments, one cannot clearly evaluate their pertinence to the accurate analysis of feeding patterns. With liquid diets, rats drink very little water. When fluid regulation and energy regulation are so thoroughly confounded, one cannot ferret out the contribution of the energy intake to the overall behavioural pattern. Clearly, consumption of liquid diets leads to different patterns of feeding than are found with dry food. Generally, meals are calorically smaller and more frequent, increasing from the typical seven to 13 meals usually found with dry laboratory chow to 16 to 20 with liquid food. In retrospect, the use of liquid diets in the analysis of feeding patterns would appear to have been injudicious.

D. *The Meaning of Postprandial Correlation*

The operation of a moderately strong proportional controller can be demonstrated within discrete segments of the circadian feeding cycle. Although the analysis of this phenomenon is an appropriate research strategy for defining short term control processes, it presently does not seem that computation of postprandial correlations for daily feeding is a powerful technique for revealing the causes of feeding. Indeed, it cannot unequivocally be assumed that the small postprandial correlation which can be teased from feeding patterns of some animals is due to the unconditional processing of the ingested food (e.g. gastrointestinal passage, rate of absorption and metabolism of food). To a degree, it may reflect the animal's capacity to learn that the satiating effects of ingested food can last certain spans of time. This may explain why weanling rats exhibit no reliable postprandial correlation and only begin to do so as they reach maturity (de Castro and Balagura, 1975).

A more serious issue which has to be considered in evaluating the small daily postprandial correlation is the extent to which it is dependent on the meal pattern criteria employed. No one has yet assessed the effect of different criteria on the relationship, but one might expect certain biasses to appear, especially when the more liberal criteria are employed. Certainly if an ongoing feeding sequence is broken up by short intervals which should not truly be considered as intermeal intervals, the probability of observing postprandial correlations could increase. Of course, if the amount consumed following the within-meal pause is also small followed by a relatively long postmeal interval, the bias could be counteracted. Although rats usually show relatively discrete continuous feeding bouts followed by long intervals free of eating, pauses of 8–12 min do occur several times a day in most animals. As an example of the worst kind of situation which may arise, consider the following arbitrarily selected example from one of our records: Following a 180-min intermeal interval, a rat eats 0·8 g (16 Noyes pellets), pauses for 13 min, eats 0·5 g, waits 10 min, eats 1 g, exhibits another pause of 8 min, consumes 0·6 g, and then does not eat again for 194 min. With a 20-min intermeal interval criterion, the animal consumed a 2·9-g meal, with a 10-min criterion the animal ate three meals of 0·8 g, 0·5 g and 1·6 g respectively. With a 6-min criterion, the animal ate four meals. Although such striking examples may be fairly rare, they highlight the type of bias which can arise merely from criteria—a bias which cannot be dealt with reasonably unless an acceptable basis for defining a meal is formulated or until it is demonstrated that such biases are negligible for the analysis employed.

Besides biases and problems of interpretation, one additional line of evidence indicates that results obtained from traditional correlative analyses do not highlight general principles which control *daily* energy balance regulation. If the postprandial correlation reflected a fundamental principle, then the relationship should not fluctuate markedly with moderate changes in experimental conditions such as changes in diet palatability and effort required to obtain food. In fact, these manipulations have a substantial effect even under conditions where the daily intake of food does not change.

Environmental factors have been studied most thoroughly by Levitsky (1974) and Collier *et al.* (1972), and their work indicates that meal sizes are increased and feeding frequency decreased by increasing palatability or effort required to obtain food. Conversely, reduced palatability and effort tend to reduce the size of meals. Levitsky found that reliable postprandial correlations emerged only under conditions where meal sizes were large and day–night differences in feeding were small—in other words, when the variability of meal patterns across the day was reduced. Clearly, environmental constraints over the patterning of feeding are powerful, and the question arises: are environmental conditions or internal ones more influential in determining how an animal patterns its daily feeding? As with any such question, the answer probably lies between the two poles, but in the face of such problems, we must be cautious in ascribing physiological meaning to specific feeding patterns that have been reported in the literature. Behavioural strategies must be differentiated from physiological imperatives. In fact, Richter's (1927) original inquiry was delightfully sensitive to such issues. Not only did Richter measure feeding patterns in the traditional sterile laboratory cage, but he also devised a complex housing system for some animals which included separate compartments for feeding, climbing, gnawing, burrowing and mating. He noted

> "that in these cages where the animal has many different diversions, the frequency of its eating period is greatly reduced. It enters the food-box once every five or six hours, and sometimes even less frequently".

Thus the causes of feeding patterns may be sufficiently different from the causes of energy balance regulation that the study of one may fail to highlight the other. Of course, this is not to assert that ongoing body energy regulation cannot be abstracted from the feeding pattern by appropriate techniques. It undoubtedly can, but the time scale may be critical. In the final accounting, a fine grain analysis may only be marginally more informative than a broader perspective, at least as far as overall regulatory questions are concerned.

IV. The Abstraction of Energy Regulatory Patterns from Ongoing Feeding

One may be tempted to say this in retrospect: after a decade of substantial effort devoted to the study of daily feeding patterns, our understanding of the processes which control energy balance regulation has not been markedly advanced by the use of this experimental procedure. Certainly as a descriptive endeavour, the analysis of daily feeding patterns is a worthwhile enterprise and provides one empirical anchor for testing precise models of feeding control, but as a research tool for analysing the basic nature of body energy regulation there is little to recommend it. Although an analysis of feeding patterns is obviously essential to address questions such as what initiates a meal and what terminates a meal, there is no clear evidence in the literature that it provides a more powerful and precise approach to unravelling underlying energy regulatory processes than is achieved by the simple measurement of food intakes over predetermined spans of time. Though it unquestionably provides a detailed picture of what is happening to daily food intake, this in itself does not make the procedure a tool of precision or insight. To be a truly useful tool, it would have to shed analytical light on causal mechanisms. Possibly with further advances, the analysis of feeding patterns may become an incisive tool, but it is also possible that the approach fundamentally misaddresses the problem of regulation. The most pertinent question for regulation may be what allows the animal to consume a stable amount of nutrients across certain spans of time rather than what governs the systematic succession of feeding bouts. If this is the case (and Richter's data on feeding patterns of environmentally enriched animals indicates it is), then the analysis of feeding patterns is a luxury which provides no praiseworthy advantages over the coarser measures of feeding.

A general knowledge of when food is eaten during the day does, however, provide rational guidelines to the general nature of underlying mechanisms which govern ongoing energy balance regulation. Though a short term proportional controller may explain a small fraction of the variability of daily feeding behaviour, the greatest variability under stable conditions appears to be due to the rhythmic fluctuation of long term signals across the day—either a circadian bias, a long-term depletion–repletion signal, or an interaction between the two.

A. *The Circadian Nature of Feeding in Normal, Diabetic, LH and VMH Rats*

When one asks the simple question—for how long will a unit of food inhibit feeding—one does not get a single answer. It depends on the time of day. There is a fundamental asymmetry in the way rats respond to food during day and night, and this provides the single most important clue to understanding the physiological causes of daily feeding patterns. At night, rats obtain much less respite from "hunger" for each mouthful than during the day. In essence, feeding during the day is more dependent on the body's endogenous regulatory signals, and evidence has been presented by Le Magnen and Devos (1970) indicating that this is due to breakdown of adipose tissue which was synthesized during nocturnal hyperphagia.

This rhythmic process of energy regulation can be summarized as a single synchronous function (Fig. 3), whether one focuses on processes occurring before a meal (i.e. successive deprivation ratios = premeal intervals/meal sizes) or after the meal (i.e. successive satiety ratios = postmeal intervals/meal sizes). Although these derived measures fluctuate synchronously in time, there is no real value to correlating the two since high concordance could be expected merely on the basis that both derived measures contain a common factor: this becomes especially problematic when the shared term is one of high variability. Thus since intermeal intervals usually exhibit more daily variability than meal sizes, one gets inevitably high correlations when satiety ratios are correlated to the following deprivation ratios (i.e. when the correlated derived measures have a common intermeal interval) but relatively low correlations when satiety ratios are correlated with the preceding deprivation ratios (i.e. when they share the less variable measure, namely, meal sizes) (Panksepp, 1973).

The correspondence between successive satiety and deprivation ratios only emphasizes that an underlying circadian signal is of cardinal importance for the

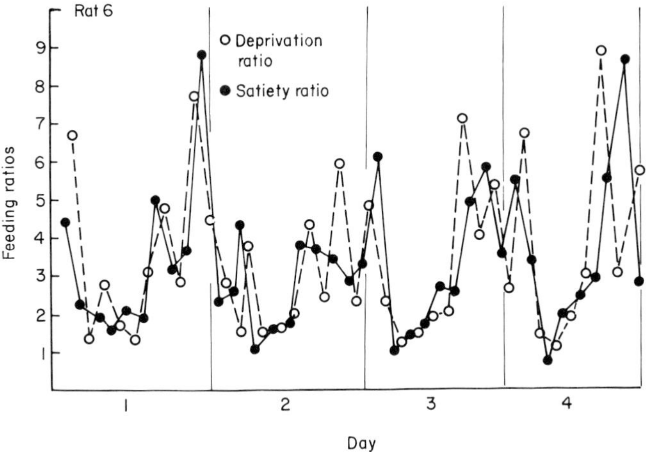

Fig. 3. Successive satiety and deprivation ratios for one animal during a four-day period.

control of daily feeding. Since the rhythmic functions depicted in Fig. 3 could be generated by a variety of feeding patterns (e.g. either small means with small intervals or large means with large intervals), the dynamics of energy regulation need not be expressed in any unique pattern of feeding but could be accomplished within a broad range of behavioural strategies. From this perspective, the essential task in understanding feeding patterns is the clarification of processes which generate the systematic circadian function of feeding ratio curves. A similar function might be obtained from an analysis of sequential intermeal interval durations since most of the variability in feeding ratios is accounted for by variability of meal frequency rather than size. However, we feel that feeding ratios are conceptually better since they incorporate all of the data in ongoing feeding into a single term with apparent face validity. Accordingly, our first order of business has been the mathematical description of this function and an analysis of how various parameters of the function vary with changes in the metabolic and neurological status of the rat.

1. *Least Squares Analysis of Daily Satiety Ratios*

We have fitted equations of the general form $Y = A + B\cos(X)$ to sequential satiety ratios for four day periods. In this equation, the Y coefficient represents the satiety ratios: A reflects the average signal intensity of the function; B is a measure of the peak to peak variability or amplitude of the function: X is time. As described in more detail elsewhere (Panksepp and Ritter, 1975), we have used two mathematical procedures to fit sinusoidal curves to the empirical data. The least squares procedure, whereby the sum of squares of the deviations of Y from a stipulated function is minimized, is, of course, the traditional procedure for accomplishing this kind of task. Figure 4 summarizes averaged curves for ten normal and ten alloxan-diabetic animals and the least squares solutions for the A and B coefficients. In diabetic rats, both the average satiating capacity of food (A coefficient) and the circadian variability around the curve (B coefficient) were reliably reduced. It should be noted that the average daily postprandial correlations for the normal animals was again a low 0·22 with three of ten animals showing statistically reliable values, and likewise for diabetics, for which the average correlation was 0·25 with four of ten animals having reliable values.

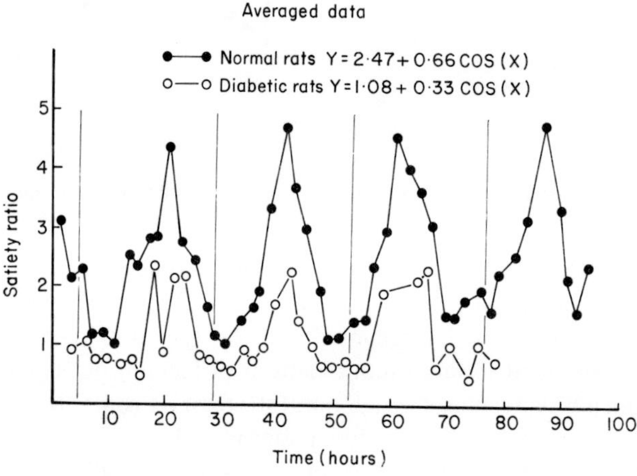

Fig. 4. Synchronously averaged satiety ratio curves for ten normal and ten alloxan diabetic rats. The least squares equations of the form $Y = A + B\cos(X)$ for each group of animals is indicated.

Unfortunately, application of the least squares technique to trigonometric functions is time-consuming and cumbersome. For instance, in our procedure, we fixed the period of the curve at 150 different set values and obtained the least squares solution for the linear residual equations. We did not attempt to shift the empirical curve on the X axis to match the maxima and minima of the mathematical curve, but rather we solved equations of very high frequencies (more than 900 periods per day). This procedure eliminated the need to match starting points of the curves while still providing a good solution for the remaining coefficients.

2. "*Hill-climbing Analysis*"

Because of possible internal flaws with our least squares solution, we also proceeded to analyse the same data with an empirical curve fitting technique. In this procedure, we set the period of each curve at 24 h and included a coefficient for shifting values along the X axis. To obtain the best solution of the equation, we employed the "hill-climbing" procedure whereby one selects the initial coefficients which appear to be close to the best fitting values. Then one systematically samples the coefficients at preset deviations around the starting point and computes the sum of squared deviations around each of the possible curves. After this systematic sampling, the values generating the lowest squared deviation are used as the starting point of another evaluation of surrounding values. By repeating this procedure, one eventually reaches a minimum value of preset tolerance which represents the best fit which can be obtained from the original starting point. By selecting different initial starting points and hence different solution trajectories, one can with the assistance of a computer rapidly reach a general minimum value which is accepted to represent the "best curve". By using this procedure, the average A coefficient of normal animals was found to be 2·2 and the B coefficient 0·9, and these values compared well with the least squares values of 2·14 and 0·92 respectively. Likewise in diabetics, the "hill-climbing" A and B values were 1·0 and 0·4—quite close to the least-squares values of 0·97 and 0·54. Because of computational ease and face validity, the "hill-climbing" procedure is deemed to be the preferred solution to the problem.

3. *Analysis of Satiety Ratios in Animals with Hypothalamic Lesions.*

Because these analytical techniques effectively differentiated the feeding cycles of normal and diabetic rats, we have extended this analysis to the feeding patterns of rats with medial and lateral hypothalamic lesions with the same techniques.

In the following unpublished work (M. Ritter and J. Panksepp), the free feeding behaviour of 16 animals was studied using procedures described in detail elsewhere (Panksepp and Ritter, 1975). After obtaining baseline measures for 4 days, eight animals received fairly small bilateral lateral hypothalamic lesions that did not produce complete aphagia, four animals received bilateral ventromedial hypothalamic lesions that increased feeding, and five animals were unoperated controls. All animals had chronically implanted electrodes so that post lesion measurements would not be marred by intervening surgery.

Four days of feeding patterns were collected immediately after placement of lesions and again 30–60 days later when the animals' body weight had stabilized. All feeding patterns were reduced to successive satiety ratios and the best-fitting sinusoidal functions were determined by the "hill-climbing" procedure. Table I summarizes these results. Lateral lesions reliably increased both the A and B coefficients and this effect, though attenuated, was still apparent during the second post-lesion test when feeding had stabilized. Ventromedial hypothalamic lesions produced the converse effects. The results of one animal whose circadian rhythm was completely abolished are depicted in Fig. 5. It should be

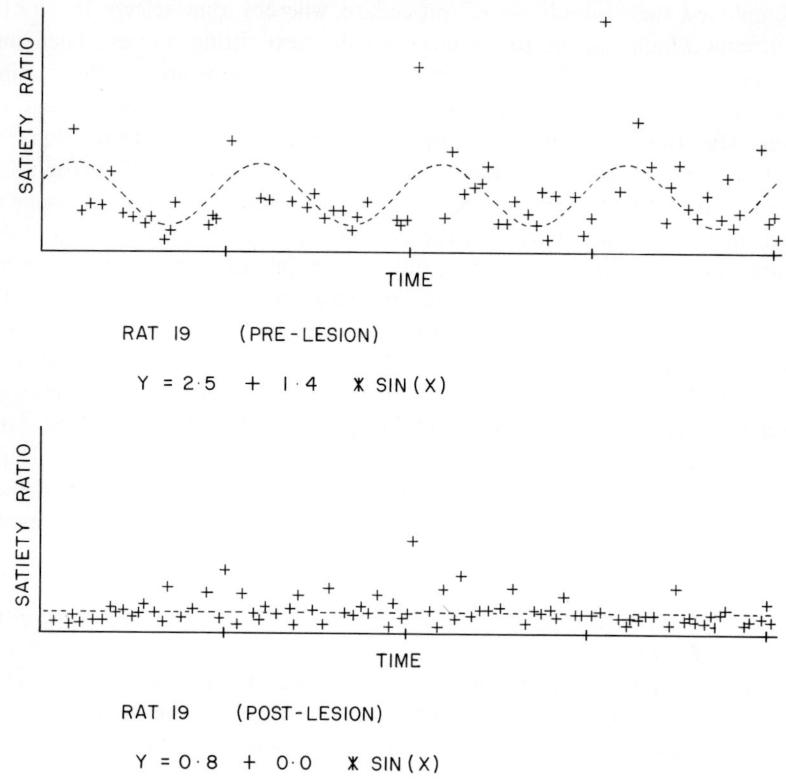

Fig. 5. A computer display of successive satiety ratios of one rat for four days prior to and four days following bilateral lesions of the ventromedial hypothalamus. Best-fitting curves according to the "hill-climbing" procedure are indicated (M. Ritter and J. Panksepp, unpublished data, 1975).

Table I.

Average "A" and "B" coefficients for equations of the form $Y = A + B\cos(X)$ fit to satiety ratios for 4-day periods before and after medial and lateral hypothalamic lesions

Group	Pre-lesion A	Pre-lesion B	Immediate post-lesion A	Immediate post-lesion B	30–60 days post-lesion A	30–60 days post-lesion B
Control	2·1 (±0·2)	1·2 (±0·2)	2·0 (±0·2)	0·9 (±0·2)	2·1 (±0·2)	0·9 (±0·2)
LHA	2·6 (±0·2)	1·1 (±0·2)	5·1 (±0·8)[a]	3·8 (±1·0)[b]	2·7 (±0·2)[b]	1·5 (±0·2)[b]
VMH	2·6 (±0·1)	1·2 (±0·1)	1·2 (±0·2)[a]	0·6 (±0·3)	1·9 (±0·2)	0·7 (±0·2)

Values are satiety ratios (minutes/45 mg Noyes pellet eaten) ± s.e. mean. [a]$P < 0{\cdot}01$; [b]$P < 0{\cdot}05$.

noted, however, that such a drastic reduction in the *B* coefficient was seen in only two of the animals. In the remaining two, the *B* coefficient was attenuated by less than 15%. Since all animals exhibited relatively large 40 to 68% reductions in the *A* coefficient, the degrees of hyperphagia and disruption of the circadian feeding rhythm might be dissociable.

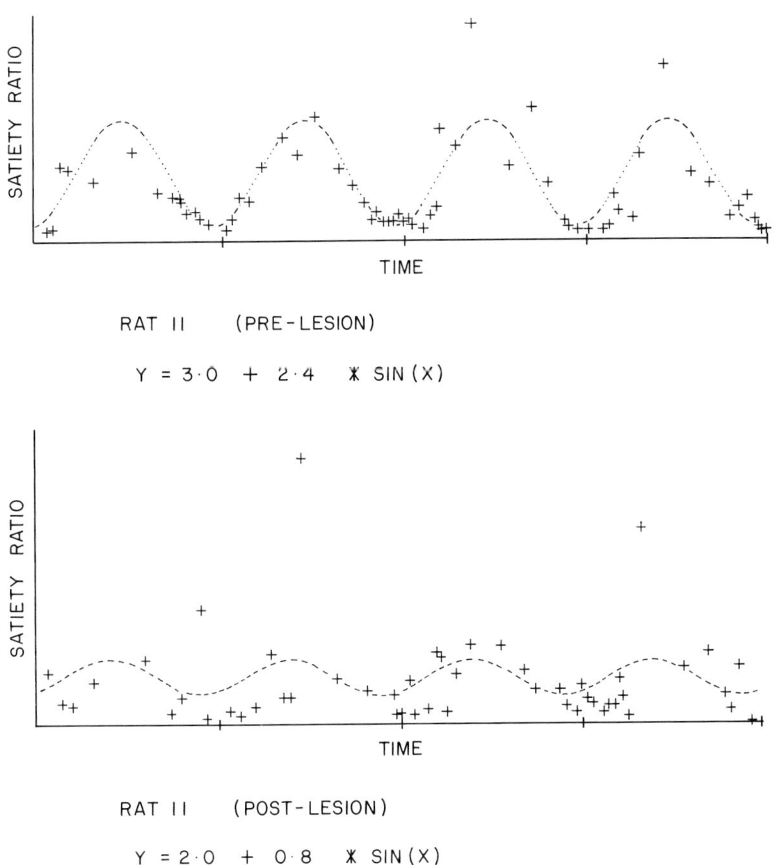

Fig. 6. A computer display of successive satiety ratios for one rat during the four days prior to and the four days following a bilateral lesions of the midlateral hypothalamus which produced overeating. Best-fitting curves according to the "hill-climbing" procedure are indicated M. Ritter and J. Panksepp, unpublished data, 1975).

One animal with lateral hypothalamic lesions was not included in the above analysis since it exhibited marked hyperphagia. The computer displays for the pre- and post-lesion results are depicted in Fig. 6. The results were similar to those following medial hypothalamic lesions, but both were situated symmetrically just lateral to the fornix columns, with no damage encroaching on the far lateral or ventromedial hypothalamus. Possibly the overeating was due to damage of the ascending ventral noradrenergic bundle (Ahlskog and Hoebel, 1973).

4. *Interrelationships Among the Coefficients and Various Measures of Feeding.*

Although it is feasible to summarize daily feeding patterns by the approach described, it is not immediately obvious how the various coefficients in our general equations should be interpreted. In probing this issue, we have computed intercorrelations of the traditional feeding parameters (i.e. average daily food intakes, meal sizes and intermeal intervals) and the *A* and *B* coefficients for the ten normal and ten diabetic animals of Fig. 4 (Table II). The number of strong interrelationships between these measures clearly indicates that they are not measuring independent processes. Daily food intake is a moderately good predictor of meal size and both the *A* and *B* coefficients. Meal size can be a good predictor of intermeal intervals and the *A* coefficients. Intermeal intervals can

Table II.
Cross-correlations between individual daily average food intakes, meal sizes, intermeal intervals, and best-fitting *A* and *B* coefficients for ten controls, ten alloxan diabetics and the two groups combined (correlation coefficient × 100)

	Meal size	Intermeal interval	*A* Coefficient	*B* Coefficient
Controls				
Food intake	39	−26	-65^{b}	−77
Meal size		57^{a}	−28	6
Intermeal interval			58^{a}	56^{a}
A Coefficient			61^{a}	
Diabetics				
Food intake	68^{b}	25	−40	−28
Meal size		60^{a}	−52	− 4
Internal interval			26	46
A Coefficient				63^{a}
Controls and diabetics combined				
Food intake	82^{c}	-58^{c}	-75^{c}	-44^{a}
Meal size		6	-73^{c}	-43^{a}
Intermeal interval			51^{b}	58^{c}
A Coefficient				75^{c}

$^{a}p < 0{\cdot}10$; $^{b}p < 0{\cdot}05$; $^{c}p < 0{\cdot}05$

predict A and B coefficients to a moderate extent. Some of these intercorrelations are, of course, inevitable consequences of shared variance, but the general pattern of results indicates that one should not even attempt to ascribe unitary functional meaning to any major parameter of feeding.

Of special importance to the present discussion is the strong relationship between A and B coefficients. In other words, when food is producing relatively little satiety, there exists relatively little circadian variability in food intake. This is consistent with the conclusion that a long term signal of regulation modulates the effectiveness of shorter term control processes during the day (Panksepp, 1973). Although no unitary meaning can be ascribed to either A or B coefficients on rational grounds, we currently assume that the A coefficient is reflective more of the long term signals of regulation while the B coefficient summarizes the interaction of long term processes with shorter term controls. Of course, these assertions are not proven and remain axiomatic in the system.

B. *Critique of the Signal Intensity Model of Energy Balance Regulation.*

The general equation which has been used here is only a first-order approximation of the actual energy regulatory function which underlies daily feeding behaviour. A strict sinusoidal curve may not be the best choice. Indeed, data from some animals suggest a sawtooth may be more appropriate, but the issue can only be resolved by comparing mathematically the fit of a variety of rhythmic functions. Also, whereas it is clear that some type of rhythmic circadian function is the major source of variation in daily feeding, other systematic influences need to be considered. An additional source of systematic variation appears to have a frequency of about one-half the number of meals per day and is usually apparent in the variation of successive data points around the circadian function. In most animals, the fluctuation of successive satiety ratios appears to reflect a systematic tracking process. A comparison of the number of times satiety ratios continue to progress in the same direction (i.e. ipsiversive transitions) versus the number of times they change directions (i.e. contraversive transitions) clearly indicates that the great majority of rats exhibit more contraversive than ipsiversive transitions (usually in a ratio of 2 to 1). We suggest that this pattern of behaviour reflects regulatory tracking, whereby an overestimate of the regulatory requirement at one meal is compensated at the next. This may again indicate how errors in short term control of feeding can be brought into line by a long-term regulatory process.

V. On the Types of Signals which Control Feeding

From the previous analysis of daily feeding, we can infer the operation of at least three classes of signals. The systematic cycling of feeding behaviour indicates the operation of a circadian generator. The fact that the average satiating capacity of food can be increased or decreased systematically by metabolic manipulations such as diabetes and hyperinsulinaemia suggests the operation of a long term regulatory signal which reflects directly or indirectly the influence of body nutrients stored across the span of many meals. The fact that animals terminate feeding and that the duration of termination can be demonstrated under special conditions to be directly related to amount ingested indicates the existence of short term satiety processes which arise as a direct consequence of food just eaten.

Of the above concepts, the long term signal of body nutrient depletion and repletion may rest on the most tenuous empirical base. One could build a credible model of feeding with only a circadian clock which modulates both meal size and the decay rate of satiety and a short term proportional controller which terminates meals and sustains the termination till the next meal. However, several facts about feeding cannot be explained readily without the inclusion of some type of dynamic long term control process.

Firstly, when an animal's body nutrient stores have been drained by starvation, the animal does not make up its deficit in a single meal but across the span of several meals. The same holds for animals which have been artificially fattened.

Secondly, one can produce patterns of feeding which are characterized by extreme overeating but very small meals—for instance, during chronic insulin treatment (Panksepp, 1973). This suggests that strong short term satiety stimuli (possibly arising from chronic stomach distension) can co-exist with a strong signal of body nutrient depletion which mandates that feeding resume when the short term signal abates by only a small extent.

Thirdly, if only a circadian signal and a short term satiety process controlled feeding, then one would expect the metabolic events preceding all meals throughout the day to be qualitatively similar. In fact, they appear to be quite different. Figure 7, adapted from Le Magnen *et al.* (1973), indicates that when rats are fed ^{14}C-glucose during the night, the expiration of $^{14}CO_2$ reaches a sustained asymptotic level which does not vary either prior to or following meals. However, when the same diet is fed during the day, the marked decline in the expiration of $^{14}CO_2$ before meals indicates that an accruing lack of immediately metabolizable substrates may be precipitating the onset of feeding. As argued by Le Magnen *et al.* (1973), this pattern of results suggests that night-time feeding is characterized by primary hyperphagia with the excess food being stored as fat, while during the day animals are hypophagic with reference to actual energy needs—the ability to undereat being sustained by metabolism of the nutrients which were stored at night. The top curve in Fig. 7 indicates this process in action. During a night-time meal, the utilization of body nutrient stores is inhibited, but as the intermeal interval progresses, recruitment of stores is resumed. Clearly, this suggests that some aspect of stored nutrients can bias subsequent feeding, and this is the essential meaning of the long term regulatory concept.

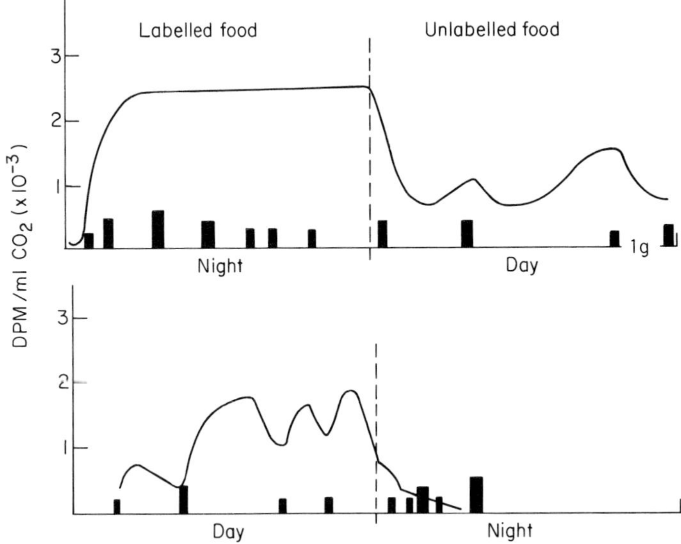

Fig. 7. Expiration of $^{14}CO_2$ in a rat fed ^{14}C-glucose adulterated diet during the night or day. Spontaneous meals indicated by solid vertical bars. Data according to Le Magnen *et al.* (1973).

Despite this evidence, it could still be argued that there is no true long term signal which acts upon the brain. The "signal" may reflect nothing more than the fluctuating patterns of body nutrient disposition across the day. For instance, circadian fluctuations of insulin may dispose cycles of lipogenesis and lipolysis which modulate energy flux through a unitary neural mechanism which does not distinguish between recently ingested food and that retrieved from body nutrient stores. Similarly, the overeating which continues across several meals following starvation may be due to temporary changes in the processing of food such as might arise from starvation diabetes. Thus, it cannot be determined presently whether the long term modulatory process is an active signal or a mere ghost of the body's nutrient disposal mechanisms. The only evidence to suggest a distinct long term signal is the finding that glucose injections into the ventromedial hypothalamus can inhibit daily food intake with no major short term effects (Panksepp, 1975). This observation awaits independent confirmation.

Beside the three types of control processes already discussed, two others may have to be incorporated into a complete model of feeding; a set point of some sort and a mechanism which relates the effective sensory properties of food (palatability) to ongoing feeding. Though the effects of taste on feeding can be extremely powerful, that fact needs no special elaboration in the present context. Whether a set-point notion is required remains unresolved and will no doubt continue so for some time. Certainly there is no incontrovertible evidence requiring the inclusion of such a process. In fact, it would be surprising if a set point existed in the engineering sense where a reference signal is compared to a feedback signal. But the lack of such a mechanism would not mean that there was no functional equivalent of a set point. In the realm of physiological mechanisms, any intrinsically stable property of the underlying system could provide a stabilizing influence equivalent to a reference signal. For instance, if neurones within a spontaneously active feeding circuit had intrinsically preferred levels of activity to which they return after external perturbations, it would tend to stabilize the output of the system in the same way a set point would, though no strict comparison was being made to error signals.

VI. In Conclusion

Even though the broad conceptual outlines of a feeding control system have been established, two major questions remain. What is the physiological nature of each of the described control processes, and how do they really combine to generate the ongoing feeding pattern of an animal? No definitive answer can be given for either at present. One could speculate that both the long term signal and the underlying circadian generator can control the amount eaten at a meal, the rate of eating and the rate at which postprandial satiety decays. One could also propose that short term signals act as threshold devices—as the final arbiters of meal onsets and offsets. The general manner in which we see the critical variables of feeding to interact has been summarized in Fig. 1 of Panksepp (1975). As an academic exercise, we have used such assumed properties to generate meal patterns that simulate quite closely those of typical rats. With arbitrary manipulation of parameters, this can be easily done, but because parameters were chosen gratuitously, I will not belabour specifics at this time. Until the actual properties of the control signals are accurately specified, such exercises can only confirm that we are dealing with a sufficient number of concepts and provide guidelines and hypotheses for further research.

Acknowledgements

This work has been supported by NSF Grant GB-40150, PHS Grant 1 RO1 AM17157-01, and Research Scientist Development Award 1-K2-MH-0086.

References

Ahlskog, E. J. and Hoebel, B. G. (1973). Overeating and obesity from damage to a noradrenergic system in the brain. *Science, N.Y.* **182**, 166–169.

Baker, R. A. (1953). Aperiodic feeding behaviour in the albino rat. *J. comp. physiol. Phychol.* **53**, 151–154.

Balagura, S. and Coscina, D. V. (1968). Periodicity of food intake in the rat as measured by an operant response. *Physiol. Behav.* **3**, 641–643.

Booth, D. A. (1972). Some characteristics of feeding during streptozotocin-induced diabetes in the rat. *J. comp. physiol. Psychol.* **80**, 238–249.

Booth, D. A. and Pain, J. F. (1970). Effects of a single insulin injection on approaches to food and on the temporal pattern of feeding. *Psychon. Sci.* **21**, 17–19.

Borbély, A. A. and Houston, J. P. (1974). Effects of two hour light–dark cycles on feeding, drinking, and motor activity of the rat. *Physiol. Behav.* **13**, 795–802.

de Castro, J. M. (1975). Meal pattern correlations: facts and artifacts. *Physiol. Behav.* **15**, 13–15.

de Castro, J. M. and Balagura, S. (1975). Ontogeny of meal patterning in rats and its recapitulation during recovery from lateral hypothalamic lesions, *J. comp. physiol. Psychol.* **89**, 791–802.

Collier, G., Hirsch, E. and Hamlin, P. (1972). The ecological determinants of reinforcement in the rat. *Physiol. Behav.* **9**, 705–716.

Cox, D. R. and Lewis, A. W. (1966). "The Statistical Analysis of Series of Events." Methuen and Co., London.

Fitzsimons, J. T. and Le Magnen, J. (1969). Eating as a regulatory control of drinking in the rat. *J. comp. physiol. Psychol.* **67**, 273–283.

Hirsch, E. and Collier, G. (1974). The ecological determinanats of reinforcement in guinea pig. *Physiol. Behav.* **12**, 239–249.

Kanarek, R. B. (1973). Availability and caloric density of the diet as determinants of meal patterns in cats. Unpublished Ph.D. Dissertation. Rutgers University, New Jersey.

Kissileff, H. (1970). Free feeding in normal and "recovered lateral" rats monitored by a pellet detecting eatometer. *Physiol. Behav.* **5**, 163–173.

Le Magnen, J. and Tallon, S. (1966). Le périodicité spontanée de la prise d'aliments ad libitum du rat blanc. *J. Physiol., Paris* **58**, 323–349.

Le Magnen, J. and Devos, M. (1970) Metabolic correlates of the meal onset in the free food intake of rats. *Physiol. Behav.* **5**, 805–814.

Le Magnen, J., Devos, Gaudillière, J. P., Louis-Sylvestre, J. and Tallon, S. (1973). Role of a lipostatic mechanism in regulation by feeding of energy balance in rats. *J. comp. physiol. Psychol.* **84**, 1–23.

Levitsky, D. A. (1974). Feeding conditions and intermeal relationships. *Physiol. Behav.* **12**, 779–787.

Nance, D. M. and Gorski, R. A. (1975). Neurohomoral determinants of sex differences in the hypothalamic regulation of feeding and body weight in the rat. *Pharmac. Biochem. Behav.* Suppl. 1, **3**: 155–162.

Panksepp, J. (1973). Reanalysis of feeding patterns in the rat. *J. comp. physiol. Psychol.* **82**, 78–94.

Panksepp, J. (1975). Central metabolic and humoral factors involved in the neural regulation of feeding. *Pharmac. Biochem. Behav.* **3**, Suppl. 1, 107–119.

Panksepp, J. and Ritter, M. (1975). Mathematical analysis of energy regulatory patterns of normal and diabetic rats. *J. comp. physiol. Psychol.* **89**, 1019–1028.

Petersen, S. (1975). The temporal pattern of feeding over the oestrus cycle of the mouse. Unpublished Ph.D. Dissertation, University of Edinburgh.
Richter, C. P. (1927). Animal behaviour and internal drives. *Q. Rev. Biol.* **2**, 397–343.
Smith, G. P., Gibbs, J. and Young, R. C. (1974). Cholecystokinin and intestinal satiety. *Fed. Proc.* **33**, 1146–1149.
Snowdon, C. T. (1969). Motivation, regulation and the control of meal parameters with oral and intragastric feeding. *J. comp. physiol. Psychol.* **69**, 91–100.
Snowdon, C. T. and Wampler, R. S. (1974). Effects of lateral hypothalamic lesions and vagotomy on meal patterns in rats. *J. comp. physiol. Psychol.* **87**, 399–409.
Thomas, D. W. and Mayer, J. (1968). Meal taking and regulation of food intake by normal and hypothalamic hyperphagic rats. *J. comp. physiol. Psychol.* **66**, 642–653.

9

Simulation of Feeding Behaviour: Comparison of Deterministic and Stochastic Models Incorporating a Minimum of Presuppositions

A. J. SCHILSTRA
Zoological Laboratory, State University of Groningen, Haren (Gr.), The Netherlands.

I. Introduction

A. *Usefulness of Modelling*

The explicit use of models has proved to be very successful in almost every field of scientific investigation. In fact, it is difficult to imagine doing anything at all without a model in mind, whether in science or in everyday life. We are constantly analysing, describing and understanding phenomena around us by relating events and finding rules of cause and effect. This boils down to the use of models, at least according to the following definition: a model is a representation of our ideas by means of some (symbolic) language, be it English, mathematics or a computer language. Many other definitions exist, but this one will serve our purpose well.

The presented ideas may concern real physical systems which are inevitably much more complicated than our ideas about these systems. We are interested in the question "how does a rat manage to maintain an approximately constant body weight when confronted with a wide range of feeding situations?". So we consider individual rats as real systems. (Like Geertsema and Reddingius (1974), "we use the concept system in the sense of something discernable from its surroundings".) Rats, however, seem to have a lot in common, and so it is useful to talk about the man-made system "the rat". Thus, in investigating the food intake control of the rat, we shall actually talk about models that are representations of our ideas of generalized food intake control mechanisms of individual rats.

As the real sytems are thought to be constructed of discrete elements interacting according to a collection of rules, we shall construct models in an analogous way from elements connected by a collection of analogous rules. For example, a certain system consists of two variable elements to which at time t the values $x(t)$ and $y(t)$ are attached. The relation between the variables x and y is found to be, at all considered times, very reminiscent of the relation between x^* and y^* in the equation $y^* = ax^* + b$ where a and b are parameters. This equation then is a model of (our ideas about) the system involving x and y. More strictly, it represents a whole family or class of models: each choice of values for a and b defines another model. The distinction between "model" and "class of models" is often cumbersome and ignored.

Physiology and ethology have amassed an enormous amount of data concerning the food intake of various animals. However, it seems that, from the same findings, more than one theory can emerge which accounts for substantial parts of them. The coexistence of glucostatic and lipostatic theories is an example of this that will be discussed below. Some of the differences in opinions could have been caused by the drawbacks of only stating the theories verbally. When too loosely formulated, theories run the danger of having too vague assumptions, unrecognized arbitrariness, unfortunate simplifications and non-rigorous reasoning. Mathematically formulated theories may have an advantage in some of these respects. Equations relating variables are defined according to fixed mathematical rules: no vagueness here. Inconsistencies are easier to spot, for example, dimensions on both sides of an equation should match. Predictions like "if such and such, then this variable will behave so and so" can actually be calculated through and tested. The simulation technique can be of great help. Apart from forcing us to be explicit on all points, it provides us with clues to interesting properties of the model that can eventually be proved analytically, or lead to experimental checks of the analogous properties of the real system. On the other hand, if we expect a certain property on grounds of a set of suppositions, and a computer simulation, while complying with the suppositions, produces a counter-example, this one counter-example is enough to do away with the generality of the hypothetical property. Moreover, models are often so complicated that simulation is the only way in which they can be investigated. Unfortunately, in general one cannot simulate a whole class of models. The parameters in the equations must be given values, so we have only one model at a time. If one then finds an interesting property of the model, it may very well be quite exceptional among the members of the class of models.

B. *The Concept of State*

To be able to compare the behaviour of animals and models, we must have some terminology in which properties of both categories can be expressed. Useful in this respect is the concept "state" (cf. Ashby, 1964). A state of a system is defined as the collection of values of all variables of the system at a particular time. In practice, this definition is far too ambitious. It is sufficient to include in the definition only those variables thought to be relevant to the problem at hand.

The state of a system is not constant. Whether or not we manipulate the animal or its environment, we can observe variables changing, behaviourally as well as physiologically. A convenient way of treating these changes which is open to mathematical treatment is to regard the system as a "black box" (Ashby, 1964). This black box transforms input (e.g. availability of food, or forced exercise, or leaving it alone) into an output (e.g. body weight, feeding behaviour). When one confronts the rat with the same input twice, the output need not be the same if the concomitant states are different. That is, input and state together determine output and change of state. As an example, consider a car as a black box. Inputs are pressures on the accelerator, brake, clutch, gear lever and steering wheel and the total resistance due to wind and friction of the tyres on the road. Direction and speed of movement are outputs, obviously depending very much at times on the internal state of the car, which includes amount of petrol left in the tank, condition of the brakes and so on.

The question we now pose is: what information can be obtained about the inner construction and working of the black box by manipulating the input and observing the output? At first we confine ourselves to the use of information about undamaged animals—absence or presence of food, the caloric value of the food and its taste value. These input variables can later be extended to include glucose infusions, electrical stimulation of the lateral hypothalamus to induce eating, and the like. Moreover, we want the models we are going to develop to have the following properties:

(i) The elements of the models and their relations must be interpretable, e.g. in terms of and in accordance with established physiological and behavioural knowledge.

(ii) given certain properties, the models should be as "simple" as possible.

C. *Simplicity*

As an example of keeping a model simple, suppose two variables in a model are associated with two physiological variables known to have a relationship as shown in Fig. 1(a). It could very well be that the investigated behaviour of the model as a whole is largely or even entirely due to the fact that variable 1 is an increasing function of variable 2. Then the introduction of the relation of Fig. 1(a) or even relation 2 of Fig. 1(b) could be superfluous to the modelling of the said behaviour. So, even while knowing Fig. 1(a) to be "true", we use relation 1 of Fig. 1(b) in order to avoid introducing more than we need into our mathematical model.

This strategy of finding out how far we can get by using only very simple assumptions has additional advantages. First, should the application of a simple relation fail to produce the desired result in contrast to the use of a less simple

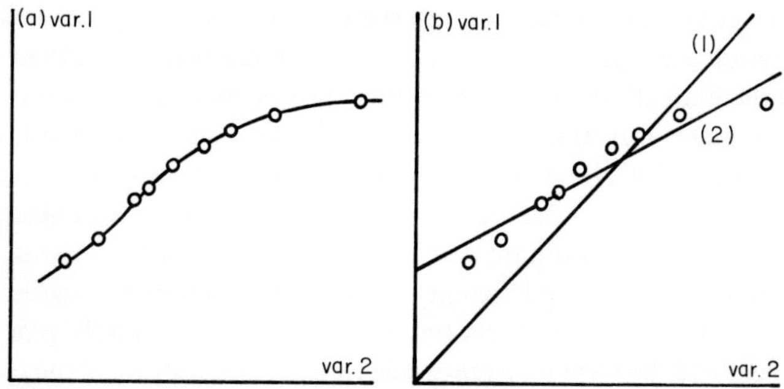

Fig. 1. In a hypothetical experiment nine points have been found that relate the variables 1 and 2 Depending on the purpose of the modelling one can either use a good fitting relation (a), or very simple relations (b) 1 or (b) 2.

one, we can appreciate more fully the meaning of the details of the latter relation. Secondly, by asking an experimentalist no more details than needed, the theorist can help to improve efficiency in experimental work.

D. *Overall Strategy of Model Development and Testing*

In the next section we will develop successive classes of models with the following scheme in mind. This scheme is not supposed to be a set of strict rules, but rather a general guide. In fact, phases may coincide, or branching may lead to parallel lines, for example at points 3 and 4 below where more than one possibility may be of interest.

0. Start with a very simple class of models.
1. Analyse its properties.
2. Compare these properties with the analogous ones of the real system.
3. Choose what discrepancy in properties most needs to be reduced.
4. Consider what would be the simplest modification within the considered class of models that should produce more realistic performance.
5. Apply this modification and go back to point 1.

The scheme does not imply, of course, that the replacement of one model by the next is done objectively; it is still the theorist's choice.

The use of models really starts to pay off when one finds it impossible to make a choice between models that account for a certain aspect of a phenomenon about equally well. At this point theoretical analysis may suggest further experiments the results of which will allow such a choice. Used in this way, models can be very powerful research instruments (cf. Reddingius, 1970; Platt, 1964).

To illustrate the points mentioned above, we shall review in the next section some selected results of the work of Geertsema and Reddingius on deterministic models of food intake behaviour. This presentation will be rather non-mathematical even though we want to emphasize the advantages of the use of mathematical models. The more mathematically inclined reader is referred to Geertsema and Reddingius (1974). Then, after a short introduction to a stochastic approach to the modelling of feeding behaviour, some drawbacks and merits of the two kinds of models will be discussed.

II. Developing Classes of Deterministic Models

A. *Feeding Characteristics of the Rat*

First we will very briefly recapitulate some findings about feeding behaviour that will be used later on. This will of course do no justice to the complexity of the phenomena involved: for more details about the available information the reader should consult Chapters 1 and 8.

The complete feeding behaviour of the rat in its natural surroundings is rather complex, involving searching, fighting, killing, swimming, waiting, gnawing, swallowing and so on (de Ruiter, 1974). The subject of our modelling, however, is the laboratory rat. In a (rather unnatural) experimental set-up like a Skinner box, it is easy to obtain information about the behaviour of the rat towards food. Upon pressing a lever in the cage, the rat is rewarded with a standard food pellet. Recording the times the lever is pressed informs the experimenter how much and when the rat has eaten. Figure 2 shows an example of such a recording. A major feature of these recordings is the clustering in time of the lever presses. These clusters have often been given the name "bouts" according to a definition like "a feeding bout is a sequence of feeding behaviour elements not interrupted by any element of non-feeding behaviour" (J. H. M. Metz, 1975). Clusters of bouts have been defined as "meals", according to a definition like "a meal is a collection of bouts of eating (ten or more pellets) separated from other bouts by twenty minutes or more" (see Panksepp, 1973 and Chapter 8).

To a good approximation the speed of eating can be considered constant during a meal. However, Wiepkema and Alingh Prins (pers. comm.) found a slight increase in the rate of intake in the initial phase of a meal, due to a decrease of intervals within the meal. This initial increase of rate was also found in mice (in that case due to an increased bout length). De Ruiter and Wiepkema (1969)

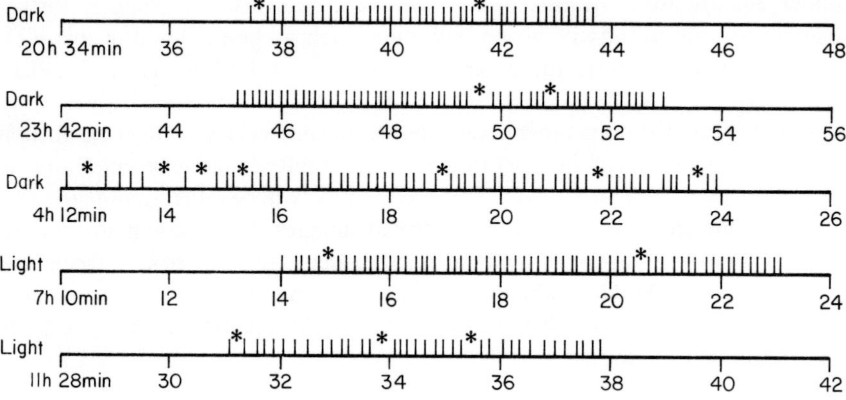

Fig. 2. An example of five consecutive meals of a rat. The vertical lines indicate the time points where the rat has pressed a bar and is rewarded with a food pellet. Intervals between "bouts" within a meal are indicated by asterisks.

suggested that the initial acceleration indicates an increased motivation to eat caused by positive feedback from pleasant sensations, or gradual release from inhibition by other motivations that compete with motivation for feeding.

It is clear that total intake is determined by the factors that govern size and frequency of meals for a given food type. The food intake and body weight of the rat is also influenced by the rate at which the absorbed energy is spent, the former keeping the latter constant for a range of exercise intensities (Mayer and Thomas, 1967). Food deprivation or overfeeding (for example produced by electrically stimulating the lateral hypothalamus) induces a change in body weight. After the normal *ad libitum* condition is restored, the animals will adjust meal size and frequency so that the deficit or excess weight is nullified. Another interesting feature of food intake is the strong circadian rhythm. During the more active half of the day, mostly the dark one, substantially more food is ingested than can be accounted for by current energy expenditure, while during the other half of the day the opposite is the case (Le Magnen and Devos, 1970).

B. *Initial Model*

The above information indicates that food intake is somehow regulated and under control of some correlate(s) of the body weight. The association of high body weight with a reduced intake, and vice versa, can be very easily described by a negative feedback loop from the energy reserves to the "meal pattern generating mechanism". Here body weight is taken as the composition of "lean body weight" and "energy reserves". Let us further assume that body weight only influences intake of food and not energy expenditure (Garrow, 1974). We can then propose the following simple class of models with a negative feedback (cf. Hervey, 1973) (Fig. 3a).

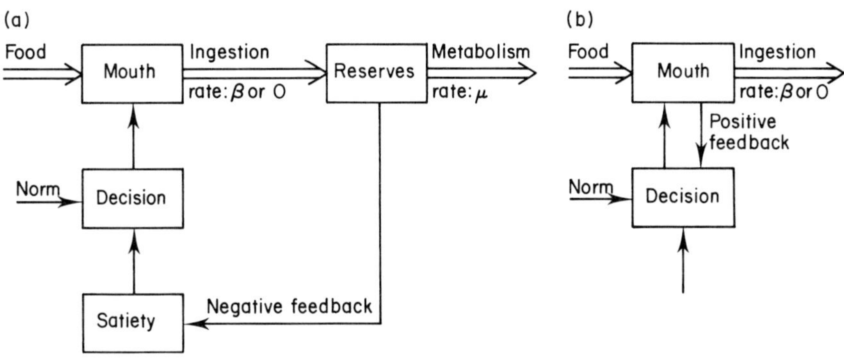

Fig. 3. (a) Initial model. See text for details of its working
(b) Insertion of a positive feedback in (a) is the first improvement and ensures prolonged on and off periods. Double arrows indicate transport of metabolizable energy, single arrows indicate the direction of information transport.

1. *Construction of model*

Let $E(t)$ be the value of a variable E at time t which is associated with the energy reserves of the rat, say expressed in calories. Metabolism causes a subtraction from E at a constant rate of say, μ calories per minute. The value of E is compared to a norm (set point) N_E. More will be said later on about the concept "norm" (Section II.C.1). Now, if E has a value greater than N_E and nothing is added to it, then, as time passes, E will become smaller than N_E. As soon as that happens, N_E-E is positive. This switches on the "feeding" at a rate β, so that $\beta-\mu$ cal/min are added to E (where $\beta>\mu$). When E has reached the value N_E again, feeding will be shut off. E will then decrease until N_E is passed again whereupon feeding will be resumed, and so on. So, reasoning loosely, the model should regulate E around a value N_E.

Unfortunately, something is very wrong: it appears to be impossible to say what state the model is in after the first switching on. As can be readily seen, the switching occurs infinitely fast; as soon as $E \geqslant N_E$, E decreases and as soon as $E < N_E$, E increases. The on/off switch is said to "dither". Clearly the model is not meaningfully defined, a most serious shortcoming of any model. Several ways are open to rectify the undefinedness:

(i) Assume the switching occurs at two norms: $N_E-\theta_1$ for switching feeding on when it is off, and $N_E+\theta_2$ the other way around (where θ_1 and $\theta_2>0$). The switching points are now separated in time and so the state of model is well defined at each instant.

(ii) Use a positive feedback: as soon as feeding starts, the norm N_E is raised by an amount π during the time feeding lasts. E then has to reach $N_E + \pi$ in order to shut off. Although the interpretation is different, this model is mathematically equivalent to the preceding one. Just put N_E instead of $N_E - \theta_1$ and $N_E + \pi$ instead of $N_E + \theta_2$. Insertion of Fig. 3b into 3a results in a block diagram of this model.

(iii) A dead time of δ time units of the on/off element also prevents the infinitely fast switching. So does

(iv) a time delay of τ time units in carrying into effect the decision to turn feeding on or off. Delays between other elements have similar effects. This modification is not mathematically equivalent to the previous one.

The improved classes of models all show a distinctive pattern of eating and non-eating, i.e. meals and pauses, the duration of which can be expressed in terms of N_E, β, μ, π, τ and/or δ. What arguments can be used to choose between these three classes (i), (ii), (iii) and (iv)? It is difficult to conceive a dead time of, say, the five minutes for which a typical meal lasts, because much shorter meals do occur. As for the time delay, the same argument applies. Also, Steffens (1975) showed that blood variables like glucose and insulin have substantially changed within one minute after the start of a meal. It seems unlikely, therefore, that the unavailability of the relevant information, by whatever signals conveyed, causes the meals to last on the average several times longer than one minute. The most promising choice seems to be the class with the positive feedback. It allows an interpretation attractively similar to the rewarding effect of oropharyngeal sensations and seems to be consistent with the warming-up early in a meal which was mentioned above.

2. *Analysis of Model*

We have now arrived at point 5 of the scheme of the preceding section and will proceed by analysing the chosen class of models. Due to the switching element, the model is nonlinear, but between the switching points the variables change in a rectilinear fashion with time. It is possible therefore to analyse the model in a relatively straightforward stepwise manner, the pieces being fitted together at the switching points.

As expected, upon analysis the model shows the desired steady state cycle of behaviour: a marked "on/off" meal pattern, while E see-saws between N_E and $N_E + \pi$. We may ask how seriously a sudden change in the inflow of energy would affect the behaviour of the model. What would happen for example, if we should bring the model in a situation equivalent to that of starvation of the rat and subsequently restore the *ad libitum* condition? Rats will then eat huge meals interspaced by short intervals, the pattern gradually changing back to normal as the body weight approaches its "should be" value. In contrast to this, the model displays an exaggerated behaviour: one enormous meal brings E back to its normal range, whereafter the steady state cycle is resumed. Likewise, after overfeeding, the model compensates by one long fast, while a real rat does eat small infrequent meals during recovery (Hoebel and Teitelbaum, 1966). Again we are confronted with unrealistic features of the behaviour of the models. After extensive deprivation a rat finishes eating the first few meals long before it has made up for the deficit. It seems as if the most recently absorbed food has a higher "satiating power" than food taken earlier. After some time the new food loses this extra satiating effect and a new meal starts. This suggests that the energy at the disposal of the rat is divided over at least two functional compartments.

Let us test the hypothesis that the model can indeed perform correctly when equipped with two compartments. Assume that the freshly ingested food enters one compartment, which gradually passes it on to the other one. The speed of entry of energy from the first to the second compartment must be higher than the speed of metabolism μ, but slower than the speed of ingestion β, in order to allow an accumulation of energy in each of the compartments. An interpretation is obvious. The gut does just this job of storing newly eaten food and passing it on to the rest of the system. Let $G(t)$ represent the amount of energy that is present in the first compartment at time t, and $R(t)$ the amount of energy in the second one, so that total energy $E(t)=G(t)+R(t)$. Assume that their combined effect, the net satiety S, may be written as $S(t)=w_G G(t)+w_R R(t)$ for all t, where w_G and w_R are non-negative constants. This S is then compared with a norm N_E (Fig. 4).

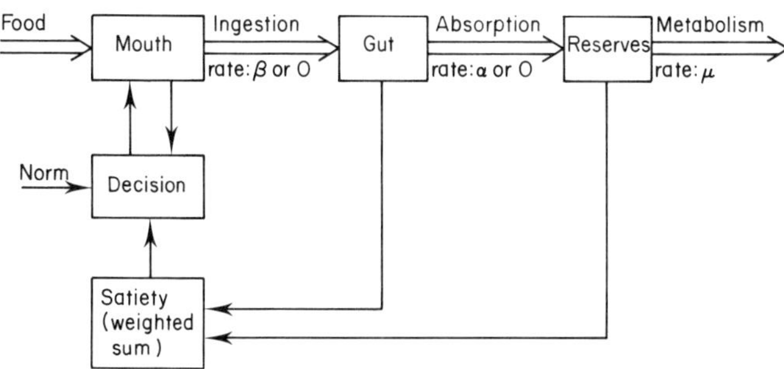

Fig. 4. The two compartments "gut" and "reserves" store energy. The contents of both contribute to the net "satiety".

As we are trying to find the most simple versions of models that show certain characteristics, we do not try to make the gut of the model empty itself with the same time course as that followed by a real gut, but we take the simplest time course that, we hope, will provide sufficient agreement between the behaviour of the model as a whole and that of a rat. We therefore assume that transport from one compartment to the other is at a constant rate, until the gut is empty. Other details, like the energy costs of transport, we shall ignore for the time being. It appears that under the condition $w_G > w_R$ the model performs satisfactorily with respect to behaviour after deprivation. The accumulation of energy in the gut shuts off feeding and then net satiety S drops until the next meal starts.

Some models of the two-compartment family also show a transient response after overfeeding if the initial condition is right. Much depends on how the excess is distributed over the compartments at time zero. However, Geertsema and Reddingius (1974) have not investigated this case further. They have added a third compartment, but by using the argument that (at least) three compartments do exist inside the rat, they have lifted the lid of the black box and peeked inside. As a consequence the use of these models outside the realm of the physiological knowledge invested in them (e.g. in other behavioural systems) is reduced. However, if we stick to feeding systems, the choice has its advantages. It is physiologically more realistic and allows experimental checks of the predictions of the behaviour of physiological variables. The three compartments can easily be associated with physiological counterparts: let the first one stand again for the caloric contents of the gut, denoted by G; the second one is thought to represent the nutritive constituents of the blood with a value $B(t)$ at time t, and the third compartment represents the energy reserves (glycogen, triglycerides, etc.), the variable R. The energy flow μ, which is needed for metabolism is subtracted from the blood variable (this choice between three compartments is again made on physiological grounds; there is no *a priori* reason). Energy reserve R must of course be able to absorb excess from the blood energy B as well as release it again.

C. *Standard Model*

1. *General Specification*

We have now arrived at the standard model depicted in Fig. 5. The models discussed below are variations of this standard model. Before going on, we will specify more fully its mode of operation, using for convenience, as we already have done, physiological names instead of their associated hypothetical variables.

When food is eaten it arrives in the gut at a constant speed of β cal/min. From there it is absorbed and added to the blood, also at a constant rate, say a_1 cal/min until the gut is empty. As mentioned before, we know this is far from realistic. If, however, this assumption (or other simple assumptions) does not cause the model to fall below the required degree of precision, we can make the point that the details of the time course of gut clearance are not necessarily very important for our present aim. A similar argument applies to the following assumptions. When blood energy $B(t)$ is greater than a norm value N_R, energy will go at a constant speed of a_2 cal/min from the blood to the reserves R. On the other hand, if $B(t)$ is smaller than or equal to N_B, a_3 cal/min will be added to the blood at the expense of the reserves. Net satiety is at all times defined as the linear relationship: $S(t) = w_G G(t) + w_B B(t) + w_R R(r)$. Feeding is controlled by comparing satiety $S(t)$ to a norm N_E and a positive feedback π.

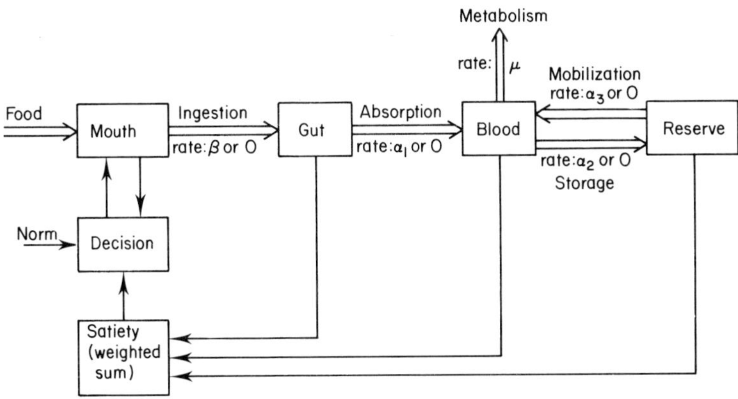

Fig. 5. The standard model. See text.

Even though a set point system has not been identified in physiology (Booth, 1976), use of the idea has a heuristic value. In our models the concept of "norm" is used in the following sense. It is postulated that the collection of all possible states of the rat can be divided into two subsets. When the rat comes into one of the states of the first set it will start eating. If in the other set it will not. The boundary between these two sets is indicated by what we call the norm N_E. In the same way a boundary is assumed between states that switch off feeding, indicated by $N_E + \pi$.

One may wonder if the introduction of three compartments would not render the positive feedback superfluous for avoiding the dithering observed in the simple class of model we start with. The answer depends on the relation between the values of a_3 (rate of influx from reserves R to blood B) and μ (rate of metabolism). Suppose $a_3 < \mu$. A little reflection will show that the model now dithers at two places: the feeding behaviour as well as the release from R will be switched on and off infinitely fast. When $a_3 = \mu$, R compensates exactly for metabolism. Soon after overfeeding is stopped, $G(t) = 0$ and $B(t)$ stays at the value N_B. Only R determines the onset of feeding, resulting in an absence of a transient period after deprivation. Furthermore, the model also dithers. However, if $a_3 < \mu$, finite meals and pauses occur under certain conditions for the parameters of the model (Geertsema and Reddingius, 1974). The duration of the meals and pauses then turn out to be dependent on the initial values of G, B and R. This case was not investigated further because of this unrealistic and complicating property. It is concluded that one cannot do away with the positive feedback in the standard model.

2. *Classes of standard model.*

We can obviously discuss only some classes of models derived from the standard model. Three classes will be selected that illustrate some points made in the Introduction.

Class A. Standard model with $a_3=\mu$.

In Fig. 6 the time course of the variables, G, B, R and S, using the parameters from the legend is illustrated. Special points in time are:

t_b=the moment a meal starts

t_s=the moment a meal stops

t_e=the moment the gut becomes empty

t_{max}=the moment the reserve is at its peak value

$t_b{}^*$ =the moment the reserve is at its lowest point. At this time, the state of the model is the same as at t_b and a new meal starts.

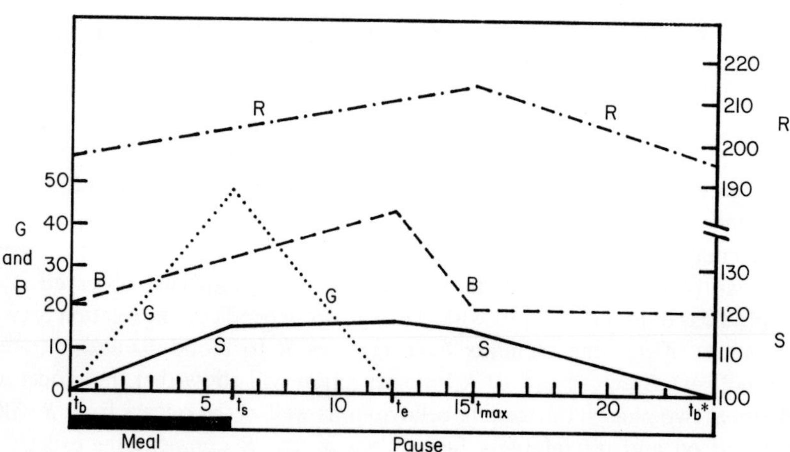

Fig. 6. Time course of variables of the standard model during one steady state cycle. $N=100{\cdot}0$, $N_B=20{\cdot}0$, $\pi=15{\cdot}0$, $a_1=4{\cdot}0$, $a_2=1{\cdot}0$, $a_3=2{\cdot}0$, $\beta=8{\cdot}0$, $\mu=2{,}0$, $w_G=0{\cdot}15$, $w_B=0{\cdot}15$, $w_R=0{\cdot}5$. R stands for the size of "energy reserves", B for the amount of "available nutritive substances in the blood" and G for the contents of the "gut".

Note how reserve energy R lags behind blood energy B, which again lags behind gut energy G. The net satiety S still rises for a while after the meal has finished. From the values of the parameters, the meal and pause lengths can be worked out by simple calculus (see Geertsema and Reddingius, 1974, appendix 1). The compartmentation was intended to allow for a transient eating behaviour while recovering from a period of deprivation or overfeeding. In Fig. 7 an

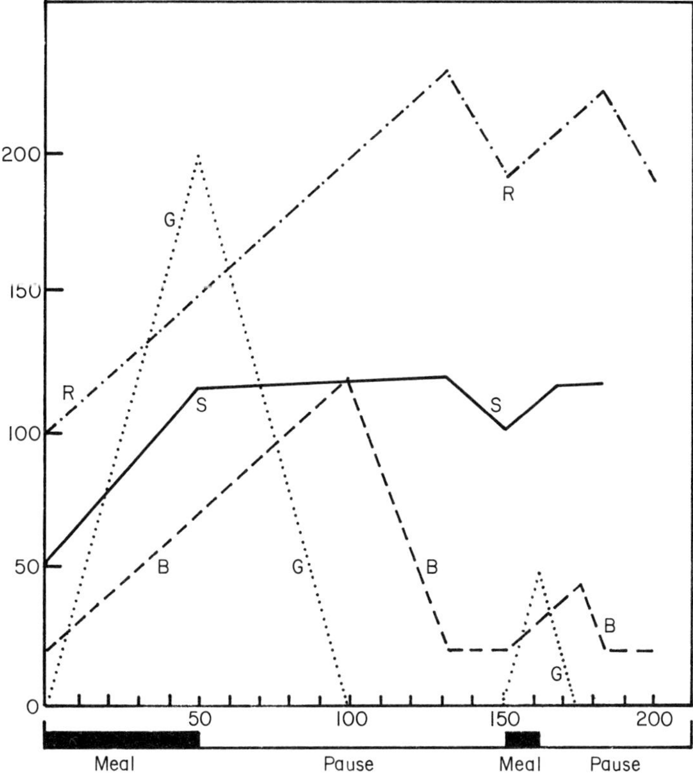

Fig. 7. Time course of variables of the standard model after deprivation. The values of Fig. 6 still let the model compensate for the deficit in one huge meal. $G(0) = 0{\cdot}9$, $B(0) = 20{\cdot}0$ and $R(0) = 100{\cdot}0$.

example is shown of the response to food deprivation. As can be seen, one meal restores the steady state. So apparently not all choices of parameters within this class guarantee an overt gradual transient response, while other choices do (see Figs 8, 9 and 10). Clearly here one should not mix up "model A" with "class A of models": only some models of class A show the desired behaviour.

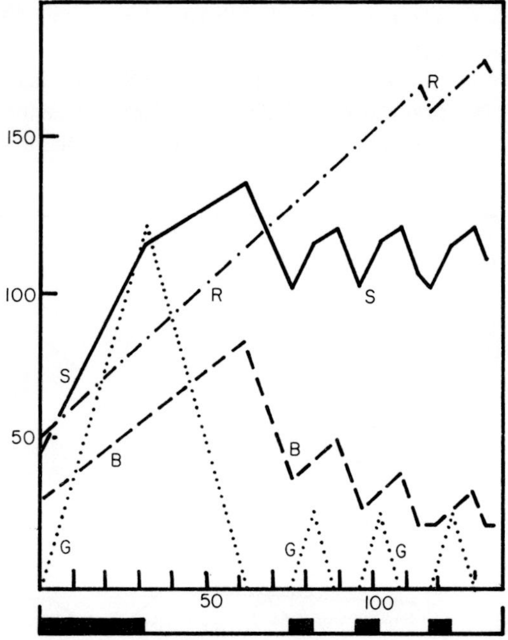

Fig. 8. Transient response of the standard model after deprivation using the same parameter values as in Fig. 7, except for the weighting factors: $w_G = 0{\cdot}2$, $w_B = 1{\cdot}0$, $w_R = 0{\cdot}5$; $R(O) = 50{\cdot}0$. Using this set of parameter values ensures the occurrence of several meals before the steady state is restored. G becomes zero between each meal.

Class B. Standard model with $a_3 < \mu$.

Some experimental evidence indicates that glucose availability may be an important factor in the regulation of food intake (see Chapter 1; Thomas and Mayer, 1968; Steffens, 1970; Strubbe and Steffens, 1977). If B represents this factor (Geertsema and Reddingius, 1974), the assumption that $a_3 = \mu$ is unrealistic. From the fact that a deprived rat increasingly uses free fatty acids as a source of energy it is inferred that the glucose availability is reduced. To allow a drop of B below N_B, a_3 must be smaller than μ. After overfeeding, B would drop to a very low value. Without a scaling of B-values to blood parameters, it is difficult to assess how serious this behaviour is for the model. Geertsema and Reddingius have improved the performance by assuming that a low glucose availability alone may induce eating. This can be incorporated as follows: When B has a value less than N_B, multiply the difference $(N_B - B)$ by a positive, constant weighting factor v_B. The product is subtracted from net satiety. For all values of

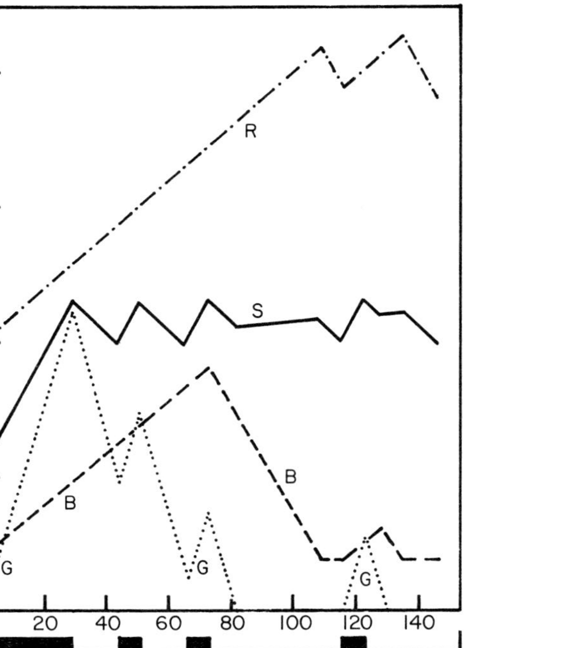

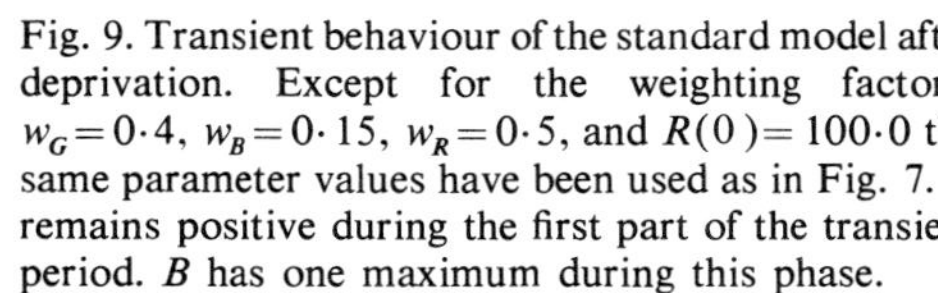

Fig. 9. Transient behaviour of the standard model after deprivation. Except for the weighting factors: $w_G = 0{\cdot}4$, $w_B = 0{\cdot}15$, $w_R = 0{\cdot}5$, and $R(0) = 100{\cdot}0$ the same parameter values have been used as in Fig. 7. *G* remains positive during the first part of the transient period. *B* has one maximum during this phase.

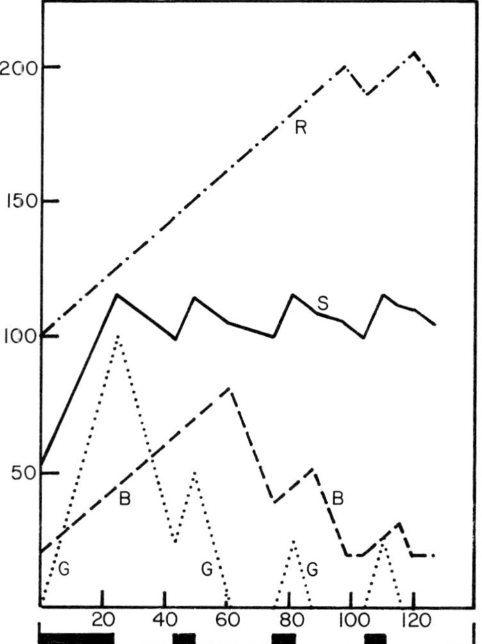

Fig. 10. Transient behaviour of the standard model after deprivation. The same parameter values have been used as in Fig. 9, except that $w_B = 0{\cdot}3$. This change results in *B* having more than one maximum in the transient phase.

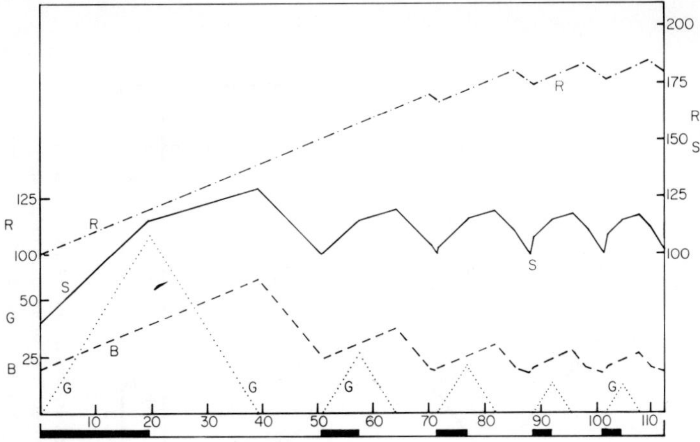

Fig. 11. Transient behaviour of a model of class B after deprivation, with $N = 100{\cdot}0$, $N_B = 20{\cdot}0$, $\pi = 15{\cdot}0$, $a_1 = 4{\cdot}0$, $a_2 = 1{\cdot}0$, $a_3 = 1{\cdot}5$, $\mu = 2{\cdot}0$, $\beta = 8{\cdot}0$, $w_G = 0{\cdot}2$, $w_B = 1{\cdot}0$, $w_R = 0{\cdot}5$, $v = 4{\cdot}0$, $G(0) = 0{\cdot}0$, $B(0) = 20{\cdot}0$, $R(0) = 100{\cdot}0$. Because $\mu > a_3$, B drops below N_B at times. Several meals occur before restoration of the steady state.

B, the middle compartment contributes $w_B B$ to S. Figures 11 and 12 demonstrate the time course of the variables of a model of this class after deprivation and overfeeding, respectively. Again, not all models of class B have the property of the gradual transient response we are looking for. Inequalities between the parameters can be worked out that indicate the subclasses of class B (as well as class A) that do. It is interesting to note that in principle these inequalities can be

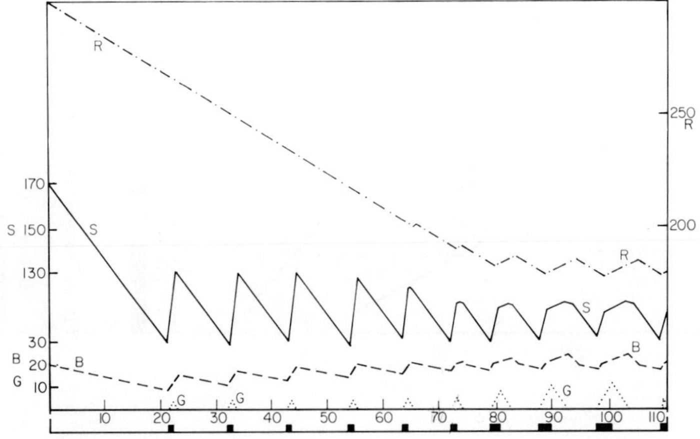

Fig. 12. Behaviour of the same model as in Fig. 11 after overfeeding: $R(0) = 300{\cdot}0$.

tested experimentally. Should the results be very much at variance with the calculated relations, we may be forced to discard one or both of these classes of models.

Class C. Standard model without a signal from the reserves R.

Among the theories about food intake regulation, some can be labelled "glucostatic", others "lipostatic" (see Chapter 1). Both the nutritional composition of the blood and the amount of adipose tissue are kept within a certain range. Since no one has succeeded so far in pinpointing an adipose tissue size receptor, one could ask if such a receptor is a necessity in order to regulate the adiposity. Artificially fattened or deprived animals do return to normal body weight if given the opportunity. A static hyperphagic rat in a similar way defends its excessive high body weight. As will be shown below, these facts are not enough warrant the conclusion that "fat size" influences the onset and/or stop meals by means of a separate receptor.

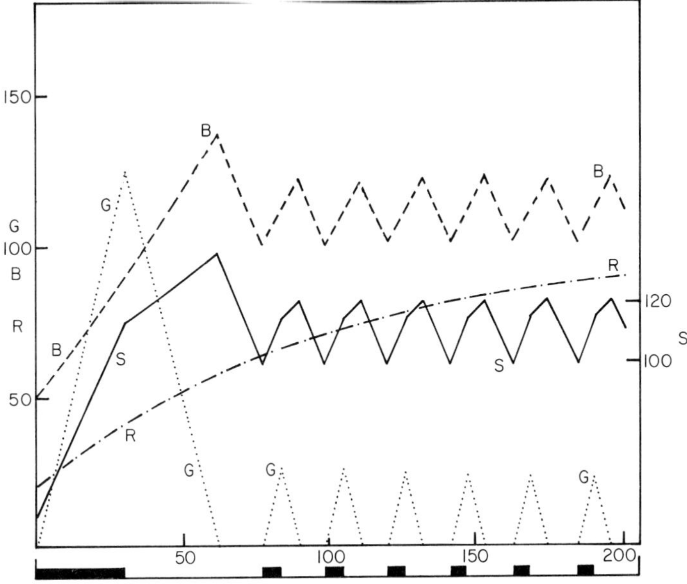

Fig. 13. Transient behaviour of a model of class C after deprivation. The parameter values are the same as in Fig. 11 except: $w_R=0{\cdot}0$, $\kappa=0{\cdot}01$, $B(0)=50{\cdot}0$, $R(0)=20{\cdot}0$. Due to the proportional release from R to B the time course of R is exponential.

Let us test the hypothesis that one cannot do without the said receptor: substitute zero for the weighting factor w_R in models of class B and check whether this abolishes regulation of R.

Depending on the parameter values, the level of reserves $R(t)$ will now increase above all bounds, decrease until zero or stay within a range of values. In the last case, where influx and efflux from R balance during one cycle, R keeps on wobbling around any value we happened to supply as initial value: there is no "preferred range". In order to be regulated, R must somehow influence the dynamics of the model. As we assume that w_R is zero, the only remaining possibility is that a_2 and/or a_3 is a function of R. I shall use the latter as an example. Assume that the rate of release of energy from the reserves is an increasing function of R for all values of B (cf. Shapiro, 1973). We assume, say,

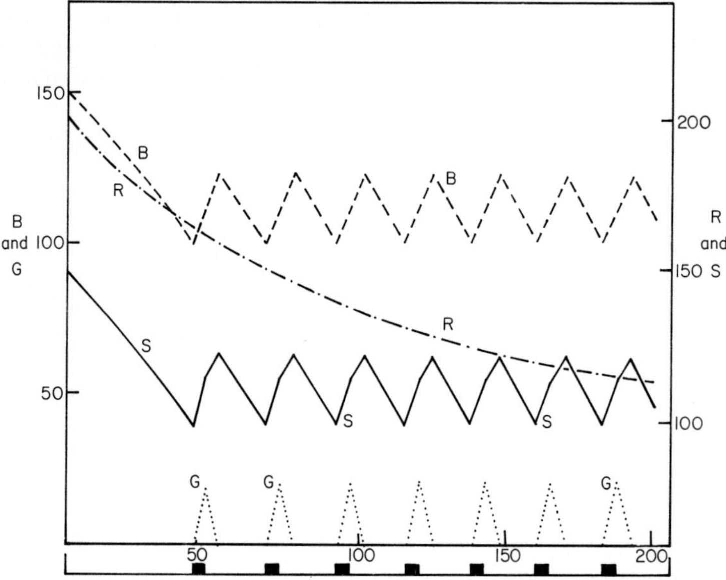

Fig. 14. Transient response of the model of Fig. 13 after overfeeding: $R(0)=200{\cdot}0$.

that $a_3=\kappa R(t)$, and that a_2 is constant for all values of B. Figures 13 and 14 demonstrate the behaviour of this model after deprivation and overfeeding. R approaches asymptotically a steady state range. Owing to the proportionality of a_3 to R, the time course of several variables is not rectilinear any more, and the easy calculation of some properties is lost. We may conclude that even though the level of reserves R is not measured by a receptor, it tends to stabilize in a certain range and to behave in a controlled manner.

D. *Models and Predictions*

The models as they stand can be used to predict or to explain behaviour in circumstances not considered during their construction. If the behaviour in such a novel situation is satisfactory, then this could be because the model has some of the logic of the real system. On the other hand, if the model's performance looks bad and cannot be improved by changing parameter values, then it misses at least an essential part of this logic. Two examples of possible explanation will be presented, the second one is rather more detail.

1. *Circadian Variation*

The circadian rhythm in the food intake of the rat is observed as an excess intake relative to the energy use during the night, compensated by reduced intake during the day. Whatever the cause of this rhythm, it may have a direct effect on some physiological variables related to food intake and an indirect effect on others. The classes of models we have developed can be used to examine and compare the consequences of hypothetical explanations.

For example, the food intake itself can be varied by factors outside the feeding system (e.g. Collier *et al.*, 1972). Here the average input of energy is modulated with a 24-h cycle while the rest of the physiological machinery follows the changing input.

Alternatively or as well, it could be that the expenditure of energy is modulated in a circadian fashion, for example by changing levels of activity. The food intake and other variables duly respond.

2. *Palatability*

Finickiness is observed in rats rendered hyperphagic by means of hypothalamic lesions (see Chapter 3). The static hyperphagic animal appears to be less prepared to work for its food and to refuse a slightly adulterated diet still completely acceptable to normal rats. Can we account for this phenomenon in terms of the classes of models discussed above, or is the introduction of a new class necessary?

We have not yet taken into consideration food qualities other than a constant caloric value and taste. Geertsema and Reddingius (1974) have offered two ways to allow for taste. First, assume the eating onset norm N_π is a function of taste: the more attractive an offered food item, the higher is N_π. This results in a higher range of compartment contents during the steady state cycle of eating and then not eating the food. Alternatively, assume π, the parameter representing the positive feedback, to be dependent on taste, suggesting the effects on eating of the accompanying pleasant sensations. Actually the second way covers the first one: any new set of switching values $N_E{}^*$ and $N_E{}^* + \pi$ belonging to a different food type in the first version can be expressed in terms of the second version by

$N_E + \pi_1$ and $N_E + \pi_2$. In order to avoid circular arguments, one must have a way of assessing the attractiveness of a food substance without using directly or indirectly an underlying varying value of N_E or π. This may be quite difficult. De Ruiter *et al.* (1969) have suggested that finickiness is due to damage of satiating mechanisms caused by hypothalamic lesions. In our models this damage can be mimicked by reducing one or more weighting factors. It can be shown that this does indeed result in an exaggerated response to taste adulteration as compared to "non-lesioned" models. After a transient period, a pattern of larger meals and pauses is produced. A higher range of reserve R-values demonstrates "obesity" in the "lesioned" model at the same time. These findings suggest that *ad hoc* hypotheses postulating special mechanisms accounting for the finickiness might be superfluous.

E. *Models and Experiments*

One of the positive aspects of constructing models in a field where much experimental work is being done, is that attention is drawn to gaps in our knowledge. Some of these gaps may have been realized before, but they persist because they do not particularly interest the experimentalist. Nevertheless, suggesting experiments to fill up the gaps and pointing out how the results could be used is obviously worthwhile. Two examples may illustrate these points.

Firstly, there are some of the differences between subclasses or between various classes of models in the on/off pattern characteristics during the transient recovery phase after a manipulation of food intake. Unfortunately, most of the fine structure of the rat's eating pattern is often not recorded or published, rendering the discrimination between models on the basis of published data rather difficult. (This may underline the importance of theorists working in co-operation with experimentalists.)

Secondly, as we have seen above, the transient and steady state behaviour of the models depends very much upon the choice of the weighting factors w_G, w_B and w_R. Much insight would be gained if we had some idea of the relative importance of gut content, blood composition and size of the reserves on the onset of meals and pauses, and the way these variables interact. Theoretically one can obtain such insight by performing the following experiments. In our models a meal starts when the equation $w_G G(t) + w_B B(t) + w_R R(t) = N_E$ holds. Suppose that G, B and R may be measured at the beginning of a meal, and suppose we could manipulate at least two of the three variables. If we could obtain in this way three linearly independent sets of values of G, B and R for three different meals, we could find values of w_G, w_B, and w_R by solving the three equations in three unknowns. Of course, matters are not as simple as that and all kinds of objections could be made against these experiments on both practical and theoretical grounds, but the value of the suggested experiments stems from the importance of a general theoretical framework covering various factors involved. The regulation of food intake is known to involve quite a lot of factors. It is therefore of little use to develop a sophisticated technique for measuring one variable if other variables are not studied at the same time. From a theoretical point of view it is sometimes more desirable to roughly measure several variables simultaneously than just one variable very precisely. The decision as to what has to be measured to what degree of precision is made easier by theoretical considerations based on research on models than just by intuition and the pursuit of the particular ideas one personally favours.

III. A Stochastic Approach

A. *Behavioural Variability*

The deterministic models discussed above appear to reproduce rather well some major properties of the eating system of the rat. They are very much at variance, however, with one such property. Even if the rat is left alone for weeks or months at a stretch, the day-to-day food intake is never quite the same, although the seemingly unpredictable differences approximately cancel each other so that the weekly averages are pretty much the same. On a greater time scale, the meal-pause pattern looks like a random mixture of a broad range of meal sizes interspaced by pauses of a wide variety of lengths. This variability is often considered a nuisance. Still, a set of raw data may well contain more information about its generating system than just the mean and standard deviation of meal sizes and pause lengths. (See also Klingsporn, 1973.)

What can be said about the cause of the variability of the observed behaviour? Several possible mechanisms suggest themselves.

(i) The physiological variables of a living system are so numerous and their interactions so complicated that we cannot hope to understand or formulate them all down to the last detail. Even in the case that all these interactions are purely deterministic, our ignorance forces us to regard details of experimental data as noise. Repetitions of experiments do not overcome this noise: all animals are different and an animal is only once naive.

(ii) Disturbances from outside the animal (like slamming of doors and distracting behaviour of other animals) cause changes in the behaviour of the experimental animal which are not predictable even from a perfect knowledge of the animal alone.

(iii) Errors occur in the information processing within the animal itself: receptors have a finite accuracy, information may be mutilated during transmission from one part of the nervous system to another, etc.

(iv) Last but not least, measurement errors are unavoidable.

For all these reasons many workers have begun to derive stochastic models of behaviour (e.g. H. Metz, 1974; Heiligenberg, 1974; Dawkins and Dawkins, 1974). "Stochastic" means here "not deterministic", i.e. some random factor is involved.

I shall now develop a number of successive classes of stochastic models of eating behaviour. The strategy used is the same as before—that is, we choose a far too simple initial class of stochastic model and compare its properties with analogous properties of the real system. We then decide what model property or properties are most seriously at variance with reality and propose ways to improve the shortcomings. One or more of the most promising variants are taken as a basis for subsequent generations of models.

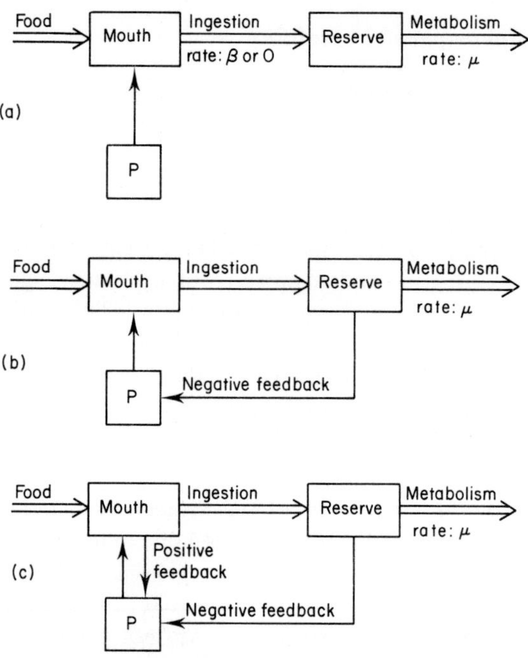

Fig. 15. Block diagram of three consecutive stochastic models. (a) Size of the reserves (R) has no influence on the chance process that shuts feeding on and off. (b) Increasing R reduces the probability of spending the next time unit eating. (c) Positive feedback increases the probability of going on eating once started.

In general, the analysis of stochastic processes is easier in discrete time than in continuous time (Cox and Miller, 1965). Moreover, as simulation on digital computers is relatively easy for discrete time models, we shall assume that changes of variables in our stochastic models take place in discrete time-jumps at integer values of time. The time unit in the models discussed in this section is the average time needed to press the Skinner box lever and consume the issued food pellet (say 5 s). In each time unit, a decision is taken whether or not to have one pellet. If a pellet is eaten, the energy content of that pellet, β calories, is added to the reserves R, while the energy need of metabolism per time unit, μ calories, is subtracted from the reserves whether or not a pellet is eaten (see Fig. 15a).

B. *Stochastic Body Weight Control*

In the beginning of this Chapter, I stated that control of body weight in the rat is evident and I omitted mention of the deterministic model without negative feedback. Thinking now in stochastic terms, one wonders if chance alone might not keep body reserves within reasonable limits.

To illustrate this idea, let us suppose that we have a population of rats which need exactly 500 pellets a day to cover their energy consumption. Suppose also that the number of pellets such hypothetical animals take each day is a random sample from the normal distribution with a mean of 500 and a standard deviation of 50 (the values are rounded to integers, and the probability of a negative value may be ignored). What can we expect for the net energy reserve gain or loss in a rat from this population after a year on this scheme? Theory of probability tells us that the expected yearly food intake of individual rats is again normally distributed with a mean of 365×500 pellets and a standard deviation of 955 pellets, an equivalent of about two days' average intake. Or, to put it another way, more than 95% of the rats can be expected to have accumulated over a period of a year a deficit or surplus of less than an average four days' intake. This behaviour is not bad, considering that a year is a substantial part of the lifetime of a laboratory rat.

It is clear, however, that this model must be quickly abandoned because it leaves the rat that is either deprived or overfed for, say, four days an unrealistically poor chance of regaining its previous weight. Nevertheless, it gives the impression that a very tight minute-to-minute or even day-to-day control is not necessary to explain the apparent long term stability of body weight. To be able to compensate systematically for an excess or deficit, the amount eaten during the next time unit must be a (probabilistic) function of the reserves already accumulated. This function must be a non-increasing function of energy reserve value E at least in an interval of E values from which the system will very probably not depart. The multitude of possible functions relating this change $p(t)$ to $E(t)$ obviously cannot be investigated exhaustively. Let us therefore as an example look at the following simple relation. Assume $p(t) = \alpha/E(t)$ for E values greater than α, otherwise $p(t) = 1$. Decrease of energy E due to metabolism increases the probability of eating a pellet in the next time unit, whereas during eating this chance diminishes because of increasing E. Fig. 15b illustrates this improved class of models where the information about the quantity of energy stored is available to the decison-generating mechanism.

Fig. 16a shows a typical result of a computer simulation of this model. E fluctuates randomly around a "preferred" value. Although any value of E greater

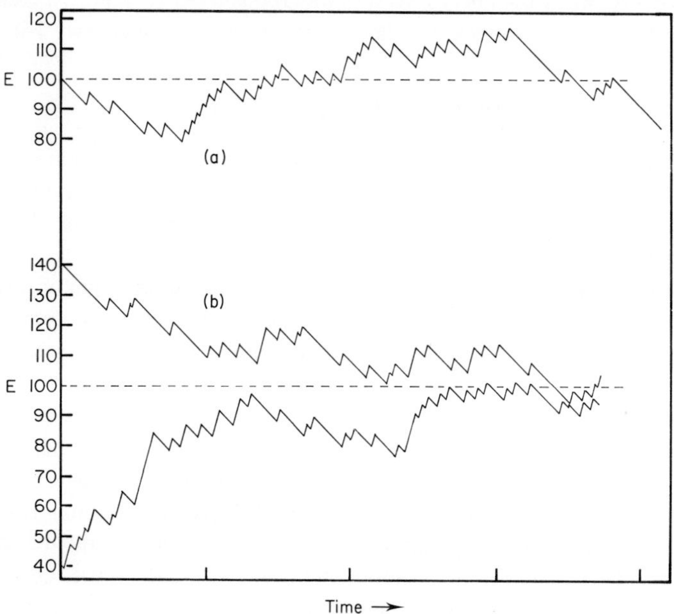

Fig. 16. (a) Sample of the time course of $E(t)$ obtained by simulating the model of Fig. 15. (b) E is kept around a "preferred" value. (b) and (c) The same model after overfeeding and deprivation. Each time unit one unit is substrated from E, while during the time spent eating five units are also added to E; $\alpha = 20{\cdot}0$.

than α has a non-zero probability of being attained at some time, the probability of E at time t having a value that differs at least by an amount r from the mean value becomes very small as r becomes larger and larger. When chance or deprivation has rendered E relatively low, $p(t)$ will be relatively high, while the converse is true when chance or overfeeding has rendered E relatively high. Examples of both cases are shown in Fig. 16b, demonstrating the tendency to restore the "proper" body weight.

A great shortcoming of this class of models is one we also encountered while discussing deterministic models. The model takes food pellets occasionally, sometimes perhaps in successive time units, but not in clusters in the sense that, after an interval, the occurrence of one pellet being eaten increases the probability of another pellet being eaten in the next time unit, as experimental data demonstrate. This apparent positive feedback can be introduced in our model by assuming that, after such a pause, the first pellet makes another stochastic decision process take over, which results in a much greater chance that the next time unit is also spent eating. Eventually a first non-eat time unit occurs and the first stochastic process takes over again. Of the two alternating stochastic processes, only one has to be a proper function of E to ensure a recovery from deprivation or overfeeding, while showing a meal pattern during the transient period. If we choose, for example, only the probability of finishing a meal in each time unit to be a function of E (e.g. $p^*(t) = \gamma \times E(t)$, where γ is a positive constant and $p^*(t) = 1$ when $E(t) > 1/\gamma$), the model compensates by changing expected meal sizes during recovery, while intermeal pauses have an unchanged distribution of lengths. Assuming both processes to be a function of E, however, ensures a realistic adjustment of meal size as well as meal frequency during transient periods (see Fig. 15c).

C. *Comparison of the Stochastic and Deterministic Models*

It is interesting to note the apparent simplicity of the stochastic models (measured in terms of the number of parameters needed to define the class of models) that perform at least as well as the deterministic standard model. The following three points illustrate this.

(i) The stochastic models generate a meal-pause pattern during recovery from deprivation or overfeeding (instead of one big meal or pause), which was all we wanted from the deterministic models.

(ii) Their output also looks far more realistic than the monotonous meal pattern of the deterministic models in the steady state.

(iii) Several investigators found a positive correlation between meal size and subsequent pause length during *ad libitum* feeding (Le Magnen and Tallon, 1966; Thomas and Mayer, 1968), while others did not (Levitsky and Collier, 1968; Panksepp, 1973).

This correlation, and also the positive correlation between pause length and subsequent meal size (which in rats is very weak or even absent), are natural features of the output of the stochastic models. These correlations of course fall completely outside the scope of the deterministic standard model. The values of the correlations can be adjusted to some extent by changing the values of parameters in the two stochastic processes. We could create models belonging to our stochastic class where the correlations have been reduced to zero. However, these would have lost their regulative behaviour: a huge $E(t)$, for instance, is no longer associated with a reduced meal size and/or an increased pause length.

On the other hand, the deterministic model may seem preferable in that it simulates the time course or variables possibly associated with physiological variables, which (except for E) the stochastic model does not. However, this is not the result of some sort of spontaneous generation of physiological insight natural to deterministic models. It results merely from the fact that in the construction of the standard model quite a lot of physiological knowledge has been invested, such as the existence of at least three compartments, each with a specific function in the system. All the standard deterministic model does is to specify what conditions those postulated physiological variables must obey for the model to have the required properties.

It should be stressed that alternative and simpler deterministic models perform about as well as the standard model of Section II.C so far as overt behaviour is concerned. For example, as already argued, a special receptor for reserve size is no prerequisite for regulatory behaviour. Similarly, a model without a gut content receptor also behaves well, provided that the gut is emptied at a rate proportional to its content. Even a model with only two compartments will succeed if certain restrictions apply to parameter values and to possible initial overfed states, as mentioned before. It would be quite arbitrary whether we gave these compartments the physiological names gut and blood, blood and reserves or gut and reserves.

In view of all this, comparison of the stochastic and deterministic models on grounds of complexity loses much of its meaning. Depending upon the assumptions made, a model of either kind may be more complex than one or the other. Both kinds have their advantages, but in different respects. The stochastic models provide a more powerful tool to answer questions that do not involve physiological details: like "if I put a lesion in this spot of the rat's brain, does it influence the feeding behaviour at all?". Stochastic models made to fit the feeding pattern before and after the lesion can then be compared. This approach does not imply anything about where and how the lesion acts. If, on the other hand, we are interested in just those physiological details (like "does this lesion influence this physiological parameter or that one; what predictions follow from these hypotheses and how could these be tested?"), then classes of stochastic models with more invested physiology become very cumbersome. Various models from this class become indistinguishable from each other as they grow more complicated: superposition of several stochastic processes soon results in a featureless output as the number of processes increases, even if these are rather regular themselves (cf. H. Metz, 1974). The unravelling of such an output is quite impossible if the time of observation is limited and if the processes are not stationary.

The above exercises with the two kinds of models have illustrated several important matters regarding the use of models in behavioural contexts. Theoretical problems have only been touched on.

> "After all, we are on a rather ambitious programme—we wish to find causal and functional explanations of animal behaviour. The models we need for that are going to be very complicated and very cumbersome to deal with. Without experience with such rough model sketches as we have dealt with, we do not think it is possible to tackle more involved ones" (Geertsema and Reddingius, 1974).

Acknowledgements

The author wishes to thank Drs J. Reddingius and L. de Ruiter for discussions that have contributed much to this chapter.

This work was made possible by a grant from the Netherlands Organization for the Advancement of Pure Research (ZWO).

References

Ashby, W. R. (1964). "An Introduction to Cybernetics". Methuen, London.

Booth, D. A. (1976). Approaches to feeding control. *In* "Appetite and Food Intake" (T. Silverstone, ed.). Dahlem Konferenzen, Berlin.

Collier, G., Hirsch, E. and Hamlin, P. H. (1972). The ecological determinants of reinforcement in the rat. *Physiol. Behav.* **9**, 705–716.

Cox, D. R. and Miller, H. D. (1965). "The Theory of Stochastic Processes". Methuen, London.

Dawkins, M. and Dawkins, R. (1974) Some descriptive and explanatory stochastic models of decision-making. *In* "Motivational Control Systems Analysis" (D. J. McFarland, ed.), pp. 119–168. Academic Press, London and New York.

Garrow, J. S. (1974). "Energy Balance and Obesity in Man". North-Holland, Amsterdam.

Geertsema, S. and Reddingius, H. (1974). Preliminary considerations in the simulations of behaviour. *In* "Motivational Control Systems Analysis" (D. J. McFarland, ed.), pp. 355–405. Academic Press, London and New York.

Heiligenberg, W. (1974). A stochastic analysis of fish behaviour. *In* "Motivational Control Systems Analysis" (D. J. McFarland, ed.), pp. 87–118. Academic Press, London and New York.

Hervey, G. R. (1973). Cybernetic models for regulation of energy balance. *In* "Energy Balance in Man" (M. Apfelbaum, ed.), pp. 329–336. Masson et Cie, Paris.

Hoebel, B. G. and Teitelbaum, P. (1966). Weight regulation in normal and hypothalamic hyperphagic rats. *J. comp. physiol. Psychol.* **61**, 189–193.

Klingsporn, M. J. (1973). The significance of variability. *Behav. Sci.* **18**, 441–447.

Levitsky, D. A. and Collier, G. (1968). Effects of diet and deprivation on meal eating behaviour in rats. *Physiol. Behav.* **3**, 137–140.

Le Magnen, J. and Devos, M. (1970). Metabolic correlators of the meal onset in the free food intake of rats. *Physiol. Behav.* **5**, 805–814.

Le Magnen, J. and Tallon, S. (1966). La périodicité spontanée de la prise d'aliments ad libitum du rat blanc. *J. Physiol., Paris* **58**, 323–349.

Mayer, J. and Thomas, D. W. (1967). Regulation of food intake and obesity. *Science, N.Y.* **156**, 328–337.

Metz, H. (1974). Stochastic models for the temporal fine structure of behaviour sequences. *In* "Motivational Control Systems Analysis" (D. J. McFarland, ed.), p. 5–86. Academic Press, London and New York.

Metz, J. H. M. (1975). Time patterns of feeding and rumination in domestic cattle. *Meded. LandbHoogesch. Wageningen* 75–12.

Panksepp, J. (1973). Reanalysis of feeding patterns in the rat. *J. comp. physiol. Psychol.* **82**, 78–94.

Platt, J. R. (1964). Strong inference. *Science, N.Y.* **146**, 347–353.

Reddingius, J. (1970). Models as research tools. *In* "Dynamics of Population" (P. J. den Boer and G. R. Gradwell, eds), pp. 64–76. Pudoc, Wageningen.

de Ruiter, L. (1974). Feeding behavior of vertebrates in the natural environment. *In* "Handbook of Physiology" Sect. 6, Vol. 1, pp. 97–116. American Physiological Society, Washington, DC.

de Ruiter, L. and Wiepkema, P. R. (1969). The goldthioglucose (GTG) syndrome in mice. *Psychiat. Neurol. Neurochir.* **72**, 455–480.

de Ruiter, L. Weipkema, P. R. and Reddingius, J. (1969). Ethological and neurological aspects of the regulation of food intake. *Ann. N.Y. Acad. Sci.* **157**, 1204–1216.

Shapiro, B. (1973). Regulation of adipose tissue size. *In* "Energy Balance in Man" (M. Apfelbaum, ed.), pp. 247–259. Masson et Die., Paris.

Steffens, A. B. (1970). Plasma insulin content in relation to blood glucose level and meal pattern in the normal and hypothalamic hyperphagic rat. *Physiol. Behav.* **5**, 147–151.

Strubbe, J. H. and Steffens, A. B. (1975). Rapid insulin release after ingestion of a meal in the unanaesthetized rat. *Am. J. Physiol* **229**, 1019–1022.

Strubbe, J. H. and Steffens, A. B. (1977). Blood glucose levels in portal and peripheral circulation and their relation to food intake in the rat. *Physiol. Behav.* **19**, 303–307.

Thomas, D. W. and Mayer, J. (1968). Meal taking and regulation of food intake by normal and hypothalamic hyperphagic rats. *J. comp. physiol. Psychol.* **3**, 642–653.

10

Semi-quantitative Simulation of Food Intake Control and Weight Regulation

MAURICIO RUSSEK *

Department of Physiology, Escuela Nacional de Ciencias Biológicas, Instituto Politécnico Nacional, México.

A version of the multifactor theory of the control of feeding has been presented as a detailed "conceptual equation" (Russek, 1976). This was a mathematical synthesis of my views on the role in the control of food intake of most of the variables that have been shown to influence feeding behaviour. This equation was a "static model" that could generate predictions only of daily food intake at different levels of the variables included.

In this chapter, I will present a "dynamic model" that exhibits a temporal course in many variables and simulates the continuous feeding behaviour of an animal. This model is based on the static one and allows one to predict the influence of all the variables included in that original equation on the size and frequency of meals and on the so-called weight "set point".

The Dynamic Model (which includes the Static) was programmed on a Wang 600–14–TP. The printed numerical output values were used to draw the graphs presented for comparison with graphs containing real data which were redrawn in the same format from results of the different authors cited.

I. Static Model

The simpler Static Model was extensively treated in an earlier article (Russek, 1976), and so only the essential parts of it will be repeated here, plus several modifications introduced since.

*The author is a fellow of the DEDICT-COFAA. The present work was done with financial help from Tecnofarmaci S. p. A. Society for the Development of Pharmaceutical Research, Rome, Italy.

This model expresses the relations between the speed of feeding (g/kg/min) and the *information* originating in a variety of receptors around the body. These include hepatic glucoreceptors, providing glycogenostatic control, and central glucoreceptors of the lateral and ventromedial hypothalamus, providing glucostatic control. Thermoreceptors and osmoreceptors are also included, without any implications about their localization. Information about the total amount of body fat is also represented, without any assumptions about the receptors that monitor it; this provides lipostatic control.

No attempt was made to obtain the best fit to experimental data. The intention was to express the influence of each factor in the simplest possible mathematical way. Therefore, nothing more than a "qualitative" fit with the experimental data was to be expected. The model reproduced the *trend* of the relation between each factor considered and food intake, but not necessarily the quantitative relations. Nevertheless, it allowed semi-quantitative predictions of the changes in the action of one factor when the level of another was modified. It also allowed the prediction of the influence of different lesions on the action of the factors considered.

Liver receptors controlling hunger. The model reflected our hypothesis that hepatic glucoreceptors are the main source of information on which the control of food intake is based. The experimental data supporting this idea have been extensively reviewed (Russek, 1971, 1975; Russek and Grinstein, 1974), and so only a very brief summary will be given here.

The existence of hepatic glucoreceptors was postulated (Russek, 1963) on the basis of a number of data obtained in our laboratory that could not be explained by the classical glucostatic hypothesis or any of the other current hypotheses (Russek *et al.,* 1968; Rodriguez-Zendejas *et al.,* 1968). A few years later their existence was confirmed electrophysiologically (Niijima, 1969). The hepatic glucoreceptors might correspond to the nerve fibres running in the Disse spaces (Russek, 1971) and to the nerve endings described as "intracellular" by some authors (Riegele, 1928; Nicolescu, 1958), and observed with the electron microscope to be "in direct contact with the hepatocyte membrane and sometimes surrounded by the hepatocyte" (Tanikawa, 1968). If we postulate an electric synapse between the innervated hepatocytes and their nerve fibres and consider that there are "gap junctions" between adjacent hepatocytes (Kreutziger, 1968), the discharge frequency of the fibres would be modulated by the hepatocytes' "average" membrane potential. This membrane potential would depend on the rate of glucose transport through the hepatocyte membrane (Daniel *et al.*, 1970; Friedman *et al.*, 1971; Haylett and Jenkinson, 1969). The outward transport of glucose from the hepatocyte depends on the rates of glycogenolysis and gluconeogenesis, and these reflect the amount of glycogen and protein reserves. The inward transport of glucose into the hepatocyte depends on the portal concentration, which reflects intestinal absorption. Thus, transport in both directions would be low when liver glycogen and protein reserves are low and no intestinal absorption is taking place. This would depolarize the hepatocytes' membranes and generate "hunger discharges" in the glucoreceptor fibres.

A. Description of the Different Components of the Static Model

1. *Hepatic Glycogenostatic Component*

This portion of the model reflects the highly significant inverse linear correlation that has been observed between food intake and (a) the hepatic concentration of reducing sugars (Russek and Stevenson, 1972), (b) concentration of liver glycogen (Péret *et al.*, 1972) and (c) hepatocyte membrane potential (Russek and Grinstein, 1974). All these relationships (Fig. 1) could be based on a linear

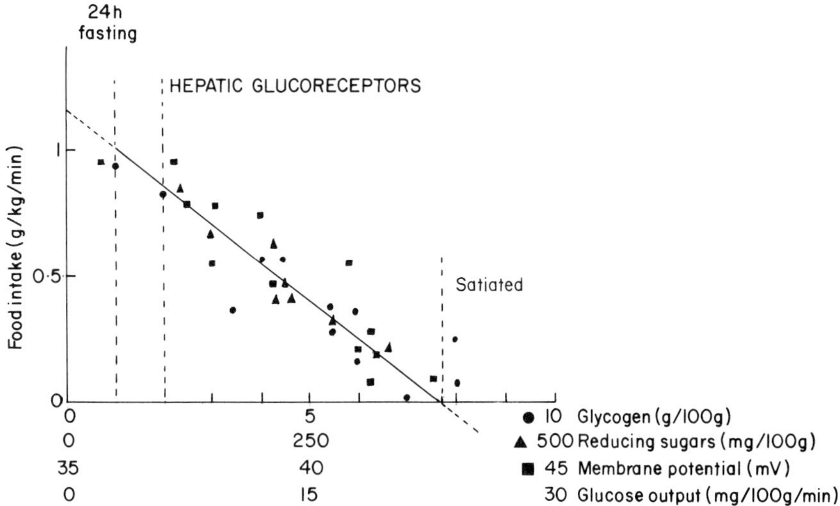

Fig. 1. The theoretical relation between liver glycogen and feeding speed calculated from the Static Model, superimposed on real data. Liver glycogen (Péret *et al.*, 1972). Liver intracellular glucose (Russek and Stevenson, 1972). Hepatocyte membrane potential (Russek and Grinstein, 1974). Glucose output data calculated from Friedman *et al.* (1967).

correlation between the rate of transport of glucose through the hepatocyte membrane and the discharge frequency of hepatic glucoreceptors (Niijima, 1969). The simplest way of expressing the control exerted by the hepatic glucoreceptors would be to subtract from the maximum possible rate of food intake (F_0) some factor which is proportional to the rate of hepatocyte glucose transport (dG/dt). That is, the actual rate of food intake (F_1) would be given by the equation;

$$F_1 = F_0 - K_0.dG/dt.$$

However, glucose transport is very difficult to measure and there are no data on it related to feeding. Nevertheless, the concentration of glycogen and the conentration of glycogenolytic substances normally determine glucose transport (Fig. 2a). When several glycogenolytic substances are acting simultaneously, their effects can be considered to be additive. The glycogenolytic actions considered in the model were those of glucagon (Gg), hypoglycaemia ($1/G$) and adrenalin (A), any of which may add to basal glycogenolysis. We have already discussed elsewhere (Racotta *et al.*, 1972; Russek *et al.*, 1974) the hypothesis that preabsorptive satiation could be due to the reflex secretion of adrenalin from intrahepatic chromaffin cells (Russek *et al.*, 1974), elicited by discharges originated in oropharyngeal and gastrointestinal receptors (anticipatory reflexes: Nicolaïdis, 1969). The alpha-hyperpolarizing effects of adrenalin (Daniel *et al.*, 1970; Haylett and Jenkinson, 1969) might be an important component of adrenalin-induced anorexia when liver glycogen is low. Therefore, the full effect of adrenalin on feeding would be:

$$F_A = F_0 - K_B \log A \; Gy - K_A A$$

where A is intrahepatic adrenalin concentration and Gy is liver glycogen.

The relative contribution of the hepatic component in controlling the total intake is much larger than that of all the other factors considered in the model put together (Table I).

Table I
Calculated Contribution of Different Factors to the Ingestion of a Normal Rat

	Food intake (g/day)	%
Hepatic glucoreceptors	24·8	85
Central glucoreceptors	7·4	25
Temperature (neutral)	0	0
Lipostasis (on "set point")	(X1)	0
Osmolarity	−3·2	−10
Total	29·0	100

Observed differences in the nocturnal and diurnal relationships between food intake and liver glycogen, and also the circadian oscillations of both variables, can be easily accounted for by assuming that the *light* produces a decrease in the sensitivity of the feeding integrating "centres" to the hunger signals from the hepatic glucoreceptors, and an increased secretion of intrahepatic adrenalin (increased preabsorptive satiation). Therefore, during the day the animal eats less for the same amount of liver glycogen (Fig. 4). It stops eating (by preabsorptive satiation) before it has ingested enough food to cover its metabolic needs, as was also noted by Le Magnen and Tallon (1966). As a consequence, the average liver glycogen is lower and lipolysis higher during the light period than during the dark period, in which the hepatic "hunger" signals become more effective and the preabsorptive reflexes become less intense.

An animal that eats around the clock (perhaps a rat subject to continuous light or darkness) would not exhibit a circadian cycle of liver glycogen contents. Nevertheless, it would exhibit smaller changes around the "threshold" for feeding, increasing above this concentration after each meal and decreasing gradually towards it during the intermeal period. The circadian cycle of food intake and liver glycogen would be accounted for by a decrease in the model's basal food intake speed (F_0), which would change the "threshold" of eating but not the slope of the curve—as was indeed observed in the actual data of Fig. 4.

2. *Central Glucostatic Components*

My idea about the central glucoreceptors is that they might play an important role in the regulation of blood glucose concentration by the control of glycogen and protein reserves, but that they play only a secondary role in the normal regulation of these reserves by the control of food intake. Only very marked hypoglycaemia, or great reduction in glucose utilization (like the effect of 2-deoxyglucose), produce a substantial increase in feeding. Large hyperglycaemia produces only mild satiation, and even this could be partially effected through the hepatic glucoreceptors.

There are two components in the model which simulate the central glucoreceptors. Those in the *lateral hypothalamus* (LH) are considered to be the ones responding to absolute glycaemia and to glucose utilization changes. A facilitatory influence proportional to the inverse of the glycaemia (G) multiplied by the utilization coefficient (u, normally taken as unity) is added to the basal feeding speed (F_0), as illustrated in Fig. 2b.

To simulate the effect of insulin on blood glucose concentration, an inverse relation between its concentration and glycaemia is included, basal glucose level being divided by $1 + \log I$ (where I is insulin concentration).

The so-called glucoreceptors of the *ventromedial hypothalamus* (VMH), for reasons discussed elsewhere (Racotta and Russek, 1974), are considered to be sensitive not to glycaemia *per se* but to the relation between the concentrations of

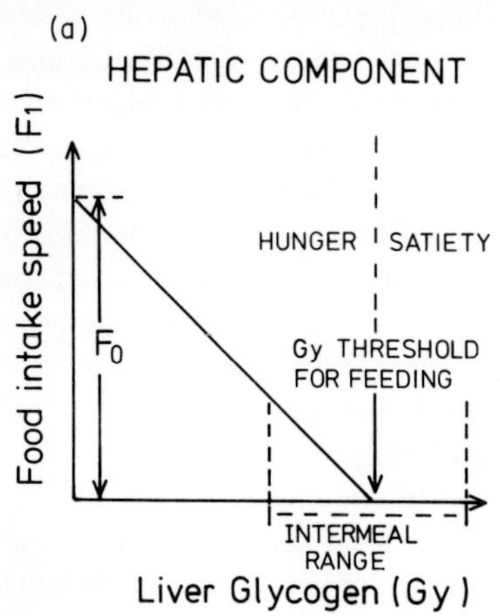

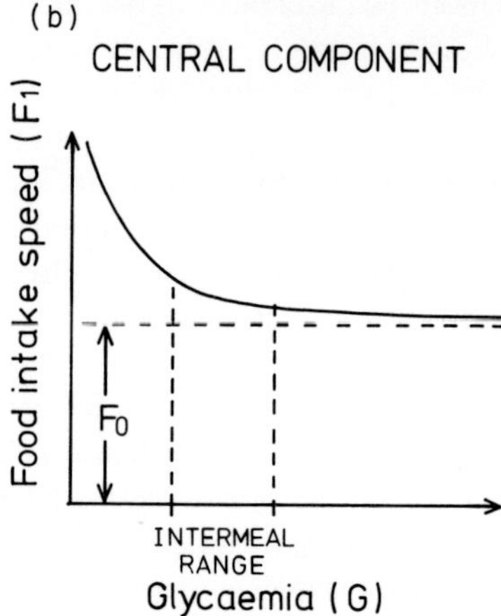

Fig. 2. Glucoreceptor components of Static Model (a) *Hepatic component* ($F_1 = F_0 - K_0 \mathrm{d}G/\mathrm{d}t$), with liver glycogen concentration substituted for glucose transport rate, i. e. $F_1 = F_0 - KGy$. In the full equation, glycogen is considered to be mobilized by several glycogenolytic substances at concentrations $S_1, S_2 \ldots$ etc. Hence the hepatic component in the final equation is: $F_1 = F_0 - (K_1 S_1 Gy + K_2 S_2 Gy + \ldots K_n S_n Gy)$. (b) *Central component*. For *LH*, $F_1 = F_0 + K_5/uG$. For an effect of insulin, $G_1 = G_0/(1 + \log I)$. The equation simulating the "glucostatic" influence of the VMH on food intake is:

$$F_1 = F_0 + \frac{\log Gg}{2 + \log I} \cdot \frac{1}{\log G}$$

where Gg is glucagon concentration and I is insulin concentration.

glucagon and insulin: the first hormone would decrease glucose entry in to the VMH, while the second would antagonize this action — that is, insulin would be needed for glucose penetration into the VMH *only* in the presence of glucagon. This information would be very important in the regulation of glycaemia by the control of these hormones (and perhaps others), but it would have even less influence on food intake than the lateral hypothalamic component.

The equation simulating the "glucostatic" influence of the VMH on food intake is given in Fig. 2.

In the resulting complete model, blood glucose concentration has two opposing mild effects on feeding — one through the hepatic glucoreceptors, and the other through the central glucoreceptors. The result is an inverse (hyperbolic) relation exhibiting a rather small range of control on food intake within the normal limits of glycaemia (Fig. 3).

Insulin has several different effects in the model: a small direct satiating effect through the VMH, an effect on liver glycogenolysis (both directly and through the effect of hypoglycaemia) whose satiating intensity depends on the amount of glycogen, and a predominant indirect hunger effect by the action of hypoglycaemia on the LH and VMH.

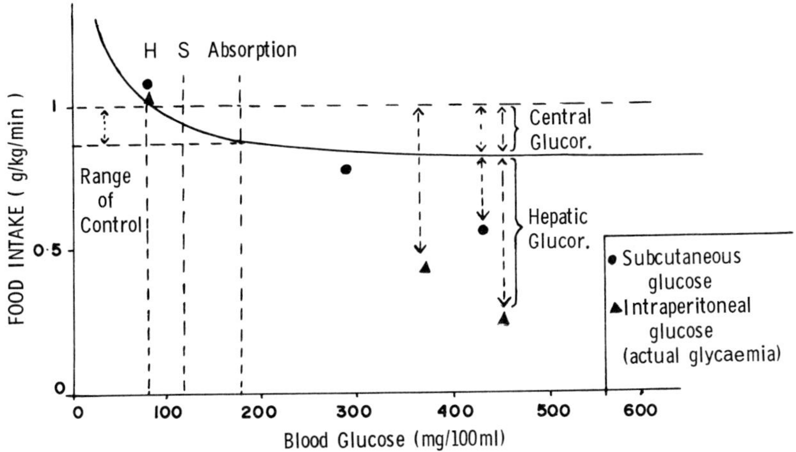

Fig. 3. Relations between glycaemia and food intake, calculated from the Static Model. The points are real data (average of 12 rats) on feeding and glycaemia after injection of glucose (Racotta and Russek, unpubl.). The theoretical contribution of the hepatic glucoreceptors to the satiating effect, as expected, is much larger for the intraperitoneal injections than for the subcutaneous. The contribution of the central glucoreceptors is always small, so the normal *range of control* of glycaemia over feeding speed is very limited (H, hunger; S, postabsortive satiation).

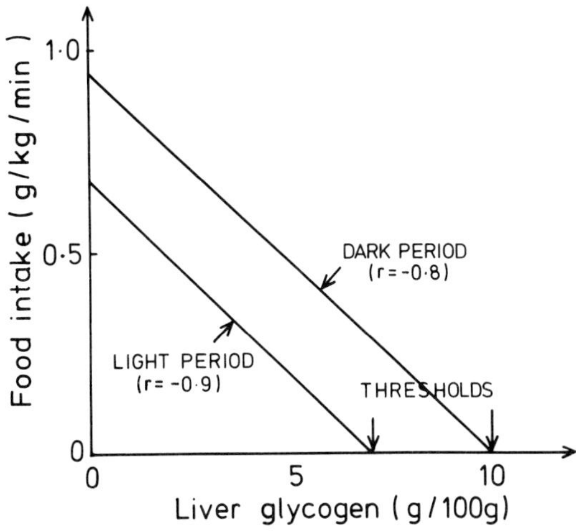

Fig. 4. Real data on liver glycogen and feeding, during the light and dark periods. It shows that during the dark period, the rat starts eating at a much higher level glycogen threshold, and eats more than during the light period at all glycogen concentrations.

Glucagon would have two opposing effects in the model: *satiation* through the hepatic glycogenolysis, dependent in the magnitude of liver glycogen concentration, and *hunger* through the VMH receptors. This might explain the contradiction between the small anorexia obtained in hungry rats (Balagura and Hoebel, 1967; Russek, 1975) whose liver glycogen is quite low, and the rather strong anorexia described in *ad libitum* human beings (Mayer, 1955, 1956) whose liver glycogen should be much higher.

The blood concentration of glucagon and insulin is very different when the animal is hungry and when it is satiated. This variation is accounted for in the revised version of the "static model" by two subsidiary empirical equations that change the concentration of the two hormones with the amount of liver glycogen, which is assumed to be the main variable defining hunger and satiety.

3. *The Thermostatic Component*

This part of the model represents the fact that, at neutral ambient temperature, there seems to be no influence of temperature on food intake (Rampone and Shirasu, 1967) while during thermoregulatory reactions to heat or cold, there is an approximately linear relation between ambient temperature and feeding (Brobeck, 1945). Thus a positive or negative term (T_A) is introduced, producing an increase or decrease of intake, which is inversely proportional to ambient temperature. This term in the calculation is a constant of proportionality multiplied by neutral temperature (T_N) minus ambient temperature (Fig. 5a).

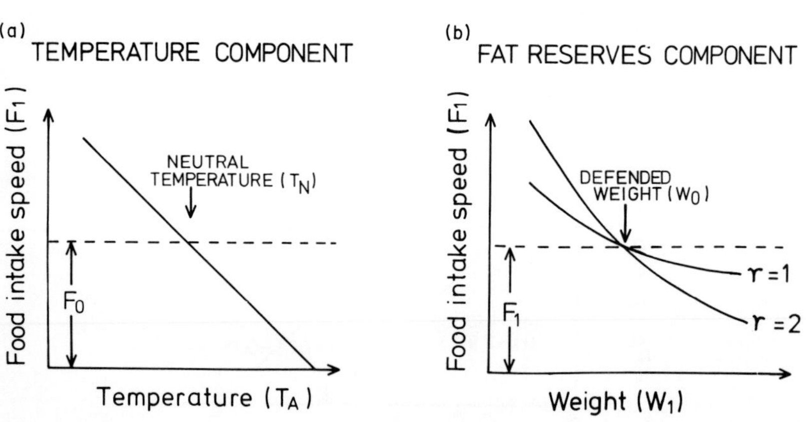

Fig. 5. (a) Thermostatic component. Food intake speed $F_1 = F_0 + K_1(T_N - T_A)$ where T_N is neutral temperature and T_A is ambient temperature. (b) Lipostatic component. Food intake speed $F_1 = (W_0/W_1)^r$ (glycogenostatic component + glucostatic component + thermostatic component), where W_0 is the defended value of body weight, W_1 is actual body weight, and r is the intensity of lipostatic control.

The calculated effect of temperature on the relation between liver glycogen and food intake is similar to the real effect produced by light and darkness: that is, a change in threshold (and in maximum intake) without a change in slope (Fig. 6, bottom). This is a prediction to be confirmed experimentally. It could be

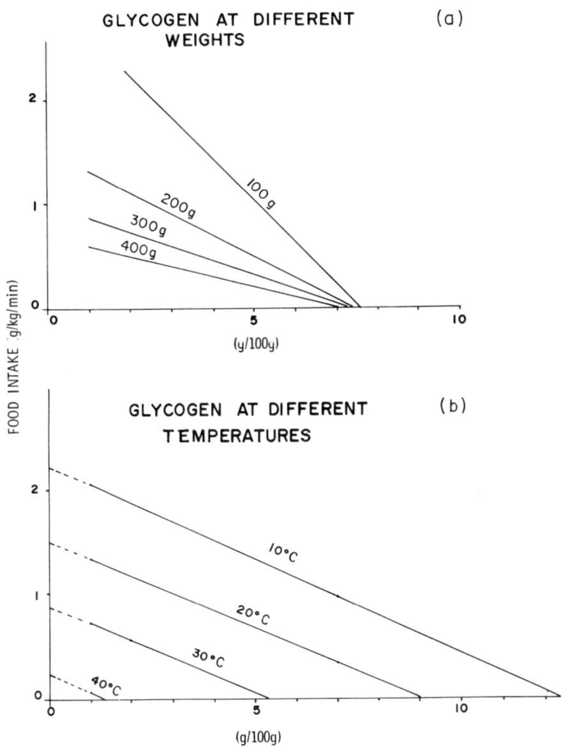

Fig. 6. Relations between liver glycogen and feeding speed, at different weights attained by overfeeding and fasting, and at different temperatures, calculated from the Static Model. Changes of glucagon and insulin with feeding and fasting were calculated according to the equations: $Gg' = Gg_0 - 11\ Gy$; $I' = I_0 + 0{\cdot}3\ Gy$.

interpreted as a change in sensitivity of the integrating nervous centres to the hunger signals from the hepatic glucoreceptors. This same interpretation would apply to all factors that have an additive effect in the model equation.

4. *The Lipostatic Component*

Some recent findings (Apfelbaum *et al.*, 1973) suggested that the regulation of "weight" (actually of fat reserves) is accomplished both by the control of energy *output* (activity and basal metabolism), and by the control of energy *input* (food intake). This modulation of feeding (Lepkovsky and Furuta, 1971; Hoebel, 1969) is exerted only when the weight is outside the "set point". I have the intuition that this effect is not *additive* but *multiplicatory*, which would mean that it does not change the threshold of liver glycogen at which feeding starts, but it would change the slope of the relation between liver glycogen and food intake (Fig. 6, top). This multiplicative factor is represented as the ratio of the "static" weight "set point" (W_0), which would depend on the number of fat cells (Hirsch and Han, 1969), to the actual weight (W_1), raised to some power (r) which defines the intensity of the lipostatic control of feeding (Fig. 5b). Again, this prediction should be confirmed experimentally. Therefore, the model shows no effect of lipostasis when the animal is at its weight "set point", and a hyperbolic relation between weight and food intake, when the animal is thinner or fatter than its "set point".

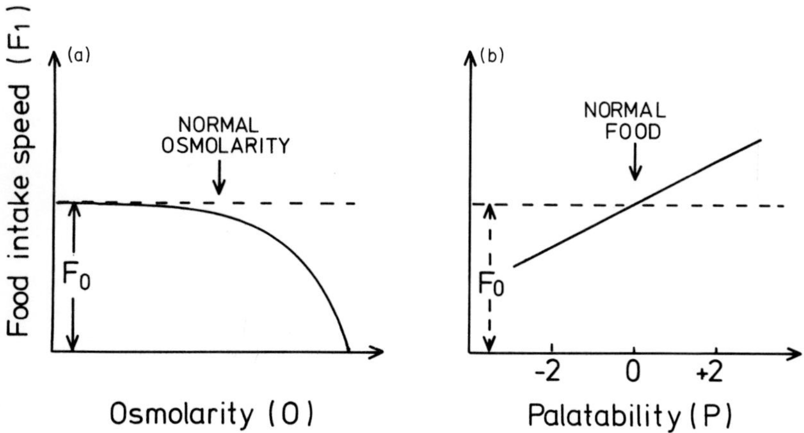

Fig. 7. (a) *Osmostatic component*. Food intake speed $F_1 = F_0 - K_6\, O^n$, where O is osmotic pressure and n is the intensity of osmotic inhibition of food intake. (b) *Palatability component*. This factor is zero for normal food, negative for less palatable and positive for more palatable food.

This multiplicatory action could be interpreted as a nonlinear change in sensitivity of the effector (motor) mechanisms of feeding, without an influence on the "triggering" mechansim (threshold). The above agrees with the fact that rats (which reach quite low levels of liver glycogen during their circadian cycle) exhibit substantial changes in food intake when thinned or fattened, while rabbits (who eat around the clock, and might be regulating glycogen close to the threshold) show a smaller change in intake when thinned, regaining weight by decreased metabolism (Levitsky *et al.*, 1974).

5. *The Osmostatic Component*

Normal body fluid osmolarity is assumed to produce a small tonic inhibition on feeding which increases exponentially with increased concentration. This is based on the fact that body dilution produces only a small increase in feeding (Kakolewski and Deaux, 1970), while concentrated saline produces strong anorexia (McCleary, 1953). Osmotic pressure (O) raised to a power (n) which defines the intensity of the osmotic inhibition of food intake is subtracted from basal food intake speed.

6. *Summary of Static Model*

Figure 8 combines all the terms defined above into a single equation.

$$F=\Bigl\{\underbrace{\Bigl[\underbrace{F_o}_{\text{Light}}-Gy\Bigl(1+\underbrace{\frac{\log Gg}{2+\log I}+\frac{20}{G}}_{\text{Glycogenolysis}}+3\ln A\Bigr)-\underbrace{\frac{A}{25}}_{\text{alpha effect}}\Bigr]}_{\text{Hepatic Glucoreceptors}}+\underbrace{(T_N-T_A)}_{\text{Temperature}}+\underbrace{\underbrace{\frac{200}{uG}}_{\text{LH}}+\underbrace{\frac{\log Gg}{2+\log I}\left(\frac{1}{\log G}\right)\Bigr\}\left(\frac{1}{2}\right)}_{\text{VMH}}}_{\text{Central Glucoreceptors}}\underbrace{\left(\frac{W_o}{W_1}\right)^r}_{\text{Fat Reserves (Weight)}}-\underbrace{10^3\cdot O^5}_{\text{Osmolarity}}+\underbrace{P}_{\text{Palatability}}$$

Fig. 8. Complete equation for the Static Model's calculations of food intake. F and F_0: feeding speed and maximum feeding speed (g/kg/min); Gy: liver glycogen (g/100 g); Gg: glucagon (ng/100 ml); I: insulin (m/100 ml); G: glycaemia (mg/100 ml); A: intrahepatic adrenalin (pg/100 g); T_N and T_A: neutral and air temperatures (°C); u: utilization coefficient (normally 1); W_0 and W_1: weight "static set point" and weight of the animal (g); O: osmolarity (Osm); P: palatability (arbitrary units; normally zero).

B. ***Effects of Lesions***

The equation can simulate the effects of different lesions, by suppressing the corresponding components.

1. *Lateral Syndrome*

My idea about lateral hypothalamic lesions is that the aphagia is due mainly to the impairment of pathways conveying information from the hepatic glucoreceptors, which is manifested in a lack of adrenalin anorexigenic effect during Teitelbaum and Epstein's (1962) phase 2 following the lesion (Russek *et al.*, 1973). The recovery (phases 3 and 4) would be caused by the reestablishment of central pathways through which the "hunger signals" from liver would again exert their influence, and is manifested by the reappearance of adrenalin anorexia. I assume that during phase 1, the pathways responsible for the thermostatic control of feeding are also temporarily impaired due to effects caused on the anterior hypothalamus by the closely located lateral lesion.

In phase 1 (suppression of hepatic, lateral hypothalamic and temperature components), the equation expressing the full model gives a negative value (satiation) and no factor is capable of eliciting feeding (Table II). In phase 2 (reintroduction of the thermostatic component), the animal might start eating some food because of sporadic decreases in temperature (caused by critical reductions of metabolic reserves as suggested by Teitelbaum and Epstein, 1962).

Phases 3 and 4 (reintroduction of the hepatic component) simulate the observed slight increase in adrenalin anorexia (Russek *et al.*, 1973) which is only a consequence of the *relative* increase in importance of the hepatic component, due to the reduction of the central glucostatic component (Table II).

Table II
Calculated Contribution of Different Factors in the Lateral Hypothalamic Lesion Aphagic Rat

	Food intake (g/day)	%
Phase 1 (Satiated)		
Hepatic glucoreceptors	0	—
Central glucoreceptors (VMH)	2·4	—
Temperature	0	—
Lipostasis	(X 1)	—
Osmolarity	−3·2	—
Total	−0·8	
Phase 2 (Thermostatic drive, hypersensitivity to dehydration)		
Hepatic glucoreceptors	0	0
Central glucoreceptors (VMH)	2·4	46
Temperature (decreased)	6·0	115
Lipostasis	(X 1)	0
Osmolarity	−3·2	−61
Total	5·2	100
Recovered (More sensitive to adrenalin)		
Hepatic glucoreceptors	24·8	103
Central glucoreceptors (VMH)	2·4	10
Temperature	0	0
Lipostasis	(X 1)	0
Osmolarity	−3·2	13
Total	24	100

2. *Ventromedial Lesions*

The suppression of the ventromedial component, with its strong inhibitory effect represented by a coefficient of 0·5 (simulating reduced lipostatic modulation and reduced preabsorptive satiation), obviously will produce a twofold increase in food intake. But the interesting result is that this is manifested as an increase in the weight "set point" or preferred value (Table III). This is the interpretation

Table III
Calculated Contribution of Different Factors in Ventromedial Hypothalamic Lesion Hyperphagic Rat.

		Food intake (g/day)	%
Dynamic Phase			
Hepatic glucoreceptors		54·6	44
Central glucoreceptors		5	9
Temperature (neutral)		0	0
Lipostasis (off "set point")		(*X* 2)	53
Osmolarity		−3·2	−6
	Total	56·4	100
Static Phase			
Hepatic glucoreceptors		24·8	85
Central glucoreceptors		5	17
Temperature (neutral)		0	0
Lipostasis ("new set point")		(*X* 1·1)	8
Osmolarity		−3·2	−10
		30·0	100

given to the ventromedial syndrome by some authors (Hoebel and Teitelbaum, 1966; Powley and Keesey, 1970). Thus, the "dynamic phase" of hyperphagia and fattening soon following the lesion is simulated by the "ventromedial lesioned" equation only while the weight (W_1) is close to the control. If W_1 is substituted by the new "set point" (the weight at which the new lipostatic relation gives the food intake prior to lesion), the behaviour of the lesion model becomes quite close to normal, which simulates observed phenomena of the "static phase". We shall see later that this change in "set point" appears even more clearly in the Dynamic Model.

3. *Hepatic De-afferentation*

The suppression of the hepatic component results in a great reduction but not complete suppression of food intake (Table IV). This is what was actually observed in the "peripheral aphagic syndrome" produced by upper abdominal denervation (Russek and Racotta, 1971), which is the closest to hepatic de-afferentation that has been technically possible to achieve. The predictions

Table IV
Calculated Contribution of Different Factors in Hepatic Deafferentation ("Peripheral Aphagic Syndrome")

	Food intake (g/day)	%
Hepatic glucoreceptors	0	0
Central glucoreceptors	7·4	175
Temperature	0 (?)	0 (?)
Lipostasis	(X 1)	(?)
Osmolarity	−3·2	−75
Total	4·2	100

(Relative hypersensitivity to hypoglycaemia, insulin and osmotic changes, all these to be confirmed experimentally).

obtained from the "hepatic de-afferented" equation, like the lack of adrenalin anorexia, relative hypersensitivity to insulin glucoprivic effects and to osmotic changes, should be tested experimentally on animals with the above-mentioned syndrome.

II. Dynamic Model

In order to introduce a time course into the static equation (Fig. 8), I had to simulate both the meal-to-meal short term glycogenostatic regulation, and the long term regulation of fat reserves. The dynamic interaction between these two mechanisms determines an apparent "set point" or "defended weight", that does not necessarily correspond to the "static set point" (W_0).

These components, plus the components of the Static Model from Fig. 4, 5 and 7, comprise the Dynamic Model summarized in Fig. 9.

A. *Short Term Regulation*

1. *Meal-to-meal Glycogenostatic Control of Feeding*

The consumption of liver glycogen was simulated by the diminution of a certain fraction of it every hour. It was chosen arbitrarily as 10% per hour in the light period and 20% per hour in the dark, but this could be varied at will. This

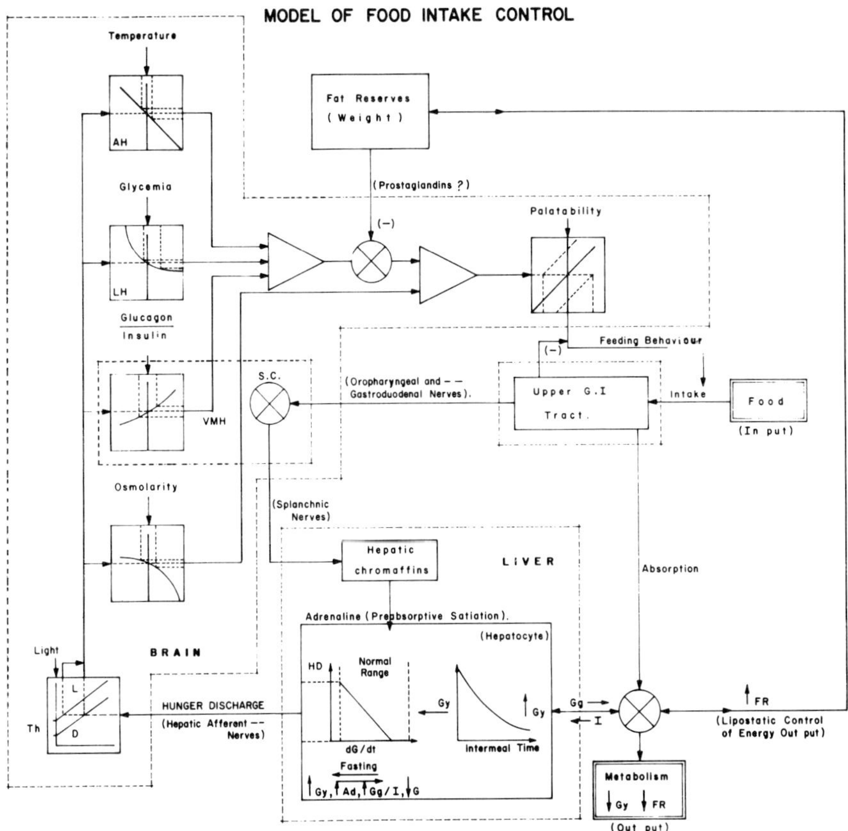

Fig. 9. Flow diagram of the Dynamic Model. Each square shows the action of one of the variables of the Static Model. AH: anterior hypothalamus; LH: lateral hypothalamus; VMH: ventromedial hypothalamus; S. C. sympathetic centre; FR: fat reserves; GI: gastrointestinal. In the square for light: Th: threshold; L: light; D: dark. In the rectangle marked "hepatocyte": HD: hunger discharge; Gy: glycogen; Ad: intrahepatic adrenaline; Gg: glucagon; I: insulin; G: glycaemia; dG/dt: glucose transport speed through the hepatocyte membrane. In the square for palatability: L: low; H: high.

parameter turned to be an important factor controlling the amount of food "ingested" by the model. Then, it was necessary to introduce a threshold of glycogen where feeding started and the influence of light on it. These thresholds were taken from Peret's actual data (Peret *et al.*, 1972: Russek, 1975) and were 7 and 10 g/100 g for the light and dark periods, respectively. When the "consumption" brings the glycogen level to the threshold, the system begins to "ingest", by calculating the amount of food intake given by the Static Model for each half-hour, and accumulating it. Preabsorptive satiation is achieved according to our hypothesis (Racotta *et al.*, 1972; Russek *et al.*, 1974) by the intrahepatic secretion of adrenalin which increases in proportion to the amount of food accumulated, and acts on the static equation according to the glycogen existing at the moment. The amount of intrahepatic adrenalin secreted was estimated on the basis of the adrenalin decrease observed in our experiments during the first half-hour of feeding in a hungry rat (Russek *et al.*, 1974; Martinez *et al.*, 1974), as 20 and 15 pg/100 g of liver, per gram of ingested food, for the light and dark periods, respectively.

Once the satiating effect of adrenalin brings the calculated feeding speed to zero (or a negative value), ingestion stops and a certain proportion of the ingested food (10% of the gross ingestion) is transformed into hepatic glycogen. The amounts which are transformed into muscle glycogen, liver and muscle protein and fat reserves, and which will be utilized during the subsequent intermeal period, are not considered in the calculations. This is because in our view the amount of liver glycogen and its consumption are tightly correlated with all these other components of the short term food reserves. That is to say, during every intermeal period, certain amounts of protein and fat reserves are consumed which are matched rather accurately to the glycogen consumption. So there is no need to take them into account in the calculations.

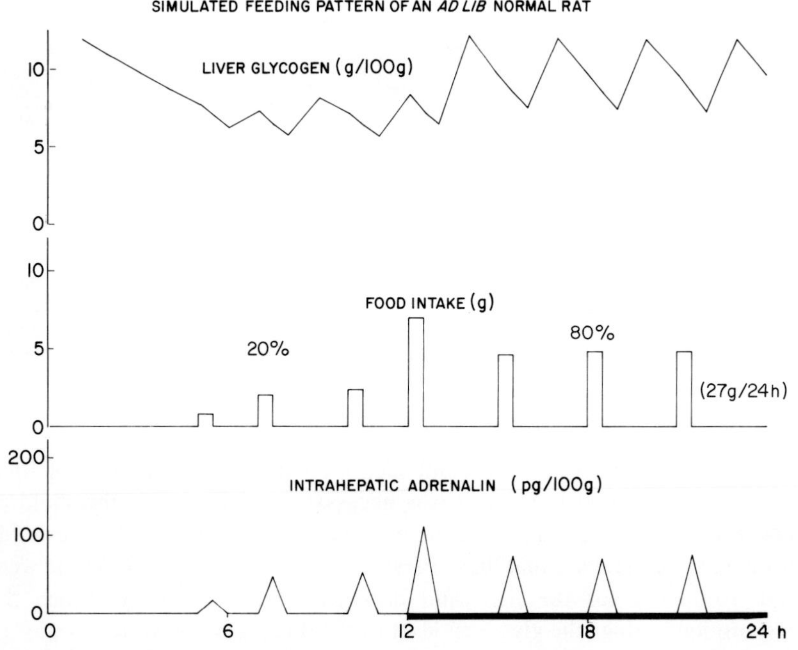

Fig. 10. Simulation by the Dynamic Model of liver glycogen changes, meal size and intrahepatic adrenalin supposedly secreted in a rat fed *ad libitum* on a lighting schedule of 12 h light and 12 h darkness.

2. *Circadian Cycles*

It is implicit in the Dynamic Model that the action of light is:

(a) to increase the threshold of the central nervous system to the incoming hunger signals from hepatic receptors;

(b) to inhibit general muscular activity and basal metabolic rate, which is reflected in a reduction of hepatic glycogen consumption rate; and

(c) to increase preabsorptive satiation (reflex secretion of intrahepatic adrenalin).

The result of all this is a well defined circadian cycle, in which meal frequency is somewhat reduced and meal size is greatly reduced during the light phase (Fig. 10), so only about 20% of the total 24–h food intake is ingested during it.

A 24–h fasting period (reducing liver glycogen to 2 g/100 g) greatly increases both the total amount eaten, and the proportion ingested during the light period (Fig. 11).

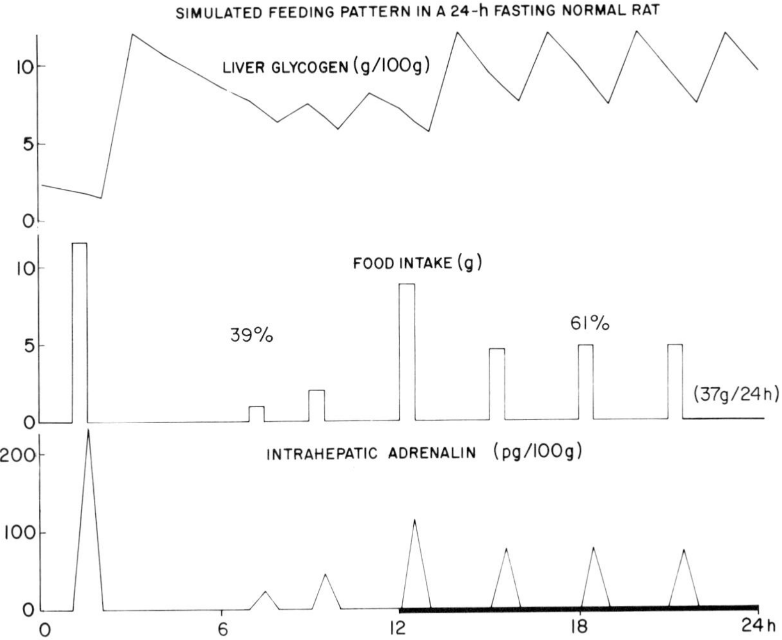

Fig. 11. Same as Fig. 10, but for a rat fasted the previous 24 h (initial liver glycogen: 2 g/100 g).

Figure 12 presents a comparison between real 24–h meal patterns obtained with a cumulative recording, and simulated meal patterns drawn in the same format.

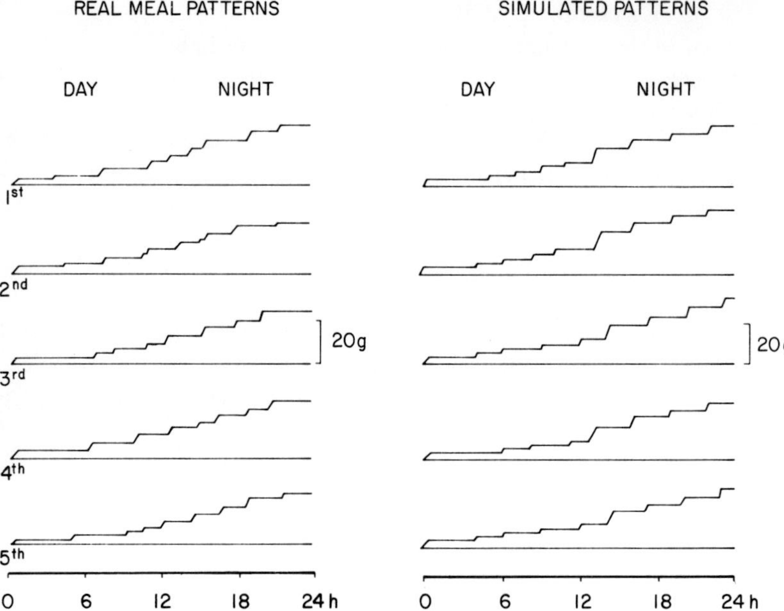

Fig. 12. Comparison between five real and five simulated 24 h feeding patterns. The simulated patterns were drawn in the same format as the real ones, from the printed data obtained with the program of the Dynamic Model. The real meal patterns were redrawn from Le Magnen, 1967.

B. *Long Term Regulation*

1. *Regulation of Fat Reserves (Weight) and Lipostatic Modulation of Feeding*

The modulation of food intake by some correlate of the total amount of fat is implicit in the Static Model. However, in the Dynamic Model the change in weight resulting from changes in intake was simulated in the following way. It was assumed that, when the amount of food ingested in a meal was not enough to bring the liver glycogen to 9 g/100 g, a certain amount of additional fat would be utilized during the following intermeal period. Therefore, an appropriate amount is subtracted from body weight. If, on the other hand, the hepatic glycogen after a meal reaches more than 12 g/100 g, the excess is added to the weight.

The lipostatic control of energy output (Apfelbaum, *et al.*, 1973; Levitsky, *et al.*, 1974) was simulated by dividing the amount added to (or multiplying the amount subtracted from) the body weight, by the same factor that exerts the lipostatic "modulation" on food intake in the Static Model. Biologically, this might correspond to opposite effects on feeding and on basal metabolic rate and/or general non-feeding activity being exerted by a substance such as a prostaglandin, secreted by the adipose cells in proportion to their fat content.

The Dynamic Model behaves quite realistically, regulating its weight around a certain apparent "set point". This defended body weight value changes in the expected way in a number of situations that will be analysed below.

2. *Force-feeding and Fasting*

The model reacts in a realistic way against increases and decreases of weight, supposedly caused by force-feeding and fasting respectively. It slowly returns to the initial weight in the course of many days, as is shown in Fig. 13. The "glycogen consumption" and the "defended weight" were adjusted to match the basal conditions of the real data. The model has no provision to simulate force-feeding, and so we simply entered the final weight and then allow the simulation to run freely until it again achieved the initial weight.

REAL DATA ON WEIGHT REGULATION.

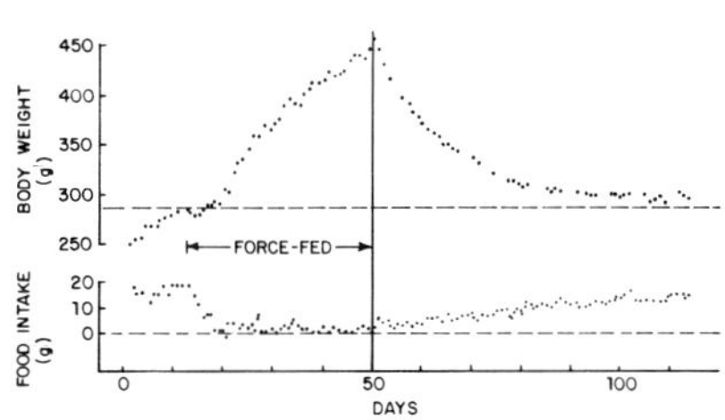

SIMULATED WEIGHT REGULATION

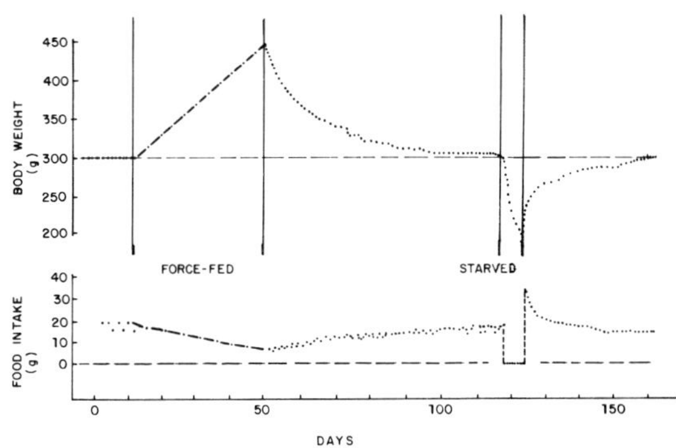

Fig. 13. Comparison between real and simulated bahaviour of an animal that increased its weight through overfeeding. The behaviour elicited by starvation and subsequent refeeding is also included in the simulation after 120 days. Real data redrawn after MacNeil, 1966.

3. *Effects of Lesions*

(a) *Ventromedial hypothalamic lesion.* When the component corresponding to the VMH is eliminated, the model fairly successfully simulates a hypothalamic hyperphagic animal, both in respect to the meal-to-meal control (Fig. 14) and to the long term regulation of weight (Fig. 15). The 24–h meal pattern exhibits a small increase in meal frequency and a large increase in meal size as observed in a real rat.

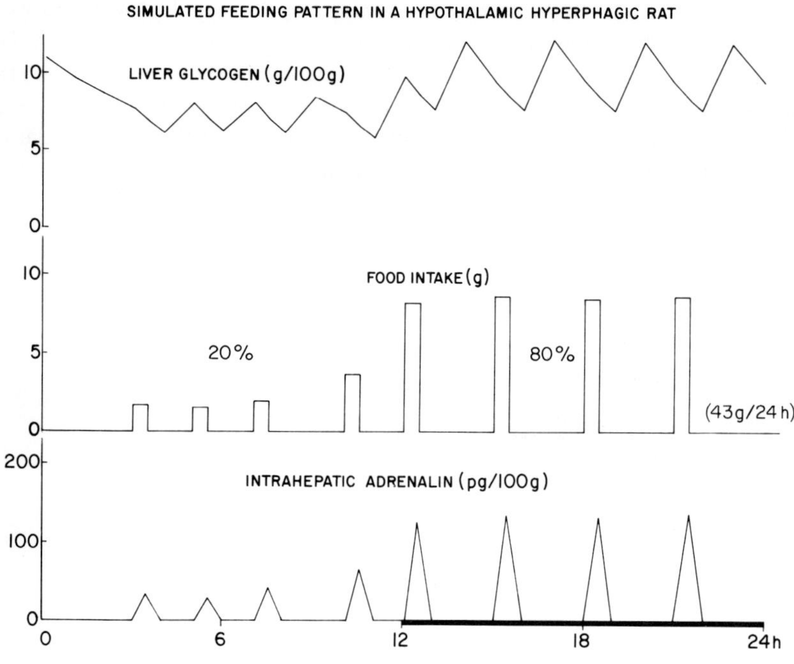

Fig. 14. A rat simulated without the ventromedial hypothalamic component (hypothalamic hyperphagia), but otherwise as Fig. 10.

In the long term regulation, the difference from the real rat's behaviour is that in the model the hyperphagia is established at its maximum from the start, while in the real animal it develops gradually during the days following the lesion.

Fig. 15. (a) Comparison between real and simulated behaviour of a rat with ventromedial hypothalamic lesions (hypothalamic hyperphagia). Both the increase in Dynamic Model's defended value of body weight and the regulation at this new level are realistically simulated. Redrawn after Hoebel and Teitelbaum, 1966. (b) Comparison between the real effects of repeated lesions of the ventromedial hypothalamus, and the simulated behaviour of an hypothalamic hyperphagic rat with three different values of the lipostatic exponent r. The decrease in weight produced by fasting and its subsequent recovery are also simulated. Redrawn from Hoebel, 1969.

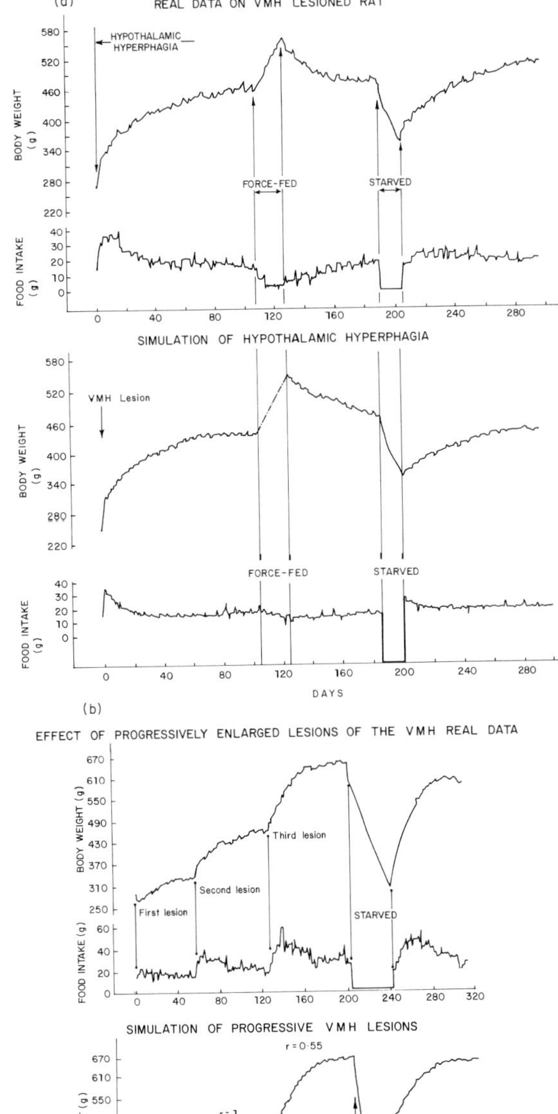
(a)
REAL DATA ON VMH LESIONED RAT
HYPOTHALAMIC HYPERPHAGIA
BODY WEIGHT (g)
FORCE-FED
STARVED
FOOD INTAKE (g)
SIMULATION OF HYPOTHALAMIC HYPERPHAGIA
VMH Lesion
BODY WEIGHT (g)
FORCE-FED
STARVED
FOOD INTAKE (g)
DAYS
(b)
EFFECT OF PROGRESSIVELY ENLARGED LESIONS OF THE VMH REAL DATA
BODY WEIGHT (g)
Third lesion
Second lesion
First lesion
STARVED
FOOD INTAKE (g)
SIMULATION OF PROGRESSIVE VMH LESIONS
r = 0·55
r = 1
r = 2.5
BODY WEIGHT (g)
1st
2rd
3d
STARVED
FOOD INTAKE (g)
DAYS

H*

In the Dynamic Model, the biological interpretation of the coefficient "$\frac{1}{2}$" (Fig. 8) is more straightforward than in the Static equation. It would represent an increase in threshold of response to the message substance from the fat reserves (which increases the apparent dynamic weight "set point") and a decrease in the amount of preabsorptive intrahepatic adrenalin (which increases meal size).

Yet the lesion could be also changing the exponent r, which defines the intensity of the modulating action of the fat message on both food intake control and energy output control. In fact, by decreasing this coefficient stepwise, one can simulate the effect of progressive lesions (Fig. 15b).

The more rapid decrease in weight during fasting in the model as compared with the fat hyperphagic (Fig. 15b) might mean that the control of energy output

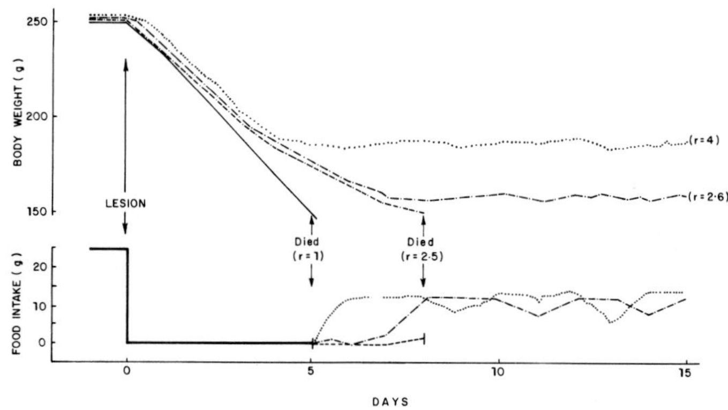

(b) SIMULATION OF A RECOVERED APHAGIC WITH DIFFERENT LEVELS OF LIPOSTATIC CONTROL

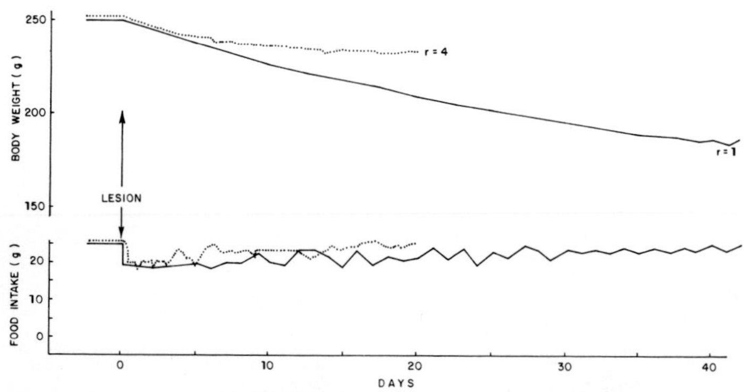

Fig. 16. Simulated behaviour of (a) the "non-recovered" lateral rat (suppression of the lateral hypothalamic and hepatic components) and (b) the "recovered" lateral rat (suppression of lateral hypothalamic component only), at different levels of the lipostatic exponent r.

is affected more than the control of feeding in such rats and it could be corrected by giving different exponents to each of them. Biologically this may just reflect the decrease in energy loss and basal metabolism as a result of the increased insulation and decreased activity in the obese rat and may not be a direct effect of the VMH lesion.

(b) *Lateral hypothalamic lesion*. To simulate a non-recovered LH aphagic rat, as has already been mentioned, the hepatic and lateral hypothalamic components were eliminated from the static equation, and a "dying mechanism" was introduced, that stops the program when the weight decreases below 150 g. An interesting finding was that the outcome of the "lesion" depends again on exponent r (Fig. 16a), that is, on the intensity of the lipostatic control. With a

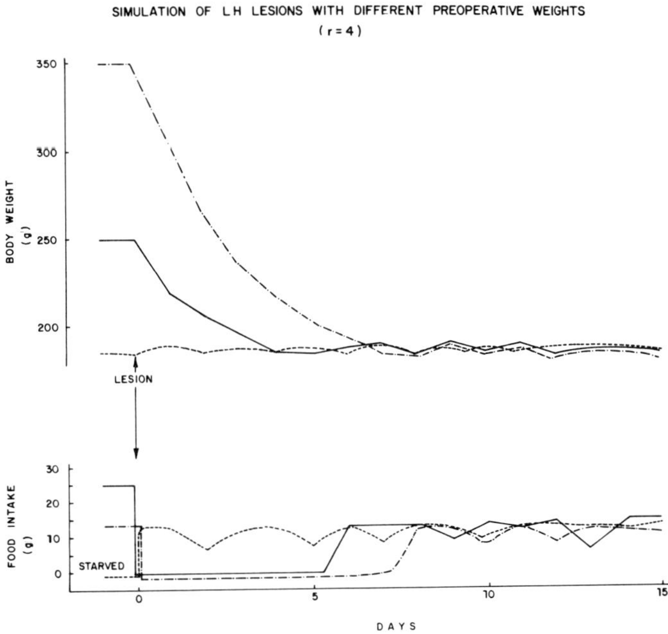

Fig. 17. Simulated effects of lateral hypothalamic lesions on animals with different preoperative weights. The duration of the aphagia is proportional to the initial weight, but the final dynamic "set point" is the same.

low r, the model does not restart feeding and dies, reproducing the Teitelbaum-Epstein (1962) type of aphagic, while with higher r, the animal begins to feed again when it decreases to a certain weight and stabilizes at this new "set point"; in this case, the duration of the aphagia depends on the inital preoperative weight (Fig. 17), thus reproducing the phenomenology of the Powley-Keesey (1970) type of aphagic.

Now, the simulations of Fig. 17 which are precariously regulating body weight at a very low "set point", with large oscillations of the daily intake, are *not* equivalent to the simulation of recovered laterals, in Fig. 16b, because the liver information pathways have not been restored. Therefore, they should not respond with anorexia to intraperitoneal injection of adrenalin or to intraperitoneal or intraportal glucose, as the recovered laterals do (Russek *et al.*, 1973). If we could produce a lesion that eliminated the information about glycaemia provided by the lateral hypothalamus, without temporarily interrupting the information from the liver receptors, the predicted behaviour should be that depicted in Fig. 16b—that is, the animal would not be aphagic but would only decrease food intake initially, and it would slowly decrease its weight to a "set point" higher than that attained by the non-recovered aphagic. Once this new, somewhat lower "set point" had been attained, the daily intake would be about the same as in the pre-operative period.

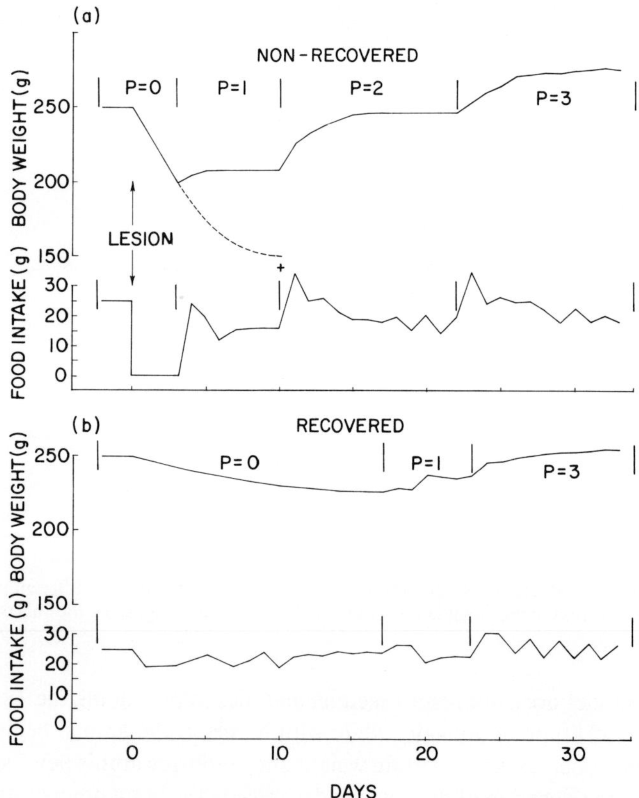

Fig. 18. Effect of increased palatability (p) on the food intake and final weight "set point" of (a) non-recovered and (b) recovered laterals, simulated in the Dynamic Model modified as in Fig. 16.

One could imagine that the lateral hypothalamic syndrome is so complicated and variable because it is a mixture of the two types of simulated aphagics described above, starting as the first type (complete aphagia) and gradually being transformed into the second type (normal ingestion, somewhat lower weight) as recovery progresses.

The syndrome is likely to be complicated further when highly palatable diets are used, for in the model these increase the food intake and weight "set point" in both the non-recovered and the recovered laterals (Fig. 18).

The comparison between the simulated hyperphagic and aphagic rats brings out a suggestive conclusion: while they show opposite effects on the weight "set point", they both may include a reduced lipostatic exponent r. Biologically this might mean that the *threshold* of the central nervous system to the substance carrying information about the amount of fat reserves changes in opposite ways when the lateral or the ventromedial hypothalamus is destroyed, but that the *effectiveness* of this substance (probably based on a recruiting action) might decrease with either lesion. Perhaps this lack of recruiting is the cause of "finickiness" in both the recovered laterals and the static phase hyperphagics, for it could mean that they require a higher palatability in order to mobilize feeding responses.

4. *Changes in Palatability*

A most profound insight into the physiological role of palatability was contained in a cartoon where Denis the Menace is saying to his mother: "How can I know if I am hungry, if you don't tell me what we are having for dinner?" (M. Cabanac, pers. comm.).

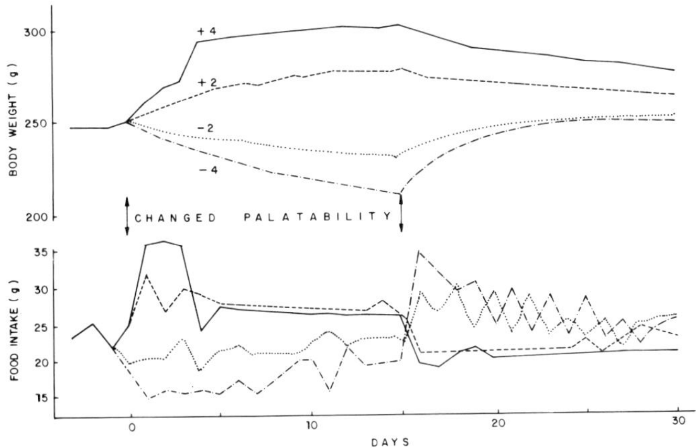

Fig. 19. Simulation of the effects of increased and decreased palatability (P), on the food intake and weight of normal rats. Factor $r = 2$.

Low palatability not only diminishes food intake and lowers body weight but it actually lowers the dynamic weight "set point", as evidenced by the difference in alliesthesia between subjects who lost weight by reduced ingestion of their normal diet and those who reduced on an unpalatable diet (Cabanac and Rabe, 1976). This palatability-induced change in defended body weight appears in the behaviour of the model simply as a dynamic balance between the opposing modulatory actions of palatability and fat reserves on the sensitivity of the central nervous sytem to the "hunger signals" from the hepatic receptors. The simulated effects of high palatability on the lateral lesioned rat have already been discussed (Fig. 17). Figure 19 shows the simulation of the effects of high and low palatabilities on the weight and food intake of a normal rat. There is a remarkable asymmetry between the effects of increased and decreased palatability: in both cases it is apparent that it is much easier to gain than to lose weight, which seems a realistic conclusion.

5. *Chronic Changes in Insulin Level*

In the Static Model, the acute effect of an increase in insulin level is realistically simulated, but a decrease in insulin, which, produces a hyperglycaemia in the model, results in a decreased food intake. The hyperphagia of the diabetic rat is not simulated because hepatic glycogen cannot be reduced in the Static Model, whereas it is our hypothesis that diabetic hyperphagia is due to just such a reduction typical of this condition.

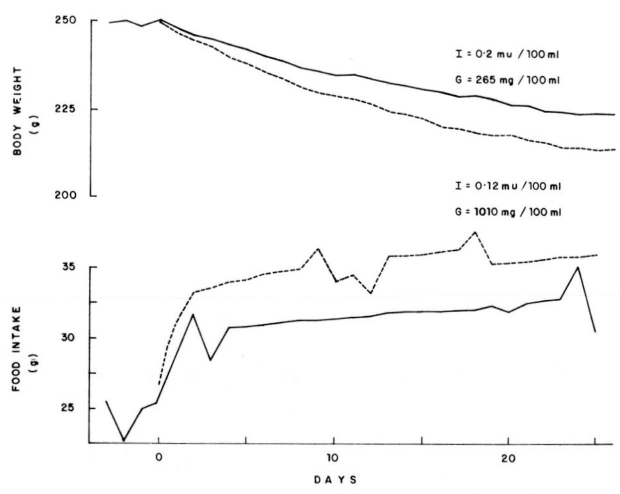

Fig. 20. Simulation of the effects of a decreased insulin level on feeding the body weight. *I*: insulin; *G*: glycaemia. Effects of insulin on glycaemia are calculated on the equation: $G_I = G/(1 + \log I)$.

In the Dynamic Model it is very easy to simulate the diabetic hyperphagia, by making the simulated storage of liver glycogen dependent on the level of insulin present at that moment. This was achieved by multiplying the amount of glycogen to be stored by the reciprocal of the coefficient used to symbolize the effects of insulin on glycaemia. The model produces a qualitatively realistic response to increase and decrease of insulin.

A decrease in insulin level induces an increase in food intake accompanied by a progressive loss of weight (Fig. 20). This would be analogous to juvenile diabetes mellitus.

A modelled increase in insulin level simulates the actual effects of a daily injection of slow-acting insulin: that is, a mild initial increase in food intake, which is progressively reduced as the weight increases (Fig. 21). The greater irregularity in the real data is expected, since a daily injection of insulin cannot produce a steady level throughout the 24 h, as is implied in the simulation. Nevertheless, the simulated food intake exhibits large oscillations that somewhat resemble the real behaviour. It is interesting to note that in order to simulate the average slope of the increase in weight, the exponent r had to be reduced. This would mean that insulin not only increases the storage of glycogen and fat, but also decreases the lipostatic control of food intake.

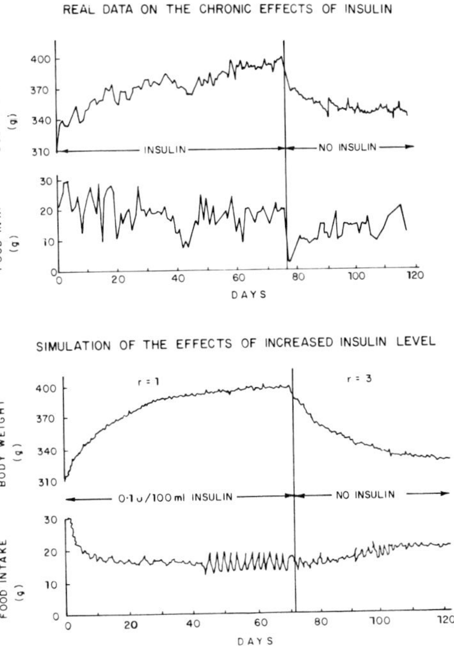

Fig. 21. Comparison between the real effects of daily injection of insulin, and the simulated effects of an increased fasting insulin level. Redrawn from Hoebel and Teitelbaum, 1966.

III. Concluding Remarks

A model is as good as the theory on which it is based. The fact that it simulates real data is no proof of the validity of the theory, but the failure to simulate experimental findings would indicate a flaw in the theory.

The usefulness of a model is that it allows one to operate formally with his ideas, providing many predictions impossible to obtain by mere intuition in a complicated system.

Perhaps the main advantage of the present model derives from the fact that I am not a mathematician, but a physiologist. Therefore, I used simple equations to simulate the trends of the relations between each factor considered and food intake, and I tried to use only parameters, coefficients and exponents with biological meaning. Thus, in the Static Model's equation (Fig. 8), F_0 would be the maximum food intake speed, determined by the maximum hepatic "hunger discharges" and perhaps by the mechanical factors involved in ingestion (speed of chewing, swallowing, prandial drinking etc.). The coefficients of the effects of glycaemia on glycogenolysis and on the LH (20 and 200) might be interpreted as the lowest hypoglycaemia attainable by insulin, and the highest hyperglycaemia normally attained during absorption, respectively. The neutral temperature (T_N) might be a function of the body's surface to volume ratio, its insulation and the metabolic rate, and can be experimentally determined. The coefficient $\frac{1}{2}$ in the VMH action and the exponent r, as already explained, can be regarded as factors affecting the threshold to, and the recruiting action of, the messenger from the fat reserves. The only coefficient and exponent without an implicit biological meaning are the ones included in the osmolarity component.

The biological meaning of all the additional coefficients included in the Dynamic Model is self-evident (glycogen consumption and storage, fat storage, control of energy output etc.). Where the actions of insulin and glucagon are involved, their action was considered to be the same as in the Static Model. This was done for simplicity and symmetry but may not be correct in all instances.

There are other aspects of the model that will have to be decided experimentally. For instance, it assumes that the action of temperature is multiplied by the lipostatic factor—rather than adding to it, for example. Under most circumstances this is irrelevant, because at normal temperature the thermostatic component is *zero* and at normal weight the lipostatic coefficient is *one*. But it will be important when simulating a starving or force-fed animal subjected to high or low temperatures. If there is no multiplicative action of weight on temperature, the temperature component should probably be placed outside the brackets where the factors affected by lipostasis are currently placed.

Both glycogen consumption and food intake are computed for fixed intervals (1 h and 0·5 h respectively). This permits the glycogen to attain different levels below the threshold before feeding starts, and produces feeding for at least half an hour before satiation stops ingestion.

These fixed periods of computation produce a variable hysteresis in the response of the Dynamic Model, resulting in a realistic lack of periodicity. The hysteresis may be interpreted biologically as resulting from the interaction between feeding and other competing drives, which results in a flip-flop or switching effect similar to the double threshold effect used by Booth and Toates (1974) and Booth *et al.* (1976) in their model of feeding behaviour, whose latest version appears in this volume. If this is the biological explanation of the hysteresis, then the Dynamic Model would be improved by introducing periods of computation for glycogen consumption and for ingestion that vary at random.

A more attractive speculation is that these periods are actually regular and are determined by the same clock mechanism that produces the cyclic variations in EEG which are observable both during wakefulness and during sleep. Letting our imagination fly a little further, we could postulate that these EEG cycles are the manifestations of a successive scanning of the drives that correspond to regulating mechanism having an external loop (a behavioural response). One could think that once a suprathreshold drive signal is detected, it continues acting until the need is satisfied. The consequence of this mechanism would be:

(i) a large variability in the latency to elicit any behavioural response, because the response will only start at the proper moment of the interval cycle when this particular drive is being "tested" by the brain;

(ii) the time interval between the starting points of two consecutive bouts of the same behaviour must be a multiple of a certain minimum interval, which may correspond to the EEG cycle.

The circadian cycle of hepatic glycogen and feeding observed by Peret *et al.* (1972) in the rat is rather poorly simulated by the model. This is because of the assumption, for simplicity, that the hepatic glycogen threshold for feeding is kept constant during the whole of the dark and light periods. The circadian rhythm could be simulated by a circadian variation of the central nervous system threshold to the hepatic "hunger discharges" (caused by a catecholamine modulation cycle), or by a circadian change in these discharges, due to an hepatic metabolic circadian cycle (caused by an hormonal cycle) that would change glucose output for the same amount of glycogen. This would be a completely *ad hoc* solution, and for that reason was not included in the model; nevertheless, it may be a physiological reality, which has to be decided experimentally.

I do hope that this chapter has demonstrated the usefulness of mathematical models in clarifying and expanding our understanding of a theory, in bringing out many of the hidden assumptions implicit in it, and providing us with a large number of predictions to be confirmed experimentally. In addition to this, I hope to have shown that a model built on the hepatic glycogenostatic theory of feeding can at least produce "a machine that belongs to the same set of machines to which the feeding animal belongs".

References

Apfelbaum, M., Bostsarron, J. and Lacatis, D. (1973). Adaptation des depenses d'énergie chez l'Homme. *In* "Régulation de l'Equilibre énergetique chez l'Homme" (M. Apfelbaum, ed.), pp. 71–81. Masson et Cie., Paris.

Balagura, S. and Hoebel, B. G. (1967). Self-stimulation of the lateral hypothalamus modified by insulin and glucagon. *Physiol. Behav.* **2**, 337–340.

Booth, D. A. and Toates, F. M. (1974). A physiological control theory of food intake in the rat: Mark 1. *Bull. Psychon. Soc.* **3**, 442–444.

Booth, D. A., Toates, F. M. and Platt, S. V. (1976). Control system for hunger and its implications in animals and man. *In* "Hunger: Basic Mechanisms and Clinical Implications" (D. Novin, W. Wyrwicka and G. A. Bray, eds), pp. 127–142. Raven Press, New York.

Brobeck, J. R. (1945). Effects of variation in activity, food intake and envrionmental temperature on weight gain in albino rats. *Am. J. Physiol.* **143**, 1–5.

Cabanac, M. and Rabe, E. F. (1976). Influence of a monotonous food on body weight regulation in humans. *Physiol. Behav.* **17**, 675–678.

Daniel, E. E., Paton, P. M., Taylor, G. S. and Hodgson, B. J. (1970). Adrenergic receptors for catecholamine effects on tissue electrolytes. *Fed. Proc.* **29**, 1410.

Friedmann, B., Goodman, E. H. Jr. and Weinhause, S. (1967). Effects of glucose feeding, cortisol and insulin on liver glycogen synthesis in the rat. *Endocrinology* **81**, 486–496

Friedman, N., Somlyo, A. V. and Somlyo, A. P. (1971). Cyclic adenosine and guanosine monophosphates and glucagon: effect on liver membrane potentials. *Science, N. Y.* **171**, 400–402.

Haylett, D. G. and Jenkinson, D. H. (1969). Effects of noradrenaline on the membrane potential and ionic permeability of parenchymal cells in liver of the guinea pig. *Nature, Lond.* **224**, 80.

Hirsch, J. and Han, P. W. (1969). Cellularity of rat adipose tissue: Effects of growth, starvation and obesity. *J. Lipid. Res.* **10**, 77–82.

Hoebel, B. G. (1969). Feeding and self-stimulation. *Ann. N. Y. Acad. Sci.* **157**, 758–778.

Hoebel, B. G. and Teitelbaum, P. (1966). Weight regulation in normal and hypothalamic hyperphagic rats. *J. comp. physiol. Psychol.* **61**, 189–193.

Kakolewski, J. W. and Deaux, E. (1970). Initiation of eating as a function of ingestion of hyposmotic solutions. *Am. J. Physiol.* **218**, 590–595.

Kreutziger, G. O. (1968). Freeze etching of intercellular junctions of mouse liver. *In* "Proceedings of XXVI Annual Meeting of the Electromicroscope Society of America" (G. J. Arsenaux, ed.). Clayton's Pub. Div., Baton Rouge, La.

Le Magnen, J. (1967). Habits and food intake. *In* "Handbook of Physiology" Alimentary Canal, Vol. I. (C. F. Code, ed.). American Physiological Society, Washington, DC.

Le Magnen, J. and Tallon, S. (1966). La périodicité de la prise d'aliments ad libitum du Rat blanc. *J. Physiol., Paris* **58**, 323–349.

Le Magnen, J. and Devos, M. (1970). Metabolic correlates of the meal onset in the free food intake of rats. *Physiol. Behav.* **5**, 805–814.

Lepkovsky, S. and Furuta, F. (1971). The role of homeostasis in adipose tissue upon the

regulation of food intake of white Leghorn cockerels. *Poultry Sci.* **50**, 573–577.
Levitsky, D. A., Faust, I. and Kratz, C. (1974). Is control of feeding necessary for the regulation of body weight? Presented at the XXIV Internat. Congr. Physiol. Sci., Jerusalem Satellite Symp., p. 88.
McCleary, R. A. (1953). Taste and postingestion factors in specific hunger behaviour. *J. comp. physiol. Psychol.* **46**, 411–421.
MacNeil, D. A. (1966). Inhibition of food intake and hypothalamic self-stimulation correlated with excess body weight. Ph. D. Thesis. Princeton University Microfilm No. 66–13332.
Martinez, I., Racotta, R. and Russek, M. (1974). Hepatic chromaffin cells. *Life Sci.* **15**, 267–271.
Mayer, J. (1955). Regulation of energy intake and the body weight. The glucostatic theory and the lipostatic hypothesis. *Ann. N. Y. Acad. Sci.* **63**, 15–43.
Mayer, J. (1956). Régulation de l'appétit. *Proc. Int. Congr. Physiol., Brussels* **20**, 138.
Nicolaïdis, S. (1969). Early systemic responses to orogastric stimulation in the regulation of food and water balance: functional and electrophysiological data. *Ann. N. Y. Acad. Sci.* **157**, 1176–1200.
Nicolaïdis, S. (1974). A possible molecular basis of regulation of energy balance. Presented at the XXIV Internat. Congr. Physiol. Sci., Jerusalem Satellite Symp., p. 97.
Nicolescu, J. (1958). "An Atlas Concerning Morphological Aspects of Visceral Nerve Endings" Editura Medicala, Bucharest, Rumania.
Niijima, A. (1969). Afferent impulse discharges from glucoreceptors in the liver of the guinea pig. *Ann. N. Y. Acad. Sci.* **157**, 690–700
Panksepp, J. (1974). Modification of daily feeding rhythms by palatability. Presented at the XXVI Internat. Congr. Physiol. Sci., Jerusalem Satellite Symp., p. 101.
Péret, J., Chanez, and Macaire, I. (1972). Consommation de protéines et rythme circadien du glycogéne hépatique chez le Rat. *C. r. hebd. Séanc. Acad. Sci., Paris* **274**, 1562.
Powley, T. L. (1971). Hypothalamic feeding centers control adipose tissue mass. Presented at the IVth International Conference on the Regulation of Food and Water Intake, Cambridge, England.
Powley, T. L. and Keesey, R. E. (1970) Relationship of body weight to the lateral hypothalamic feeding syndrome. *J. comp. physiol. Psychol.* **70**, 25–36.
Racotta, R. and Russek, M. (1974). Possible hypothalamic control of hormonal regulation of glycaemia. *Proc. Inter. Union Physiol. Sci.* **11**, 367 abs.
Racotta, R., Vega, C. and Russek, M. (1972). Liver catecholamines and preabsorptive satiation. *Fed. Proc.* **31**, 309 Abs.
Rampone, A. J. and Shirasu, M. R. (1967). Temperature changes in the rat in response to feeding. *Science, N. Y.* **144**, 317.
Riegele, L. (1928). Uber die feinere Verhalten der Nerven in der Leber von Mensch und Saugetier. *Z. mikrosk.-anat. Forsch.* **14**, 73.
Rodriguez-Zendejas, A. M., Vega, C., Soto-Mora, L. M. and Russek, M. (1968). Some effects of intraperitoneal glucose and intraportal glucose and adrenaline. *Physiol. Behav.* **3**, 259–264.
Russek, M. (1963). An hypothesis on the participation of hepatic glucoreceptors in the control of food intake. *Nature, Lond.* **197**, 79.
Russek, M. (1971). Hepatic receptors and the neurophysiological mechanisms controlling feeding behaviour. *In* "Neurosciences Research" (S. Ehrenpreis and O. C. Solnitzky, eds), Vol. 4, pp. 213–282. Academic Press, New York and London.

Russek, M. (1975). Current hypotheses in the control of feeding behaviour. *In* "Neural Integration of Physiological Mechanisms and Behaviour" (J. A. F. Stevenson Memorial Volume), (G. J. Mogenson and F. R. Calrescu, eds), pp. 128–147. Toronto Univ. Press, Toronto.

Russek, M. (1976). A "conceptual" equation of intake control. *In* "Hunger: Basic Mechanisms and Clinical Implications" (D. Novin, W. Wyrwicka and G. A. Bray, eds), pp. 327–347 Raven Press, New York.

Russek, M. and Grinstein, S. (1974). Coding of metabolic information by hepatic glucoreceptors. *In* "Neurohumoral Coding of Brain Function" (R. D. Myers and R. R. Drucker-Colin, eds), pp. 81–97. Plenum, New York.

Russek, M. and Racotta, R. (1971). A peripheral aphagic syndrome. *Proc. Union Physiol. Sci.* **9**, 445.

Russek, M. and Stevenson, J. A. F. (1972). Correlation between the effect of several substances on food intake and on the hepatic concentration of reducing sugars. *Physiol. Behav.* **8**, 245–249.

Russek, M., Rodríguez-Zendejas, A. M. and Pina, S. (1968). Hypothetical liver receptors and the anorexia caused by adrenaline and glucose. *Physiol. Behav.* **3**, 249.

Russek, M., Rodriguez-Zendejas, A. M. and Teitelbaum, P. (1973). The action of adrenergic anorexigenic substances on rats recovered from lateral hypothalamic lesions. *Physiol. Behav.* **10**, 329–334.

Russek, M., Racotta, R. and Martinez, I. (1974). Hepatic chromaffin cells: Possible keystone in preabsorptive satiation. Presented at the XXIV Internat. Congr. physiol. Sci., Jerusalem Satellite Symposium. p. 115.

Tanikawa, K. (1968). "Ultrastructural Aspects of the Liver and its Diseases". Igaku Shoin Ltd., Tokyo.

Teitelbaum, P. and Epstein, A. N. (1962). The lateral hypothalamic syndrome: recovery of feeding and drinking after lateral hypothalamic lesions. *Psychol. Rev.* **69**, 74–90.

11

Prediction of Feeding Behaviour from Energy Flows in the Rat

D. A. BOOTH
Department of Psychology, University of Birmingham, England

The components of our model of hunger processes in the rat (Mark 3 version) and some of the results of simulation have been stated in reviews elsewhere (Booth *et al.*, 1976; Booth, 1976). This chapter records how the model developed. That is a way of describing the model itself which may help it be comprehensible to someone who happens to be unfamiliar with either computer simulation or our theoretical orientation, or perhaps both. Indeed, an unfamiliar systems analysis of any complexity is daunting to almost anyone in its final form, and a good route to the "inside" of any system is to follow its elaboration from some simple precursor along a series of "natural" modifications. Such an account also illustrates our views as to the relationships one should endeavour to maintain between modelling, theorizing, use of the experimental literature, and the design of new experiments.

I. Background Concepts and Theory

A. *The Physiological Control Systems Approach*

Oatley (1967) presented an account of the physiological basis of mammalian thirst using the concepts of control engineering. These had been used previously in physiological analysis but Oatley extended the analysis of a system of physiological components to include what any psychologist would categorize as motivational behaviour. The components of his model represented the current understanding of the physiology and psychology of those aspects of the real animal which control its water intake and the disposal of water throughout its body. Toates and Oatley (1969) presented a digital computer simulation for the rat of a quantitative version of Oatley's analysis and put it to use to examine the plausibility of certain differing theoretical accounts of rats' drinking responses. The quantitative predictions of water intake were tolerably realistic, with some instructive differences between modelled behaviour and results from real rats. Later developments of this approach to computed theory of drinking control are discussed by Oatley (1973, 1974) and Toates (1974, 1975).

Between 1967 and 1972, Oatley and I discussed several ways in which a computer simulation of feeding and its physiological basis might be constructed for the rat. We never quite convinced each other that we yet had an adequately realistic and fully workable analysis of the system. However, in early 1973 Toates became keen to work on the construction of an "eating computer". We were not aware of any other computer simulation of food intake, although when I presented our model at Ermenonville later in the year, Panksepp called my attention to Hirsch (1972)—reprinted as Chapter 4 in this book. His model was in a more abstract style, without directly and independently measurable component functions. Also it worked on daily jumps, not on meal-to-meal real time processing. At a still later stage, at the Jerusalem conference in 1974, Barnwell presented neural network equations he had constructed a couple of years previously (see Chapter 5), and—most relevant of all—Schilstra drew my attention to Geertsema's (1973) PhD Thesis, a summary of which had just become available in English (Geertsema and Reddingius, 1974); Geertsema's modelling work is reviewed here in Chapter 9. These models were also more conceptual than the attempt Toates and I envisaged. We wanted to use simple but measurably realistic models of actual components of the body and behaviour, interconnected in the simulation in the way they are in the real rat, and see if we could predict feeding behaviour which was quantitatively realistic—for example, meal sizes and intervals between them of the right size and typically distributed around the clock.

B. *The Energy Supply Theory of Satiety/Appetite*

The enterprise might be viable only if we had sufficiently realistic characterizations of the main components of the system, if these were programmable, and of course if the theory informing the selection of relevant components and their interconnections was somewhere near the truth.

I had become convinced in the previous couple of years that at one level of analysis the theory of hunger physiology could be considerably simplified. I had suggested that there was a set of satiety signals or a single signal which reflected the current supply of readily metabolized energy (Booth, 1972a, b, d). The initial evidence for this view was the finding that a wide variety of energy-yielding nutrients or metabolites had a suppressant effect on food intake following their absorption, and their satiating effect was related to their energy yield independently of their convertability to glucose (Booth, 1972d). Additional considerations (see pp. 270–271) encouraged the extension of this idea to the hypothesis that feeding in the rat was under the control of a single main factor—an "energostatic" or energy supply stabilizing system (Booth, 1972a, d), better termed "ischymetric" or power measuring (Nicolaïdis 1974).

To assert that a more or less unitary complex of stimuli from energy metabolism directly or indirectly exerts the most important single influence on feeding is not to deny that feeding can be affected by a change in one or more of a multitude of variables. From a single-factor viewpoint, these variations are either extraneous constraints within which the basic energy control system has to work or variations which are correlatable with events in the energy control system and so can be incorporated into it by learning mechanisms.

Once the notion that energy supply ruled appetite had been formulated, glimmerings of how to calculate energy supply began to take form and the range of experimental design that seemed likely to be usefully relevant narrowed sharply.

1. *Direct and Indirect Control*

The supply of energy to the relevant tissues would be in direct control of feeding if there was an invariant consequence for onset, offset or selectivity of food intake when energy supply was in a particular state. Most experiments on the relation of physiology or biochemistry to behaviour in appetite are built on the assumption of direct control. The results can be meaningless if control is indirect (e.g. amino acid aversion: Booth and Simson, 1974; conditioned satiety and appetite: Booth, 1977).

The influence of energy metabolism may be indirect in two ways. Firstly, learning to predict energy effects of imposed, or organism-controlled situations, provides anticipatory control. Anticipatory actions can greatly influence the performance of the system, but then current energy supply is no longer the only influence of energy metabolism on feeding. Experience of states of energy metabolism which consistently follow both the organism's current state of metabolism and other aspects of its current state (external and internal) is important in interpreting the current metabolic state.

Secondly, at least some of the information which reflects energy metabolism may be provided to the nervous system not by metabolism itself, but by hormones or tissue innervation signalling events which are normally tightly connected with metabolism.

2. *Unitary but Fractionable Control*

The influence of energy metabolism may not from all points of view be strictly unitary. At one level of analysis and to a certain degree of approximation, the flow of energy to a functional satiety/hunger transducer system may account for observed feeding behaviour and changes in body content under many conditions. At a more detailed or lower level of analysis, or under some unusual conditions, the transducer system will be seen to have component parts. Different aspects of energy metabolism may be sensed in different ways and by effects which are not exactly proportional to energy.

Metabolic control of feeding is unlikely to be restricted to energy metabolism, although I believe that hunger is normally dominated by current energy. Amino acid supply and the balance in the pattern of amino acids available to tissues can affect feeding independently of energy (Booth, 1974) again possibly largely via learning (Booth and Simson, 1974). Vitamin deficiencies, which disrupt metabolism, can also have marked effects on food intake (Harris *et al.,* 1933). However, the rat's feeding behaviour will not often be subject to such influences—in the laboratory because a single complete diet is provided and energy control brings all other necessary nutrients with it, and in the wild because many mixtures of foodstuffs consumed on an energy control basis provide sufficient vitamins and minerals, and often adequate protein too. A theory that considers only energy metabolism may therefore suffice for a wide range of circumstances. The model in this chapter is built on this basis. The information we have on behavioural and physiological effects of protein, vitamins and salts may be sufficient to elaborate the model to cover situations in which they become important independent variables, but we have only just begun to work on that.

Evidence for energy flow theory, its current paradigmatic advantages, and the relations between energy and other influences on hunger and satiety are reviewed elsewhere (Booth, 1978).

II. An Elemental Control Loop

Feeding affects energy flow. Energy flow, according to the theory, affects feeding. This implies that there exists a recurrent loop between the body and feeding behaviour. We might be able to calculate the loop's performance. Furthermore, feeding increases energy flow, whereas, on the energy supply theory of satiety and hunger, energy flow should inhibit feeding. Thus the loop has negative feedback characteristics. That is, there might on calculation of a model of the loop prove to be an elemental system capable of controlled or relatively stable performance. Not any negative feedback loop would do. The characteristics of the components would have to prove suitable. The system might oscillate continuously between feeding and not feeding, without staying in one or other state for any appreciable time. Even if the system modelled meals, it might very rapidly reach a cumulative state of energy content which would correspond to death by starvation or by explosion!

Toates and I therefore started designing a computer programme for the most elemental model, consisting of three components:

(i) a simulation of the process we believed to be most influential in the short term effects of feeding on energy flows within the rat;

(ii) a simulation of the effect of energy flow on the tendency to feed or not;

(iii) a simulation of the process of food intake itself.

A. *A Gut Clearance Function*

From what is known of rat physiology, we thought that the largest variation in energy flow to the tissues—and often the largest single category of energy flow in the body—was intestinal absorption. So the first aspect of energy processing we chose to simulate was gastrointestinal transit of food. During a year's collaboration in 1971, Davis had taught me to attend to the details of what normally happened to food between the mouth and the blood and to be sensitive to the inadequacy of the measurements and manipulations of gastric and intestinal processing then current in physiological psychology (Davis and Booth, 1974).

The rate of absorption is not limited by the rate of transport of digested nutrients across the intestinal wall, nor in normal circumstances by the rate of digestion. Absorption rate is usually determined by the rate at which chyme is pumped from the stomach into the duodenum. Thus, at least under steady state conditions, the way the stomach empties will largely determine the flow of energy to the tissues.

1. *Gastric Emptying Data*

At the time Toates and I started to build the elemental model, I had some data on gastrointestinal transit of glucose loads which approximated in energy the size of the rat's normal meals (Booth, 1972a, fig. 8), and Jarman had more detailed observations (Booth, 1971) since published (Booth and Jarman, 1976: fig. 3). From Hunt's theory of control of gastric emptying by an osmoreceptor in the duodenal wall (Hunt and Knox, 1968), I was disposed to believe that glucose loads and the starch and protein from a meal would pass from the stomach according to very similar functions, except perhaps for some initial transients. Laboratory chow for the rat is typically about half starch and one-fifth to one-quarter protein by weight, with only a few per cent of fats of all sorts. Later preliminary data on chow clearance did not discourage this view (Booth *et al.*, 1976: fig. 2). Furthermore, Hunt and Stubbs (1975) later adduced a variety of data consistent with the notion that—at least with fluid diets in man—gastric emptying was controlled according to the energy content of the stomach as it affects the duodenal wall osmoreceptors and fatty acid receptors, independently of the relative composition in carbohydrate, protein and fat. They also showed that gastric emptying rate was a function of the energy density of the meal. Our glucose clearance data were mainly with 40% glucose (1·5 kcal/ml), which is similar in energy density to a mixture of chow and water taken in the proportion of about 1 g to 1 ml which is usual for an *ad libitum* meal (i.e. 1·6–1·7 kcal/ml), a coincidence which was lucky for the fate of the early version of the model.

The characteristics of the initial stages of gastric emptying were ill-defined and remain so, at least for intubated fluid loads in both rat and man. Hunt and Knox (1968) drew attention to the variations in the extrapolated intercept on the gastric contents co-ordinate when an exponential function was fitted to plots of gastric contents against time for about the first hour in different human subjects. The extrapolated "starting times" for the load given, and the appearance in some circumstances of a phase of very rapid emptying compensated by a limited period of very slow emptying, represent deviations from an exponential emptying function in the first minutes following a load. Toates and I spent some time trying to settle on a calculation of initial transients, because they appeared likely to have a considerable effect on absorption rate towards the end of a meal, and hence on meal size. In the end we despaired of coping with the general ignorance of the details of earlier emptying and gave up that at this stage—perhaps fortunately, because these transients may be negligible or even absent with voluntarily ingested solid nutrients (Booth *et al.,* 1976: fig. 2; see Fig. 1 of this chapter), unless the animal takes a large meal or has been starved (Oatley and Toates, 1969; Wiepkiema *et al.,* 1972). In these circumstances an initial rush of food into the duodenum may occur before digestion can become sufficiently adapted to the meal to provide an appropriate strength of stimulus to the duodenal wall receptors inhibiting gastric emptying. When the digestive products of this undercontrolled rush are seen, they are abundant enough to stop gastric emptying almost completely until the excess has been absorbed.

2. *Gastrointestinal Processing of Chow* ad libitum

Newman and Nolan are currently collecting systematic data in my laboratory on gastric and intestinal contents in the rat following voluntary ingestion of a normal sized meal under close to *ad libitum* feeding and drinking conditions. The results put those earlier interpretations onto a much firmer basis. Stomach contents decline in a smooth curve, and the contents of intestinal segments vary little if at all under these conditions (Fig. 1). The rate of stomach emptying decreases with amount in the stomach, giving a much better fit by a quadratic equation than a linear equation, and no significant improvement on adding cubic or higher polynomial components. The quadratic function in time has an almost exact root—that is, the square root of amount in the stomach gives a stright line when plotted against time. When the curve is fitted to a power function, the exponent of time is almost exactly two, i.e. again, square root of stomach contents is linear against time. Finally, linear regression accounts for more of the variance and gives a much more realistic extrapolation to stomach contents at zero time when carried out on the square root of stomach contents against time than on the logarithm of contents against time—i.e. the emptying function is not truly exponential when its whole time course is considered.

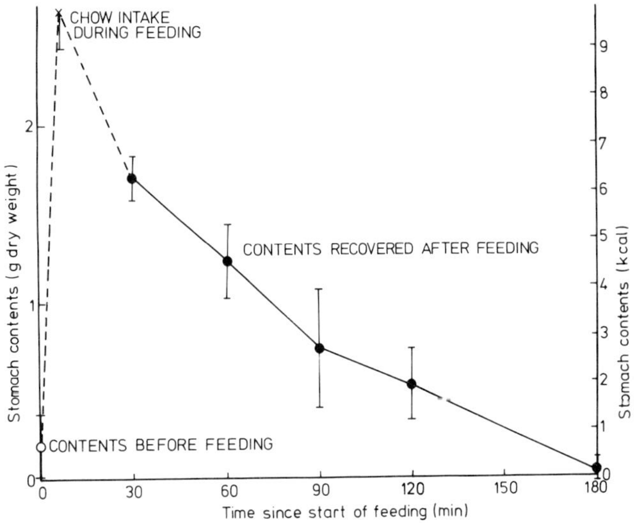

Fig. 1. Contents of stomachs at intervals following the ingestion of 3 g of chow by 325-g male rats in the middle of the dark phase of the lighting cycle. Solid circles represent amount recovered from the fed rats, and the cross their chow intake. The open circle is the amount recovered from rats identically pretreated but killed instead of being given food. A 240-min point was deleted for curve fitting calculations. The best quadratic fit ($F=97{\cdot}6$) was $A=9{\cdot}5-0{\cdot}075t+0{\cdot}000\,14t^2$ (where A is amount in the stomach in kcal and t is time in minutes). The linear, exponential and square root regression best fits were respectively $A=7{\cdot}89-0{\cdot}046t$, $\log A=1{\cdot}69-0{\cdot}0158t$, and $A^{\frac{1}{2}}=3{\cdot}24-0{\cdot}0165t$, with F-ratios of 101, 42·8 and 154·2. If the square root function is taken to represent this curve, then emptying rate as a function of amount in the stomach is simply derived as follows. Take $A^{\frac{1}{2}}=c-mt$. Squaring, $A=c^2-2mct+m^2t^2$. Differentiating, $\mathrm{d}A/\mathrm{d}t=-2mc+2m^2t=-2m(c-mt)=-2mA^{\frac{1}{2}}$. Thus, under the conditions of the data in this Figure, the energy rate of gastric clearance is the square root of the energy in the stomach multiplied by $(-2)(-0{\cdot}0165)=0{\cdot}033$ in kcal units. Data of Dr J. C. Newman with the assistance of Mrs Veronica Nolan.

If we measure the slope of the curve of gastric contents against time at any particular level of energy content, this gives the rate of gastric emptying for that stomach content. The simple mathematical statement of the same point is that the rate of change of amount in the stomach ($\mathrm{d}A/\mathrm{d}t$) is the first differential of the function which relates amount in the stomach (A) to time (t). Conveniently or confusingly, the first differential of a square root function is also a square root function (see caption to Fig. 1). That is, the rate of gastric emptying at any moment is proportional to the square root of the amount in the stomach. The proportionality factor (or rate constant) is minus two times the slope of the straight line to which the curve of Fig. 1 is converted by plotting the square root of gastric energy contents against time. There is a tradition, from both Marbaix and Cannon at the turn of the century to Hopkins recently, that in so far as the stomach approximates to an elastic cylinder, its wall tension (which might well determine gastric emptying rate) should be proportional to the square root of the volume of gastric contents (Hunt and Knox, 1968). When we known more about the mechanisms by which gastrointestinal contents influence gastric and duodenal contractions and the propulsive power which is thought to arise from the pressure differences the contractions create, it may well become possible to reduce the description of gastric clearance to a lower level of analysis. Until that time, it appears to be a robust and accurate representation of the data on chow *ad libitum* to take the energy rate of gastric emptying to the proportional to the square root of gastric energy content over the whole of the period of emptying. If Hunt and Stubbs' (1975) analysis of human data proves to apply also to the rat, then the rate constant for chow clearance will apply to other nutrient mixtures of similar energy density, but different rate constants will apply to calorifically more dilute or more concentrated diets.

Other conditions under which different emptying rate constants apply will be mentioned later in this chapter.

3. *Calculation of Absorption Rate from the Gastric Clearance Function*

The stomach is emptying while it is being filled during a meal, as well as after the end of the meal. The calculation of emptying can be updated sufficiently frequently on the computer to mimic the continuity of the real process. Emptying is simply negative filling. Emptying and filling cumulate to yield the amount in the stomach which in turn determines emptying. This calculation of model stomach contents is represented diagrammatically in Fig. 2.

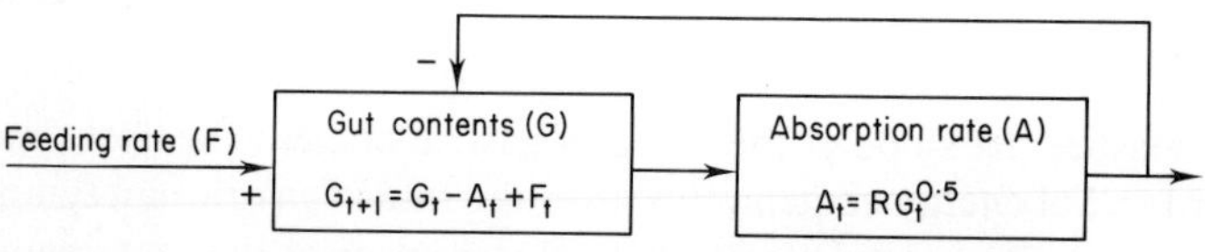

Fig. 2. Flow diagram for simplified gut clearance model. This can be simply represented in a series of calculations reiterated for intervals of real time sufficiently short to mimic the results of continuous differential equations. Thus, calculate the amount absorbed since the last calculation using the rate of absorption corresponding to the amount in the gut; from the rate of ingestion calculate the amount ingested since the last calculation; alter the amount in the gut by subtracting the absorption and adding any ingestion. Under the night time conditions of Fig. 1, the proportionality factor $k = 0{\cdot}033 \times \sqrt{1000} = 1{\cdot}04$ in small calorie units. In our first simulations, the night factor was 0·9 and the day factor 0·6.

We considered representing gastrointestinal processing as two compartments, stomach and intestine. However, the amount of computation and the number of variables on which there were few or no data seemed very large compared with the loss of accuracy involved in regarding the intestine contents as negligibly small in energy and in energy flow variance compared with the stomach contents. Therefore we used the square root function to cover the whole of gastrointestinal processing from ingestion to absorption. This is to make the implicit assumption that there is a very brief delay between ingesting a morsel of food and the absorbed digestion products reaching the tissues in which energy flow acts on the nervous system to affect feeding. We were aware at the time that Pilcher, Jarman and Booth (1974) had data on transfer of carbon to the brain and other tissues at 5 and 10 min after oral ingestion of radioactively labelled starch, extrapolation of which to zero transfer coincided with zero time within a resolution of a minute or so. There was already evidence that part (Rupe and Mayer, 1967) or all (Steffens, 1969b) of the glucose contributing to the hyperglycaemia which arises within a few minutes of ingestion arises from free glucose incorporated in the diet. Pilcher's data showed further that food can pass from the mouth to the tissues within a couple of minutes, even if digestion is required as it normally is. However, the inadequacy of neglecting even a 2-min delay is to be tackled below (Section IV.B.l.a.).

B. *A Hunger and Satiety Thresholds Function*

1. *The Two-Threshold Concept*

The basic idea of any energy supply theory of hunger/satiety would be expressed in its most primitive form by the statement that the propensity to feed appears when the flow of energy from absorption becomes too small and disappears again when absorptive flow becomes adequate or too great. As will be seen from later development of the model, I do not believe that either the flow from absorption alone or any uninterpreted energy flow is the determining factor. Nevertheless, additional energy flows could be incorporated later, as well as interactions with external conditions such as sensory qualities of the food and the time of day. The first step was to make a calculation on direct sensitivity to the major flow, absorption.

The simplest representation of this energy flow theory would be the rule that feeding started when absorption fell below a certain rate and stopped again when absorption rose above a certain rate. The step-function characteristic of the energy thresholds for the start and end of the meal was a computational convenience. Not only was the threshold likely to be probabilistic, but in our view even a classical logistic function would have been an oversimplified epiphenomenon of the signal detection problems the animals has of discriminating its internal states of high and low energy flow.

There were more fundamental problems than the characteristics of the function for feeding and non-feeding. Was the same decision function involved in starting and stopping feeding? We formed the impression from data mentioned above that increase in energy supply to tissues at the end of a meal was detectable. For that matter, if homology between physiology and experience has any weight, hunger sensations are easily separated from satiety sensations, and it was reasonable to suppose that these might be experiences of different bodily states, rather than some misreference or illusion generated purely by differences in brain processing. In any case, a single decision function operating on information generated promptly on ingestion might produce unrealistically short meals and intermeal intervals. A positive feedback effect of the taste of food had been invoked by McFarland (1971), Weipkema (1971), Le Magnen (1971) and others, which would serve to lock the rat into feeding behaviour. However, there was no obvious way in which the attenuation of this positive feedback effect, which would largely determine meal size, could be adjusted to relate amount eaten to contents of the gut at the start of eating, the nature of the diet, and other significant conditions. Another possible way of operating with a single threshold was to postulate pretuned oral metering: Toates and Oatley (1969) have a feedforward loop in their thirst model which predicts (from mouth and gut signals by unspecified mechanisms) the eventual parenteral yield of water from the drinking bout. On balance, it seemed to us less arbitrary to think in terms of two thresholds on the same variable, i.e. a starting decision at one level of energy supply and a stopping decision at a higher level of the same energy supply.

We were aware that we were not dealing with the reality of competing motivation and behaviours. With Oatley (1967) and McFarland (1971), we believed that a desire to feed had to interact with other behavioural needs—no doubt weighted according to their biological or psychological functions; and also that several currently strong desires possibly share time in behavioural expression. The combination of this feeding model with a drinking model is described by Toates in Chapter 14. McFarland treates the question of behavioural priorities more generally in Chapter 15, and Booth and Mather refer to some interactions in the human case in Chapter 12. The simulations described in this Chapter treat feeding propensity as rigidly determining feeding behaviour. Some minor inaccuracies and major limitations on predictive range no doubt arise in consequence.

2. *Data on Threshold Absorption Rates*

The type of experiment needed to estimate absorption flows which permit or suppress feeding is not easily performed. (Indeed only now at the time of writing is it being started: a proper design appears even more daunting now the model has been more fully elaborated.) However, we had access to the results which

Campbell and Davis (1974a,b) had obtained in my laboratory in 1971. They showed that short term duodenal or portal (but not jugular) infusion of modest doses of glucose could slow or suppress nutrient ingestion in the rat. From some of their dose-response data using a glucose drinking measure, it was possible to estimate very roughly, a glucose delivery rate which was not quite high enough to affect feeding and another higher rate at which feeding was just about completely suppressed: these were around 15–20 cal/min and 50–80 cal/min respectively.

Such rough and ready calculations from data obtained for other purposes would be worth corroborating from any direction available. The otherwise partly circular move of estimating thresholds from amounts found in the gut at the start and finish of meals did in fact yield estimates in the same ranges. Twelve rats were killed in the second half of the light phase, each as it started to eat a meal undisturbed with free access to chow of energy density 3·43 kcal/g. The stomach contents averaged 0·26 g dry weight, excluding hair and faeces. With a rate constant of 0·6 on a square root stomach clearance function, this corresponds to an absorption rate of 18 cal/min. With a meal size of 2·5 g, stomach contents would approach 2·8 g, which would correspond to an absorption rate of 59 cal/min.

Threshold values of 18 cal/min for feeding onset and 60 cal/min for feeding offset were therefore used in the Mark 1 version of the modal (Booth and Toates, 1974b; Toates and Booth, 1974).

It should be emphasized that even a procedure of estimating thresholds solely by measuring amounts in the stomach and using the model's gut clearance function would not be viciously circular: the model would only work realistically if the concept of a threshold energy flow were applicable, if constant thresholds could validly be assumed, and if the conditions of stomach sampling were representative of all other conditions being simulated on the basis of the resulting threshold estimates.

The threshold functions are presented diagrammatically in Fig. 3. The procedures include the loop's third component, specification of feeding rate when feeding occurs.

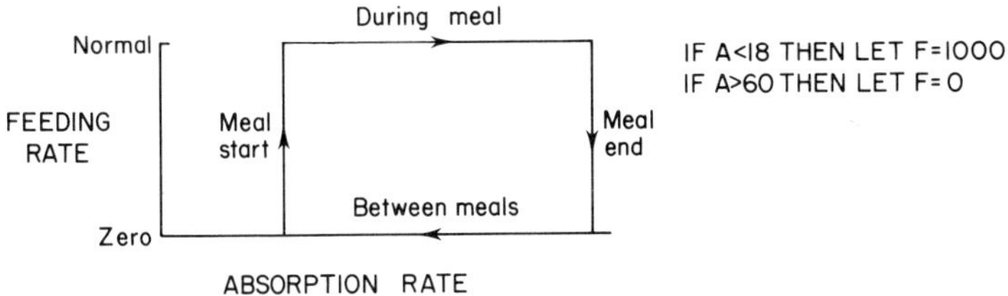

Fig. 3. Double threshold function. Between meals the absorption rate decreases until it reaches the hunger threshold value of 18 cal/min, and feeding is started, at a rate of 1000 cal/min. Absorption rate increases during the meal up to the satiety threshold value when feeding stops.

C. *A Feeding Rate Function*

Given that food is present and that there is a propensity to feed, the simplifying assumption in the present model is that food is taken at a constant rate until there ceases to be a propensity to feed. I believe that in fact the propensity to feed is a consequence of some interaction between internal state and the external situation including sensory characteristics of the food. However, in the situation where there is only one foodstuff, freely available and always presented in the same way, this interaction does not have to be made explicit. The internal state alone (or predictions of it) can determine whether feeding occurs or not. The external situation alone can determine the rate at which food intake occurs. The physical accessibility of the diet (on the floor, in a grid basket, down a tunnel, ease of responding in the case of operant delivery) and the form in which it is presented (blocks, pellets, powder, fluid) can affect the rate of ingestion. Texture, smell and taste (probably in that order) can affect the enthusiasm of mastication and ease of swallowing, both innately and as a result of familiarization and conditioning (Booth *et al.*, 1974) but these effects can be lumped into a constant intake rate with a single diet *ad libitum*. In the rat, there appear to be no systematic data on the effects of different levels of food deprivation or energy flow deficiency on the rate of intake of laboratory maintenance diet.

Constant feeding rate is of course a convenient approximation, but we chose it initially and we have maintained that choice because it appears to be a very close approximation to reality for many situations. Of course, rats do often eat in a series of short phases—mouthfuls, pawfuls, bursts of licking. However, the transit and circulation characteristics of the gut and blood have a considerable smoothing effect. Even if a swallow is sometimes the start of a peristaltic wave extending across the stomach along the intestine, eating bursts within meals probably generate no postabsorptive transients. Major transients at the start and towards the end of meals have also been emphasized by some workers. An acceleration of intake in the early stages of the meal has been observed under some conditions (Wiepkema, 1971; Le Magnen, 1971) and used as a basis for the concept of positive feedback at the start of the meal. Slowing of intake in the latter half of the meal is also widely supposed to occur, and to reflect incipient satiety. However, if one looks at data for individual meals of individual rats, the most one sees is a few runs of feeding at increasing intervals—a stepwise rather than smooth slowing, the smoothness being an artefact of grouping data. Furthermore, the stepped slowing may be more characteristic of fluid diets than solid diets, and of some rats or feeding conditions than others. When a 45-mg food pellet is continuously available and directly accessible to the rat, neither accelerative nor decelerative transients are generally seen in our experience (Table I).

Rates as varied as 0·1 g/min (Le Magnen and Tallon 1966) and 0·5 g/min

Table I.
Interpellet intervals and average feeding rates on the eatometer.

Rat	Day	Phase	Interpellet interval record	Mean feeding rate (mg/min)
1	3	Light	55922 48 33 42 35 45 42 36 30 44 74 32 1 78 60 27 31 41 43 35 55 40 44 64 27 40 44 64 27 40 46 51 81 46 37 80 72 24 27 90 65 46 63 82 39 65 42 53 62 52 68 42 41 53 55 45 44 85 36180	251
		Dark	18170 12 39 33 49 27 31 27 27 26 37 25 27 29 47 26 27 35 33 40 40 39 27 30 38 52 38 0 41 44 31 481 31 35 28 36 53 28 42 27 39 43 33 43 31 29 37 49 51 34 26 273 61 24 25 42 45 61 24671	264
	8	Light	46092 61 47 38 44 31 43 42 47 34 61 27 50 98 37 61 28 44 152 83 37 60 136 37 120 49 80 66 140 29 50 83 50 143 44 71 50 54 49 68 38986	215
		Dark	23337 36 35 32 54 35 30 28 35 47 30 28 26 40 51 41 81 65 24 33 58 23 253 48 33 46 56 30 31 77 36 69 29 75 95 135 44 132 53 83 29 32 50 856 40 28 88 28 42 31 71 26 25 47 184 27 34 43 53 48 1739 38 60 36 82 35 34 30 46 45 29 39 69 36 54 42 7337 41 32 33 204 57 28 32 35 27 39 62 30 34 31 38 34 14534	194 (156) (169)
	9	Light	57490 48 42 34 72 30 37 38 33 43 34 43 27 40 33 66 33 35 37 36 50 71 42 31 53 29 59 25771	295
		Dark	16246 33 45 37 50 26 46 34 38 39 31 31 35 47 39 21 32 35 38 40 36 38 37 63 28 46 35 46 36 29 9682	317
4	4	Light	37402 52 45 32 35 39 33 22 38 38 29 31 35 36 35 18 31 35 1420 26 46 16 36 47 33 34 28 32 28 34 27 31 33 32 21 38 44 37 35 37 22 36 55 31 26 85 37 35 30 42 53 39 40 19148	205
		Dark	14076 18 52 49 29 37 40 31 57 26 33 40 43 18 31 41 41 30 34 43 34 35 45 31 36 32 46 29 39 374 28 40 41 53 25 38 30 43 42 950 15 53 18 50 66 14 63 15 168 108 28 26 21 38 35 46 49 31 103 35 6192	207
7	5	Light	37288 69 55 62 50 51 38 116 53 38 33 54 44 31 34 49 44 48 30 115 20 29 46 37 40 48 64 61 32 22772	255
		Dark	16832 76 34 36 34 44 59 26 30 95 27 45 25 47 33 42 30 41 62 55 31 131 33 43 47 53 31 34 54 36 50 27 54 43 54 46 42 55 53 44 30 44 7313 55 35 33 43 51 30 36 45 23 51 18243	285 (75)

Intervals between 45-mg Noyes pellets taken were printed out in 0·2-s units, with 1·0 sec of dead time for printing. Thus a printout of 45 corresponds to 10 s and a local rate of 270 mg/min. The meals just before midnight and midday respectively are tabulated with their pre- and postmeal intervals from such a record which had no built-in criteria (Booth and Campbell, 1976).

(Levitsky, 1970; Kissileff, 1970) have been reported, but around 0·3 g/min is typical with pellet eatometers and for many laboratory maintenance diets in block or powder form (Table I; De Castro and Balagura, 1975). The feeding rate in g/min or ml/min has to be multiplied by the energy density of the diet in cal/g or cal/ml respectively for the purposes of the model. Some lab chow is quoted as 3·2 kcal/g (Le Magnen and Devos, 1970), other chow at 3·43 kcal/g (Booth, 1972a). When gastric distension is modelled, water content of the diet can be ignored (except when water intake is being modelled, as in Chapter 13) on the assumption that salivation and gastric secretion even up the differences between dry and wet diets. In SI units, our values for standard chow, where better are not available, are 5 mg/s intake weight rate and 13·4 J/mg energy density. This corresponds to an energy intake rate of about 1 kcal/min.

D. *Performance of the Loop*

This elemental model (Fig. 4) was bound to produce meals, because of the double-threshold component. So long as clearance during the meal proved not to be disproportionately great, we also expected meal sizes to be fairly realistic, because of the cross-checking we had done in the thresholds data bases and because absorption was modelled as instantaneous. The prediction of interval between meals was less trivial, because (once the feeding onset threshold was set) the inter-meal interval was critically dependent on the gut clearance function. The model's inter-meal interval for a 2·5-g meal was in fact 230 min (gut rate constant 0·6; absorption onset and offset thresholds 18 and 60 cal/min; eating rate 0·3 g/min; chow density 3·2 kcal/g).

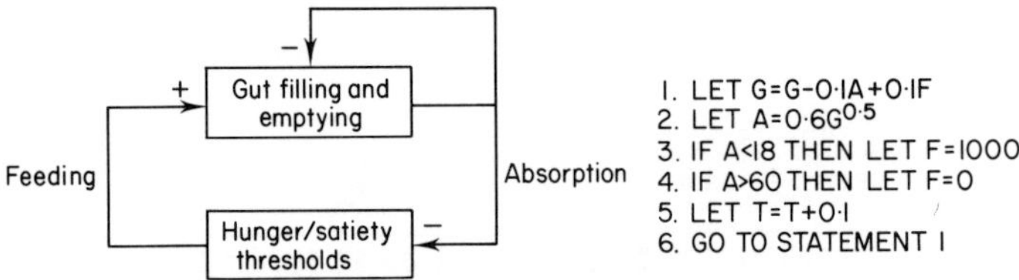

Fig. 4. The elemental loop of absorption from the gut, an energy-flow thresholds system, and entry of food into the gut. The calculation cycle is outlined in the list of statements to the right, where G is gut contents A is absorption rate and F is feeding rate (as in Fig. 2), and T is time in minutes. The 6-s interval between calculations, as well as substantive parameter values, can be reset if better values become available.

We proceeded then to consider elaborations and perturbations of the elemental loop. The first question we set ourselves was whether known perturbations would account for the circadian variations in the rat's meal pattern. We also considered what perturbations might produce the currently studied changes in food intake and feeding pattern induced by manipulations such as damage to the hypothalamus or to the pancreas or physiological changes such as rise or fall in environmental temperature.

III. Circadian Pattern

A. *Variation in Gut Clearance Rate*

Jarman's data on the passage of a glucose load through the gut had clearly shown that the rat's stomach empties considerably faster in the dark phase of the lighting cycle than in the light phase (Booth and Jarman, 1976). We expected the incorporation into the model of this daytime reduction in the value of the gut clearance rate constant to lengthen the time that the system would take for rate of absorption to fall from the satiety threshold to the hunger threshold during daylight. That is, the model should at least make a prediction in the correct direction, that meals are less frequent by day than by night in the rat. The question was how much more or less of a day–night difference would be predicted by this computation than is in fact observed, and what other effects the gut clearance variation might have on the meal pattern, e.g. on meal size. Any progress in this direction would provide an interesting comparison with the Oatley—Toates modelling of drinking in the rat. There they found it best to simulate the circadian drinking pattern by a set-point change. Here a major contribution could be made by a peripheral processing change. However, there was and is a difficulty with modelling circadian variation. The feeding rhythm observed appears to be quite sensitive to the conditions of housing, as well as no doubt being affected by differences in strains etc. Even laboratories all using a cycle of 12h dark and 12h light report a wide range of ratios of night-time intake to daytime intake, varying at least from 1·5:1 to 3:1. Possibly the main variable in this is how much the animals are disturbed by extraneous stimuli during the light phase (Booth and Campbell, 1976). Night/day ratios tend to be higher in reverse-cycle conditions than in conditions were the nocturnal rat has to compromise with diurnal human beings.

In fact, a change of gut clearance rate constant has several consequences even in the elemental model. The daytime slowing does increase the ratio of intermeal interval to size of the preceding meal. It also increases the amount in the stomach at the start of a meal, because the absorption rate low enough to release feeding corresponds to a greater gut energy contents when the rate constant is lower. This makes it a greater strain on the mathematical intuition to anticipate ahead of computation whether meal sizes will change much from night to day: if stomach contents at the start of meals were the same by day as by night, then modelled daytime meals would certainly be bigger—because the lower rate constant would require a larger gut content to reach an absorption rate high enough to switch off feeding. The higher starting contents and the nonlinear relationship between gut contents and absorption rate makes a simple non-mathematical scientist like myself turn with relief to a programmed calculating machine. How important is the clearance during the meal? How critical are the values of hunger and satiety thresholds we have chosen?

At an eating rate of 1 kcal/min (i.e. about 0·3 g/min), hunger and satiety thresholds of 18 and 60 cal/min and gut rate constants of 0·9 by night and 0·6 by day (derived from Jarman's glucose data), the model predicts 1·5-g meals at 110-min intervals by night and 2·5-g meals at 245-min intervals by day.

B. *Variations in Thresholds*

We had yet to incorporate another substantial known circadian influence in the elemental loop (see Section III C), but we paused to consider a qualitatively unrealistic aspect of this prediction. Meal sizes are occasionally found to be almost identical by day and by night in the rat. Usually night-time meals are somewhat larger than daytime meals, e.g. mean values in the range 2·5–3 g as opposed to 1·5–2·5 g by day. We were not aware of any report of smaller meals by night. Introducing the gut rate variation had produced predictions of the right order in other respects—meal sizes and intermeal intervals in the right ranges, and a meal size/intermeal ratio difference between night (0·014) and day (0·010) in the right direction. What was wrong with the simulation of day–night difference? Did something else vary that was already represented in the model, or was there another factor determining meal size which was yet to be represented? We were not too concerned about this failure at this stage, for two reasons. Firstly, the failure was only partial: the predicted total intakes by day and by night were close to reality, i.e. meals were timed appropriately for their size. Secondly, larger meals by day seemed at the time to be the right prediction in the context of ventromedial hypothalamic hyperphagia (Section III. C. 1.b.(ii)).

In the light of his thirst modelling, one possibility was obvious to Toates: maybe the hunger threshold or the satiety threshold or both thresholds varied between night and day. He found that in simulations only the satiety threshold value was critical for meal sizes, although varying the hunger threshold did have some effect. However, both satiety and hunger thresholds were critical for intermeal intervals. So if we introduced the complexity of a circadian variation in satiety threshold to explain the usually observed day–night meal size difference, the intermeal intervals were changed too—smaller daytime meals meant smaller meal size/intermeal interval ratios by day, and the circadian feeding rhythm almost disappeared altogether! If thresholds were varying, the elemental model had to include a reduction in both thresholds to produce smaller meals by day with high size/interval ratios. Could behaviour be hard to get going and easy to stop by day when the rat is less active and more sleepy? In the absence of either direct evidence or strong theoretical conviction, we were not disposed to establish such a postulate in the model at this early stage. Later I found it was unnecessary anyway (Section IV. B. 2. a).

Nonetheless, we anticipated that one day the threshold functions would have to be elaborated to permit motivational interactions. Feeding may have to share time with sleeping, especially by day. Feeding and drinking may compete at times during meals, It appears from Oatley's (1971) result and Toates' simulation of combined feeding and drinking systems (Chapter 14) that the circadian drinking rhythm is not purely secondary to the feeding rhythm. It is not clear yet whether the primary drinking rhythm is an aspect of an arousal rhythm or a variation to some extent specific to thirst. More precise data to determine the components of the full model of feeding may yet revive the question of circadian threshold variation in the energy-based system.

C. *Variation in Metabolic Diversions of Absorbed Energy*

The theory that energy supply controls appetite does not permit one to be restricted to the flow of energy from intestinal absorption. Variations in absorption rate will affect a feeding control system only relative to variations in other energy flows, in particular the consumption of energy by all tissues in the body, or all except perhaps the energy flow detector cells themselves. However, energy is not only converted to external work and to heat, but is also converted to potential energy, predominantly as triglyceride fat. Elaboration of the debit and credit accounts for loss, storage and release of energy were a major part of successive extensions to the elemental model just described.

1. *Circadian Lipogenesis–Lipolysis Rhythm*

(a) *Energy flow and the fat store.* If one entertains the hypothesis that hunger and satiety reflect energy supply with little regard to substrate, then for consistency one should suppose that energy released from storage will add to energy absorbed from the gut to inhibit feeding. This deduction from an energy flow hypothesis has an attractive corollary: if the tendency to mobilize fat increases at all as the amount of fat stored increases, then a powerful mechanism for stabilizing body fat content exists. This would avoid postulating more complicated or more accurate fat-measuring devices such as some proposed in recent years. It would be neatly symmetrical to assume that deposition of fat subtracted from the absorptive energy flow and so attenuated satiety. At the time we were building the first version of the model, Le Magnen kindly provided an advance copy of the paper from his laboratory on short term measurements of oxygen consumption and carbon dioxide production which illustrated the correlation between frequent, larger meals and net lipogenesis and less frequent, smaller meals and net lipolysis (Le Magnen *et al.,* 1973). By making some conventional although approximate assumptions, Le Magnen and Devos (1970) had estimated the net rate of energy flow into fat synthesis or from fat mobilization over a given period of time: this involves calculating from the proportion of carbon dioxide production to oxygen consumption how much oxidation energy the rat was deriving from food and how much from fat over that period. Le Magnen *et al.* (1973) calculated the night-time total excess in energy intake from the cumulative diversion of energy into lipogenesis and a largely compensatory total deficit in daytime intake permitted by mobilization of that energy excess. Our model provided a way to use Le Magnen's data more precisely, relating each short term estimate of lipogenesis/lipolysis to feeding behaviour occurring at the same time.

Many radioisotope incorporation studies show that a re-fed animal moves promptly to fast fat synthesis, and human respiratory calorimetry has shown the shift from preprandial net lipolysis to postprandial net lipogenesis. We would expect the same rapid changes around meals in the rat. Le Magnen and Devos (1970; Fig. 11) provided some 20-min average estimates indicating shifts towards faster lipogenesis after meals, although the results were not sufficiently complete for use on our model nor arithmetically well matched to their other data in the same paper. The bulk of the data published from Le Magnen's laboratory consisted of 2-h averages, unfortunately lacking the temporal resolution or more particularly the meal relatedness that our model's absorptive flow calculations had. However, the data did represent the smoothed trends in the circadian variation from lipogenesis by night to lipolysis by day. The 1973 paper presented respiratory data for a greater number of animals than the 1970 paper, but when the equations of Le Magnen and Devos (1970) are applied to

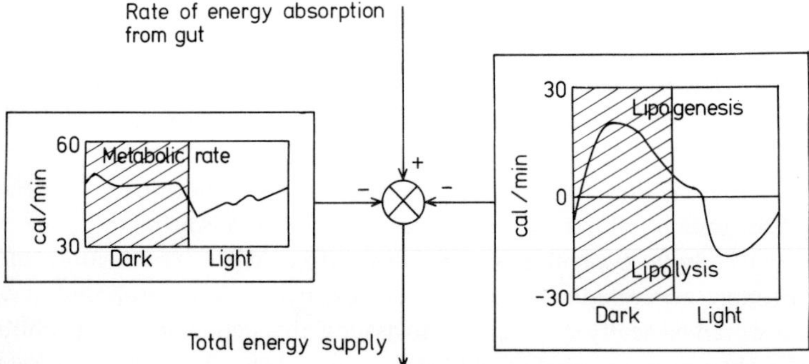

Fig. 5. Metabolic components of the energy flow summation. Mark 1 included only lipogenesis–lipolysis ("lipoflow"). Mark 2 included metabolic rate in the calculations as well. The curves represent estimates made by Le Magnen and Devos (1970) from respiratory data averaged over period of 2 h around the clock. The computer programs used linear interpolations between the mid-2-h data points originally reported.

the 1973 data a much more modest circadian rhythm of lipogenesis–lipolysis is seen. We decided to represent as strong a circadian rhythm of fat storage and mobilization as had been evidenced, therefore taking Le Magnen and Devos (1970) 2-h averages around the clock and adding an interpolated value for the appropriate time of day to the absorptive flow estimates with the model (Fig. 5).

This addition was rather absurd as the absorption calculation was updated every 10 s in our model, and the estimated flow often changed more in a few minutes than the highly smoothed 2-h average lipogenesis–lipolysis estimate did in hours. We consoled ourselves with the thought that this was another component whose values were soundly based on data, and that its inclusion gave the model a chance to reflect a general tendency that varied around the clock. In fact, the lipogenesis–lipolysis cycle helped to correct the disparity in meal sizes in the wrong direction between night and day that was introduced into the elemental model by the circadian variation in gut clearance rate (Fig. 6). However, later simulations in the Mark 3 version showed this to be a misleading viewpoint.

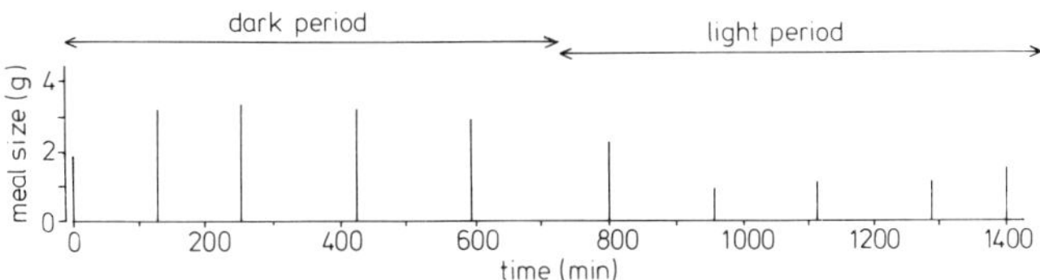

Fig. 6. Meal pattern on a representative day when the circadian lipoflow cycle is included in the calculations, but no circadian variation in the gut clearance rate factor (constant at 0·75 throughout the 24 h). (This is not a realistic simulation as lipoflow variation is likely to be strongly dependent on gut clearance variation. It is intended only to indicate the relative contributions of lipoflow and gut clearance rhythms when compared with Fig. 7A and C).

(b) *Feeding model: Mark 1.* At this stage we thought the model had become interesting enough to submit a brief account for publication and to talk about it at meetings (Booth, 1973; Booth and Toates, 1974a, b). Our first summary was eventually judged too specialized for a general science journal or a local psychological journal and so Jack Davis kindly sponsored it in the Psychonomic Society bulletin (Booth and Toates, 1974b). This had the spin-off that Davis programmed the model from our brief verbal account and got exactly the same results—so we had the comforting assurance that we had at least been programming what we intended to. Later in the year, *Nature* took a brief account with a more general introduction and several additional types of simulation included (Toates and Booth, 1974).

This simple model had a considerable predictive range. If available observations or reasonable assumptions were applied to specify the states of components of the system, the model made quantitative predictions over the conditions now listed. The predictions were generally in approximate agreement with reality, which was even more encouraging.

(i) Intact rat. The envelope of the lipogenesis–lipolysis rhythm was neatly reflected in the meal sizes and intermeal intervals of a simulation of the freely fed rat (Fig. 7). As lipogenesis intensified in the dark, so meals increased in size and came closer together. Conversely, as lipolysis increased during the light period,

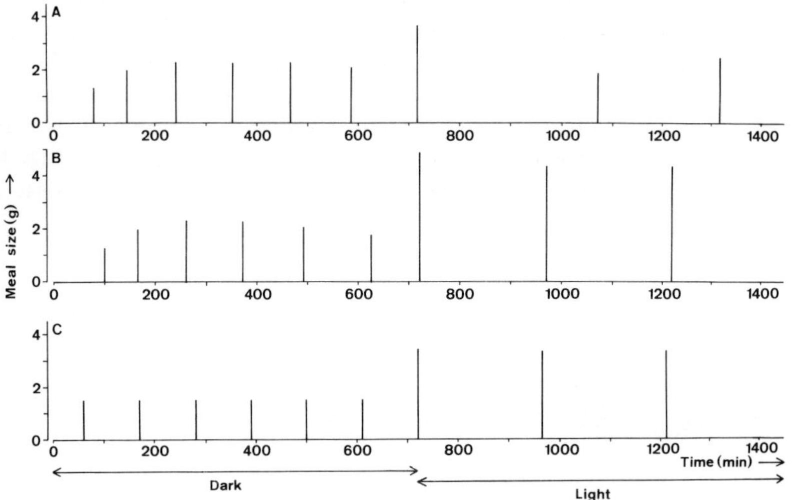

Fig. 7. A, Intact rat. B, Ventromedial hypothalamic lesion—dynamic phase (daytime lipoflow lipogenic as at night). C, VMH static phase (no net lipoflow at any time). These are meal pattern predictions from day 2 of computer runs whose day 1 outputs were given in fig. 2 of Booth and Toates (1974b). The day 1 outputs always started with a meal as the simulations were set with an empty stomach initially.

meal size decreased and the meal-to-meal interval (already lengthened by slowed gastric clearance) increased. Total intakes by day and by night were in the right range, and so long as the relation between meal size and meal-to-meal interval differed in the correct direction also between night and day, we were less concerned that daytime meals were still predicted wrongly to be larger than night-time meals. Despite the variation imposed on the effects of constant gut rate by the circadian fat rhythm, the variance of meal size was unrealistically low. Again, this was attributable to a conveniently but arbitrarily deterministic model and so did not bother us. The sudden slowing of gut clearance at dawn precipitated meals unrealistically close in time to change of lighting. We therefore decided, rather than change the value of the gut rate constant instantaneously at dawn and dusk (which was unlikely to be realistic), to allow the value to change linearly over an hour before and an hour after lighting changeover. Data on the time course of shifts in gastric clearance rate around lighting changes are now being obtained (Newman and Booth, in prep.).

(ii) Rats with ventromedial hypothalamic lesions. Rats with bilateral destruction of the area of the ventromedial nucleus of the hypothalamus do most of their well known overeating and extra fat deposition in the light phase (Balagura and Davenport, 1970; Kakolewski *et al.,* 1971; Le Magnen *et al.,* 1973). Indeed, Le Magnen *et al.,* (1973) had respiratory data indicating a constant high level of lipogenesis around the clock. We simulated VMH lipogenesis either as a daytime repeat of the night-time lipogenesis reported in the intact rat by Le Magnen and Devos (1970) or on the basis of their 1973 data.

The daytime lipogenesis almost doubled the food intake total predicted by the model for that period. However, this was not as large an intake as reported by Le Magnen *et al.* (1973), and so it seemed likely that some additional factor(s) also contributed (see Section IV.B.2.b.). The model predicted that the greater intake was achieved by a great increase in daytime meal size, with a slight decrease in intermeal interval (Fig. 7B). Our impression from Le Magnen's report was that this was not unrealistic. However, Kissileff assured us at Ermenonville that the VMH daytime meal pattern was in fact similar to the night-time pattern (Becker and Kissileff, 1974). This made it obvious that something was wrong with the assumptions of this VMH simulation. The remaining difference between day and night, within the model, was the values of the gut rate constant. Over the coming months we were to formulate the hypothesis that a major abnormality following VMH lesions was the loss of slowed clearance by day (Booth *et al.,* 1976; see Section IV below).

The elemental loop without net lipogenesis or lipolysis was reincarnated by Booth and Toates (1974b) as a simulation of the static phase of the VMH syndrome (Fig. 7C), in which the animal's obesity has reached a plateau and total food intake is practically normal, although the intake ratio between night and day remains abnormally near unity. The accumulation of now unacceptable assumptions in the components of this simulation (Section IV.B.2.b.) make it seem even more of a joke now than it did initially.

(iii) Rats with lateral hypothalamic lesions. We ran simulations with much slower feeding rates (Toates and Booth, 1974). These might have reflected at least some aspects of the lateral hypothalamic syndrome—in particular, the apparent aversion to food even when the initial loss of sensory reactivity in this preparation has attenuated, and also the abnormal tendency to drink frequently during meals which persists even when the lateral rat has otherwise fully recovered from its initial failure to eat. Given the absorption smoothing effect of gastrointestinal processing, we assumed that there was no need to represent in the model the distinction between slow uninterested feeding and much interrupted feeding.

With a net feeding rate as low as about one-tenth of normal, the model never stopped eating during the night and hardly ate at all by day. This has a qualitative similarity to the recovered lateral rat. At less severely reduced feeding rates, the meal sizes and intervals between meal starts were more normal, although of course meals took much longer and intermeal intervals were reduced.

Once again, simulation with only one component changed is not a fair test of the fully developed model's power to explain a real syndrome. Use of a normal lipogenesis–lipolysis rhythm was obviously likely to be incorrect. Later there appeared good reason to simulate the recovered lateral hypothalamic rat as also suffering from an increased metabolic rate (Keesey, 1976) and from a slowed stomach (Booth, 1976; notwithstanding the results of Ralph and Sawchenko, 1975), with liquid diet, which can be misleading.

(iv) Food intake after food deprivation. A rat deprived of food for a period such as 6–24 h eats a larger than average meal when access to food is restored, and returns to take a second meal sooner than a freely fed rat would do on average. An adjustment in the lipogenesis–lipolysis input to the model was sufficient to stimulate these effects: if a meal started at the fastest observed level of lipolysis (10 cal/min) and this was changed over about half an hour to the highest level of lipogenesis and maintained at that level (35 cal/min), then a larger meal (4·0 g) and shorter meal-to-meal interval (116 min) than the *ad libitum* average was predicted (Booth and Toates, 1974b; Booth *et al.*, 1976), real rats taking 4·0 g followed by 110 min (Le Magnen and Tallon, 1968).

However, this simulation mainly served to sensitize us to the need for further additions to the model. If switches from lipolysis to lipogenesis around meals were to be represented, they should also be included in the simulation of freely fed rats. Also, rats which are repeatedly deprived according to a schedule show a steady increase in size of the first meal when access is restored (Le Magnen and Tallon, 1968). Deprivation schedules augment lipogenic capacity (Cohn and Joseph, 1960), but even this further adjustment of the fat synthesis component of the simple model (Fig. 8) would not produce realistic predictions: rats

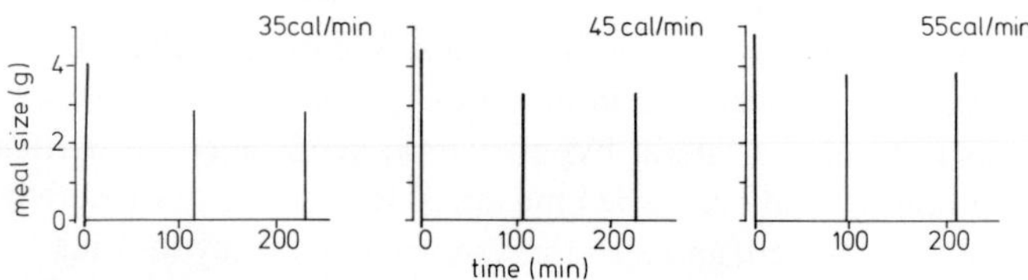

Fig. 8. Simulations of the meal pattern following food deprivation. Lipoflow was taken to be 10 cal/min of lipolysis at the start of the meal in all cases, but to rise shortly after the meal to lipogenic asymptote of the value indicated in each case. Greater lipogenesis causes larger meals, but the effect on the first meal is very modest compared with the 6–10 g meals typical on restoring food to a rat which has been adapted to the deprivation schedule.

adapted to deprivation schedules take a first meal of 6–10g. If the model was along the right lines at all, a major component was missing—such as perhaps learned behaviour as well as adapted physiology (Section IV A).

(v) Insulin-induced eating. The increase in food intake elicited in the rat by injection of a large dose of insulin (Booth and Brookover, 1968; Steffens, 1969a) is generally attributed to a failure to support glucose metabolism (cytoglucopoenia) in the brain during insulin-induced hypoglycaemia. However, as Le Magnen and Devos (1970) and Le Magnen *et al.*, (1973) emphasized, the possible contribution of the large lipogenic effect of the insulin injection must be considered. This is part of the cause of the hypoglycaemia, of course, and so this consideration may prove only to treat the problem of insulin-induced eating at another level of analysis—total energy distribution rather than purely glucose distribution. Nevertheless, such an analysis of the phenomenon brought it within the range of the Mark 1 model: set at a temporary high level of lipogenesis, it could make a prediction as to the effect of insulin injection on feeding. This simulation was qualitatively identical to simulating the dynamic phase of the VMH syndrome as in (ii) above. Overeating was predicted in the light phase but not in the dark phase (Fig. 7B)—unless the already strong night-time lipogenesis was supposed to be further intensified. In fact we had just obtained data, later published by Booth and Campbell (1975) showing that insulin does induce additional food intake at night in the rat, although the effect is more modest than by day. This finding was not consistent with a view that insulin induces feeding by reversing net lipolysis to net lipogenesis, but it was accommodated by an interpretation that insulin adds a lipogenic tendency to pre-existing net lipolysis or lipogenesis, except on occasions when lipogenesis is already maximal as it sometimes probably will be at night in the freely fed rat.

Quantitative simulation of the lipogenic effect of insulin to predict its effect on food intake had to await realistic modelling of normal periprandial lipogenesis by day and night, just as with deprivation effects. If increased lipogenesis did prove to explain insulin-elicited eating, this would support the view that the phenomenon can be regarded as an unphysiological acceleration of postprandial nutrient processing (Booth and Pain, 1971), while satiety-augmenting effects of smaller doses better represent the physiological role of insulin in feeding (Lovett and Booth, 1970; Booth and Jarman, 1975).

(vi) Variation in heat loss. A simulation of control of feeding by net energy flow to a satiety/hunger receptor system readily accommodates semi-quantitative predictions of the effects of increased loss of energy by the demands of exercise or of temperature maintenance in the face of reduced environmental temperature, or conversely a reduced cost of thermoregulation when the environmental temperature is raised to a modest extent.

For example, we calculated the effect of subtracting a constant drain of 5 cal/min in the Mark 1 model, or adding a constant economy of 5 cal/min (Table II).

Table II
Feeding model Mark 1: percentage changes in food intake on change in energy losses

	Change in metabolic rate	
	Up by 5 cal/min[a]	Down by 5 cal/min[b]
Amount eaten in light	+18%	−33%
Amount eaten in dark	+7%	−10%
24-h intake	+11%	−18%

[a]Cf. moderate exercise or cooling.
[b]Cf. warmer environment.

The purely behavioural effect of subtraction by heat loss is of course identical to subtraction by increased lipogenesis, as with insulin injection. "Cooling" or "exercise" increased intake substantially, "warming" decreased it. In reality, the behavioural picture is complicated by varying time courses of such changes in food intake. Effects not well enough understood to be readily incorporated in a model include the transient hyporexia following vigorous exercise (Baile *et al.*, 1971), the stress of rapid large change in external temperature, and the energy costs of different ways of keeping cool in very warm environments.

Again, the most important effect of running these variations on Mark 1 was to focus our attention on a missing component—a general representation for heat loss. This was incorporated in subsequent marks (Section III. C.2a).

(vii) Diabetes mellitus. In chronic diabetes, large amounts of energy are lost as sugar and other substrates in the urine. Nevertheless, there are substantial amounts of energy circulating to the tissues as glucose, amino acids and ketone bodies. Booth (1972b, c) provided evidence that the large food intake generally seen in chronically diabetic rats was attributable to a satiety deficit—the rats did not respond to the postabsorptive action of glucose loads, and they showed an abnormally low proportion of longer time intervals between meals. The reduced meal sizes seen by Booth (1972c) are not typical of experimental diabetes mellitus (Panksepp, 1973; De Castro and Balagura, 1975), and after that report was published the food pellets were found to have been formulated using industrial spirits and to be aversively bitter. The diabetogenic drug was streptozotocin rather than alloxan, whose destruction of pancreatic beta cells is more extensive while its specificity is less; the rats were also eating considerably more than De Castro and Balagura (1975) report: so the ketoacidosis they invoke is less likely to have reduced meal sizes than the poor acceptability of the diet, especially given the slowing of feeding rate which occurs in any case in diabetes (Booth, 1972c; De Castro and Balagura, 1975). The satiety deficit interpretation is not dependent on any correlation between meal size and interval to the next meal; indeed Booth (1972c) reported the loss of the modest correlation which appeared before injection.

Large meals and relatively reduced intervals between meals were indeed predicted by a simulation of the diabetic satiety deficit as a failure of absorbed energy to have its full effect plus a failure ever to deposit fat—indeed a continual mobilization of fat as the scrawniness of chronic experimental diabetes develops (Table III). However, the meal sizes were impossibly large—30 g of food (with a

Table III
Model Mark 2 and 2D: feeding in a diabetes-like state

	Total 24-h intake (g)	Number of meals	
		Light	Dark
Without distension	90	1	2
With distension	63	2	4

Effective energy flow from gut = 0·3 of actual flow. Lipolysis = 10 cal/min (constant). Cited by Toates and Booth (1974) and Booth and Toates (1974b).

similar volume of fluid) would literally burst the rat's stomach if it actually went in. This seemed an obvious context in which to invoke the interpretation of gastric and/or intestinal distension as a safety mechanism, high in threshold and not normally operative. We decided to add a loop which represented an inhibition of feeding when gut contents became very large in volume. Russek (1971) had suggested that distension elicits a reflex breakdown of liver glycogen via sympathetic innervation, in which case the mechanical stimulus was indirectly producing an energy flow at the liver. Even if this was not the case, it was computationally convenient to represent the inhibitory effect of distension as an energy flow, if only "virtual" not real.

Unfortunately, we could find no experiments in which gastric (or intestinal) volume had been measured while an inhibitory effect on feeding behaviour was measured in the absence of possible postabsorptive consequences of the gut manipulations. The simplest procedure we could think of was to take Paintal's (1954) neatly linear relation between larger values of stomach volumes and firing in vagus nerve afferents in the cat and assume that the vagal firing was in direct proportion to the satiety effect. We divided the volumes by ten to scale down the cat to the size of a rat. We assumed that the prevention of feeding by gastric distension acting alone would arise near the physical limit, i.e. around 40 ml. This gave the distension satiety function of Fig. 9. We believe that the direct satiating effect of distension is very small except under conditions of large meals. Also the data base is behaviourally inadequate and the physiological mechanisms remain indeterminate, and so the distension loop rather spoils the philosophy of the rest of the model. Therefore we omit distension, except when specifically mentioned. Another way of rationalizing this strategy is to profess the suspicion that the volume threshold is considerably higher than even the 5 ml in the model loop of Fig. 9. An increase in slope to compensate for a higher threshold would produce broadly similar predictions in many circumstances.

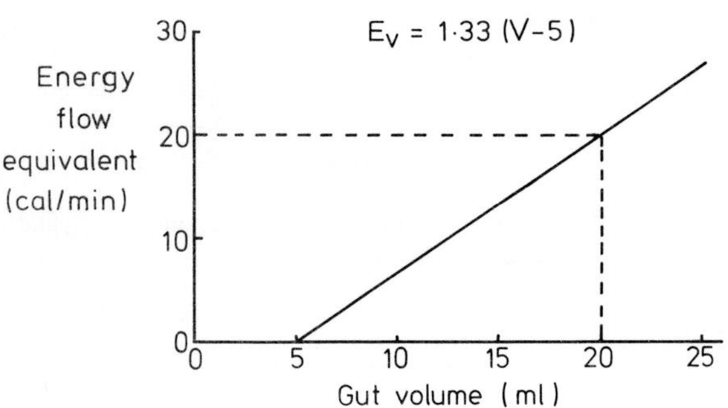

Fig. 9. A satiating influence of gut distension at high threshold. Distension-induced satiety is represented in the calculations as equivalent to a real flow of energy to the hunger/satiety receptor system.

Table III shows predicted meal sizes became more than moderate when the distension loop of Fig. 9 was incorporated in this primitive model of diabetes. A less drastic attenuation of the satiating effect of absorption, plus an adjustment in the energy loss component added in the next Section, would produce still more realistic meal sizes.

(viii) Dehydration anorexia. Toates began to relate the Toates–Oatley simulation of thirst physiology to the hunger model, by representing any water deficit calculated in the drinking model as an inhibitory influence on feeding—for convenience as "virtual energy" like the representation of distension satiety anorexia. This model marriage, and its children, are presented by Toates in Chapter 14.

2. *Circadian Metabolic Rate Rhythm*

(a) *Lumped estimate of energy consumption in non-receptor tissue.*

(i) Short term metabolic rate. Heat loss is a very large flow of energy which has to be supplied by the animal from absorption, fat mobilization, and sometimes other endogenous energy supplies. However, the loss is relatively constant and so it was not represented in the Mark 1 model. Nevertheless, even as background diversion of energy from the satiety/hunger receptor system, it could not be ignored entirely, because circadian variation was clearly observable in the data from Le Magnen's laboratory. The cause of this variation bears further analysis—and receives some later in the chapter. But at this stage we wanted to make use of the metabolic rate data since they were available from Le Magnen's respiratory exchange data exactly in parallel to the lipogenesis–lipolysis estimates. Inclusion of metabolic rate, i.e. heat output, would also enable calculation of the model's energy balance, by difference from energy input as food. Le Magnen's lipogenesis–lipolysis cycle gave a small cumulative fat gain over 24 h. The cumulative difference in feeding rate and metabolic rate gave a total energy gain, and the difference between total gain and fat gain was an estimate of non-fat energy gain, which approximates to lean body mass growth.

Le Magnen's 2-h average metabolic rate estimates around the clock were therefore subtracted from the sum of absorption and lipolysis (Fig. 5). Strictly logically, we should probably take 99% or some large fraction of metabolic rate, which is heat flow to the environment, to represent energy lost by all tissues except the receptor cell itself—if the assumption is correct that the system looks at its energy input and not its net energy supply. However, we assume that this correction, if appropriate at all, would be negligibly small.

(ii) Threshold values. The original hunger and satiety thresholds were estimates of absorption rates at which feeding was begun and suppressed, against a hitherto unspecified background of lipogenesis–lipolysis and heat loss. When a background metabolic rate of about 35–40 cal/min and a modest few cal/min of lipogenesis were subtracted from the Mark 1 threshold values of 18 and 60 cal/min, the hunger and satiety threshold values became about equal and opposite in sign, around −20 cal/min and +20 cal/min respectively. The infusion data and the gut contents data on which the absorption threshold estimates were based had margins of error of at least five cal/min either way. Furthermore, the estimates of metabolic rate came from another laboratory, different in strain of rat, type of chow and the housing conditions for the experiments. So the data base had a degree of approximation which permitted modest indulgence of predilections for symmetry and for nicely rounded numbers. There was also the general theoretical preconception that organisms like rats might build their feeding control around the detection of decline in energy supply and of incipient excess in energy supply. Such an organism need have only one type of detector system, namely one that is inactive when its energy supply is in a null range, but triggers feeding when the supply gets noticeably low and stops it once supply becomes rapid again. Such a detector could well have thresholds which were symmetrical around a net zero flow of energy into the type of tissue in which it is contained.

The particular threshold values chosen do of course have a substantial effect on details of meal size and intermeal interval (Table IV). However, a few cal/min in either direction leaves the meal size predictions within the range of means reported from different laboratories. There is little effect on total food intake or cumulative increase in body energy contents so long as the threshold values are varied symmetrically around zero. However, daily intakes and energy increments are sensitive to changes to threshold values which are asymmetic around zero (Table IV, bottom half).

Table IV
Model Mark 2: Effects of various hunger and satiety threshold values

Thresholds (cal/min)		Amount eaten (g)		Approx. meal size (g)	Number of meals		24-h energy increment (cal)
On	Off	Light	Dark		Light	Dark	
−20	20	7·5	16·3	2·4	3	7	4500
−15	15	7·7	15·3	1·7	4	9	4000
−25	25	7·0	17·1	2·9	2	6	6500
−30	15	4·5	14·6	2·0	2	7	−8360
0	40	12·2	22·6	3·0	3	7	34 000
0	25	11·7	19·7	1·8	5	11	30 000
−15	10	7·2	15·2	1·5	5	11	1280

Cited by Booth and Toates (1974b) and Booth *et al.* (1976).

Threshold values are less adequately specified by experimental data than are many other components of the model. On the basis of the above considerations we decided (until such time as better data were available on energy flows at the start and end of meals) to use threshold values approximately symmetrical around zero net flow of energy to the non-lipid components of parenteral mass, and in the region of 20 cal/min or slightly less. These values were compatible with the fragmentary data directly available. They were also compatible with data indirectly, in that they kept reasonably realistic the predictions from a whole model in which the other components were fairly tightly data-determined.

(b) *Feeding model: Mark 2.* The addition of metabolic rate and the energy accumulation calculations, with the distension loop if desired (Mark 2D), yielded a version of the model which was presented at the Jerusalem and Los Angeles hunger conferences near the end of 1974 (Booth and Toates, 1974c; Booth *et al.*, 1976). As well as collaborating in the incorporation of literature data into the model, Toates had carried out all the computations cited above while he was in Odense. He was then interrupted by the turmoil of a move in the summer of 1974 and I had the help of Steve Platt to write a program for the Mark 2 version of the model to run in Birmingham. Fig. 10 gives a block diagram of Mark 2D, with the key equations from the computer program to which it corresponds.

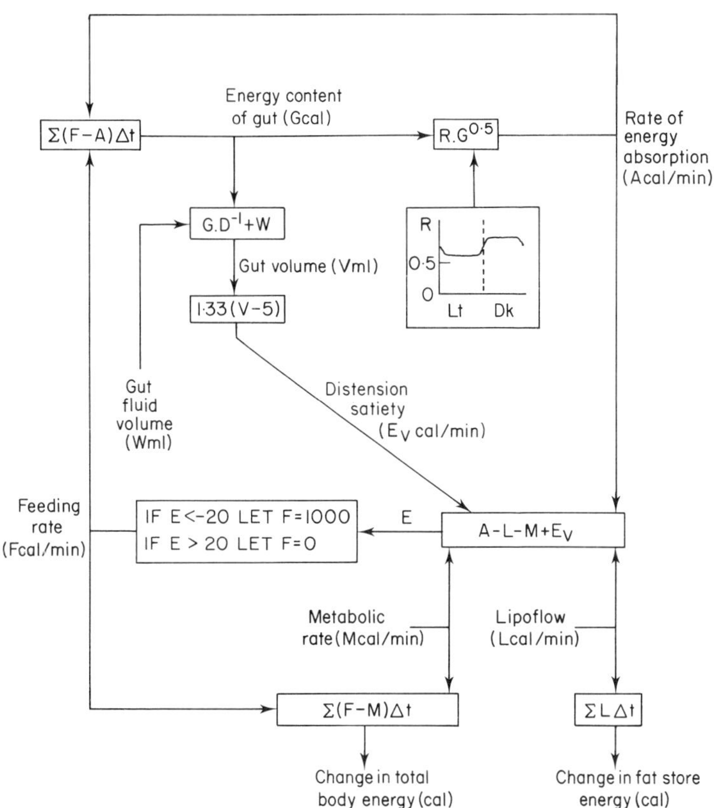

Fig. 10. Feeding control model, Mark 2D. E is the net rate of energy supply (cal/min) to non-lipid parenteral tissues which contain the hunger/satiety receptor system; other symbols are defined in the diagram. $\Sigma \times \Delta t$ is an approximation to integration carried out by successive additon at short intervals of simulated time.

(c) *Derivation of metabolic rate from other data.* If one is able to specify the environmental temperature, the rat's body weight, the amount of exercise it is taking, and the heat lost by processing its diet, it is possible to estimate metabolic rate from known empirical equations (Wunder, 1975). At the time of writing, we do not go all the way down this path, even with the Mark 3 simulations, because useable activity data are not generally available. It is qualitatively clear, however, that rats are much more active in the dark than they are in the light, relatively independently of feeding schedule and type of caging (Norton *et al.*, 1975). This factor probably dominates the increase in metabolic rate by night. Faster processing of food and hence an average higher thermic effect ("specific dynamic action") is a relatively minor contribution. In line with Le Magnen's data, we generally add an activity increment of about five cal/min to the metabolic rate at night over the daytime rate.

3. *Absorption-contingent Metabolic Variations*

The current rate of absorption not only should determine the component of metabolic rate attributable to the thermic effect of food processing, it should also be a major determinant of the current rate of lipogenesis. Indeed, given a particular individual in a particular state of endocrine adaptation, the secretion of hormones affecting fat deposition and mobilization and also increase in lean mass will generally be determined by the current absorption of glucose, amino acids and fatty acids. Even though attention to the insulin secretory response alone, plus perhaps hormone secretion during sleep, might suffice, I had until recently assumed that the feeding model would have to be plunged into details of enzyme and hormone dynamics (calculations which after all are well established for simulation of blood glucose control). Indeed we are currently engaged on biochemical estimation of major substrate flows in the rat *in vivo*. However, noting Ackerman *et al.*'s (1965) experience of parameter lumpings, during 1975 I explored the viability of modelling with all the endocrine and substrate control of fat synthesis and mobilization lumped into two appallingly simple linear functions of current energy supply. The constraints on the parameter values in such equations prove to be fairly strict. They have to do more than merely predict a realistic feeding pattern. They will play a large part in determining growth and fattening, although we have so far attended to this consideration more in the human model than in the rat model (see Chapter 12). Most directly of all, they have to predict the 2-h average respiratory exchanges measured in Le Magnen's laboratory when the model is simulating rats of the type he used.

I chose the variables on which to base lipogenesis and lipolysis equations on the general view that the deposition and mobilization of fat depends on the current supply of energy substrates which varies according to absorption but is presumably set against the background of energy consumption. So the rate of absorption less metabolic rate was chosen as the variable to which net lipogenesis or net lipolysis was proportional. I have tried using absorption rate alone, or absorption rate minus one constant for lipogenesis and another constant for lipolysis, but there may be less rather than more realism introduced into the predictions from such simulations, and the theoretical basis for such variables seems more arbitrary. It might be still more rational to determine lipogenesis or lipolysis by the net energy flow which also affects satiety/hunger, i.e. subtract current lipogenesis or add current lipolysis as well as subtracting metabolic rate from absorption rate to estimate pressure for lipogenesis or demand for lipolysis. After an adjustment of the proportionality factors, the results would be almost identical.

Lipolysis cannot be over about 10 cal/min in an energy flow model of hunger with symmetrical threshold values, or the prediction will be no eating by day or even no eating ever. The proportionality constant for lipolysis as absorption falls below metabolic rate was therefore set at one-quarter, giving 7–8 cal/min at zero absorption. Much of the excess of absorption over consumption is presumably deposited in fat, that is, net lipogenesis involves a larger proportionality constant (Fig. 11). A simulation with the proportion set at three-quarters closely

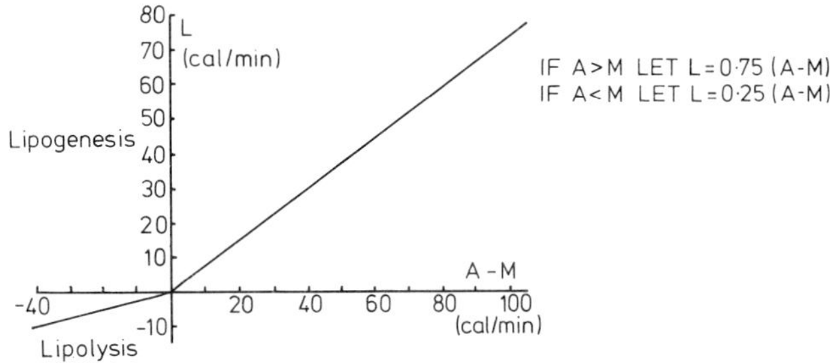

Fig. 11. Lipoflow functions in feeding model Mark 3, normal rat *ad libitum*. Lipogenesis is proportional to the excess of absorption over metabolic rate, taking three-quarters of the excess. Lipolysis is modelled to occur when absorption is less than metabolic rate, in proportion to the deficit, but not exceeding 10 cal/min even when absorption drops to zero, giving a deficit of 30–40 cal/min.

mimicked Le Magnen's lipogenesis estimates (Fig. 12). With a "basal" metabolic rate of 27 cal/min, to which 5 cal/min of activity expenditure is added in the dark, the generally accepted heat loss of 10% of the food energy produces a series of 2-h average metabolic rate predictions which also match Le Magnen's data tolerably well (Fig. 12).

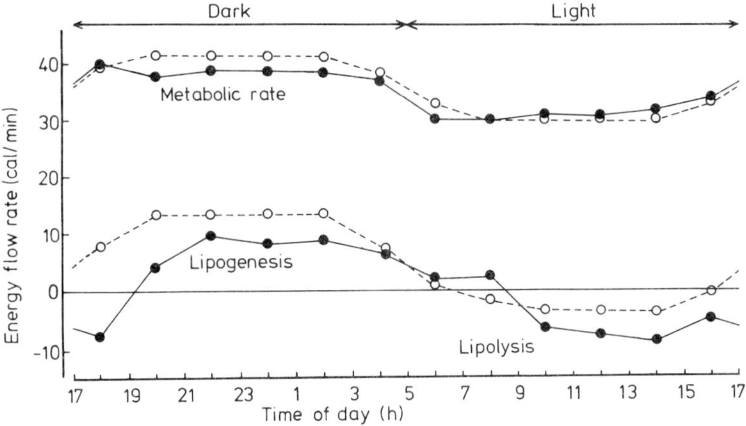

Fig. 12. Observed and simulated metabolic parameters in intact rats fed *ad libitum*, from Le Magnen and Devos (1970) and Mark 3 calculations.

These simulation results suggest that the circadian rhythm of lipogenesis and lipolysis is entirely secondary, and one does not have to seek a clock controlling the pancreas, although one may exist within the limits left by the parameter estimations for the modelling. The circadian rhythm of gastric clearance rate is a major determinant by its direct effect on absorption rate for a given amount in the stomach. The gastric rate function variation and the circadian motor activity rhythm also contribute indirectly to the lipogenesis–lipolysis rhythm, via their effects on the size of meals (Section V).

IV. Improved Model of Satiety

A. *Integration of Two Aspects of the Theory of Satiety*

The predictive success of the Mark 1 and 2 models Toates and I had developed was something of an embarrassment to my general theoretical stance on feeding control. While it was very encouraging to find the physiological hypothesis that energy flow determined feeding did work well in a physiological control model, I also believed that learning was very important in the control of feeding. Indeed, so had many other people for a long time, but in addition a considerable number of recent results had directly demonstrated major contributions to normal food intake both from the conditioning of aversions or preferences (Simson and Booth, 1973; Booth *et al.,* 1974) and from the conditioning of behaviour at the end of meals which was independent of the conditioning of choice or of rate of eating at the start of meals (Booth, 1972e; Booth and Davis, 1973). Evidence for this latter—acquired desatiating properties of arbitrary orosensory cues—had also been seen by Davis and Campbell (1973) and since by Kraly and Carty (1976) in rats in which food was removed from the stomach as fast as it entered by feeding. The acquired orosensory desatiating effect has a large influence on the size of a meal, doubling or even tripling it, and could be learned or relearned (when aversions did not interfere) after the experience of one or at most a few meals (Booth, 1972e; Davis and Campbell, 1973). How could a model predict feeding behaviour directly from current energy flow without reference to the oral properties of the food when experimental results showed such a strong influence of acquired oral control?

The way to a reconciliation is not readily seen unless an important point is noticed. Conditioned satiation or desatiation was a powerful effect in the context of relatively normal feeding, when other satiating influences were likely also to be present. For example, some postabsorptive satiation remained from the previous meal because the rats were only moderately deprived (Booth, 1972e; Booth and Davis, 1973), or possibly some postabsorptive satiation was created by the sham meal because a small fraction escaped the withdrawal procedures of Davis and Campbell (1973) or Kraly and Carty (1976). When the absence of all other satiating influences is ensured by extended prior deprivation and efficient drainage of food from the stomach as it enters, there is at most a modest contribution from orosensory satiation which is extinguished by the very first sham feeding experience (Smith and Gibbs, 1976). One thing systems analysis teaches us is the foolishness of trying to understand the role of one mechanism in a system by running experiments designed to remove all other mechanisms: some, perhaps most, normally operative mechanisms must remain but their operation dissociated from the mechanism of interest by carefully designed and monitored manipulations. Specifically here, acquired oral satiation acts against the background of some degree of direct satiation. Indeed direct satiation effects may be presumed to work against a background of acquired orosensory satiation when they are imposed on free intake of a familiar diet (Booth, 1972a). An entirely successful demonstration of one category of effect is simply irrelevant to the question whether the other effect is also operative in that situation. Satiety may be assumed to be simultaneously learned and at least part postintestinal.

Now, by the end of 1974, the seriousness of an oversimplification in the gut component of Marks 1 and 2 was beginning to bear in on me. For all the speed with which absorption began, it was certainly not true that the current contents of the stomach were instantaneously affected by passage of food into the mouth and instantaneously reflected in the flow of energy into tissues. Even if oscillations arising from the delays in the duodenal–gastric control of gastric emptying were ignored, there was always present a delay between energy leaving the stomach and it entering the liver or the brain. The data on time of onset of rises in tissue radioactivity following the start of ingestion of radioactive starch showed that the lag for digestion, absorptive and circulation to tissue could be much less than 5 min in deprived rats (Pilcher *et al.,* 1974). However, such an experiment has yet to be reported in freely feeding rats, whose digestion and absorption dynamics might conceivably be slower; food in stomach certainly makes the gastric emptying of a saline load slower (Poulakos and Kent, 1973).

A delay of only two or three minutes between passage of energy into the duodenum and its arrival at the energy receptor system would have serious consequences for the feeding predictions in the Mark 2, exactly in the way that the delay in absorption has classically been the theoretical stumbling block over which glucostatic and similar hypotheses have tripped when pursued as far as to explain satiety. If absorption alone has to switch off feeding, meals seem certain to have to last a much longer time, and therefore (unless intake rate is somehow reduced) meals become larger in energy content. Within the Mark 2 model, feeding at a rate of 0·3 g/min, a simple delay of 3 min adds about 1 g to the predicted size of the meal, and so on in proportion. Total intake is little affected, as the predicted intermeal intervals lengthen approximately in compensation, but the point is that the real system has found a way of taking in that total in a fashion which yields smaller meals.

One possibility should now appear obvious: by summation or some other interaction, orosensory satiation on top of absorptive partial satiation provides the full intensity of satiety sufficient to stop feeding.

Nothing in a principle of simple summation requires that the orosensory satiation be acquired. However, such a system with experimentially independent oral satiety would have similar functional disadvantages to the substitution of a positive feedback, single-threshold system for a double-threshold system (discussed in Section II.B.1): meal sizes would be strongly subject to the vicissitudes of interaction between the temporal characteristics of the innate oral satiety system and variation in the timing of partial satiation due to variations in diet, feeding circumstances and so on. Sensory satiety, apparently some form of habituation, certainly exists in the rat for any familiar food stimulus, and the dysregulatory nature of such a mechanism is illustrated by the way that repeated dishabituation by change of food stimulus can cause marked overeating (reviewed in Booth, 1976).

Yet even if for such reasons one considers that useful control of meal size must depend on orosensory satiating influences acquired by experience of the effects of a food, there are still theoretical problems with simple addition of acquired and absorptive influences. By what behavioural process does a food stimulus suppress the intake of food? Conditioned satiety in the rat has usually been demonstrated with the food stimulus present from the start of the meal. Indeed it is hard to detect a satiating after-effect on removal of the stimulus (Booth and Davis, 1973, experiment 2; Holman, 1973). Does some sort of sensory inhibition accumulate as feeding proceeds? It is difficult to find any precedent for such a combination of habituation-like processes and associative control of performance. Furthermore, the oral stimulus which at the end of the meal is critical to inhibit (or, in the desatiation case, facilitate) feeding behaviour is the same stimulus that at the start of a meal is often facilitating (inhibiting in the converse case) food intake (experiments 2 and 3 of Booth, 1972e; experiments 1 and 2 of Booth and Davis, 1973). The behavioural effect could conceivably depend on the stage in the meal because of some timing process, but again this would not be well regulated, even if a plausible clock or counter could be found in the rat's behavioural organization. Alternatively, the direction of effect could depend on the internal stimuli which change as ingestion proceeds. That is, a stimulus which has conditioned attraction when the rat is hungry could have conditioned aversiveness when the rat is partly satiated (or vice versa on a conditioned desatiating diet). To put it another way, the mechanism is not *summation* of response tendencies to separate stumuli, but the generation of a response tendency by a *particular combination* of oral and postingestional stimuli which has been conditioned by the postingestional stimuli that eventually follow as digestion progresses.

A simple conception of such a combinatory mechanism would be that the orosensory stimulus comes to select a particular (low) intensity of direct satiety as sufficient to stop feeding. The associative mechanism which establishes this selection would be some aspect of the postabsorptive consequences of the meal which contained that oral stimulus—the duration of satiety or its intensity. A formulation more precisely in terms of learning theory is discussed elsewhere (Booth, 1977; also Chapter 12, Section IV A).

B. *Feeding Model: Mark 3*

1. *Improvements on Mark 2*

Further to the changes I made in the calculation of lipogenesis and lipolysis (mentioned in Section III.C.3.) Mark 3 was created by adding three components to Mark 2: gut lag, conditioned satiety, and a feedback from fat store—all first programmed by Platt. We also altered the threshold variability routines.

(a) *Gut lag.* Toates and I had experienced the difficulties of even the crudest attempt to model the dynamics of digestion and intestinal absorption (Section II). At present the postulate of a simple delay between gastric clearance and energy flow detection may be realistic enough for many situations. With the conditioned satiety algorithm described next, the duration of the delay is not critical to the predictions by the model over a wide range of delay times. We commonly use what I believe to be a realistic value, say four minutes. The program empties the stomach according to the clearance function of Marks 1 and 2, but calculates the postabsorptive effects of a particular gastric emptying rate value with the prespecified delay after that rate occurred.

(b) *Conditioned satiety.* The rate of energy flow to the satiety/hunger receptor system which is sufficient to stop a particular meal is preselected at the start of the meal according to the record of the peak energy flow following the last meal with the same sensory characteristics. The "target" peak of energy flow remains 20 cal/min, the Mark 2 satiety threshold. If the last meal having the same sensory characteristics produced a peak energy flow over 20 cal/min, then the energy flow value at which feeding is stopped is lowered; if the last peak undershot target, the effective threshold is raised. For simplicity, the effective threshold is changed by the amount the target was misssed: the changes in energy flow rate following meals are sufficiently close to linear for such an equation generally to produce nearly all the conditioning or reconditioning of satiety after one meal, as the data indicate can indeed occur (experiment 2 extinction phase, Booth, 1972e). Lighting conditions are included among the sensory characteristics of a meal and so the effective satiety threshold settles to a value by day which differs from that by night because differences in clearance function and activity energy expenditure produce differing postprandial consequences of a given amount in the stomach. Mark 3 has no provision for choice between diets, but the effects of changes in diets between or even within meals could be simulated: the sensory qualities of the diet would then also determine satiety threshold. They could also be programmed to determine feeding rate.

(c) *Threshold variability.* The detection of low and high threshold levels of energy flow, and the retrieval of the acquired satiety threshold value from memory, are all exact in simulations where only mean values of meal parameters and body parameters are required. In the real organism all these values will be subject to perceptual variability, and we introduced this as an option in the model. Platt and I represented this variability by adjustable normalized ranges of random numbers around the determinate threshold, but the stochastic properties of energy flow make such a routine yield a very skewed distribution of thresholds used. Mather and I have substituted random walks of the threshold value to be used. The effective threshold goes up or down on each calculation cycle by, say, one cal/min. At the hitherto determinate threshold value, the probability of a shift up or down is equal. At the limit set for the walk in any one direction, it becomes certain that the shift will be towards the central tendency. Between these extremes, probability varies linearly.

(d) *Feedback from stored fat.* Neither increments in lean body mass (growth) nor increments in adipose body mass, or its ratio to lean body mass (adiposity), are rigidly determined in the rat. Indeed it has been argued elsewhere that even the notion of some preset reference value determining body weight or fat store size is more misleading than helpful (Booth *et al.,* 1976; Booth, 1976; Garrow, 1975; Peck, 1976; Toates, 1975). This is not to deny that the degree of long term stability on body energy content is remarkable compared with the amount of energy that passes through the body. It is rather to point out that the organism has well known types of mechanism which could be used to maintain this stability and are considerably simpler in physical organization that the engineer's simplest set point machine, e.g. a thermostat. These are the mechanisms of compensating energy flows between compartments of the body.

If the present theory is right in identifying the hunger signal as net flow of non-lipid energy and the satiety signal as anticipated equivalent net gain of non-lipid energy, then the meal pattern should (if allowed to run freely) rather tightly control the long term gain in non-lipid energy according to the pre-existing structure of the body—sizes of stomach, muscles, brain etc. Indeed, there is evidence that lean mass turnover and feeding are tightly coupled (Pullar and Webster, 1974; Garrow, 1975). Fat mass is more easily displaced. However, there is evidence that large excursions of fat mass do have an inhibitory effect on feeding. The phenomena are clearer with increases in fat induced by overfeeding enforced by gastric intubations, electrical brain stimulation or insulin injections—when the forcing is removed from the fattened rat, it eats little or nothing until fat mass returns to within a modest fraction over the original, and food intake still remains low until body composition is in the normal range. In the case of ventromedial hypothalamic obesity, the size of the fat store is in equilibrium with food intake: forced excursions below the postsurgical stable value on a particular diet are corrected by overeating, and excursions above that stable value are corrected by undereating (Kennedy, 1953). A system would show these properties if the bias was more towards delivering energy to inhibit feeding the larger were the fat stores, and more to depositing energy the smaller the fat stores (Cohn and Joseph, 1962). The main energy flows into and out of fat are known biochemically, although quantitative details are unsettled. Clearly these flows are strongly affected by hormones. A simple feedback mechanism would involve some hormone-independent or "basal" characteristic. Basal lipolysis may in fact increase with size of fat cell (Smith, 1970; York, 1975). The resultant bias on glycerol supply to other tissues, or on the widely varying supply of non-esterified fatty acids, would in the long run produce a cumulated compensatory adjustment in food intake. The speed and robustness of the compensation would depend on characteristics of this component of energy flow *in vivo* which have yet to be measured. A systems analytic viewpoint makes it clear that signal persistence is the secret of long term control, not high precision or large magnitude.

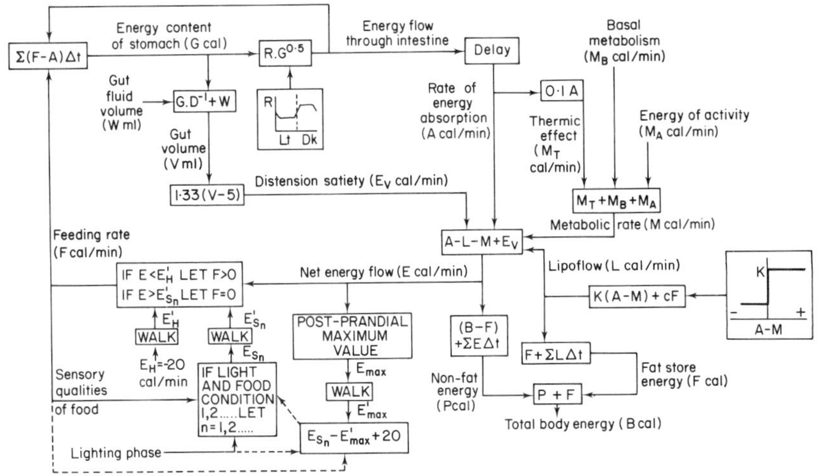

Fig. 13. Feeding model. Mark 3. The flow diagram defines the letter symbols used. "Walk" refers to the probabilized walk of hunger threshold, acquired satiety threshold and maximum energy flow recorded after a meal: these values shift around their mean values to represent the noise in the measurement of energy flow level by the hunger/satiety receptor system. Broken lines represent the retrieval of information from memory of the lighting conditions and sensory qualities of the food at the last feeding or of the acquired satiety value ($E_{S,n}$) which was established for the current lighting and foodstuff.

On these grounds, I wrote a fat feedback equation into Mark 3 which has no noticeable effect from one day to the next, as fat stores do not change that fast, but does ensure that an extra 30 or 50 g of adipose tissue on a 300–400 g rat almost completely inhibits feeding. The calculation simply adds one cal/min of lipolysis to the net energy flow to satiety for every 10 g of fat gained.

With these additional components incorporated, the Mark 3 version of the feeding model reached in 1975 can be represented diagrammatically as Fig. 13.

2. *Predictions from Mark 3 Modelling*

(a) *Freely fed intact rats*. Le Magnen and Devos (1970) and colleagues (1973) are the only ones as yet to report metabolic estimates from respiratory dat in conjunction with meal pattern statistics in the freely fed rat. The Mark 3 predictions of the lipogenesis–lipolysis and metabolic rate cycles were given in Fig. 12. The feeding pattern predicted by the same simulation is given in Table V. A rather different pattern of meal sizes and intervals was reported by Becker and Kissileff (1974); a modest adjustment in gut clearance constants produces predictions close to the meal pattern and weight gain they observed (Table VI). This would of course be unremarkable if the values of most parameters in the model had to be changed. On the other hand, it could hardly have been objectionable to do that, considering the great differences between measurement and treatment conditions in the two laboratories. In particular the Americans used liquid food.

Table V
Characteristics of intact Wistar rats from Le Magnen's laboratory

	Reported characteristics				
	1968	1970	1973M	1973F	Simulated
Total intake in dark (g)	13·0	17·3	13·8	12·6	12·8
Meal size in dark (g)	2·6	3·1	—	—	3·2
Total intake in light (g)	8·5	5·1	4·4	3·5	4·2
Meal size in light (g)	2·0	1·6	—	—	2·1
Daily weight gain (g)	—	—	1·95	—	2·0

Data taken from Le Magnen and Tallon (1968), Le Magnen and Devos (1970) and Le Magnen *et al.* (1973), males of Exp. 1 and females of Exp. 3. The simulation has gut clearance factors of 0·8 and 1·1 by day and night respectively, and a basal metabolic rate of 27·5 cal/min.

(b) *Rats with ventromedial hypothalamic lesions*. Mark 3 simulations of data from Becker and Kissileff (1974) are given in Table VI. The maintenance of lipogenesis during the day, and indeed the frequent meals, could only be

Table VI
Characteristics of female Wistar rats reported by Becker and Kissileff (1974)

	Pre-lesion ($n = 15$)		1–3 days after WMH lesions ($n = 7$)	
	Observed	Simulated	Observed	Simulated
Total intake in dark phase (g)	17·1	16·4	18·9	19·0
Average meal size in dark (g)	2·6	2·7	3·6	3·5
Total intake in light phase (g)	4·2	4·2	20·2	20·6
Average meal size in light (g)	2·1	2·1	3·8	4·2
Daily weight gain (p)	2·75	2·9	10·8	12

Simulations were based on a day gut factor of 0·8 changing to 1·25 after lesions and a night gut factor of 1·1 changing to 1·25. Basal metabolic rate was 27 cal/min throughout. The lipogenesis factor was raised from 0·75 to 0·85 after lesions.

simulated by including the assumption of a fast gastric clearance function in daylight. In fact, a somewhat faster clearance than normal by night as well seemed necessary to reach the total intake observed. However, changes in the gastric clearance function alone were not sufficient to produce realistic predictions of meal size by day (the conditioned satiety algorithm drove them very small by interaction with the gut lag). A good simulation was achieved by assuming that the lesion caused an increase in the proportionality constant of the lipogenesis equation, as in Mark 1 VMH lesion simulations (Section III.C.1.b.(ii)). The effect of this assumption was tested because hyperinsulinaemia is one of the best established physiological abnormalities in the ventromedial syndrome, and would be expected to augment lipogenesis. Of course the developing obesity also implies augmented lipogenesis (and/or reduced lipolysis). At present it is not possible to tell whether the hyperinsulinism is secondary to speeded absorption, and after some time adaptation of the pancreas to give a larger secretory response to a given absorption rate, or whether the changed pancreatic control is primary as some believe. Even if primary, an increased insulin response would still also require an abnormally fast gastric clearance constant to give the full VMH syndrome, according to variations I have run of this simulation, and the speeded gastric emptying and absorption would be mainly, though perhaps not exclusively (Gold, 1975), by day. More detailed data are needed on the physiological and feeding-pattern responses immediately after the VMH lesion. In particular, after surgery carried out with the stomach empty of food we need tests for hyperinsulinism or hyperinsulinaemic response to food cues before any food has been ingested.

(c) *Rats with lateral hypothalamic lesions.* The average feeding pattern of the classical recovered lateral rat may be a blurred composite of a complex and variable conjunction of abnormalities induced by such a diffuse lesion. The slowed feeding rate of the Mark 1 lateral simulation (Section III.C.1.b.(iii)) was combined with a slowed stomach clearance constant to give the simulation of Table VII. An increase in basal metabolic rate and the circadian pattern of energy expenditure would also be worth simulating.

Table VII
Preliminary simulation of recovered lateral hypothalamic rat

Total intake in dark phase	9·4g
Average meal size in dark	4·6g
Total intake in light phase	2·3g
Average meal size in light	4·6g
Daily weight gain	0g

This simulation was based on a feeding rate lowered to 0·1 g/min, and gut factors lowered to 0·6 at night and 0·4 by day. Metabolic rate was nor raised, not its circadian rhythm changed.

(d) *Rats on a deprivation schedule.* At least at some values of other parameters, simulations which include adaptive hyperlipogenesis show augmented meal sizes via the conditioned satiety mechanism. However, this effect does not seem nearly strong enough to produce 8-g meals. Probably the stomach clearance function also adapts to the deprivation schedule. Also the expectation of feeding after extended deprivation may produce such strong receptive relaxation of the stomach that neither postabsorptive satiety from pumped chyme not gastric or duodenal distension-induced distress are generated within the meal, even though when tone returns to the gastric musculature the stomach's large contents would cause very fast emptying and absorption and hence a very high rate of lipogenesis even without pancreatic or adipose adaptation. It remains to be seen whether some combination of such adaptations and learning mechanisms can account quantitatively for the large first meal following deprivation on a schedule. No other theory yet has.

(e) *Rats in the cold.* Since our first attempt to simulate the feeding of cooled rats with nothing more than a raised heat loss in a Mark 1 model (Section III.C.1.b.(vi)), Kraly and Blass (1976) have found evidence of increased gastric emptying within 1·5 h of rats being placed in the cold. Less of a liquid meal was recovered via a fistula from the stomach when rats which had been deprived at room temperature were transferred to 5°C than when they remained at room temperature. The square root rate constant (calculated from the meal size and the last recovery measurement) increased by 45%. They also observed an increase in intake rate in the cold by about 40%.

The first meal on presentation of the milk diet is particularly difficult to simulate as the adaptations to the 24-h deprivation cycle remain unspecified (subsection (d), above). Hence, a Mark 3 simulation was started at the end of the first meal, taking as input the observed somewhat larger first meal in the cold. Both the reduced meal sizes and also the proportionately even further reduced intermeal intervals are predicted. Slow eating and fast gastric clearance cause the small meals, and fast gastric clearance reduces the intermeal interval for a given meal size. The increased metabolic rate in the cold, estimated from Wunder's (1975) equations, tends to increase meal size but to reduce intermeal interval still further.

The increased metabolic expenditure to maintain body temperature will also keep animals which have been deprived immediately previously under the same conditions at a lower net energy flow to the satiety/hunger system, assuming that lipolysis does not completely counteract this effect. This greater deficit in energy flow below hunger threshold would presumably be reflected in more vigorous appetitive behaviour. Thus, although the parameter values for a computer simulation would be fairly arbitrary, such an extension of the model would predict the increased operant rate in the cold observed by Kraly and Blass (1976).

Kraly and Blass (1976) adduce a peripheral sensation of cold as the motivating stimulus. These simulations suggest that heat loss could be the sufficient stimulus, and it could trigger the gastric change too. These two accounts are quite compatible, although it is not clear whether one should say the sensation mediates the effects of heat loss or vice versa—or should reject the implicitly over-linear view of causation involved in such verbal formulations.

(f) *Other states.* Short light–dark cycles have been found to entrain the rat's activity, vigilance and sleep rhythm to a large extent, although a residual free-running circadian variation can still be seen (Borbely and Huston, 1974; Borbely, 1975). The simulation of such conditions is critically dependent on the time course of changes in the gastric clearance rate factor from one lighting phase to the other. Progressively stronger entrainment of feeding to light change could indeed reflect an adaptation which produces more rapid changes in clearance rate constant.

Changes in the palatability or accessibility of the diet will be represented in the present model as constraints on feeding rate. Without close physiological specifications of the adaptation and learning consequent to initial exposure, it would not be wise to attempt to simulate the observed feeding patterns. Booth (1972f) showed that the responses to changes in palatability and access duration involved several distinct mechanisms, in interaction with the energy density of the diet. Hopefully, the results of all the above modelling will educate others as they have me into doubting that mere behavioural observation of the effects of dietary manipulation is going to advance our understanding of the control mechanisms operative in intact rats or in experimental preparations of various sorts. Gastrointestinal, hormonal and systemic metablic processing must also be monitored while the rats are under maintenance conditions.

V. Conclusions

A. *There the Glove Lies*

This model of feeding is a steed fit for a good few more jousts yet. Give me the data on the rat's physiology and diet and I'll put the values into the model which will yield a prediction of the rat's feeding behaviour. Wrong predictions will interest me more than right ones—although a right prediction is more satisfying than a wrong one until the reason for the wrong prediction has been diagnosed!

The beast runs backwards too. If we have the details of a deviant feeding pattern, the model can be used to provide a qualitative or even quantitative analysis of possible causes—orosensory, gastrointestinal, hormonal-metabolic, satiety or hunger biases, associative operations.

The simulations just described impress one less with their accuracy than with their exposure of our ignorance of the relevant details of what is happening in the rat on a deprivation schedule or suffering from obesity, diabetes or any specific cerebral knife-cut, catecholamine depletion or whatever. Even if an experimenter is interested only in observing the conveniently large behavioural abnormalities resulting from unphysiological disruptions of the system, there is still no substitute for experimentally controlled physiological, biochemical and psychological analyses of the critical processes behind the behaviour. It is to be hoped that the model will draw attention to useful experimental designs.

A systems analysis that covers the phenomena of current and past interest is a *paradigm*—a structure within which to experiment, and unlikely to be refutable by any one single finding. Hopefully the present analysis is an approximation whose eventual dismissal will identify it as a special case or simplification, not as erroneous through and through. The particular Mark 3 model described in this chapter is of course only one family of simulations out of a potential tribe of mechanical embodiments of a theory of hunger, or of feeding in the rat in particular. If the variety of models becomes too great, it can be a serious problem to determine whether the models do have a family resemblance. At the moment, to my mind connection between the model and the theory is clear, but even that is not to claim that the model uniquely represents my theory. Indeed, I suspect that the model could be adjusted to be compatible with many of the physiological or psychological hypotheses put forward by other authors in this book. The question which can then be asked is whether one adjustment fits all the data on components and overall performance better than another adjustment.

B. *What have we Learnt?*

1. *Generalities*

One moral might be that we cannot afford to ignore the fine details in time or quantity of behavioural and physiological process. This, out of context is an almost useless aphorism, for the problem is choosing the significant detail our of the infinitie flux of collectable data. In context, however, there are specific pointers to what might be worth measuring in addition to daily food intakes and body weights.

Another abstract conclusion would be that simple principles which are already well established explain more than some of our more complicated theorizing seems to allow. Also the workability of the Mark 3 model has several general implications as to the status of the theorizing behind it.

(a) *Coherence.* I am sceptical of my ability to work our intuitively the implications of my physiological and learning process theory of hunger. I know from experience that I am too stupid to co-ordinate more than two or three definite hypotheses at once without sometimes committing logical fallacies. The attraction of mechanized synthesis of an explicitly analysed system is that it can release scientific understanding from the limited capacity of the individual human mind. There remains the need to keep a feel for the overall system, and to keep the management of model development tightly disciplined. Fast serial calculation can keep track of interactions too numerous to hold in mind at once, but it will mechanically follow up as many as you give it; so they must be kept to a minimum.

The computability of a model of a theoretical system establishes the absence of several incoherences that can afflict verbal or diagrammatic analysis.

(i) *Consistency.* Unnoticed self-contradiction can creep in, for example between the account of one phenomenon on one page and the account of another on the next. If the same computer program provides a simulation of both phenomena with only a change in input values, this sort of error does not exist.

(ii) *Explicitness.* As any programmer knows, it is all too easy to have a specification turn out to be ambiguous. Despite all the polemics in psychology about definition and operationalizability, hypotheses about feeding control are not often programmable without a lot more work to tie then down to useable procedures.

(iii) *Completeness.* The author and the reader can find a systematic verbal theory convincing, when in fact their intuition carries them over unnoticed gaps in the analysis. From the elemental loop onwards, our modelling was centred on the analysis of those consequences of feeding behaviour which seemed likely to have major effects on feeding behaviour. An experimentally or even metaphysically blinkered analysis of consequences or causes is hardly likely to be complete. On the other hand, a rough-and-ready outline analysis of likely major processes or their correlates can prove robust enough for a working model to survive the fires of detailed refinement.

(b) *Adequacy.* The model does not merely succeed in crunching numbers *ad libitum* without dying. In additon, all the numbers are about right. More precisely, the simulations generally can produce output values within the range of values observed in reality, from functions and parameter values in the components which are again within the range of empirical plausibility. That is, the model shows that the theory behind it is adequate to the available data, at least for phenomena which have been simulated to date.

One can bandy words for hours, even years, on the relevance of particular processes or the power of a systematic set of hypotheses. Program a version of the systematic hypotheses and show mechanically what follows. Mere argument can then be briefer, or at least more cogently directed.

(c) *Verisimilitude.* Adequacy does not imply truth. There might be theories incompatible with mine for which models could be constructed which were also adequate to the data. Let us hope that there will soon be another example of a quantitatively predictive model of feeding patterns which relies on components with independently empirically measurable characteristics. It is hardly likely that a critical experiment will decide between the models or the theories, but one paradigm should prove more productive than the other, sooner or later. Compare the evidence for, and performance of, rival programmed feeding systems and you are almost bound to have learned something about hunger.

2. *Specifics*

The present theory and the Mark 3 version of the computable model of it have particular aspects which relate to other workers' theories. Metabolic control of feeding is a notion which has been in the field for a very long time, and indeed in the form of Mayer's glucose utilization theory of satiety/hunger has dominated the field for more than 20 years. The present theory is unusual in combining metabolic control and learning, each being essential to the successful operation of the other. Lip service has also long been paid to the role of learning in feeding, although not generally by those interested in metabolic factors—Le Magnen being the main exception. However, his work of the 1950s and early 1960s and the last decade of work on conditioned aversions does not extend experimentally to conditioning effects of normal foods *ad libitum,* a gap I have been attempting to fill since the late 1960s (Booth, 1969; 1977), inspired by Le Magnen (1956) and mildly aggravated by Rozin and Kalat (1971) and Garcia *et al.* (1974).

I was also encouraged to stop looking for hunger signals, and to lose any major interest in interfering with blood composition and tissue metabolism, by

Le Magnen and Tallon's (1966, 1968) analyses of feeding patterns in the rat, and instead to look for satiating effects of normal food, particularly postabsorptive effects. We found that we could identify postabsorptive satiation and that it developed as energy was delivered to the tissues relatively independent of the chemical nature of the energy-yielding substrate, and so I formulated the view that it was the nutrient utilization rates in critical tissues which cause satiety (Booth, 1969, 1971, 1972a,d; Booth and Jarman, 1976). It seemed a very obvious step for a biochemist to take, to invoke the Krebs tricarboxylic acid cycle to explain the similarities in satiating power of starch, protein and fats. A translation of Ugolev and Kassil (1961) I saw two years later showed that it was obvious enough to have been anticipated by at least nine years. I have only recently noticed that Kleiber's (1936) hydraulic model of energy flow through the organism includes a link to "regulation of appetite", which takes the basic idea far further back, although Kleiber seems never to have exploited it, and the homeostatic theorists of the 1950s ignored it.

(a) *Integration of fat in feeding control.* Le Magnen himself had gone on to measure metabolic correlates of feeding (Le Magnen and Devos, 1970; Le Magnen *et al.,* 1973) over the same period. Also around this time, Panksepp (1971) was studying the equivalence of different foodstuffs in their effects on food intake. Nicolaïdis was also considering the potential signalling power of the rate and acceleration components of absorption transients after a meal, and formulated his ischymetric theory (Nicolaïdis, 1974). The ideas of these three workers and myself on the metabolic control of feeding seem identical in many respects. Detectable differences arise when we suggest how fat might be integrated into the system. My idea is that fatty acids delivered physiologically are additive with other substrates according to their energy yield, to the tissues such as the liver. The model is written in this way and includes both phasic and basal components of lipolysis in the energy flow account. Le Magnen has invoked the Randle cycle, however, in support of a concept of modulation of glucose metabolism by free fatty acids. This modulation would not, I think, necessarily be proportional to energy, but could give free fatty acids an effect stronger than their energy yield. The model shows that, on the assumptions it incorporates, the lipolysis flow rates Le Magnen has observed can account for the correlated feeding pattern as he has suggested but purely by an additive effect of the modest energy supply rate from fat mobilization. Furthermore, a purely subtractive effect of lipogenesis has a substantial influence postprandially at the parts of the day when the stomach empties quickly. Postulates of long term regulatory mechanisms provide a major difference between both Panksepp and Nicolaïdis and myself. The same integration of energy flow appears sufficient from the model simulations, if energy flow from adipose fat stores is modulated slightly by the size of those stores. Panksepp (1972) and Nicolaïdis (1974), on the other hand, posit a hypothalamic specialization which "witnesses to" or "parallels" to the peripheral adipose store by its own triglyceride content or fat metabolism (Panksepp and Pilcher, 1973; Nicolaïdis *et al.,* 1974). These postulates seem to me theoretically cumbersome, and experimentally it will be extremely difficult to demonstrate that a "fat head" actually mediates long term regulation, even if a cerebral correlate of normal variations in peripheral adiposity is in due course substantiated.

Hopefully the long term stability characteristics of Mark 3 simulations will dispel a number of misconceptions which appear to have confused some discussion on long term regulation in connection with control of feeding. The level or the direction of movement of fat mobilization, plasma non-esterified fatty acids, glycerol, or whatever, just before or just after meals is no basis for diagnosing "the role of free fatty acids in hunger". These transients may bear little relation to the instantaneous utilization of fatty acids by the relevant tissues, and the current utilization which is postulated to control feeding may in fact be averaged over a period of the order of the blood circulation time in the rat (about 1 min). Even the moment-to-moment relation between effective current utilization rate and propensity to feed may not reveal the most important role of fatty acids in feeding control. Current utilization could vary widely (no doubt usually compensated by co-ordinate variations in supply of other substrates) but the net effect averaged over a couple of meals or a day be nil. If however, in addition to influences tending to yield a null balance of free fatty acid supply, there is an influence tending to mobilize or deposit fat, the model predicts suppression or facilitation of feeding in consequence. If this bias is small, it will be difficult even to detect without very careful experimental design, let alone measure the mobilization bias or the food intake reduction. Yet the long term effect of the slightest bias will be for free fatty acids to reduce meal size, increase intermeal interval, or (generally) both, and to slim down the animal. Water flows over a waterfall with no perceptible effect on the rock, and a widely varying rates between dry and wet seasons; nonetheless, the retreat of the waterfall upstream over the decades is highly predictable while the bedrock is constant in composition. Even a simple dynamic equilibrium has an equilibrium point, partly set by "external" conditions, but well defended at its stable value without any mechanism for comparing the current value with an equilibrium value preset by some other mechanism. The mere interaction of the anatomically separated sets of chemical equilibria around the body provides even more strongly defended stabilities in the long term average values of many overall chacteristics of the system. Witness the stability or the mere three of four equilibria which constitute the Mark 3 model.

(b) *Parenteral receptors.* Russek's elegant model of feeding control (Russek, 1976; Chapter 10) is built round a hepatic glucoreceptor mechanism which he has long argued is the main control of satiety and hunger. Oomura (1976) and colleagues have been accumulating evidence that hypothalamic neurones have at least two types of sensitivity to glucose as well as responding to insulin and fatty acids. It remains to be seen whether these are rivals to an energy flow theory or forerunners of a reduction of the overall theory by biochemical fractionation. Any specialized cellular receptor mechanism will still need the metabolic "frontage" which our modelling has presupposed (Booth and Toates, 1974b), recently reviewed by Friedman and Stricker (1976). Physiological and biochemical modelling are succinctly reviewed by Garfinkel *et al.* (1974). Although none of our modelling descends yet to the molecular, enzymic or cellular level, the key physiological parameter, energy substrate flux, is biochemically meaningful—indeed, currently being measured in our laboratory. The biochemical reduction will come when the relevant processes have been located and their normal operations measured.

(c) *Brain processing*. This model says a lot about guts and blood and tissues, and a little about mouth and nose and eyes. A lateral hypothalamic appetite centre and a ventromedial hypothalamic satiety centre have not been mentioned. This is because I do not believe they exist(Booth, 1976). However, it would be perverse to take the model to give no major role for the brain in feeding control. Feeding rate, however little or much an expression of nutrient-conditioned preference/aversion, is undeniably a product of sensorimotor control. Conditioning itself requires a change in cerebral properties serving to permit retrieval of past contingencies. The gastric and hormonal functions that can vary in the model probably do so largely under central control.

A neurophysiological reduction of the implied central processes would include, for example, the substitution of feeding rate by transfer functions across sensory receptors and brainstem motor, orosensory and sensorimotor relays concerned with gnawing, chewing and swallowing. Activation of the receptor system by low energy flow would be transformed into net facilitatory influences perhaps relying heavily on catecholaminergic neurones, while activation by high energy flow might facilitate serotoninergic systems having a net inhibitory behavioural effect on sensorimotor and appetitive systems.

The lesson from the realism of a model replete with peripheral processing is that we should not hasten unduly fast to invoke central processing mechanisms to explain characteristics of behaviour which can be explained by well known changes in non-neural processes without any change in the input–output characteristics of the neural feeding system. The simpler, or at least the more explicit, our specification of what the brain has to do, the more chance neuroscience has to begin solving the problem that certainly is there to be solved—how neuronal systems interrelate to organize behaviour within specified external and internal environments.

REFERENCES

Ackerman, E., Gatewood, L. C., Rosevear, J. W. and Molnar, G. D. (1965). Model studies of blood-glucose regulation *Bull. math. Biophys.* **27**, Special issue, 21–37.

Baile, C. A., McLaughlin, C. L., Zinn, W. and Mayer, J. (1971). Exercise, lactate, hormones and gold thioglucose lesions of the hypothalamus of diabetic mice. *Am. J. Physiol.* **221**, 150–155.

Balagura, S. and Devenport, L. D. (1970). Feeding patterns of normal and ventromedial hypothalamic lesioned male and female rats. *J. comp. physiol. Psychol.* **71**, 357–364.

Becker, E. E. and Kissileff, H. R. (1974). Inhibitory controls of feeding by the ventromedial hypothalamus. *Am. J. Physiol.* **226**, 383–396.

Booth, D. A. (1969). Metabolic factors affecting feeding and their regulatory role. Paper presented to British Association for Advancement of Science, Exeter, September 1969.

Booth, D. A. (1971). The control of feeding in metabolic regulation. Paper presented at IVth International Conference of the Regulation of Food and Water Intake, Cambridge, August 1971.

Booth, D. A. (1972a). Satiety and behavioural caloric compensation follow intragastric glucose loads in the rat. *J. comp. physiol Psychol.* **78**, 412–432.

Booth, D. A. (1972b). Feeding inhibition by glucose loads, compared between normal and diabetic rats. *Physiol. Behav.* **8**, 801–805.

Booth, D. A. (1972c). Some characteristics of feeding during streptozotocin-induced diabetes in the rat *J. comp. physiol. Psychol.* **80**, 238–249.

Booth, D. A. (1972d). Postabsorptively induced suppression of appetite and the energostatic control of feeding. *Physiol. Behav.* **9**, 199–202.

Booth, D. A. (1972e). Conditioned satiety in the rat. *J. comp. physiol. Psychol.* **81**, 457–471.

Booth, D. A. (1972f). Caloric compensation in rats with continuous or intermittent access to food. *Physiol. Behav.* **8**, 891–899.

Booth, D. A. (1973). Feeding and the regulation of body energy. Paper presented at the International Symposium "Hunger and the Regulation of Body Energy", Ermenonville, France, October, 1973.

Booth, D. A. (1974). Food intake compensation for increase or decrease in the protein content of the diet. *Behav. Biol.* **12**, 31–40.

Booth, D. A. (1976). Approaches to feeding control. *In* "Appetite and Food Intake" (T. Silverstone, ed.). Dahlem Konferenzen, Berlin.

Booth, D. A. (1977). Satiety and appetite are conditioned reactions. *Psychosom. Med.,* **39**, 76–81.

Booth, D. A. (1978). Metabolism and the control of feeding in man and animals. *In* "Chemical Influences on Behaviour" (K. Brown and S. J. Cooper, eds). Academic Press, London and New York.

Booth, D. A. and Brookover, T. (1968). Hunger elicited in the rat by a single injection of crystalline bovine insulin. *Physiol. Behav.* **3**, 439–446.

Booth, D. A. and Campbell, C. S. (1975). Relation of fatty acids to feeding behaviour: effects of palmitic acid infusions, lighting variation and pent-4-enoate, insulin or propranolol injection. *Physiol. Behav.* **15**, 523–535.

Booth, D. A. and Davis, J. D. (1973). Gastrointestinal factors in the acquisition of oral sensory control of satiation. *Physiol. Behav.* **11**, 23–29.

Booth, D. A. and Jarman, S. P. (1975). Ontogeny and insulin-dependence of the satiation which follows carbohydrate absorption in the rat. *Behav. Biol.* **15**, 159–172.

Booth, D. A. and Jarman, S. P. (1976). Inhibition of food intake in the rat following complete absorption of glucose delivered into the stomach, intestine or liver. *J. Physiol., Lond.* **259**, 501–522.

Booth, D. A. and Pain, J. F. (1970). Effects of a single insulin injection on approaches to food and on the temporal pattern of feeding. *Psychon. Sci.* **21**, 17–19.

Booth, D. A. and Simson, P. C. (1974). The rejection of a diet which has been associated with a single administration of a histidine-free amino acid mixture. *Br. J. Nutr.* **31**, 285–296.

Booth, D. A. and Toates, F. M. (1974a) A computer model of hunger. Paper presented to the Experimental Psychology Society, Bristol, April, 1974.

Booth, D. A. and Toates, F. M. (1974b). A physiological control theory of food intake in the rat: Mark 1. *Bull. Psychon. Soc.* **3**, 442–444.

Booth, D. A. and Toates, F. M. (1974c). Control of food intake by energy supply. Paper presented at Vth International Conference on Physiology of Food and Fluid Intake, Jerusalem, October 1974.

Booth, D. A., Stoloff, R. and Nicholls, J. (1974). Dietary flavor acceptance in infant rats established by association with effects of nutrient composition. *Physiol Psychol.* **2**, 313–319.

Booth, D. A., Toates, F. M. and Platt, S. V. (1976). Control system for hunger and its implications in animals and man. *In* "Hunger: Basic Mechanisms and Clinical Implications" (D. Novin, W. Wyrwicka and G. A. Bray, eds), pp. 127–143. Raven Press, New York.

Borbely, A. A. (1975). Circadian rhythm of vigilance in rats: Modulation by short light–dark cycles. *Neurosci. Letters* **1**, 67–71.

Borbely, A. A. and Huston, J. P. (1974). Effects of two-hour light–dark cycles on feeding, drinking and motor activity of the rat. *Physol. Behav.* **13**, 795–802.

Campbell, C. S. and Davis, J. D. (1974a). Licking rate of rats is reduced by intraduodenal and intraportal glucose infusion. *Physiol. Behav.* **12**, 357–365.

Campbell, C. S. and Davis, J. D. (1974b). Peripheral control of food intake: interaction between test diet and postingestive chemoreception. *Physiol. Behav.* **12**, 377–384.

Cohn, C. and Joseph, D. (1960). Effects on metabolism by the rate of ingestion of the diet, 'Meal eating' versus 'nibbling'. *Am. J. clin. Nutr.* **8**, 682–689.

Cohn, C. and Joseph, D. (1962). Influence of body weight and body fat on appetite of "normal" lean and obese rats. *Yale J. Biol. Med.* **34**, 598–607.

Davis, J. D. and Booth, D. A. (1974). Vagotomy in the rat reduces meal sizes of diets containing fat. *Physiol. Behav.* **12**, 685–688.

Davis, J. D. and Campbell, C. S. (1973). Peripheral control of meal size in the rat: effect of sham feeding on meal size and drinking rate. *J. comp. physiol. Psychol.* **83**, 379–688.

De Castro, J. M. and Balagura, S. (1975). Meal patterning in the streptozotocin-diabetic rat. *Physiol. Behav.* **15**, 259–263.

Friedman, M. I. and Stricker, E. M. (1976). The physiological psychology of hunger: a physiological perspective. *Psycho. Rev.,* **83**, 409–431.

Garcia, J., Hankins, W. G. and Rusiniak, K. (1974). Behavioral regulation of the milieu interne in man and rat. *Science, N.Y.* **185**, 824–831.

Garfinkel, D., Achs, M. J. and Dzubow, L. (1974) Simulation of biological systems at the level of biochemistry and physiology. *Fed. Proc.* **33**, 176–182.

Garrow, J. S. (1975). Regulation of body weight. *In* "Obesity: Its Pathogenesis and Management" (T. Silverstone, ed.), pp. 3–27. Medical and Technical Publishing, London.

Geertsema, S. P. (1973). Ontwikkeling analyse en toepassingen van enige modellen der regulatie van voedselopnamel. Ph.D. Thesis, University of Gronigen.

Geertsema, S.P. and Reddingius, H. (1974). Preliminary considerations in the simulation of behaviour. *In* "Motivational Control Systems Analysis" (D. J. McFarland, ed.), pp. 355–405. Academic Press, London and New York.

Gold, R. M. (1975). Hypothalamic hyperphagia despite imposed diurnal or nocturnal feeding and drinking rhythms. *Physiol. Behav.* **14**, 861–866.

Harris, L. J., Clay, J., Hargreaves, F. J. and Ward, A. (1933). Appetite and choice of diet. The ability of the vitamin B deficient rat to discriminate between diets containing and lacking the vitamin. *Proc. Roy. Soc. Lond.* **113**, 161–190.

Hirsch, J. (1972). Discussion. *Adv. psychosom. Med.* **7**, 229–242.

Hunt, J. N. and Knox, M. T. (1968). Regulation of gastric emptying. *In* "Handbook, of Physiology: Alimentary Canal, Vol. 4: Motility" (C. F. Code and W. Heidel, eds), pp. 1917–1935. American Physiological Society, Washington, DC.

Hunt, J. N. and Stubbs, D. F. (1975). The volume and content of meals as determinants of gastric emptying. *J. Physiol., Lond.* **245**, 209–225.

Kakolewski, J. W., Deaux, E., Christensen, J. and Chase, B. (1971). Diurnal patterns in water and food intake and body weight changes in rats with hypothalamic lesions. *Am. J. Physiol.* **221**, 711–718.

Kennedy, G. C. (1953). The role of depot fat in the hypothalamic control of food intake in the rat. *Proc. Roy. Soc., Lond., B* **140**, 578–592.

Kissileff, H. R. (1970). Free feeding in normal and recovered lateral rats monitored by a pellet-detecting eatometer. *Physiol. Behav.* **3**, 163–173.

Kleiber, M. (1936). Problems involved in breeding for efficiency of food utilization. *Proc. Am. Soc. Anim. Prod.* 247–258.

Kraly, F. S. and Blass, E. M. (1976). Increased feeding in rats in a low ambient temperature. *In* "Hunger: Basic Mechanisms and Clinical Implications" (D. Novin, W. Wyrwicka and G. A. Bray, eds), pp. 77–87. Raven Press, New York.

Kraly, F. S. and Carty, W. J. (1976). Pregastric stimuli are sufficient for short-term satiety in 3-h deprived rats. Paper presented at Eastern Psychological Association meetings, New York.

Le Magnen, J. (1956). Effets sur la prise alimentaire du Rat blanc des administrations post prandiales d'insuline et le mécanisme des appétits caloriques. *J. Physiol., Paris* **48**, 789–802.

Le Magnen, J. (1971). Advances in studies on the physiological control and regulation of food intake. *In* "Progress in Physiological Psychology" (J. Sprague and E. Stellar, eds), Vol. 4, pp. 204–261. Academic Press, New York and London.

Le Magnen, J. and Devos, M. (1970). Metabolic correlates of the meal onset in the free food intake of rats. *Physiol. Behav.* **5**, 805–814.

Le Magnen, J. and Tallon, S. (1966). Le périodicité spontanée de la prise d'aliments ad libitum du rat blanc. *J. Physiol., Paris* **58**, 323–349.

Le Magnen, J. and Tallon, S. (1968). L'effect du jeûne préable sur les caracteristiques temporelles de la prise d'aliments chez le rat. *J. Physiol., Paris* **60**, 143–154.

Le Magnen, J., Devos, M., Gaudillière, J.-P., Louis-Sylvestre, J. and Tallon, S. (1973). Role of a lipostatic mechanism in regulation by feeding of energy balance in rats. *J. comp. physiol. Psychol.* **84**, 1–23.

Levitsky, D. A. (1970). Feeding patterns of rats in response to fasts and changes in environmental conditions. *Physiol. Behav.* **5**, 291–300.

Lovett, D. and Booth, D. A. (1970). Four effects of exogenous insulin on food intake. *Q. J. exp. Psychol.* **22**, 406–419.

McFarland, D. J. (1971). "Feedback Mechanisms in Animal Behaviour". Academic Press, London and New York.

Nicolaïdis, S. (1974). Short-term and long term regulation of energy balance. Paper presented at XXVI International Congress of Physiological Sciences, New Delhi, October 1974.

Nicolaïdis, S., Petit, M. and Polonowski, J. (1974). Etude du rapport entre la régulation de la masse adipense corporelle et la composition lipidique de ses "centres régulateurs". *C. hebd. Séanc. Acad. Sci., Paris* **278**, 1393–1396.

Norton, S., Culver, B. and Mullenix, P. (1975). Development of nocturnal behavior in albino rats. *Behav. Biol.* **15**, 317–331.

Oatley, K. (1967). A control model of the physiological basis of thirst. *Med. biol. Engng.* **5**, 225–237.

Oatley, K. (1971). Dissociation of circadian drinking pattern from eating. *Nature, Lond.* **229**, 494–496.

Oatley, K. (1973). Simulation and the theory of thirst. *In* "The Neuropsychology of Thirst" (A. N. Epstein, H. R. Kissileff and E. Stellar, eds), pp. 199–223. Winson, New York.

Oatley, K. (1974). Circadian rhythms and representations of the environment in motivational systems. *In* "Motivational Control Systems Analysis" (D. J. McFarland, ed.), pp. 427–459. Academic Press, London and New York.

Oatley, K. and Toates, F. M. (1969). The passage of food through the gut of rats and its uptake of fluid. *Psychon. Sci.* **16**, 225–226.

Oomura, Y. (1976). Significance of glucose, insulin, and free fatty acid on the hypothalamic feeding and satiety neurons. *In* "Hunger: Basic Mechanisms and Clinical Implications" (D. Novin, W. Wyrwicka and G. A. Bray, eds), pp. 145–157. Raven Press, New York.

Paintal, A. S. (1954). A study of gastric stretch receptors. Their role in the peripheral mechanism of satiation of hunger and thirst. *J. Physiol., Lond.* **126**, 255–270.

Panksepp, J. (1971). Effects of fats, proteins, and carbohydrates on food intake in rats. *Psychon. Monog. Suppl.* **4**, 85–95.

Panksepp, J. (1972). Hypothalamic radioactivity after intragastric glucose-^{14}C in rats. *Am. J. Physiol.* **223**, 396–401.

Panksepp, J. (1973). Reanalysis of feeding patterns in the rat. *J. comp. physiol. Psychol.* **82**, 78–94.

Panksepp, J. and Pilcher, C. W. T. (1973). Evidence for an adipokinetic mechanism in the ventromedial hypothalamus. *Experientia* **29**, 793.

Peck, J. W. (1976). Situational determinants of the body weights defended by normal rats and rats with hypothalamic lesions. *In* "Hunger: Basic Mechanisms and Clinical Implications" (D. Novin, W. Wyrwicka and G. A. Bray, eds), pp. 297–311. Raven Press, New York.

Pilcher, C. W. T., Jarman, S. P. and Booth, D. A. (1974). The route of glucose to the brain from food in the mouth of the rat. *J. comp. physiol. Psychol.* **87**, 56–61.

Poulakos, L. and Kent, T. H. (1973). Gastric emptying and small intestinal propulsion in fed and fasted rats. *Gastroenterology* **64**, 962–967.

Pullar, J. and Webster, A. J. F. (1974). Heat loss and energy retention during growth in congenitally obese and lean rats. *Br. J. Nutr.* **31**, 377–392.

Ralph, T. L. and Sawchenko, P. E. (1975). Hypothalamic lesions modify gastrointestinal transit in the rat. Paper presented at Eastern Psychological Association meetings, New York.

Rozin, P. and Kalat, J. W. (1971). Specific hungers and poison avoidance as adaptive specializations of learning. *Psychol. Rev.* **78**, 459–486.

Rupe, B. D. and Mayer, J. (1967). Endogenous glucose release stimulated by oral sucrose administration in rats. *Experientia* **23**, 1009–1010.

Russek, M. (1971). Hepatic receptors and the neurophysiological mechanisms controlling feeding behavior. *In* "Neurosciences Research" (S. Ehrenpreis and O. C. Solnitzky, eds), Vol. 4, pp. 213–282. Academic Press, New York and London.

Russek, M. (1976). A conceptual equation of intake control. *In* "Hunger: Basic Mechanisms and Clinical Implications" (D. Novin, W. Wyrwicka and G. A. Bray, eds), pp. 327–347. Raven Press, New York.

Simson, P. C. and Booth, D. A. (1973). Olfactory conditioning by association with histidine-free or balanced amino acid loads. *Q. J. exp. Psychol.* **25**, 354–359.

Smith, G. P. and Gibbs, J. (1976). What the gut tells the brain about feeding behaviour. *In* "Appetite and Food Intake" (T. Silverstone, ed.). Dahlem Konferenzen, Berlin.

Smith, U. (1970). Effects of glucose and insulin on lipolysis rates in human fat cells of different sizes. *FEBS Letters* **11**, 8–10.

Steffens, A. B. (1969a), The influence of insulin injections and infusions on eating and blood glucose level in the rat. *Physiol. Behav.* **4**, 823–828.

Steffens, A. B. (1969b). Rapid absorption of glucose in the intestinal tract of the rat after ingestion of a meal. *Physiol. Behav.* **4**, 829–832.

Toates, F. M. (1974). Computer simulation and the homeostatic control of behaviour. *In* "Motivational Control Systems Analysis" (D. J. McFarland, ed.), pp. 407–426. Academic Press, London and New York.

Toates, F. M. (1975). "Control Theory in Biology and Experimental Psychology". Hutchinson Educational, London.

Toates, F. M. and Booth, D. A. (1974). Control of food intake by energy supply. *Nature, Lond.* **251**, 710–711.

Toates, F. M. and Oatley, K. (1969). Computer simulation of thirst and water balance. *Med. biol. Engng.* **8**, 71–87.

Ugolev. A. M. and Kassil, V. G. (1961). Fiziologiia appetita. *Uspekhi Sov. biol.* **51**, 352–368. [Translation 9-23-63, Library Branch, Division of Research Services, N.I.H.].

Wiepkema, P. R. (1971). Positive feedbacks at work during feeding. *Behaviour* **39**, 266–273.

Wiepkema, P. R., Prins, A. J. A. and Steffens, A. B. (1972). Gastrointestinal food transport in relation to meal occurrence in rats. *Physiol. Behav.* **9**, 759–763.

Wunder, B. A. (1975). A model for estimating metabolic rate of active or resting animals. *J. theor. Biol.* **49**, 345–354.

York, D. A. (1975). Lipid metabolism in genetic models of obesity. *Proc. Nutr. Soc.* **34**, 249–255.

12

Prototype Model of Human Feeding, Growth and Obesity

D. A. BOOTH AND P. MATHER
Department of Psychology, University of Birmingham, Birmingham, England

I. Presuppositions

A. *Tentativeness of the Approach*

Some recent experimental results (Booth, 1977a; Booth *et al.*, 1976b) suggest that the outlines of the biological and learned bases of hunger in man are similar to those already elucidated in somewhat more detail in the rat. This should not be too surprising in so far as the rat is similar to man in being an omnivore species and possessing the basic mammalian equipment viscerally and cerebrally that is more elaborate in us. Indeed, not just because we already know a good deal about the rat, but purely on homocentric grounds, the physiology and learning mechanisms involved in appetite in the intact rat, particularly when fed on a variety of diets, should be considered worthy of intensive study.

Despite this, and despite the relative success of our systems analysis of feeding control in the rat (Chapter 11), we had considerable reservations about attempting to extend such modelling to man. In the first place, although functions and parameter values for human beings could be roughly specified, precise relevant data were even more sparse than in the rat. As in the animal laboratory, over-restrictive notions of scientific rigour have dominated the design of experiments. The traditions of human physiological experimentation have until very recently failed to provide us with good measurements in subjects taking their normal diet on a normal schedule during a normal day's work, and the role of learning in normal feeding has hardly been a topic of experimentation at all. Secondly, social determinants would presumably be dominant in the human case, however great the importance of the biological substructure of

K*

human appetite and learned accommodations to it. A simulation not taking account of social influences on feeding might therefore be most unrealistic in its predictions.

Nevertheless, an attempt to build a human version of our systems analysis of feeding should at least expose the limitations of an approach with a focus restricted to biological determinants of human appetite and so point to new lines of experimental or clinical investigation. At best, it could pave the way for a theoretically well founded and clinically useful model of a realistic combination of biological, cognitive and social controls.

B. *General Theory: The Energy Flow Cycle*

We assumed that appetite is the expression of an incipient deficiency in the net supply of energy to working tissues, in behavioural tendencies or attitudes which favour means of correcting that deficiency. Satiation, i.e. loss of appetite during feeding, is an anticipation of what would without a change in behaviour be an over-correction of the deficiency. The sensations that an individual habitually experiences either when he has an appetite or when he has satisfied it are identifiable subjective correlates of a potentially low or high energy supply. Motivation to eat food results from effects on cerebral activity of states of the stomach, intestines and body tissues which reflect their content or net input of metabolizable energy.

Knowledge about the body and the effects of food on it could be based on initially undifferentiated distress states of gross energy deficiency or excess. Unlearned reaction patterns could ensure feeding occurs during nursing, when control may not be needed. The characteristics and relevance of bodily sensations or particular foodstuffs could then be progressively discriminated during infancy and childhood by means of natural experience of feeding in relation to need. The pleasantness of a foodstuff is assumed to be at least in part an anticipation of the effects of ingesting it on the supply of energy to critical tissues.

It would of course be extremely difficult to specify every physiological or cognitive detail of energy-related information possessed by an individual from one moment to the next. However, such detail might not be needed in order to calculate the relation of behaviour to energy need. The particular flavours that rich foods have in a given culture, the precise physical or chemical effect of a meal in the gut or the tissues which serves as a satiety signal, or the speed or other characteristics of learning—this might all be information which is redundant for the purpose of generating some major predictions of feeding behaviour, and its consequences for body compositon.

The energy requirement is not of course the only need met by feeding. It is however by far the largest nutrient requirement apart from water, particularly if each essential amino acid is considered separately. Furthermore, when no extreme ecological, cultural or economic constraints are operative, mixed diets supply adequate amounts and balances of amino acids, salts, fatty acids and vitamins if the dietary mixture is taken in a calorically sufficient quantity. Thus, normal hunger may be purely an energy appetite. Even if in fact other specific appetites can and do operate, they may only be influential in unusual conditions or in the fine details of foodstuff selection. A representation for acquired protein appetite could in due course be included in a model of human feeding, if it proves to be more realistic to complement energy-specific appetite in that way.

A detailed development of this view of hunger has been put into one of many possible specific forms or models suitable to be programmed for computer simulation.

II. A Computer Program for a Basic Model

A model is typically represented by a family of related computer programs. Each particular program may be used for a variety of simulation runs: values of some parameters in the model can be changed from run to run to simulate different conditions in the real system. To help in exposition of the workings of our prototype model of human feeding control, a stripped-down version has been constructed. Statements which comprise a program for this basic model are listed in Figs 1–6. The remainder of this section is an explanation which does not require knowledge either of programming or of the details of the theory of hunger on which the model is based. Some readers may be interested to see the exact computational procedures in this case, particularly as a working computer program is not given in any other chapter in this book.

A. *Starting Data*

1. *Computational Declarations*

(a) *Arrays*. The program uses two one-dimensional tabulations during the calculations. One stores a continuously updated list of what is roughly speaking the contents of the successive portions of a notionally segmented small intestine (GUTLAG). The other lists the fraction of work output to be added to basal metabolic rate as activity varies around the clock (FMETAB). These dimensions have to be declared at the beginning of a program list (statement 1, Fig. 1).
(b) *Real and integer variables*. The programming language Fortran treats variables which are meant always to be whole numbers (INTEGER) differently from variables whose values are always to be regarded as going to at least one decimal place (REAL). The characteristics of each variable have to be declared

```
      C COMPUTATIONAL DECLARATIONS

0001        DIMENSION GUTLAG(20), FMETAB(3000)
0002        REAL MAXFLO, LIPO, MINFLO, INFAT, METABR, LEAN, OUTFAT, STOMAK
0003        REAL DENSIT, ERATE, WORK, FATFBK, ACQOFF, WEIGHT, FAT
0004        REAL T2, T3, T4, T5, HUNGER, CONT, ABSOR, PERIOD, STOP, FMETAB(3000)
0005        REAL T1, GUTLAG(20), FLO, START, SINCE
0006        REAL DAYFAT, DYLEAN, ACON, AFA, ALEA, FATDAY, LEANDY
0007        INTEGER SECOND, DAY, DAYS, MINUTE, HOUR, CYCLE, DIGEST, D1GEST, COUNT
0008        INTEGER N, NEND, MMI, MSIZE
```

Fig. 1. Initial declarations of dimensions and numerical types of variables. This is the first part of a program list written in Fortran for a basic version of the prototype human feeding model. The rest of the program is given in Figs 2–6. Lines beginning "c" are comments not used by the computer. The statement numbers on the far left are also not part of the program proper.

at the start of the program (statements 2–8, Fig. 1). The meanings of all the variables are explained below.

2. *Values of Parameters and Variables*

The simulation requires boundary and initial conditions to be set and also values for the various parameters in the mathematical functions to be used in the calculations. In interactive versions of the model, the program can be written so that the computer asks the user to choose a value in the case of any values that are frequently varied from one simulation to the next. Such preliminary questions are not included in this program but the structure of variables underlying them is maintained for clarity of exposition.

(a) *Body composition.* The weight of the person being simulated is stated in kilograms (statement 9, Fig. 2). As WEIGHT is a real variable (statement 3, Fig. 1), it must be stated to at least one decimal place even if the value is in fact an integer. Adipose tissue is taken to comprise 15% of body mass in this instance, and in effect all fat is supposed to reside in adipose. The energy density of

```
      C VALUES OF PARAMETERS AND VARIABLES

0009        WEIGHT=75.0
0010        FAT=WEIGHT*15.0*7700.0/100.0
0011        LEAN=WEIGHT*85.0*3000.0/100.0
0012        WORK=1.4
0013        T2=900.0
0014        T3=1080.0
0015        T4=2040.0
0016        T5=2820.0
0017        NEND=2880
0018        DENSIT=1.9
0019        ERATE=25.0
0020        STOMAK=.193
0021        DIGEST=12
0022        INFAT=.56
0023        OUTFAT=.43
0024        FATFBK=-1.0E-06
0025        MINFLO=-1.07
0026        MAXFLO=1.46
0027        ACQOFF=1.08
0028        STOP=0.0
```

```
      C INITIAL CONDITIONS

0029        HUNGER=0.0
0030        CONT=0.0
0031        ABSOR=0.0
0032        SECOND=0
0033        MINUTE=0
0034        HOUR=0
0035        DAY=-1
0036        DAYS=3
0037        N=0

      C CALCULATION PARAMETERS

0038        CYCLE=30
0039        PERIOD=0.5
0040        COUNT=DIGEST+1
0041        D1GEST=DIGEST+1
0042        FATDAY=FAT
0043        LEANDY=LEAN
```

Fig. 2. Setting parameters to their standard values, variables to their initial values, and fixing calculation parameters.

adipose is taken to be 7·7 Mcal/kg. Thus statement 10 (Fig. 2) calculates the fat energy of the body in kilocalories. The remaining mass is designated lean, and its energy content is calculated from an average density of 3 Mcal/kg (statement 11).

(b) *Daily activity pattern.* This version of the model includes a very crude specification of the variation in energy loss around the clock. The energy costs of posture, movement and external work are supposed to run at a constant maximum for the working period of the day, and are assumed to be zero during sleeping hours. In this particular instance, very low activity costs of 1·4 kcal/min are specified (statement 12, Fig 2). Statements 13–17 specify times of waking, starting full work, stopping work, and going to sleep, respectively, ending with the time at which the 24-h period ends. The time unit here is 30 sec, because this is the time base on which all the calculations are done in this version: there are 2880 half-minutes in 24 h (statement 17). Waking is at 900 half-minutes, i.e. 7.30 a.m. (statement 13), and so on.

(c) *Alimentary parameters.* The energy density of the diet is taken to be 1·9 kcal/g (statement 18, Fig. 2). This version of the model does not distinguish component foodstuffs within the diet. Eating rate is also taken to be a constant, namely 25 g/min (statement 19). Both these parameters could easily be programmed to vary independently during meals, e.g. water content affecting density, and textures or flavours affecting eating rate. In this basic version there is probably little point, as we believe that learning processes not represented in it (see Section VI.A) would be important in calculating the effects of major variations of that sort. In fact, this program needs only an energy rate of ingestion, which could have been specified in a single statement.

The major determinant of the rate of energy flow to the body is the rate of gastric emptying. This is calculated in kcal/min from the amount of food energy (kcal) in the stomach, according to the equation in statement 55 (Fig. 4). STOMAK (statement 20) is the proportionality factor in this gastric emptying function. The larger that this parameter STOMAK is, the higher the rate at which the stomach pumps out nutrient for a given amount in the stomach.

It may be noted that this and the following six parameters hae been adjusted to provide approximately stable body composition (see Section IV.A.1 and B).

Digestion, and to a lesser extent transit between the mouth and stomach and between intestinal lumen and tissues, take a significant time compared with the duration of a meal. In this prototype model, these delays are represented simply as a lag (DIGEST) between gastric clearance and the energy reaching the hunger/satiety receptor system which transduces net energy flow to lean tissues into neural activity controlling feeding onset and offset. In a more advanced model it might be possible to simulate the molecular and cellular processes of digestion and replace a simple delay by more realistic functions. DIGEST (statement 21) is here set equal to 6min.

(d) *Fat deposition and mobilization.* The flow of energy into or out of fat is calculated on the simplifying assumptions (discussed later in the chapter, Section IV.C.2) that net lipogenesis occurs in proportion to the excess of energy supply over energy consumption and that net lipolysis is in porportion to deficit of supply relative to consumption. The proportionality factors INFAT and OUTFAT (statements 22 and 23, Fig. 2) are assumed to differ.

A small continuous addition to lipolysis is assumed to arise from a basal level of fat mobilization in proportion to total fat energy. FATFBK (statement 24) is the proportionality factor in the equation (statement 70, Fig. 4) used to calculate this negative feedback signal from fat store size into the satiating energy flow. FATFBK is negative because it is a loss of energy from total fat. It is a very small number because it translates tens of thousands of kilocalories of fat store energy into a fraction of a kcal/min of fat mobilization. In statement 24, "E-06" means an exponent or power of minus six, i.e. FATFBK $= -1 \times 10^{-6}$.

(e) *Hunger and satiety thresholds in this basic version of the model.* The onset and offset of feeding is determined directly by particular values of the rate of flow of energy into non-fat components of the body. Feeding starts when this energy flow goes below the value of the parameter MINFLO (statement 25, Fig. 2). Feeding ends when energy flow goes above a satiety threshold which has been acquired by past experience of the energy flow following the end of a meal. MAXFLO (statement 26) sets a target for the flow maximum which is reached as absorption peaks after the delay for digestion to catch up with the rate of gastric emptying. The acquired satiety threshold ACQOFF is adjusted up or down after a meal to approximate the next postprandial peak to the target value (statement 99, Fig. 5). In statement 26, ACQOFF is given a starting value which approximates to the value it would acquire for the second meal: this removes the possibility that first simulated meal would be very abnormal and the simulation would take longer to stabilize. Of course, if just such a transient were of interest, ACQOFF could be made equal to MAXFLO, or given any other relevant starting value.

STOP (statement 28) is a tag which is used to calculate meal sizes (statements 81 and 89–90, Fig. 5). It must be set to zero for the start of the simulation.

3. *Initial Conditions*

A number of tags and variables have to be declared before they are invoked during calculations, and have to be given some value. The very first cycle of calculation would rectify any anomalies in the values given here. HUNGER (statement 29) is a tag set to unity by the onset of the tendency to feed and reset to zero by the offset of feeding. Stomach contents (CONT) and the rate of intestinal absorption (ABSOR) are set to zero initially. This is consistent with zero hunger, because the simulation is started at midnight (statements 32–34) when the person is asleep and there is no tendency to feed even if the gut is empty. The number of the day before the start (DAY) and the number of days after which the simulation is to stop (DAYS) are set to give three days of output (statements 35 and 36). Statement 37 sets to zero (midnight) the count which is increased by one at each iteration of the calculation cycle (see statement 100, Fig. 6), until another 24h has elasped (statements 108 and 109).

4. *Calculation Parameters*

Finally, some computational "housekeeping" has to be done before the simulation proper can begin.

(a) *Calculation cycle.* The model works on the principle of calculating a new state of every variable at a fixed interval of simulated time after the last calculated state. This procedure of successive addition makes the mathematical operations in the program much easier to understand for those of us to whom differential equations are something of a mystery. Furthermore, it bypasses difficulties which may arise in constructing or using the appropriate continuous mathematics. If the time interval between the calculated states is short enough relative to the rates of changes in states within the real system, successive addition will give results not appreciably different from integration.

There are changes every few seconds in the physiological and psychological processes which are critical at the level of systems analysis on which this model is operating. However, the changes are probably slow enough to be approximately constant in rate for a quarter or half a minute at least. We have generally run simulations of human feeding on a calculation cycle of 30 seconds or less. When the basic model given here is run on calculation cycles of 10 seconds or less the results are very similar. The duration of the time step is specified in seconds (CYCLE, statement 38) and minutes (PERIOD, statement 39). COUNT and D1GEST (statements 40 and 41) are tags used to detect the postprandial energy flow maximum (statements 95–99, Fig. 5) which is simply the energy flow value after the digestion lag DIGEST. Midnight values of fat and lean energy (FATDAY and LEANDY) are given the starting values of these body energy components (statements 42 and 43).

Statements 44–50 (Fig. 3) fill the FMETAB array with a list of values of the activity component of metabolic rate corresponding to each half-minute around the clock (=2800 calculation cycles). Between waking and the start of the working period these values are fractions linearly increasing from zero to full working rate (statement 47). They are linearly decreasing from the end of work until bedtime (statement 49). During the sleep period, zero values are entered in

```
0044        DO 100 I=1,2880
0045        FMETAB(I)=0.0
0046        T1=FLOAT(I)
0047        IF(T1.GT.T2.AND.T1.LT.T3) FMETAB(I)=(T1-T2)/(T3-T2)
0048        IF(T1.GE.T3.AND.T1.LE.T4) FMETAB(I)=1.0
0049        IF(T1.GT.T4.AND.T1.LT.T5) FMETAB(I)=(T5-T1)/(T5-T4)
0050    100 CONTINUE
0051        DO 1 I=1,D1GEST
0052        GUTLAG(I)=ABSOR
0053      1 CONTINUE
0054        GO TO 10
```

Fig. 3. Filling the arrays of the fractional work metabolism pattern and the digesting intestinal contents.

places in the array corresponding to the sleep period. This array could in principle include values which represented any pattern of activity for which it was of interest to test the model.

Statements 51–53 fill the array of intestine contents with zeros, to displace any values which might otherwise be created by the initial state of the computer.

Statement 54 then specifies a jump to the labelled statement 111 (Fig. 6), which sets the day number to zero. This in turn permits statement 112 to be used for the first and last time, leading to statements 120–126 which print the titles of the columns on the output and a dummy line reporting the states of variables (see Fig. 7), before starting the first calculation cycle at the labelled statement 55.

B. *Main Calculations*

The part of the program list concerned primarily with calculating values of energy flow rates is given in Figs 4 and 5.

```
      C           CALCULATION CYCLE

      C STOMACH CONTENTS

0055      2 CONT=CONT+PERIOD*(HUNGER*DENSIT*ERATE-STOMAK*SQRT(CONT))
0056        IF(CONT.LT.0.0)CONT=0.0
0057        ACON=CONT/1000.0

      C INTESTINAL LAG IN ABSORPTION

0058        DO 3 I=2,D1GEST
0059        GUTLAG(I-1)=GUTLAG(I)
0060      3 CONTINUE
0061        GUTLAG(D1GEST)=STOMAK*SQRT(CONT)
0062        ABSOR=GUTLAG(1)

      C METABOLIC RATE

0063        METABR=WEIGHT/60.0+FMETAB(N+1)*WORK+ABSOR*0.05

      C LIPID FLOWS

0064        IF(ABSOR-METABR)101,102,103
0065    101 LIPO=OUTFAT*(ABSOR-METABR)
0066        GO TO 105
0067    102 LIPO=0.0
0068        GO TO 105
0069    103 LIPO=INFAT*(ABSOR-METABR)
0070    105 LIPO=LIPO+FAT*FATFBK
0071        FAT=FAT+PERIOD*LIPO
0072        AFA=FAT/1000.0
```

Fig. 4. Start of the main calculations.

1. *Stomach Contents*

The energy content of the stomach (CONT) is updated by statement 55 (Fig. 4). This adds to the pre-existing gastric contents the amount of energy which might have been eaten since the last calculation cycle (PERIOD min ago) while subtracting what has been cleared from the stomach in that time.

The computational variable HUNGER is set at unity when feeding occurs and at zero when there is no feeding. The energy rate of feeding is the multiple of the diet's energy density (DENSIT) and the weight rate of feeding (ERATE). Thus HUNGER times DENSIT times ERATE is the current energy rate of feeding.

The current rate of energy clearance from the stomach is calculated from the energy content (CONT) remaining from the last calculation cycle. As discussed in Chapter 11, stomach emptying rate is generally close to proportional to the square root of stomach contents. Therefore, the rate of loss of energy from the stomach is the square root ("SQRT") of its contents multiplied by the rate constant specified at the start of the simulation (STOMAK, statement 20, Fig. 2).

The difference between rate of energy loss from the stomach and any energy gain by feeding, expressed in kcal/min, is multiplied by the simulated time since the last calculation in minutes (PERIOD, statement 39, Fig. 2). This gives the net gain or loss of energy which, when added to the original value for stomach energy content, gives the new value.

After the stomach has become practically empty the equation of statement 55 might occasionally give values of CONT very slightly less than zero. This is not merely physically unrealistic; it creates the computational fault of attempting the square root of a negative number at the next use of 55. Therefore statement 56 sets the value for stomach contents exactly to zero immediately if it happens to become negative. Statement 57 merely scales stomach contents to megacalories for output (statements 124 and 128, Fig. 6).

2. *Intestinal Contents and Absorption*

The delay between energy leaving the stomach and reaching tissues after digestion and absorption is handled by storing a series of recent flow values from the stomach in an array. The series is as long as the simple delay representing digestion which was specified before calculation cycles began (DIGEST, statements 21 and 41). Statements 58–61 (Fig. 4) update this array. Each flow value is moved along one step (statements 58–60) and the current rate of energy flow from the stomach is entered in the newly vacated first step in the array (statement 61), using the square-root clearance function as in statement 55. The most ancient stomach clearance rate value, from the other end of the array (at DIGEST + 1), is then taken as the current rate of absorption (statement 62).

3. *Metabolic Rate*

Statement 63 (Fig. 4) calculates current metabolic rate in the conventional manner by adding its several components. Basal metabolic rate is calculated from current body weight (WEIGHT) by simple proportion, a reasonable approximation over the range of body weights usually considered during modelling with this prototype. Further energy expenditure is added to allow for posture, movement and external work at times of day when the modelled subject is not in bed: the fractional level of activity for the current half-minute time unit ($N+1$) is read from the activity pattern listed in the FMETAB array (statements 44 to 50) and multiplied by the full working rate of expenditure (WORK, statement 12). Finally, the energy lost in processing food (thermic effect, formerly called "specific dynamic action") is added, estimated in this case as 5% of the rate of absorption. Failure to absorb a small fraction of metabolisable energy, and consequent faecal energy loss (plus any insensible and urinary energy losses), should be represented in the most accurate model.

4. *Fat Deposition and Mobilization*

On the assumption that net lipogenesis occurs in proportion to the excess of energy supply over energy consumption and that net lipolysis is in proportion to deficit of supply relative to consumption, metabolic rate is taken to represent the main component of energy consumption. The proportionality factors are assumed to differ between lipogenesis and lipolysis, with a large fraction of any excess being diverted into fat deposition, but a more modest fraction of any deficit being met from lipolysis. Thus, one equation is used during deficit (statement 65, Fig. 4) and another during excess (statement 69). These equations give lipolytic energy flow a negative value and lipogenic flow a positive value. Statement 64 uses a Fortran algorithm to specify which equation is used: which of the three labelled statements listed (101, 102, 103) is used depends on the value of the IF function. If metabolic rate is greater than absorption rate (ABSOR-METABR is negative), 101 is used (statement 65: lipolysis). If the rates are equal, 102 is used (zero lipoflow). If absorption is faster than metabolism, 103 (statement 69: lipogenesis) is used.

If it is supposed that the amount of fat in adipose cells influences their lipogenic or lipolytic characteristics, this coupling of fat store size to current energy flow can also be represented at this stage of the calculations. In this program, statement 70 represents a lipolytic bias which increases with adiposity, as strongly or as weakly as the limited stability of body fat content may imply (see Section V.C.1): the strength of this feedback is set by the proportionality factor FATFBK of statement 24 (Fig. 2).

The fat content of the body is then increased or diminished according to the current flow of energy into or out of fat (statement 71) and adipose energy scaled to megacalories for output (statement 72).

5. *Non-fat Energy Flow and Storage*

The net energy flow to parenteral tissues excluding fat (FLO) is calculated by statement 73 (Fig. 5). Lipogenesis (or the negative flow of lipolysis) and total metabolic rate are subtracted from absorption.

```
      C FLOW INTO AND OUT OF LEAN TISSUE

0073        FLO=ABSOR-LIPO-METABR
0074        LEAN=LEAN+PERIOD*FLO
0075        WEIGHT=LEAN/3000.0+FAT/7700.0
0076        ALEA=LEAN/1000.0

      C MEAL START

0077        IF(HUNGER.GT.0.5) GO TO 5
0078        IF(FLO.GT.MINFLO) GO TO 7
0079        HUNGER=1.0
0080        START=FLOAT(N)
0081        SINCE=(START-STOP)*PERIOD
0082        IF(SINCE.LT.0.0)SINCE=SINCE+1440.0
0083        MMI=IFIX(SINCE)
0084        WRITE(6,4)HOUR,MINUTE,MMI
0085      4 FORMAT(/1H0,12HMEAL STARTED,4X,4HTIME,2I3,
           14X,18HMEAL-MEAL INTERVAL,I5,3X,7HMINUTES)

      C END OF MEAL

0086        IF(HUNGER.LT.0.5) GO TO 7
0087      5 IF(FLO.LT.ACQOFF) GO TO 7
0088        HUNGER=0.0
0089        STOP=FLOAT(N)
0090        SINCE=(STOP-START)*PERIOD
0091        MSIZE=IFIX(SINCE*ERATE)
0092        WRITE(6,6)HOUR,MINUTE,MSIZE,ACQOFF
0093      6 FORMAT(1H ,12HMEAL STOPPED,4X,4HTIME,2I3,
           14X,9HMEAL SIZE,I6,2X,5HGRAMS,11H   OFF USED,F5.2)
0094        COUNT=0

      C CONDITIONING OF SATIETY

0095      7 IF(COUNT-DIGEST)201,202,9
0096    201 COUNT=COUNT+1
0097        GO TO 9
0098    202 COUNT=DIGEST
0099        ACQOFF=ACQOFF-(FLO-MAXFLO)
```

Fig. 5. Decisions to start and to stop feeding.

The last calculated non-fat energy flow rate is used to calculate the latest addition to or loss from non-lipid body energy (statement 74), scaled to megacalories by statement 76. This change in non-fat energy would roughly correspond to growth or wasting of lean body mass. Current fat energy and non-fat energy are both converted from kilocalories to kilograms and added to give current body weight (statement 75), ignoring the weight of current gut contents.

The net postintestinal flow of energy to non-fat mass is assumed to be sampled by the receptor system which controls appetite and its satiation. Thus the value of FLO is critical to the rest of the calculations.

6. *Deciding to Start or to Stop Feeding*

(a) *Meal Start.* Competing motivations and social and other external constraints are not represented in this simplified model. Also the diet is treated as a single unit of fixed availability and palatability. Under such conditions, the decision to start feeding is assumed to be determined entirely by the current supply of energy to lean tissues.

The relevant statements are given in the continuation of the program list in Fig. 5. Unless the system is already feeding (i.e. HUNGER has already been set equal to unity and is greater than 0·5, statement 77), the current energy flow (FLO) is compared with the hunger threshold (MINFLO) (statement 78, Fig. 5). If energy flow is below threshold, then the feeding tag is activated (statement 79) and the meal start-time tag is set at the current time in half-minute calculation cycle units (statement 80).

Statements 81–85 then calculate the interval since the end of the last meal (START minus STOP) and specify a print-out of the time at which the meal has started and of the meal-to-meal interval (MMI).

(b) *Meal finish.* If, on the other hand, the system is already feeding (HUNGER is unity and *not* less than 0·5, statement 86), energy flow is compared with another threshold (statement 87, Fig. 5), and if flow is above threshold the tendency to feed is stopped (the HUNGER tag is zeroed, statement 88) and the time of stopping noted (statement 89). This effective satiety threshold (ACQOFF) has a value which has been established on previous calculation cycles following the occurrence of meals (see next section).

The time from START to STOP (statement 90) gives meal size when multiplied by eating rate (statement 91). Statements 92 and 93 then print out the time of the end of the meal, the meal size and the satiety threshold value used.

7. *Conditioning of Satiety*

A tag (COUNT) counts the number of calculation cycles from the end of a meal (statement 94) until the count corresponds to the length of the digestion lag (DIGEST). Then on that cycle the program no longer skips over a statement which will adjust the satiety threshold (statement 99, Fig. 5). In statement 95 before then, COUNT minus DIGEST is negative and label 201 is followed, merely adding one to COUNT (statement 96). After then, COUNT minus DIGEST is positive and label 9 is followed, skipping the conditioning of satiation threshold and going to statement 100 (Fig. 6).

After the period of the digestion delay following the end of a meal, the peak gastric clearance rate generated by peak gastric contents will have worked through to a peak absorption rate. This in turn will have brought net energy flow (FLO) to a peak. Thus the conditioning adjustment of the satiety threshold by statement 99 only occurs on the calculation cycle when FLO is at its postprandial maximum. The adjustment is to add the difference between the energy flow at maximum (FLO) and standard target maximum energy flow (MAXFLO, statement 26, Fig. 2). The effect of this is that if energy flow overshoots target, the satiety threshold is reduced, tending to produce a smaller meal and a lower maximum at the next meal. On the other hand, if energy flow undershoots, the threshold is raised and the next meal is bigger.

C. *Time Monitoring and Output Routines*

1. *Updating*

The calculation cycle is completed by adding one to the cycle number before starting a new cycle (statement 100, Fig. 6) and updating all components of the

```
         C UPDATE TIME

0100           9 N=N+1
0101             SECOND=SECOND+CYCLE
0102             IF(SECOND.NE.60) GO TO 2
0103             MINUTE=MINUTE+1
0104             SECOND=0
0105             IF(MINUTE.NE.60) GO TO 14
0106             HOUR=HOUR+1
0107             MINUTE=0
0108             IF(N.NE.NEND) GO TO 14
0109             N=0
0110             HOUR=0
0111          10 DAY=DAY+1

         C DAILY CONDITION REPORT

0112             IF(DAY.EQ.0) GO TO 12
0113             DAYFAT=FAT-FATDAY
0114             DYLEAN=LEAN-LEANDY
0115             WRITE(6,11)DAY,DAYFAT,DYLEAN
0116          11 FORMAT(1H0,10X,10HEND OF DAY,I3,3X,3HFAT,F6.1,
               13X,4HLEAN,F6.1)
0117             FATDAY=FAT
0118             LEANDY=LEAN
0119             IF(DAY.EQ.DAYS) STOP

         C PAGE TITLES

0120          12 WRITE(6,13)
0121          13 FORMAT(1H1,' TIME     METABR     GUT      ABSOR    LIPO
               1    FLO      FAT     LEAN    WEIGHT ',/)

         C REPORT DECISION STATEMENTS

0122          14 IF(HUNGER.GT.0.5) GO TO 16
0123             IF(MINUTE.NE.0) GO TO 2

         C ROUTINE HOURLY REPORTS

0124             WRITE(6,15)HOUR,MINUTE,METABR,ACON,ABSOR,LIPO,FLO,AFA,ALEA,WEIGHT
0125          15 FORMAT(1H0,2I3,F8.2,F8.3,3F8.2,2F8.2,F8.2)
0126             GO TO 2

         C FEEDING REPORTS (FIVE MINUTELY INTERVALS)

0127          16 IF(FLOAT(MINUTE)/5.0-FLOAT(MINUTE/5).GT.PERIOD/5.0) GO TO 2
0128             WRITE(6,17)HOUR,MINUTE,METABR,ACON,ABSOR,LIPO,FLO,AFA,ALEA,WEIGHT
0129          17 FORMAT(1H ,2I3,F8.2,F8.3,3F8.2,2F8.2,F8.2)
0130             GO TO 2

         C END OF WORKING PROGRAM

0131             END
```

Fig. 6. Time adjustments and reports of current values of variables.

real time clock (statements 101–111). Thus statement 101 increases the clock seconds (SECOND) by the calculation cycle duration (CYCLE sec, statement 38). When SECOND reaches 60, statement 102 no longer causes the program to skip over statement 103 and 104 which increase clock minutes (MINUTE) by one and reset SECOND to zero. Similarly, when MINUTE reaches 60 (statement 105–107) and the number of calculation cycles (N) reaches the number for 24h (statements 108–111), they are reset to zero and the clock hours and the clock days are advanced accordingly.

When the specified number of days (statement 36, Fig. 2) has been run, the program stops (statement 119).

2. *Daily Reports*

Each time a new day starts (i.e. statement 111 has been reached), statements 113 (Fig. 6) onwards are reached. The last day's increases in fat energy (statement 113) and non-fat energy (statement 114) are calculated and reported with the day number in typed output (statements 115 and 116). The fat and non-fat energy tags are reset to current energy values (statements 117 and 118) for the coming day's increments.

If another day is to run, titles for a new page of data columns are printed (statements 120 and 121).

3. *Other Output Routines*

The program puts out regular reports of the current values of key variables. If no feeding tendency exists, statement 122 (Fig. 6) permits statement 123 to be read, which permits statements 124–126 to put out a report of the current time, metabolic rate (kcal/min), stomach contents (Mcal), absorption, lipoflow, and net non-fat energy flow rates (kcal/min), fat and non-fat energy (Mcal) and body weight (kg) when the clock minutes have been reset to zero by statement 107, i.e. on the hour every hour between meals. Because flow values change much faster during meals, the program is constructed to report every 5 min (statement 127) while feeding is going on (statement 122). Other parts of the program bound these meal reports with output at the start (statement 85) and finish (statement 93) of the meal.

D. *Output From a Sample Run*

Matrix printer output from this program is given in part in Fig. 7.

The first line of values in the output precedes the first calculation cycle, but the second line reports the values calculated for 1 a.m., at basal metabolic rate with the gut empty. As was seen on later days of simulation and is often the case in reality, the stomach is empty by the small hours of the morning. LIPO was negative, i.e. there was lipolysis. FLO was also negative, i.e. there was utilization

```
TIME     METABR    GUT      ABSOR    LIPO     FLO      FAT      LEAN     WEIGHT

 0  0    0. 00    0. 000    0. 00    0. 00    0. 00    0. 00    0. 00    75. 00

 1  0    1. 25    0. 000    0. 00   -0. 62   -0. 63   86. 59   191. 21   74. 98

 2  0    1. 25    0. 000    0. 00   -0. 62   -0. 63   86. 55   191. 18   74. 97

 3  0    1. 25    0. 000    0. 00   -0. 62   -0. 63   86. 51   191. 14   74. 95

 4  0    1. 25    0. 000    0. 00   -0. 62   -0. 63   86. 47   191. 10   74. 93

 5  0    1. 25    0. 000    0. 00   -0. 62   -0. 63   86. 44   191. 06   74. 91

 6  0    1. 25    0. 000    0. 00   -0. 62   -0. 63   86. 40   191. 02   74. 90

 7  0    1. 25    0. 000    0. 00   -0. 62   -0. 62   86. 36   190. 99   74. 88

 8  0    1. 71    0. 000    0. 00   -0. 82   -0. 89   86. 32   190. 95   74. 86

MEAL STARTED     TIME  8 20     MEAL-MEAL  INTERVAL   500     MINUTES
  8 25     2. 10    0. 206    0. 00    -0. 99    -1. 11    86. 30   190. 92    74. 85
  8 30     2. 30    0. 427    2. 45    -0. 00     0. 15    86. 30   190. 92    74. 85
  8 35     2. 45    0. 642    3. 78     0. 66     0. 67    86. 30   190. 92    74. 85
  8 40     2. 57    0. 854    4. 73     1. 12     1. 03    86. 30   190. 93    74. 85
MEAL STOPPED     TIME  8 40     MEAL SIZE     512  GRAMS    OFF USED 1. 08

 9  0    2. 92    0. 789    5. 53    1. 37    1. 23    86. 33   190. 95   74. 86


MEAL STARTED     TIME 19 10     MEAL-MEAL  INTERVAL   325     MINUTES
 19 15     2. 17    0. 206    0. 07    -0. 99    -1. 11    86. 44   191. 06    74. 91
 19 20     2. 27    0. 427    2. 45     0. 02     0. 17    86. 44   191. 06    74. 91
 19 25     2. 32    0. 642    3. 78     0. 73     0. 73    86. 44   191. 06    74 91
MEAL STOPPED     TIME 19 29     MEAL SIZE     475  GRAMS    OFF USED 1. 10

 20  0    2. 26    0. 671    5. 11    1. 51    1. 34    86. 49   191. 11   74. 94

 21  0    1. 99    0. 405    3. 99    1. 04    0. 97    86. 57   191. 18   74. 97

 22  0    1. 72    0. 205    2. 87    0. 56    0. 60    86. 62   191. 23   74. 99

 23  0    1. 45    0. 072    1. 76    0. 09    0. 22    86. 64   191. 25   75. 00

          END OF DAY  1    FAT   2. 5    LEAN    1. 4


MEAL STARTED     TIME 18 59     MEAL-MEAL  INTERVAL   320     MINUTES
 19  0     2. 23    0. 000    0. 19    -0. 96    -1. 07    86. 45   191. 07    74. 92
 19  5     2. 20    0. 229    0. 10    -0. 99    -1. 11    86. 44   191. 07    74. 91
 19 10     2. 31    0. 449    2. 62     0. 08     0. 22    86. 44   191. 06    74. 91
 19 15     2. 36    0. 664    3. 88     0. 77     0. 76    86. 44   191. 07    74. 92
MEAL STOPPED     TIME 19 19     MEAL SIZE     487  GRAMS    OFF USED 1. 11

 20  0    2. 25    0. 640    5. 00    1. 45    1. 29    86. 51   191. 13   74. 94

 21  0    1. 98    0. 381    3. 88    0. 97    0. 92    86. 58   191. 19   74. 98

 22  0    1. 71    0. 188    2. 76    0. 50    0. 55    86. 63   191. 24   75. 00

 23  0    1. 44    0. 063    1. 64    0. 02    0. 17    86. 64   191. 26   75. 01

          END OF DAY  3    FAT  -3. 9    LEAN   -2. 6
```

Fig. 7. Output from the basic model as programmed in Figs 1–6, showing the start and finish of the first simulated day and the finish of the third day.

of liver glycogen and/or muscle amino acids and other non-fat energy sources. While metabolic rate was at its resting value (1·25 kcal/min), this energy flow to the non-fat compartment was not deficient enough to trigger feeding. However, the 0800 report shows that, as waking activity increased on a still empty stomach (GUT = 0), FLO fell deeper into deficiency. When FLO reached the hunger threshold, feeding began at 0820, 500 min from the start of the simulation).

Nothing metabolic improved for the first few minutes of the meal (0825 report). After the delay period for digestion, however, a little absorption began and net energy flow began to be ameliorated. In this program, the activity level somewhat unrealistically continued to rise during the meal, on its ramp from sleeping to working. The thermic effect of food also contributed to this rise in METABR. Despite that, the deficit of absorption (ABSOR) relative to metabolism was eliminated and lipolysis ceased, some of the increasing excess energy then being diverted into fat synthesis (LIPO becomes positive by 0830). When the cumulative food intake 6 min previously was great enough to provide absorption sufficient to bring non-fat energy flow to the satiety threshold, the meal stopped after a not unrealistic 20 min and moderately hearty 512 g. The initial value given to the satiety threshold was close to the value the simulation would acquire when it settled down, and so this first breakfast was similar to that on later days of simulation.

The next segment of output in Fig. 7 shows the simulated first evening meal and the first 24-h increments in fat and lean energy (kcal). The final segment is the last lines of this simulation, giving the third day's supper and energy increments.

Figure 8 gives the complete output from the second day of this simulation. The metabolic parameters up to the end of breakfast were identical to those on day 1. However, supper on day 1 had conditioned satiety to a slightly lower threshold and so the meal was a little smaller. As breakfast was passed from the stomach, so absorption showed, and—helped somewhat by the energy expenditure at a full working level (METABR = 2·7)—the net energy flow became low enough to trigger the start of lunch at 1317. In this highly determinate system, always eating the same menu, all meals are of fairly similar size.

Rather less had to remain in the stomach for supper to be triggered at 1904, because work had ended and activity was on its slow downward ramp through the evening, creating less energy loss.

Some food was still left in the stomach at bedtime, 2330, and so net energy flow to the non-fat compartment (FLO) was not even slightly negative. Once the system was simulating sleep, energy flow became substantially negative when the stomach had emptied, as has been seen from the early morning hours in both Figs 7 and 8. Yet the sleeping metabolic rate was low enough not to create an energy flow shortfall severe enough to reach the usual hunger threshold. So the empty stomach does not under these conditions trigger a midnight binge. Subjects with a lower effective hunger threshold or with higher activity levels when they should be asleep would be predicted to behave differently: such may

```
TIME      METABR    GUT      ABSOR    LIPO      FLO      FAT     LEAN     WEIGHT
 0  0      1.28    0.007     0.63    -0.37    -0.28    86.63   191.25    75.00

 1  0      1.25    0.000     0.00    -0.62    -0.63    86.59   191.22    74.99

 2  0      1.25    0.000     0.00    -0.62    -0.63    86.56   191.18    74.97

 3  0      1.25    0.000     0.00    -0.62    -0.63    86.52   191.14    74.95

 4  0      1.25    0.000     0.00    -0.62    -0.63    86.48   191.11    74.93

 5  0      1.25    0.000     0.00    -0.62    -0.63    86.44   191.07    74.92

 6  0      1.25    0.000     0.00    -0.62    -0.63    86.41   191.03    74.90

 7  0      1.25    0.000     0.00    -0.62    -0.63    86.37   190.99    74.88

 8  0      1.71    0.000     0.00    -0.82    -0.89    86.33   190.95    74.86

MEAL STARTED     TIME  8 20     MEAL-MEAL INTERVAL   771     MINUTES
  8 25     2.10    0.206     0.00    -0.99    -1.11    86.31   190.93    74.85
  8 30     2.30    0.427     2.45    -0.00     0.15    86.30   190.93    74.85
  8 35     2.45    0.642     3.78     0.66     0.67    86.31   190.93    74.85
  8 40     2.57    0.854     4.73     1.12     1.03    86.31   190.93    74.85
MEAL STOPPED     TIME  8 40     MEAL SIZE    500  GRAMS    OFF USED 1.06

 9  0      2.92    0.767     5.46     1.33     1.20    86.34   190.96    74.87

10  0      2.87    0.479     4.34     0.74     0.73    86.40   191.02    74.89

11  0      2.81    0.259     3.22     0.14     0.27    86.43   191.05    74.91

12  0      2.75    0.106     2.10    -0.37    -0.29    86.42   191.05    74.91

13  0      2.70    0.020     0.98    -0.83    -0.89    86.38   191.01    74.89

MEAL STARTED     TIME 13 17     MEAL-MEAL INTERVAL   277     MINUTES
 13 20     2.68    0.123     0.60    -0.98    -1.10    86.37   190.99    74.88
 13 25     2.73    0.346     1.70    -0.53    -0.50    86.36   190.99    74.88
 13 30     2.82    0.564     3.36     0.22     0.32    86.36   190.99    74.88
 13 35     2.87    0.776     4.40     0.77     0.76    86.36   190.99    74.88
 13 40     2.91    0.985     5.23     1.21     1.11    86.37   190.99    74.88
MEAL STOPPED     TIME 13 40     MEAL SIZE    575  GRAMS    OFF USED 1.12

14  0      2.94    0.890     5.87     1.55     1.37    86.40   191.02    74.89

15  0      2.89    0.578     4.75     0.96     0.91    86.47   191.09    74.93

16  0      2.83    0.333     3.63     0.36     0.44    86.51   191.13    74.95

17  0      2.77    0.155     2.51    -0.20    -0.06    86.52   191.14    74.95

18  0      2.50    0.044     1.39    -0.56    -0.55    86.50   191.12    74.94

19  0      2.23    0.001     0.27    -0.93    -1.03    86.45   191.08    74.92

MEAL STARTED     TIME 19  4     MEAL-MEAL INTERVAL   324     MINUTES
 19  5     2.21    0.000     0.17    -0.96    -1.07    86.45   191.07    74.92
 19 10     2.19    0.229     0.08    -0.99    -1.12    86.44   191.07    74.91
 19 15     2.29    0.449     2.62     0.09     0.23    86.44   191.06    74.91
 19 20     2.34    0.664     3.88     0.78     0.77    86.44   191.07    74.91
MEAL STOPPED     TIME 19 24     MEAL SIZE    487  GRAMS    OFF USED 1.10

20  0      2.26    0.665     5.09     1.50     1.33    86.50   191.12    74.94

21  0      1.99    0.400     3.97     1.02     0.96    86.58   191.19    74.97

22  0      1.72    0.201     2.85     0.55     0.59    86.63   191.24    75.00

23  0      1.44    0.070     1.73     0.07     0.21    86.64   191.26    75.01

         END OF DAY  2    FAT   7.1   LEAN   7.1
```

Fig. 8. The complete second day from the simulation programmed by Figs 1–6.

be some of the causes of unusual amounts of feeding late at night. As the time during sleep at which the stomach empties does not affect the timing or size of breakfast, late night binges would not be compensated in the short term and the system could rely only on long term feedback to avoid gaining weight. Conversely, too little activity by the time food was presented after waking would leave the system above hunger threshold—possibly one reason why some people can only take coffee at breakfast.

The pattern of gastric contents and metabolic flow rates around the clock on day 2 is given in Fig. 9.

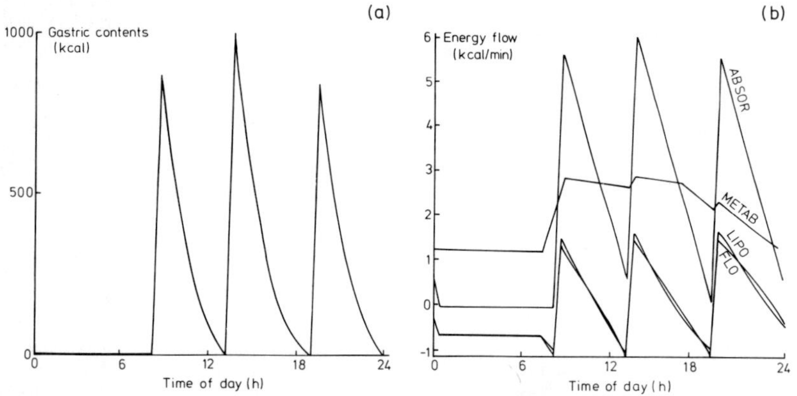

Fig. 9. Output from the basic model, reprogrammed to record the values of variables at every calculation cycle of day 2 and to plot them graphically: a, gastric contents (kcal); b, rates of absorption, total metabolism (heat output), lipogenesis–lipolysis and flow into or out of the non-fat compartments (kcal/min).

III. Programming and Computer Use

The program given in the previous section is written in the language Extended Fortran IV as used on an ICL 1906A computer. Fortran is a versatile scientific programming language to which computer operating systems on both departmental and university computers here are well adapted and in which model optimizing and testing routines are readily available.

This and other versions of the present model have also been written in the language Basic. Both that language itself and the systems available to us for operating with it are particularly suitable for introductory teaching purposes. Most of the program statements read naturally even to those not familiar with Basic or any other programming language. A program in Basic can even be edited in a number of ways by someone who is not fluent in constructing programs. We find it convenient to use time-shared systems in Basic, on a departmental computer when only a few terminals are needed as in the tutorial situation, and on an inter-university system when each student in a class is using a terminal. However, a relatively high-level and simple language like Basic is at present available only at an appreciable cost in flexibility and computing speed. On a small computer like our department's PDP-11, the few days of real life that might take a night's run to simulate in Basic take only a few minutes in Fortran. When the computer is not being used over the weekend for other work, 15 years of a human lifetime can be simulated using a Fortran program.

Languages like Basic and Fortran can be learned very quickly—almost painlessly if one works with an already operative program which has a familiar scientific basis. Someone using a model like the present one for a while should be able to modify it radically to his own needs, or might even throw it away and build his own model. Short programming courses are widely available, however, and it can be better to take one: they provide a systematic introduction into all aspects of use of a programming language, and the user is less likely to find himself lost at times in the manuals for the local language or operating system or to be a pest to his colleagues who are programming literate.

IV. Some Tests of Properties of the Model

A. *Adjustment Procedures*

Our approach to modelling is primarily empirical, in the sense that each component function and parameter value in the model could in principle be derived from independent experimental data. However, at present there are some components in the human model for which quantitative data are almost totally lacking. Furthermore, there seems likely to remain for some time a considerable latitude within which parameter values and even function characteristics for most components could be varied and remain consistent with data. In this situation, we should seek the numbers that work best, within the ranges that data permit.

1. *Optimization*

If some criterion can be specified for the overall performance of a version of the model, the values of major parameters can be adjusted to meet this criterion. We have used an optimizing routine from the Nottingham University Algorithm Library (No. EO4CCF). This minimizes a general function of the required number of independent variables, using a Simplex method (Nelder and Mead, 1965). The reiterative calculations adjust the variables—the parameter values chosen from the model for optimization—to meet the criterion of optimum performance, for example a minimum change in body weight over a given number of days.

2. *Sensitivity Testing*

Even if the elements of the model were entirely determined by empirical data, and not in part by optimizing considerations, it would still be instructive to see the effects on the model's output when the values of some parameters were varied. The results provide an analysis which can indicate which parts of the model are most critical to the output generated, whether the "predictions" put out be realistic or not. That is, merely computational "experiments" can elucidate the sensitivity of the model to variations in its different components.

3. *Adaptation*

The basic model presented here has a limitation which would be expected to narrow the range of useful sensitivity tests to small deviations from the optimized (or experimentally precisely determined) values of variables and to short term effects of such deviations. None of the functions in the model *adapts*. That is not to say that the basic model as a whole fails to show adaptive responses to disturbance or that its undisturbed operation is maladaptive in some way. It is to say that there is not a *parameter* in any function whose value is dependent on the value of the output variables from another function. Functions are not interdependent or dependent on changes in external conditions, even though the values of *variables* calculated according to the various functions are of course highly dependent on the values of variables input from other functions. For example, the level of the metabolic rate variable influences the level of the momentary rate of gastric emptying, another *variable,* by affecting the timing of meals and hence the contents of the stomach. However, a persisting high level of metabolism (e.g. because of hard work or a cold environment) does not in the basic model adapt the gastric emptying rate constant, which is the main *parameter* in that gastric clearance function. This non-adapting gastric emptying rate constant is almost certainly unrealistic. Changes in eating rate may also adapt the gastric emptying rate constant. Persistently high absorption rates may adapt the proportionality factors (which reflect hormone secretory responses) controlling fat synthesis or mobilization. And so on around the model. Quantitative experimental determinations of the adaptive relations between persisting values of variables and values of functions' parameters will obviously be important in the development of a model to give realistic output in simulations of long term effects.

One qualification must be entered on the above: one function in the basic model does adapt, in the sense that all learning is adaptive—the conditioned satiety function. In this case, the maximum postprandial value of the FLO variable resets the value of the parameter which determines at what FLO value the next meal will be ended. It remains to be seen whether conditioning, i.e. adaptation of interneuronal relations, is important in any of the physiological adaptations mentioned above. It is generally expected that such adaptations will be systemic (e.g. in the pancreatic or intestinal cell) but recent evidence that anticipatory responses of pancreas (Woods and Porte, 1974) and intestine wall (Saito *et al.*, 1976) are neurally mediated may serve to warn that this presupposition should be modified.

B. *Optimization for Constant Body Composition*

Most mature adults change in body composition very slowly compared with the rate of flow of energy through the body, and for that matter compared with the variations in composition of the diet and intensity or quality of motor activity. The basic model contained one simple function specifically designed to achieve long term stability (statement 70). Nevertheless, it seemed sensible at this stage to exclude from the model any powerful short term influence tending to change body composition.

We therefore chose six key parameters whose values were to be adjusted to minimize changes in the fat and non-fat energy of the body over several days of simulated processing (Section IV.A.1). These parameters were the rate constants for gastric emptying (STOMAK), lipogenesis (INFAT), lipolysis (OUTFAT) and lipolytic feedback from fat store (FATFBK), the hunger threshold (MINFLO) and the target satiety level (MAXFLO). The body stability criteria were changes less than 0·33 kcal in lean energy and 1 kcal in fat energy totalled over 7 days. When the optimization procedure had gone through sufficient iterations to produce no further change, values of about 0·19, 0·55, 0·4, 0·2, 1·5 and −1·1, respectively, were obtained. At the values given in Fig. 2, as can be seen in Figs 7 and 8 the simulation gained on average over several days no more than about 1 kcal/day of either fat or non-fat energy. This would amount to about 5 lb (2·3 kg) in 20 years, less than the population average rate of weight increase around middle age (Garrow, 1974). These optimized parameter values were in fact close to those we had originally chosen by scaling the rat up to human size. In an earlier version of this human model, without feedback from fat stores, the optimum values were also similar. That is, short term control by itself could be tuned to give a long term average effect of constancy in body composition while the conditions specified for that optimization were not disturbed.

The optimizations were run by varying the parameters of a given set of functions while leaving one particular constant set of values assigned to other parameters. The effect of varying these latter functions and values remains to be investigated. In particular, the activity pattern and metabolic rates were those used in the example of Section II.A.2.b—sleeping from 2300 to 0730, and working at 1·5 kcal/min between 0900 and 1700. Also assumed were a dietary energy density of 1·9 kcal/g, an eating rate of 25 g/min and a digestion lag of 6 min. With other values of these parameters, different values of the optimized parameters would no doubt be required to keep body composition constant. Such calculations might therefore provide some basis for suggestions as to the types of adaptation of parameter value which might be used in the real person to help to preserve constant body composition. This would be an example of simulation work *generating* theory.

C. *Sensitivity of Body Constancy-Optimized Model*

To test how critical a parameter was to the food intake and body composition predictions of this example of the model, optimized and other parameter values were varied by at least 10% and in some cases by much more. The effects calculated on the timings and sizes of meals and on gain in fat and non-fat energy were averaged over a simulated 4 days, which followed 4 days from the start of run to ensure the simulation had had time to adapt fully to the conditions specified. A model without feedback from fat was used.

1. *Gastric Emptying Rate Constant*

As to be expected, the model was quite sensitive to modest variations in the characteristics of gastric clearance. These are represented by the rate constant and the exponent in the equation which is used to calculate current emptying rate from current gastric energy content (statement 55, Fig. 4). In this simplified

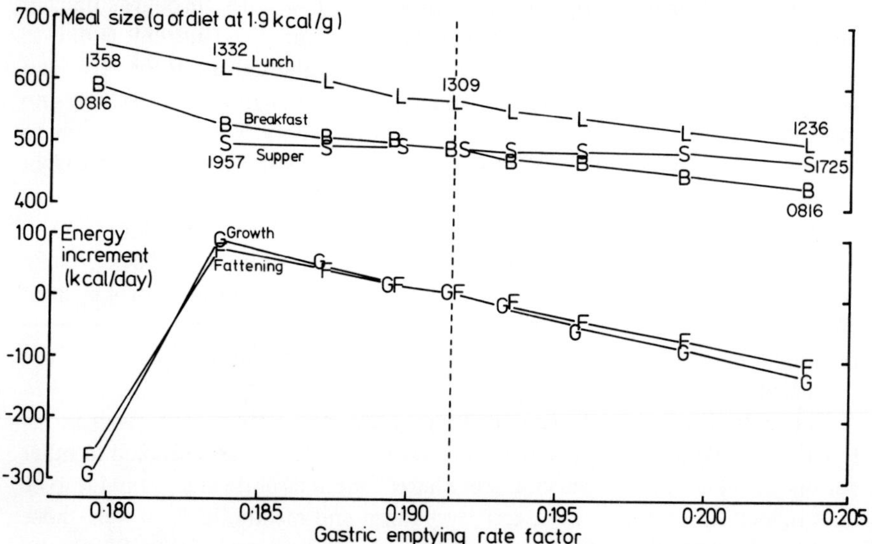

Fig. 10. Variation of gastric emptying rate factor around an optimized value of 0·1915. Average meal sizes and 24-h clock timings are given for the first (B), the second (L) and (when it occurs) the third (S) meal of the day and for the 24-h gain (or loss) of energy in fat (F) or non-fat (G) components of the parenteral mass.

model, the rate constant (STOMAK) would have to be adjusted according to the energy density of the diet if the simulation was to allow for the observed variations in emptying rate with energy density of stomach contents (Hunt and Stubbs, 1975). Faster emptying after ingestion of more concentrated diet may account for a correlation between chubbiness and energy density of the diet (Hunt *et al.,* 1975). Trowell (1975) has summarized evidence that lack of dietary fibre, not concentration of the diet, is a major cause of obesity because it makes for more efficient absorption. Booth (1976) argued that individual's gastric emptying characteristics as such, independently of energy density or fibre content, could be an additional factor in the varying propensities different people have to remain lean or to tend to obesity.

Meals decreased in size with faster rate factors and increased in size with slower rate factors, particularly at breakfast and lunch (Fig. 10). This is because the strength of satiety in the model ultimately depends on the relation between amount in the stomach and rate of gastric emptying: the less needed to get fast absorption, the smaller is the satiating amount of food. Larger meals are not rapidly compensated by smaller meals on other days (even with the long term feedback of the model of Section II), because the total amount eaten in a day (within wide limits) only determines when during sleep the stomach becomes empty and absorption stops—this having no behavioural effect. Therefore, larger meals generate net energy deposition and smaller meals permit net energy loss (Fig. 10). Breakfast stayed at 0816 and lunch stayed around the lunch hour, but supper became so late with the slower stomach that at a rate factor of 0·18 it dropped out altogether. This of course overwhelmed the energy depositing effect of the larger breakfasts and lunches which occurred with the slower stomach, and energy was lost rapidly (Fig. 10).

The direction of this effect is the opposite of that seen in the rat model, in which a fast stomach fattens (Chapter 11). The size and direction of the effect may be quite sensitive to the values of lipoflow parameters, particularly the point of changeover between lipolysis and lipogenesis and hence the stage towards the end of the meal at which the changeover occurs and affects meal size. More rapid emptying might falter if inoperative during meals or if ineffective at conditioning satiety.

2. *Lipoflow Parameter Values*

(a) *Changes in one value at a time.* Small variations in the factors in the equations which determine the proportion of spare energy deposited as fat (INFAT) or the proportion of energy shortfall covered by fat mobilization (OUTFAT) had effects on body composition which would be very substantial when cumulated over the long term (Fig. 11a,b). The effects on the meal pattern were minute, and yet of course a systematic small increase (or decrease) in meal size and slight consequential changes in meal timing occurred which were the

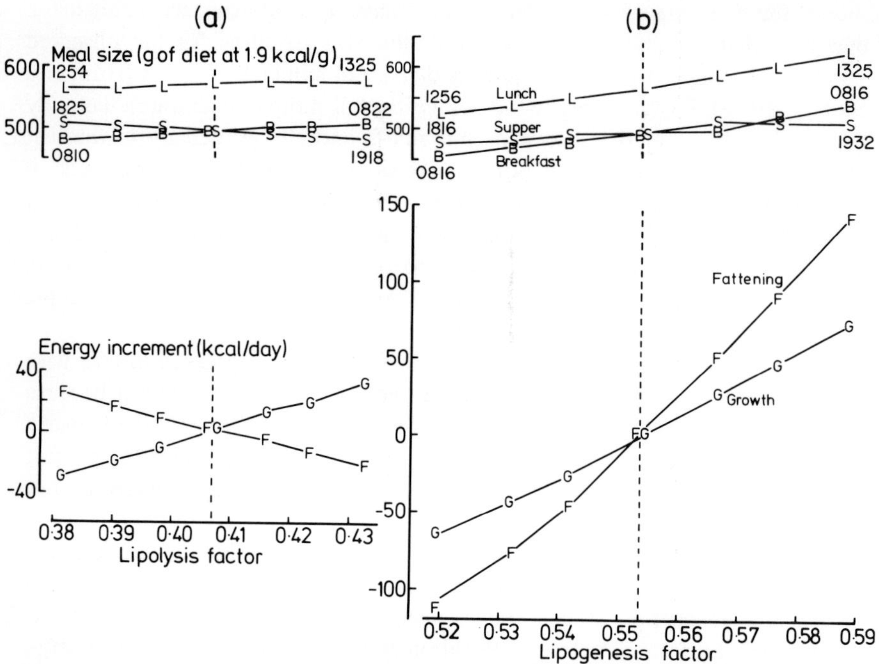

Fig. 11. Variation of lipoflow proportionality factors: a, lipoflow; b, lipogenesis. Symbols as in Fig. 10.

input on which the net body energy gain (or loss) was based. This is the all too familiar truism of weight control thermodynamics: a persistent minute "error" in meal size and total food intake will cumulate dramatically over the months and years. There is naturally an increase in delay to the next meal while a slightly larger meal is absorbed. Yet this does not compensate for the increase in meal size in the human subjects as modelled. The reason is the same as in the case of changes in gastric emptying characteristics—the behavioural irrelevance of the time the gut becomes empty during sleep means that (at least in the short term) one day's intake is disconnected from the next. In reality, people may have some mechanism to help the size of breakfast reflect, say, the time since the gut became empty: yet such a mechanism would have to be implausibly powerful to provide immediately the appropriate degree of full compensation. Thus the modelling encourages us to diagnose our long period of sleep as one of the weaknesses in the human feeding control system considered as a stabilizer of energy balance.

(b) *An elementary account of growth and obesity.* The pattern of effects on body composition of changes in the proportionality factors for lipogenesis and lipolysis suggests a summary analysis of mechanisms which could contribute to normal growth and to the development of obesity. These suggestions also bring out how the lipoflow proportionality factors INFAT and OUTFAT could have physiological and biochemical meaning as parameters which lump together the effects of hormonal control of substrate distribution to tissues.

Table I.
Approximate body composition effects of varying the proportionality factors in the lipogenesis and lipolysis equations, in which lipoflow is set to be proportional to the differences between absorption and utilization rates

Lipoflow	Change in proportionality factors	Long term energy increment (arbitrary units)		
		Non-fat	Fat mass	Total mass
1. Lipolysis	Decrease	-1	$+1$	0
2. Lipolysis	Increase	$+1$	-1	0
3. Lipogenesis	Decrease	$-\frac{1}{2}$	-1	$-1\frac{1}{2}$
4. Lipogenesis	Increase	$+\frac{1}{2}$	$+1$	$+1\frac{1}{2}$
Lipogenesis Lipolysis	Increase Increase	$+1\frac{1}{2}$	0	"Pure growth"
Lipogenesis Lipolysis	Increase Decrease ($\frac{1}{2}$)	0	$+1\frac{1}{2}$	"Pure fattening"

Table I summarizes the effects of variations in lipoflow factors such as those graphed in Fig. 11. In the range tested, increases and decreases in the lipolysis factor (OUTFAT) have relatively negligible effects on total body energy content. However, this is because the changes have complementary effects on fat and non-fat components, or—to use more conventional categories, introducing only slight inaccuracy— on adipose and lean body masses. That is, a reduced lipolysis factor fattens at the cost of wasting (loss of lean mass), and an increased lipolysis factor slims but increases lean mass, i.e. causes a form of "growth". On the other hand, changes in the lipogenesis factor (INFAT) do produce changes in total body energy content, according to the model. Reduced lipogenesis has a slimming effect but it also has a wasting effect, although the wasting is less in energy value than the slimming. Increased lipogenesis fattens but also to a lesser extent generates growth.

In reality, action of a hormone or some other control mechanism may be best represented by coordinate changes in both lipoflow factors. Insulin, for example, independently both augments lipogenesis and inhibits lipolysis. Growth hormone and/or other anabolic hormones may not merely augment lipolysis but directly or indirectly increase the turnover of fat. Alternatively, the anabolic hormones could be largely lipolytic but endocrine controls introduce lipogenic tendencies alongside that lipolytic effect by augmenting both the anabolic secretions and the secretion of insulin. In either case, the anabolic controls may be critical to whether energy is put into growth or fattening.

Growth without fattening or slimming would be generated by conjoint increases in both lipogenesis and lipolysis factors: addition of lines 2 and 4 of Table I gives 1·5 increments of lean mass with no net change in adipose mass. This is a simulation of a classical view of the role of growth hormone, with a proviso that insulin sufficiency is also necessary. Indeed, insulin has a somatomedin-like role.

Fattening without growth or wasting would result if an increase in the lipogenesis factor were co-ordinate with a decrease in the lipolysis factor to around half the extent. Line 4 of Table I plus half of line 1 would give 1·5 increments of adipose mass with no net change in lean mass.

The implications of this simple analysis need exploring for the techniques of body weight control which involve dietary control and the modification of feeding behaviour. One suspects that according to the model there would be no problem about sustaining growth (as in an immature human being) so long as no economic or other social constraints prevent intake from being adequate in amount and balance, and so long as the normal childhood hormonal pattern is present. For obesity, in contrast, one has the intuition that the model would require relatively heroic reductions in total intake to conteract a markedly fattening hormonal pattern or cellular response abnormality. This pessimistic analysis seems all too realistic in the light of what we know about the aetiology and therapy of obesity in many cases. However, for this and the several other aetiologies of obesity which are possible within the model, the simulation technique may at least provide a way of calculating the minimum required heroics—that is, the changes in feeding pattern which would be least hard to maintain in the face of their physiological, cognitive and social conditions and consequences.

3. *Energy Thresholds*

(a) *Hunger Threshold* (*MINFLO*). The model's output was relatively insensitive to minor variations in the level of energy flow shortfall which was sufficient to trigger feeding (Fig. 12a).

(b) *Target Satiety Level* (*MAXFLO*). The effective satiety threshold is adjusted in the model by a learning mechanism which predicts which level of energy flow at the end of a meal should, following a meal, produce a maximum energy flow at the target satiety level (cf. statement 99, Fig. 5). Thus although the satiety threshold is not a set parameter, its value is strongly determined by the target for postprandial maximum satiety.

Not surprisingly, changes in satiety target had substantial effects on meal size (Fig. 12b). The lower the target the smaller are the meals, and the higher the larger. There follows the effect of meal size on energy storage which is familiar by now. The storage effects are similar in lean and adipose mass: a more detailed

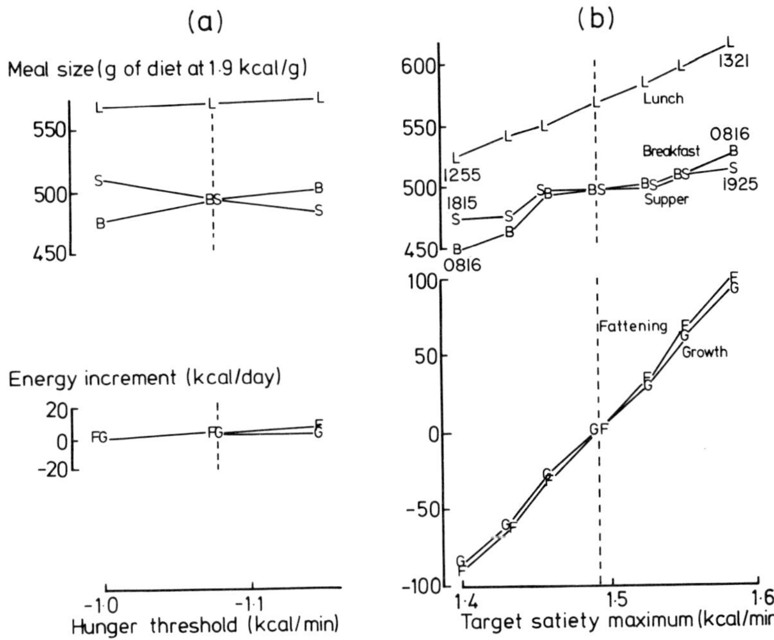

Fig. 12. Variation in meal onset and offset control parameters: a, hunger threshold; b, target satiety maximum.

model may be necessary to give an account of the differences between fattening and body-building effects of extra-hearty meals.

4. *Non-optimized Parameters*

(a) *Digestion delay*. The delay between gastric emptying and circulation of energy to the tissues proved not to be critical to performance of the model. This is partly because the learning mechanism for adjusting the satiety threshold is not programmed to show any effect of CS-US interval. It is also contingent on relatively linear characteristics of the increase in lipogenesis as absorption gathers pace.

(b) *Metabolic rate*. Substantial variations in the rate of energy expenditure during the simulated working day have considerable effects on feeding and body energy. It will be important to re-optimize parameter values for different basal and working metabolic rates. Indeed, adaptation of gastric clearance and lipoflow functions to metabolic rate would probably be realistic. Nevertheless, Fig. 13a shows simply the effects of variations in work output around the level of very light work which was used in these first simulations and in the optimization around which these sensitivity tests range.

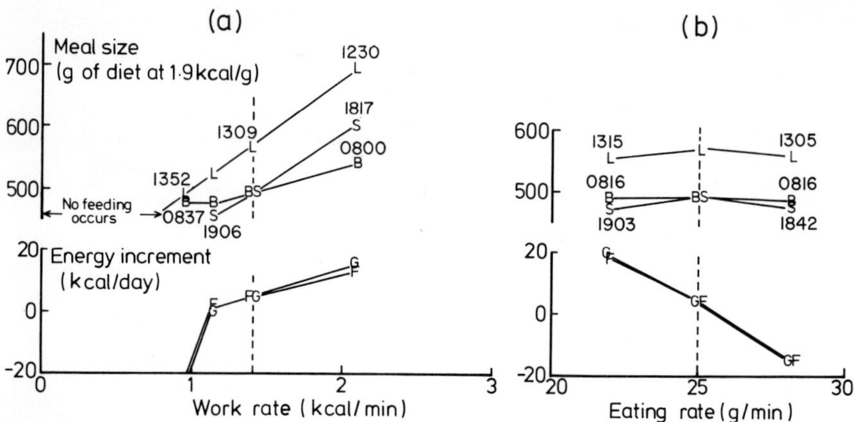

Fig. 13. a, Changes in rate of energy expenditure in external work and motor activity. b, Changes in feeding rate.

The model's predictions provide an interpretation of the saying "He who does not work shall not eat" which is different from that which St Paul intended. If the working rate is below about 1 kcal/min, the assumed decreasing metabolic rate in the evening becomes so low that a somewhat delayed third meal of the day never begins. Indeed at 0·7 kcal/min working rate, the hunger threshold is never reached at any time of day. These unrealistic predictions are partly contingent on having optimized the programmed parameters for a work rate of 1·4 kcal/min. In particular, the hunger threshold may be too extreme. As discussed later, the concept of a simple threshold is highly questionable. Furthermore, even if it is used, a threshold should not be a determinate value as in this program, but should be subject to internal and external "noise" (as in the rat feeding model, Mark 3, Chapter 11). Eating would then tend to occur on occasion even at low work rate, in reaction either to an apparent slight shortfall in energy flow or to a high incentive feeding situation.

With increasing work rate, this optimization increases meal size and, despite the larger meals, starts feeding again earlier (Fig. 13a). At still higher energy expenditures, the simulations predict more than three meals a day. This may not be an unrealistic view of the situation where heavy work can be interrupted for refreshment breaks and food is readily available during such breaks. The simulation gains stored energy despite increased work, but the gain of non-fat energy is similar to that of fat energy, and so the cumulative effect would be "body-building", not increased adiposity.

(c) *Eating rate.* Reducing the feeding rate from the 25 g/min on which the program was optimized caused slight variations in meal sizes with no clear trend, but a consistent tendency to put on lean and fat mass (Fig. 13b). Modest increases in feeding rate tended to decrease meal size slightly, with resulting losses in both lean and fat mass. It remains to be seen how robust this result is when optimization has been carried out according to other criteria and when the model has been improved to reflect more realistically the effects of food energy density on gastric emptying. As it stands, the result raises a question about the widespread belief that fast eating contributes to obesity. This presupposition to the behaviour modification strategy of slowing feeding has been challenged on ground of lack of evidence (Mahoney, 1975). It has frequently been observed that on average obese subjects eat faster than standard weight subjects, but simplistic physiological hypotheses as to satiety mechanisms are not a justification for concluding forthwith that the rapid feeding causes obesity, rather than some other factor causing both characteristics. For example, high density food conditions a relative palatability into the flavour of the food (Booth *et al.,* 1972). Thus, when dense foodstuffs are available, they will tend to be selected increasingly over lighter foods and the rate of their ingestion may accelerate. Higher energy densities in the stomach will speed absorption and so deposit more fat energy. There is evidence that high food density does indeed contribute to chubbiness (Hunt *et al.,* 1975), but the many factors operative preclude a very strong correlation between food energy or carbohydrate density and eating rate.

It must be emphasized that at the very most these simulations raise a question about the conventional wisdom that slow eating slims. Without improved modelling and much more detailed analysis of model performance there would be no basis for suggesting that people *should* eat fast to slim. Nevertheless, insofar as the mechanisms modelled are an acceptable theory of satiation, the intuition that gobbling should fool the satiety mechanism is refuted by systems analysis computed within the indicated presuppositions.

V. Long-term Stability via Short Term Control

There has been considerable factual and conceptual confusion about so-called regulation of body weight. Mogenson and Calaresu analyse the problems in Chapter 1 of this book. In fact, in man there is no conclusive evidence that energy balance is kept constant on a day-to-day basis or even from one month to the next (Garrow, 1974). Furthermore, human body weight and adiposity do not on average stay strictly constant, but increase slowly even between 25 and 40 years of age. Nevertheless, the approximation to constancy from one year to the next is very close relative to the cumulative quantities of energy ingested as food and lost as external work, heat and excretion.

However, this degree of stability over the very long term does not in principle require a very precise feedback control mechanism of the type that an engineer would construct, in terms of which Brobeck (1965) defined the physiological concept of regulation and Hervey (1969) has discussed the specific problem of the control of the amount of fat stored. There is a great variety of types of possible stabilizing influence, and many of them biologically more plausible than a thermostat-like control mechanism (Toates, 1975; Booth *et al.*, 1976a). As the point becomes more widely appreciated, so the uses of terms such as regulation, homeostasis and set point are qualified. They are offered as merely descriptive of the observed stability characteristics, allegedly losing their specific mechanistic implications. In contrast, our approach is to avoid the use of special words that tend to create unnecessary realities in the minds of their users or hearers. Rather we try to account for the observed degree and quality of stability by invoking known influences or by postulating biologically plausible mechanisms which are the simplest that can do the job.

A. *Control of Appetite and Satiety by Energy Flow*

However directly or indirectly the brain measures energy flow to non-fat tissues, as postulated in the theory behind the present model (Booth, 1972a,b), and by whatever combination of learned or direct effects the energy flows control feeding behaviour (Chapter 11, Section I.B.1), the short term control of timing and size of meals by their energetic interactions with utilization creates a powerful stability in the longer term. Providing that natural variation in the values of quantities in the system has a central tendency, variability in short term effects will tend to average out into a much less variable cumulative effect (Schilstra makes an analogous point in Chapter 9). The body may process relatively huge amounts of energy but it is a more or less fixed structure of viscera, bones, muscle and skin which carries out the processing. There are firm physical limits as well as narrower and subtler physiological limitations on what many body compartments can store or even process. Just a large tank filled from a tap and emptied from a drain will, within wide limits of inflow and outflow, find and roughly maintain a steady content for particular orders of inflow rate and drain diameter. The pond on the village green has no cistern mechanism.

B. *Basal Metabolic Rate*

The biochemistry of energy utilization adjusts to changes in conditions in a number of ways which tend to stabilize energy exchange and shift energy balance closer to the null point than it would otherwise be.

Heat loss increases with lean body mass. This is numerically a relatively tiny stabilizing effect. Nevertheless, the greater energy cost of maintaining more tissue is a limitation on tissue accretion.

Energy utilization becomes more efficient as a period of restricted intake lengthens. This effect normally asymptotes. Nevertheless, it limits the rate of tissue wastage under transient insult.

Some have suggested that overfeeding reduces the efficiency of energy utilization. This effect of "luxuskonsumption" has never been proven to physiologists' general satisfaction, but it may yet turn out that some people show such an effect under some circumstances (Garrow, 1978). This could be a more substantial limit on energy accumulation.

Basal metabolic rate and the energies of posture and movement are complex functions of adipose mass or adiposity (adipose as proportion of total). Some relations (e.g. the insulating properties of fat) are destabilizing. An effect of sense of effort on tendency to move would also be dysregulatory, and the inactivity of some obese people is well known. On the other hand, given (say) the maintenance of a certain speed of movement, the energy cost of distorting and carrying adipose tissue would be a restraining effect on its accumulation.

Probably none of these effects is particularly powerful, but they should be represented in a full model so far as each is evidenced.

It should be noted that there may be large individual differences in efficiency of energy utilization or in basal metabolic rate relative to body weight. These differences are not regulatory mechanisms for individuals but they should produce large individual differences in total intake and feeding pattern. Where social influences based on average intake or pattern hold sway over an individual who otherwise might be at an extreme of low (or high) intake, the low (or high) metabolic rate can be dysregulatory and fattening (or anorexigenic).

C. *Bias of Energy Flow by Size of Energy Store*

1. *The Feedback Mechanism*

One very simple form of negative feedback, which is to some extent already experimentally supported, could in principle be sufficiently powerful to provide a greater degree of stability of adiposity or body weight than is in fact observed in man. This is because, although at a given moment the feedback influence might be mixed with large short term variations, the feedback would be persistent at an average level which was monotonically related to the deviation of the amount of stored energy from a value which would be in equilibrium with fat-depositing tendencies and so would exert a strong long term control.

The general form of such a feedback would be a change in the energy store (i.e. a flow of energy into or out of it) which is proportional to some power function (exponent c) of the size (S) of the store:

$$\Delta S = kS^c$$

The store could be lean mass, in which case we are talking about a bias to growth or to wasting. More relevantly to the adult human case, the store could be adipose mass, and the bias be lipolytic or lipogenic (and both may exist simultaneously). In the arithmetically simple case where $c = 1$, lipolytic and lipogenic functions can be added to give a single equation which may be net lipolytic or lipogenic. Positive exponents on wasting or lipolytic functions and negative exponents on growth or lipogenic functions provide negative feedback—that is, tend to stabilize body energy.

A background lipolysis in proportion to adipose energy content (or a background lipogenesis in inverse proportion) would severely restrain tendencies to put on fat and would help take it off in the absence of such tendencies. Such background could be local, depending on cell structure, or it could be distributed, for example in a phenomenon such as insulin resistance. In fact, basal lipolysis *in vitro* increases as human adipose cell size increases (Goldrick and McLoughlin, 1970). As it has turned out, the basic prototype model happens to operate in such a way that the direction of short term effects on fat storage depends largely on lipolysis or turnover rather than on modulation of absolute lipogenic flow (Section IV.C.2.b).

Until such time as experiments in man *in vivo* under normal conditions provide an estimate of basal lipolysis as a function of adipose energy, and this in turn is related to feeding behaviour, the properties of such a stabilizing mechanism will have to be explored merely by conceptual experiments. The basic prototype model of Section II includes a lipolytic feedback equation in the energy flow calculation. Its proportionality factor (and exponent) could be set at other values, the other parameter values optimized to give equilibrium adiposity in the normal range and then the sensitivity tested of these models to prefattening, preslimming and imposed fattening or slimming influences.

The long term stabilizing properties of the program of Section II have been preliminarily tested simply by altering the initial body fat content and running the simulation for many months. As expected, the feedback from fat stores does tend to return body weight, and particularly its fat component, to a value which is preferred under the other conditions of simulation (Fig. 14). However, with the FATFBK parameter value used, which is of an order compatible with data on basal lipolysis in human adipose cells *in vitro*, the loss of excess fat and the correction of fat deficit is interestingly slow—taking years to lose or gain 10kg, not days or even months. If this is a realistic computation of the quantitative effect of this type of negative feedback in man, then it may prove beyond the power of existing data to discriminate between such an equilibrium theory of weight control and a theory of "buffered" levels of energy store (Garrow and Stalley, 1975). The body weight changes were achieved by relatively miniscule changes in food intake. Very small changes in lean mass occurred along with the large changes in adipose mass.

Garrow (1974) has argued that excursions in human energy balance can be so large and their corrections where they occur (whether in part or whole) are so delayed that the observed stability characteristics can be attributed to the individual's perception of his own weight or form and his deliberate control of food intake and/or energy expenditure. Nevertheless, people differ greatly in the speed and extent of weight change and even a change in adiposity which is very large, relatively rapid and never fully corrected is not a phenomenon that is evidence against a simple physiological feedback from fat store to appetite. Such a feedback has to operate in the context of many other influences. If it is not the

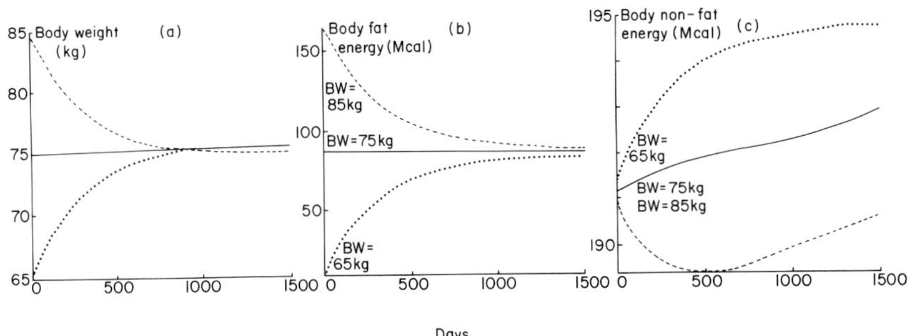

Fig. 14. Longterm stability of: a, body weight; b, fat energy; and c, non-fat energy in the basic model when the initial body composition is normal or is increased or decreased in adipose tissue content by 10 kg. Note that the scale for non-fat energy is 30 times more expanded than the scale for fat energy, and that the fat gain of the simulation starting at 75 kg, although also miniscule, is three times greater than the graphically more more obvious gain in non-fat energy over about four years.

type of feedback that involves assessment of deviation from some particular pre-set privileged value of fat store size, then the stable value of fat store will depend on other conditions in the system, or under some unfortunate circumstances there may be no permanently stable value towards which fat store size tends. As discussed in Section IV.A.3, a particularly important possibility is that components of the system adapt as the system is persistently operated under new conditions. Whatever feedback from fat store to appetite might exist could itself adapt to persistently high storage rate, turnover or amount—adaptation which is as likely in principle to attenuate the negative feedback effect as to strengthen it.

Thus, the fact that someone has grossly increased in weight and shows no sign of losing weight, or even appears to be continuing to get fatter indefinitely and has extreme difficulty in stopping weight increase at any level, is not evidence against the existence of the kind of feedback function proposed above. The evidence against it would be (the very difficult) measurement of the quantitative relation between adipose triglyceride content or cell size and long-term net mobilization and then the calculation of the effects of the operation of such a functional relation in a feeding control system with other defined characteristics. That is, systematic computation not only aids the formulation of experimental design. It is likely also to prove essential to definite interpretation of the results.

2. *Short Term Set Point and Long Term Equilibrium Point*

In the present model the energy flow rate to non-fat tissues at which feeding stops is about equal and opposite to the rate at which feeding starts. That is, the short term control system has a preferred value of energy flow (approximately zero), even though the flow is never more than transiently at that value because of the considerable inflow which builds up towards the end of a meal and the considerable utilization of non-fat energy which is occurring by the time a meal starts. Thus the short term control mechanism performs similarly to a closed-loop system with a set point or reference value of zero energy inflow into non-fat tissues, although the delays in this "energostat" make for large oscillations in energy flow rate. As just emphasized, a major long-term control could be merely an equilibrium system, of open loop construction and without fixed set point characteristics. To this extent the model is in contrast to the common assumption that short term control is open loop while long term control has very precise set point characteristics (Hervey, 1969).

Whether or not the description of the model's characteristics as long term equilibrium-like and short term set point-like proves to be broadly accurate, and whether or not this model is realistic to the observed phenomena, this point illustrates the potential value of any detailed analysis of a system. The general terms used to describe the system's behaviour often prove to be "chapter headings" for characteristics which are not attributable to any one discrete mechanism but are properties whose generation is distributed diffusely through a number of processes. The more abstract concepts of the present model (e.g. "energy flow") are themselves subject to such reduction in due course. This does not in any way imply that the abstract control characteristics of internal variables do not exist. However, it does imply that there is a limit to the usefulness of repeated demonstrations of those functional characteristics by experiments which do not also provide evidence as to the mechanisms by which they are achieved. It would be more profitable to elucidate the mechanisms of stabilization of body weight or energy flow than to refine in great detail the data on their set point- or equilibrium-like properties.

Also, current theories of obesity might be more realistic if they used equilibrium-type stabilization concepts. Accounts of the hyper-reactivity of moderately obese and some normal-weight individuals to highly salient (and presumably therefore usually external) stimuli, in terms of relative deprivation (Nisbett, 1972) and restraint (Herman and Mack, 1975), do not require a body weight or adipose weight set point. Any displacement of equilibrium between feeding and fat in the direction of less feeding than would otherwise occur will release a stronger tendency to feed which is monotonically related to distance of fat store size from equilibrium. Furthermore, to the extent that an energy flow deficiency has undifferentiated distress components (as well as components learned to be ameliorable by feeding), restrained subjects will be more reactive to all strong stimuli (arousal or general drive) as well as to strong feeding-related stimuli (specific conditioned drive and incentive), as has been observed (Schachter and Rodin, 1974). Indeed, where the distinctive distresses of hunger and oversatiation have been poorly discriminated (Slochower, 1976) or bias against response to them introduced (Griggs and Stunkard, 1964), then this general hyperemotionality or externality will be stronger relative to specific feeding reactivity than in subjects with better detection or lower response criteria, even though these normal subjects may be less reactive to food.

VI. Additions to Give the Full Prototype Model

A number of elements in the basic model of human feeding are very easily filled out for greater realism. Examples include improving the gastric emptying and intestinal digestion functions, adding a plausible level of noise to the detection of energy flow level, calculating basal metabolic rate more precisely, varying the pattern of activity and work done around the clock, and imposing variations in the composition and availability of food or the speed and continuity of feeding within the meal. Our general policy is to change the program as better data about components of the model become available. The incorporation of human fluid intake control might also be attempted, along the lines described by Toates for the rat in Chapter 14.

A. *Metabolic Expectancies*

One elaboration has been given high priority. In the basic version of the prototype model (Section II), the only role for learning is adjustment of the effective satiety threshold to create a target maximum energy flow after the meal. If the model were augmented to allow for feeding under varying conditions or on a variety of foodstuffs, each sensory condition of intake should determine its own acquired satiety threshold.

Learning certainly has a greater role than this in human appetite. Eating rate varies from one foodstuff to another, and where there is choice some foodstuffs are selected while others are rejected. Some, possibly most, of these variations in acceptability during or before ingestion of a foodstuff are acquired reactions to the appearance or orosensory qualities of the food, established by conditioning (Booth, 1977a). That is, we react enthusiastically to some foods in part because we have had long experience of the increases in supply of energy-yielding substances or amino acids to tissues which resulted when these foods were ingested while the supply was low. We may be unenthusiastic about other foods when we are hungry because they have failed to repair such current deficiencies in supply.

It must be noted that such effects remain to be demonstrated in man by formal experimentation. It would then be necessary to assess their importance relative to unlearned preferences and aversions, and to the intake-stimulating effect of variety, which depends on sensory adaptation, habituation or some other foodstuff-specific mechanism (Booth, 1976). However, conditioning of preferences and aversion to normal foods in infancy has been seen in animals (Reisbick, 1973; Booth *et al.*, 1974; Hogan, 1975). Furthermore, there are indications of importance of conditioned acceptability in man, even in adulthood. For example, loss of craving for carbohydrate foods is reported following ileojejunal bypass in the early phase when carbohydrate absorption is disrupted (Bray *et al.*, 1976).

Although the existence of nutrient-conditioned appetites and aversions in normal human feeding remains to be established, conditioned satiation and desatiation have been demonstrated in man using starch loads in relation to normal meals (Booth *et al.*, 1976b).

Indeed, the same starch load procedure has also been used to show the influence on human food intake and attitudes to food which is possessed by various internal states generated following ingestion, probably by the absorption of carbohydrate energy at differing rates (Booth, 1977b). The difficulties of showing suppression of intake or hunger sensations following ingestion of energy-rich foodstuffs under some conditions (Wooley, 1976) may arise from the variations in dietary composition not altering the relevant energy flow stimulus sufficiently, relative to the strong conditioned sensory qualities of the familiar foodstuffs used and the likely broad generalization over internal stimuli. Now, the intake suppression which is seen most strongly at about 20–30 min after a concentrated starch load corresponds to a peak in glucose absorption rate (Booth *et al.*, 1976a) which would come a few minutes after the meals had ended in the conditioned satiety experiment of Booth *et al.* (1976b). Thus energy flow rate change is a good candidate as the unconditioned stimulus with the associative property of creating appetitive or aversive conditioned stimulus value (anticipatory motivational power) in the conjunction which is experienced late in a meal of a particular dessert foodstuff and modestly positive values of energy flow (or the sensed correlates thereof).

So we come to the view that satiety generally and conditioned satiety in particular is a state-dependent selective aversion or rejection, where the state is an internal stimulus which occurs towards the end of a meal. This incipient satiety state could be a metabolic one (such as a particular energy flow rate), in whatever way it is detectable to the brain. Hungry behaviour on this view is also a state-dependent preference or acceptance, conditioned or not. Indeed, because the changes resulting from ingestion of a food depend on when during a meal it was taken, the same rich diet can come to be preferred in the state of low energy flow rate at the start of a meal and rejected in the state of high energy flow at the end of the meal (Booth, 1977a, b), while conversely a poor diet may be rejected during hunger and accepted during incipient satiety. (These suggestions are formulated in terms of respondent behaviour, but intake could in part be operant—the analysis is concerned with stimulus–stimulus association, not with the details of response organization.)

Another way of stating this view is to say that internal and external states relevant to feeding are used to interpret each other and to predict the consequences of such a conjunction of cues. Remembered contingencies amongst foodstuffs and body sensations dominate the attribution of appetite and its satisfaction to one's own current state and the attribution of current acceptability or unacceptability to the particular food or drink.

This analysis has been programmed for the case of energy flow states in the full version of the prototype human feeding model. [Amino acid flow rates are due to be programmed in a separate representation of protein appetite acquisition (Booth, 1974)]. Correction of a negative energy flow, following experience of a foodstuff during low energy flow, conditions a preference in future for that foodstuff in the presence of that low energy flow. Failure to correct a low energy conditions an aversion to the food in that low flow state. Excessive energy flow conditions an aversion to the foodstuff in the presence of high energy flow.

Such a program performs very similarly to the basic model, at least in the version tested so far. The state-dependent conditioned responding provides an account of the start and stop of feeding which eliminates the thresholds used in the simplified model. With a variety of foods available, feeding starts when the unconditioned and conditioned acceptability for any one of them in compound with current energy flow becomes positive. Feeding stops when there ceases to be any food-plus-energy-flow compound stimulus eliciting acceptability. An availability parameter can also be incorporated, to represent the extent to which food is not immediately present and ingestable.

B. *Biochemical Reduction*

The energy flows in this model are literal sets of fluxes of specifiable energy-yielding metabolites. So, given sufficient information, the energy flow variables can be reduced to the biochemical level of particular substrates moving between particular organs or tissue types in the body. At present we have the impression that the experimental literature is insufficiently complete to permit the construction of the biochemical systems analysis of the freely feeding ambulant human subject which would be needed to make a realistic reduction to explicitly biochemical physiology. Understandably, biochemical physiologists have to date concentrated on simplified preparations such as postabsorptive man and the effects of specified loads such as glucose administered intravenously or perhaps orally. Some reasonable guesses can be made as to the distribution and remobilization of dietary carbon between normally spaced meals, but firm data would establish the superiority of the biochemical reduction over our current simplification in terms of flows of metabolizable energy into fat and non-fat compartments. The strategic time to resolve the specification of energy flows into their substrate components would probably be when one of the many blood glucose regulation models manages to cover the case of periprandial man. Then hopefully that model could be integrated with ours with very little trouble. One major snag could be that we would have had to have identified the locations and characteristics of the satiety-hunger (i.e. metabolic conditioner or reinforcer) "transducer" or "receptors" before the detailed biochemical processing could be grafted onto the cognitive processing. It would certainly be necessary to have these functions detailed quantitatively, as well as much other neuronal processing, before realistic neurophysiological modelling could be included.

VII. Value of the Model

A. *Potential Uses of Simulation in the Obesity Clinic*

1. *Diagnosis*

A systems analysis based on measurable components could in principle be used to identify and to characterize the variables which are critical to an individual's weight control problem. Many other analytical techniques, e.g. most current varieties of multivariate statistical analysis, are inapplicable because the system does not perform by linear combination of independent variables.

At the very least, acquaintance with a realistic simulation tends to expose inadequacies in the preconceptions behind some clinical experimentation. For example, our simulations often emphasize once again how small an abnormality in gut function or hormonal control of fat metabolism could be sufficient cause of gross obesity in the long term. It may be possible to calculate how much the precision or sensitivity of current physiological, biochemical or behavioural measurements must be increased before we have a chance of identifying such a defect in a patient or a group of patients.

Simulation may also be necessary to the resolution of questions of primary or secondary causation. It may to some extent weaken their cogency, or at least expose the poverty of their therapeutic implications. Without quantitative systems analysis, the experimental approach to identification of a primary factor is somehow to eliminate or at least hold constant all other factors. Such simple designs are not generally practicable, and often are in principle fallacious. In contrast, data obtained by measured alteration of variables within a normal range can be fed into a computer model to identify (given a specification of current functional contexts within the rest of the system) which variations are more critical than others. The conclusions then may be relevant to questions of how to begin to move the system from its current (mal)functioning.

2. *Therapy*

Accurate calculation of the processing in a single individual would require much better founded functions in the model. It would also require greater precision than is often currently available in the techniques for estimating the parameter values in those functions for an individual. Thus diagnosis and therapy by literally individual simulation may be a long way off.

However, a reasonably realistic general model of the control of human feeding and body composition could provide qualitative and semi-quantitative analyses of obesity in various classes of internal and external circumstances. The effects of various combinations of treatments on different types of obesity would be calculable in advance in no other way. Simulations of types of therapy would never justify by themselves firm recommendations as to clinical practice. However, they may yield general suggestions which would be sufficiently soundly based to justify proper clinical trial, or to raise serious questions about current clinical procedures.

3. *Theory of Obesity*

What is the point of trying out such a crude model of obesity? It is the first which can be used to test the very rough quantitative plausibility of particular theories of the aetiology or therapy of obesity, against a background of quantifiable assumptions which are as reasonable as can be constructed from the available data. Any particular assumption within such simulations is open to criticism and can be replaced by a more realistic assumption as soon as the basis of the criticism can be made accurately quantitative or at least computably operational.

Similar points could be made for the model of growth suggested in Section IV.C.2.b but not detailed further here. Framing theory in the form of a quantitative systems analysis provides an additional tool to determine what might be worth looking for in an infant, child or adolescent to relate to clinical problems of body composition or feeding (whether or not distinctive to youth), or to ensure the general provision of conditions within the range for normal healthy growth.

B. *Modelling as an Aid to Scientific Understanding*

Computer simulation, especially of a realistic interdisciplinary and reductive sort, is expensive in effort, time and money. A verbal statement of the theoretical analysis behind such a model, augmented with diagrams, might be sufficient to direct experimental investigation of various component processes of the human feeding system. So, is the expense of simulation worthwhile?

The answer depends on a judgment whether we have begun to understand anything about the processes underlying human appetite and body change. If we consider that we do have a few plausible facts, then we are faced with the problems of putting these facts together predictively. One major problem is that, however well judged the simplifying assumptions and approximations, a realistic analysis of the processes by which feeding behaviour and nutrient utilization are determined will inevitably have a considerable complexity. Pre-programmed mechanized calculation is the only way to cope beyond some degree of complexity. Other problems with realistic verbal theories of hunger mechanisms will be unnoticed looseness, hidden inconsistencies and unintended implications. The discipline of specifying the processing with sufficient precision and coherence to generate predictions mechanically, whether they fit the facts or not, brings out these deficiencies in the theorizing. Once the model is specified adequately, the labour and unreliability of human intuition or even human calculation are avoided—or, rather, they are transferred to the more appropriate task of managing the use of scientists' time and computer costs involved in testing and applying the theory as modelled.

One of the trick questions to ask a modeller is what his model has told us that we did not know before. The question is tricky because modelling is a species of theory construction and not a species of empirical observation, and so a model can never tell us the sort of thing an experimental result can, which is what an illogical questioner wants. We are content for the modelling to be judged by the empirical work it will guide. If we find the model enables us to state better the thinking which informs experimental design, that will be everybody's gain if the theorizing embodied in the model is as adequate as any alternatives.

What a theory can do as a theory is deal with some theoretical problems. There follow a couple of illustrations, both concerning relations between scientific disciplines or levels of reality in human feeding control, and both related to trick questions which we have posed ourselves as well as had posed of us by others.

Does the model show that metabolism affects feeding or merely that feeding affects metabolism? This is intended as a criticism of the analysis for being fallaciously circular. All the question achieves is a complaint against reality—that is, it exposes unrealistic preconceptions about behavioural and biological causation. In general physiology, in cognition and in behavioural neurology, the rule is re-entrant causal sequences, not one-way causation. A system description which (if necessarily only in outline) is complete in the sense of autonomously workable will not be able to describe what is going on without very often implying that one process affects another and also this other process affects the former. The present model is specified in terms of physiological and psychological variables which are in principle measurable. It couples the behavioural and the biological levels of phenomena together in a (probabilistically) determinate system. If therefore we had a set of assumptions or data which specified all the behavioural functions and all the physiological functions but one, the model could be used to predict physiology from behaviour and physiology together, even though it was originally constructed to predict feeding patterns from physiological and behavioural elements.

Another trick question is whether human feeding is biologically or socially determined. Our thinking on this was clarified by early runs of the prototype model. It was a considerable shock to find that a model of biological processes and cognitive adjustments to them predicted three meals a day and none at night—a pattern we had believed to be maintained by social convention and socially acquired individual habit. On consideration, however, this result does not justify a shift from the view that when (and even how much) an individual eats on a particular occasion can be strongly determined by immediate social, perceptual and physical exigencies. What the result does suggest is that the social conventions as to meal timings, and the cuisines and economics determining meal composition, have adapted to the biological demands generated by the pattern of life of the type of people in the society in question. Three major meals a day may be the most appropriate pattern when physical work at modest levels continues through 6–8 hours of the day without long breaks, under conditions where food can be readily obtained although generally in non-work locations.

Nevertheless, precisely when and where and what we next eat is a decision within a multilevel system in which a person's body and his own information processing are only two segments among several. The model should be elaborated so that the food availability parameter in the meal onset equations is susceptible to external influences, as also the food acceptability should be opened to interaction with motivations unrelated to feeding. Decisions as to the individual's location, companions, scheduling of activities and other social and physical choices may have a structure which can be specified. Then our cognitive feeder can be socialized, as well as given other things to do with his time.

In conclusion then, we present a model in a basic form with elaborations, which amounts only to a prototype because it operates only at the levels of physiology and learning, and with simplified algorithms even at those levels. A fully operational model would include social-cognitive functions as limiting conditions on the effective availability of foods and the relation of hunger to actual acceptance of food. It would also have biochemical functions to complement and in some cases to replace the prototype's physiological functions.

The model could in principle also have a neural level. In this prototype, and even in a fully operational model, perceptual, associative, motivational and motor processing can all be represented as functions at the behavioural level with no explicit reference to brain processing. Indeed, contrary to some current stories, the improvement in predictive power for the behaviour of the normal organism to be made from incorporating brain processing equations should be expected to be negligible. However, the effects of drugs or of course brain damage on feeding behaviour are unlikely to be predictable without neural process components in the model. Furthermore, if the nutrient content of normal meals directly affects brain metabolism and hence synaptic transmitter function as has recently been suggested, however unlikely that would seem *a priori*, then some aspects of neural processing may be directly implicated in the detection of the current flow rate of energy-yielding or other critical nutrients (Booth and Stribling, 1978).

The results of even this prototype model suggest that the underlying theory of the energy flow cycle, unlike prior theories of hunger, may contribute to appetite physiology in particular and to psychosomatics generally an elucidation that could at best compare with that provided by the tricarboxylic acid cycle concept of Krebs for the biochemistry of intermediary metabolism. Beginning to test the model has at least been fun.

References

Booth, D. A. (1972a). Satiety and behavioural caloric compensation following intragastric glucose loads in the rat. *J. comp. physiol. Psychol.* **78**, 412–432.

Booth, D. A. (1972b). Postabsorptively induced suppression of appetite and the energostatic control of feeding. *Physiol Behav.* **9**, 199–202.

Booth, D. A. (1972c). Conditioned satiety in the rat. *J. comp. physiol. Psychol.* **81**, 457–471.

Booth, D. A. (1974). Acquired sensory preferences for protein in diabetic and normal rats. *Physiol. Psychol.* **2**, 344–348.

Booth, D. A. (1976). Approaches to feeding control. *In* "Appetite and Food Intake" (T. Silverstone, ed.), pp. 417–478. Dahlem Konferenzen, Berlin.

Booth, D. A. (1977a). Satiety and appetite are conditioned reactions. *Psychosom. Med.* **39**, 76–81.

Booth, D. A. (1977b). Appetite and satiety as metabolic expectancies. *In* "Chemical Senses and Food Intake" (Y. Katsuki, M. Sato, S. Takagi and Y. Oomura, ed.). University of Tokyo Press, Tokyo and University Park Press, Baltimore.

Booth, D. A. and Davis, J. D. (1973). Gastrointestinal factors in the acquisition of oral sensory control of satiation. *Physiol. Behav.* **11**, 23–29.

Booth, D. A., Lovett, D. and McSherry, G. M. (1972). Postingestive modulation of the sweetness preference gradient. *J. comp. physiol. Psychol.* **78**, 485–512.

Booth, D. A., Stoloff, R. and Nicholls, J. (1974). Dietary flavor acceptance in infant rats established by association with effects of nutrient composition. *Physiol. Psychol.* **2**, 313–319.

Booth, D. A. and Stribling, D. (1978). Neurochemistry of appetite mechanisms. *Proc. Nutr. Soc.*, in press.

Booth, D. A., Toates, F. M. and Platt, S. V. (1976a). Control system for hunger and its implications in animals and man. *In* "Hunger: Basic Mechanisms and Clinical

Implications" (D. Novin, W. Wyrwicka and G. A. Bray, eds), pp. 127–143. Raven Press, New York.

Booth, D. A., Lee, M. and McAleavey, C. (1976b). Acquired sensory control of satiation in man. *Br. J. Psychol.* **67,** 137–147.

Bray, G. A., Barry, R. E., Benfield, J., Castelnuovo-Tedesco, P. and Rodin, J. (1976). Food intake and taste preferences for glucose and sucrose decrease after intestinal bypass surgery. *In* "Hunger: Basic Mechanisms and Clinical Implications" (D. Novin, W. Wyrwicka and G. A. Bray, eds), pp. 431–439. Raven Press, New York.

Brobeck, J. R. (1965). Exchange, control and regulation. *In* "Physiological Controls and Regulation" (W. S. Yamomoto and J. R. Brobeck, eds), pp. 1–13. W. B. Saunders, Philadelphia.

Garrow, J. S. (1974). "Energy Balance and Obesity in Man". North Holland, Amsterdam.

Garrow, J. S. (1978). The regulation of energy expenditure in man, *In* "Recent Advances in Obesity Research II" (G. A. Bray, ed.) Newman, London, in press.

Garrow, J. S. and Stalley, S. (1975). Is there a "set point" for human body weight? *Proc. Nutr. Soc.* **34**, 84A.

Goldrick, R. B. and McLoughlin, G. M. (1970). Lipolysis and lipogenesis from glucose in human fat cells of different sizes. Effects of insulin, epinephrine and theophylline. *J. clin. Invest.* **49**, 1213–1223.

Griggs, R. C. and Stunkard, A. J. (1964). The interpretation of gastric motility. II. Sensitivity and bias in the perception of gastric motility. *Arch. gen. Psychiat.* **11**, 82–89.

Herman, C. P. and Mack, D. (1975). Restrained and unrestrained eating. *J. Personality* **43**, 647–660.

Hervey, G. R. (1969). Regulation of energy balance. *Nature, Lond.* **223**, 629–631.

Hogan, J. A. (1975). Development of food recognition in young chicks: III. Discrimination. *J. comp. physiol. Psychol.* **89**, 95–104.

Hunt, J. N. and Stubbs, D. F. (1975). The volume and energy content of meals as determinants of gastric emptying. *J. Physiol., Lond.* **245**, 209–225.

Hunt, J. N., Cash, R. and Newlands, P. (1975). Energy density of food, gastric emptying and obesity. *Lancet* **ii**, 905–906.

Mahoney, M. J. (1975). Fat fiction. *Behav. Ther.* **6**, 416–418.

Nelder, J. A. and Mead, R. (1965). A Simplex method for function minimization. *Computer J.* **7**, 308–313.

Nisbett, R. E. (1972). Hunger, obesity and the ventromedial hypothalamus. *Psychol Rev.* **79**, 433–453.

Reisbick, S. H. (1973). Development of food preferences in newborn guinea pigs. *J. comp. physiol. Psychol.* **85**, 427–442.

Saito, M., Murakami, E., Nishida, T., Fujisawa, Y. and Suda, M. (1976). Circadian rhythms of digestive enzymes in the small intestine of the rat. II. Effects of fasting and refeeding. *J. Biochem.* **80**, 563–568.

Schachter, S. and Rodin, J. (1974). "Obese Humans and Rats". Wiley, New York.

Slochower, J. (1976). Emotional labelling and overeating in obese and normal weight individuals. *Psychosom. Med.* **38**, 131–139.

Toates, F. M. (1975). "Control Theory in Biology and Experimental Psychology". Hutchinson Educational, London.

Trowell, H. (1975). Obesity. *In* "Refined Carbohydrate Foods and Disease" (D. P. Burkitt and H. C. Trowell, ed), pp. 240–245. Academic Press, London and New York.

Woods, S. C. and Porte, D. (1974). Neural control of the endocrine pancreas. *Physiol. Rev.* **54**, 596–619.
Wooley, S. C. (1976). Psychological aspects of feeding. *In* "Appetite and Food Intake" (T. Silverstone, ed.), pp. 331–354. Dahlem Konferenzen, Berlin.

13

Models of the Control of Food Intake and Energy Balance in Ruminants

J. M. FORBES
Department of Animal Physiology and Nutrition, University of Leeds, Leeds, England.

I. Introduction

A. *Ruminant Intake Control*

The ruminant is characterized by a capacious multicompartmented stomach in which bacteria and protozoa live symbiotically, digesting part of the food and supplying unusual substrates, e.g. volatile fatty acids, to the metabolic systems of the host animal. One major feature, which makes ruminants of such great economic importance, is the partial digestion of cellulose and other structural carbohydrates which cannot be broken down in the non-ruminant digestive tract. Hence the importance of grass and grass products in the agricultural economy and the widespread research interest in the digestive physiology, metabolism, grazing behaviour and microbiology of the ruminant.

It has long been realized that the rate of breakdown of plant material in the rumen is slow, particularly with high fibre diets, and that this might lead to the physical capacity of the digestive tract being reached before the animal's nutritional requirements were satisfied. The rather scattered reports on this aspect have been summarized by Balch and Campling (1962) in the first comprehensive review of the control of food intake in ruminants. With the advent of the use of high cereal, low fibre diets on commercial farms, and the concurrent experimental study of the digestion of such feeds, it was realized that cattle and sheep could regulate their energy balance by controlling food intake, as long as the physical bulk of the diet was not excessive. Perhaps this was first made clear by the work of Conrad, Pratt and Hibbs (1964) which will be referred to later in this chapter. The last 15 years have seen a rapid expansion in research into factors affecting and controlling food intake which has been comprehensively reviewed by Baile and Forbes (1974).

We find ourselves with a wealth of knowledge about many aspects of digestion and metabolism on the one hand (e.g. Phillipson, 1970), and grassland ecology on the other (e.g. Spedding, 1965), but with gaps in our understanding of the links between the two–that is, how the amount of food eaten is controlled so as to supply the appropriate quantity of substrates to the metabolic processes within the ruminant tissues. Some of these gaps will become clear during the following discussion of attempts at modelling and prediction.

B. *Varieties of Quantitative Analysis*

We will deal first with prediction equations, where the animal is treated as a "black box" and the aim is not primarily to try to explain the reasons for correlations between food intake and, for example, weight of grass available per acre, or digestibility of a number of diets. Then we will consider attempts to put together numerous quantitative relationships between component variables (e.g. sunlight and grass growth, protein content of diet and activity of rumen microorganisms) in order to predict intake and/or productive processes (growth, lactation) from given environmental inputs.

These "models" have been constructed primarily for investigation of herbage/animal interactions when under variable conditions of weather and management. None of them takes the control of food intake as its central theme.

The author's current attempts to construct models with particular emphasis on physiological changes within the animal are presented in the hope that the "black box" can be made at least slightly translucent. We do not deal with qualitative, descriptive schemes, such as the complex diagram of Baile and Forbes (1974, p 169). These may be useful summaries of the current state of knowlege, but they do not otherwise advance our understanding of the control of food intake.

II. Regression Equations Predicting Intake

A. *Simple Regression*

The simplest type of equation is one derived from a closely controlled experiment in which there is one variable and the effect of this on voluntary food intake is observed.

1. *Live Weight*

The intake of hay by sheep of different weights was found by Blaxter *et al.* (1961) to vary in proportion to live weight to the power 0·73; and similar relationships between intake and live weight have been derived from multiple regressions (see below). When the weight of food eaten is monitored as cattle grow, it is found that 0·6 is the appropriate power to which live weight must be raised to predict intake most accurately (Forbes, 1971).

The relationship between fresh herbage intake and live weight is more difficult to study because of the errors associated with the indirect methods of measuring pasture intake and the difficulty of assessing live weight accurately when up to one quarter of that weight is digesta which, by its very nature, varies in weight at different times of day. Hodgson and Wilkinson (1967), using cattle of widely differing weights and careful measurement of intake of grass by individual cattle, found the best relationship between intake and live weight when the latter was raised to the power 0·61, in close agreement with the indoor feeding experiments. The regression coefficients and intercepts for the various observed relationships between live weight and food intake in ruminants differ quite widely, probably due to the different diets used in the experiments.

2. *Food Quality*

The physical and nutrient density of the diet has long been known to affect the amount voluntarily consumed by ruminants. Lehmann (1941) observed that the lower the yield of digestible nutrients per unit weight of a particular feed, the lower was the intake of this feed by cattle and he proposed a "ballast" theory to explain this. He calculated that, for the range of roughage offered to his cows, 4·3 kg per day of indigestible organic matter was consumed by a cow of 500 kg. Later Kruger and Schulze (1956), still stressing the importance of the physical bulk of roughage feeds in limiting the amcunt eaten, used satiety units [10 × (dry wt × vol. of dry wt) + water vol.] to predict with some success the intake of roughage by cows. A remarkably close correlation between intake of a range of feeds by sheep (X, ml/Wkg$^{0\cdot66}$/day) and feed density (p, g/ml) was found by Baile and Pfander (1967):

$$X = 73p^{-1\cdot20} \quad (r = -0\cdot99) \tag{1}$$

In the 1960s it was gradually realized that, with low fibre, cereal-based rations, intake was more closely related to nutrient requirements than to physical properties of the diet or its indigestible residues. Experiments were designed to investigate the effect of variation of diet quality on feed intake by ruminants.

One of the main problems is, of course, that increasing the level of inclusion of one constituent of the diet automatically reduces the content of one or all the other constituents. Another problem is to avoid selection of certain dietary constituents in the *ad libitum* feeding situation; this is commonly overcome by pelletting the mixed ration, which entails prior grinding of the roughage portion and thus alteration of its physical properties and rate of disappearance from the rumen.

With pelletted hay diets containing 0 to 60% of barley, with a range of digestibilities from 54 to 69% of the dry matter, Donefer *et al.* (1963) found intake by sheep to fall with increasing digestibility so as to maintain a constant intake of digestible energy. Montgomery and Baumgardt's (1965) work with cattle yielded similar results and a tabulated summary of the results of 15 experiments of this type is included by Baumgardt (1970) in his review of compensation for dilution of the caloric content of the diet. In one particularly extensive study, Dinius and Baumgardt (1970) diluted a cereal-based diet with several levels of sawdust and clay and found that, with rations of up to 2·5 kcal digestible energy (DE) per g, dry matter (DM) intake (Y, kcal DE/W kg 0·75) was positively related to caloric density (X, kcal DE/g):

$$Y = 148X - 154 \quad (r = 0{\cdot}85). \tag{2}$$

On the other hand, with rations of greater than 2·5 kcal De/g there was not a significant relationship:

$$Y = 241 - 12X \quad (r = 0{\cdot}18). \tag{3}$$

That is with these rations, where physical capacity was though not to be a limiting factor, intake was controlled to give a constant level of DE (Fig. 1).

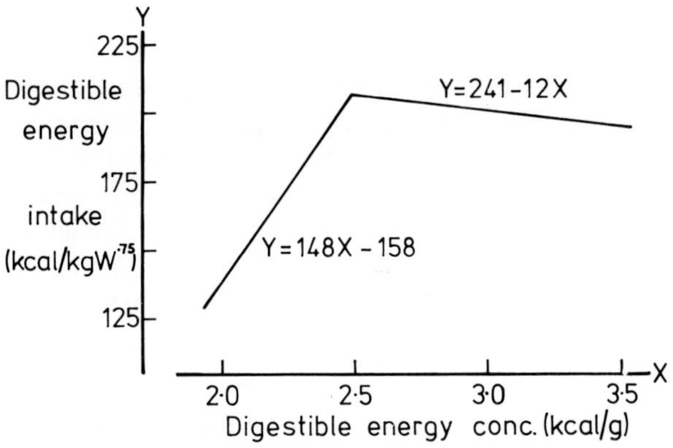

Fig 1. Voluntary intake by sheep of diets of different energy concentration, prepared by mixing feed and inert fillers in different proportions (Dinius and Baumgardt, 1970).

Baumgardt (1970) points out that the digestibility at which the two types of relationship intersect is approximately 56% when the rations have included diluent in a ground form, whereas with long roughages, the intersection is at approximately 67% DM digestibility. We will return to this point later.

3. *Nutrient Requirements*

A third independent variable which affects voluntary food intake is the level of energy demand of the animal (see Baumgardt, 1970, p. 247). There is a rapid rise in nutrient requirements at the start of lactation, particularly in the dairy cow where, at the peak of lactation, energy losses can be up to three times greater than just before parturition. In all reported observations on food intake of ruminants in early lactation there is an increase, which is correlated with milk yield in most cases (summarized by Forbes, 1970a). The increased energy intake is not usually sufficient to supply the full requirements of milk secretion, especially in high yielding cows, and the mobilization of fat reserves normally occurs in the first two months of the ten month lactation. A further complication is the probability that the quantity of food eaten by the non-lactating cow is not of sufficient bulk to limit intake by physical means, whereas an attempt by the cow to meet the huge increase in energy output in milk and heat by increasing her food intake brings the intake of indigestible matter up to the physical limit.

B. Multiple Regression

It becomes clear that we must consider the interacting effects of live weight, physical and chemical characteristics of the diet, and nutrient requirements. We can use multiple regression analysis for this purpose.

Such a study was reported in the classic paper by Conrad *et al.* (1964). They collected together data gathered over many years at the Ohio Agricultural Experiment Station during the testing of the nutritive value of a wide range of roughage and concentrate feeds for lactating dairy cows. Preliminary analysis showed a weak positive relationship between DM intake and the digestibility of the DM, although digestible DM intake tended to be constant with feeds with digestibilities above 66%. The data were therefore regrouped into a low digestibility group (52 to 67%) and a high digestibility group (67 to 80%).

1. "*Physical*" *Limitation on Intake*

With the low digestibility group intake was best predicted by live weight, digestibility and faecal DM output (postulated to be an index of gut capacity):

$$\log I = 1{\cdot}53 \log D + 1{\cdot}01 \log F + 0{\cdot}99 \log W - 5{\cdot}3 \qquad (4)$$

($r = 0{\cdot}997$), where I = DM intake [lb (0·45 kg) per day], D = DM digestibility (%), F = faecal DM per 1000 lb (454 kg) live weight, and W = live weight (lb).

2. "*Metabolic*" *Limitation on Intake*

With roughage-based feeds of 67% and greater, faecal DM played no part in predicting intake, whereas productive energy (in milk and estimated requirements for live weight gain) accounted for a significant part of the variation in food intake:

$$\log I = -0{\cdot}46 \log D + 0{\cdot}51 \log W + 0{\cdot}25 \log E + 0{\cdot}55 \qquad (5)$$

($r = 0{\cdot}833$), where E = productive energy (Mcals per day). Figure 2 shows DM intake adjusted for body weight and faecal DM output in the case of feeds of less than 67% digestibility and adjusted for weight $^{0{\cdot}73}$ and productive energy for

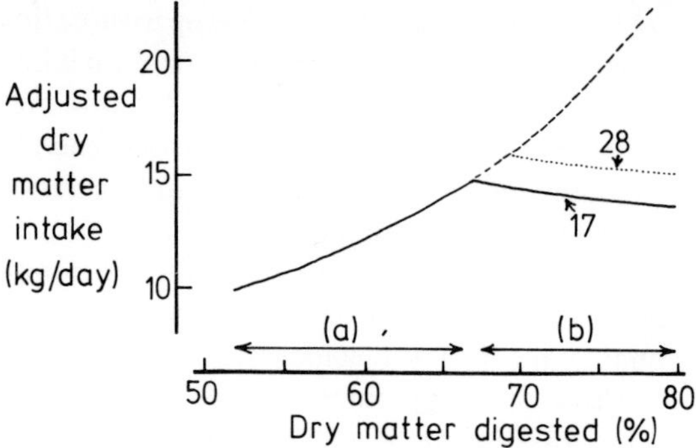

Fig 2. Relationship between food intake of lactating cows and digestibility for a wide range of feeds (from fig. 4 of Conrad *et al.*, 1964). (a) Corrected for variations in body weight and faecal DM; (b) Corrected for variations in body weight 0·73 and productive energy. 17, 28: milk yield in kg per day.

feeds with digestibilities of 67% or over (Conrad *et al.*, 1964). It is of particular interest to note the observed higher level of intake with high yielding cows when fed on highly digestible diets.

3. *Combinations of Limitations*

Equations 4 and 5 have been used to produce matrices in which each cell is occupied by the food intake at a particular combination of body weight, digestibility, faecal DM and productive energy. Faecal DM could be increased by increasing the rate of passage of undigested feed particles (e.g. by grinding a roughage prior to feeding) or by increasing gut capacity (e.g. by a reduction in the volume of abdominal fat). The level of intake predicted by equation 4 ("physical" limitation) was compared with the solution of equation 5 ("metabolic" limitation) for each set of independent variables and the lower of the two values was used. Figure 3 shows food intake for wide ranges of productive energy and faecal DM at four digestibilities in cows of 454 kg body weight, using a modification of the technique of Dirkx and Dufour (1975). The interaction between the positive effects of lifting physical restriction and increasing the nutrient requirements can be seen. At low levels of faecal DM, a high yielding cow cannot reach the level of intake necessary to meet its requirements; it must either draw on its body reserves or reduce its milk yield—in practice it probably does both.

In order to test the applicability of the equations of Conrad *et al.* (1964) to other situations, I have used the data of Monteiro (1972) which include milk yields, body weights and weight changes at regular intervals during long and short lactations of Friesian and Jersey cows. Faecal DM was estimated on the assumption that the value at the beginning of lactation (i.e. at calving) was 4·5 kg (the mean for Conrad's cows) and that it subsequently varied in proportion to half of the change in body weight; as abdominal fat was mobilized or deposited,

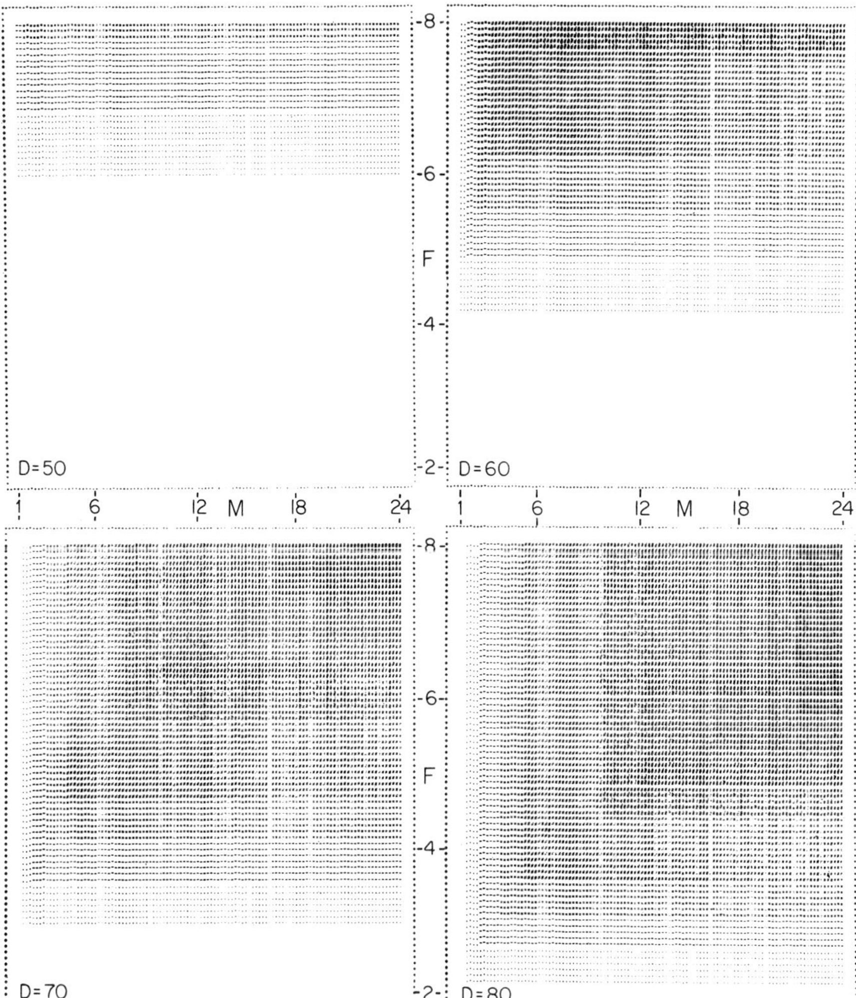

Fig 3. Generalized relationships between food intake, productive energy (M, Mcals/day) and faecal dry matter (F, kg/day) at DM digestibilities of 50, 60, 70 and 80% in 454 kg cows, based on the multiple regressions of Conrad *et al.* (1964). Food intake is proportional to density of print and is below 9·1 kg in blank areas, increasing by 1·2 kg steps with each grade of darkness, to a maximum of 20 kg DM/day.

so gut capacity, and therefore faecal DM, increased or decreased. The results are shown in Fig. 4 for two contrasting situations: long Friesian and short Jersey lactations. With a feed of 80% digestibility there is reasonable overall agreement with the observed intakes. The equations predict that intake is limited physically only briefly in early lactation at a time when observed intake is much lower, not reaching a peak until about the tenth week of lactation. The feed actually offered

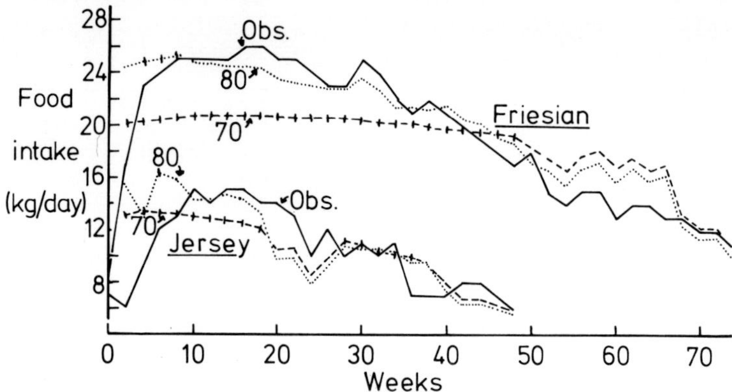

Fig 4. Predictions of food intakes of dairy cows using the equations of Conrad *et al.* (1964) and the data of Monteiro (1972). 70, 80, digestibility of DM in feeds used in model. Obs., observed intakes.

to Monteiro's cows was certainly of a lower digestibility, probably no more than 70% (Gibson, 1969). The equations predict physical limitation of a 70% digestible diet for a considerable part of lactation, which results in a voluntary intake considerably lower than that observed. Application of the equations to short Friesian and long Jersey lactation also gave intakes which were higher than observed in early lactation.

The data used by Conrad *et al.* (1964) were obtained only from cows in established lactation and it is not justifiable to extrapolate the relationships found in such animals to predict intake quantitatively in non-lactating cows, or animals in very early lactation. Curran *et al.* (1970) extracted results from several of their earlier experiments, for cows in the last four weeks of pregnancy and first 16 weeks of lactation, and used multiple regression analysis to find the factors most closely associated with food intake. Live weight was not a useful predictor of food intake; live weight change was of limited use because of the difficulty of weighing ruminants accurately (and in any case, it would be impracticable to weigh cows frequently even on farms with suitable weighing equipment). Roughage intake was most effectively predicted by roughage digestibility (a positive relationship) and weight of concentrates fed (a negative relationship). The list of independent variables which were most usefully included in prediction equations varied with different stages of pregnancy and lactation, however, and no useful generalized model emerges from their regressions. One useful aspect of the work of Curran *et al.* (1970) is their estimates of the variability of their predictions, a point so often lacking in predictive models. Their work was then extended (Curran and Holmes, 1970) to cover the voluntary intake of herbage by lactating grazing cows, measured by a marker dilution technique. Milk yield was highly correlated with intake of grass and live weight, particularly when the 0·73 power was used. The digestibility of the ingested herbage had little value in explaining variation in intake, probably because of the small range in digestibilities recorded. Herbage availability, measured as the amount of grass cut by a standard mechanical method, approached a 5% level of significance in equations where digestibility was not included as an independent variable.

4. *A Multiple Regression Model*

A more sophisticated use of multiple regression analysis was adopted by Monteiro (1972), who first proposed a simple model for the positive-feedback control of food intake and from this developed a series of theoretical equations linking food intake with live weight change, milk yield and maintenance requirements. Food intake was assumed to respond either immediately to changes in energy demand, or to lag behind changes in nutrient requirements. Data collected from the Friesian and Jersey cows mentioned above were fitted to

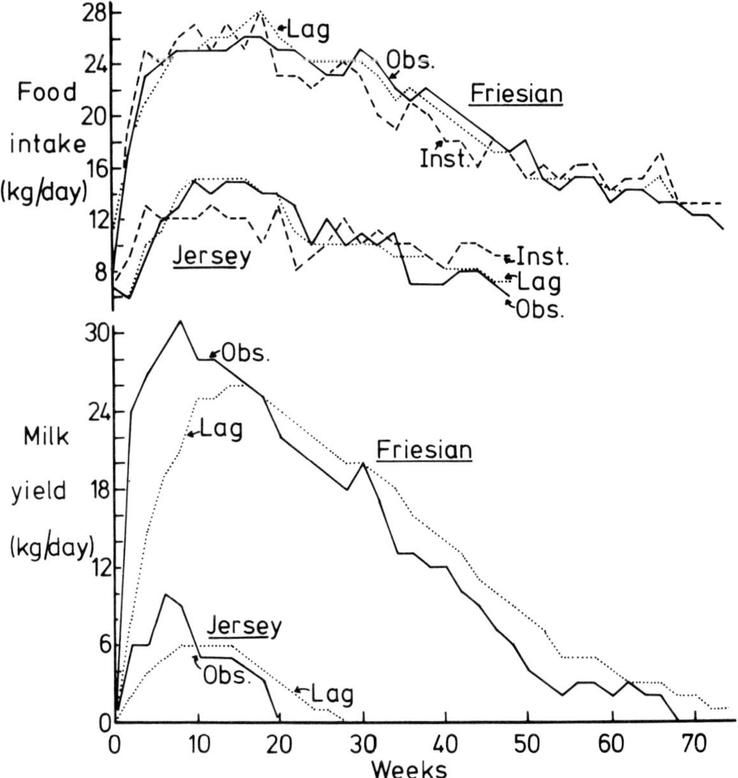

Fig 5. Observed and predicted food intakes and milk yields of lactating cows redrawn from figs 2 and 3 of Monteiro (1972). Obs., observed; Inst, instantaneous response model; Lag, delayed response model.

the equations by iterative procedures using least squares techniques until stable values of the constants were reached. The instantaneous response model predicted food intake with reasonable accuracy but for each type of lactation it tended to overestimate in the first few weeks of lactation, to underestimate in mid-lactation and again to overestimate at the end of lactation (Fig. 5). This inability to account for the observed lag of the increase in food intake soon after parturition, when milk yield rises to a peak and body reserves are usually called on, is overcome by the use of the delayed response model which predicts food intake during the whole of lactation with considerable accuracy (Fig. 5). It must be noted, however, that the milk yields predicted by this more complex model fall far short of those actually observed in the first few weeks of lactation. Thus, forcing the close agreement between calculated and observed food intake also forces a depression in milk yield in early lactation.

The accuracy of predicting food intake depends on the long delay factors which were calculated and which indicate that it would take almost 100 days for a food intake response to reach 95% of that required for full compensation for a change in milk yield or movement of body reserves. A possibility is that rumen capacity increases too slowly after parturition to allow an immediate increase in food intake to meet the rapid increase in energy output (Tulloh and Hughes, 1965; Ronning and Laben, 1966); that is, there is physical limitation of intake during early lactation. This cannot be tested by Monteiro's approach. Evidence on the delay between change in energy requirements and response in energy intake in man (Edholm, *et al.*, 1955) and rats (Adolph, 1947) suggests a much more rapid response than that deduced for cows by Monteiro (1972). Lofgren and Warner (1972) suggested that their sheep responded within 15 minutes by adjusting intake when the concentration of digestible energy was changed, and although this is not the only interpretation of their results (Forbes and Blair, 1974), the sheep had certainly adjusted fully within a few days. We should not necessarily assume that a cow can adjust to changes in her nutrient requirements as quickly as a sheep can adjust to changes in dietary energy concentration, and there is clearly need for further work in this area.

5. *Restriction on Multiple Regression Predictions*

The usefulness of the numerical values of coefficients determined by multiple regression is reduced by the probability, discussed by Curran and Holmes (1970), that one or more of the independent variables are themselves correlated with other variables which are not included in the regression. Such considerations prevent the application of prediction equations to situations in which one or more of the factors affecting food intake differ significantly from those existing in the experimental situation from which the model was derived. Thus we are restricted to using such models in a qualitative manner, to suggest trends. We should not seriously expect them to predict intake accurately.

III. Programmed Iterative Models

The prediction regression approach tries to fit equations as accurately as possible to values of many parameters measured simultaneously. An alternative approach is to "synthesize" situations of feed/animal interaction, using simple cause-and-effect relationships obtained in controlled experiments. The "black box" approach of the regression analyst becomes an attempt to treat the animal as a "grey box". Unfortunately, as we will see, most models have concentrated on herbage growth and food/animal interactions, using a one-day cycle for recalculation of variables and therefore making no attempt to model the actual, minute by minute changes occurring within the animal which are presumably closely linked with the control of meal size, meal interval and rate of eating.

A. *Systems Models Incorporating Prediction of Food Intake*

The most comprehensive iterative model so far described is that of Rice *et al.* (1974). Meteorological and soil data are used to predict herbage growth and composition, based on the model of Smith and Williams (1973). The authors assume that voluntary intake of grass by sheep is limited by the physical capacity of the digestive tract, which is a reasonable assumption under range conditions. To allow a one-day iteration cycle, this capacity is calculated by notional extrapolation from acutal gut capacities recorded in the literature. That immediately exposes the main weakness of this model in that if forces the "animal" to take its food in one meal per day, an obviously unphysiological situation. The particular strength of the model of Rice *et al.* (1974) is, however, that it does not stop with the ingestion of grass by the sheep, but uses known relationships between dietary quantity and quality and rumen fermentation to predict yields of nutrients available for absorption and to predict the rumen capacity available to receive ingested food at the next "daily meal." Absorbed energy and nitrogen (as in index of protein) are apportioned to maintenance, pregnancy, lactation and growth, in that order, growth being negative (i.e. live weight loss) if food intake is insufficient to meet the requirements of the other processes. A new live weight is calculated and the calculations repeated daily.

Isolating the animal section of the model and "feeding" this with diets of different digestibility results in a linear increase in food intake as digestibility is increased from 48 to 70%. This relationship differs from the curvilinear relationship usually obtained from real animal experiments. Also with a non-pregnant, non-lactating sheep such as the one used in the production of these results from the model, we would expect to see a change-over to metabolic control of feeding and a distinct change to a negative relationship between intake and digestibility, well below 70% digestibility. That does not occur because Rice *et al.* (1974) did not consider the possibility of metabolic control of intake in this model.

They demonstrate that weight gains predicted by the model are well correlated ($r = 0{\cdot}93$) with actual weight gains by sheep. This is an indication of the success of the modelling techniques used but, again, all the weight gains are below the low value of 100 g per day, indicating that the only feeds tested were of poor or moderate quality, in the range of digestibilities where we would expect intake to be positively correlated.

When the model is used for its stated purpose, that of predicting animal responses to long term changes in factors affecting herbage growth, it is shown to produce realistic results for food intake and live weight change throughout an annual cycle.

The work of Smith and Williams (1973) on prediction of herbage availability deals more briefly with animal factors than does that of Rice *et al.* (1974). Thus herbage intake is predicted solely from the weight per hectare and height of grass available and it is not surprising that at high levels of availability food intake is grossly overestimated. This model was then used to predict the effects on live weight gain of different systems of sheep grazing management (Smith and Williams, 1976) as a guide to the planning of future grazing experiments. Armstrong (1971) includes the concept of potential intake in his model of a sheep grazing system in order to overcome the limitation of using herbage availability alone to predict intake. Although this is a useful feature it is apparently calculated by a purely theoretical process, in distinct contrast to the approach of Rice *et al.* (1974). The main purpose of Armstrong's model is to simulate grazing management systems and this it seems to do with reasonable success.

An even more comprehensive system model, incorporating economic considerations of fat lamb production, has been developed by Edelsten and Newton (1975). Again iteration is once per day and intake of herbage is related to herbage availability, but allowance is made for higher intake, at any given level of availability, in animals with high potential intakes (e.g. at the peak of lactation), and for the depressing effect on herbage intake of supplementary feeding with silage or cereal concentrates.

Systems models of grazing dairy cows have been developed recently by T. H. Booth (1975). Intake of grass was initially predicted from potential intake, with the preconception that this rose slowly until reaching a peak 100 days after calving, and from herbage allowance and its digestibility. In the second model, however, Booth more logically based the potential intake on the milk yield predicted from the statistical analysis of lactation curves (Wood, 1969), with depression of milk yield when intake failed to match requirements due to low herbage allowance or digestibility.

de Wit's (1968) observation that "grazing cows have the habit of walking and disposing of their waste on their own dining table" was quoted by Brockington (1972), introducing his model of the interaction between pasture contamination by faeces and herbage intake. Introduction of cows to uncontaminated pasture gave initial high voluntary intakes, but the gradual reduction in herbage available per unit area and the reduction in the area available for grazing, as more of the field became contaiminated, led eventually to an equilibrium, where lower food intake and lower faeces production were balanced. Brockington used a relationship obtained experimentally, relating intake to area of contamination, and made no assumptions about the nature of the control of food intake.

In each of the approaches considered so far in this section, the authors' aim has been to simulate a complex plant/animal relationship, and voluntary intake has been calculated from empirical formulae, except in the case of Rice *et al.* (1974) who have partly included physiological relationships. In no case was the main aim to predict intake from physical and physiological changes within the animal.

B. *The Interactions between Physical and Metabolic Control of Intake*

1. *Lactating Cows*

I have attempted to incorporate the idea of dual control of food intake by ruminants ("physical" and "metabolic" limitations) into a simple iterative model in the lactating dairy cow (Forbes, 1977 b). The physically limited level of intake is calculated from equation 4 above (Conrad *et al.*, 1964). The metabolically limited level is calculated as the metabolic energy (ME) requirements for maintenance, milk production and movement of body reserves (ARC, 1965). Body weight is assumed to increase by 0·5 kg per day unless physical limitation of intake intervenes; no "lipostat" is assumed other than the physical embarrassment of gut capacity by increasing deposition of abdominal fat, which is taken to be half the total labile body fat. Gut capacity is assumed to be depressed by 0·5 l per kg increase in abdominal fat and to be the direct determinant of faecal DM which is used in equation 4. Milk yields were taken from the work of Monteiro (1972) for the four classes of cow and it was assumed, for the sake of this simple model, that milk yield was unaffected even when energy intake was very much lower than energy output; a future development will be to make milk yield to some extent dependent on current food intake.

Daily iterations were carried out for 500 days with feeds of several digestibilities. Some results are shown in Fig. 6.

With high yielding Friesian cows offered a feed with a digestibility of 55% (2·0 kcals ME per g DM), intake was limited physically for at least 10 months and extreme losses in body weight occurred during lactation.

A feed with a digestibility of 65% gave body weight changes which followed similar patterns to those observed by Monteiro (1972), except that the initial

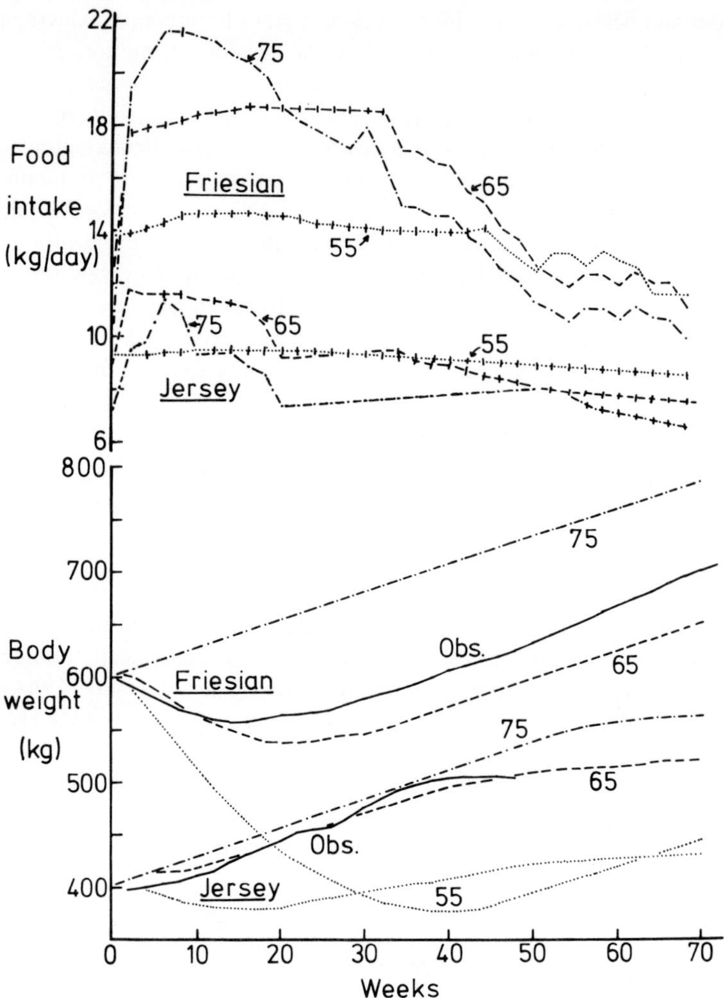

Fig 6. Predictions of food intake and body weight of dairy cows by the iterative model COWMKIII. 55, 65, 75: digestibility of DM in feeds used in model. Obs., observed intakes.

decline in weight was not as steep as that observed, probably because the model does not at this stage account for the loss of weight associated with involution of the uterus. This model, in common with other predictive devices, gives in the first few weeks a more rapid rise in food intake than the observed rise, even though a "physical" limit to intake is reached as soon as the second week of lactation.

With a 75% digestible feed, intake is always able to keep up with metabolic demands, except for a very short period at the peak of the long Friesian lactation.

The intakes predicted from the ME requirements are in almost all cases lower than the observed intakes, suggesting that intake is systematically higher than nutrient requirements as assessed by the ARC working party (ARC 1965). These higher observed intakes should however, lead to higher weight gains than were actually observed. The cause of this anomaly remains to be resolved; I probably made a false assumption about the ratio of digestibility to metabolizable energy in the feed.

The Jersey cows with short lactations are predicted to approach a plateau in body weight approximately one year after calving, due to physical limitations. This agrees reasonably well with the observed plateau which was reached at about 10 months. The body weight at which equilibrium is reached is predicted to vary with the concentration of available energy in the feed. Unfortunately I know of no experimental observations with which to compare this finding. Both real and model cows with long lactations lose more weight than those with short lactations and show no signs of reaching a plateau in body weight after 15 months of observation or iteration.

One development of this model has been to remove its dependence on actual milk yield data by substituting an "ideal" milk yield curve derived from Wood's (1969) statistical analysis of large numbers of lactation curves (Forbes, 1977b). When physical limitations intervene and energy output is not matched by energy intake, milk yield is depressed in proportion to the energy deficit. Current knowledge of the control of the partition of energy between milk and body stores is, however, not yet sufficient to make such predicted corrections to milk yield with a great deal of confidence.

2. *Sheep in Various Physiological States*

My interest in the decline in food intake often seen in late pregnancy in ewes encouraged me to adopt with sheep an approach similar to that described above for the lactating and post-lactating cow, but to incorporate non-pregnant and pregnant phases in addition (Forbes, 1977a). It is assumed that food intake is related directly to nutrient demands, as set out by the ARC working party (ARC, 1965), unless physical limitation intervenes. Rumen capacity depends on abdominal capacity, volume of abdominal fat and volume of uterus. Physically limited intake (PI, g/day) is related to rumen capacity (RV, litres), with an allowance for faster disappearance of diets of higher digestibility (D, %DM) by the formula:

$$PI = (500 + 30RV) \times D/65 \quad (6)$$

derived from non-pregnant and pregnant ewes of various degrees of fatness (Forbes, 1969). The weight of abdominal fat was initially set at 2kg, and it was assumed that half of any fat mobilized or deposited subsequently was abdominal.

(a) *Mature fattening sheep.* The model (SHEEPMK 1) was used to predict intake by moderately thin sheep (2 kg abdominal fat) at four rates of fattening offered a range of feeds. The digestibilities at which physical limitation was predicted to change to metabolic control, for animals depositing 50, 100, 150, and 200 g fat per day, were 56, 64, 70 and 76% respectively. I am not aware of any experimental results with which to compare these directly. When the model is developed for growing lambs it will be possible to compare predictions with the extensive data of Baumgardt and his colleagues (Baumgardt, 1970) obtained with lambs fed on a wide range of diets.

SHEEPMK 1 was then run for 500 days with two target rates of fattening (50 and 200 g/day) and three feeds (digestibility and ME concentration: 55, 2·0; 65, 2·4; 75%, 2·8 kcals/g). Food intakes and empty body weights (body weight minus gut contents) are shown in Fig. 7. The animals failed to achieve the higher

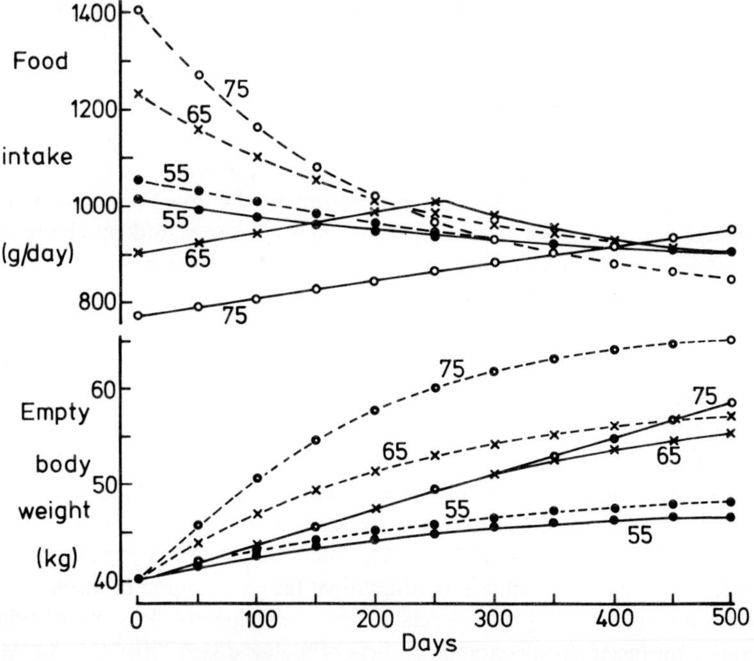

Fig 7. Predictions of food intake and empty body weight changes in mature fattening sheep by SHEEPMK 1. 55, 65, 75: Digestibility of dry matter in feed; ———— target fat deposition of 50 g per day; – – – – – target fat deposition of 200 g per day.

rate of fattening, even with the highly digestible feed, as physical limitation of intake was predicted. Abdominal fat did accumulate, however, and voluntary intake declined until, by 500 days, a situation of equilibrium was being approached with body weight positively related to digestibility. With the synthesis of 50g fat per day, food intake was able to keep pace with energy requirements for at least 500 days with the 75% digestible diet, for 250 days with the medium feed, but not at all with the 55% digestible feed. Body weight changes reflected these patterns of food intake. Sheep and cattle are rarely allowed to fatten excessively in practice, and although I have heard it said that ruminants can become extremely fat if fed on concentrate diets for long periods, there is little published evidence on this. It has been noted that

> "prolonged *ad libitum* feeding of non-pregnant sheep on a wide variety of diets has eventually let to partial or complete inappetance, followed, in the latter instance by the death of the animal, and this only occurs after a fat or very fat condition has been attained, regardless of the period on the diet" (Reid and Hinks, 1962).

SHEEPMK 1 predicts that gross fatness can eventually be attained on good quality feeds, but not the fatal consequences (unless rate of fat deposition was so slow that old age intervened!). Gibson (1969) found that cows tended to become fat on *ad libitum* feeding of the diet used by Monteiro (1972) but that this could be "counteracted to some extent by the introduction of a modified form of the diet with a higher percentage of chopped straw and a lower nutrient density".

(b) *Pregnant and lactating ewes.* The basic model was adapted for pregnancy and lactation by the inclusion of data on the increase in weight of the uterus in ewes bearing single and twin fetuses (Forbes, 1968), the increased energy requirements of pregnant ewes (ARC, 1965), oestrogen secretion in late pregnancy (Challis *et al.*, 1973), the effects of oestrogens on concentrate intake by sheep (Forbes, 1971), and the milk yields of lactating ewes (Forbes, 1968). A target rate of fat deposition of 50g per day was adopted and the program was run with daily iteration for five weeks before conception, through the 21 weeks pregnancy and for 17 weeks *post-partum*, the lambs being weaned at 10 weeks of age, for single and twin bearing ewes offered three types of feed.

The results in Fig. 8 show that the model predicts a continuous decline in intake of the low digestibility diet during pregnancy, with a rise to the initial value after parturition and a slight fall at weaning, with physical limitation throughout, except after weaning in ewes that had suckled twins. When I fed ewes on either hay (60% digestible) or silage (54% digestible) from the 10th week of pregnancy until parturition there were continuous declines of intake in both groups (Forbes, 1968).

With the diet of 65% digestibility, intake was predicted to rise until the 15th week of pregnancy, when physical limitation took over and intake declined until parturition, the decline being steeper for twin-bearing ewes. This is comparable with changes in food intake of ewes on good quality silage (77% digestibility as measured by an *in vitro* technique), and with those fed on hays of 65 and 68% digestibility (measured *in vivo*) (Forbes, 1970b), and with the results of Reid and Hinks (1962) who fed ewes on a hay of unspecified quality. During lactation, intake was predicted to be physically controlled, but after weaning metabolic control was resumed. The ewes of Reid and Hinks did not show such a large increase in intake after parturition, possibly because Merino ewes usually have low milk yields. My hay-fed ewes did show the increase predicted, but with a steady rise during the first six weeks of lactation, rather than the sudden

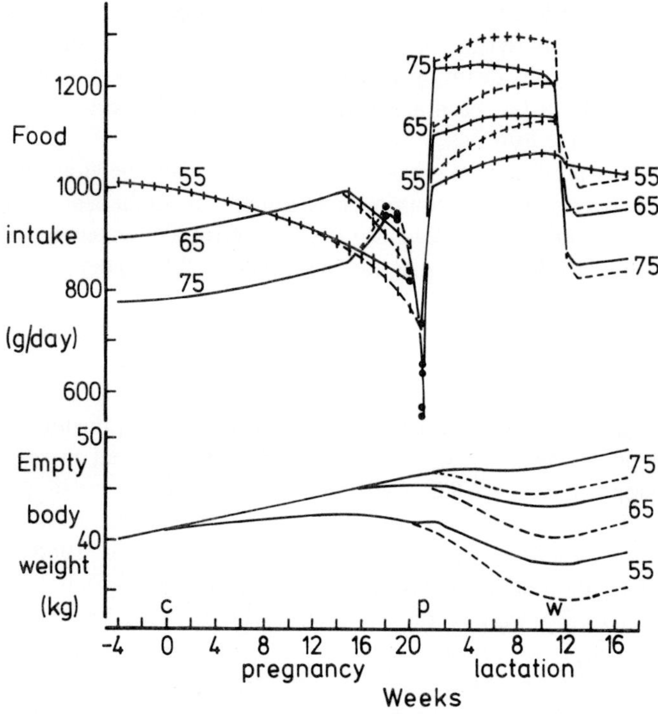

Fig 8. Predictions of food intake and empty body weight changes in pregnant and lactating ewes by SHEEPMK 1. 55, 65, 75: Digestibility of dry matter in feed; ———— ewes with single lambs; ----- ewes with twin lambs. c, conception; p, parturition; w, weaning.

increase that was predicted by the model. The 75% digestible diet was eaten according to nutrient demands by the model ewes i.e. at a lower level of DM than the 65% digestible diet, until oestrogen limitation was encountered at the 18th week of pregnancy. Observations on ewes fed barley (82% digestible), in the same experiment as those offered the 68% digestible hay mentioned above, showed a lower DM intake than hay fed ewes and a decline during the last five weeks of pregnancy (Forbes, 1970b). During lactation the high quality feed allowed model ewes to maintain their body weight, while at weaning there was a precipitous fall in intake.

SHEEPMK 1 seems to be a reasonably successful predictor of the intake of various qualities of feed by sheep in different physiological states, and gives a sounder theoretical basis for the planning of future experimental work to elucidate the interactions between metabolic and physical control of food intake in ruminants.

C. *Towards a More Physiological Model of Feeding in Ruminants*

All the regression and iterative approaches so far discussed have been based on the day as a time unit, which is a very convenient, though quite artificial, way of dealing with long term changes such as pregnancy, lactation and fattening. If we wish to understand the control of feeding during the day we must study the factors which cause both the initiation and cessation of each meal. Experimental work has tended to emphasize the cessation of feeding; for example, in much of Baile's work (summarized by Baile and Forbes, 1974) sheep or goats were allowed to start feeding spontaneously, but this resulted in intraruminal or intravenous infusion of possible suppressors of feeding causing, in many cases, premature cessation of feeding. The concept that cessation is more important than initiation is supported by the model of Metz (1975) who collected data on the daily time pattern of eating and ruminating in cows. He found that the length of a meal was correlated with the interval since the last meal but not with the time to the next meal and concluded that meals do not start at some fixed level of depletion. Similar observations with sheep offered a 60% concentrate diet (Baile, 1975) showed no correlation between meal size and either pre- or post-meal interval, whereas when the same animals were accustomed to a 24% concentrate (i. e. 76% roughage) diet there were significant relationships of meal size to both intervals. Hay feeding was associated with more meals per day and it was suggested the physical limitations were responsible for the observed correlations. Both hunger ratio (premeal interval/meal size) and satiety ratio (postmeal interval/meal size) declined significantly with increasing meal size and Baile concluded from this that "sheep do not initiate a meal and determine its size by simply repleting some store". An alternative theory would be that, because of more rapid digestion and absorption, small meals are more satiating, per unit weight, than are large meals.

If hunger does not initiate feeding, then what does? Ruminants are by instinct gregarious animals and, even when kept in individual pens, all sheep within sight or sound of each other have a strong tendency to start feeding at the same time (unpubl. obs.), triggered by some external stimulus, or by the start of feeding of one animal. Any model which is intended to predict within-day feeding patterns in ruminants should not, therefore, assume that a meal only starts when a fixed level of depletion is reached, unless it can be checked against animals kept completely isolated from any external stimuli.

We are currently developing a model of feeding in sheep on the same general lines as Booth's rat model (Toates and Booth, 1974; see Chapter 11), with the proviso that the start of feeding will in some cases be triggered by external stimuli. Preliminary experimentation involving infusion of a physiological mixture of volatile fatty acids into the portal vein of sheep suggests that the flow of energy into the liver which prevents feeding (equivalent to Booth's "upper threshold") is around 1 kcal per minute (Anil and Forbes, unpubl. obs.) and this is incorporated in the model.

The rate at which the products of digestion of each "bite" of food are absorbed at any particular time after ingestion was initially calculated from curves of cumulative absorption against time, derived from the literature. Predicted meals were much larger than observed, and thus much less frequent, due to the slow rate of absorption predicted during the 15 minutes or so normally taken by real sheep to eat an average meal. Three lines of investigation are currently underway to overcome the problems encountered in the prediction of cessation of a meal.

(i) Further searching of the literature, and if necessary, animal experimental work, to get more information on minute-by-minute absorption rates during and shortly after feeding; feeds high in soluble carbohydrates (e.g. concentrates, young grass) could yield a rapid initial peak of absorption.

(ii) Examination of the possibility that the "spike" of insulin secreted at the start of feeding or sham feeding in sheep (Basset, 1975) would cause those cells which might transduce energy flow (e.g. in liver, hypothalamus) to "see" more metabolites during feeding than at other times, and signal to the satiety controller in the brain accordingly.

(iii) Perhaps physical limitation occurs temporarily even with feeds of high digestibility, but by the time digestion has released space in the rumen to allow further intake, sufficient metabolites have been absorbed to exceed the upper threshold and thus prevent further feeding for some time. None of these approaches is sufficiently well developed to comment on results at this stage.

IV. Discussion

The advantage of the regression equation approach to predicting the voluntary food intake of ruminants is that realistic estimates can be given, with indications of variability. Such estimates are limited, however, to situations close to that in which the statistical relationship was obtained. The iterative model, on the other hand, is more flexible but not as accurate. Prediction of variability has not been attempted, except by Edelsten and Newton (1975) who generated a flock of model sheep at the start of each run with individuals whose herbage intake, milk yield, initial body weight and date of lambing were set randomly within a normal distribution with standard deviations appropriate to each parameter.

One major discrepancy between observed intake and predictions both by regression and iterative modelling is in early lactation, when observed intake takes several weeks to reach predicted levels. One possibility, that the uterus is sufficiently large to occupy a significant amount of abdominal capacity for several weeks, has already been mentioned. Another idea worthy of further investigation is the intake depressing effect of very high levels of circulating oestrogens. Challis (1971) showed that in the last two days of pregnancy in sheep and goats, plasma oestrogen concentration rises to levels up to ten times greater than a few days earlier, suggesting a rate of secretion of oestrogens equivalent to three mg oestradiol per day. Progesterone secretion declines sharply in the last few days of pregnancy (Challis *et al.*, 1971), and its likely protective role against the effects of oestrogens on food intake (Muir *et al.*, 1972; Forbes, 1974) will therefore diminish at that time. When we injected 10 mg oestradiol benzoate on two consecutive days into four moderately fat non-pregnant ewes, their intake of the highly digestible diet fell by 60% and took at least two weeks to return to pretreatment levels (unpublished observations). One animal at the time of writing, six weeks after injection, is still eating little more than half of her pre-injection intake and has become quite thin. Could a similar, but less extreme, situation exist after parturition?

The construction of a model often depends to some extent on the modeller's prior knowledge of observed results, and I cannot deny that this is the case in my models. There has, however, been one major prediction which I did not anticipate. I could not incorporate quantification of my preconceived idea of "lipostatic" control of food intake because I did not know either the mechanism of such control, or the set point for body weight at which it might operate. I was surprised, then, to find that without such a constraint my models predict that physical limitation of intake by abdominal fat eventually limits the ruminant to body weights similar to those attained in real sheep and cattle allowed unrestricted access to food for many months. This is not proof of the absence of a metabolic or endocrine lipostat, but, for the ruminant at least, an alternative theory worthy of experimental study.

Acknowledgements

I thank the Centre for Computer Studies for advice and the use of the Leeds University ICL 1906A computer. Professor G. R. Hervey and Dr D. A. Booth gave invaluable advice in the early stages of development of the ruminant models. The British Society of Animal Production kindly gave permission to quote from the paper of Dr L. S. Monteiro and Professor H. R. Conrad allowed similar access to his group's paper in the Journal of Dairy Science. The programs described in this Chapter are written in Fortran and copies are available from the author.

References

Adolph, E. F. (1947). Urges to eat and drink in rats. *Am. J. Physiol.* **151**, 110–125.

Agricultural Research Council, (1965). "The Nutrient Requirements of Farm Livestock". No. 2, Ruminants. Agricultural Research Council, London.

Armstrong, J. S. (1971). Modelling a grazing system. *Proc. Ecol. Soc. Austral.* **6**, 194–202.

Baile, C. A. (1975). Control of feed intake in ruminants. *In* "Digestion and Metabolism in the Ruminant" (I. W. McDonald and A. C. I. Warner, eds), pp. 333–350. Univ. New England, Australia.

Baile, C. A. and Forbes, J. M. (1974). Control of feed intake and regulation of energy balance in ruminants. *Physiol. Rev.* 160–214.

Baile, C. A. and Pfander, W. H. (1967). Ration density as a factor controlling food intake in ruminants. *J. Dairy Sci.* **50**, 70–80.

Balch, C. C. and Campling, R. C. (1962). Regulation of voluntary food intake in ruminants. *Nutr. Abstr. Rev.* **32**, 669–686.

Basset, J. M. (1975). Dietary and gastro-intestinal control of hormones regulating carbohydrate metabolism in ruminants. *In* "Digestion and Metabolism in the Ruminant" (I. W. McDonald and A. C. I. Warner, eds), pp. 383–398. Univ. New England, Australia.

Baumgardt, B. R. (1970). Regulation of feed intake and energy balance. *In* "Physiology of Digestion and Metabolism in the Ruminant". (A. T. Phillipson, ed.), pp. 235–253. Oriel, Newcastle upon Tyne.

Blaxter, K. L., Wainman, F. W. and Wilson, R. S. (1961). The regulation of food intake by sheep. *Anim. Prod.* **3**, 51–61.

Booth, D. A., Toates, F. M. and Platt, S. V. (1976). Control system for hunger and its implications for animals and man. *In* "Hunger: Basic Mechanisms and Clinical Implications". (D. Novin, W. Wyrwicka and G. A. Bray, eds), pp. 127–142. Raven Press, New York.

Booth, T. H. (1975). Systems analysis of grazing dairy cows. Ph. D. Thesis, University of Reading.

Brockington, N. R. (1972). A mathematical model of pasture contamination by grazing cattle and the effects on herbage intake. *J. agric. Sci., Camb.* **79**, 249–258.

Challis, J. R. G. (1971). Sharp increase in free circulating oestrogens immediately before parturition in sheep. *Nature, Lond.* **229**, 208.

Challis, J. R. G., Harrison, F. A. and Heap, R. B. (1971). Uterine production of oestrogens and progesterone at parturition in the sheep. *J. Reprod. Fert.* **25**, 306–307.

Challis, J. R. G., Harrison, F. A. and Heap, R. B. (1973). The kinetics of oestradiol–17β metabolism in the sheep. *J. Endocr.* **57**, 97–110.

Conrad, H. R., Pratt, A. D. and Hibbs, J. W. (1964). Regulation of feed intake in dairy cows. 1. Change in importance of physical and physiological factors with increasing digestibility. *J. Dairy Sci.* **47**, 54–62.

Curran, M. K. and Holmes, W. (1970). Prediction of the voluntary intake of food by dairy cows. 2. Lactating grazing cows. *Anim. Prod.* **12**, 213–224.

Curran, M. K., Wimble, R. H. and Holmes, W. (1970). Prediction of the voluntary intake of food by dairy cows. 1. Stall-fed cows in late pregnancy and early lactation. *Anim. Prod.* **12**, 195–212.

Dinius, D. A. and Baumgardt, B. R. (1970). Regulation of food intake in ruminants. 6. Influence of caloric density of pelleted rations. *J. Dairy Sci.* **53**, 311–316.

Dirkx, J. and Dufour, P. (1975). A subroutine to represent tridimensional surfaces on a printer. *Comp. Prog. Biomed.* **5**, 61–65.

Donefer, E., Lloyd, L. E. and Crampton, E. W. (1963). Effect of varying alfalfa: barley ratios on energy intake and volatile fatty acid production by sheep. *J. Anim. Sci.* **22**, 425–428.

Edelsten, P. R. and Newton, J. E. (1975). A simulation model of intensive lamb production from grass. Grassland Research Institute Technical Report No. 17. Grassland Research Institute, Berkshire.

Edholm, O. G., Fletcher, J. G., McCance, R. A. and Widdowson, E. M. (1955). The energy expenditure and food intake of individual men. *Br. J. Nutr.* **9**, 286–300.

Forbes, J. M. (1968). The effect of pregnancy on rumen volume and voluntary feed intake in the ewe. Ph. D. Thesis, University of Leeds.

Forbes, J. M. (1969). The effect of pregnancy and fatness on the volume of rumen contents in the ewe. *J. agric. Sci., Camb.* **72**, 119–121.

Forbes, J. M. (1970a). The voluntary food intake of pregnant and lactating ruminants: A review. *Br. vet. J.* **126**, 1–11.

Forbes, J. M. (1970b). Voluntary food intake of pregnant ewes. *J. Anim. Sci.* **31**, 1222–1227.

Forbes, J. M. (1971). Physiological changes affecting voluntary food intake in ruminants. *Proc. Nutr. Soc.* **30**, 135–142.

Forbes, J. M. (1974). Feeding in sheep modified by intraventricular estradiol and progesterone. *Physiol. Behav.* **12**, 741–747.

Forbes, J. M. (1977a). Interrelationships between physical and metabolic control of voluntary food intake in fattening, pregnant and lactating mature sheep: A model. *Anim. Prod.* **24**, 91–101.

Forbes, J. M. (1977b). Development of a model of voluntary food intake and energy balance in lactating cows. *Anim Prod.* **24**, 203–214.

Forbes, J. M. and Blair, T. (1974). Lack of effect of intraruminal loading on short-term intake of a concentrate feed by sheep. *Proc. Nutr. Soc.* **33**, 77A.

Gibson, D. (1969). The development of a complete diet for cattle. Animal Breeding Research Organisation Report, Edinburgh.

Hodgson, J. and Wilkinson, J. M. (1967) The relationship between live-weight and herbage intake in grazing cattle. *Anim. Prod,* **9**, 365–376.

Kruger, L. and Schulze, G. (1956). Feed intake and consumption in milk cows. III. The satiety value of feeding stuffs. *Züchtungskunde,* **28**, 438–450.

Lehmann, F. (1941). *Z. Tierernä. Futtemittelk.* **5**, 155. (Quoted by Balch and Campling, 1962.)

Lofgren, P. A. and Warner, R. G. (1972). Relationship of dietary caloric density and certain blood metabolites to voluntary feed intake in mature wethers. *J. Anim. Sci.* **35**, 1239.

Metz, J. H. M. (1975). Time patterns of feeding and rumination in domestic cattle. Mededelingen Landbouwhogeschool, Wageningen, Nederland, **75**, No. 12.

Monteiro, L. S. (1972). The control of appetite in lactating cows. *Anim Prod.* **14**, 263–282.

Montgomery, M. J. and Baumgardt, B. R. (1965). Regulation of food intake in ruminants. I. Pelleted rations varying in energy concentrations. *J. Dairy Sci.* **48**, 569–574.

Muir, L. A., Hibbs, J. W., Conrad, H. R. and Smith, K. L. (1972). Effect of estrogen and progesterone on feed intake and hydroxyproline excretion following induced hypocalcaemia in cows. *J. Dairy Sci.* **55**, 1613–1620.

Phillipson, A. T. (ed.) (1970). Physiology of Digestion and Metabolism in the Ruminant. Oriel, Newcastle upon Tyne.

Reid, R. L. and Hinks, N. T. (1962). Studies on the carbohydrate metabolism of sheep. XVII. Feed requirements and voluntary feed intake in late pregnancy, with particular reference to prevention of hypoglycaemia and hyperketonaemia. *Aust. J. agric. Res.* **13**, 1092–1111.

Rice, R. W., Morris, J. G., Maeda, B. T. and Baldwin, R. L. (1974). Simulation of animal functions in models of production systems: ruminants on the range. *Fed. Proc.* **33**, 188–195.

Ronning, M. and Laben, R. C. (1966). Response of lactating cows to free-choice feeding of milled diets containing from 10 to 100% concentrates. *J. Dairy Sci.* **49**, 1080–1085.

Smith, R. C. G. and Williams, W. A. (1973). Model development for a deferred grazing system. *J. Range Mgt* **26**, 454–460.

Smith, R. C. G. and Williams, W. A. (1976). Deferred grazing of Mediterranean animal pasture for increased winter sheep production. *Agric. Systems.* **1**, 37–46.

Spedding, C. R. W. (1965). "Sheep Production and Grazing Management". Baillière, Tindall and Co, London.

Toates, F. M. and Booth, D. A. (1974). Control of food intake by energy supply. *Nature, Lond.* **251**, 710–711.

Tulloh, N. M. and Hughes, J. W. (1965). Physical studies of the alimentary tract of grazing cattle. II. Techniques for estimating the capacity of the reticulo-rumen. *N. Z. J. Agric. Res.* **8**, 1070–1078.

de Wit, C. T. (1968). Plant production. Miscellaneous papers. *Landb. hogesch. Wageningen,* No. 3, 25–50.

Wood, P. D. P. (1969). Factors affecting the shape of the lactation curve in cattle. *Anim. Prod.* **11**, 307–316.

14

A Physiological Control Theory of the Hunger–Thirst Interaction

F. M. TOATES
Division of Psychology, Preston Polytechnic, Preston, England.

I. Introduction

A. *Mechanisms of Homeostasis*

The concept of homeostasis has long held a strong attraction not only for biologists and physiologists, but in one form or another for psychologists also. It is perhaps not difficult to see why. We owe to Claude Bernard the first detailed and formal statement of the fact that life is only possible if the essential functions of the body do not venture far outside rather narrow limits. A frail organism, if it is to survive in what is often a hostile environment, must therefore be able to take measures to oppose the effect of forces pulling it away from its normal state. At one time "vital spirits" might have seemed a suitable candidate to explain this apparently intelligent and purposeful behaviour of the organism, but these were academically exorcized by the Berlin school of materialists who insisted that only physico-chemical explanations were permissible in physiology. In one very real sense this was tantamount to saying that the problem is essentially one of engineering.

Even though the ideas and tools of control engineering as we now know them did not exist at that time, nonetheless there were available some good mechanical examples of automatic regulation. This, or possibly just insight, gave rise to explanations of physiological regulatory processes in mechanistic terms. Thus if an excess of water is taken into the body the excretion of water by the kidney is accelerated until body water volume returns to normal. If a water deficit exists, the animal drinks until the deficit is eliminated, at which point drinking is automatically switched off. Such a mechanism holds an intuitive attraction as an explanation of a biological function, and it not only seems to work in the sense that it allows verifiable predictions to be made but it also enables some of the philosophically difficult problems of purpose in biology to be answered (see Oatley, 1972, 1973).

Homeostatic types of system also have a place in the psychological literature. It might be worth noting in passing the resemblance, at least superficially, which even cognitive theories such as achievement motivation and cognitive dissonance have to this concept. Both involve reduction of disparity between some ideal state of affairs and its actual state, as do existential and self-actualization models. Homeostasis perhaps more convincingly comes into its own, however, when one needs to relate some aspect of behaviour to a proposed physiological state. Freud was often occupied with pressure regulator analogies, and descriptions of neural mechanisms seeking an activity level of zero, and this is not far from the thinking of present-day European ethologists.

The American psychologist Hull adopted the idea of homeostasis and made it the core of his behaviour theory. It should be noted that in Hull's as well as the other models it is some physical quantity which we are asked to consider, whether it be the deficit in body fluids giving rise to thirst, the vitamin C content of the body, or even the amount of sublimated energy needed to paint the Mona Lisa.

When an investigator has sufficient confidence in his proposed system to be able to draw a model in control systems language, it commonly involves a set point—such as the temperature set point which helps determine sweating, or the fluid volume set point which plays a role in thirst. Set point refers to that value which the controlled variable should have and which action is directed towards attaining. The German expression *Sollwert* (should-value) describes it somewhat better than the English equivalent. The set point concept is very attractive, perhaps at times to the point of being seductive, and this is probably true in the case of hunger (the present writer not having been immune from this in the past). Investigators in the area of hunger almost from intuition appeal to a set point concept, be it eating to hold body weight constant or the pressure on the soles of the feet constant, or eating in response to a drop in temperature below normal, a reduction in uptake of sugar from the blood, or a fall in fat deposits. Figure 1 shows how such a theory of feeding could be translated into systems terms. When the actual value of body weight content or blood glucose level or whatever falls below a set point level, an error signal arises which, if greater than a threshold, causes eating. Eating then forms an input to the integrator which represents body energy while energy consumption is a negative input to the same integrator.

We have however proposed (Booth and Toates, 1974; Toates and Booth, 1974; Booth *et al.*, 1976; see also Chapter 11 by Booth) a radical departure from the conventional set point model in so far as we argue that the immediate cause of eating is not body energy level falling below a set point but rather the rate of energy supply coming to below a threshold. Whether this should simply be redefined as an energy rate set point is perhaps more a semantic and philosophical question than a physiological one, the important point being that our feeding control is anchored to an energy rate rather than to a quantity.

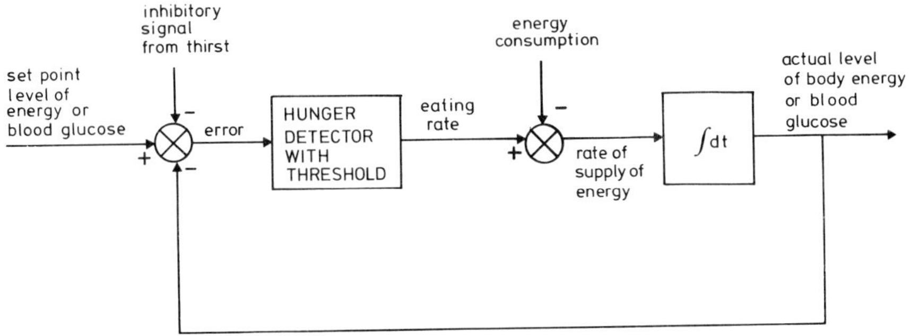

Fig. 1. Model of hunger based upon homeostatic regulation of energy flow.

B. *Thirst and Hunger*

The main theme of this chapter is the interaction between the controllers of water and food intake. The body's various controllers do not exist in isolation from one another but rather show a profound interdependence. This may be due either to the peripheral interaction of one system's response with an effect of another controller's operation or to some built-in cross-coupling between the two controllers. An example of the former is provided by the person in the middle of a desert who may die of water loss as a consequence of the sweat glands pouring out precious fluid in an attempt to keep the body temperature down. The only consolation for such a person is that his life expectation would be even shorter were it not for the work of the sweat glands. The ultimate purpose of any biological control system is the survival of the organism, and this may mean one controller taking a subordinate position in a hierarchy. For example a thirsty animal eats less food than a non-thirsty one, not because its need for food is less but because the appearance of food in the gut with its associated osmotic pull could seriously embarrass the body fluids if they were already depleted of water. Nature has therefore provided an inhibitory link from thirst to hunger. A free-for-all between hunger and thirst would not represent good biological economy.

The specific goal of this chapter is the demonstration of where control theory and simulation methods can illuminate our understanding of the hunger–thirst interaction. Before such techniques are employed it is important to survey the experimental literature thoroughly in order to establish exactly what it is that we should be modelling. Awkward results must never be passed over, not just because of scientific integrity but also because they may prove to be the salvation of a model.

II. Experimental Literature on the Hunger–Thirst Interaction

We will consider first the way in which eating affects drinking, then the question of the thirst to hunger interaction.

A. *The Dependence of Drinking on Eating*

In a situation where food is rationed but water is allowed *ad libitum*, animals (with one or two exceptions) drink in the steady state an amount of water proportional to the quantity of food eaten (Cizek, 1959). The relatively enormous quantity of water drunk by a food-deprived rabbit appears to be non-homeostatic but it may represent a desperate attempt to hold extracellular volume constant in the face of an electrolyte imbalance and in this sense is homeostatic after all. It is abolished by allowing sodium chloride solutions to drink (Cizek, 1961). Since the hungry animal usually drinks less than the animal having food available, this poses the question whether hunger exerts some kind of inhibition on thirst. Verplanck and Hayes (1953) suggested that this was indeed the case. However, Oatley and Tonge (1969) tested this suggestion by measuring the effect of hunger on the drinking caused by giving rats injections of salt and found no evidence of any such inhibition. An inhibition would indeed seem to be redundant since it is difficult to envisage that a hungry rat should need to reduce its water intake, except as a result of a peripheral interaction such as a reduced rate of urine production.

However, this is no subject area nor time for acceptance of the obvious—as was demonstrated by Kutscher (1972), whose results were rather difficult to fit to any such simple model. He compared the water loss suffered during a period of deprivation with the amount drunk in 1 h without food following the water deprivation period and found the latter to be only about 10% of the former if food was not available during water deprivation, and only 30% if food was available. The difference of 20% between the two treatments cannot be explained in terms of a greater water loss by the fed rats, since for any given deprivation period the water loss is the same irrespective of whether or not food is available. At least two questions arise from these results;

(i) why did rats drink so little?

(ii) why is there a difference between rats receiving food and those deprived of food?

An explanation in terms of abnormal stomach distension caused by drinking is not adequate, since if this were true the 24-h deprived rats would be expected to drink a larger percentage of their deficit than the 96-h deprived. This was not the case in practice.

Kutscher advanced the argument that hunger inhibits thirst, being aware of course that rats which are deprived of water only, as well as those which are food- and water-deprived, will suffer food deprivation, the former voluntarily (in so far as we are allowed to describe any behaviour as voluntary!). The rat experiencing total food deprivation is hungrier than that having food available and voluntarily restricting its intake, and so one can argue that the drinking of the totally deprived rat is less because it is more inhibited by hunger than that of the rat having food *ad libitum*. Such an interpretation though is quite incompatible with the conclusions of Oatley and Tonge (1969).

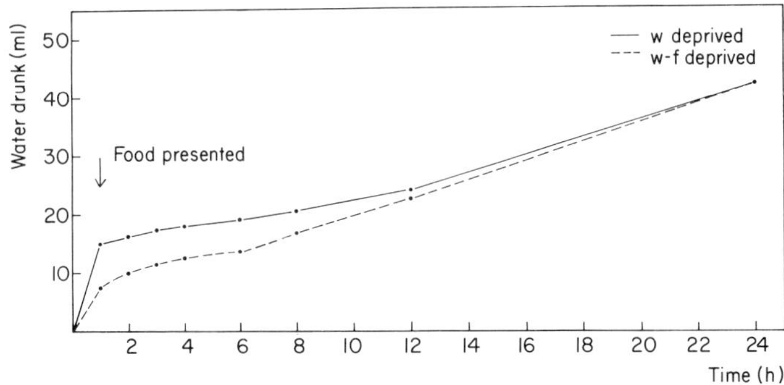

Fig. 2. Amount drunk by rats following 48h of either water deprivation or water and food deprivation. One hour's drinking the the absence of food was followed by drinking in the presence of food. Subjects were of mean weight 427g and had lights on from 0800 to 2000. Deprivation began and water was presented at 0800.

If in fact drinking is being inhibited by hunger, then presentation of food ought to abolish hunger fairly rapidly and thereby allow the rat to drink an amount appropriate to its deficit. (This would certainly be the case if the interaction is in fact as it is described in systems terms later in this chapter.) Since both food–water- and water-deprived animals suffer a deficit of the same magnitude over any given deprivation period, the imbalance in 1-h drinking between the two treatments should be corrected after presentation of food.

Figure 2 shows the result of a study by myself. Rats were either deprived of food and water or just water for 48h and then water was allowed but food withdrawn for 1h. After 1h, food again was returned. It is clear that the drinking curves only very slowly converge as a function of time. This would appear to be evidence against the argument that the difference between the two treatments is due to a difference in intensity of an inhibition from hunger to thirst, since one might expect that the food–water deprived rats would rapidly catch up with the water deprived. Furthermore, the amount drunk by rats following both treatments is quite inappropriate to their deficit, which for this size of animal is some 40ml after 48h of deprivation. This amount of water is taken only after about 24h has elapsed, by which time of course some 20ml will have been lost from the body. In other words, any coupling of the deficit correction to hunger correction is unconvincing.

In fact it is possible to offer a different answer to the question why the rats drink so little. During a period of water deprivation, accompanied as it invariably is by a reduction of food intake if not total food deprivation, breakdown of cell contents will occur. The number of molecules of solid matter in the body will be less. Collier and Levitsky (1967) showed, in an experiment that may bear a similarity to the present one, that when rats suffer water deprivation during a period when they are allowed food they maintain a constant ratio of lean body mass to water in the various organs of the body. This, of course, involves reduction in the size of the organs in order to match the loss of water. The rat shrinks in size but maintains the same lean mass to water ratio as before. Let us take a cell of weight x which will comprise approximately $0 \cdot 7x$ of water and $0 \cdot 3x$ of solid matter, since the water content of the organs of the body such as muscle, liver, etc. is between 60 and 80% (Collier and Levitsky, 1967). Because of breakdown of this particular cell's contents, the rat will loose $0 \cdot 7x$ of water from the cellular compartment. However, when drinking is allowed one would not expect the rat to compensate for this quantity by its drinking mechanism, since the cell contents are not what they were before. Only after food intake has allowed cellular rebuilding to occur would the rat compensate—hence the slow response shown in Fig. 2.

The deficit as defined by Kutscher is calculated as follows. Rats are killed when having water and food available, and other rats of the same original weight are killed after deprivation. The water content is obtained in each case by weighing the carcass after it has been dried in an oven. The difference between the two values of water content is called the deficit. This procedure can give a misleading impression, and a somewhat macabre example serves to illustrate the point. A person having had a limb amputated would appear to suffer a body water deficit, but one would not expect the subject to experience thirst. In the present experiment and in the one reported by Kutscher, the water-deprived rat presumably drinks more than the water–food-deprived rat because breakdown of cell contents will be greater in the water–food-deprived animal, despite the fact that total loss of water is the same in each case. That is, in the water deprived animal a greater share of the insensible and urine loss would be obtained from a source other than the cells (the plasma for example).

It is a well known, but unexplained, phenomenon that during the first day or so of food deprivation rats exhibit a high rate of urine production. We are now in a position to account, at least in part, for this effect in terms of the water made available by cellular breakdown. Another contributing factor would be that water held in the gut is free to migrate into the body fluids proper with the cessation of feeding.

Why, though, do rats continue to drink almost normally during the first day of food deprivation? Oatley (1971) advances the argument that this is due to a mechanism which generates drinking in a pre-programmed sequence in food-deprived rats. Frustration may well be involved. Morrison (1968) found that rats are reluctant to work to obtain water under these conditions. This suggests that drinking over and above a certain level is not regulatory.

B. *Effect of Thirst on Hunger*

Turning the discussion in the opposite direction, to the effect of thirst on hunger, there is good evidence for an inhibitory link. Working with rats, Oatley and Toates (1973) showed that hypertonic saline injections drastically reduced subsequent eating. The effect is abolished very rapidly by allowing the animal water to drink, thus partly although not completely answering the possible charge that it is due to discomfort. However, a comparable reduction in feeding occurs in response to the presumably less traumatic stimulus of water deprivation (Toates and Oatley, 1972).

Kakolewski and Deaux (1970) investigated the effect of water deprivation on rats and found that drinking 3 ml or more of water always resulted in the initiation of eating following a latent period. The latency was increased if solutes were added to the drinking water, a rather strong argument for an osmotically sensitive thirst receptor exerting an inhibition which may be disinhibited by drinking. Similarly, Toates in an unpublished study found that, follwing 48 h of water deprivation in the presence of food *ad libitum*, rats given 8 ml of isotonic saline to drink did not increase their food intake in a 1-h observation. Amounts eaten were 0·07 g (no fluid), 0·05 g (8 ml of isotonic saline) and 2·21 g (8 ml of water). However, food deprived rats, which would eat even when no fluid was available, did eat more in a 1-h test if allowed isotonic saline, although not as much as if water was available.

Renal excretion of sodium in the 1-h test was not measured, but it is tentatively concluded that, while feeding can be disinhibited by relief of osmotic thirst, the animal which is feeding in any case is aided even by isotonic saline and therefore by a factor other than a reduction in osmotic pressure.

Under *ad libitum* conditions, feeding and drinking occur closely together in time (Fitzsimons and Le Magnen, 1969). There may be several reasons for this.

(i) One reason is that, as we have seen, thirst restrains feeding. If the thirst needed to reach the drinking threshold is sufficient to exert an inhibition on feeding, then there will be a rather rapid disinhibition of feeding when the drinking threshold is exceeded and the consequent water intake returns thirst to zero.

(ii) Another reason why one would expect meals and drinks to be closely associated under *ad libitum* conditions is that a rat takes a quantity of water appropriate to its future needs arising from the meal. For example, if the diet is changed from one low in protein to one rich in protein then, because of increased loss of water in the urine, the rat's daily water intake increases and this appears to be achieved by the animal recalibrating the amount of water it drinks in association with each meal. When the diet is reduced in protein content, there is an inertial lag but after a few days the water to food ratio at each meal decreases to a new steady state level. This, together with the finding of Oatley and Toates (1969) that the movement of fluid into the gut following a meal is not sufficiently fast to account for the drinking which is done in association with a meal, implies that eating food is in its own right a thirst stimulus.

(iii) Possibly the association of eating and drinking is simply the result of an attention mechanism. Drinking arouses the animal and it pays attention to any hunger signal. Nicolaïdis and Rowland (1975) showed that even if the animal's water needs are met by infusion they still drink to some extent and this is common immediately prior to meals (see their Fig. 8, middle histogram). The close association between eating and drinking may easily be disrupted if the animal is forced to take meals at times other than at its own choosing. Fitzsimons and Le Magnen (1969) showed that, if food is allowed only for two 1-h periods during the day, the rat continues to drink a large amount of water at night when no food is being eaten. Similarly, Oatley (1971) found that if a rat is allowed access to food pellets regularly every 2·4 h during the day and night it continues to drink most of its 24-h intake of water in the 12 h of darkness. In other words, there is an independent circadian rhythm which controls drinking and this is normally entrained with the eating rhythm. The close hunger-thirst association has caused some confusion in the past, at least one author having argued that the drinking rhythm is simply a reflection of the hunger rhythm and is caused by their interaction. Nevertheless, the relationship between hunger and thirst may be mutual in this respect, for a very preliminary study by Oatley and the present author (reported by Oatley, 1973) indicated that, if access to water is allowed only at fixed intervals, eating still shows a circadian rhythm.

III. A Model of Hunger, Thirst and Their Interaction

A. *Hunger*

Figure 3 shows a proposed model of the hunger system which was presented by Booth and Toates (1974) and Toates and Booth (1974). More sophisticated models are now being used (Booth *et al.*, 1976; Booth, 1976; Chapters 11 and

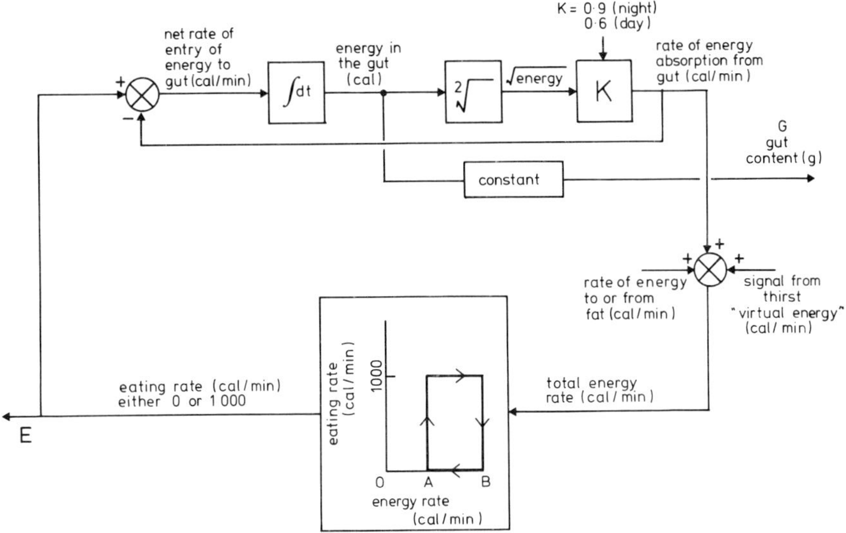

Fig. 3. A model of feeding, showing the interaction with thirst.

12) but for our present purposes the Mark 1 version of the model will suffice. The net rates of energy input to and output from the gut (cal/min) are integrated to give a total gut energy content (calories). Energy in the gut will be absorbed at a rate which is proportional to the square root of the energy content of the gut, i.e.

$$\text{rate from gut} = K \times (\text{gut content})^{\frac{1}{2}}.$$

In fact the proportionality factor K is constant during any given 12-h period of the day, but is higher in the dark phase than in the light. In other words, in the rat the gut empties faster by night than by day (see Booth *et al.*, 1976 and chapter 11). At the output of the block marked K, we have rate of energy absorption from gut (cal/min). If this is fed back and subtracted from eating rate we obtain net rate of energy to the gut (cal/min). Rate of absorption of energy from the gut is added at a summing junction to rate of energy flow to or from fat in order to give total rate of supply of energy. If this falls below ON, i.e. appetite threshold value A, eating is initiated. This continues until the energy rate rises to OFF, i.e. satiety threshold value B, at which point eating is switched off. Based on observations of rats in an eating situation, eating is represented as having a rate of either zero or 1000 cal/min.

Note two things about this model.

(i) Absorption of energy is taken to be sufficiently prompt to be the factor which switches off eating. Although distension of the stomach at large volumes is a sufficient condition to inhibit eating, it is not a necessary condition, and our model seemed to get on alright without it under *ad libitum* feeding conditions.

(ii) Energy rate not energy quantity determines feeding.

B. *Thirst*

A model of thirst in the rat has been constructed, simulated on a digital computer and shown to have considerable explanatory and predictive power (Toates and Oatley, 1970; Oatley and Toates, 1971; Oatley, 1973, 1974; Toates, 1974, 1975). The full details of the model will not be elaborated here. The interested reader is referred to either Toates and Oatley (1970) for the full program or to Toates (1975) for a detailed discussion of the simulation method employed. The essentials of the model are shown in Figs 4–11 which are based on Oatley's (1974) revision.

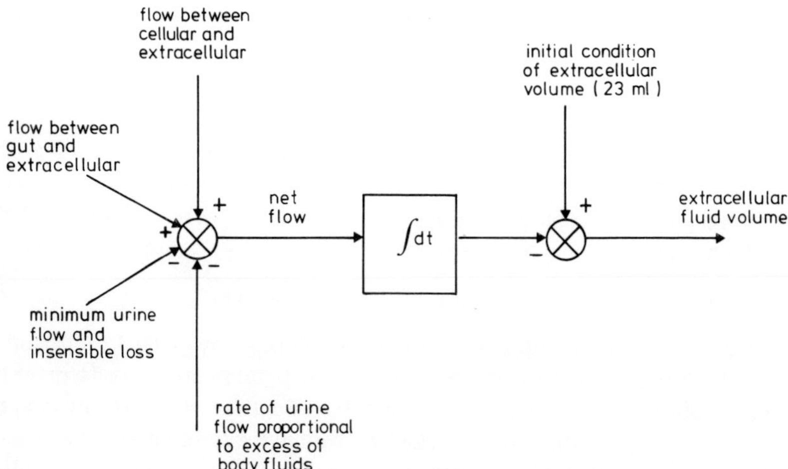

Fig. 4. Model of the extracellular fluid compartment.

Figure 4 shows the water in the extracellular compartment of the rat. The model refers to a rat of 100 g weight, and the initial condition of extracellular fluid volume (ECF) is 23 ml. The term $\int dt$ refers to the integral of flow with respect to time. In other words, ECF volume will be given by the sum of the initial condition (23 ml) and the integral of all the net flows into the extracellular compartment with respect to time. As the summing junction shows, the net flow of water into the extracellular space is given by the rate of absorption of water from the gut, plus the rate from the intracellular space, minus the rate lost as urine and insensible loss.

The equations defining the passage of water from the gut to the blood were presented by Toates (1974) and are shown in Fig. 5. If the ratio of water (ml) to food (g) in the gut is less than 1·1, water moves from the blood. If the ratio is greater then it moves in the opposite direction. Thus in the model, gut water is

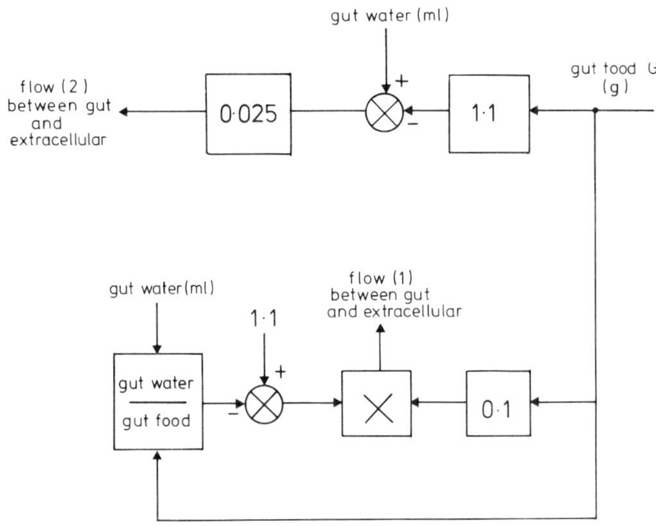

Fig. 5. Model of the water exchange between gut and extracellular space.

divided by gut food and the ratio compared with 1·1 in order to give the concentration gradient. The rate of flow of water will be proportional to the gradient times the amount of food present. This multiplication operation is shown together with a constant proportionality term of 0·1. The output of the multiplier is flow rate of water.

Of course, water introduced into the stomach without food will also migrate into the blood. This is represented by subtracting from gut water that amount (if any) which is attached to gut food. Thus, gut food (G) is multiplied by 1·1 and subtracted from gut water. The difference is multiplied by 0·025 and gives an additional flow from gut to blood. This will handle water loads on an empty gut, but also gives an additional expression for moving excess water out of a stomach holding food. The mathematics fits the physiology sufficiently well but it is hoped in the future that the equations can be rationalized.

Loss of water from the body is shown to be made up of a constant excretion rate plus a rate proportional to fluid excess, the latter representing a negative feedback effect employing antidiuretic hormone (Fig. 4). Intracellular fluid volume (ICF) is made up of its initial condition minus the integral of the flow from the intracellular space to the extracellular space (Fig. 6).

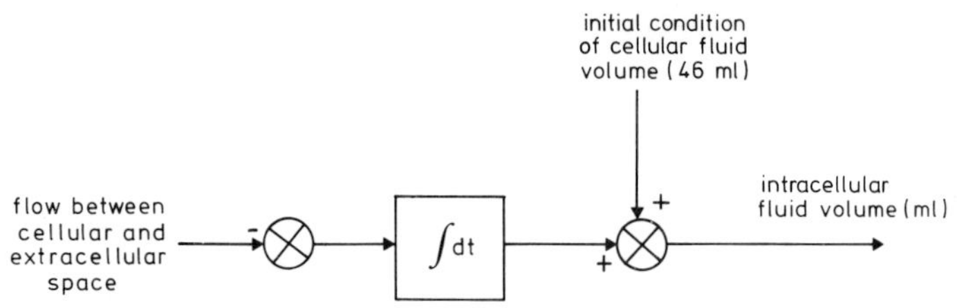

Fig. 6. Model of the intracellular fluid compartment.

The ionic concentration in each compartment is assumed to be proportional to the principal ion divided by water volume. Thus extracellular sodium (Na) is divided by ECF to give ECF Na concentration and cellular potassium (K) is divided by ICF volume to give ICF K concentration (Fig. 7). If one of these is subtracted from the other we obtain the relative ionic concentration difference across the cell boundary. The constants 30 and 37·5 are present simply to balance the mathematics so that the normal sodium concentration is in equilibrium with the normal potassium concentration. Any imbalance in concentration gives rise to a gradient which means a flow of water between the two compartments.

It is believed that the thirst signal is made up of the sum of signals proportional to extracellular and cellular deficit minus inhibitory signals from the gut and from a decaying memory of the amount of water drunk. Thus, in Fig. 8, ECF is subtracted from its normal value of 23 ml to give an extracellular error signal, this being the work of an extracellular volume receptor. Similarly, ICF volume is subtracted from its normal value of 46 ml to give an ICF error signal, and this is the work of an osmoreceptor. These two signals are joined by an eating to thirst signal (discussed shortly), and added together to give a total thirst signal. Note the existence of a pass gate between the error detector and the

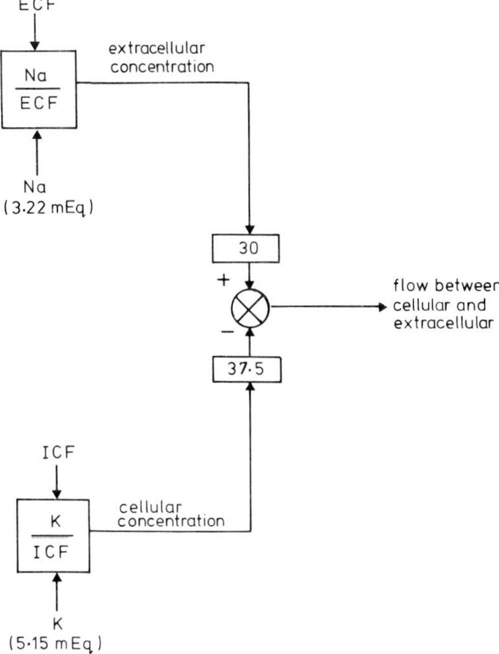

Fig. 7. Model showing the mechanism for the exchange of water between the intracellular and extracellular spaces.

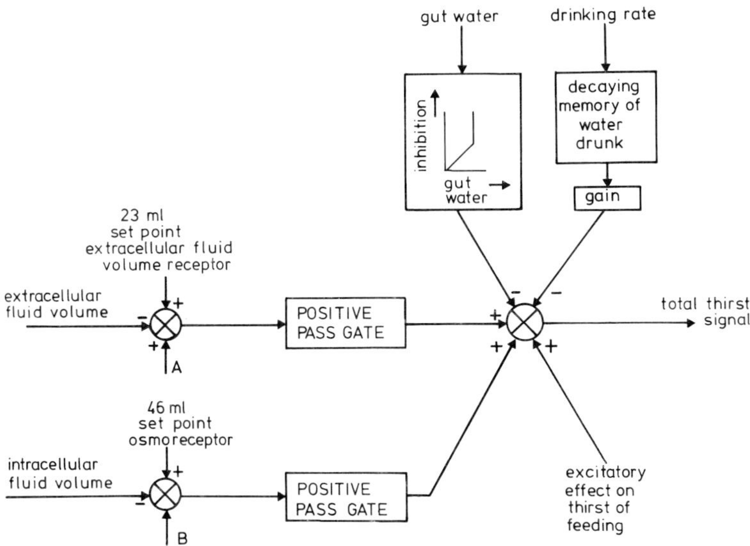

Fig. 8. Model showing how the thirst stimulus arises.

summing junction. This is because it is known that an extracellular surplus does not cancel out a cellular deficit as far as stimuli to thirst are concerned. It is presumed that the same applies to a cellular surplus. At the summing junction a signal derived from gut volume and another from the memory of the amount drunk inhibit the excitatory thirst stimuli.

Immediately following the summing point is a threshold with hysteresis (Fig. 9). As the thirst signal increases from zero, the drinking rate is zero until the threshold is exceeded. At this point drinking switches into the ON state and the animal drinks. It continues to do so until thirst is returned to zero.

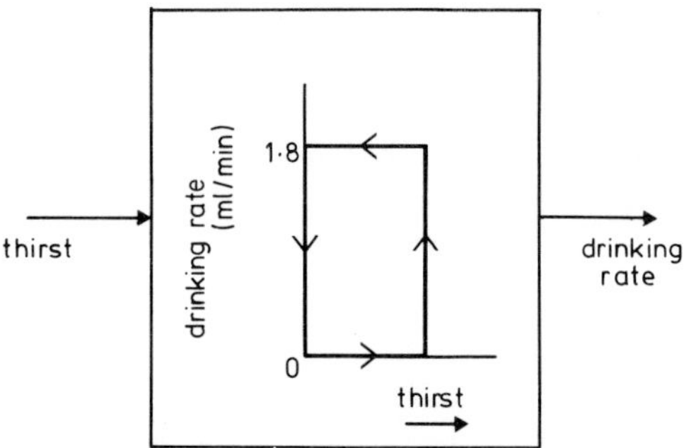

Fig. 9. Model of the thirst-drinking threshold, showing hysteresis effect.

In Fig. 8, *A* and *B* represent the influence of a circadian rhythm on the thirst controller. An animal does most of its drinking by night and very little by day. Somehow the model must account for this, and Oatley (1974) proposed that in fact the cellular and extracellular set points go up and down with a circadian frequency. Thus a circadian oscillating signal is added or subtracted at *A* and *B*. (It makes little difference whether we add or subtract, since the important point is that the set point should rise and fall with a 24-h cycle.) Although I fully agree with Oatley that this represents the best guess as to the nature of the interaction, Oatley's description may possibly be misleading in one respect. He seems to imply from his proposed experiment that the rat drinks when the set point is high and refrains from drinking when it is low, and this would indeed be the case if the system were proportional control. In fact, though, since the body fluids act as an integrator of the amount of fluid drunk, the animal will drink when the set point is increasing. After the set point reaches its maximum the animal will stop drinking and refrain from further drinking until after the set point reaches its minimum and starts the upward journey again, unless of course water losses from the body are such that during the downward journey the actual value of body fluids falls below the set point.

The thirst model has two obvious features in common with the hunger model. First, during the day the animal is able to make use of what was consumed during the previous night—in the one case energy stored as fat and in the other case water held in the body fluids. Because of these two systems the animal is spared activity during the day. As far as drinking is concerned, this arises from the rather cunning operation of bringing the set point down to match the loss from the body. Of course it implies that at the end of the night the rat contains a larger volume of body fluids than at the end of the day. Apparently this remains to be tested experimentally, as does Kissileff's (1973) suggestion that a difference in insensible loss between the day and night plays a role. However, urination continues by day and presumably so does some insensible loss, though rats drink very little. So the proposal that body fluid volume exhibits a circadian rhythm would seem reasonable.

The second parallel between the systems is the existence of a threshold. It is not difficult to see that it could be of survival value to an animal not to be distracted too often by the regulatory needs of the body. The threshold takes care of this, although how realistic the value measured in the laboratory is to the animal in the wild remains a subject of speculation. In the light phase, the interaction between the circadian rhythm and the physiological controller means that the distraction to the animal is minimal.

C. *The Hunger–Thirst Interaction*

In Fig. 3 a signal is shown coming from thirst and entering the hunger system. It may at first appear somewhat odd that this signal has a positive sign attached to it since it represents an inhibitory influence. The mathematics are however correct: for thirst to inhibit feeding is mathematically equivalent to it mimicking an energy rate which is not really present, i.e. the thirst inhibition provides what we might call virtual energy.

The gain of the pathway of thirst inhibition on hunger was adjusted until the model ate approximately 14 g of food in 24 h of water deprivation (quotation marks are not added to the words "ate" and "water deprivation" as a gesture of confidence in simulation!). This compares with the 22 g which the model would normally eat, these figures being taken from experimental data on rats (Toates, 1971).

In the opposite direction, the excitatory effect of feeding on thirst (Fig. 10), the gain was adjusted until about 1·3 ml of drinking was caused by eating 1 g of food in the dark phase. This effect has a decay attached to it: in other words, food is potent as a direct stimulus to drinking only for a limited time following feeding. After this time has elapsed, the thirst-producing effect of eating relies upon the ability of food to pull water into the stomach or the need to excrete the breakdown products of metabolism.

In Fig. 8 the eating to thirst interaction is shown going into the thirst summing junction just like any other thirst stimulus. The question arises as to what if anything can inhibit the drinking which is normally caused by eating dry food. According to the model an excess of body fluids is unable to do so because we have a pass gate in the pathway which blocks the signal representing a surplus.

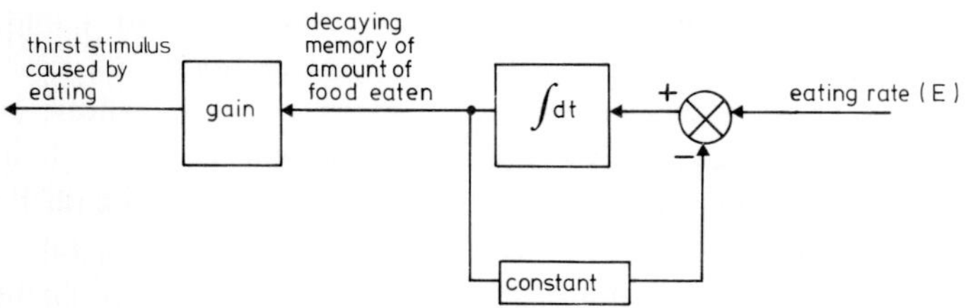

Fig. 10. Model showing the excitatory effect of eating on thirst.

Evidence which suggests that fluid excess in the body is not effective in inhibiting meal-associated drinking is to be found in the results of Fitzsimons (1957, 1971), who showed that slowly infusing the rat's normal daily water intake did not prevent the rat from drinking a considerable quantity of water. However, Kissileff (1969) demonstrated that drinking is suppressed if water is infused into the stomach of intact rats at the time of eating. Toates (1974) showed that immediately following a session of schedule-induced polydipsia, when both the stomach and body fluids might be expected to hold a considerable load of water, meal-associated drinking is reduced. The model of course allows for this, since stomach water volume exerts an inhibitory effect on drinking, irrespective of the nature of the excitatory stimulus. One aspect not shown here, which will be included in future simulations, is water of metabolism.

IV. Simulation Results

A. *Feeding and Drinking* ad libitum

Figure 11 shows the complete model and Fig. 12 the *ad libitum* eating and drinking pattern of a simulated 300-g rat. The simulation was run on a digital computer using an extension of the method described by Booth and Toates (1974). It is clear that drinking and eating usually occur rather closely together in time, although occasionally a drink occurs unrelated to a meal. Drinking usually follows eating in a realistic fashion, as would be expected from the construction of the model. Yet this sequences does not occur every time. Sometimes a meal follows rather soon after drinking, indicating the disinhibiting

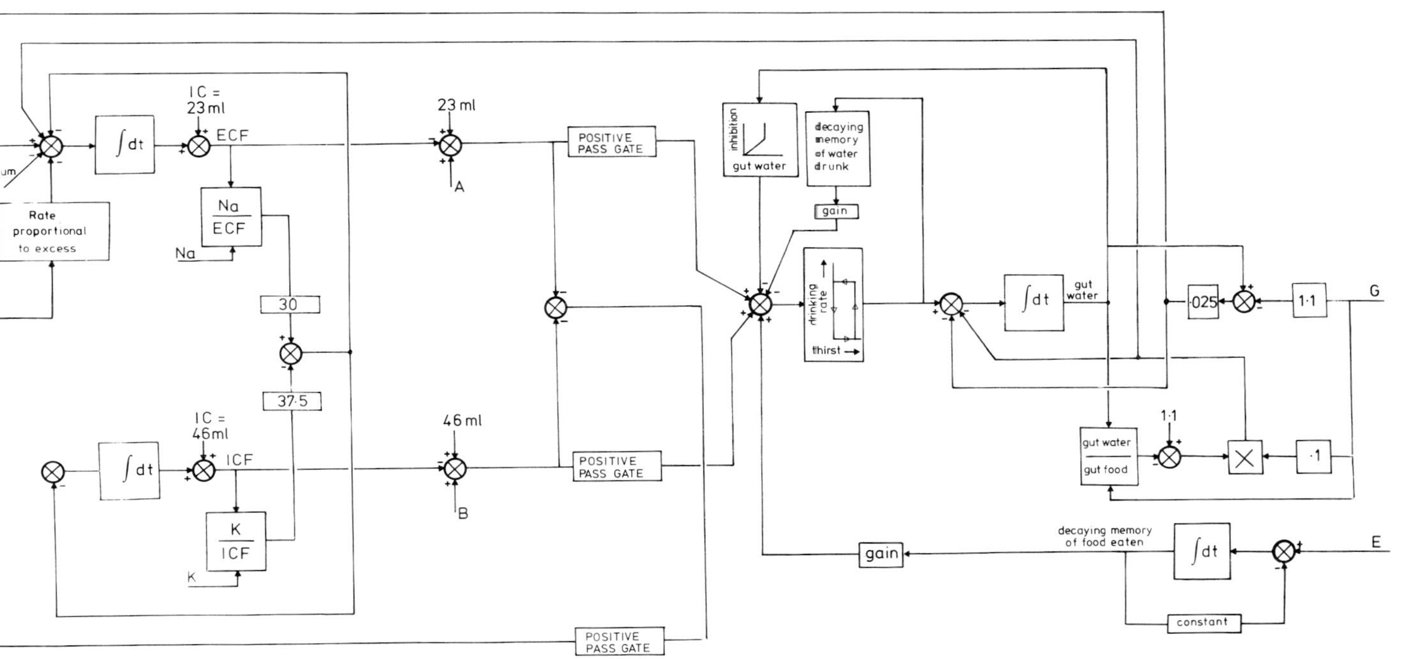

Fig. 11. Complete thirst model

effect of water on feeding. The pattern of meals and drinks is a reasonable approximation to what occurs in rats, as are the quantities consumed which were 12·3 g and 18·7 ml by night and 7·4 g and 7·4 ml by day.

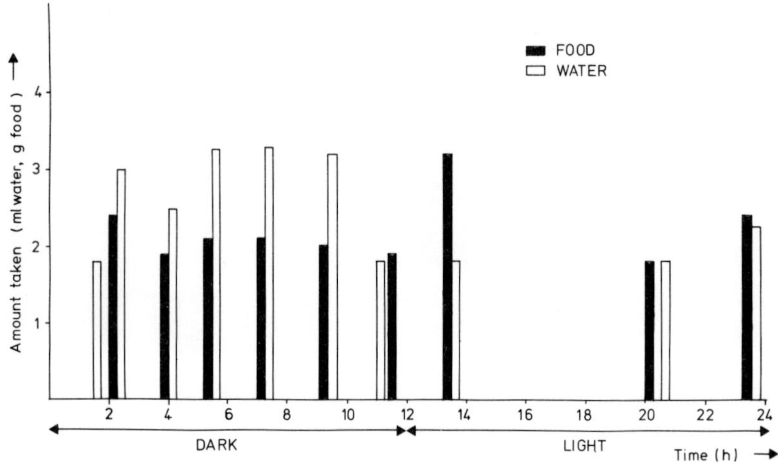

Fig. 12. Simulation of 24-h food and water intake for a 300 g rat.

B. *The Nature of the Thirst to Hunger Inhibition*

One reason why we feel it is worth extending the present simulation and including a more sophisticated hunger model is that this line of modelling may cast some light on the nature of the interaction of thirst on hunger. Already the model makes one quite specific prediction and that is that the reduction in food intake brought about by thirst is because the animal takes smaller meals and not fewer of them. Incorporation of feeding model Mark 3 (Chapter 11) into the simulation may show that this remark should be qualified. However, Levitsky (1970) found that the thirsty rat does indeed take smaller meals rather than a lesser number of meals.

According to the model, thirsty and non-thirsty animals should diverge in their cumulative eating over a period of time even if the thirst stimulus remains constant. This was not found to be the case by Oatley and Toates (1973) for salt-injected rats. Clearly, further thought needs to be given to this problem. It is interesting to note that the conventional set point system shown in Fig. 1 would predict that, for a fixed level of thirst, rats should lag behind their non-thirsty controls by a fixed amount rather than diverging from them.

V. Some Theoretical Implications

A. *Advantage of a Close Temporal Association Between Eating and Drinking*

According to the model, the thirst signal generated by eating adds to any thirst signal that may already be present because of fluid loss and therefore should be effective in pushing the thirst signal over the threshold and thus synchronizing eating and drinking. One would expect that drinking would seldom occur in the absence of a meal. There ae at least two benefits which the animal might derive from such a close coupling. As was pointed out by Toates (1974), if drinking occurs immediately after a meal, this serves to supply the stomach directly with water which would otherwise have to be pulled from the body fluid pool. Were the animal to drink only in response to the dehydration caused by loss of body fluids to the gut, the gut would have to accommodate a double load of water: that removed from the body fluids plus that drunk to replace them. This would not represent good biological economy. In addition, there may be an ecological and survival factor to consider: as Rowland and Nicolaïdis (1974) point out, both plants and prey are likely to be found in the vicinity of water.

B. *Is Meal-associated Drinking Non-homeostatic?*

The argument advanced is that drinking caused by eating acts through the normal thirst channel, which adapts following the passage of food through the mouth and serves an anticipatory role in the timing of drinks. According to the model, the only influence of the thirst-provoking effect of eating is one of timing, and even here it appears to be rather limited in what it can do without the co-operation of the circadian thirst rhythm. To test this, the circadian oscillator which pushes the body fluid set points up and down was omitted from the simulation, all else being left intact. This completely abolished the circadian rhythm in drinking despite the existence of the eating rhythm and its connections to drinking. The result supports Oatley's (1973, 1974) interpretation of the importance of an independent thirst rhythm. According to this simulation, the rat drinks no more water than is necessary to replace the minimum urine and insensible losses as defined in the simulation. Following a meal the body fluids are not flooded with excess fluid which then needs to be excreted.

One must hasten to add that the system behaves in this homeostatic fashion only under normal circumstances. If the animal is infused with water, then, although drinking is reduced, this is not to the extent of 1 ml for every 1 ml infused, which is what a strictly homeostatic interpretation would demand. From the model described above one would not expect perfect regulation to occur under these circumstances. A deficit in the body fluids is not needed for feeding to initiate drinking, since feeding is a thirst stimulus in its own right (Fig. 8). Presumably, if the meal size is large enough, it can push thirst above the threshold even in the presence of a body-fluid surplus. It helps of course if there is already some fluid deficit to add to the feeding-induced thirst. This will indeed be the case in the night phase for all but the last of the four stomach infusion conditions described by Fitzsimons (1971) in his Table VIII, so long as the infusion given by day has been excreted by night–which may well occur since the stomach would not be expected to retain it in the absence of a comparable quantity of food. One would expect meal-associated drinking to be reduced by a stomach infusion of water and this clearly is the case from Fitzsimons' results.

C. *The Effect of Meal Size on Drinking Behaviour*

The model might throw some light on Oatley's (1971, 1973) experiments (see also Kissileff, 1973). When rats are forced to take meals of 1·6g at 2·4-h intervals regularly during the day and night, Oatley found that, although they continued to drink the same proportion of their intake at night, the close temporal association between meals and drinks was relaxed. If a rat is free to choose the size of its meal, it will on average eat meals of about 3 g in the dark phase, and Oatley's rat appears to have been doing something like this when it had food *ad libitum*. However, during the periods of scheduled feeding the rats were never allowed a meal of more than 1·6g, so it is quite possible that this size was not enough to push thirst regularly over the threshold. The rat's water requirements would be unchanged by the schedule, and so presumably between meals thirst would reach threshold due to fluid loss and without any assistance from eating. Such a conclusion depends on the assumptions that (a) thirst is proportional to meal size [Fitzsimons and Le Magnen (1969) showed that drinking is proportional to meal size] and (b) feeding-induced thirst passes through the threshold.

In the light phase the association between eating and drinking is not as close under *ad libitum* conditions as it is in the dark. The food to water ratio is higher in the light phase than in the dark (Zucker, 1971). Oatley (1973) reports that some rats even drink as much as 100% of their intake during the night, though the average is nearer 80 to 90%. I have heard of only one condition under which a rat eats 100% of its *ad libitum* food intake by night (P. Mather, pers. comm.) and the average seems to be around 70%. The reason for the loose associaton by day may be that (a) meal sizes are smaller by day, averaging 1·9 g according to data collated by Booth (1976), and this is insufficient to exceed the threshold and (b) since the set point is on its downward journey, the chance of an error in body fluids being present is less by day than by night. The figures given by Booth are accurately predictable by the Mark 3 version of the hunger model (see Chapter 11) and presumably, when that is coupled to the thirst model in place of Mark 1, the joint hunger–thirst model will give a more realistic simulation by day. In fact Fig. 2 of Oatley (1971) shows that drinks are just as likely to follow meals in the light phase during scheduled eating as during *ad libitum* eating.

That meal size may well be a decisive factor is indicated in an experiment reported by Fitzsimons and Le Magnen (1969). If rats were allowed access to food for only two periods of 1h during the day, considerable quantity of water was drunk following and during these meals. During the night, when no food was available, intake of water dropped. One possible explanation for this effect would be that the gut may hold a large quantity of water by virtue of the enormous meals taken by day and that this is made available during the night phase. It is however difficult to believe that this could bring down night-time drinking quite to the extent that Zucker (1971) found in an experiment very similar to that of Fitzsimons and Le Magnen. This matter will be examined in future simulations. The drastic reduction in dark phase drinking on some schedules is not seen for the first day or so, and it may require some kind of physiological adaptation or a circadian rhythm phase-shift explanation which at present is not at all obvious. It is interesting to note that total food deprivation has little effect on the drinking rhythm (see Fig. 8 of Fitzsimons and Le Magnen, 1969).

D. *Effect of Diet Compositon*

Another question which future simulation work will need to ask is that of the effect of the composition of the diet. When this is changed from one low in protein to one rich in protein, the water intake associated with each meal increases (Fitzsimons and Le Magnen, 1969). This effect is usually attributed to relearning. At first the additional water is not drunk in association with meals but after a day or so has elapsed the water-to-food ratio increase at each meal accounts for the increased water consumption. When the diet is changed back to one low in protein, the animal does not reduce its water intake immediately but exhibits some inertia. It would be rather easy to make the model behave in this way, since all one would need to do is slowly to increase the gain associated with the pathway from eating to drinking over a period of a few days of simulated time. One would then need to decrease it slowly to simulate a change from a high protein diet to one low in protein. This would, of course, represent the effect of learning. Before simulated learning was complete one would expect the model to drink at times other than meals in order to make up for the losses brought about by the higher excretion rate.

However, one also needs to ask whether any change in the model is needed to account for the result, apart from the changes in urination rate and possibly in meal patterns. It could be the case that it takes a while for the two controllers to get into synchrony again when the meal pattern is changed. This is of course pure speculation and without more information there would be little point in pursuing either argument. Nevertheless, it is probably worth noting that, if the rats shown in Fig. 9 of Fitzsimons and Le Magnen (1969) are typical, a very interesting adaptation to the protein diet occurs, on which the authors make no comment. Rats on the first three days of the high protein diet drink some 35 ml daily, whereas those on the last two days drink only about 20 ml.

E. *Schedule-induced Polydipsia*

Although one must resist the kind of parameter twiddling and component shuffling which means that one ends up with as many simulations as there are situations to be simulated, it is highly tempting to by-pass the threshold in the path of the excitatory effect of feeding upon drinking in the present model. This would have the disadvantage that Oatley's (1971) scheduled meal experiment could no longer be neatly explained, but it would have the potentially enormous bonus that the model would exhibit polydipsia in response to interval food schedules.

The model incorporates a rapid decay with time in the excitatory effect of feeding on drinking. Despite this decay, following a meal of 3 g (which takes about 9 min to complete) the animal/model still manages to drink as much as 3–4·5 ml of water. This requires a powerful message to be sent to the drinking areas of the brain during the course of feeding, a message which is not normally put into action for some time because the animal can only do one thing at a time. The persistence in eating may be due to a stronger hunger than thirst signal, possibly because of positive feedback effects from feeding.

Acquisition of schedule-induced polydipsia may reflect learning on the part of the animal that no more food is available for the rest of the interval. The drinking signal, which is relatively enormous for the size of pellet, directs the animal to the water spout immediately after the pellet has been eaten, before there is time for much decay of the drinking signal to occur. Note that the model shows no inhibition of drinking by excess body fluid volume, only a stomach volume inhibition. The model would explain the rather rapid disappearance of polydipsia when food is removed from the delivery apparatus.

It is hoped that in the future this thirst–hunger model can be extended to give a fully adequate explanation of schedule-induced polydipsia and other phenomena. In particular attention needs to be directed at ways in which the model may alter in the presence of a very strong hunger signal: attention factors require investigation (see also Chapter 15 by McFarland).

F. *Species Differences in Feeding–Drinking Interaction*

In the area of feeding–drinking interaction, work has been almost exclusively carried out on rats, in so far as examining the timing of meals and drinks is concerned. However, it appears from recent experiments carried out in my laboratory (F. M. Toates and B. Ewart, to be submitted) that there would be much to gain in this area from considering some species differences with a view to further connections between computer simulation and experimentation.

We found that under *ad libitum* conditions gerbils eat and drink in close temporal proximity. Although some meals and drinks are taken in isolation, there is a very strong tendency for a meal to follow immediately after a drink. We have observed no animal which drank immediately after a meal; the usual interval was 20–50 min. The association obviously cannot be explained in terms of the animal making an exploratory mission and taking care of any existing deficits at the same time, for in such a case a random order would result.

Rats behave quite differently. Although there is a tendency for a drink to occur before a meal, there is still a stronger tendency for it to occur immediately following a meal. Oatley and Toates (1969) proposed that meal-associated drinking in rats anticipates the dehydrating effect of food appearing in the gut. Even postprandial drinking follows too rapidly to be caused by dehydration. As was explained earlier, by "anticipates" it is meant that the act of feeding has an excitatory effect on drinking. This clearly does not occur in the gerbil.

How might one explain the consistent patterns of drinks coming immediately before meals in the gerbil? It could reflect some very clever anticipation of future dehydration. More likely it is due to the influence of an inhibitory linkage from the thirst system to feeding. Kept in the laboratory, gerbils (like rats) cut down on food when deprived of water. It is possible that, even under *ad libitum* conditions, a sufficient fluid deficit builds up between drinks to restrain feeding. Drinking then disinhibits feeding. Given that there is no excitatory linkage from feeding to drinking, the inhibitory thirst–feeding interaction holds full responsibility for the time association between the two activities. Because of the absence of postprandial drinking, the chances are that the animal approaches the time of each meal with a larger fluid deficit than is the case for the rat. Drinking therefore has a large chance of triggering feeding. It is worth noting that the gerbil generally takes drinks which are rapid, uninterrupted and of large volume. Rats are much less distinct in the patterns and interrupt their drinking to feed.

It is necessary to consider the gerbil in its natural habitat. Water for drinking will be unavailable and must be obtained in the food. Therefore the absence of a feeding to drinking excitation is perhaps not surprising. It is interesting that in the laboratory the gerbil cuts down on food when it is water deprived. There is room for considerable speculation as to the use of such an interaction in the natural habitat—could it be to steer the animal towards moist food?

The severe polydipsia which the gerbil exhibits when food deprived could be due to a physiological imbalance involving, for example, sodium, potassium or proteins, as in the rabbit (see Section IIA). If this were the case there is every reason to suppose that it could be simulated by extensions of the kind of modelling described in this chapter. However, the physiological explanations which have up to now been proposed have been shown to be inadequate when the appropriate experimentation has been carried out on the gerbil.

It is often argued that one of the strengths of model construction is that even if it fails to produce an entirely convincing simulation it at least raises questions that might otherwise have escaped attention. In considering how one might adapt the rat simulation to the gerbil, and in doing the necessary experimentation, we believe that we can ask a fundamental question. Could the peculiar timing of drinks and meals in the gerbil provide a vital clue in understanding why it exhibits polydipsia when food deprived and the rat does not? Do we need to abandon an explanation of the association between drinking and feeding in terms of a disinhibition of feeding by drinking in making an explanation of polydipsia? Let us entertain the idea that a "psychological" rather than "physiological" explanation is appropriate in the case of starvation polydipsia. Suppose that for some reason food seeking missions are always preceded by drinking, which puts the onus for the association of the feeding side, and let us suppose that the frequency of such food seeking missions goes up when the animal is hungry. Polydipsia may then be the result. We are now devoting time (both real and simulated!) to answering these questions. We are asking if it is possible that both a timing sequence and a thirst to feeding inhibition play a role in determining the nature of the gerbil's feeding and drinking patterns.

VI. Addendum

A. *Incorporation of a More Advanced Feeding Model*

The model of feeding has been considerably developed beyond the simple first approximation which was employed in the simulations reported in this chapter. Fortunately the time before going to press has allowed a very preliminary examination of the results predicted from a coupling of a more sophisticated Mark 3 rat feeding model (see Chapter 11) to the present drinking model.

The first 24 h of the simulation are shown in Fig. 13. The pattern seems clear. Drinking is strongly circadian, generally some 1–2 ml being taken in association with each gram of food during the dark phase and very little drinking taking place during the light phase.

Even though the meal sizes are more realistic than in the previous simulation (in other words, larger meals in the dark than in the light), the circadian rhythm of drinking was found to be primarily dependent upon the rhythm in the body-fluid set point. Omission of this set-point rhythm from the program resulted in there being absolutely no circadian drinking rhythm, despite the change in meal size between day and night. Again, this argues that meal-associated drinking serves a very short term timing function only, and is not responsible for the circadian rhythm in drinking, a view held by Oatley (1971, 1973).

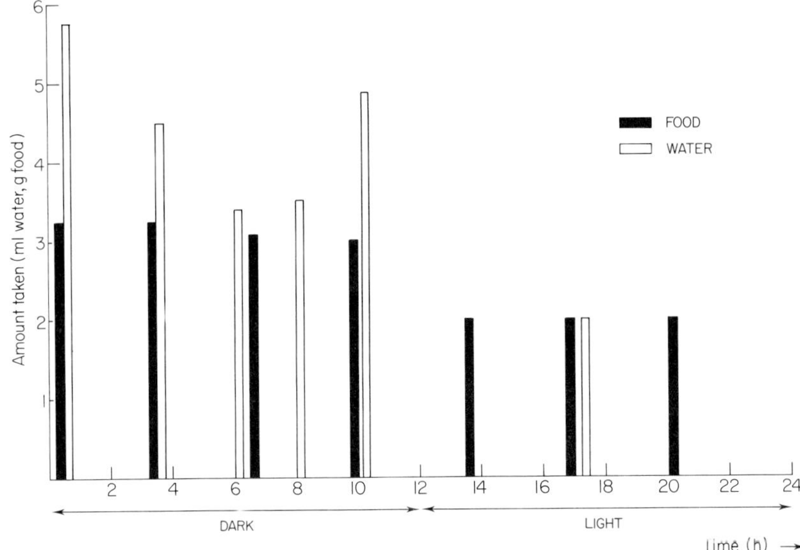

Fig. 13. Simulation of 24-h of food and water intake for a 300 g rat, using the advanced model of feeding.

Work is now in progress to develop also the drinking and fluid regulation part of the program, and when this has been achieved further simulations in the area of feeding–drinking interaction will be reported.

References

Booth, D. A. (1976). Approaches to feeding control. *In* "Appetite and Food Intake" (T. Silverstone, ed.), pp. 417–478. Dahlem Konferenzen, Berlin.

Booth, D. A. and Toates, F. M. (1974). A physiological control theory of food intake in the rat. *Bull. Psychon. Soc.* **3**, 442–444.

Booth, D. A., Toates, F. M. and Platt, S. V. (1976). Control system for hunger and its implications in animals and man. *In* "Hunger: Basic Mechanisms and Clinical Implications" (D. Novin, W. Wyrwicka and G. A. Bray, eds), pp. 127–143. Raven Press, New York.

Cizek, L. J. (1959). Long term observations on relationship between food and water ingestion in the dog. *Am. J. Physiol.* **197**, 342–346.

Cizek, L. J. (1961). Relationship between food and water ingestion in the rabbit. *Am. J. Physiol.* **201**, 557–566.

Collier, G. and Levitsky, D. (1967). Defence of water balance in rats: Behavioral and physiological responses to depletion. *J. comp. physiol. Psychol.* **64**, 59–67.

Fitzsimons, J. T. (1957). Normal drinking in rats. *J. Physiol., Lond.* **138**, 39P.

Fitzsimons, J. T. (1971). The physiology of thirst: a review of the extraneural aspects of the mechanisms of drinking. *In* "Progress in Physiological Psychology" (E. Stellar and J. M. Sprague, eds), pp. 119–201. Academic Press, New York and London.

Fitzsimons, J. T. and Le Magnen, J. (1969). Eating as a regulatory control of drinking in the rat. *J. comp. physiol. Psychol.* **67**, 273–283.

Kakolewski, J. W. and Deaux, E. (1970). Initiation of eating as a function of ingestion of hypoosmotic solutions. *Am. J. Physiol.* **218**, 590–595.

Kissileff, H. R. (1969). Oropharyngeal control of prandial drinking. *J. comp. physiol. Psychol.* **67**, 309–319.

Kissileff, H. R. (1973). Nonhomeostatic controls of drinking. *In* "The Neuropsychology of Thirst: New Findings and Advances in Concepts" (A. N. Epstein, H. R. Kissileff and E. Stellar, eds), pp. 163–198. V. H. Winston, Washington, DC.

Kutscher, C. L. (1972). Interaction of food and water deprivation on drinking: Effect of body water losses and characteristics of solution offered. *Physiol. Behav.* **9**, 753–758.

Levitsky, D. A. (1970). Feeding patterns of rats in response to fasts and changes in environmental conditions. *Physiol Behav.* **5**, 291–300.

Morrison, S. D. (1968). Regulation of water intake by rats deprived of food. *Physiol. Behav.* **3**, 75–81.

Nicolaïdis, S. and Rowland, N. (1975). Systemic versus oral and gastrointestinal metering of fluid intake. *In* "Control Mechanisms of Drinking" (G. Peters, J. T. Fitzsimons and L. Peters-Haefeli, eds), pp. 14–21. Springer-Verlag, Berlin.

Oatley, K. (1971). Dissociation of the circadian drinking pattern from eating. *Nature, Lond.* **229**, 494–496.

Oatley, K. (1972). "Brain Mechanisms and Mind". Thames and Hudson, London.

Oatley, K. (1973). Simulation and theory of thirst. *In* "The Neuropsychology of Thirst: New Findings and Advances in Concepts" (A. N. Epstein, H. R. Kissileff and E. Stellar, eds), pp. 119–223. V. H. Winston, Washington, DC.

Oatley, K. (1974). Circadian rhythms and representations of the environment in motivational systems. *In* "Motivational Control Systems Analysis" (D. J. McFarland, ed.), pp. 427–459. Academic Press, London and New York.

Oatley, K. and Toates, F. M. (1969). The passage of food through the gut of rats and its uptake of fluid. *Psychon. Sci.* **16**, 225–226.

Oatley, K. and Toates, F. M. (1971). Frequency analysis of the thirst control system *Nature, Lond.* **232**, 562–564.

Oatley, K. and Toates, F. M. (1973). Osmotic inhibition of eating as a subtractive process. *J. comp. physiol. Psychol.* **82**, 263–277.

Oatley, K. and Tonge, D. A. (1969). The effect of hunger on water intake in rats. *Q. J. exp. Psychol.* **21**, 162–171.

Rowland, N. and Nicolaïdis, S. (1974). Periprandial self-intravenous drinking in the rat. *J. comp. physiol. Psychol.* **87**, 16–25.

Toates, F. M. (1971). Thirst and body fluid regulation in the rat. D.Phil. thesis, University of Sussex.

Toates, F. M. (1974). Computer simulation and the homeostatic control of behaviour. *In* "Motivational Control Systems Analysis" (D. J. McFarland, ed.), pp. 407–426. Academic Press, London and New York.

Toates, F. M. (1975). "Control Theory in Biology and Experimental Psychology". Hutchinson Educational, London.

Toates, F. M. and Booth, D. A. (1974). Control of food intake by energy supply. *Nature, Lond.* **251**, 710–711.

Toates, F. M. and Oatley, K. (1970). Computer simulation of thirst and water balance. *Med. biol Enging* **8**, 71–87.

Toates, F. M. and Oatley, K. (1972). Inhibition of *ad libitum* eating by salt injections and water deprivation. *Q. J. expl. Psychol.* **24**, 215–224.

Verplanck, W. S. and Hayes, J. R. (1953), Eating and drinking as a function of maintenance schedule. *J. comp. physiol. Psychol.* **46**, 327–333.

Zucker, I. (1971). Light–dark rythms in rat eating and drinking behaviour. *Physiol. Behav.* **6**, 115–126.

15

Hunger in Interaction with Other Aspects of Motivation

D. J. MCFARLAND
Animal Behaviour Research Group, Department of Zoology, Oxford, England

I. Introduction

The traditional approach to motivation is to study a particular system, which is usually envisaged as a system controlling a group of functionally related activities. It is convenient to refer to such systems in general terms, as "feeding system" or "aggression system", although it should be realized that such a classification has no logical or biological validity, and contains a number of dangerous hidden assumptions. This view of a motivational system is largely a matter of convenience, and most investigators recognize that interactions between such systems occur at many levels. It is not commonly realized, however, that in analysing motivational interaction new concepts and properties emerge, which could not have been discovered within the analysis of a single system.

To give a simple example: an animal cannot always satisfy all its needs in the face of environmental ambivalence. For instance, if an animal has to expose itself to the hot sun in order to obtain food, then hyperthermia may become a consequence of feeding behaviour. If the animal cannot satisfy both hunger and thermal requirements, it has somehow to be able to compare the merits of reducing hunger with those of reducing hyperthermia, and choose an optimal compromise solution. The introduction of optimality considerations into problems of motivational theory introduces a whole new range of concepts, and necessitates a sophisticated systems analysis approach to motivation.

In general, systems analysis has developed into three main approaches.

(i) *The classical approach* developed from the study of simple servo-mechanisms, and based on the use of differential equations and their operational equivalents. This approach has been applied to various aspects of biology, including behaviour (e.g. Milsum, 1966; McFarland, 1971), and has been found to be particularly useful in analysing the relationships between particular chosen variables (i.e. input–output relationships).
(ii) *The state-space approach* is much more general in its applicability, being well suited to the study of multivariable systems. Its application in biology has so far been relatively restricted, but the state-space approach promises to be more powerful in the analysis of complex biological systems.
(iii) *The stochastic approach* has been developed to meet the need to handle the variability inherent in real-life systems. Biological systems are variable in their behaviour by virtue both of their complexity and of their design. In this chapter I discuss some problems associated with the classical approach to the analysis of the systems controlling feeding, and attempt to show how the state-space approach may help to solve some of these problems.

II. The Classical Approach

The early studies, which applied classical systems analysis to behavioural problems, concentrated primarily on problems of orientation (e.g. Mittelstaedt, 1957) and of homeostasis (e.g. McFarland, 1965; Oatley, 1967). The lessons learned from these studies have led to the development of more sophisticated methods of analysis, and have shown that homeostatic mechanisms are much more complex than had previously been realized.

A. *Negative Feedback*

In the traditional view,

> "Homeostatic drives are believed to arise as a direct consequence of internal stimulation that results when an essential physiological process deviates from some optimal level of functioning" (Grossman, 1967).

It is a *sine qua non* of this view of homeostasis that the CNS be able to monitor the state of the blood, though this was not appreciated by early investigators. Hypothalamic sensitivity to changes in temperature, osmosity and blood glucose, has been demonstrated, and the roles of these variables in the regulation of feeding and drinking implicated. The means by which the brain obtains information concerning water and energy balance are not fully understood, and it appears that a number of different mechanisms act in parallel. In addition to regulation of the internal environment, the CNS acts as a controller of negative feedback loops which encompass the external environment. In particular, hunger and thirst differ from some other aspects of homeostasis in that appropriate behaviour is essential for maintenance of the *status quo*. The deprived animal cannot compensate for loss of water or energy, it can only reduce the rate of loss. Thus feeding and drinking behaviour can be regarded as an essential part of homeostasis.

The classical view of feeding and drinking as regulatory processes implies that feeding and drinking are initiated by monitored systemic changes, which can be regarded as inputs to the mechanisms controlling the behaviour. In other words, the output of the control mechanism is changed in response to a change in input. Certain consequences of the output—for example, the oral, alimentary and systemic consequences of drinking—serve to alter the input, so that a number of feedback loops are formed. Thus feeding and drinking may be said to be under feedback control. However, recent work suggests that, in addition to feeding and drinking in response to systemic changes, these activities may occur in anticipation of such changes. In such cases feedforward control can be said to exist (McFarland, 1970a).

B. *Feedforward*

Feedforward can be seen as a phenomenon which enables the animal to anticipate the long term consequences of behaviour, and to take appropriate action to forestall deviations of the internal steady state. Thus the long term digestive consequences of food intake generally increase thirst, but instead of drinking as a result of such a thirst increase, many animals drink in advance and thus anticipate the effects of food ingestion (Fitzsimons and Le Magnen, 1969). Similarly, thermoregulation involves water loss, but instead of allowing thirst to build up as a result of this loss, many animals drink in anticipation and thus have water available for thermoregulation (McFarland, 1970a; Budgell, 1970, 1971). It appears that the simple picture of homeostasis as a negative feedback mechanism does not adequately account for the results of these studies.

C. *Adaptive Control*

If we ask what principles are involved in the execution, by the animal, of the behaviour patterns that are required to achieve certain physiological consequences, the answer that has traditionally been given is fairly clear. The behaviour is governed by a conventional type of negative feedback mechanism, by which the physiological consequences of behaviour, or their short term neurological representatives, progressively reduce the level of motivation as the animal becomes more satiated. This is the type of thinking that underlies Cannon's (1932) concept of homeostasis and governs much current research into physiological and behavioural aspects of regulation. However, the simple negative feedback model is not adequate to account for the complexity of the situation that arises in nature. Even the introduction of refinements to the classical regulatory model, such as positive feedback and feedforward (McFarland, 1970a), does little to account for the problem of ambivalence in the consequences of behaviour.

The ambivalence problem arises because there may not always be a one-to-one relationship between a particular activity and its physiological consequences. Thus in behavioural thermoregulation the animal may associate a particular activity with a one-dimensional (univalent) consequence, namely a change in body temperature. Feeding behaviour, however, has multidimensional consequences relating to the many nutrients involved. These consequences will be ambivalent when a particular food has a number of components. When the consequences of behaviour are ambivalent, constraints may be set up such that the animal cannot achieve its "goal" even though the necessary "commodities" are available in the environment (McFarland and Sibly, 1972). There must be some sort of adaptive control (McFarland, 1971) by which the animal is able to change the properties of its regulatory mechanisms to suit environmental circumstances. The adaptive control can occur, either through the medium of physiological acclimatization, or by means of changes in behavioural strategy.

An animal that relies on short term satiation mechanisms to tell it how much to eat or drink at a particular time, must be able to recalibrate consequences of ingestion. Although animals may sometimes be able to detect changes in the constitution of food by taste, this could account for only a few of the many changes that are possible. It seems more probable that animals learn how much to eat as a result of experiencing the physiological consequences of eating particular foods. In addition to learning how much to eat, animals also have to learn what to eat. As Rozin and Kalat (1971) point out:

> "It is hard to believe that the rat comes equipped with prewired recognition systems for each of the many substances for which it can show a specific hunger".

Indeed, it is now known that many animals can learn to avoid or select particular foods, as a result of physiological consequences occurring hours after ingestion (Revusky and Garcia, 1970; Rozin and Kalat, 1971; McFarland, 1973). As another example of learned modification of homeostatic mechanisms, Richter and his associates showed that when physiological regulators were surgically eliminated ". . . the animals themselves made an effort to maintain a constant environment or homeostasis" (Richter, 1943). The evidence shows that rats given a suitable environment could compensate behaviourally following parathyroidectomy, adrenalectomy, pancreatectomy and thyroidectomy. In essence, Richter's thesis is that animals deprived of physiological regulation resort to behavioural measures in maintaining the stability of the internal environment.

Suppose we invert Richter's argument: animals deprived of behavioural opportunity, by suitable alterations to the environment, resort to physiological regulation and acclimatization in achieving internal stability. Moreover, if an animal can survive under such conditions, by virtue of physiological adaptation, it will no longer be motivated to do all its former behaviour. For example, an animal acclimatized to the heat is no longer motivated to sit in the shade. An animal which is short of food may cease to indulge in the expensive luxury of sexual behaviour, and will eventually cease to be sexually motivated.

D. *Implications*

So far I have argued that, to account for the control of such classical "homeostatic" aspects of behaviour as feeding, drinking and thermoregulation, it is necessary to take account not only of the negative feedback mechanisms involved, but also of feedforward anticipatory mechanisms, of adaptive control mechanisms permitting changes in behavioural strategy, and of acclimatory mechanisms providing long term physiological adjustment. These are all aspects of the control of feeding, to which classical control theory has been, and is being, applied, as evidenced by many of the contributions to this volume. However, when we come to consider the nature of motivational interactions, it becomes apparent that the classical approach is not a satisfactory tool with which to analyse motivational systems with a repertoire of more than one type of behaviour. In general, this is due to the fact that motivational systems are multi-input–output systems with a nonlinear output, only one type of behaviour being evident at any one time. This raises problems of a fundamental nature, which are very difficult to handle by the classical approach. Before going into possible alternative ways of describing motivational systems and their interactions, we need to have a picture of the types of interactions that can occur in motivational systems.

III. Motivational Interactions

A. *Primary and Secondary Motivational States*

1. *Motivational States*

An alternative to the traditional motivational concepts of drive and incentive is the concept of motivational state, by which all motivational variables are combined into a single system. The concept of motivational state is essentially analogous to the concept of state used in physical sciences and in systems theory in general (McFarland, 1970, 1971). The state variables correspond to the stored quantities in the system, the outputs of "integrators". The identification of storage processes within the system must, therefore, be a prime consideration in the analysis of motivation.

McFarland (1971) distinguishes between storage effects associated with the potentiality of the animal to perform certain types of behaviour and those associated with ongoing behaviour. The change in motivational state induced in an animal deprived of appropriate external stimuli may lead to an increase in the animal's potential to carry out the behaviour, and when the external stimuli are presented, the intensity of the behaviour is often an increasing function of deprivation time. On the other hand, an animal prevented from continuing with its ongoing behaviour, in the presence of the external stimuli, is generally said to be in a state of frustration rather than deprivation (Yates, 1962). In such cases an increase in the intensity of the behaviour can often be observed when the obstruction is removed, a phenomenon generally known as the "frustration effect" (Amsel, 1958).

These two aspects of motivation can also be differentiated by the methods employed in their study. Generally, the procedure employed in studies of "primary" feeding and drinking, for example, is to take food and/or water deprivation time as an independent variable and to keep physiological and behavioural measures as standardized as possible. Conversely, the "secondary" aspect of motivation is studied by means of standardized deprivation schedules, whilst manipulating variables directly related to ongoing behaviour during recovery from deprivation. The distinction between primary and secondary aspects of motivation leads to the definition of two types of motivational state, analogous to displacement and momentum in mechanical systems (McFarland, 1971).

2. *A General Homeostatic Motivational System*

The distinction between these two aspects of motivation can also be made on other grounds, perhaps best illustrated by reference to the homeostatic type of motivational system, such as thirst. A general picture of a homeostatic motivational system is given in Fig. 1.

Physiological imbalances occur both as a result of the action of environmental factors, such as temperature, and as a result of influences from other motivational systems, such as the feeding system. These imbalances are monitored by the central nervous mechanisms, which in turn actuate two types of corrective mechanism. The latter may be conveniently classified into physiological and behavioural mechanisms, which essentially act in parallel to correct the imbalance. An example of a physiological corrective mechanism would be the pituitary–kidney antidiuretic axis.

Mechanisms of this type act to conserve the commodity which is in imbalance, but are not always able to restore the balance. This is the prime function of the behavioural mechanism, the action of which results in intake of the required commodity. Such intake can have three types of effect.

(i) It can have purely behavioural consequences, which feed back to the behavioural mechanism, and subserve satiation, reward, etc.

(ii) It can have physiological consequences which act to restore the balance.
(iii) It can influence other motivational systems. For example, ingestion of cold water can have thermoregulatory consequences.

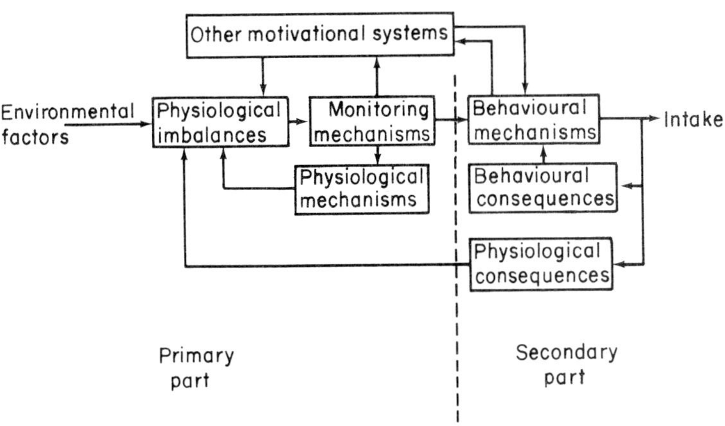

Fig. 1. General picture of a motivational system. (From McFarland, 1971.)

This outline of a motivational system falls into two distinct parts, separated by a dotted line. The primary part is continuously active and its state at any time represents a situation that can be called the *primary motivational state.* The secondary part is active only when the animal is engaged in the appropriate type of behaviour. The *secondary motivational state* thus refers to those aspects of motivation involved in ongoing behaviour.

3. *Levels of Motivational Interaction*

Interactions between motivational systems can exert their effects on either the primary or the secondary parts. Thus the state of the feeding system can affect the degree of build-up of motivational potential for drinking, but feeding behaviour itself can also affect drinking directly by its action on the secondary part. Thus it is useful to make a distinction between primary drinking, and secondary drinking (see Fitzsimons, 1958).

In terms of the type of system illustrated in Fig. 1, three main levels of motivational interaction may be distinguished. These may be called the primary level, the secondary level, and the level of the "final common path" (McFarland, 1971; McFarland and Sibly, 1975). These are summarized in Fig. 2.

At the primary level, influences may come directly from the environment, as instanced by the effect of ambient temperature upon the temperature regulation system, but more commonly they come from other motivational systems. Thus the effect of ambient temperature upon feeding and drinking operates via the thermoregulatory system. There are two main ways in which such interactions occur.

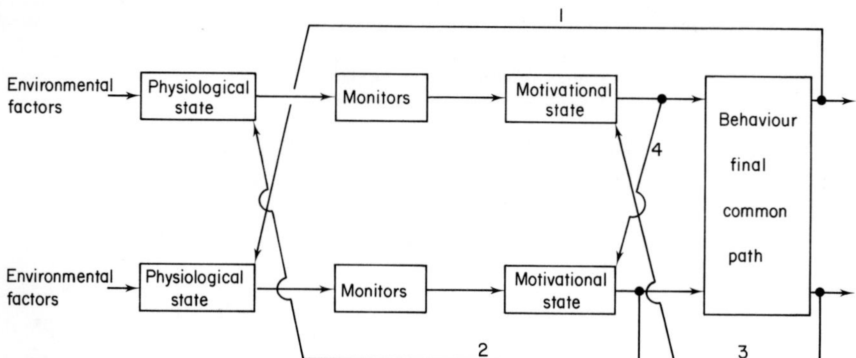

Fig. 2. Generalized representation of the possible types of interaction between motivational systems. Feedback loops within systems have been omitted for clarity. The numbers 1–4 refer to the types of interaction mentioned in the text.

(1) There may be physiological changes in one system, which result from behaviour controlled by another system. For example, increased water loss can be a direct consequence of food intake (McFarland and Wright, 1969).
(2) Physiological changes in one system may result from changes in motivational state in another system. Thus, particular motivational states can effect the release of hormones relevant to other systems. In some birds, for instance, incubation facilitates the production of prolactin, thus providing the hormonal background necessary for parental behaviour (Lehrman, 1961).

At the secondary level, there are also two main types of interaction.

(3) There may be changes in motivational state in one system, consequent upon behaviour in another system. For instance, water ingestion may lead to changes in brain temperature (McFarland and Budgell, 1970), or consequences of reproductive behaviour may lead to shifts in motivation by providing relevant external stimulation. Thus the condition of a bird's nest, and the presence of eggs in the nest, may contribute to shifts in motivational state (Lehrman, 1959; Hinde and Steel, 1966).
(4) There may be a direct interaction between motivational states in different systems. Thus there is evidence to suggest that the depressive effect of thirst on feeding is due to inhibition within the CNS (McFarland, 1964; Oatley and Tonge, 1969; Rolls and McFarland, 1973). Interaction of this type must be shown to be independent of motivational competition at the level of the final common path. For example, Epstein *et al.* (1970) observed that a starving rat, which has just been allowed to start eating, changed to vigorous drinking

when injected with angiotensin intracranially. To demonstrate that angiotensin genuinely inhibits feeding, it is necessary to show that the effect will occur in the absence of external stimuli associated with drinking, attention to which could compete with those of feeding (McFarland and Rolls, 1972).

B. *Constraints from Natural Selection*

This type of problem involves some consideration of the decision-making processes by which animals choose between motivational alternatives. Before going on to discuss this complex topic, however, it may be helpful to reconsider the primary and secondary levels of motivational interaction from the point of view of the constraints likely to be inherent in the design of motivational systems by natural selection.

1. *Stability of Internal Environment*

One type of constraint is provided by the necessity for maintenance of stability in the internal environment. The relevance of this principle to feeding and drinking behaviour is obvious, but its relevance to other types of behaviour is less clear. However, every activity must affect the stability of the internal environment, because every activity uses energy and obligates various physiological regulatory mechanisms. Moreover, the performance of one activity postpones the performance of others and thus accentuates those aspects of instability that the other activities are designed to minimize. The stability of the internal environment must, therefore, act as a constraint on the way in which motivational systems are designed by natural selection.

Consideration of stability is particularly important in the study of interactions between motivational systems, and in the relation between physiological regulation, acclimatization, and behaviour, which are the three ways in which internal stability is maintained. A formal mathematical approach along these lines has been developed by Sibly and McFarland (1974), and this has some indirect implications for the present study.

2. *Structure of External Environment*

The consequences of an animal's behaviour are an important determinant of future behaviour, and these partly depend upon the nature of the environment. The structure of the environment, in so far as it determines these consequences, can be seen as a constraint which helps to shape the structure of the behavioural control system itself. When the consequences of behaviour affect motivational state in a non-unitary manner, the environment is said to be ambivalent. For example, if hunger state could be defined in terms of measurements for carbohydrate, protein and fat, then the consequences of eating a food containing more than one of these constituents would be ambivalent. McFarland and Sibly

(1972) showed how certain consequences of behaviour, and therefore certain goals, can be unrealizable, in the sense that they cannot be attained by the animal, as a result of environmental ambivalence. In such situations, stability can only be maintained by a combination of acclimatization and some (probably learned) behavioural optimization procedure.

C. *The Behavioural Final Common Path*

1. *The Third Level of Interaction*

The constraints mentioned above stem largely from the nature of the environment, and its roles in determining the "climate" in which the animal finds itself, and in determining the consequences of the animal's behaviour. Another form of constraint is provided by the fact that the animal must use a limited set of muscles to carry out a wide range of activities. The term "behavioural final common path" is appropriate here, because all influences upon behaviour converge at this point. This term should be strictly confined to the consideration of motivational control in behavioural terms, rather than the structure of the nervous system. von Holst and von Saint Paul (1963) used the term "initial common path" for competition at the perceptual level, and "final common path" (after Sherrington, 1906) for competition at the motor level. Both these types of competition are envisaged as operating in the behavioural final common path, which thus involves the last type of interaction (see McFarland, 1971) in the causal chain—the final "decision" before a potential activity becomes overt.

2. *The Trading-off Level*

At any particular time, the potentiality for many incompatible behaviour patterns will exist simultaneously. These must in some senses compete for the "behavioural final common path". The potentiality for some types of behaviour will at any time be greater than that of others, so that the animal may be said to have a set of motivational priorities. To this extent there must be some degree of separability between the various motivational control variables. Moreover, decisions among different courses of action must be made in terms of a common currency, and weighted among a common set of criteria. (The animal must have some means of comparing the "merits" of feeding, courting, sleeping, etc.). The necessity for comparing the merits of different courses of action implies that there must be some "trade-off" mechanism built into the motivational control system.

Since the trade-off process must take into account all relevant motivational variables, it is clear that the mechanism responsible must be located at a point of convergence in the motivational organization. This point is provided by the behavioural common path. A description of the structure of the common path can be achieved in terms of mathematical expressions which are a consequence of the necessity for some trade-off mechanism. In other words, however the mechanism is described, it can always be redefined in terms of these mathematical expressions (McFarland and Sibly, 1975). This approach has proved to be particularly useful in the analysis of hunger–thirst interactions, and will be discussed later in this chapter.

The tendency to perform some activities will at any particular moment be greater than that of others, so that the animal may be said to have a set of motivational priorities. Thus feeding might be top priority, grooming the second priority, and sleep the third. We can expect the order of priority to be related to the sequence of overt activities that are observed in a particular situation, especially when there is little change in external stimulation. The question is: what factors determine which tendency is to have priority in the behavioural final common path, and thus gain overt expression?

Traditionally, the answer has always been that the "strongest" tendency is the one which gains overt expression, by direct competition with the other tendencies. However, this is now known not to be the only way in which one activity can succeed another. When an animal feeds or drinks, it does not always indulge exclusively in feeding or drinking behaviour, but intersperses its behaviour with other activities, such as grooming. For example, observations (McFarland, 1970b) show that the normal course of feeding or drinking behaviour in doves is characterized by pauses during which other types of behaviour occur. The type of behaviour appearing during these pauses is influenced both by the second-in-priority motivation, and by relevant external stimulation. Experimental manipulation of such factors can influence the type of behaviour that occurs as an adjunct to feeding or drinking behaviour. However, such manipulation does not affect the temporal position of the adjunctive behaviour, or the overall course of the dominant feeding or drinking behaviour. These findings provide strong evidence for the view that the adjunctive behaviour occurs by disinhibition (McFarland, 1969), and not by competition with the ongoing behaviour. If the occurrence of pauses in ongoing feeding or drinking behaviour is not due to competition from other motivational systems, it must somehow be preprogrammed in the control of ongoing behaviour itself.

Under natural conditions, many animals habitually pause during feeding behaviour, and this has obvious survival values when there are predators around. Experimental studies show that complex programming and interleaving of different activities is widespread in the animal kingdom, and that simple competition is by no means the rule (McFarland, 1974a). Some of the implications of these discoveries, especially in relation to feeding behaviour, will be discussed later in this chapter. For the present, we should note that the behavioural final common path probably represents the most complex level of motivational interaction, and that special methods of analysis and representation are required to deal with such complexity.

III. The State-space Approach

A. *A Space of State Variables*

The state-space approach differs from traditional methods of representing feedback systems in being both more abstract and more general. It is better able to handle complex systems, and principles of organization, which are difficult to formulate by conventional methods. The state-space approach, when incorporated into a computer simulation, can be used to generate precise quantitative descriptions and predictions. In this chapter, however, we concentrate upon its general characteristics.

The internal environment of an animal can be viewed as a system of interacting variables, which is subject to influences resulting from changes in the animal's behaviour. The state of any biological system can in principle be characterized in terms of the state variables of the system, the minimal number of state variables necessary for a complete description of the system being the same as the number of degrees of freedom of the system (McFarland, 1971; Milsum, 1966; Rosen, 1970). The state of the internal environment can thus be described in terms of a finite number of physiological state variables, each of which can be represented as an axis of an n-dimensional hyperspace. We can represent the state of the physiological environment as a point in an n-dimensional Euclidean space, the axes of which are independent.

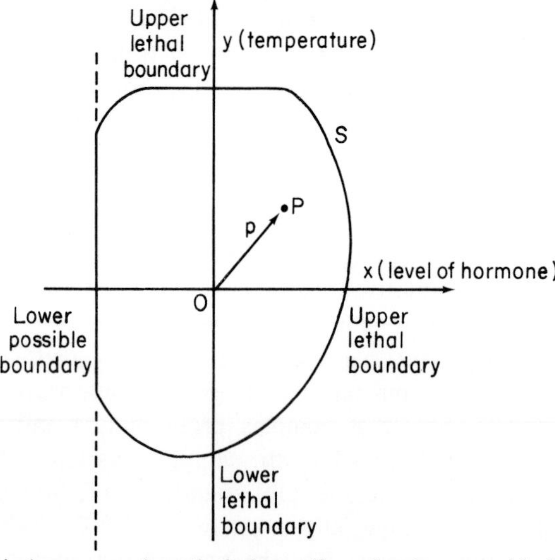

Fig. 3. Physiological space: an hypothetical two-dimensional space, with the origin 0 corresponding to optimal body temperature y and hormone level x. The physiological state is indicated by the position of the point P, specified by its coordinates, or by the vector $\mathbf{p}$. The boundary to the states in which the animal can survive, S, delineates the possible and lethal limits to the values of x and y. (From Sibly and McFarland, 1974.)

In this space there are boundaries determined by the physical possibilities (e.g. negative hormonal levels are impossible), and by values of state variables beyond which the animal cannot live (e.g. certain temperature extremes are lethal). For convenience we might choose as the origin of this physiological space the ideal optimal point on each axis. That point is the value of each state variable which is optimal in the biochemical or physiological sense. It may be that this is the state that would be attained were external conditions such as to allow the attainment of any of the states within the boundary. This physiological space is illustrated in Fig. 3.

B. *Movements Through State-space*

The adaptive processes, which oppose displacement of physiological state, range between rapid physiological reflexes and slow-acting acclimatization mechanisms. There will generally be a spectrum of such processes, as illustrated in Fig. 4. A physiological displacement results from the sudden transportation to high

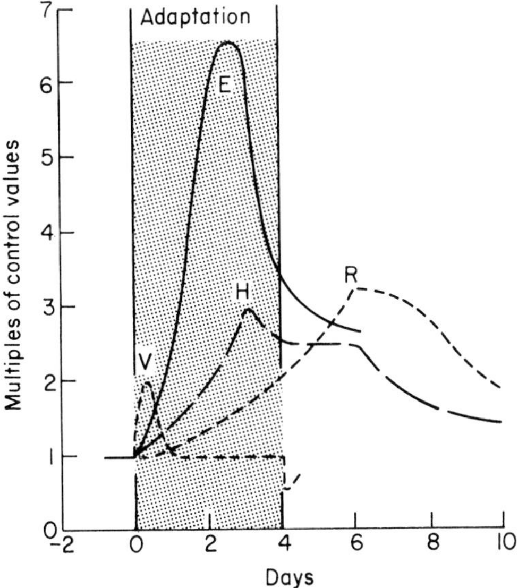

Fig. 4. Adaptive modifications in a man breathing rarefied air during four days, followed by six additional days of deadaptation. V = lung ventilation; E = serum erythropoietin; H = rate of hemoglobin synthesis; R = fraction of reticulocytes in circulating blood. (From Adolph, 1972.)

altitude, and this is initially counteracted by increased rate of breathing. This type of physiological reflex involves a high level of energy expenditure, and such high cost can be alleviated by means of relatively slow-acting acclimatization mechanisms. An increase in the number of circulating red blood corpuscles is the ultimate response involved in acclimatization to high altitude. Such acclimatization does involve some increased cost, but it alleviates the necessity for extreme behavioural or regulatory measures.

We can distinguish three types of process serving to maintain the physiological state of an animal within lethal boundaries: acclimatization, regulation and behaviour. How do these three processes interact? Sibly and McFarland (1974) show that these processes will generally be vectorally additive, and are therefore alternatives. In the process of adaptation, various combinations of regulation, behaviour and acclimatization may occur.

Thus in adapting to high altitudes, the processes regulating respiration initially function with respect to their normal optima. Stability may be maintained through behavioural measures, such as avoiding heavy work, but gradually the individual will become acclimatized, so that the behavioural measures may be relaxed. At the same time regulation may occur directed towards new optima.

As another example, consider a man moving from a cold to a hot climate. He may be able to expose himself to the sun, acclimatize quickly, and thus obviate any special behavioural measures. On the other hand, he may seek the shade, and thus postpone his acclimatization.

These examples emphasize the point that the degree of regulation, acclimatization, or behavioural response, depends upon the degree of displacement or drift from the adapted or optimal state. The different processes act in parallel, their effects are additive, but at the same time the success of one mechanism obviates the necessity for another.

A consequence of this representation of motivational space is that shifts in the origin of the space due to acclimatization will be reflected in behavioural changes. For example, an animal deprived of water may attempt to adapt by eating less food, seeking a cooler environment, and reducing its activity. It may sacrifice large portions of its behavioural repertoire, such as reproductive behaviour. The possibility that acclimatization may induce marked changes in motivational systems has received very little attention from research workers, though there is some support for this hypothesis in the field of acclimatization to temperature in fish. Many fish show temperature preferences related to acclimatization temperature (Fry and Hochachka, 1970).

C. *Characterizing the State Variables*

1. *Principles*

We can deduce, from considerations of physiological regulation and acclimatization, that motivational systems are stable under certain conditions. Moreover, under such conditions motivational state can be deduced from the animal's behaviour, provided that the structure of the environment is known. In order for motivational state to be specified, two questions have to be answered: how many state variables are necessary to describe the state, and what are the values of such variables at any particular point in time? The first question is discussed by McFarland and Sibly (1972) and Sibly and McFarland (1974). Their answer is that the number of state variables that are required to specify the motivational state under any particular set of conditions can be determined from knowledge of the consequences of behaviour, provided that certain conditions hold. The second question will be discussed later in this chapter.

The physiological state of an animal is, to some extent, monitored in the brain. The representation of the physiological state in the brain is sometimes called the "command state" (McFarland, 1971), because it represents a set of "instructions" to the behaviour control system. To carry out commands, and achieve objectives, the animal has to assess the state of the external environment. We can represent the animal's estimate of the relevance of the various environmental stimuli as a "cue state" (McFarland and Sibly, 1975) in a space similar to the command space, but representing the external environment as monitored by the animal. The command state and cue state together represent the sum of the causal factors controlling the behaviour of the animal. An advantage of the state space approach is that it can combine the internal and external influences upon behaviour without prejudice to the particular combination rules that may operate in any given set of circumstances. This general representation is summarized in Fig. 5.

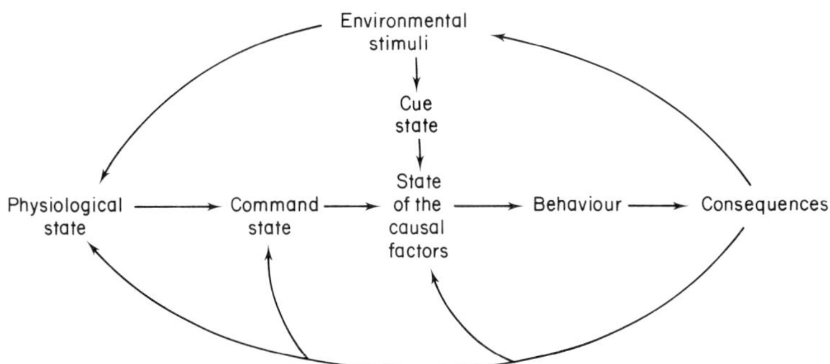

Fig. 5. Relations between the causal factor state, other system states, and behaviour.

McFarland and Sibly (1975) argue that any model of the motivational (i.e. reversible) process governing the behaviour of an animal can be represented by means of isoclines in a multidimensional causal factor space. The argument is axiomatic, based upon the two prime assumptions: That

(i) it is always possible to classify the behavioural repertoire of a species in such a way that the classes are mutually exclusive in the sense that the members of different classes cannot occur simultaneously,

(ii) these incompatible actions are uniquely determined by a particular set of causal factors.

Isoclines join all points in the space which represent a given "degree of competitiveness" of a particular "candidate" for overt behavioural expression. The competition between candidates is an inevitable consequence of the fact that animals cannot "do more than one thing at a time".

When we come to the problem of how the various incompatible activities are related to the motivational state of the animal, we can see that each is controlled by a set of causal factors. The causal factors will include variables describing the animal's "estimate" of the stimuli present in the external environment (e.g. cues to the availability of food), and variables relevant to the animal's internal state. McFarland and Sibly (1975) represent the total motivational state in a *causal factor space* (Fig. 5), in which there is an axis corresponding to each class of causal factor, with the classes defined in terms of some suitable arbitrary criterion.

For example, an (hypothetical) animal might have a motivational state that

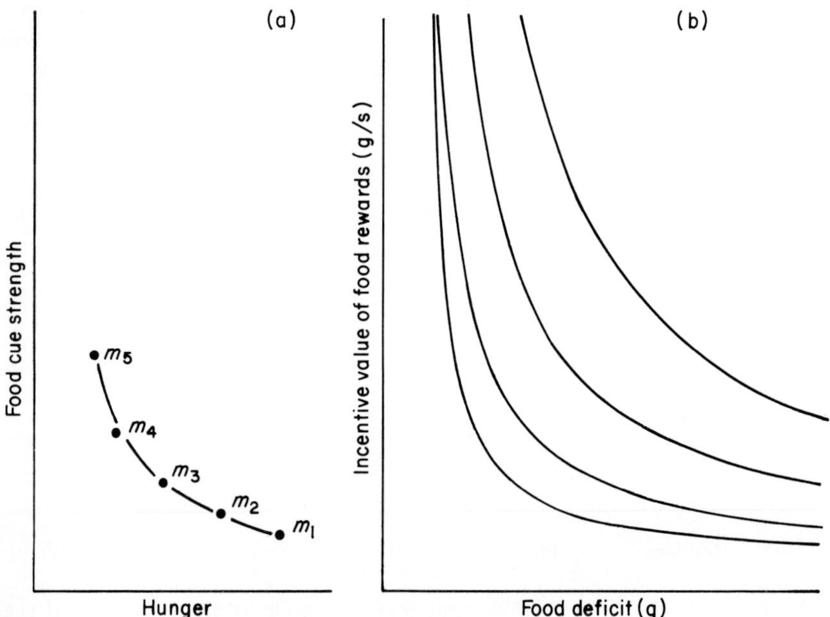

Fig. 6. (a) Two-dimensional causal factor space for feeding. The feeding strength is the same for points $m_1 \ldots m_5$ and the line joining these points is a motivational isocline. (From McFarland and Sibly, 1975.)
(b) Hypothetical causal factor space showing isoclines of equal feeding tendency. (From Sibly, 1975.)

can be represented in a two-dimensional space (Fig. 6a), with one axis corresponding to the degree of hunger, and the other to the strength of food cues (i.e. the animal's estimate of the availability of food). Thus the causal factor space has some axes corresponding to each class of causal factor. It is clear that there are likely to be a number of motivational states that will map to the same feeding tendency. For example, an animal may have a high hunger but low cue strength (m_1), giving the same feeding strength as if it had a low hunger and high cue strength (m_5). The line joining all those motivational states ($m_1 \ldots m_5$) which give the same behavioural tendency, is an example of a *motivational isocline.*

A simple example is provided by the work of Sibly (1975) on feeding in the Barbary dove (*Streptopelia risoria*). The animals were tested in an operant situation in which they characteristically alternate between feeding and drinking. Sibly found that, when an animal is deprived of both food and water, its choice of one over the other depends on whether the product of deficit times incentive is greater for food or water. Deficit is defined as the quantity of food or water that the animal will ingest, if allowed to become satiated. Incentive is defined as the maximum rate (grams per second) at which rewards can be obtained. This result means that, when deficit is plotted against incentive, as in Fig. 6b, the isoclines joining points of equal feeding tendency are hyperbolae. If we take this figure to represent the part of the causal factor space that is relevant to feeding (in reality there will be more than two dimensions), then a point in this space represents the motivational state with respect to feeding. The strength of feeding tendency is given by the value of the isocline passing through the point, and this strength enters the "behavioural final common path" and competes with the other tendencies, such as the drinking tendency, etc.

The importance of motivational isoclines is that their shape is a design feature, which is intimately related to the animal's ecological circumstances. Any decision-making process, in which there is "totally decidable logical preference", can be expressed as a set of isoclines, or "indifference curves" (Kaufmann, 1968). The essence of the argument is that, because animal behaviour can always be classified into mutually exclusive and exhaustive categories (i.e. the animal is always doing something), a totally decidable logical preference always exists, albeit inherent in the design of the decision-making machinery (McFarland and Sibly, 1975).

Corresponding to every trajectory in causal factor space is an overt behaviour sequence. Each trajectory crosses a series of regions bounded by the isoclines, so that a corresponding series of changes in behaviour results from any particular trajectory. However, the characteristics of a trajectory are determined largely by the consequences of the behaviour, while the characteristics of the corresponding behaviour sequence are determined jointly by the path of the trajectory and the shape of the isoclines which the trajectory crosses. The trajectories vary from occasion to occasion, but the isocline shape is a design feature, moulded by natural selection, and presumably adapted to the animal's natural way of life. Knowledge of the shape of the isoclines, therefore, is the key to understanding the way in which a particular behavioural system works. Moreover, the hypothesis that the decision rules, which we represented by isoclines, are designed by natural selection to produce optimal behaviour sequences, is truly an hypothesis in that it is testable. Sibly and McFarland (1976) have shown how optimality theory can be used to predict the families of behaviour sequences that should correspond to any hypothesis about the design of decision rules. Such predictions can be tested by direct observation of behaviour. Before going on to discuss the implications of this approach for the study of feeding and drinking, we need to have a clearer idea of the way in which motivational variables appear to behave when represented in the state space.

2. *Laboratory Analysis of Motivational State*

Changes in motivational state can in principle be represented by a trajectory in a state space. Such changes result either from "exafferent" factors from outside the system, or from the consequences of the animal's own behaviour, "reafferent" factors. The problem is to know how to interpret observations of animal behaviour in terms of these factors; i.e. how can a motivational trajectory be constructed from observed behaviour?

(a) *Basic Phenomena of Hunger–Thirst Interaction* The problem is greatly simplified when the animal is kept under controlled conditions in the laboratory. Where the animal's environment is under the control of the experimenter, much can be done to determine the dimensionality of the space within which the trajectory is to be drawn (see above). For an animal maintained on a homogeneous diet and pure water in a controlled environment, only two axes are necessary to represent all possible primary states of hunger and thirst. When such an animal is deprived of food and water, the values of the two state variables become much larger than the values of other motivational state variables. When placed in an environment where both food and water are available, the states of hunger and thirst become so overriding that the animal restricts itself to feeding and drinking for a period of time, during which its motivational state can be represented in a hunger–thirst state plane (Fig. 7a). The point in this plane, representing the motivational state at any time, may move under the influence of "exafferent" factors, but in a controlled environment these can be minimized. In such situations, changes in motivational state can be ascribed almost entirely to the consequences of observed behaviour. The problem has now become one of interpreting observed behaviour in terms of its motivational consequences. Let us see how the possible consequences of feeding and drinking might be portrayed.

The motivational consequences of eating may decrease hunger, a negative

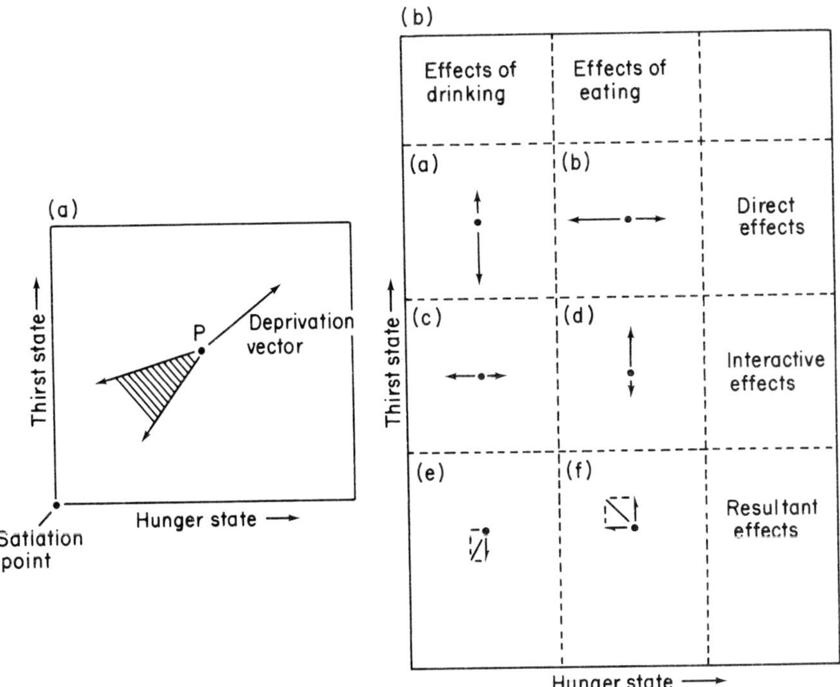

Fig. 7. (a) Hunger–thirst plane in which the overall motivational state is represented by a point *P*. This point may move away from the origin under the influence of "exafferent" factors, such as water and energy loss during deprivation. This possibility is shown as a deprivation vector. The point *P* may move towards the origin under the influence of "reafferent" factors resulting from the consequences of the animal's own behaviour. The shaded area represents the "cone of realizable consequences" (McFarland and Sibly, 1972) within which a behavioural trajectory must lie. (From McFarland, 1974b.)
(b) Possible effect of feeding and drinking. (a) Drinking may increase and/or reduce thirst, (b) feeding may increase and/or reduce hunger, (c) drinking may increase and/or reduce hunger, (d) feeding may increase and/or reduce thirst, (e) possible resultant effects of drinking, (f) possible resultant effects of feeding. (From McFarland, 1974b.)

feedback effect, or increase hunger, a positive feedback effect. Similarly, following drinking there may be negative and positive effects upon thirst. These feedback effects may operate through a number of routes, such as oral monitoring, loading of the alimentary tract, and changing the state of the blood. These routes may involve different time courses, but they essentially act in parallel and their effects are therefore additive at the level of the motivational command (see McFarland, 1971, pp. 239–249 for a demonstration of this type of additivity). In addition to these straightforward feedback effects, feeding may have positive or negative effects on thirst, and drinking may affect hunger. It is well known that eating dry food increases thirst in many animals (Bolles, 1961; McFarland,

1965; Oatley and Tonge, 1969), and feeding may also reduce thirst by virtue of the water content of the food. Drinking is not normally thought to affect hunger, but some such effects in certain species cannot be ruled out.

(b) *Hunger–Thirst Trajectory*. Feeding and drinking thus have four possible types of consequence, and in the state-plane these appear as vectors (Fig. 7b). Each diametrically opposed pair of vectors can be resolved into a single resultant, the direction of which depends upon the relative magnitudes of the positive and negative consequences. This cancelling effect leaves two orthogonally related vectors, which can in turn be represented by a single resultant (Fig. 7b). The direction of the resultant depends not only upon the values of the two vectors from which it is derived, but also upon the scaling of the hunger and thirst axes. Since the scaling is an arbitrary matter, no great importance can be attached to the absolute direction of a vector, but relative differences between vectors are meaningful. In these circumstances, it is useful to represent a standard situation by orthogonal vectors, and this has been done (McFarland, 1971; McFarland and Lloyd, 1973) in the case of feeding and drinking in the Barbary dove (*Streptopelia risoria*) which is to be used as the primary example in this chapter.

In this particular case, the negative consequences of feeding and drinking are generally greater than the positive consequences, and deprived animals reliably satiate when given access to food and water (McFarland and Lloyd, 1973). The consequences of feeding and drinking can be therefore represented by a pair of orthogonal negative vectors, of unit length corresponding to each unit of food or water ingested. The satiated state can be represented as the origin of the state space, and if the satiated condition can be established reliably, the trajectory will always terminate at the origin. The amounts of food and water intake required to reach satiation can always be worked out *post hoc*, and upon this basis a complete trajectory can be drawn (Fig. 8).

Although this "direct" type of trajectory has proved quite useful (McFarland, 1971; McFarland and Lloyd, 1973), it involves a number of unsatisfactory assumptions. Firstly, a satiated condition cannot always be reliably established. An animal may overshoot or undershoot the satiation point, because of the existence of unrealizable states within the system (McFarland and Sibly, 1972), or because of the action of positive feedback from the consequences of behaviour (McFarland and Sibly, 1975). Secondly, the direct method involves an implicit assumption that a unit of observed behaviour can always be represented by a unit vector, regardless of the time of its occurrence. In practice, the correspondence between behaviour and its internal consequences may change with time. Thus the effect of feeding upon thirst may be delayed and built up with time, so that trajectories that are orthogonal at the outset may not remain orthogonal. The relation between negative and positive feedback may also vary in time, thus altering the length of vector per unit of behaviour.

A number of methods of overcoming these difficulties have been devised. These are not reported here, because they are fairly complicated in themselves, and have been reported elsewhere. Some of these methods involve manipulation and interruption of behaviour, and these have been particularly useful in the analysis of feeding and drinking behaviour in doves (McFarland, 1974b; Sibly, 1975), pigs (Sibly and McCleery, 1976), and rats (McCleery, unpubl. obs.). Other methods involve manipulation of data from natural observations, or uninterrupted laboratory experiments, and these may involve computer simulation (e.g. Houston *et al.*, in press), calibration of motivational variables (Houston and McFarland, in 1976), and optimality calculations (Sibly and McFarland, 1976).

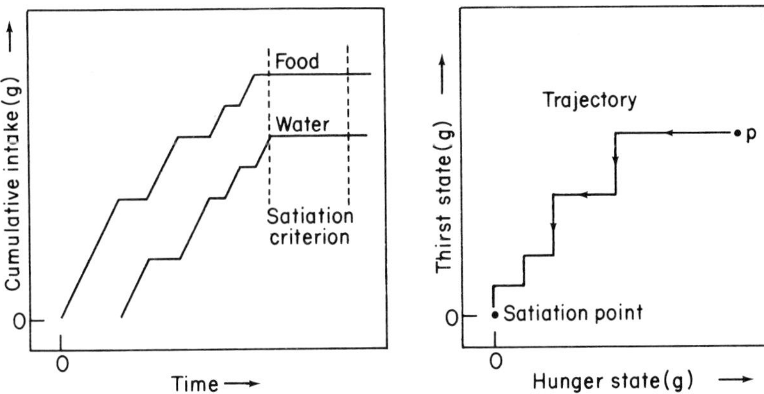

Fig. 8. Hypothetical cumulative intake of food and water plotted as a function of time (left), and corresponding trajectory in the hunger–thirst state-place (right). (From McFarland, 1974b.)

(c) *Motivational Dominance Boundary.* At this point it may be helpful to paint a brief picture of the changes in state that are envisaged as taking place when an animal feeds and drinks. Given that the animal is initially both hungry and thirsty, its motivational state can be represented as a point in a hunger–thirst space, as indicated in Fig. 9a. This initial state will have been reached during a period of food and water deprivation, during which it will have been moving away from the saturation state. Because the period of feeding and drinking is short compared with the deprivation period, further movement in this outward direction can be ignored. When the animal is allowed to feed and drink, the motivational state will change and a trajectory will be traced in the general direction of the satiation point. The exact trajectory will depend upon the precise environmental circumstances, particularly the constitution and availability of food and water, as discussed above.

We can expect that the state space will be divided by a "dominance boundary", or "switching line", on one side of which hunger is dominant over thirst and vice versa on the other side (Fig. 9b). Simple competition between hunger and thirst results in a trajectory that aims for the nearest point on the switching line that is compatible with the constraints inherent in the situation. When the switching line is reached, a simple competition theory predicts dithering between

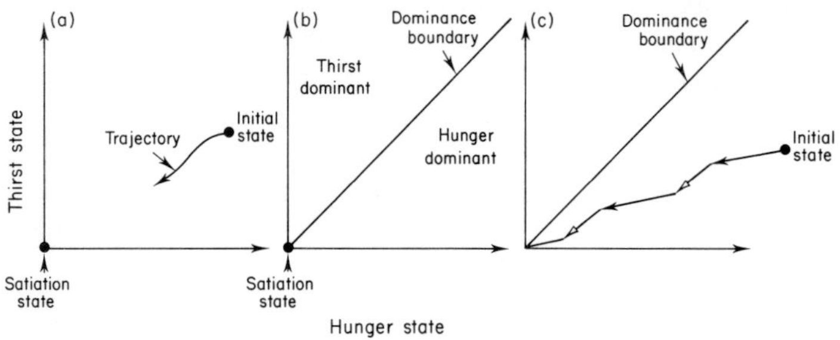

Fig. 9. (a) Features of the hunger–thirst plane of the causal factor space.
(b) The dominance boundary in the hunger–thirst state-space.
(c) Trajectory resulting from feeding and drinking. Black arrowheads indicate termination of feeding bout. White arrowheads indicate termination of drinking bout.

feeding and drinking. This feature of simple control models has been commented on by a number of workers, and two main solutions have been proposed. One possibility is that there is an element of positive feedback in feeding and drinking, which gives "momentum" that carries the trajectory well over the switching line (Wiepkema, 1971; McFarland, 1971, 1974a). Another possibility is that there is hysteresis involving two thresholds in the state space (Geertsema and Reddingius, 1974; Booth 1976). Experiments with doves suggest alternative possibilities.

(i) Time-Sharing. There is considerable evidence that drinking can occur well to the hunger side of the dominance boundary, and vice versa (McFarland and Lloyd, 1973; McFarland, 1974a; Sibly and McCleery, 1976). This "subdominant" drinking (or feeding) is under the control of the dominant control system in that both its onset and duration is determined from within the feeding system. This is a typical "time sharing" situation (McFarland, 1974a), and it would appear to have certain advantages for the animal. For instance, by introducing bouts of subdominant drinking, the primarily hungry animal can achieve satiation without the trajectory ever crossing the dominance boundary, as illustrated in Fig. 9c. In other words, satiation can be achieved without loss of control by the feeding system. It appears that hunger and thirst compete for dominance, but that the dominant system, by employing a time-sharing strategy, can retain its dominance for longer than would otherwise be the case.

(ii) Hysteresis or Catastrophe. There is evidence, however, that hysteresis is also involved, particularly in the competition for dominance. It has been suggested (McFarland and Sibly, 1975) that the problem of switching between activities may be appropriately handled by catastrophe theory. In fact, almost any hysteresis phenomenon can be described in terms of catastrophe theory (see also Chapter 16). It has been applied to the analysis of feeding and drinking in doves by Houston and McFarland (unpublished), in summary as follows.

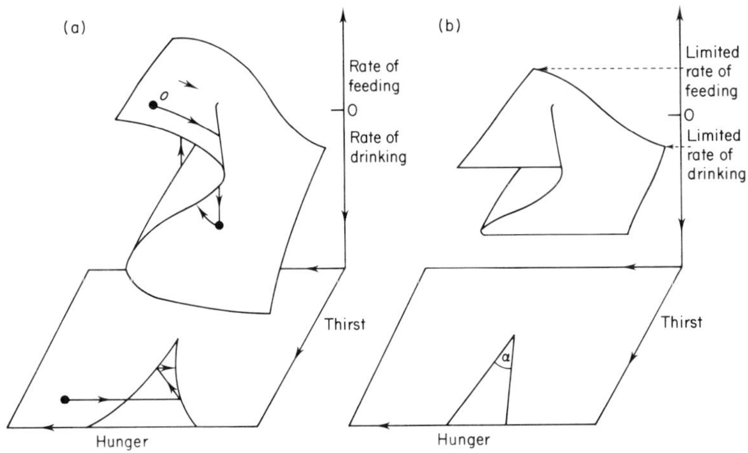

Fig. 10. (a) Cusp catastrophe (see text for explanation).
(b) Deformed cusp catastrophe (see text for explanation).

Figure 10a shows a simple cusp catastrophe for a feeding and drinking situation. Starting at point *o* on the folded surface, we assume that the hungry and thirsty animal starts by feeding, and we trace a trajectory on the upper surface of the fold, representing a reduction in the degree of hunger. At a certain point, marked by the projection of the cusp onto the lower figure, the trajectory flips to the lower surface, and the animal starts drinking. The trajectory then reduces thirst until a point is again reached where a catastrophic flip occurs, and feeding starts again. The switching lines for feeding and drinking appear as curved lines, when the cusp is projected onto the hunger–thirst plane.

We must take account of the fact that there is a limit to the rate at which an animal can obtain food and water in any particular situation. Such limits act as constraints upon behaviour, and must be taken into account in any type of model. Imposing such limits in the catastrophe model has the effect of deforming the folded surface, in such a way that the switching lines projected onto the hunger–thirst plane appear as straight lines, as illustrated in Fig. 10b. Experimental manipulation of the rates of feeding and drinking in a situation in which it is possible accurately to measure the shape and position of such switching lines

(McFarland, 1974; Sibly and McCleery, 1976) shows that in doves the switching lines are indeed straight lines in the hunger–thirst plane. Moreover, catastrophe theory predicts that the angle between the switching lines should be a linear inverse function of the rates of feeding and drinking, and the positions of the two lines should correspond to the respective constraints upon feeding and drinking. Both these predictions have been confirmed in numerous experiments involving precise quantitative measurement of switching line position (McFarland and Sibly, 1975; Sibly, 1975). The upshot is that, although catastrophe theory is not the only way in which these findings can be accounted for, it does provide a parsimonious description of this complex aspect of the behavioural final common path.

A lesson to be learned from study of switching phenomena is that the thresholds responsible for turning on/off a particular activity, such as feeding, cannot be considered in terms of the factors controlling that activity alone, but that the position of switching lines depends upon the way in which the animal trades off the costs and benefits of the various activities in its repertoire. To understand this, we have to consider the situation as it is likely to occur in the animal's environment.

3. *The Natural Environment and Optimal Behaviour Sequences*

(a) *Costs and Benefits of Feeding*. In the natural environment, animals have to take account of many aspects of motivation in addition to hunger. In deciding whether to eat or not, they have to evaluate the costs and benefits of the alternatives. For example, red deer stags may not eat at all for five or six weeks during the rut, when reproductive behaviour takes priority. Similar facultative changes in feeding occur prior to and during hibernation, migration and pregnancy, and may occur at particular points in the life history.

In evaluating the costs and benefits of feeding, animals must take into account probable future feeding opportunities, the handling time of particular food items, and the spatial distribution of prey (Holling, 1965, 1966). Thus both external stimuli and "cognitive" strategies play an important role in determining when an animal eats in the natural environment. For example, "sit and wait" strategists typically pass over small prey because it is not worth their while to spoil their camouflage, and pass over large prey because the handling-time is long and other more efficient opportunities may be missed. Moreover, many animals may not eat possible foods, either through altruism to their kin, through provision for the future, to avoid competition with other species, etc. (Wilson, 1975).

(b) *The General Optimality Analysis*. The decisions to start and stop feeding involve a complex balance of costs and benefits, encompassing much more than the traditional ideas of regulatory physiology. For this reason, classical control models are not suitable for this type of behavioural analysis. By representing motivational systems in terms of a state-space, it is possible to overcome many of the difficulties inherent in the traditional approach. In particular, the state-space approach lends itself naturally to optimality considerations, so that it becomes possible to test whether the deployment of behavioural options is optimally related to environmental conditions, for a given species in a particular situation.

In applying optimality concepts to animal behaviour, we are considering what an animal ought to do in a given situation. In doing this we have to remember that the various possible behaviour patterns differ in their consequences, and have different costs and benefits attached to them. For example, a white-tailed deer (*Odocoileus virginianus*), in sitting down to reduce exposure to the cold wind, is gaining considerable benefit in terms of energy conservation (Moen, 1973). At the same timc it is accruing costs due to its reduced range of vision and possibility of detecting predators. There will also be costs associated with the lost opportunities for other activities such as feeding. At any particular time the relative advantages of standing and sitting will depend upon various factors, such as the environmental temperature, the wind speed, the likelihood of predators approaching, and their probability of visibility and ease of detection. We can imagine the animal weighing all these factors in its mind every time it stands up or sits down, but it is more likely that the animal uses decision-rules of thumb which are inherent in the "design" of the animal.

In considering decision-making in animals, we must distinguish between design and execution. The design involves a balance of costs and benefits, while the execution involves evaluation of the situation and carrying out procedures designed to fit the situation. Generally, the design will have been carried out by natural selection during the process of evolution, whereas the execution is the business of the individual animal. We may, however, wish to allow for the possibility that in more intelligent species a certain amount of weighting of costs and benefits can be carried out by the individual animal.

Since natural selection is the designing agent, we must regard fitness as the ultimate criterion of benefit. Although it is permissable, in the analysis of specific and clear-cut problems, such as optional foraging problems, to regard time or energy budgets as objective functions (Krebs, 1973), in the analysis of the global problem, involving the animal's total behaviour repertoire, fitness is the only satisfactory optimality criterion (McFarland, 1976). Recently it has become possible to calculate the way in which fitness is maximized throughout the life history of a given species (Leon, 1976), and throughout a particular behaviour sequence in a given environment (Sibly and McFarland, 1976). Although it is the latter which concerns us here, the prospect of calculating optimal life histories is also an exciting one, because it may provide a way of understanding the functional relevance of changes in feeding behaviour with age.

To say that a behaviour sequence should maximize fitness is to imply that not only are the species-typical characteristics of behaviour patterns subject to natural selection, but so also is the order and precise timing of their performance. The costs and benefits attributable to an activity depend partly upon the internal state of the animal, and partly upon the consequences of its behaviour. The consequences are largely determined by the environment, so that the net benefit or fitness change, accruing to the performance of a particular activity at a particular time, will depend upon the environmental circumstances. Figure 11 shows how fluctuating environmental circumstances can affect the advantages of performing various activities.

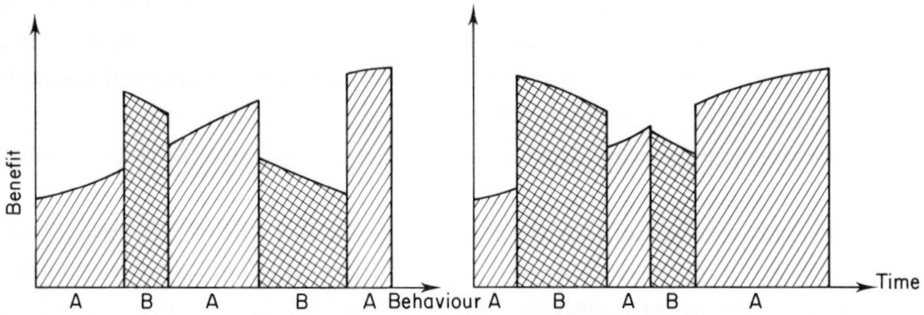

Fig. 11. Benefit gained from two hypothetical behaviour sequences under one set of environmental circumstances. The benefit gained from activity A, in a certain period of time, is represented by the area under the curve. The benefit gained from activity B is the area under a different curve. These "opportunity" curves are characteristic of the environment, and are repeated in the two cases illustrated in this figure. The total benefit gained from a behaviour sequence of a given length is obtained by summing the shaded areas. Of the two hypothetical behaviour sequences illustrated, that on the right yields the greater benefit, even though they both occur under the same environmental pattern of changing benefit from A and from B.

To obtain the optimal behaviour sequence, the animal should maximize a mathematical function which takes account of the motivational state of the animal, the state of the environment, and the balance of costs and benefits likely to result from any particular action. It can be shown (Sibly and McFarland, in 1976) that if the optimality criterion is Darwinian fitness, and the animal is attuned to its environment in the sense that its motivational state is appropriately affected by environmental stimuli, then the mathematical function which the animal should maximize is a

$$\text{Hamiltonian} := \text{plant equations} - \text{cost function}.$$

The plant equations describe the changes in the motivational state of the animal that are determined by the environmental circumstances and by the consequences of the animal's behaviour. The cost function represents the precise manner in which the costs and benefits of behaviour are counterbalanced.

Whereas the cost function summarizes the costs and benefits that should be counterbalanced in general terms, the Hamiltonian takes account of the specific situation in which the animal finds itself at a particular time.

The argument is that the animal is designed by natural selection to deploy its behavioural options in a manner that continuously maximizes the Hamiltonian. By so doing it achieves that behaviour sequence which maximizes fitness in the prevailing circumstances.

Given complete freedom of action, the animal could always attain the optimal sequence. There would be no room for improvement and, for an animal adapted to its environment, there would be no need for learning. However, animals do not have complete freedom of action, and there are inevitable constraints upon behaviour. In particular, animals cannot indulge in negative behaviour, they can carry out only one activity at a time, and there is a limit to the rate at which they can behavc. These may seem to be trivial and obvious constraints, but they mean that the animal can rarely achieve the ideal optimal solution. There will always be room for improvement by learning, and the application of optimality theory to behaviour will have to be extended to take account of learning. However, the present theory is adequate for situations in which the animal is near learning asymptote, and some progress has been made in this type of research (Sibly and McFarland, 1976; McFarland, 1976).

(c) *Optimality and Time-Sharing.* In conclusion, let us attempt to relate optimality considerations to the notion of the behavioural final common path outlined earlier in this chapter. In Section III.C.1 it was mentioned that Sibly (1975) found evidence for the following decision rule in the dove (*Streptopelia risoria*) for situations in which food and water were of limited availability: "food and water should be taken at the maximum possible rate, and the choice of food over water should depend on whether the product of deficit times incentive is greater for hunger or for thirst". As mentioned above, this decision rule corresponds to an hyperbolic isocline in the causal factor space. By using optimality theory, Sibly and McFarland (1976) showed that a particular cost function was concordant with the well known feeding or drinking exponential satiation curve, characteristic of doves and other species. Moreover, this same cost function predicts the feeding–drinking decision rule found by Sibly (1975). On this basis it is possible to calculate the optimal trajectory in a hunger–thirst space for an animal deprived of both food and water, and allowed to eat and drink under specific circumstances of food/water availability. These optimal trajectories are similar to those obtained from doves during periods of uninterrupted feeding and drinking. The most interesting thing about them, however, is that they necessitate a certain amount of subdominant feeding and drinking, as illustrated in Fig. 12. This observation suggests that time-sharing is a strategy by means of which an animal attains an optimal behaviour sequence, even though one type of motivation may be dominant. Studies of feeding and foraging patterns in natural situations (e.g. Smith, 1964) seem to reinforce this view. Many animals pause frequently during feeding, and look around. Some studies (e.g. Kenward and Sibly, in press) suggest that this is a time-sharing strategy designed to counterbalance the benefits of feeding against the risks from predators, etc. This research is very promising in that it now seems possible to build a theoretical bridge between feeding behaviour studied in the laboratory and that observed in the natural environment.

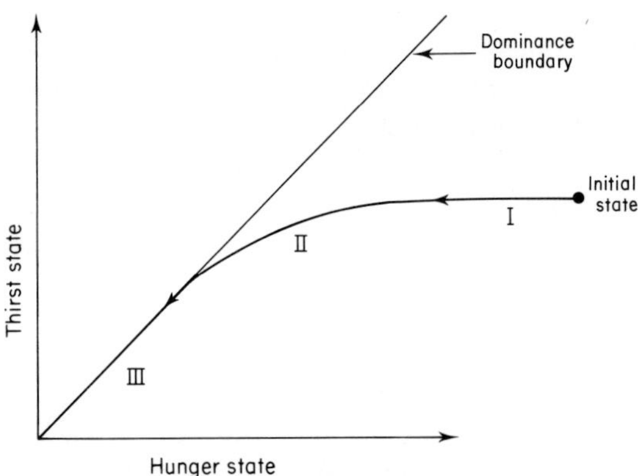

Fig. 12. Optimal trajectory in the hunger–thirst state plane. In phase I only feeding behaviour occurs; in phase II there is time-sharing between feeding and drinking (hunger dominant); in phase III hunger and thirst compete for dominance.

References

Adolph, E. F. (1972). Some general concepts of physiological adaptations. *In* "Physiological Adaptations" (M. K. Yousef, S. M. Horvath and R. W. Bullard, eds). Academic Press, New York and London.

Amsel, A. (1958). The role of frustrative nonreward in noncontinuous reward situations. *Psychol. Bull.* **55**, 102–119.

Bolles, R. C. (1961). The interaction of hunger and thirst in the rat. *J. comp. physiol Psychol.* **54**, 58–64.

Booth, D. A. (1976). Approaches to feeding control. *In* "Appetite and Food Intake" (T. Silverstone, ed.), pp. 417–478. Dahlem Konferenzen, Berlin.

Budgell, P. (1970). The effect of changes in ambient temperature on water intake and evaporative water loss. *Psychon. Sci.* **20**, 275–276.

Budgell, P. (1971). Behavioural thermoregulation in the Barbary dove (*Streptopelia risoria*). *Anim. Behav.* **19**, 524–531.

Cannon, W. B. (1932). "The Wisdom of the Body." London, Kegan Paul.

Epstein, A. N. Fitzsimons, J. T. and Rolls, B. J. (1970). Drinking induced by injection of angiotensin into the brain of the rat. *J. Physiol., Lond.* **210**, 457–474.

Fitzsimons, J. T. (1958). Normal drinking in rats. *J. Physiol., Lond.* **138**, 39.

Fitzsimons, J. T. and Le Magnen, J. (1969). Eating as a regulating control of drinking in the rat. *J. comp. physiol. Psychol.* **67**, 273–283.

Fry, F. E. J. and Hochachka, P. (1970). Fish. *In* "Comparative Physiology of Thermoregulation" (G. C. Whitlow, ed.), Vol. I. Academic Press, London and New York.

Geertsema, S. and Reddingius, J. (1974). Preliminary considerations in the simulation of behaviour. *In* "Motivational Control Systems Analysis" (D. J. McFarland, ed.), pp. 355–405. Academic Press, London and New York.

Grossman, S. P. (1967). "A Textbook of Physiological Psychology". John Wiley and Sons, New York.

Hinde, R. A. and Steel, E. A. (1966). Integration of the reproductive behaviour of female canaries. *Symp. Soc. exp. Biol* **20**, 401–426.

Holling, C. S. (1965). The functional response of predators to prey density and its role in mimicry and population regulation. *Mem. Ent. Soc. Canada* **45**, 1–59.

Holling, C. S. (1966). The functional response of invertebrate predators to prey density. *Mem. Ent. Soc. Canada* **48**, 1–86.

von Holst, E. and von Saint Paul, U. (1963). On the functional organisation of drives. *Anim. Behav.* **11**, 1–20.

Houston, A. and McFarland, D. J. (1976). On the measurement of motivational variables. *Anim. Behav.* **24**, 459–475.

Houston, A., Halliday, T. and McFarland, D. J. (in press). Towards a model of the courtship of the smooth newt *Triturus vulgaris*, with special emphasis on problems of observability in the simulation of behaviour. *Med. biol. Engng.*

Kaufmann, A. (1968). "The Science of Decision-making". Weidenfeld and Nicolson, London

Kenward, R. E. and Sibly, R. M. (in press). Wood pigeon feeding at brassica sites. *Anim. Behav.*

Krebs, J. (1973). Behavioural aspects of predation. *In* "Perspectives in Ethology" (P.P. G. Bateson and P. H. Klopfer, eds). Plenum Press, New York.

Lehrman, D. S. (1959). Hormonal responses to external stimuli in birds. *Ibis* **101**, 478–496.

Lehrman, D. S. (1961). Hormonal regulation of parental behaviour in birds and infrahuman mammals. *In* "Sex and Internal Secretions" (W. C. Young, ed.). Williams and Wilkins, Baltimore.

Leon, J. A. (1976). Life histories as adaptive strategies. *J. theor. Biol.* **60**, 301–335.

McFarland, D. J. (1964). Interaction of hunger and thirst in the Barbary dove. *J. comp. physiol. Psychol.* **58**, 174–179.

McFarland, D. J. (1965). Control theory applied to the control of drinking in the Barbary dove. *Anim. Behav.* **13**, 478–492.

McFarland, D. J. (1969). Mechanisms of behavioural disinhibition. *Anim. Behav.* **17**, 238–242.

McFarland, D. J. (1970a). Recent developments in the study of feeding and drinking in animals. *J. psychosom. Res.* **14**, 229–237.

McFarland, D. J. (1970b). Adjunctive behaviour in feeding and drinking situations. *Rev. Comp. Anim.* **4**, 64–73.

McFarland, D. J. (1971). "Feedback Mechanisms in Animal Behaviour". Academic Press, London and New York.

McFarland, D. J. (1973). Stimulus relevance and homeostasis. *In* "Constraints of Learning" (R. A. Hinde and J. Stevenson-Hinde, eds). Academic Press, London and New York.

McFarland, D. J. (1974a). Time-sharing as a behavioural phenomenon. *In* "Advances in the Study of Behaviour" (D. S. Lehrman *et al.,* eds), Vol. V. Academic Press, New York and London.

McFarland, D. J. (ed.) (1974b). "Motivational Control Systems Analysis" Academic Press, London and New York.

McFarland, D. J. (1976). Form and function in the temporal organisation of behaviour. *In* "Growing Points in Ethology" (R. A. Hinde and P. P. G. Bateson, eds). Cambridge University Press, London.

McFarland, D. J. and Budgell, P. (1970). The thermoregulatory role of feather movements in the Barbary dove (*Streptopelia risoria*). *Physiol Behav.* **5**, 763–771.

McFarland, D. J. and Lloyd, I. H. (1973). Time-shared feeding and drinking. *Q. J. exp. Psychol.* **25**, 48–61.

McFarland, D. J. and Rolls, B. J. (1972). Suppression of feeding by intracranial injection of angiotensin. *Nature, Lond.* **236**, 172–173.

McFarland, D. J. and Sibly, R. (1972). "Unitary drives" revisited. *Anim. Behav.* **20**, 548–563.

McFarland, D. J. and Sibly, R. M. (1975). The behavioural final common path. *Phil. Trans. Roy. Soc. B.* **270**, 265–293.

McFarland, D. J. and Wright, P. J. (1969). Water conservation by inhibition of food intake. *Physiol. Behav.* **4**, 95–99.

Milsum, J. H. (1966). "Biological Control Systems Analysis". McGraw-Hill, London and New York.

Mittelstaedt, H. (1957). Prey capture in Mantids. *In* "Recent Advances in Invertebrate Physiology" (B. T. Scheer, ed.), pp. 51–71. University of Oregon Publications, Eugene.

Moen, A. N. (1973). "Wildlife Ecology". W. H. Freeman, San Francisco.

Oatley, K. (1967). A control model for the physiological basis of thirst. *Med. biol. Engng* **5**, 225–237.

Oatley, K. and Tonge, D. A. (1969). The effect of hunger on water intake in rats. *Q. J. exp. Psychol.* **21**, 162–171.

Revusky, S. and Garcia, J. (1970). Learned association over long delays. *In* "Psychology of Learning and Motivation" (C. H. Bower and J. T. Spence, eds), Vol. IV. Academic Press, New York and London.

Richter, C. P. (1943). Total self-regulatory functions in animals and human beings. *Harvey Lectures* **38**, 63–103.

Rolls, B. J. and McFarland, D. J. (1973). Hydration releases inhibiton of feeding produced by intracranial angiotensin. *Physiol Behav.* **11**, 881–884.

Rosen, R. (1970). "Dynamical System Theory in Biology". Wiley, New York.

Rozin, P. and Kalat, J. W. (1971). Specific hungers and poison avoidance as adaptive specialisations of learning. *Psychol. Rev.* **78**, 459–486.

Sherrington, C. S. (1906). "The Integrative Action of the Nervous System." Yale University Press, New Haven, Conn.

Sibly, R. M. (1975). How incentive and deficit determine feeding tendency. *Anim. Behav.* **23**, 437–446.

Sibly, R. M. and McCleery, R. H. (1976). The dominance boundary method of determining motivational state. *Anim. Behav.* **24**, 108–124.

Sibly, R. M. and McFarland, D. J. (1974). A state-space approach to motivation. *In* "Motivational Control Systems Analysis" (D. J. McFarland, ed.), pp. 213–250. Academic Press, London and New York.

Sibly, R. M. and McFarland, D. J. (1976). On the fitness of behaviour sequences. *American Naturalist.* **110**, 601–617.

Smith, J. N. M. (1964). The food searching behaviour of two European thrushes. I. Description and analysis of search paths. *Behaviour* **48**, 276–302.

Toates, F. M. and Oatley, J. (1972). Inhibition of *ad libitum* feeding in rats by salt injections and water deprivation. *Q. J. exp. Psychol.* **24**, 215–224.

Wiepkema, P. R. (1971). Positive feedbacks at work during feeding. *Behaviour* **39**, 2–4.

Wilson, E. O. (1975). "Sociobiology—the New Synthesis". Harvard University Press, Cambridge, Mass.

Yates, A. J. (1962). "Frustration and conflict". Methuen, London.

16
*A Catastrophe Theory of Anorexia Nervosa**

E. C. ZEEMAN
Mathematics Institute, University of Warwick, Coventry, England

I. Introduction

Catastrophe theory is a new mathematical method for describing the evolution of forms in nature. It was created by René Thom who recently wrote a revolutionary book expanding the philosophy behind the ideas (Thom, 1972). It is particularly applicable where gradually changing forces produce sudden effects. We often call such effects catastrophes, because our intuition about the underlying continuity of the forces makes the very discontinuity of the effects so unexpected, and this has given rise to the name. The theory depends upon some new and deep theorems in the geometry of many dimensions, which classify the way that discontinuities can occur in terms of a few archetypal forms; Thom calls these forms the *elementary catastrophes*. The remarkable thing about the results is that, although the proofs are sophisticated, the elementary catastrophes themselves are both surprising and relatively easy to understand, and can be profitably used by scientists who are not expert mathematicians.

In physics many classical examples can now be seen to be special cases of low-dimensional catastrophes, and as a result the higher dimensional catastrophes are beginning to suggest new experiments and offer understanding of more complicated phenomena. However in the long run the more spectacular applications may well be in biology, providing models for the developing embryo, for evolution and for behaviour. Much of Thom's book concerns embryology. Models in psychology and sociology suggest new insight into the complexity of

*An extract from Zeeman (1977), reprinted by permission of the author and publisher.

human emotions and human relationships, and offer new designs for experiments. Catastrophe theory provides a new qualitative mathematical language for servicing the hitherto "inexact" sciences.

This chapter is the second part of an article published elsewhere (Zeeman, 1977). The first part of that article introduced some simple applications of catastrophe theory to elasticity, aggression, emotions, war and economics, and led up to a precise mathematical statement of one of the classification theorems, together with Thom's list of the seven elementary catastrophes having a control space of dimensions fewer than or equal to four. In a third part of that article we selected some familiar examples from classical physics, in order to illustrate the generality and quantitative power of the new language in the physical sciences. Selected for this book, however, is the part in which we go more deeply into one particular application, namely a model for the nervous disorder anorexia nervosa, in order to illustrate the profundity and qualitative power of the new language in the human sciences. Another application is given by McFarland (Chapter 15, pp. 397–398).

II. Anorexia Nervosa

Anorexia is a disorder suffered mainly by adolescent girls and young women, in whom dieting has degenerated into obsessive fasting. It generally begins between the ages of 11 and 17, although it can start as early as nine or as late as 30. It can lead to severe malnutrition, withdrawal and even death.

The proposed model is the joint work of the author and J. Hevesi, who is a psychotherapist specializing in anorexia. Hevesi has spent some 5000 hours during the last five years talking to over 150 anorexics and the model is based on his close observations. Of these 150, over 60 agreed to undertake his course of treatment, and of those treated he has achieved an 80% success rate of complete cure. His innovation is the use of trance therapy. The Anorexic Aid Society in Britain recently conducted a survey of over 1000 anorexics, and the secretary of the society, Mrs P. Hartley, who is a psychologist, writes:

> "I first read of Mr Hevesi in several letters from patients who responded to my appeal for information about anorexia nervosa, and their experience re treatment. These patients are the only ones who claim that they have recovered completely—i. e. those whose *attitude* to life itself has changed since undergoing Hevesi's treatment. They are not just eating properly (only the awful surface problem anyway) but living a full life as a *complete* personality." (her italics).

III. Cusp-catastrophe Model

A. *Psychopathology*

The advantage of using mathematical language for a model is that it is psychologically neutral; it permits a coherent synthesis of a large number of observations that would otherwise appear disconnected, and in particular enables us to place the trance states in relation to other behavioural modes. As yet the model is only qualitative, in the sense that the predictions that have been verified by observation have been qualitative rather than quantitative. Nevertheless it does provide a conceptual framework within which the theory could also be tested quantitatively by monitoring patients. Meanwhile we hope that it may not only give a better understanding of anorexia and its cure, but also provide a prototypc for understanding other types of behavioural disorder.

A striking feature of anorexia is that it sometimes develops a second phase after about two years, in which the victim finds herself alternately fasting and secretly gorging; the medical name for this is bulimia, and anorexics often call it stuffing or bingeing. If we regard the normal person's rhythm of eating and satiety as a continuous smooth cycle of unimodal behaviour, then we can interpret this second phase of bimodal behaviour as a catastrophic jumping between two abnormal extremes. Therefore by the main theorem we can model the anorexic's behaviour by a cusp-catastrophe, in which she is trapped in a hysteresis cycle, as in Fig. 1.

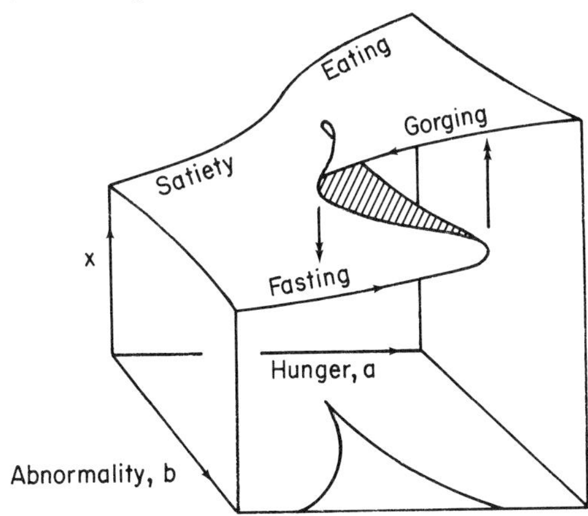

Fig. 1. Initial behaviour model for anorexia.

Before we begin to analyse the model, we can immediately draw one important conclusion: *the victim will be denied access to the normal modes in between.* This denial of access to normal modes occurs during the first phase of only fasting. Thus the main thrust of our approach will be to explain anorexia not as the complicated behaviour of a perverse neurotic, but as the logical outcome of a simple bifurcation in the underlying brain dynamics. If this is the case, then catastrophe theory at once indicates a theoretical cure: if we can induce a further bifurcation according to the butterfly catastrophe (Thom, 1972; Zeeman, 1976), then this should open up a pathway back to normality. The practical problem is to devise a therapy that will induce such a bifurcation, and this is what Hevesi's treatment achieves.

In Fig. 1 we have chosen hunger and abnormality as the two control factors (a, b). Hunger is the normal factor because hunger normally governs the rhythmic cycle between eating and satiety: there are various known methods for measuring hunger, but we do not yet know which will be best to use for quantitative testing. We postpone the discussion on the measurement of abnormality unitl later. Meanwhile to measure the behaviour, x, it would be necessary to find some psychological index that correlates with the scale of wakeful states shown in Fig. 2.

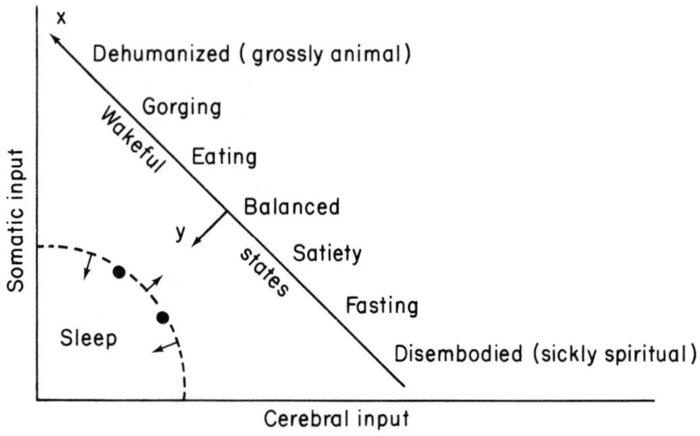

Fig. 2. The x-axis measures both wakeful behaviour, and the relative weight given to the cerebral and somatic inputs to the limbic brain. The dotted line shows the boundary of the sleep basin, and the arrows show the movement of this boundary due to anorexia, leaving fixed the two nodal points.

What actually governs the behaviour is the underlying brain state, and if it is true, as MacLean (1973) suggests, that emotion and mood are generated in the limbic brain, then it is likely that x is measuring some property of limbic states. Since the limbic brain receives both cerebral inputs from the neocortex, and somatic inputs from the body, we might conjecture that x is some measure of the relative weight given to those inputs as shown in Fig. 2. Of course such a conjecture must remain speculative until it is confirmed or rejected by future brain research. Nevertheless the conjecture has already proved useful in explaining many of the symptoms of anorexia, and, what is perhaps more important, it has enabled us to identify what may be the key operative suggestions in the therapy, as we shall see. Meanwhile the conjecture implies that the main neurological feature of anorexia is that during wakefulness the limbic brain is dominated either by cerebral inputs or by somatic inputs, while the balanced states have become unstable, and therefore inaccessible.

Before leaving Fig. 2 notice that it is two-dimensional. From the psychological point of view the natural axes to use are x and y, which are inclined at 45° to the neurological axes, cerebral and somatic. Here x measures the different wakeful states, while y measures the difference between wakefulness and sleep, and y exhibits the familiar healthy catastrophes of falling asleep and waking up. For a more complete model we ought really to use both the behaviour variables x and y, five controls, and a seven-dimensional catastrophe called E_6 (Callahan, 1977). However this is beyond the scope of this article, and so for simplicity of presentation we shall sacrifice y and use only x.

We now introduce a third control factor, c, which will play the role of the bias factor in the butterfly catastrophe. Define c to be *loss of self-control*, measured by loss of weight. Geometrically the effect of bias is to swing the cusp to and fro. The resulting effect on the behaviour surface is shown in Fig. 3.

During the first phase of the disorder the anorexic is firmly in control of herself, and so $c < 0$ as in Fig. 3a. The normal person has learnt to perform the regular smooth cycle at the back, socially structured by mealtimes. The anorexic however finds herself trapped on the lower sheet at the front by the abnormality; in other words the limbic brain oscillates continuously in states underlying a fasting frame of mind all the time she is awake, even when she goes through the motions of eating. The frame of mind is predominantly cerebral, and the victims often speak in terms of "purity"; it tends to smother instincts and produce excessive verbalization. During the first phase, victims often deny being ill, and refuse treatment.

Then as the anorexic loses weight, she gradually loses control of herself; the bias factor c gradually increases, causing the cusp to swing gradually to the left, as in Fig. 3b. How far the cusp will eventually swing in relation to the cycle will depend upon the individual. If it swings sufficiently far for the right-hand side of the cusp to cross the right-hand end of the cycle, then this will cause the sudden onset of the second phase. For now, instead of being trapped in the smooth fasting cycle on the lower sheet, the victim finds herself trapped in the hysteresis cycle, jumping between the upper and lower sheets. The catastrophic jump from fasting to gorging occurs when she "lets go": in the victim's own language, she watches helplessly as the apparent "monster inside herself" takes over, and devours food for several hours. Some victims vomit and gorge again, repeatedly.

The catastrophic jump back occurs when exhaustion, disgust and humiliation sweep over her, and she returns to fasting for a day or several days. Some anorexics refer to this as the "knock-out". At each of the two catastrophes the

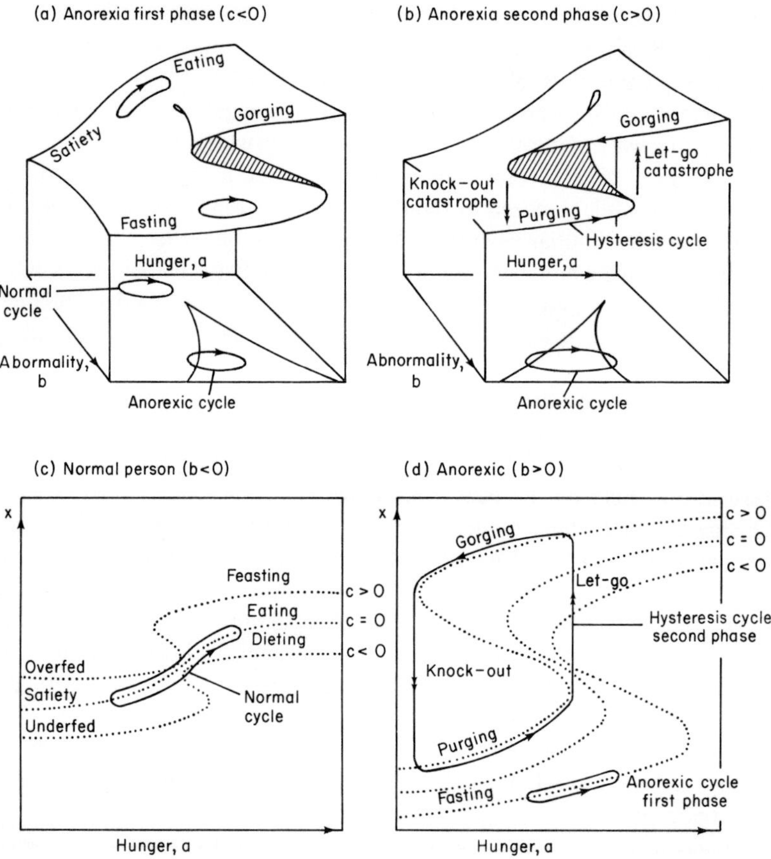

Fig. 3. The effect of the bias factor, c. (a) Anorexia first phase ($c < 0$). Strong self-control swings the cusp to the right, and abnormality displaces the normal cycle into fasting; (b) Anorexia second phase ($c > 0$). Loss of self-control swings the cusp to the left, causing the anorexic to jump into the catastrophic hysteresis cycle of alternately gorging and purging; (c) Normal person ($b < 0$). Changes in bias modify the behaviour slightly; (d) Anorexic ($b > 0$). Changes in bias modify the bahaviour dramatically.

limbic brain jumps from one set of states to the other, denying the victim access to the normal states between. Some anorexics even ritualize the catastrophes. The hysteresis cycle can be much longer than the previous cycle, because the after-effects of the gorge tend to prolong the fasting period.

Figure 3c and d show how the different cycles fit onto sections of the cusp surface. Notice that we have labelled the fasting period of the hysteresis cycle as "purging": this is because it occurs at a different value of x to the "pure" fasting of the first phase. Indeed the two limbic states underlie quite different frames of mind; fasting is cerebrally dominated, not allowing food to enter, while purging has the somatic element of getting rid of bodily contamination.

It is not known what proportion of anorexics switch into the second phase. Sometimes the switch occurs after a hospital treatment with drugs that are used to persuade the starving first-phase anorexic to eat. If the effect of such drugs is to reduce cerebral inputs to the limbic brain in favour of somatic inputs, which is consistent with observed side-effects, then the drugs would be reinforcing the bias and therefore *causing* the switch. Thus the long term harm caused by the use of such drugs may be greater than the short term benefits.

B. *Therapy*

Now we come to the cure. The strategic problem is how to persuade the anorexic to relinquish her abnormal attitudes, but this cannot be done directly. Therefore the tactical problem is how to break the vicious circle:

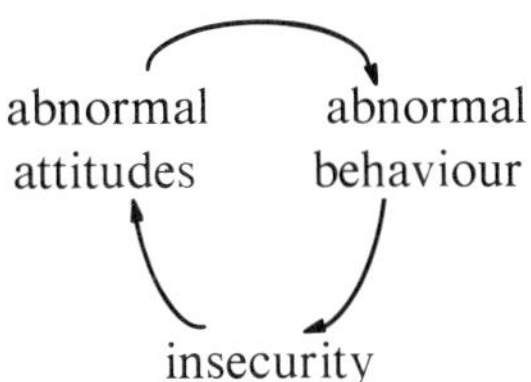

The idea is to break in at the behavioural corner, by creating a third abnormal behaviour mode, during which the insecurity can be treated with reassurance. We will later show how this in turn causes a catastrophic collapse of the abnormal attitudes.

The new behaviour mode must lie between the abnormal extremes if it is going to provide a context within which reassurance can be effective. Therefore the butterfly catastrophe in Fig. 4 tells us the geometric relationship that this mode must have (i.e. the dynamic relationship that the underlying brain states must have) in relationship to the existing modes.

Meanwhile Fig. 2 shows that we must look for such a mode in the twilight zone between waking and sleeping for the following reasons. In the huge dynamical system modelling the limbic states of a healthy person, sleep is an attractor (i.e. a stable oscillation) with a stable boundary to its basin of attraction, separating it from wakefulness. In Fig. 2 we have symbolically indicated the boundary by a dotted line. In the anorexic the boundary becomes

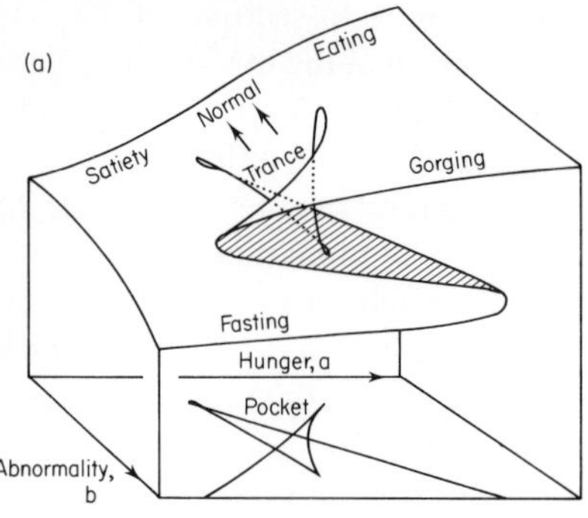

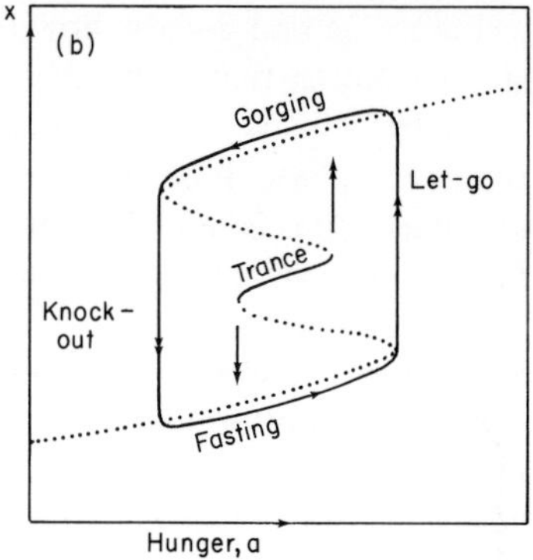

Fig. 4. The effect of the butterfly factor, $d > 0$. (a) When therapy starts the trance states appear as a new triangular sheet of stable behaviour over the pocket, in between the upper and lower sheets. The new sheet opens up a pathway back to normality; (b) The trance states sit inside the hysteresis cycle; initially they are fragile, and coming out of trance is a catastrophic jump into either a fasting or a gorging frame of mind.

fuzzy because the basin is being shifted, as indicated by the arrows; on either side the basin is being eroded by the increasing stability of the abnormal extremes, while in between it is being enlarged by the decreasing stability of the balanced states. These changes cause the sleeping patterns to be disturbed: sleep is fragmented, shifted around and edges of the fragments become fuzzy: the anorexic goes to bed late, wakes at night, sleeps little, finds herself lounging about in her night clothes. Moreover, for exactly the same mathematical reason that temporary lakes sometimes appear on the boundaries of river basins near the nodal points in between erosion and growth, so fragile attractors may appear at the boundary of the sleep basin, particularly near the two nodal points marked in Fig. 2. Therefore the anorexic finds hereself spontaneously falling into fragile trance-like states, in the twilight zone between waking and sleeping, between dreaming and perceiving. At the somatic node these trance-like states are filled with thoughts about food, and lists of food, while at the cerebral node they are shot through with schemes and plans of how to get through the day, how to manage social occasions and avoid set mealtimes, their preparations and aftermaths, shopping, cooking and washing up.

It is these confused trance-like states that are utilized by the therapist; *therapy builds upon naturally occurring processes*. Hevesi's treatment consists of about 20 sessions of trance therapy over a period of six to eight weeks, each lasting two to three hours. When the sufferer asks for help, the therapist begins by pushing aside the inconclusive and confusing contents of these states, pushing them away in their respective directions so as to create a new more balanced trance. Because of the state of the sufferer, quite casual remarks can carry the force of suggestions, and thus the operative suggestions are actually made quite marginally, almost incidentally. First, a casual but firm announcement is made at the beginning (and adhered to throughout the treatment) such as: "I don't care what you eat—we are not going to talk about eating or food", because this reduces the somatic input. Secondly, after the formal step of going into the trance, a suggestion is made such as "Let your mind drift—don't think—look", because this reduces the cerebral input.

Thus the patient's mind is cleared of both food and scheming, and is free to look at itself. By contrast, when she is fasting she is looking all the time at the outer world with anxiety, and when she is gorging she is overwhelmed by this same world, but during the trance she is cut off and isolated. By suspending the threats, the rules, the resistance and the hunger the trance gives temporary freedom from anxiety. She is able to look at the products of her own mind, and contemplate its images and memories. In this state she is open to reassurance, and, more importantly, *able to work out her own reassurance.*

The more the patient practises trance, the easier it becomes: reinforcement causes an increase in the stability of the new attractor, and an enlargement of its basin of attraction. The trance states begin to emerge as the new middle sheet of Fig. 4a. Therefore we introduce the last control factor, d, as *reassurance,* measured by time under trance.

Summarizing the four control factors:

(a) normal factor: hunger;

(b) splitting factor: abnormality (measurement discussed below);

(c) bias factor: loss of self-control, measured by loss of weight;

(d) butterfly factor: reassurance, measured by time under trance.

Going into trance is a catastrophic jump from the lower sheet (because therapy usually takes place during the fasting part of the cycle) onto the middle sheet. Therefore the patient tends to *fall* into trance. What causes this jump? In fact the jump has two components, a relatively small one in the x-direction, and a larger one in the y-direction towards sleep, which is the second behavioural variable of Fig. 2 that we have omitted from Fig. 4 for simplicity. And it is not caused by a reduction in the abnormality, b, but by an increase in drowsiness, which is the fifth control factor, again omitted for the same reason; this is the only point where the simplification has caused a slight geometrical inaccuracy in our pictures. For more complete pictures see Callahan (1977).

Coming out of the trance is another catastrophe, and causes the reverse jump back onto the lower or upper sheet, depending upon whether the left or right side of the pocket is crossed, as shown in Fig. 4b. The patients confirm that when they awake from the first few trance sessions they find themselves sometimes in a fasting and sometimes in a gorging frame of mind.

We now come to what happens during the trance. As the therapy progresses Hevesi's patients report that they experience three phenomena, of which the third is observable from the outside. Of course what the mind sees in trance it has put there and interpreted in its own fashion, even though the images will naturally be made according to past experiences, and the feelings will be such as are stored up from the past. The experiences in trance may be compared to the steps in which an actor approaches a role. The first step is to envisage the part in a few simple strokes or characteristics; the second is to hear the lines the character is allotted to speak (say in a first reading through of the script); the third is to get into the part and play it, to act it in front of an audience.

The first phenomenon is an experience of herself as a double personality: one personality is usually described as the "real self" and the other is called various names by different patients such as "the little one", "the imp", "the demon", "the powers", "the spirit", "the voice" or merely "it". Possibly the suggestion by the therapist to look rather than to think may prepare the way for the appearance of "persons", but usually the latter appear by themselves, and we shall argue below that the patient is in fact giving a logical description of herself. It is the voice, or however she describes it, that is apparently issuing the prohibitions over food: "The little one says I mustn't eat". Typically the first appearance may occur about the third session: "I've got a voice", and then perhaps a couple of sessions later "This is the first time the voice has spoken in public".

The second phenomenon is an apparent transfer of important messages between the two personalities, such as the real self promising to "pay attention" to the little one, reassuring the little one that she "will not be forgotten", while the latter in return agrees to relax the prohibitions. Sometimes the little one is symbolically given a gift, such as a teddy-bear that she once longed for and never got.

The third phenomenon is a "reconciliation" or "union" or "fusion" of the two personalities, a "welcome possession" as opposed to the earlier malignant possession. Typically "She is coming out", or "She is very near the front", and then "The voice just seems to be part of myself". This third phenomenon is accompanied by a manifestation that can be witnessed by the therapist, such as speaking with a strange voice, and usually happens after about two weeks in around the seventh session (depending of course upon the individual). When the patient awakens from this particular trance, she discovers that she has regained access to normal states, and is able to eat again without fear of gorging; she speaks of this moment as a "rebirth". Therefore during this trance the cure has taken place, a catastrophic drop in the abnormality, b, which we shall explain in a moment. Thus the trance states have opened up a path in the dynamics of the brain back to normality, indicated by the arrows in Fig. 4a. Subsequent trance sessions re-enact the reconciliation in order to reinforce normal states and buffer them against the stresses of everyday life. At the same time the trance technique is itself reinforced, so as to provide a reliable method of self-cure, should the patient ever need to use it again at a later date.

C. *Aetiology*

Having dealt with the behavioural point of view, we now turn to the heart of the problem: what causes anorexia? Why can most slimmers diet without becoming anorexic? Why is there such a slow, insidious, apparently irreversible escalation of the disorder? How can we measure the abnormality, b? Why is the resulting neurosis/psychosis so rigid? How can there possibly be such a dramatically sudden cure?

We shall add one more cusp catastrophe to the model that will answer these questions except the first. The reason that it cannot answer the first is that the model refers to what can be observed, whereas the original causes are probably hidden much earlier in childhood. We can offer an analogy, which may give some insight, but is not strictly part of the model. The metaphor is to describe anorexia as an "allergy to food"; of course it is *not* an allergy, but it does show some qualities similar to those of an immune system being set up, switched on, and inducing exposure-sensitivity. The origin of anorexia may occur in early childhood, when, perhaps for want of love or due to the inability to obtain the attention that it needs, the child retires into its shell. In other words, the personality sets up an immunity against disappointment by turning inwards, and leaving the shell to act out the game of life. This immunity works well enough until the shell begins to grow and get out of hand, when the encapsulated core of the personality finds that it can no longer manage. It is then that the anorexia is switched on, instinctively identifying food as the cause of growth. This may be why anorexia so often begins at the onset of puberty, or after a period of obesity. From now on the victim is exposure-sensitive to food, and being presented with food raises deep-seated anxieties. The logical reaction is to avoid stressful situations, and so the core begins to issue prohibitions to the shell concerning food. Consequently the victim begins to feel an urge to avoid food, which she cannot explain. When she attempts to explain it, she tries to capture in words some quality of the urge: e.g. "the little one" is a recognition of its origins in childhood, "the imp" describes its bad quality, "the voice" its unidentifiableness. Usually such attempts are met with disbelief, and she soon stops trying to explain.

Our metaphor breaks down when the anorexia begins to escalate. This can be observed, and so can be put into the model, as follows. Increasing insecurity is observed, associated with a gradual escalation of abnormalities over food. A typical escalation might include the following stages, but of course each anorexic will differ in the details of her own particular escalation.

	tummy-aches at school
	give up carbohydrates
	give up cooked meat
escalating	elaboration of diet (weight watching, calorie counting)
stages of	excessive diet (e.g. only cheese, peanuts, black tea)
abnormality	excessive activity
over food	deception (e.g. secret purging after each meal)
	manipulation (of rest of family)
	nocturnal eating only
$b \downarrow$	"I don't need to eat"

The important observations for our purpose are

(i) there is an escalation of stages;

(ii) at each stage a bimodal attitude is possible, normal or abnormal;

(iii) when the anorexic reaches each stage, she will already have adopted abnormal attitudes towards all the previous stages, but as yet maintains normal attitudes towards the subsequent stages;

(iv) increasing insecurity is associated with the escalation.

Interpreting these facts geometrically gives the graph in Fig. 5a showing the normality of attitude as a function of insecurity level, i, and abnormality stage, b. Abnormal attitudes begin at stage b_0 when insecurity has reached level, i_0. By the time insecurity has reached level i_1 the anorexic will have adopted abnormal attitudes towards all stages up to b_1, but will so far have maintained normal attitudes towards stages beyond b_1. Thus b_1 measures the level of abnormality. Then, as the insecurity increases, so does the abnormality, following the curve in the horizontal plane, confirming that the onset of anorexia is a continual escalation by a succession of little catastrophes, little changes of attitude.

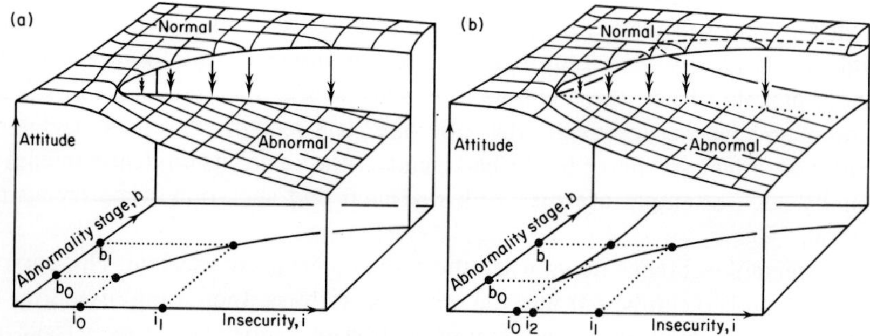

Fig. 5. Abnormal anorexic attitudes. (a) The graph showing the escalation of anorexia by a succession of little individual catastrophes, as abnormal attitudes are adopted towards each stage; (b) The graph embedded in a cusp catastrophe. The left branch of the cusp indicates how far the insecurity must be reduced in order to effect a cure.

Moreover as the disorder deepens, the individual catastrophes become bigger, and the attitudes towards earlier stages more abnormal (carbohydrates are at first avoided, and later feared).

We now appeal to the main theorem. The stability of memory and habit implies the existence of an implicit dynamic that holds the attitudes stably on the graph. The existence of a dynamic allows us to deduce that the graph is part of a cusp catastrophe. The right branch of the cusp marks the points where the stability of normal attitudes breaks down, and the attitude switches to abnormal, causing the gradual escalation of the disorder, while the left branch marks the points where the stability of abnormal attitudes breaks down, and the attitude switches back to normal. Thus the left branch (whose existence is a consequence of the theorem) predicts the possibility of a complete cure.

The left branch also explains why the disorder is rigid and seemingly irreversible, as follows. Suppose that after reaching i_1 the insecurity level drops again. Then the abnormality will *not* drop, but will stay fixed at b_1 until the insecurity has dropped to i_2 (where i_2 is given by the intersection of the line $b = b_1$ with the left branch), because all the abnormal attitudes will be held stably on the lower sheet, up to the boundary of that sheet. Then as the insecurity drops from i_2 to i_0, there is a sudden turn of attitudes switching back to normal, along the left branch of the cusp.

Notice that the worse the anorexia is, the more rigid and irreversible it is, because as b_1 increases, so does the length of the interval i_1–i_2, and hence the greater the reduction in insecurity that must be achieved before any improvement can take place. The model also explains why reasoning with the victim about her eating habits may be worse than useless, because it can only reinforce her insecurity and cannot change her attitudes; what is needed is the more fundamental reassurance about the source of insecurity. But the anorexic is not open to such reassurance while she is obsessed with, and transparently aware of, her abnormal behaviour. Hence the utilization of the trance states, in order to give a temporary freedom from that obsession and awareness. Figure 6, which is deduced from Fig. 5, shows how the therapist under these conditions can, by gently reducing the insecurity, trigger a dramatically swift catastrophic cure. Figure 6 also illustrates the difference between slimming and anorexia, showing how a quantitative difference in the initial insecurity can lead to a qualitative difference in the eventual outcome, that will enable the slimmer to achieve her slimness without danger, but prevents the anorexic from escaping from her prison without help.

We have used the word "cure" in the sense of the fundamental change of attitude to life, referred to in the very revealing testimony from Mrs Hartley quoted at the beginning; the actual physical recovery from the accompanying malnutrition and amenorrhoea will then follow naturally over the next few months. It is doubtful if this type of cure could be achieved while administering drugs that disrupt cerebral activity, because the recapturing of the whole delicate network of normal attitudes must depend not only upon reassurance, but also upon harnessing the full power of the cerebral faculties rather than suppressing them.

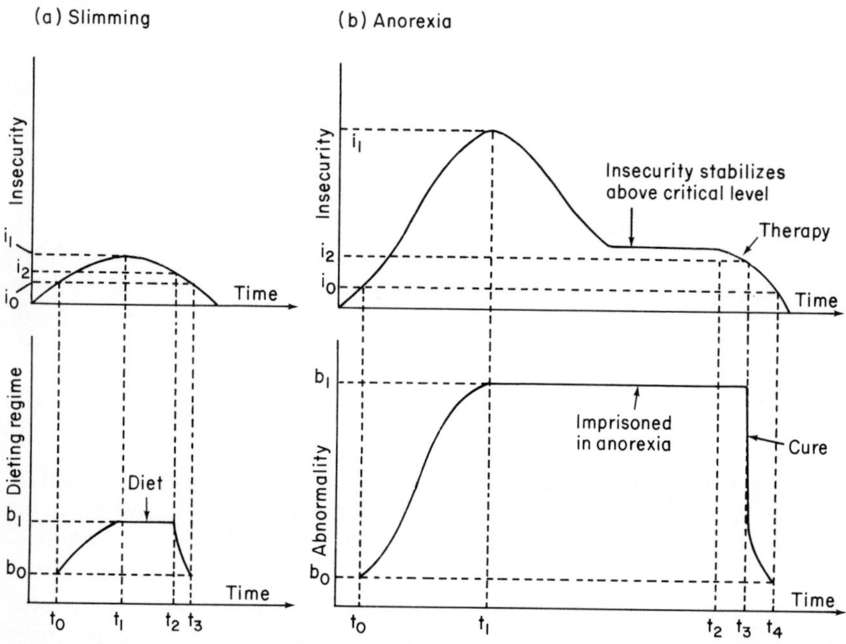

Fig. 6. Comparison between slimming and anorexia. (a) The *slimmer*, anxious about her size, reaches insecurity threshold i_0 at time t_0, and therefore begins to diet with regime b_0; reaches maximum insecurity i_1 at time t_1, and therefore stabilizes dieting regime at strictness level b_1; finds, as dieting succeeds, that insecurity drops to the critical level i_2 by time t_2, and therefore rapidly relaxes her dieting regime; finds that insecurity drops to threshold i_0 by t_3, and therefore gives up dieting; (b) The *anorexic* begins the same, except that due to deep-seated anxieties reaches a much higher maximum insecurity i_1, causing her abnormality to develop and stabilize at level b_1; is prevented from reducing her insecurity to the critical level i_2 by the feedback from the abnormal behaviour forced on her by the anorexia, and therefore remains locked in the disorder; begins therapy at time t_2, which, by reassurance during trance, reduces the insecurity to the critical level i_2 by t_3, thereby effecting the catastrophic cure by t_4.

One of the most interesting points made by Paul MacLean is that the limbic brain is non-verbal, being phylogenetically equivalent to the brain of a lower mammal. Therefore the problem of describing its activity in ordinary language is like trying to describe the conversation of a horse; no wonder anorexics have difficulty in explaining their symptoms. The patient can perceive that certain subsets of states are connected, and have boundaries, and so for her the most logical approach is to identify those subsets as "dissociated subpersonalities", and give them names. In the model these subsets are represented by the different sheets, and the structural relation between them is defined by the unique geometry of the catastrophe surfaces. Therefore we may identify those sheets with the patient's descriptions of her subpersonalities. For example the upper sheet of Fig. 1 is often called the "monster within", and the lower sheet the "thin beautiful self". When she goes into trance the reduction of sensory input causes a shift in focus, from the close-up to the long distance, from the immediacy of mood and behaviour to the long term perspective of personality and insight. In terms of the model there is a shift from the perception of the states represented by the sheets of Fig. 1 to those of Fig. 5. Therefore the "monster" and "thin self" recede in importance, and are replaced by the "real self" and the "little one" corresponding to the normal and abnormal sheets of Fig. 5. More precisely, it is the dynamic holding the attitudes stably on the abnormal sheet that is dimly perceived and interpreted as "prohibitions" by the voice or as "malignant possession" by the little one. The "reconciliation" refers to the left branch of the cusp, which marks the boundary of the abnormal sheet, where the stability breaks down and the catastrophic cure takes place. Thus the apparent nonsense spoken by some patients makes perfectly good sense within the framework of a complete model.

IV. Testing the Model

Finally comes the question of how the model can be tested scientifically. It already satisfies Thom's criterion for science, because by its coherent synthesis it reduces the arbitrariness of description. Furthermore it has survived a number of qualitative experiments between myself and Hevesi of the following nature. From the mathematics I would make some prediction, or get depressed about some failing of the model, and then when we next met Hevesi would confirm the prediction, or confirm that what I had thought to be a failing was in fact another correct prediction. Let me give some examples. The mathematics predicted the location of the trance state as the middle sheet of the butterfly. However at one stage I thought the model had failed because bias destroys the middle sheet, meaning that for those patients the trance was not accessible, but to my surprise Hevesi revealed that he found very confirmed fasters or very confirmed bingers more difficult to cure. Another prediction of the mathematics was the qualitative difference between the "fasting" and "purging" frames of mind, illustrated in Fig. 3d; the correctness of this prediction concerning the operation of the bias factor gave further evidence in favour of using the butterfly catastrophe.

Perhaps our most striking experiment concerned the identification of the suggestions which were operative in the trance procedure. Hevesi says that the trance is not like hypnosis, because the therapist does not attempt to control the patient. I was curious to know what he actually did during the trance, but when I asked him he maintained that he did not do very much. Meanwhile the mathematics was insisting that we ought to look at the underlying neurology as well as the psychology, even if only implicitly, in order to locate the dynamic; consequently we formulated the conjecture about inputs to the limbic brain in terms of MacLean's theories. It was only then, after watching himself with new eyes, that Hevesi was able to lay his finger on the operative suggestions that were reducing those inputs. Thus the model facilitated the communication of the therapeutic technique.

To test the model quantitatively would require monitoring a patient in different states; the prediction would be that the psychological data would give catastrophe surfaces with the same bifurcation set as those extracted from the accompanying neurological and physiological data. Also, different patients would have similar bifurcation sets, or parts of them similar.

References

Callahan, J. (1977). "Geometry of E_6 and Anorexia" Warwick University preprint.

MacLean, P. D. (1973) "A Triune Concept of the Brain and Behaviour". University of Toronto Press, Toronto.

Thom, R. (1972). "Stabilité Structurelle et Morphogénèse". [English transl. by D. H. Fowler, 1975.] Benjamin, Paris.

Zeeman, E. C. (1976). Catastrophe theory. *Sci. Am.* (April 1976), 65–83.

Zeeman, E. C. (1977). "Catastrophe Theory." Addison-Wesley, Reading, Mass.

17

The Regulation of General Evolving Systems: Needs and Hunger in a Formal Ecology

G. PASK
Systems Research Ltd., Richmond, Surrey, England

I. Introduction

The argument in this paper is as follows: science is characterized by cycles of redefinition. In behavioural science (all branches of biology, ethology, psychology, as well as the allied disciplines of anthropology and social studies), the basic terms, like "behaviour", acquire new meanings as a result of a fairly systematic process consisting in analogical reasoning backed up by empirical support.

Specifically, two cycles of redefinition are used as examples. One of the two, bearing upon "drive" and "motivation" (especially hunger-reduction mechanisms) is spelled out in some detail in section II.A. The second, which is more fundamental, concerns the definition of organisms and populations—their regulation, their integrity and, ultimately, their characterization as recognizable entities. This cycle, being familiar, is merely outlined in Section II.B. It is typical of all such cycles of redefinition that they cross the usual disciplinary boundaries. For example, what used to be in the province of psychology appears in new guise as a physiological construct or, equally well, as a sociological one. This fact, if no other, suggests the approach of general systems theory.

Some features of general systems theory are outlined and applied to both cycles of redefinition. So far as the second cycle is concerned, the pay-off is fairly obvious. Organisms, populations, and cultures can be usefully regarded as general self-reproducing systems, having properties in register with the properties manifest by particular psychological or biological systems of many different kinds.

Later on, the train of argument returns to the cycle of redefinition implicating drive and motivation. Using some fairly recent concepts of general systems theory, a partially successful attempt it made to furnish a better definition of hunger than "appetitive drive", however complex the mediating mechanism might be. For, even though one might not wish to deny that there are hunger and satiation centres in the brain, the mere statement that these functionally distinguished regions are or are not active says little about hunger, as the term is ordinarily understood—as an *awareness* of *being* hungry. Furthermore, this conception of hunger as awareness appears to be mandatory if we are to unify or even plausibly explain the various symbolic regulating systems which are known to exist and are exemplified in this chapter.

The imperfect (but plausible) attempt is to identify hunger as a special variety of consciousness which (with due qualifications) is a systemic property asserted without commitment to the particular type of fabric out of which the system is built.

II. Cycles of Redefinition

A cycle of redefinition has no direct connection with fact; it is to do with observers, and the perspectives they choose to adopt. True, as more facts are established (whatever *that* means) observers become more discriminating and (if the facts really *are* facts) more knowledgeable. So, also, these more discriminating perspectives engender more informative experimental methods. But, in essence, the redefinitions form part of a metatheory, about one or more sciences. Their cyclic character bears witness to the reincarnation of old ideas in modern forms.

A. *Drive and Motivation*

The psychology of drive and motivation excellently illustrates such a cycle of redefinition and recurrence. "Motivation" means a specific type of cognition or activity, for example, "searching for food"; and "drive" means the undifferentiated quantity ("hunger" for example), reduced or satiated by the motivational mechanisms. For instance, Bindra and Stewart (1966) provide an authoritatively guided tour through the literature on drive and motivation, and reveal a pattern of scientific development, which is discernable in a much wider survey. It is a pattern of successive and cyclic redefinition which goes (illustratively) as follows:

(i) Our notion of an organism is fashion-bound, insofar as fashion influences the choice of "simple" or "most parsimonious" units. For example, some 50 years ago the organism was conceived as a stimulus–response mechanism, an idea refined and generalized, with inception of information theory, into an input–output device. Such a thing was essentially passive; it reacted to stimulation (for example, it ate food) and it could be unambiguously demarcated from its environment, or from other organisms just because of an apparently well specified sensory motor interface.

(ii) Intervening variables, mediators or internal conditions of the entity so demarcated (i.e. by a sensory–motor interface) are admitted to account for the fact that organisms (so distinguished from their environment) do not always react. For example, the organism does not eat when it does not need food.

(iii) To overcome the manifest counterfactuality of passive reaction (organisms *do* behave autonomously), various internal stimuli were imported; amongst them, Skinner's notion of an operant, "drives" to be reduced and "goals" to be achieved (an attempt to avoid "purpose").

(iv) Ashby's (1956) homeostatic construct of "essential variables" [referring back to Cannon's (1932) work on the automatic regulatory mechanisms and Tolman's (1932) "goal directedness"] reflect these refinements. Typical specializations are Lorenz's (1950) idea of cumulative states and Thorpe's (1956) specific action potential.

(v) It was recognized that this swing, towards an organism forced into motion by an internal drive state, had been misplaced. The simple reinforcement and reward theory is unmanageably enriched (or, if you prefer it, hopelessly marred) by the fact that almost anything can become a "higher level" reinforcer ("money", for instance, is one of Skinner's examples).

(vi) On scrutiny of the mediating mechanisms involved, or the sheer logic of observation, it became evident that there were drives [Berlyne's (1960) "curiosity drive" for example] that served, within limits, to create autonomous activity. Notice the circularity involved: drives were originally imported to account for a manifest dynamism.

(vii) Generalized drives were reified, physiologically, in terms of mechanisms of activation and arousal. This development led to a reappraisal of the notion of drive in which generalized and specific components were distinct but compatible.

(viii) It became apparent that "releasers" (in ethology) or simply "stimuli" (in psychology) figured as quite different events from those posited in (ii). Thus, any effective stimulus has a component which influences a specific modality (the original meaning), an attention-directing component, and (usually) a mood-specific component, able to act upon more or less specific arousal and activation mechanisms.

Less obviously, perhaps, the reappraisal led to a very fundamental redefinition of an organism [specified as in (ii) with structures and mechamisms introduced as refinements], since the organism of (ii) is specified as an integral unit *in terms* of simple (not augmented) stimuli.

This cycle of redefinition, as yet only partly completed, is relevant to the main theme of hunger. Moreover, it is hoped to add to the redefinition sequence by redefining "hunger" as something more than an appetitive drive, however complex or differentiated it may be.

B. *Programmatic Organizations and Biological Mechanisms*

Not many years ago, fashion ordained that the ritual displays of animals and symbolic interplays of civilized human beings were "epiphenomena" basically caused by complex combinations of said-to-be simple processes such as food seeking, mating and so on. The caustic allusions to "fashion" and"said-to-be simple" are not altogether unjustified, since to an ordinary (rather than specially scientific) observer, the "epiphenomena" in question are the most obtrusive phenomena of all. For example, gamekeepers usually see posturing over a limited territory and territorial marking as salient; commentators upon human beings have always been impressed by cultural invariants and symbol-laden artifacts. But these are not easy to explain within explanatory schemata which conform to the traditional stereotypes, even though such stereotypes are entirely defensible as *one* of *many* alternatives.

Wynne-Edwards (1962) and Carr-Saunders (1922) (in slightly different contexts) were probably the first to question and make a specific case against the epiphenomenal doctrine as applied to animal populations. Bateson (1972), Rappaport (1967) and Wilkins (1963) make an equally specific case against the doctrine as it appeared in anthropology and social science.

Broadly, the arguments are as follows. Epiphenomena are manifestations of social or species-oriented control programs without which the society or species could not exist. In this sense, they are fundamental phenomena. For example, Wynne-Edwards, using a plethora of instances, demonstrated the fact that programs in which epidiectic (density regulating) and epigamic (breeding regulatory) displays play a signal-abstracting part serve to regulate population density in an ecological niche and thus maintain an organization and distribution viable within limited supplies of available food and space. Rappaport says the same of the Tsembega rituals: they maintain a proper balance between man and pigs in the tribal territories. Bateson paints a similar picture with the Naven ritual, and elaborates the underlying mechanisms in his later work. Nor is the regulation always of the negative feedback variety. Evolution is a prerequisite to survival and certain events [reallocation of tribal membership amongst the Tsembega; the programs of cargo cultures and other Messianic movements, described by Schwartz (1972); role allocation, in social homeostasis] effect both positive feedback and structural modifications. In particular, the systems are not only *regulative* (dynamically stable) but conceived as *self-reproductive* and *evolutionary*. They are thus of interest because they produce their own reproduction (subject to certain resource constraints and various organizational constraints).

Precisely the same comments apply to the *components* of a self-reproducing and regulating system (and for that matter, to the systems in which the original acts as a component part). So, for example, the individual (Tsembega) tribe member is a component of the ritual regulator of the tribe; and the tribe, so conceived, is a similarly related component of the Tsembega as a culture. The same is true, it is suggested, of an organism with certain innate or imprinted symbol-processing operations, its immediate neighbours and its species.

Quite obviously, in speaking thus of an "individual Tsembega" we refer to a coherent system of beliefs with a name ("Joe", for example) attached to it—that is, an "individual" in the sense of transactionalist psychology—a unique role, or in Kelly's personal construct psychology a person, or in my own jargon (Pask, 1973, 1975a, b, for example) a "Psychological Individual". These are the entities which are regulated by the ritual program, and the ritual program itself is an entity of the same sort (of which the individuals are components). Given these identifications, a respectable recursive (chicken-and-egg type) formulation of self-reproduction is possible and the systems that do self-replicate may be recognized.

To speak thus in no way denies that it is also possible (in fact, necessary) to adopt a different perspective in which the members of tribes can be head counted, the protein intake of the population measured, and so on. Nor does this way of speaking deny that the heads which are counted are reproduced by the usual biological/genetic mechanisms, which lead to learning and maturing brains or, more commonly in animal populations, brains open to imprinting or specific adaptive modification at various stages of development. But the argument does entail a systemic eclecticism, to the extent that the following assertions (or pairs of similar assertions) are not contradictory and are both necessary.

(i) The systems identified from *one perspective* (for example, sexually reproducing individuals, brains, etc.) and the systems identified from *another perspective* (for example, roles, personae, psychological individuals or whatever, reproduced in a ritual cycle) are *rarely in one-to-one correspondence* with each other; the same applying at any level of micro or macro description.

(ii) The *processes* (biological, symbolic or whatever) involved in reproducing and regulating these different sorts of recognizable entity are *systems of the same kind.*

We conjecture, also, that an indefinite number of perspectives will lead to well specified and recognizable units having regulative and reproductive properties but that an adequate description involves the coherent fusion of only a finite number (greater than unity) of the perspectives that might possibly be adopted by an external observer.

III. Systemic Viewpoint

In contrast to the original (essentially reductionist) "epiphenomenal" doctrine, the dogma which emphasizes symbolic reproduction is based upon the general systemic proposition that certain properties of man and animals are common to any system of a given class, whatever kind of system it may be, for example, biological, symbolic or mechanical.

A. *An Interpretation*

Under systemic interpretation, we shall consider systems that persist and, perhaps, evolve in the process, as abstract or programmatic self-replicable systems. Their replicability is contingent upon certain constraints upon their surroundings which, like the abstract systems, will be represented as programs and formal relations. Frequently, the surroundings will consist primarily or even exclusively of other (perhaps similar, perhaps quite different) self-replicable systems so that the "surroundings" embody some features of a niche or ecological environment and some features of its biological inhabitants.

The systems said to be self-replicable are (as noted earlier) recursively specified and may represent organisms or populations or stylistic invariants (cultures, rituals and the like).

1. *The Concept of Resource*

In order to reproduce, persist or evolve, the self-replicable programs must be compiled and executed. For this purpose there must be a computing medium and a supply of negentropy (ordered energy). These prerequisites for actual replication, evolution, etc. are lumped together as a *resource,* specified with respect to whatever self-replicating subsystem is under discussion.

Occasionally, the consequences of this definition, though consistent, seem bizarre. For example, consider the role, or personality, or psychological individuality of a hermit living in isolation and with brain storage of experiences that are carried over from his previous existence in civilized society (these are stipulated as there is some doubt as to whether or not a wolf child, for example, *is* a psychological individual). The surroundings of the hermit, *qua* psychological individual, include the symbolic structures in brain storage and the symbolic constraints of an immediate environment. The resources include the brain as a computing mechanism as well as the nourishment required for brain metabolism.

As a result, our resource should not be imagined as a necessarily simple or scalar valued quantity, though with respect of some subsystems it might be sufficiently quantified in this manner. A crucial and not altogether obvious feature of any resource that acts as a computing medium (and, as a result of our definition a resource does so) is deductive capability. In my own jargon (Pask 1970), I am asserting that the medium called a resource can accommodate "language oriented" systems though, with respect to them, the resource may act as a "taciturn system" not necessarily involving linguistic information processing in the execution of self-replication.

2. *Realizability of General Self-reproducing Systems*

It is possible to demonstrate the existence of many quite general self-reproducing systems, with subsystems that are reproduced and self-reproducing, given adequate resources. Moreover, under the correspondences just outlined, these general systems can be placed in register with the particular biological systems or with biological phenomena which are features of their activity. True, the former expedient is more readily adopted for biologically primitive systems with well specified life cycles, for example, the cellular slime moulds (Bonner, 1958) imaged in Pask, *et al.* (1961) and Pask (1962). Yet in principle the same technique can be extended to systems of arbitrary complexity; thus placing features of systems in register with ubiquitous biological or social phenomena.

The literature is replete with working models in this category (bounded by certain important caveats to be discussed in Section IV). For example, at one extreme, there are realistic models for primitive populations—Kauffman (1971) is typical. At the other extreme, there are realistic models, operating at a detailed level, for social processes. For example, Cartledge and Rejac (1970) have written an interactive computer program that images the Tsembega ritual cycle. Robinson (1975), having detected similar regulatory and reproductive cycles as characteristic of "deviant" social groups, has written programs that image their behaviour. Ben Eli (1976) has recently modelled urban society, and its development, in similar terms.

B. *Points of Controversy*

Even the most die-hard reductionist is unlikely to criticize the mechanisms involved (provided, of course, they are shown to work and to react appropriately to parameter changes). The whole exercise is just as uncontentious at this level as, for example, statistical modelling of groups and development—the accepted statistical epidemological models (on the one hand) or the mathematical models of molecular biology (on the other).

The points of debate and potential objection appear to be more fundamental and are of two interestingly different kinds. (1 and 2, below).

1. *Validity of a Systems Theoretical Approach*

One kind of issue is implicit in the previous discussion. It was stated that some ritual regulatory systems are reproduced and are necessary for the reproduction and survival of real populations. The truth of this assertion is undeniable in some particular cases (though clearly it is open to dispute in other particular cases). But there are certain ingrained (and, I submit, irrational) dispositions to prefer special types and directions of causal argument which are built into the conventional wisdom of science. Not uncommonly, the asserted primacy of a symbolic regulation system (for example, one of Wynne-Edwards' proposals) meets with the reaction: "but *really* that regulator arose from (or it was caused *by*) the pre-existence of the regulated organisms". This utterance is merely the expression of an attitude. The disposition appears to stem from two sources.

First, there is the assumption that the said-to-be simple must cause the said-to-be complex. This belief is predicated upon a familiar (but by no means universally optimal) frame of observational reference in which cells are simpler than organs, and organs are simpler than organisms. It is bound up, too, with hoary disputes about teleology, that hinge upon mistaking the legitimate circularity of recursion for the (surely illegitimate) circulatory of a vicious regress.

Secondly, there is an innate distrust of multiple (as against unique) causality. That is, many scientists at present feel more comfortable with necessary and sufficient (or biconditional) arguments than with the implicative mode of argument which Singer (1946) and Somerhoff (1950) called a producer–product relation. The distrust is no more than a feeling (proper enough in classical mechanics) that there "ought" to be unique causes for specific effects, even though such uniqueness seldom arises.

Now, the general systemic formulation is useful because it encourages neither of these dispositions. Its definitions are often circular and the notion of simplicity is relative to an observer's frame of reference which can shifted, *ad libitum*. Whereas unique causality *may* be the case, the entire philosophy of general system theory takes multiple causality as the rule, unique causality as the exception. Further, there is a deep and interesting sense in which the units (atoms, particles, or whatever the building blocks are called) are themselves systems—thus permitting the relativism and the shifting perspectives noted previously.

Criticisms of general systems precepts are largely a matter of taste. Pure reductionists may or may not welcome the systemic approach, but I believe it is fair to say that this approach has now been adequately formulated in at least two ways: in terms of category theory (Goguen *et al.*, 1974, Goguen, 1975) augmented by certain topological concepts, and in terms of generative algebraic schemes and their interpretation within non-classical model theory (Andreka *et al.*, 1973a,b, 1975). By the criterion of a foundation or clear formulation, general systems theory is as valid a view of science as any other.

2. *Usefulness of a Systems-theoretical Approach*

The other issue of debate is less well stated, not at all a matter of disposition and far less decidable. Pragmatically, but crudely, the issue is: can we get anything from a general systemic view which could not be obtained without it (discounting mere convenience, which, in this context, is a trivial justification for upsetting the status quo)? Frankly, I do not know the general answer to this question.

What I wish to do in this paper is to point out some respectable self-replicating systems, which produce and interact with other self-replicating systems. On that basis, the more ambitious aim is to derive a meaning for "hunger" which supercedes the notions of drive, motivation, and so on, exhibited within the definition cycle of Section II.A. But I am acutely aware that a non-trivial essay in this direction depends upon distinguishing simulation from doing, and introducing the idea that mutiple causes may be of different kinds.

IV. Simulation and Reality

Various arrangements exist which exhibit features that are in register with ubiquitous biological phenomena (density regulation, induction, interspecific co-operation and competition, predator prey fluctuation, role differentiation and sexuality, amongst others). All of the arrangements are, however, simulations (usually computer simulations) of reality.

Since simulation is used so commonly and successfully in different fields of science and technology (for example, operational research, or economics) we are prone to forget that a simulation is not an actuality. Only under special circumstances (those pertaining, as a rule, in the field of application mentioned) is it possible to say "anything can be simulated with sufficient trouble".

A. *Unrealistic Uniformity*

In a simulation, there is necessarily (by edict) a uniformity which does not usually apply to reality as a whole.

(i) There is a uniform semantic interpretation, insofar as entities in the simulation are indexed (perhaps by an elaborate scheme such as Godel numbering) so that the universe of the simulation is fixed. Within the universe there may, of course, by symbolically distinguished subordinate universes.

(ii) The interpretation given to implication or derivation is a uniform kind of action. The programmatic instructions, in register with these syntactic operators, are actions or (in the last resort) time steps. By edict, these actions are of the same kind: that is, either the time-determined doings occur in sequence and one at once, or, if not, then all of them are synchronized. The existence of concurrency and asynchronicity is simulated in various ways (random number tagging, or random searching, for example) but in any case concurrency is simulated, i.e. *imitated,* but not *done.*

B. *Unrealistic Restrictedness*

A simulation, or mimicry of what *is,* can demonstrate that certain arrangemens of self-replicating systems must develop structures in register with communication channels and that they must develop resource sensors and resource predictors. All of this is intriguing enough in its own right. Yet, because the arrangements are simulations, we have precluded the emergence of certain features. The rules of the simulation do not admit their interpretation. For example, though it is possible to show division of labour in respect of achieving a goal and the communicative acts that underline this organization, it is improper (because of the presupposed simulation rules) to say that the arrangement is conscious, even though consciousness might be inferred if an isomorphic process were observed in a population of real organisms. By the same token (and of greater immediate relevance), it is possible to show that a need for resource leads to something like a drive state of hunger and, consequently, the motivation for food seeking. Similarly, if the searches are successful, there exists a condition not unreasonably identified with satiation. However, simulations are (as a matter of definition) not aware of anything, even though they mimic the concomitants of awareness quite realistically. That is, because the arrangement is a simulation with rules which preclude such an inference, one cannot say that its "hunger" is really an awareness of the need for food.

The crucial point to be stressed at this juncture is that the difference between a simulation and a reality, or between imitation and doing, is a matter of logic, not of material fabric. *A priori,* the distinction between mechanical computing elements and bits of protoplasm is irrelevant. There is no *a priori* reason to believe it is impossible to construct a real, non-biological, system which is *hungry* and does not just, like its simulated counterpart, *seem to be hungry.* The intriguing possibility of doing just this is considered in the following sections.

V. Types of Self-Reproducing Simulations

Modern concern with self-reproduction dates back to work by Von Neumann (1966), Baricelli (1962) and Penrose (1962). It is quite closely connected with a concept of "self organization" [due to Von Foerster (1960), and the statistical analogue of self-reproduction]. As Ashby (1964) points out, it is essential to distinguish between genuine self-reproduction and copying or replication, as in a printing press, or in numerous elegant examples which he cites. The distinction has the same quality as the better known distinction between growth and crystallization or allied phenomena.

We are interested in systems that reproduce systems capable of reproducing (and usually evolving as well). These systems can be mathematically characterized in terms of a Turing machine—that is, a paradigmatic *abstract* "stripped down to the essentials" computer. There exists a universal Turing machine which, given the description of any Turing machine that includes a description of itself, can produce a copy description and can produce a copy of this machine (which could be a copy of itself) if provided with a constructor (program writer). In this particular representation, the universal machine and the copy maker must be controlled by a further abstract device that regulates and punctuates (or cuts off as discrete entities) the product machines and descriptions. Such an arrangement is minimally able to self-reproduce in specified surroundings, provided that the resources are available for executing the computations and converting the abstraction into a particular kind of actuality permitted by the simulation rules.

There are various ways of simulating this type of system. For the most part the mathematicians assume unlimited, but very narrowly specified, resources—the infinite tape of a Turing machine and the postulate that instructions are, willy nilly, obeyed. Other simulations, including Von Neumann's original "kinetic model", impose a constraint upon the construction: it has to search, in a "sea of parts", for the components it requires. Much the same is true of Löfgren's (1962, 1968, 1972) work, though the constraints of the surroundings are formalized and made especially explicit.

Another type of simulation involves a so-called "tesselation" surface. This surface is usually, though not necessarily, a plane. It consists of adjacent cells each occupied by one or more distinct finite state machines. The cells are indexed and labelled by the current state of the machine(s) in each one. State transitions depend upon the current state of a cell and the states of any specified neighbouring cells. Von Neumann's "tesselation model" is of this kind and Conway's "life" is probably the simplest and most familiar example (Conway, 1970). Gardner's (1971) commentary is particularly illuminating and indicates the possibilities (Fig. 1). Tacitly, perhaps there is the idea of the tesselation surface functioning as a resource, which is a computing medium as in Section III.A.1.

As state transitions go on within the tesselation surface, patterns of state labelling develop and are known as "configurations". Some persist, move around, and interact, in the plane. Clearly, in this case, it is the configurations that are (or are not) reproduced in the surroundings afforded by neighbourhood and transitions rules. The finite state machines are part of the resource and are not reproduced. Cellular finite state machines as a rule also have the resource of an unlimited supply of negentropy. It is crucial that all state transitions are synchronous and that ambiguities (due to interacting configurations, for example) are resolved by some appropriate simulation expedient. By these or other means, the total resource is restricted. As a result, interesting phenomena of competition and co-operation are observable as configurations interact.

One well-known result is that the equivalent of a reproductive Turing machine can be realized as a configuration. Some configurations are and others are not of this type. The perpetuation of those that are constitutes non-trivial self-reproduction (Gardner, 1971; Burkes, 1970).

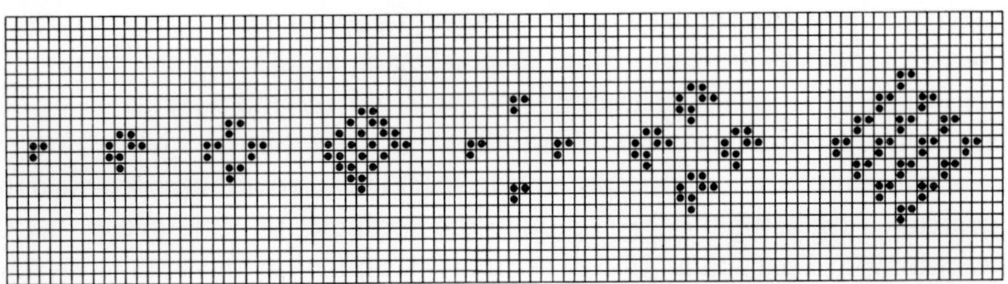

Fig. 1. A simple example of self-replication discovered by E. Fredkin. Each cell has two states, empty or filled, and the four orthogonally adjacent cells are its "neighbours". Each cell with an even number of filled neighbours (0, 2, 4) at time t becomes or remains empty at time $t+1$, and each cell with an odd number of filled neighbours (1, 3) at time t becomes or remains filled at time $t+1$. After 2^n moves (where n varies for different patterns) any initial pattern of filled cells will reproduce itself four times—above, below, left and right of an empty space that it formerly occupied. The four replicas will be displaced 2^n cells from the vanished original. The new pattern replicates again after another 2^n steps, so that the duplicates keep quadrupling in the endless series 1, 4, 16, 64 . . . The figure shows two quadruplings of a "right tromino". More subtle and complex examples are cited in Gardner (1971). From Gardner (1971), with permission.

A somewhat different class of simulations makes a definite and useful distinction between the supply of negentropy (as "food" or "money" or whatever) and the structure of the computing medium. A few artifacts, constructed to *do* operations rather than *mimic* them, illustrate the same distinction. For example, one instance is a collection of Walter's "tortoises" interacting competitively and co-operatively for sustenance on a plane surface (a floor, not a tesselation surface) and vying also for the space they need in which to perform motions, interactions, acts of communication, and like operations which are all part of their kind of "computation". The same distinction applies in Andreae and Cashin's "Stella" (1969) and its descendants (Andreae, 1975), in a colligation of Angyan's (1959) "turtles" or in the work of Svoboda (1958) continued and expanded by his students and colleagues, notably Klir and Vallach. Such "artifacts" carry around with them the finite state machines which are located in the "cells" of a tesselation plane and are peculiarly well illustrated by Toda's (1962) models or (at the level of computer simulations, necessarily rather than voluntarily bound to serial and synchronous operation) by Apter (1966). The significance of spatial motion of a toy animal or spatial extension of a plant-like structure is evidenced by a long-established equivalence between the phenomena called in one sphere "reproduction and evolution" and the phenomena known in a different sphere as "learning, insight, invention and innovation". The publications in support of this view are many and are not cited here but the

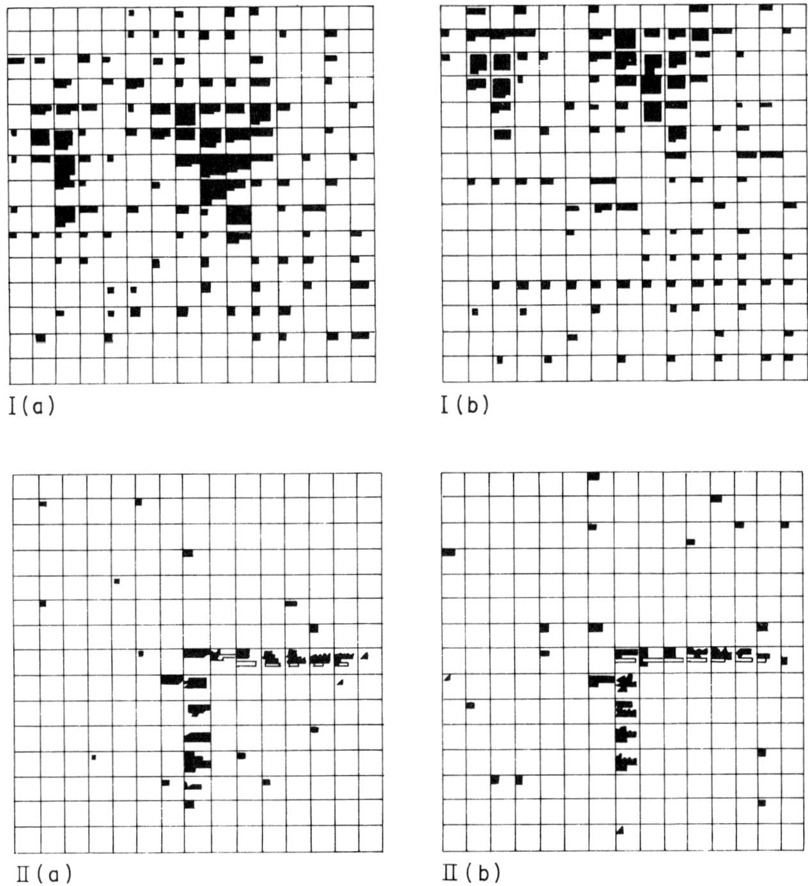

Fig. 2. Computer simulation of automata "feeding" off 15 × 15 cells in the centre of a large planar space.

(I) Distribution showing density of a fairly complex automaton in which "decisions" regarding movement and survival depend on "memory" of automata [(a) is step 50 in simulation, (b) is step 60].

(II) Distribution of simple automata of four types characterized by possible motion (vertical, horizontal, vertical and horizontal, diagonal). The function of "memory" is replaced by co-operative interaction between types and simple "breeding" rules for combination and disintegration, i.e. in this model, "decisions" regarding movement and survival are necessarily distributed [(a) is step 50 in simulation, (b) is step 60)]. From Pask (1975a) with permission.

interested reader may consult the reference lists of Pask (1962, 1965, 1966, 1968, 1969, 1970, 1975a,b) which indicate my (lamentably incomplete) knowledge of what has been written. The relevant references include papers such as those of Beurle (1954, 1959), Pringle (1956), Farley and Clarke (1962), Walter (1956), Aleksander (1969), Hebb (1949) and many others couched in terms of neurone-like aggregates where (roughly) evolution of a type of creature is equated with phenomena of learning and innovation in a brain.

In the compass of one chapter, it is impossible to overview the results obtained from all these generalized studies. In fact we sum up the discussion by commenting that all of the self-reproducing systems so far mentioned (configurations, automata, or the like) are vying for a limited resource, and that the amount of this resource is constant, although it may be more or less providently deployed.

For example, each cellular automaton of the tesselation surface may be regarded as receiving a constant influx of negentropy (food, money or some other more specialized surrogate) permitting one and only one state-transition at once. Further, the medium is homogeneous: cell neighbourhoods are uniform in the tesselation surface, as are the rules which relate the next state of a cell to the states of its neighbours. Reproducing configurations thus compete for a uniform resource consisting in states of the cellular automata and the negentrooy needed to effect state transitions.

It is thus possible to infer that:

(i) a reproducing configuration is recognized by an invariance of form, not by its location on a tesselation surface;

(ii) if a reproducing configuration can be recognized, the underlying reproducible organization (program) has a "need" for the medium;

(iii) distortion of the form of the reproducing configuration will in general change this "need";

(iv) if there is more than one reproducing configuration in proximity so the medium is limiting, the configurations compete for the medium;

(v) either one configuration may distort the form of the other, or they may coalesce into a different configuration, which is also reproducible.

VI. Self-reference and Control Over the Resource

Varela *et al.* (1974) consider a self-referential phenomenon which they call "autopoiesis".

> "The autopoietic organization is defined as a unity by a network of productions of components which (i) participate recursively in the same network of productions of components which produced these components, and (ii) realize the network productions as a unity in the space in which the components exist" (Varela *et al.* 1974).

Maturana and colleagues hold autopoiesis to be characteristic of living systems. They regard reproduction and evolution as the division of an autopoietic system into systems (replicas or not) that are also autopoietic:

> "In living systems the organization reproduced is the autopoietic organization, and reproduction takes place in the process of autopoiesis, that is, the new unity arises in the realization of the autopoiesis of the old one. Reproduction in a living system is a

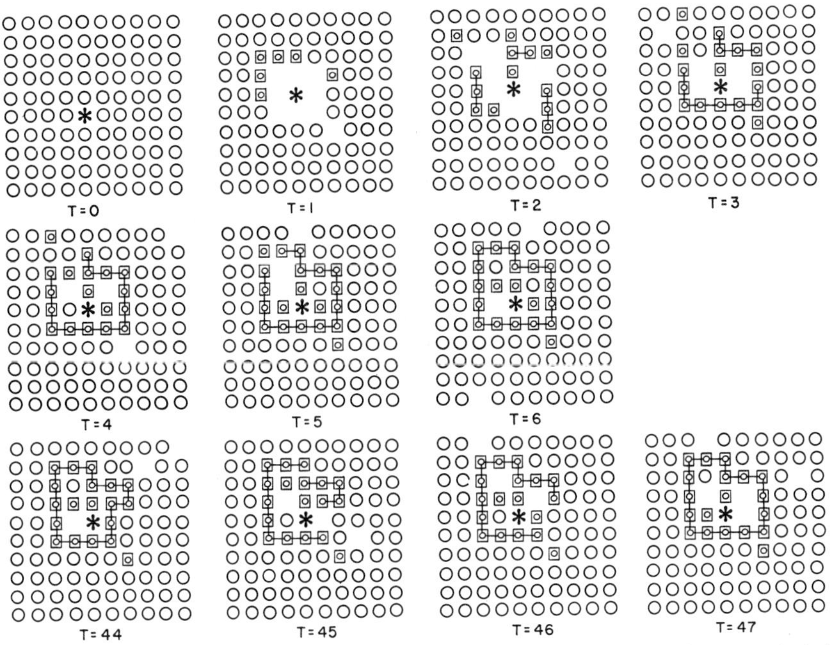

T=0 T=1 T=2 T=3

T=4 T=5 T=6

T=44 T=45 T=46 T=47

Fig. 3. Representation of the output of a computer program minimally imaging autopoiesis in terms of the rules.

(1) Composition: $* + 2\ 0 \rightarrow * + \ o$.

(2) Concatenation: $\underbrace{o - o \ldots - o}_{n} + \underbrace{o\ o\ o - \ldots - o}_{n+1}$
(Bonding)

$n = 1, 2, 3, \ldots$

(3) Disintegration: $o \rightarrow 2\ 0$.

Interaction [1] between the catalyst * and two substrate elements 2 0 is responsible for the composition of an unbonded link o . These links may be bonded through interaction [2] which concentrates these links to unbranched chains of o . A chain so produced may close upon itself, forming an enclosure which we assume to be penetrable by the o's, but not for *. Disintegration (Interaction [3]) is assumed to be independent of the state of links o . i.e. whether they are free or bound, and can be viewed either as a spontaneous decay or as a result of a collision with a substrate element 0. The figure shows two representative sequences. The first ($T = 0 \rightarrow 6$) shows the spontaneous generation of an autopoietic unity. Interactions between substrate 0 and catalyst * produce chains of bonded links which eventually enclose the catalyst, thus closing a network of interactions which constitute an autopoietic unity within this universe. The second sequence ($T = 44 \rightarrow 47$) shows compensation in the boundary broken by spontaneous decay of links. Ongoing production of links re-establishes the unity under changes of form and turnover of components. From Varela *et al.* (1974) with permission.

process of *division* which consists, in principle, of a process of fragmentation of an autopoietic unity with distributed autopoiesis such that the cleavage separates fragments that carry the same autopoietic network of production of components that defined the original unity. Yet, although self-reproduction is not a requisite feature of the living organization, its occurrence in living systems as we know them is a necessary condition for the generation of a historical network of successively generated, not necessarily identical, autopoietic unities, that is, for evolution".

"Autopoietic" systems can be simulated as abstract entities by simple production schemes. Consider for instance, a rectangular grid of cells which may be occupied by motile elements (called, suggestively, "substrate") or by relatively rare elements ("catalysts"), or which may be void. The following scheme can, with suitable rules of movement and other conditions, give rise to autopoiesis if the properties of the "bonded substrate" (specified below) differ from those of a "substrate" element—for example, if a line of bonded elements is impermeable to a catalytic element.

(i) Catalyst + 2 substrate → catalyst + bonded substrate.

(ii) Bonded chain length m + bonded substrate → bonded chain length $m+1$.

(iii) Bonded substrate → 2 substrate.

Of these (iii) is the resource limiting rule (from which it will be evident that the resource organization and the negentropy needed to maintain it are obtained by executing "→"). The surrounding of the autopoietic structures that develop (and that may divide to form other autopoietic structures) is the geometry of the grid. (Fig. 3).

Arrangements using different rules have been simulated by Wells (1975). Varela (1975, 1976) has independently formalized the notion of self-reference, in terms of Spencer-Brown's (1969) logic of distinctions.

The critical trick is that the self-reference which is latent in the definition of autopoiesis regulates the resource available to the system. We comment that the notion of "need", even in the loose and scarcely satisfactory sense of Section V, is of consequence only if an autopoietic system does reproduce so that there are several potentially independent autopoietic systems. In this case, need (without qualifying quotes–i.e. need with awareness) may arise as a result of the *actual* interaction between self-referential systems (not *simulated* interaction) in the sense of Section IV. That is, need is genuine if a system which *may refer* to itself *does refer to* some other system.

Studies of reproductive systems which regulate their own resources (within overall limits set upon the entire population of systems) started many years ago. General references are given in Section V and at this point attention is restricted to those studies in which I have been directly involved. For example, Von Foerster and Pask (1960, 1961) considered various society-like communication models, with these properties. They argued, amongst other things, that quantal states exist in which an aggregate of a given complexity is stable only within certain discrete bands of obtainable resource.

A. *A Simulation of Feeding Self-reproducing Automata*

In a later series of simulation experiments, Feldman, Lewis and I (Pask *et al.* 1961, 1963) examined populations of automata able to move around in a plane of cells, T (rather like the cells of Maturana's simulation, and not, strictly, a tesselation surface). From a few primitive types of automaton and a reproductive act involving combination, it was possible to generate various complex automata of different types (a particular automaton of type U being U_i, or of type V being V_i). Each type of automaton is characterized by its possible motions in the plane and a sensory field (and, in some experiments, by inheritable data allowing for simple preduction).

Each cell in the plane T (a particular cell being T_j) is a locus for injecting into the universe the negentropy required to engender action. We called this negentropy quality "food" and allowed it to accumulate, either in T cells or in "stomachs" carried around by different automata U_i, V_i, ... The sensory field of an automaton is the set of adjacent T cells to which an automaton of its type can move and hence in which the automaton can determine the food accumulated. Under the conditions of our simulation, an automaton could not be sessile. Its integrity depends upon moving which, in turn, depends upon removing "food" from the cell T_j, which the automaton currently resides, and placing it in the automaton's stomach. Hence, the presence of an automaton (U_i say) imposes a pattern of food depletion on the surrounding T cells, which in isolation would be characteristic of U_i's motion pattern. Normally, there are many automata and (unlike the cells in Maturana's simulation), a T cell is usually occupied by several (often many) automata U_i, V_i.

The structure of an automaton is taken to decay unless it is maintained by adequate food supply. Thus, for survival, automata are programmed to seek food. If an automaton is unsuccessful and as a result decays, then its structure is converted into food available in the T cell where it does decay. Hence, the limiting resource (as in Maturana's simulation) is a complex of food and organization.

It soon becomes evident that the food-sensing and motion mechanisms give rise to a communication process as well as an energetic process and that automata of different types are signalled by the depletion patterns they impose upon the T cells. It is also clear the automata, acting under our (co-operative) simulation rules, form aggregates, X. Apart from some limiting cases, a viable population depends upon the reproduction of aggregates which may seek out either particular types of automata (U, V, . . .) required to form the organized aggregate, or regions in the T plane that fit the requirements of the aggregate. In general, also, there are several aggregates, often of different composition, coexisting in the cell plane. Any one of these aggregates (called X_r), although potentially independent, may nevertheless interact with the others, coalesce with or interfere with them. Stable X_r are self-reproducing.

Some of the behaviours of this system are now quite well understood (for example, Shimura and Pask, 1974). The more interesting and fully investigated characteristics are summarized in Pask (1975a), Chapter 3 (where, incidentally, the caption to Fig. 28 should be augmented by "10 non-reproducing automata of type X added at points A and B as induction stimuli"). Regarding the notion of "need", it is legitimate to say of proximal pairs or aggregates such as U_i, V_i, or U_i, X_k or V_i, X_k, that if food is scarce in the T cells, due to their joint presence, then they have a "need for food", which, if not satisfied, leads to their decay and conversion into food.

Since an X aggregate is a colligation of U automata, V automata or automata that are combination products in interaction, an X aggregate also has a "need" for food, without which it could not reproduce and maintain its integrity.

In the case of a pair of more of aggregates, say X_r, X_s, the resource constraint is different. Depending upon the interactions (computations) which determine reproduction and evolution, X_r and X_s have a relative "need" for U automata or V automata—that is, these units form the main resources for X_r or X_s.

Proceeding one step futher leads to a peculiarly lifelike self-referential system, which according to my understanding is also autopoietic. The step is as follows. Let the reproducing aggregates X_r, X_s, be the cells in a heterogeneous tesselation surface—that is, the aggregates are finite state machines, the tesselation cells, but the finite state machines are in general of different capability and the tesselation surface is no longer homogeneous. Suppose, as a result of the interaction between the reproducing aggregates, there is a self-reproducing configuration (Y) of aggregates on the new tesselation surface. Let the overall food influx be constant, as before, but now apportion the influx rate to the tesselation cells supporting the X_r and X_s aggregates at this instant in such a manner that a configuration of aggregates Y does exist; for X automata in the new tesselation surface now serve as resource for the configuration, Y. The apportioning rule or relation is precisely the surrounding (cf. Section III.A) in which the configuration Y *can* exist.

A system of this type has been realized and is also at the roots of Ben Eli's (1976) model which does the job more elegantly. I would like to say of the configuration Y that "Y is hungry" insofar as the automata X's are available in short supply. I would also say that Y is "aware of being hungry" because it is a self-referential system sustaining and sustained by a relative need for aggregates such as X_r and X_s which mediate actions and generally actions of different kinds. Unfortunately, this statement is no more than metaphorical (with "hunger" or "need" in quotes), becuase of the argument in Section IV. The whole system is a simulation, in which the actual independence (or asynchronicity) and interaction (or partial or local synchronization) are quite arbitrary. Both independence and interaction are determined at points of ambiguity by simulation tricks such as relaxation, averaging and priority orderings to select which of the automata move first. As a result of that, we are imitating rather than achieving the crucial distinctions between individual aggregates (X_r, X_s), their individual universes of interpretation and their kinds of action; in that sense the "awareness" of hunger is phoney. It remains phoney whilst the distinctions depends upon us, the external observers outside the system. To a participant (automaton or observer as preferred), awareness of hunger is genuine.

VII. An Alternative Method of Distinguishing Between "Need" and Need

The essential distinction between "need" or "hunger" and awareness of need (or hunger) can also be retrieved by a route different from that of the last section. One can start from the work of Petri (1965) and Holt (1968), who provide a fundamental specification of information transfer which is quite unlike the familiar selective and statistical notions of information (Ashby, 1956, Shannon and Weaver 1949, for example), concerned with reduction in an observer's uncertainty or an increment in an observer's state of information.

The specification relies instead on reference to systems (α, β) regarded as potential participants. Initially, these systems are independent or, equisignificantly, they are asynchronous. Information transfer takes place between them insofar as they become locally or partially dependent (or synchronized). Probably "partial synchronicity" is the clearest manner of speaking, since synchronicity is an obvious prerequisite for program-sharing between systems. To begin with, because they are asynchronous systems and will be seen as distinct by an external observer, the critical event of information transfer between them will be visible as the creation of a further system, γ. Systems α and β share programs with system γ and, in particular, engage in regulatory or resource-oriented co-operation with it. I have argued elsewhere in detail (Pask 1975b, for example) that if systems α, β and γ are all organized as Psychological Individuals (alias, in the biological domain, autopoietic systems) then system γ may be referred to normally and non-trivially as a *conversation* and the information transfer between α and β is the *observable consciousness* of α with β of whatever is computed by the programs they share which are under execution in γ. Whereas the awareness (or status as a self-referential system) of α alone, or β alone, is not externally observable, the consciousness of something by α with β *is* observable and implies also their awareness in the conversation system*.

*In the field of neural activity, attention and learning (rather than the field of evolving populations), much the same idea is used by Walter (1956, 1964) where "abcission" is partial synchronicity and in the simulation SRETIC (Kilmer *et al.*, 1969) which has also been realized in terms of special-purpose computing modules. The general concept "redundancy of potential command" is enunciated in McCulloch (1965).

This is, of course, the peculiar significance attached to the construction in which aggregate X_r is α, X_s is β, and configuration Y is γ (all of them autopoietic). An awareness of hunger is observable as the sharing of programs that are concerned with resource preservation, due to co-operative activity. If, and only if, these observability conditions have been satisfied are we in a position to remove the qualifying quotes from "hunger" or "need" and this, in turn, calls for a realization rather than a simulation of systems X_r, X_s, and Y.

A. *Realization of Self-regulating Feeding Automata*

Let me illustrate a realization and its properties by a artifact called the "Colloquy of Mobiles". This is not a controlled laboratory study but a public exhibition piece. The colloquy and several other contrivances of the same ilk are described in Pask (1971), the Appendix to which contains details of its manufacture and operation at the Institute of Contemporary Arts in London over a six week period (Figs. 4, 5).

The colloquy of mobiles was a dynamic model or piece of sculpture consisting of a society of automata in the form of a man-sized powered mobiles. The idiom was chosen partly for aesthetic reasons and partly to avoid forms (rather than behaviours) which suggested animism. To most people a mobile is merely a piece of more or less attractive artwork. A powered mobile with partly controlled motions has the configuration of either artwork or robot.

The colloquy consisted of five mobiles, three of one kind and two of another, each with many degrees of freedom of motion but constrained overall by suspension beams. States of "satisfaction" (accumulation of a composite food-like resource) were displayed by levels of illumination. The motions and other activities of the five mobiles were controlled by five asynchronous programmable machines (these days they would be called "microcomputers"). One minicomputer was used to regulate resources in an artificial environment. Resources could be maximized if and only if the individual mobiles acted co-operatively. That this requirement is not trivial will be evident from the following comments upon the system.

Apart from motion, the mobiles signalled and showed learning. The signalling was carried out by means of light beams, motor-driven reflectors and light-sensitive vanes—that is, there was basic language but many different modalitites of expression, some or all of which might be used by any one mobile. Learning about the environment, or about the motions and signals of the other mobiles in the colloquy, was a modification of the collection of inbuilt scanning and resource-searching routines. A mobile both could and did build up an independent representation of its world. (Uncut film of the salient transactions is available for inspection.)

Co-operation need not take place. However, it may take place insofar as some of the (learning-modified) routines are executed synchronously as a result of signalling interactions that entail information transfer and the programs adapted by one mobile are used by others in a coalition. This type of program-sharing occurred periodically, and tended to persist as the establishment of ritual regulation cycles, reminiscent of the Tsembega ritual regulation noted in Section II.B.

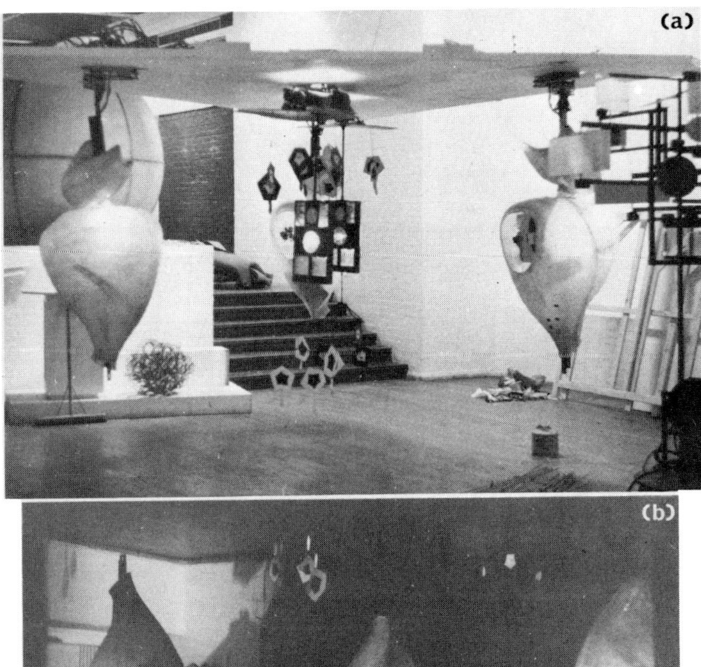

Fig. 4. (a) and (b). "Colloquy of Mobiles", a practical ecosystem in which powered mobiles are "organisms" in the environment provided by mechanical constructions of the suspension beams rotational motions, etc. and a computer program that organises the *a priori* independent adaptive machines built into each mobile (two "males" and three "females"). (a) During assembly. (b) Interacting through light signals, photocells and servo driven reflectors, during operation in the dark. From Reichard (1971) with permission.

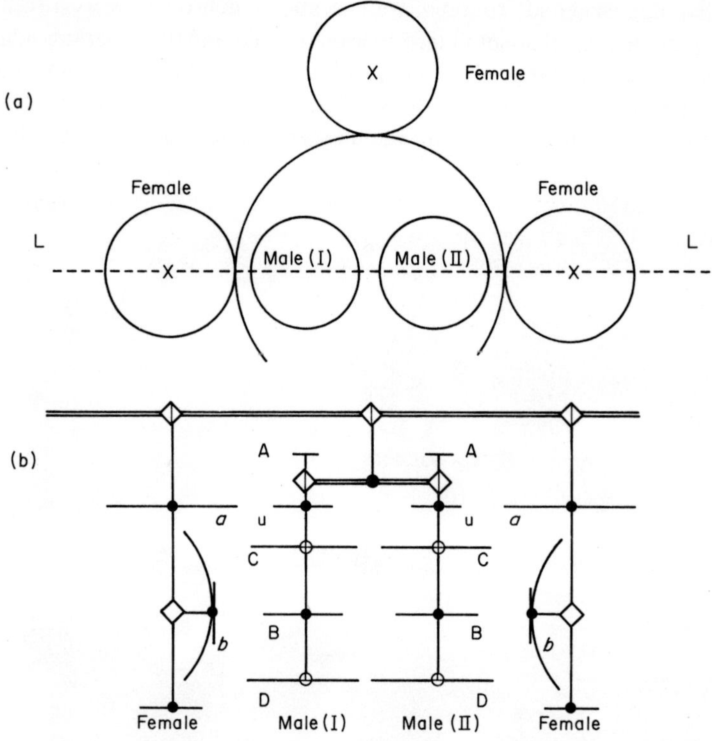

Fig. 5. A sketch showing the construction of the powered mobiles in Fig. 4. From Reichardt (1971) with permission. (a) Horizontal plan. (b) Vertical section taken through line L in horizontal plan.

Key

A Drive state display for male.
B Main body of male, bearing "energetic" light projectors.
C Upper "energetic" receptors.
D Lower "energetic" receptors.
u Non "energetic" intermittent signal lamp.
a Female receptor for intermittent positional signal.
b Vertically movable reflector of female.
/ Bar linkage bearing male I and male II.
◇ Drive motor.
⊕ Free coupling
+ Fixed coupling.
= Bar linkage.

In the context of the overall ecosystem, the existence of such a regulation, under the resource constraints determined by the mini-computer and in the surrounding (Section III.A) determined by the degrees of freedom of motion, permitted the existence of more inhabitants, i.e. some of the transactions should have reproduced mobiles. Although it is physically possible to assemble fresh mobiles, this expedient would have been too expensive. Instead, we allowed members of the public to enter the system of mobiles. (The colloquy area was 15 × 12 ft (4·6 × 3·7 m) and the suspension points were 11 ft (3·4 m) from floor level). People necessarily interrupt the signalling and in a mobile's view are seen as mobiles, especially if they are provided with signalling devices (torches and mirrors) like those used by the mobiles, and give meaning to the (displayed) resource. In fact, such interactions took place spontaneously (notably with groups of 11- to 15-year-old people) and some have been recorded. With a system like this, you may act as an observer or as a genuine participant.

VIII. Summary

It is easy to simulate self-reproducing and evolving regulators of the type proposed in the definition cycle of Section II.B. Further, it is not too difficult to overcome the obstacles of Section IV and consequently to furnish realizations rather than mere simulations of a very general and not necessarily biological type. Such systems are autopoietic and have autopoietic parts. However, as a point of terminology, Maturana, being a biologist, is chiefly concerned with living matter and it may be wise to reserve the word "autopoietic" for biological systems. I, being more of a psychologist and general system theorist, recognize isomorphic self-referential systems and allude to them as psychological individuals; hence, the peculiar definition of resource in Section III. A.

Such systems, either simulated or realized, exhibit characteristics that tally with the notions of drive, motivation and "hunger" obtained in the definition cycle of Section II.A.

Against a background of general system theory, some aspects of Varella's self-referential calculus, and self-reproduction as a whole, can be tractably conceived in terms of a Petri–Holt type of information transfer which takes place when initially independent (and hence asynchronous) systems come into partial or local synchronicity. It is suggested that awareness, observable as consciousness, is equivalent to this (fundamental) type of information transfer, in cases where the event of dependency (synchronicity) involves the interaction of two or more self-reproducing and self-referential systems. In particular, awareness of being hungry is a special variety of awareness, occurring when two or more such systems are observably conscious with one another of a need for a resource.

The interpretation of this statement, formally respectable in Varella's scheme, depends upon whether or not an external observer will relinquish his external role and admit to participation in the joint system. If so, the statement in the last paragraph is no longer a philosophical curiosity, but a piece of sound sense.

Unbiassed observers (the 11- to 15-year-old groups noted in Section VIII) do act as participants in "inanimate" systems. Professional ethologists must reserve one side of their mind for the same purpose. The run of scientific observers might be encouraged to countenance participation and to be explicit about it, by noting that the definition cycle of Section II.A yields (in II.A.6) certain innovative or exploratory propensities such as Berlyne's (1960) "curiosity drive", or Morris's (1966) "neophyllic tendency". The definition cycles of Section II.A and Section II.B are indeed themselves manifestations of an awareness of and desire for innovation and explorations to which scientists are especially prone and in the realization of which they are the participants; there are informational resources for which an individual may hunger.

References

Aleksander, I. (1969). Some psychological properties of digital learning nets. *Int. J. Man-Machine Studies* **2**, 189–213.

Andreae, J. H. (1975) (ed). "Man machine studies". Progress Report UC-DSE/6 and UC-DSE/7, to the Defence Scientific Establishment.

Andreae, J. H. and Cashin, P. M. (1969). A learning machine with monologue. *Int. J. Man-Machine Studies* **1**, 1–21.

Andreka, H., Gergely, T. and Nemeti, I. (1973a). "Toward a General Theory of Logics." Part 1, On universal algebraical construction of logics. Hungarian Academy of Sciences, Central Research Institute for Physics, Budapest.

Andreka, H., Gergely, T. and Nemeti, I. (1973b). "Purely Algebraical Construction of First Order Logics". Hungarian Academy of Science Central Research Institute for Physics, Budapest.

Andreka, H., Gergely, T. and Nemeti, I. (1975). "Easily Comprehensible Mathematical Logic and its Model Theory." Hungarian Academy of Sciences Central Research Institute for Physics, Budapest.

Angyan, J. (1959). Machina reproducatrix. *In* "Mechanisation of Thought Processes" pp. 933–945. HMSO, London.

Apter, M. (1966). "Cybernetics and Development". Pergamon, London.

Ashby, W. R. (1956). "Introduction to Cybernetics". Chapman and Hall, London.

Ashby, W. R. (1964). The self reproducing system. *In* "Aspects of the Theory of Artificial Intelligence" (C. A. Muses, ed.), pp. 9–18. Plenum Press, New York.

Baricelli, M. (1962). Numerical testing of evolution theories. *Acta bio-theor.* **16**, 69–126.

Bateson. G. (1972). "Steps to an Ecology of Mind". Chandler Publishing Co. and Paladin, New York.

Ben Eli, M. (1976). Unpublished thesis. Brunel University, England.

Berlyne, D. E. (1960). "Conflict, Arousal and Curiosity". McGraw Hill, New York.

Beurle, R. L. (1954). Activity in a block of cells capable of regenerating impulses. Royal Radar Establishment Memoranda 1942 and 1943.

Beurle, R. L. (1959). Storage and manipulation of information in the brain. *J. Inst. Elect. Engrs.* **5** (new series).

Bindra, D. and Stewart, J. (1966) (eds). "Motivation". Penguin, Harmondsworth, England.
Bonner, J. T. (1958). "The Evolution of Development". Cambridge University Press, Cambridge.
Burkes, A. W. (ed). (1970) "Essays on Cellular Automata". University of Illinois Press, Chicago.
Cannon, W. B. (1932). "The Wisdom of the Body". London.
Carr-Saunders, A. M. (1922). "The Population Problem: a Study in Human Evolution". Oxford University Press, Oxford.
Cartledge, J. W. and Rejac, G. C. (1970). "Simulation of the Tsembega Ritual Cycle". Term Thesis, IC. 5625, School of Information Science, Georgia Inst. of Technology.
Conway, J. H. (1970). The game of life. *Sci. Am.* (Oct), 62–68.
Farley, B. and Clarke, R. (1962). Activity in a network of neurone-like elements. *In* "Procedures of the 4th London Symposium of Information Theory" (C. Cherry, ed.). Butterworth, London.
Gardner, M. (1971). Cellular automata, self-reproduction, the Garden of Eden and the game of Life. *Sci. Am.* (Feb.) 112–118.
Goguen, J. A. (1975). Objects. *Int. J. gen. Systems* **1**, 237–243.
Goguen, J. A. *et al.* (1974). Initial algebra semantics. Presented at New Orelans; also as RC 5243, Watson Research Centre of IBM.
Hebb, D. O. (1949). "The Organization of Behaviour". Wiley, London.
Holt, A. W. (1968). Final report for the information system theory project. Rome Air Development Centre, Contract No. AF30(602)-4211.
Kauffman, S. A. (1971). Cellular homeostasis, epigenesis and replication in randomly aggregated macromolecular systems. *J. Cyb.* (*Trans. Amer. Soc. for Cyb.*) **1** (Jan-Mar), 71–96.
Kilmer, W. T., McCulloch, W. S. *et al.* (1969). A model of the vertebrate central command system. *Int. J. Man-Machine Studies* **1**, 279–310.
Löfgren, L. (1962). Limits for automatic error correction. *In* "Principles of Self-Organisation" (H. Von Foerster and G. W. Zopf Jr., eds), pp. 181–228. Pergamon Press, London.
Löfgren, L. (1968). An axiomatic explanation of complete self-reproduction. *Bull. Math. Biophys.* **30**, 415–425.
Löfgren, L. (1972). Relative explanation of systems. *In* "Trends in General Systems Theory" (G. J. Klir, ed.), pp. 340–407. Wiley, New York.
Lorenz, K. (1950). The comparative method in studying innate behaviour patterns. *Symp. Soc. exp. Biol.* **4**, 221–268.
Maturana, H. R. (1969). Neurophysiology of cognition. *In* "Cognition, a Multiple View" (P. L. Garvin, ed.), pp. 3–24. Spartan Books, New York.
McCulloch, W. S. (1965). "Embodiments of Mind". MIT Press, Cambridge, Mass.
Morris, D. (1966). "Biology of Art". Methuen, London.
Pask, G. (1958). The growth process inside the cybernetic machine. *In* "Proceedings of 2nd Congress of International Association of Cybernetics," Gauthier Villars, Namur, pp. 765–794.
Pask, G. (1961). The cybernetics of evolutionary processes and of self-organising systems. *In* "Proceedings of 3rd Congress of International Association of Cybernetics", Gauthier Villars, Namur, pp. 27–74.
Pask, G. (1962). A proposed evolutionary model. *In* "Principles of Self-Organisation" (H. Von Foerster and G. W. Zopf Jr., eds), pp. 229–254. Pergamon Press, London.

Pask, G. (1964). Learning machines. *In* "Automatic and Remote Control" (Proceedings of the 2nd Congress of the International Federation of Automatic Control), pp. 393–411. Butterworths, London.

Pask, G. (1966). Comments on the cybernetics of ethical, sociological and psychological systems. *In* "Progress in Biocybernetics" (N. Wiener and J. P. Schade, eds), Vol. III, pp. 158–250. Elsevier, New York and Amsterdam.

Pask G. (1968). A cybernetic model for some types of learning and mentation. *In* "Cybernetic Problems in Bionics (Bionics Symposium, 1966)" (H. L. Oestreicher and D. R. Moore, eds), pp. 531–585. Gordon and Breach, New York and London.

Pask, G. (1965). Man/machine interaction in adaptively controlled experiment conditions. *Bull. Math. Biophys.* **27**, Special Issue, 261–273.

Pask, G. (1969). Cognitive systems. *In* "Cognition: a Multiple View" (P. L. Garvin, ed.), pp. 349–405. Spartan Press, New York.

Pask, G. (1970). The meaning of cybernetics in the behavioural sciences. *In* "Progress of Cybernetics" (J. Rose, ed.), Vol. I, pp. 15–45. Gordon and Breach, London. [Reprinted in *Cybernetica* No. 3 (1970), 140–159 and No. 4 (1970), 240–250. Reprinted in *Artorga Communications* (1971), 146–148.]

Pask, G. (1971a). Interaction between individuals: its stability and style. *Math. Biosci.* **11**, 59–84.

Pask, G. (1971b). A comment, a case history and plan. *In* "Cybernetics, Art and Ideas" (J. Reichardt, ed.), pp. 76–99. Studio Vista, London.

Pask, G. (1973). Learning strategies, memories and individuals. *In* "Cybernetics, Artificial Intelligence and Ecology Proceedings IVth Annual Symposium of the ASC." (H. W. Tobinson and D. E. Knight, eds). Spartan Books, New York.

Pask, G. (1975a). "The Cybernetics of Human Learning and Performance". Hutchinson, London.

Pask, G. (1975b). "Conversation, Cognition and Learning". Elsevier, Amsterdam and New York.

Pask, G., Lewis, B. and Feldman, R. J. (1961). Cybernetic investigation of learning and perception. Scientific Report on Contract AF61 (C52) 640 USAF.

Pask, G., Lewis, B. and Feldman, R. J. (1963). Cybernetic models for the learning process. Scientific Report on Contract F61(051) 964, USAF.

Penrose, L. S. (1962). On living matter and self-replication. *In* "The Scientist Speculates" (I. J. Good, ed.), pp. 258–72. Heinemann, London and New York.

Petri, G. A. (1965). Communication with automata. (Tr. by F. Greene, Jr.). Supplement to Technical Documentary Report 1, Rome Air Development Centre, Contract AF30(602)3324.

Pringle, J. W. S. (1956). On the parallel between learning and evolution. *In* "General Systems Yearbook" Vol. I, pp. 90–110. Society for General Systems Research.

Rappaport, R. A. (1967). "Pigs for the Ancestors". Yale University Press, New Haven and London.

Reichardt, J. (ed.) (1971). "Cybernetics, Art and Ideas". Studio Vista, London.

Robinson, M. (1975). Unpublished thesis, Brunel University, England.

Schwartz, T. (1972). Comments and discussion. *In* "Our Own Metaphor" (M. C. Bateson, ed.). Knopf, New York.

Shannon, C. E. and Weaver, W. E. (1949). "Mathematical Theory of Communication". University of Illinois Press, Urbana.

Shimura, M. and Pask, G. (1974). Some properties of transmission lines composed of random networks. *Math. Biosci.* **22**, 155–178.

Singer, E. A. (1946). Mechanism, vitalism and naturalism. *Phil. Sci.* **13**, 81–99.

Somerhoff, G. (1950). "Analytical Biology". Oxford University Press, Oxford.

Spencer-Brown, G. (1969). "The Laws of Form" George Allen and Unwin, London.

Svoboda, A. (1958). Un modèle d'instinct de conversation. *In* "Proceedings of 2nd International Congress on Cybernetics, Namur 1958" pp. 866–872. International Association of Cybernetics.

Thorpe, W. H. (1956) (2nd edn. 1963). "Learning and Instinct in Animals". Methuen, London.

Toda, M. (1962). Design for a fungus eater. *Behav. Sci.* **7**, 15, 87–115.

Tolman, E. C. (1932). "Purposive Behaviour in Animals and Man." New York and London.

Varela, F. (1975). A calculus for self-reference. *Int. J. gen. Systems* **2**, 5–24.

Varela, F. (1976). The grounds for a closed logic. Report BM87306776, University of Colorado Medical School.

Varela, F., Maturana, H. R. and Uribe, R. (1974). Autopoiesis: the organisation of living systems, its characterisation and a model. *Biosystems* **4**, 187–196.

Von Foerster, H. (1960). On self-organising systems and their environments *In* "Self Organizing Systems" (M. C. Yovitts and S. Cameron, eds), pp. 31–50. Pergamon, New York.

Von Foerster, H. and Pask, G. (1960). A predictive model for self organizing systems, Part I. *Cybernetica* **3**, 258–300.

Von Foerster, H. and Pask, G. (1961). A predictive model for self organizing systems, Part II. *Cybernetica,* **4**, 20–55.

Von Neumann, J. (1966). "Theory of Self Reproducing Automata" (A. Burks, ed.). University of Illinois Press, Urbana.

Walter, W. Grey (1956). Studies on activity of the brain. *In* "Cybernetics: Circular, Causal and Feedback Mechanisms" (Transactions of the 1953 Josiah Macy Jr. Foundation Conference), pp. 18–32.

Walter, W. Grey, *et al.* (1964). Contingent negative variation: An electric sign of sensotimotor association and expectancy in the human brain. *Nature, Lond.* **203**, 380–384.

Wells, C. (1975). Listing available from Columbia University School of Business Administration, New York.

Wilkins, L. (1963). "Social Deviance". Tavistock, London.

Wynne-Edwards, V. C. (1962). "Animal Dispersion in Relation to Social Behaviour". Oliver and Boyd, Edinburgh and London.

18

Hunger Modelling: A Discussion of the State of the Art

G. A. BRAY, D. A. BOOTH, L. A. CAMPFIELD,
G. J. MOGENSON AND A. J. STUNKARD

I. Scientific Merits and Demerits of Quantitative Systems Analysis

D. A. BOOTH. Bray and Campfield (1975) reviewed endocrinological and metabolic factors in the control of food intake from the point of view of physiological systems analysis. They integrated the data in a qualitative model in the form of a block diagram and called for experimental and theoretical development on which to base quantitative computer simulations of feeding and energy storage. I was keen therefore to get their comments on this collection of computable and often quantitative hunger models.

Mogenson (1976) reviewed the current status and future prospects for the neuroscience of hunger and has himself contributed substantially to recent developments in this field. Neural processing has not featured strongly in this book, and even Mogenson's introductory chapter with Calaresu dealt more with general regulatory principles of feeding and body weight control. So it seemed important to have his comments on the connection between current hunger modelling and the preoccupation of mainstream physiological psychology—no doubt justifiable in the long term—with brain mechanisms controlling behaviour and somatic processes.

Stunkard (1976) has an unusually clear perspective on both physiological and behavioural factors in human feeding control and an enthusiastic concern to promote our understanding of and capacity to deal with the clinical problems of weight control. He would bring another distinctive viewpoint to the discussion.

A. *Usefulness in Principle of Systems Analysis*

Let's consider first the optimism in principle that most chapter authors express about computer models. Stunkard had an acquaintance with modelling in its early days in a related field. I shall ask him first whether he thinks that we can expect (even expect *a priori*) that systems analysis could help appetite science.

A. J. STUNKARD. Some years ago I was introduced to the marvels of computer simulation in attempting to construct a mathematical model of glucose metabolism (Seed *et al.*, 1962). I was impressed at the time with the power of a systems approach and the remarkable approximations to experimental results which could be produced by very rough approximations of individual parameters. But I had not expected that such modelling could be applied so soon to the vastly more complex field of the control of food intake.

My first reading of this volume left me quite enthusiastic. It reminded me of the early days of the glucostatic theory, when Jean Mayer was organizing large quantities of disparate data and bringing coherence to an inchoate field. I sensed in this volume the same *elan*, the same joy in synthesis, the same disregard for conflicting evidence or, alternatively, the same systematic and often successful search for flaws in such evidence. I could not help but share the authors' delight that it had been possible to model, among other things, meals instead of continuous eating, meal sizes which manifested circadian rhythms, meal sizes which corresponded to periods of weight gain and weight loss, and to asymptotes of weight gain and loss. Here was heady wine indeed. Who can argue with success?

Caught up in this wave of enthusiasm I could only agree with the authors' accounts of the virtues of computer simulations. At the cost of some redundancy, let me list a few. Booth, for example, in describing the value of such assistance to our limited abilities noted that

> "I am sceptical of my ability to work out intuitively the implications of my physiological and learning process theory of hunger. I know from experience that I am too stupid to co-ordinate more than two or three definite hypotheses at once without sometimes committing logical fallacies. The attraction of mechanized synthesis of an explicitly analysed system is that it can release scientific understanding from the limited capacity of the individual human mind".

Davis, Collins and Levine point out the virtue of quantitative explicit models in generating specific predictions:

> "Starting with a few quite reasonable assumptions about the nature of some of the major variables which control fluid intake and the ways in which they interact, the model makes unambiguous predictions about the pattern of drinking—predictions which can be tested quantitatively".

Mogenson and Calaresu provide the most systematic account of the virtues of systems analysis and of modelling:

> "(i) A very complex system can be looked at in functional terms in its entirety and the properties of the system that emerge from its organization because of connectivity relations will become obvious.
> (ii) Gaps in knowledge and imprecise thinking are easily detected under the demands of a precise mathematical formulation.

(iii) When the model is completed more experiments may be suggested either because gaps in knowledge become obvious, or because the model makes predictions about the mode of operation of the system which can be tested experimentally.
(iv) Models introduce a new theoretical way to look at systems using powerful computational techniques. One of the goals . . . is to produce a symbolic representation of functional relations based on experimental findings that can be represented by a computer program. Testing on a computer may thus produce predictions that were not initially obvious and that may be tested experimentally".

Schilstra states:

"From the same findings more than one theory can emerge that accounts for substantial parts of them. The coexistence of glucostatic and lipostatic theories is an example. Part of the variance between opinions could have been caused by the drawbacks of only stating them verbally. When too loosely formulated, they run the danger of too vague assumptions, unrecognized arbitrariness, unfortunate simplifications and non-rigorous reasoning. Mathematically formulated theories may have an advantage in some of these respects".

He goes on to state that

"The use of models really starts to pay off when one finds it impossible to make a choice between models that 'explain' certain aspects of a phenomenon about equally well. At this point theoretical analysis may suggest further experiments, the results of which will allow such a choice. Used in this sense, models can be very powerful research instruments".

So, models help, at least in the abstract. But when we descend to the concrete, the problem of coexistence of different or even incompatible theories, which Schilstra ascribed in part to the drawbacks of verbal statements, seems hardly affected by their elaboration into mathematical statements. The use of models precisely did *not* distinguish between theories. Evidentally a great many permutations of variables can produce quite similar and quite plausible results.

B. *Difficulties in Deciding Between Models*

Consider first the grand models of feeding control, those of Booth and colleagues and of Russek. Each relies heavily upon one special mechanism and one method of measuring it. But Booth's energostatic mechanism, derived in such large part from gastric emptying has little in common with Russek's hepatic glycogenostatic mechanism with its dependence upon hepatic glucoreception. Yet both models produce engagingly authentic simulations and neither gives a moment's thought to the further experiments that might allow a choice between them.

Just as in the case of the grand models, so also in the finer details, the different models all too frequently provide no basis for decision between them. For example, Booth's model treats intestinal distenson as a negligible factor in all but the most extreme cases. Davis, on the other hand, makes such distension one of the two critical variables in his model. And neither gives any basis for choice between two quite incompatible views.

As we consider the heuristic value of computer simulations, we are forced to look at the other side of the coin of their success. For this very success limits their usefulness. Booth notes that

> "the predictive success of the Mark 1 and 2 models . . . was something of an embarrassment to my general theoretical stance on feeding control. While it was very encouraging to find the physiological hypothesis that energy flow determined feeding did work in a physiological control model, I also believed that learning was very important in the control of feeding . . . and how could a model predict feeding behaviour directly from current energy flow without reference to the (learned) oral satiating properties of the food?"

Davis and colleagues had the same problem.

> "One must observe caution in model building, for probably one of the most serious problems of all with a model such as ours which gives good first approximation to data is that one begins to take it too seriously. Our initial success was seductive, and there is a strong tendency under these circumstances to believe that the model really does represent reality and that all that is needed is a little patching up here and there when discrepancies appear between theoretical predictions and experimental data . . . It can also lead the model-builder astray and obscure the subtleties and complexities of behaviour which do not fit easily into the model".

So the models which we have seen have not yet proved particularly useful in deciding between alternative theories.

J. D. DAVIS. I tend to agree with Stunkard. I don't think that in their present state of development there is a basis on which a decision between various theories can be made, and I am not sure that trying to make a decision is appropriate. Each of the models does well when applied to the problem which it was intended to clarify. We make no claims for comprehensiveness, and in fact we specifically make that point in our chapter. Our model works well in the situations for which it was designed to be applied. Therefore, I think that it is useful in that context. It was not designed to predict meal patterns, sex differences, circadian rhythms, the effects of liver glucoreceptor activity, etc. and therefore should not be compared with models which are designed to handle these variables.

C. *Pointing to Experiments*

D. A. BOOTH. Mather and I said that "we would be content for the modelling to be judged by the empirical work it will guide", rather than deciding between rival theories purely by modelling itself. Do we have examples of experiments suggested by models in the book?

A. J. STUNKARD. As yet the number of examples of this is limited. But those that do exist are instructive.

Toates has proposed the quite counter-intuitive notion that the circadian drinking rhythm may be independent of the circadian eating rhythm. Now the close relationship between drinking and eating makes such a proposition by no means apparent; in fact it would seem that circadian drinking patterns can be quite adequately explained by the linkage of individual drinking bouts to individual meals with their circadian rhythms. Toates suggested instead that the thirst-provoking effect of eating is limited to the timing of the drinking bouts of an independent circadian thirst rhythm and he has modelled quantitative parameters of such a system. It seems likely that only this kind of provision of quantitative estimates would embolden researchers to design experiments to distinguish between these two hypotheses and we are probably still a long way from finding anyone that bold. Yet in the absence of such simulation, this hypothesis would seem untestable.

A second example of the manner in which modelling can guide research is provided by Davis *et al.* In their treatment of the so-called Garcia effect—the establishment of learned taste aversions with long CS–US intervals. The typical finding is that the draught size is reduced when ingestion is followed by a variety of procedures designed to induce gastrointestinal illness, such as the injection of lithium chloride or apomorphine. As Davis notes, there are at least two possible explanations of this effect; the aversion may be mediated either by a decrease in palatability or by altered postingestional cues. The traditional measure—the total volume ingested—cannot distinguish between these two alternatives. Davis's model, however, provides a way to distinguish between the two by their differing cumulative intake curves. For an alteration in palatability alone would influence only the asymptote of the cumulative ingestion curve.

Clearly an outcome favouring altered palatability alone as the explanation would have been the more elegant. Unfortunately, this was not what happened although Davis and colleagues keep open the possibility of further studies which might save the palatability-alone hypothesis. But what seems important here is the manner in which the model lives up to its heuristic potential. For it forces us to go beyond current understanding of the Garcia effect as a special kind of aversion with a special origin, to look at the mechanisms by which it exerts its effect.

D. A. BOOTH. We turn now to Bray and to Campfield, for comments on the varieties of style of modelling represented in the book.

D. *Inexplicitness of Model Specification*

G. A. BRAY. I think that the book should serve a very useful purpose in encompassing both basic science concepts of feeding control and the work of people who understand what modelling is all about.

Its real lack though—from my point of view, a serious lack—is that few of the models are actually programmed and so available to be experimented with. A novice in modelling might be inclined to ignore chapters which do not include a computer program, or at least a model stated in a way which is very easily programmable. The easiest way to communicate this type of information is by listing equations, initial conditions and parameter values as Barnwell and Davis *et al.* have done, or supplying a detailed computer program listing as Booth and Mather have done. The determined reader should also be able to extract the models from the block diagrams and parameter values provided by Hirsch, Schilstra, Russek, Booth, Toates and Forbes.

D. A. BOOTH. In fairness to contributors it must be pointed out that I asked them to use verbal and graphical descriptions as much as possible and to confine algebra to the caption or the face of a figure or to an appendix. I suggest that an author who obviously is running programs should be approached with a request for a program listing or tape. There would be economic and aesthetic snags to publishing programs routinely, but undoubtedly there are problems that need to be solved generally about publication of simulation work (Garfinkel, 1976).

G. A. BRAY. A second general reaction I have is that the book as a whole has a very heavy behavioural orientation and is weak on the internal workings. For example, it is surprising that the model that Booth and colleagues have developed for the rat works so well without including endocrine and metabolic factors. It is clear from Booth's and others' chapters that this indeed happens, but it is equally clear to me that insulin and metabolism have a profound influence on feeding and indeed are its underpinnings.

Perhaps this puzzling success can be attributed to the level of analysis employed. Nearly 100 years ago, the monk Gregor Mendel described the basic laws of inheritance. In the process of doing this he defined a genetic character as the unit of heredity, leading directly to the later concept of the "gene". Charles Darwin even earlier had noted the capacity of animals and plants to adapt to their environment by survival of the "fittest". Yet neither Mendel nor Darwin had any biochemical understanding of genetics. It was not until the discovery of nucleic acids and the final expostulation of the double helix for the genetic material in the chromosomes that we had the biochemical basis on which to explain the process of evolution and of genetics.

A similar analysis can no doubt be applied to the study of feeding behaviour, although the time span must be shortened. We know that there is a periodic process of energy ingestion and a continuous but somewhat variable process of energy consumption in the living animal. The control of feeding can no doubt be defined in these terms (i.e. energy flow), as Booth and colleagues have done, without implying a specific metabolic or endocrine substrate. On the other hand, the endocrine and metabolic substrate which underlies these processes will in due course be described as precisely as the genetic code and allow a new level of understanding of the behaviour of eating.

E. *Criteria for Evaluating Hunger Models*

When we turn to more specific evaluation of the different models, problems of criteria arise. Mogenson and Calaresu (Chapter 1) reviewed the data base from which mathematical models of food intake must be developed and offered a classification of the system as a controller of food intake. Campfield and I, on the other hand, adopted the point of view in our review that the output or controlled variable of the system is body energy storage rather than food intake, and a different classification of the elements of the control system resulted (Bray and Campfield, 1975). Since at least these two ways of looking at this system exist, how can mathematical models of food intake and/or body energy storage be judged?

In fact it is not whether food intake is called the output of the control system or the output of one of several subsystems which really matters. There is no disagreement about the importance of the signal we call "food intake", or the fact that it results from the complex interactions of a large set of signals. What does matter are the criteria we should use to judge the performance of the mathematical models. We would suggest—apparently in broad agreement with authors in this book—that a minimum set of criteria arises from the existing experimental data base. A mathematical model of "short term" food intake should predict meal sizes and inter-meal intervals for both light and dark periods and the observed perturbations induced by lateral and ventromedial hypothalamic lesions in these variables. A mathematical model of "long term" food intake and body energy storage should predict daily food intake, daily body weight and fat mass, and the observed perturbations induced by lateral and ventromedial hypothalamic lesions in these variables. If desired, additional criteria such as the anticipatory aspect of food intake, effects of 2-deoxyglucose, glucose, insulin, environmental temperature and exercise on food intake, body weight and fat mass could also be imposed. A less global but no less important test of a mathematical model of food intake is whether the model fulfills the explicitly stated purpose for which it was developed.

By these criteria, the models of Schilstra (standard model), Russek, Booth and Booth/Mather are acceptable short term models and the models of Hirsch, Forbes, Russek, Booth and Booth/Mather are acceptable long term models. Although the models of Barnwell, Campfield and Davis *et al.* do not meet these criteria, they are successful with respect to the stated purposes for which they were developed. Therefore, each model presented can successfully reproduce the essential elements of the experimental data base in intact and lesioned animals or the specific data base for which it was developed.

However, can a "best all-round" or optimal mathematical model be selected from among these candidates? The answer is an emphatic *no*, because each model was developed for a specific purpose based on a specific hypothesis about the feeding control system. These models are embodiments of several different theories about the control of feeding and/or body energy storage and the relative degree of success implies that each of these competing theories has some merit. The ability of these models to explain an ever-expanding experimental data base should now be tested. In the search for a more comprehensive model of feeding control, some of these models will surely fall by the wayside and the others will be extensively modified.

II. Characteristics of the Models

L. A. CAMPFIELD. To take this evaluation into more detail, I would like first to characterize the differing styles of modelling represented in the book according to the analysis I offered in Chapter 6, and then to comment on some selected examples.

A. *Types of Model*

This volume includes many different types of models designed for different purposes. However, they can be grouped as parametric and non-parametric as defined above. The models presented by Thurmond and Cromer (Chapter 3), Barnwell (Chapter 5), Panksepp (Chapter 8) and Schilstra (Chapter 9) are non-parametric or empirical in the sense that no information about the structure and connectivity is assumed in their development. The models of Hirsch (Chapter 4), Davis *et al.* (Chapter 7), Russek (Chapter 10) and Forbes (Chapter 13) can be classified as non-parametric models that are constrained by the experimental observations about the system. Although the parameters of these models do not correspond to potentially measurable quantities in the biological system, a rudimentary structure or at least connectivity is utilized in the development of the model. The models presented by Booth (Chapter 11), Booth and Mather (Chapter 12) and Toates (Chapter 14) are examples of isomorphic, parametric mathematical models, because an explicit structure with a direct correspondence to the biological system is assumed and the parameters of the model correspond directly to physical quantities in the system.

The non-parametric models range from the linear combination of factors modifying food intake of Thurmond and Cromer, to the trigonometric function relating "satiety ratios" to time of Panksepp, to the rate equations of Schilstra and finally to the two nonlinear first-order differential equations of Barnwell. The model of Davis *et al.* is a first-order linear differential equation, while Russek's conceptual equation and Forbes' regression equations are rate equations. Hirsch's model can be reformulated as a first-order differential equation. The parametric models of Booth, Booth and Mather, and Toates are formulated as algebraic difference equations. The rate equation models of Schilstra, Russek, Forbes, Hirsch, Booth, Booth and Mather and Toates are solved by successive summation over fixed time intervals during which all rates are assumed to be constant. If the time interval is small relative to the dynamics of the system, the solution generated by this method will approach that obtained by numerical integration of the corresponding differential equations.

B. *Methods of Systems Analysis Used*

All of the models except those of Thurmond, Barnwell and Panksepp were developed using closed loop feedback control system block diagrams. Negative, and in some cases positive, feedback was included in all models. The model of Barnwell is the only model to use the state variable approach and the models of Thurmond and Panksepp are empirical input-output relationships. The models of Hirsch, Davis *et al.* and Forbes are linear models; all others contain one or more nonlinear terms. The model of Davis *et al.* was analysed using the method of linear control systems theory. The models were all time-invariant (stationary), continuous and lumped parameter; all were deterministic except those of Schilstra and Booth. Stability, in the sense of control theory, was not specifically discussed in any of the chapters. However, the simulated responses of models presented were consistent with the response of stable systems. Although identifiability analysis was not utilized to design experiments with these models, the more general parameter estimation problem was discussed and illustrated. The issue of the existence of a feedback loop between body energy storage and feeding was discussed but not resolved.

Let us now go through some specific cases, using the criteria that Bray and I are suggesting. The importance of the control system model of feeding presented by *Hirsch* in Chapter 4 is that, in addition to being the first model of its kind, it demonstrates the validity of the application of systems analysis approach to long term control of feeding and body energy storage. Central to its approach was the notion of set point. In fact, three separate set points were proposed to represent the range of drives from “taste” to “metabolic” hunger. The amount of stored calories generates a feedback signal that is compared to three set points, with the resultant error signals causing the initiation of feeding. Satiety is modelled by a signal, PF, which is generated as a function of caloric intake divided by the metabolic error signal; the hypothesis is that satiety is a function of caloric intake and total amount of stored calories. The outputs of the model are the amount of stored calories, the amount eaten and the taste and metabolic error signals. The time scale of interest is 50 days. The model simulated ventromedial hypothalamic lesions by reducing peripheral satiety factors, lateral hypothalamic lesions by reducing the metabolic set point, overfeeding or starvation by increasing or decreasing the amount of stored calories, genetic obesity by reducing the feedback signal, and changes of activity by changing energy expenditure. These simulations are excellent examples of the use of a mathematical model for hypothesis testing. However, the success of these simulations could have been more easily judged by the reader if experimental data had been presented for direct comparison. The model would have been easier for others to use if the equations of the model and computational details had been supplied. This mathematical model of the long term control of food intake and body energy storage exceeds the minimum criteria proposed above.

The models described by *Schilstra* in Chapter 9 are good examples of the philosophy of proposing the simplest or "minimal" model, testing it and then proposing a more complex model for a biological system. The objective was to include in the model a degree of complexity sufficient to reproduce the observed system behaviour. The development of the "standard model" was traced from a liner negative feedback block diagram, assuming constant rates for metabolism (μ) and food intake (β), and the existence of a "norm" for feeding. The feeding behaviour predicted by this model was oscillatory; this led to the addition of positive feedback modelled as two thresholds or "norms" for the initiation and cessation of feeding. The model was then extended to two and then three compartments: gut, blood and reserves. Satiety was modelled as a weighted linear combination of the energy content of these compartments. The standard deterministic model was completed by the addition of a norm for blood energy and the assumption of constant overall transfer rates between compartments. The criteria for testing the model were normal meal patterns over a two-hour period, and the transient response of the starved or overfed model on return to *ad libitum* feeding. Three hypotheses were tested represented by three classes of the model, based upon the relative magnitudes of the rates of metabolism and the reserve exchange with the blood, and the existence of a receptor for the size of reserves. Although not presented formally, the parameter estimation and identifiability problems for the standard model were mentioned by the author. Some "predictions" of the model follow directly from the assumptions. For example, the model predicts a circadian rhythm in food intake if "the average input of energy is modulated with a 24-hour cycle." It also predicts the finickiness and increased energy reserves of ventromedial hypothalamic obesity by changing the weighting factors in the satiety equation.

A. J. SCHILSTRA. I entirely agree with Campfield's general point that a result which is implied in all its detail under any conditions within the model should not be called a prediction. However, it is not correct to apply the point to our treatment of circadian rhythms (Chapter 9, Section II.D). We imposed 24-h cycles as a manipulation, not as a prediction, and then we examined the consequences of introducing this additional complexity.

L. A. CAMPFIELD. In the latter part of his chapter, Schilstra presented three discrete non-parametric stochastic models for feeding control. First, an open-loop model incorporating a stochastic decision process for eating was presented. This model failed to reproduce the deprivation/overfeeding transient response and was rejected. In the second model, the amount eaten was modelled as a probabilistic function of the accumulated reserves. This model reproduced steady-state and transient responses following starvation and overfeeding. However, it did not predict clustering of meals. A third model incorporating positive feedback was proposed to deal with this shortcoming. In the discussion, the author commented on the different uses of the deterministic ("physiological details") and stochastic (curve fit of feeding data) models. The issue that is discussed, however, does not involve any particular characteristic of deterministic or stochastic models as a group but rather the difference between parametric (standard model), and the non-parametric (stochastic) models. Schilstra concludes that a third-order closed-loop, positive feedback control system can reproduce the daily meal pattern of the rat following starvation or overfeeding and that simple stochastic empirical models can reproduce the variability observed in food intake data from individual rats. In terms of the utility of the models presented, the standard deterministic model satisfies the minimal criteria proposed above for a mathematical model of the short term control of food intake, while the stochastic model does not.

Another excellent example of the development, testing and use of an empirical model that is constrained by the physiological and behavioural knowledge is the model of *Davis et al.* for the short term control of drinking of flavoured fluids by non-hungry and non-thirsty rats presented in Chapter 7. This minimal model was developed to test quantitatively the hypothesis that the intake of flavoured fluids is controlled by the interaction of the palatability of the fluid and the gastrointestinal consequences of its ingestion. The model is a linear, deterministic, continuous, time invariant, closed-loop feedback control system, modelled by a first-order differential equation that is solved analytically for the resulting exponential intake rate $I(t)$ and the cumulative intake $C(t)$. The time interval of interest was 30 minutes. The equations contain two parameters that characterize a particular fluid (input): g, the magnitude of the flavour, and r, the retention coefficient, which is a measure of the rate of its intestinal absorption. The other parameter, d, is a lumped system parameter representing the transformation of a step input of flavour to the output, drinking rate. The effect of changes in these parameters on the exponential time course of both drinking rate and cumulative intake were studied and these outputs were predicted under different experimental conditions and compared to experimental data. The agreement was very good and the authors proposed that drinking rate and cumulative intake curves may be analysed using their model. Although the assumptions, limitations, development, testing and use of the model were well presented, its utility as a model of food intake and body energy storage is limited because it is a model developed for a specific experimental situation—satiated rats who are drinking for taste over a 30-minute interval. Also, it does not satisfy the minimal criteria proposed above for a mathematical model of short term control of food intake because it does not predict discrete meals and intermeal intervals. However, it remains as an excellent example of the interaction of mathematical modelling and experimental studies of feeding control.

The model of the interactions between a "feeding circuit" and a "satiety circuit" that *Barnwell* presents in Chapter 5 is an example of an empirical model which was developed by utilizing the fact that neurones form multiple inhibiting or excitatory synapses with other neurones. Although the two first-order, ordinary nonlinear differential equations of the model contain the lumped parameters α, β, δ, η, these parameters do not correspond to physically measurable entities and they have no structural significance and, therefore, the model is classified as non-parametric. The development of the model equations is well presented and exemplifies an important general theoretical approach to neurophysiology. The author concludes that the model is useful "in showing how such reverberatory, mutually inhibitory circuits can integrate incoming information and make decisions that change an animal's behaviour". Unfortunately, the presentation of the computer simulations does not allow the reader fully to appreciate the power of the model (Figs 4–8, Chapter 5). It is clear, however, that magnitudes of the activities of the feeding and satiety circuits do change with time and simulation conditions. It is difficult to judge the utility of the model because it is in a preliminary stage and many interesting extensions are promised by the author. The model presented does not meet the proposed minimum criteria of a model of the short-term control of feeding because its output (activity) was not related to feeding, nor were cycles of activities that might have represented meals presented. This model is also an example of "predictions" following directly from assumptions. For example, if an oscillatory input is applied, the observation of an oscillatory response is not totally unexpected from two coupled first-order nonlinear differential equations. Also, the assumptions about the coupling between the two circuits in the model lend themselves to the possibility of the reversal of relative magnitude for some set of parameter values. It might be more precise to call these verifications of the model rather than predictions.

Both the static and dynamic models of food intake control proposed by *Russek* are examples of non-parametric, minimal models that are constrained by the connectivity of the food-intake/body energy storage control system. These models were developed to simulate both short term and long term control of food intake and body weight for a period up to 150 days. The static model only calculates daily food intakes using an algebraic rate equation. The dynamic model, which calculates meal sizes and meal frequencies, is presented as a block diagram which can be recast as two coupled first-order differential equations.

The dynamic model consists of the static conceptual equation plus short term "glycogenostatic" control of feeding and long term fat reserves, both of which are controlled by hepatic glycogen content. Decreased glycogen content causes increased food intake. Body weight decreases if the calories ingested are not sufficient to increase hepatic glycogen above a threshold level. Conversely, body weight increases if glycogen content exceeds a second threshold level. Lipostatic control of energy storage was also modelled. The strength of this model is a large number of simulated experiments (circadian rhythm, forced-feeding, fasting, VMH and LH lesions, changes in palatability and insulin concentration) and the graphical comparison with experimental results. In most of the simulations, at least the directions of changes in model variables are indiciated, so that the reader is aware of the explicit hypothesis that is being tested. This chapter also contains some "predictions" which follow directly from the many assumptions of the model. For example, circadian rhythm is "predicted" as a result of an assumption that hunger thresholds and basal metabolic rate are a function of illumination. Also, if food intake is a function of glycogen which in turn is dependent upon insulin concentration, then it follows that if insulin concentration is reduced (as in diabetes), less glycogen will be stored and, thus, food intake will increase. As suggested above, these simulations could be called verifications of the model (and its several hypotheses) rather than predictions and the term "prediction" reserved for the simulation of an experiment not yet conducted or for an estimate of an unmeasurable internal variable under specified experimental conditions. Despite its ability to simulate both short and long term control of food intake and body weight and its extensive successful testing, the usefulness of the dynamic model would have been enhanced if equations, assumptions and enough detail about the individual simulations had been given so that an interested reader could reproduce these simulations. However, in spite of these omissions, the Russek model should be a very useful research tool in the study of the control of feeding.

In Chapter 13, *Forbes* presented a review of non-parametric regression and systems models for extrapolating the intake of feed as a function of digestibility in the ruminant and describes a non-parametric but biologically constrained model of the interactions of "physical" and "metabolic" control of intake in cows and sheep. In the model, the intake of feed is assumed to match energy expenditure unless limited by the geometry of the gut. Daily food intake and body weight are predicted as a function of time and digestibility of the feed, over a period of 500 days. Forbes discussed the distinction between an empirical, non-parametric ("regression") model that has no predictive value and a model based on the connectivity of feeding control system ("iterative") that has predictive ability.

Booth presented two complex, isomorphic, parametric mathematical models for both the short and long term control of food intake and body energy storage, one for rats and one (with *Mather*) for human beings. The importance of these is that they are parametric models which propose a specific structural hypothesis with potentially quantifiable parameters. They also make explicit the functional dependence of behaviour on a metabolic consequence of that behaviour. These models are based on the hypothesis that the energy flows from the gut to the blood and between the blood to adipose tissue are major control signals for feeding. The Mark 3 model of feeding in the rat (Chapter 11) consists of representations of the following processes: gut accumulation, distension time lag and clearance, a feeding rate function with random hunger and satiety thresholds, fat storage/breakdown rates, circadian rhythms for gut clearance rates and energy output of activity, metabolic rate, conditioned satiety, and feedback from fat stores. The models are presented in block diagram form and are represented mathematically by algebraic rate equations and inequality constraints. The time interval of interest is several days. These equations are solved for feeding rate and energy flows by successive summation over fixed intervals of 0·5 min during which all rates are assumed to be constant. The Mark 3 model successfully simulates meal sizes, intermeal intervals and daily weight gains in rats with VMH or LH lesions or diabetes and in intact rats with dehydration anorexia, treated with insulin or exposed to low temperature. The presentation of the development, testing and use of the model emphasizes the necessary interaction between hypothesis formulation and testing, model formulation and testing and experimental studies.

The feeding model for the human subject presented in Chapter 12 is similar to the Mark 3 model in the rat. The basic model contains representations of stomach contents, rate of absorption, metabolic rate, fat deposition and mobilization, non-fat energy flow and storage and threshold for meal start and finish and feeding meal size, interval and body weight. The time interval of interest is several days. The unique features of this chapter are: the statement by statement discussion of the computer program listing used to solve the model equations as a function of time; the detailed discussion of the computational method of successive addition with a step size of 0·5 min; the example of parameter estimation to minimize the error between the output of the model and experimental data; and the calculation of the sensitivities of the model output to changes in parameter values. The chapter ends with an important discussion of the role of mathematical models in the study of the control of feeding.

The parametric mathematical model of hunger–thirst interactions presented by *Toates* in Chapter 14 is unique because it deals quantitatively with the interaction of two complex biological control systems. The chapter is a good example of a review of the experimental data on which a model is based and the presentation of the development of each model subsystem and synthesis into the complete fourth-order nonlinear block diagram. The model is tested for *ad libitum* eating and drinking of a 300-g rat over a 24-h period and the implications of the model simulations for the theory of the interactions of eating and drinking are discussed.

The conjunction of these very diverse models, differing both in methods and in underlying theories, should facilitate comparisons and evaluations which may provide a basis for a more comprehensive understanding of this control system and its related systems.

III. Neural Substrates of Feeding

D. A. BOOTH. Now we shall turn to Mogenson for comments specifically on central processing in computable theories of feeding control. I believe you want to enter a note of caution, speaking as a neurophysiologist.

G. J. MOGENSON. Yes, I do. Since food intake is controlled by the central nervous sytem, one of the important goals of systems analysis must be to understand the neural mechanisms which initiate and terminate feeding behaviour. The first point I wish to make looking back on the book is that, although a number of brain structures have been implicated, definitive evidence concerning these neural mechanisms is lacking. This is in part because the central nervous system is very complex, as is feeding behaviour, but also in part because of the way the field has developed.

A. *Brain Processes*

Since experimental studies of the neural substrates of feeding behaviour began in the early 1940s the field has been dominated by a "centralist" approach, as I have detailed elsewhere (Mogenson, 1976) and as Booth (1976) also has emphasized. Reports of aphagia and of hyperphagia following lesions of the lateral hypothalamus and ventromedial hypothalamus respectively and subsequent demonstrations of the initiation and cessation of feeding by electrical stimulation of these regions were taken as evidence of central integrative sites for "hunger" and "satiety" signals. Early qualitative models—for example, the dual-mechanism model—assumed that the lateral hypothalamus and the ventromedial hypothalamus integrated hunger and feedback signals (e.g. gastric distension) and were possibly the site of receptors for hunger and/or satiety signals (e.g. glucoreceptors). More recent investigations have suggested alternative interpretations of lesion and stimulation experiments, however, and the status of the hypothalamus in the control of food intake—for some years considered the locus of feeding and satiety centres of integrative mechanisms—is now regarded as uncertain. Space does not permit a discussion of these recent developments; they are dealt with in the proceedings of two international conferences (Novin *et al.,* 1976; Silverstone, 1976). The point is that with the demise of the hypothalamic dual-mechanism model is has become apparent that the neural substrates of feeding behaviour are largely unknown.

Some of the models described in this book, although more quantitative and rigorous, share the limitations of the earlier qualitative models referred to above. It is assumed by several authors that the LH and VMH control appetite and satiety, perhaps in association with limbic structures to form reverberatory neural circuits that are mutually inhibitory. However, most of the neurophysiological evidence on which this assumption is based is not definitive.

Lesions, stimulation and other techniques used by neurobiologists interested in the neural substrates of behaviour are frequently not sufficiently discrete for the investigations of neural pathways and neural integrative mechanisms. Unfortunately this has not, in the past, been recognized sufficiently. Lesions destroy and electrical stimulation activates multiple neural pathways. Furthermore, these techniques may destroy fibres of passage (e.g. nigrostriatal pathway: Ungerstedt, 1971; ventral noradrenergic pathway: Ahlskog and Hoebel, 1973) in addition to or instead of a hypothalamic integrative mechanism.

B. *Signals to the Brain*

Assumptions have also been made in previous chapters as to which signals—integrated by central appetite and satiety systems—are of fundamental importance in the control of food intake. Some of the putative "hunger" and "satiety" signals come from the external environment, some provided by the food itself, others occurring as the food passes along the gastrointestinal tract and as nutrients are absorbed into the blood stream and reach the liver, the brain and other organs. It is clear from previous chapters that systems analysis is a valuable conceptual approach in dealing with the dynamic influence of the multiple signals which seem to contribute to the control of feeding behaviour. However, the value of this approach depends on selecting the appropriate signals; this is the second point I wish to make. An essential prerequisite for the effective use of systems analysis and for developing models which will guide the neurobiologist in localizing receptors and in investigating neural pathways and central integrative mechanisms is to identify those signals that are *biologically significant* to the animal. Behavioural and ethological studies are also needed to determine *under what conditions* the various signals contribute to the control of food intake.

The neural structures (such as lateral hypothalamus, amygdala, ventral tegmental area) implicated by lesion and stimulation techniques in the control of food intake, may be investigated with more elegant techniques. For example, the microelectrode, electrophysiological recording technique is highly discrete and has been used to identify hypothalamic neurones that are responsive to glucose, free fatty acids and insulin (Oomura, 1976). Since these experiments were performed in anaesthetized animals, however, the results do not show that these glucoreceptive neurones contribute to the initiation and/or termination of feeding behaviour. They could instead provide glucostatic signals for the autonomic-endocrine mechanisms involved in the regulation of blood glucose levels. The promise of these techniques, especially when used to investigate the neural substrates of feeding behaviour in unanaesthetized, behaving animals (Rolls *et al.*, 1976) will only be realized when the relevant signals and peripheral mechanisms have been identified.

In summary, from available experimental evidence, little is known about where the signals which initiate and terminate feeding behaviour are integrated in the central nervous system and, in fact, the physiologically relevant signals are not known with certainty. It appears that extensive behavioural studies and investigations of relevant peripheral signals and mechanisms may be needed before the systems analyst can tell the neurobiologist what sort of central neural mechanisms to look for.

IV. Clinical Implications

D. A. BOOTH. There is little in the book relating modelling to medical or psychological problems of feeding control.

Of course, there is Zeeman's and Hevesi's (Chapter 17) remarkable application of catastrophe theory to the treatment of anorexia nervosa. It will be important to see how successful different therapists are if they use procedures carefully derived from Zeeman's model. I turn to Stunkard for a comment in conclusion from the point of view of feeding behaviour modification in obesity.

A. J. STUNKARD. When I first heard about this book I was delighted by the opportunity to find out what mathematical modelling could contribute to the complex and confusing field of hunger. More specifically, as a clinician and clinical researcher, I was eager to find out what kind of help might be on the way for someone whose periodic looks over his shoulder reveal a large and growing number of obese people who seem to be gaining on him.

The current interest in behaviour therapy of obesity has led to several efforts to determine whether obese persons manifest a distinctive "obese eating style" (Stunkard and Kaplan, 1977). Most of these efforts have serious flaws. At least three, however, have produced reliable estimates of the rates of food intake of obese and non-obese people and, in the associated effort to control the conditions of the study, have also taught us a great deal about other influences upon eating rates. The results of these studies could have a significance far beyond that of their original purpose of discriminating between obese and non-obese persons. For they could provide vital quantitative estimates of parameters necessary for the construction of general models of human eating behaviour. For example, when considered only in the context of a comparison of eating rates of obese and non-obese people, the results of the three studies are almost trivial: one found that the obese ate slightly faster, one found no difference and one found that the obese are faster under some circumstances and not under others. But the numbers potentially tell us much more.

Hill and McCutcheon (1975) reported that obese young white men ate at a rate of 57 g/min compared to 44 g/min for non-obese men ($P < 0{\cdot}05$) in the laboratory when they were permitted to eat as much as they wished of a standard meal (and when they ate about the same amount of it). On the other hand, we have found identical rates of eating by obese and non-obese old, white women when they were provided with a completely standardized meal in a restaurant (46 g/min) (A. J. Stunkard, M. Colland and A. Myers, unpubl. obs.). Dodd *et al.* (1976) similarly found no difference in the rate of eating of obese and non-obese women when they were matched on the size of the meals they chose in a quick-food restaurant (24·5 versus 24·0 g/min). When, however, these investigators studied randomly selected subjects, they found that obese women chose larger meals than the non-obese and that they ate them at a more rapid rate (27 versus 20 g/min; $P < 0{\cdot}05$).

These studies permit the unremarkable conclusion that obese people tend to eat a bit more rapidly than do non-obese ones. But what they tell us about the influence of the circumstances of eating is much more important. The influence of obesity pales into insignificance beside the influence of circumstances. In just three studies we have learned that these circumstances can result in eating rates that differ by 100%. Clearly human eating involves a highly plastic response repertoire. Behaviour therapists have taken advantage of (presumptions about) this plasticity to construct improved treatment programmes. Enough may now have been learned about the quantitative aspects of human eating to begin to explicate this repertoire and build mathematical models of its role in the whole human system. If so, the interaction between model and real man, between theory and data, may have brought us to the threshold of the kind of understanding that will permit the prediction and control of human eating behaviour.

D. A. BOOTH. In some fields of physical medicine, it is possible to have a computer on-line (or at least conveniently off-line) to the clinic, to provide a diagnosis and hence the selection of patients suitable for the available treatment package or the design of a treatment regime for an individual patient. Obviously, there is a long way to go before we have such computation on-line to the obesity clinic. On the other hand, nothing like that will ever happen unless the scientists have managed to build realistic computable theory.

A. J. STUNKARD. I was delighted to be introduced to catastrophe theory by the

Zeeman article and particularly because I agree that anorexia nervosa is a singularly good candidate for such analysis. But my reason for thinking so arises from a clinical feature which Zeeman does not mention and therein lies an added attraction of his theory. The introduction of a social learning approach to the treatment of anorexia nervosa has led to a finding as striking as any in the long history of this curious disorder and one as striking as any in the field of psychopathology: the use of a simple behavioural paradigm can reverse—often with two days—a condition which has defied all therapeutic endeavours for a period of years. Simply making a highly preferred activity—access to physical activity is a notable example—contingent upon small daily weight gains resulted in prompt and rapid weight gains of as much as four pounds a week (Blinder *et al.*, 1970). When we first began this work at the Univerity of Pennsylvania over a decade ago we were concerned that we were merely exerting some subtle form of coercion which, while it produced weight gain (an imperative with the life-threatening emaciation of our patients), might be neutral or even damaging to their psychological well being. Much to our surprise we found improvements in the psychological state of the patients which were as striking, and as prompt, as those in their eating behaviour.

These finding have since been replicated and extended, especially by Agras *et al.* (1974). Why and how such a simple reward works is still unclear. Agras suggests that the most important element is the feedback of information as to caloric intake and body weight and he has produced some elegant support for this thesis. Why it should be so effective is still unclear. Perhaps catastrophe theory will help provide an answer.

References

Agras, W. S., Barlow, D. H., Chapin, H. N., *et al.*(1974). Behavior modification of anorexia nervosa. *Archs. gen. Psychiat.* **30**, 279–286.

Ahlskog, J. E. and Hoebel, B. G. (1973). Overeating and obesity from damage to a noradrenergic system in the brain. *Science, N.Y.* **182**, 166–169.

Blinder, B. J., Freeman, D. M. and Stunkard, A. J. (1970). Behaviour therapy of anorexia nervosa: effectiveness of activity as a reinforcer of weight gain. *Am. J. Psychiat.* **126**, 1093–1098.

Booth, D. A. (1976). Approaches to feeding control. *In* "Appetite and Food Intake" (T. Silverstone, ed.), pp. 417–478. Abakon Verlagsgesellschaft, West Berlin.

Bray, G. A. and Campfield, L. A. (1975). Metabolic factors in the control of energy stores. *Metabolism* **24**, 99–117.

Dodd, D. K., Birky, H. J. and Stalling, R. B. (1976). Eating behavior of obese and non-obese females in a natural setting. Unpublished manuscript, Guardian Angel Home, Peoria, IL.

Garfinkel, D. (1976). Methods of publication of large metabolic models. *Biosci. Commun.* **2**, 49–55.

Hill, S. W. and McCutcheon, N. B. (1975). Eating responses of obese and non-obese humans during dinner meals. *Psychosom. Med.* **37**, 395–401.

Mogenson, G. J. (1976). Neural mechanisms of hunger: current status and future prospects. *In* "Hunger: Basic Mechanisms and Clinical Implications" (D. Novin, W. Wyrwicka and G. A. Bray, eds), pp. 473–485. Raven Press, New York.

Novin, D., Wyrwicka, W. and Bray, G. A. (eds) (1976). "Hunger: Basic Mechanisms and Clinical Implications". Raven Press, New York.

Oomura, Y. (1976). Significance of glucose, insulin, and free fatty acid on the hypothalamic feeding and satiety neurons. *In* "Hunger: Basic Mechanisms and Clinical Implications" (D. Novin, W. Wyrwicka and G. A. Bray, eds), pp. 145–157. Raven Press, New York.

Rolls, E. T., Burton, M. J. and Mora, F. (1976). Hypothalamic neuronal responses associated with the sight of food. *Brain Res.* **111**, 53–66.

Seed, J., Acton, F. and Stunkard, A. (1962). A model for the appraisal of glucose metabolism. *Clin. Pharmacol. Ther.* **3**, 191–215.

Silverstone, T. (ed.) (1976). "Appetite and Food Intake". Abakon Verlagsgesellschaft, West Berlin.

Stunkard, A. J. (1976). "The Pain of Obesity". Bull, Palo Alto, CA.

Stunkard, A. J. and Kaplan, D. (1977). Eating in public places: a review of reports of the direct observation of eating behavior. *Internat. J. Obesity,* **1**, 89–101.

Ungerstedt, U. (1971). Adipsia and aphagia after 6-hydroxy dopamine induced degeneration of the nigro-striatal dopamine system. *Acta physiol. scand. Suppl.* **367**, 95–122.

Index

E

F

G

N

O

P

Q

R

S